EXPLORING MICROSOFT® OFFICE 97 PROFESSIONAL

Volume II

Robert T. Grauer / Maryann Barber

University of Miami

Prentice Hall, Upper Saddle River, New Jersey 07458

Acquisitions Editor: Carolyn Henderson
Assistant Editor: Audrey Regan
Editorial Assistant: Lori Cardillo
Executive Marketing Manager: Nancy Evans
Editorial/Production Supervisor: Greg Hubit
Project Manager: Lynne Breitfeller
Senior Manufacturing Supervisor: Paul Smolenski
Manufacturing Coordinator: Lisa DiMaulo
Manufacturing Manager: Vincent Scelta
Senior Designer/Interior and Cover Design: Suzanne Behnke
Composition: GTS Graphics

ISBN 0-13-754250-X NB21

PRENTICE-HALL INTERNATIONAL (UK) LIMITED, *LONDON*
PRENTICE-HALL OF AUSTRALIA PTY. LIMITED, *SYDNEY*
PRENTICE-HALL CANADA INC., *TORONTO*
PRENTICE-HALL HISPANOAMERICANA, S.A., *MEXICO*
PRENTICE-HALL OF INDIA PRIVATE LIMITED, *NEW DELHI*
PRENTICE-HALL OF JAPAN, INC., *TOKYO*
PEARSON EDUCATION ASIA PTE. LTD., *SINGAPORE*
EDITORA PRENTICE-HALL DO BRASIL, LTDA., *RIO DE JANEIRO*

Printed in the United States of America

10   9   8   7   6   5

CONTENTS

EXPLORING MICROSOFT® WORD 97

1

Advanced Features: Outlines, Tables, Styles, and Sections   1

2

Desktop Publishing: Creating a Newsletter   55

3

Creating a Home Page: Introduction to HTML   91

EXPLORING MICROSOFT® EXCEL 97

1

List and Data Management: Converting Data to Information   1

2

Consolidating Data: 3-D Workbooks and File Linking   53

3

Automating Repetitive Tasks: Macros and Visual Basic   93

CHAPTER OBJECTIVES   93
OVERVIEW   93

Exploring Microsoft® Access 97

1

One-to-Many Relationships: Subforms and Multiple Table Queries   1

CHAPTER OBJECTIVES   1
OVERVIEW   1

2

Many-to-Many Relationships: A More Complex System   53

3

Building Applications: Introduction to Macros and Prototyping   115

Exploring Microsoft® PowerPoint 97

1

Enhancing a Presentation: The Web and Other Resources   1

Exploring Microsoft® Outlook 97: A Desktop Information Manager

To Marion, Benjy, Jessica, and Ellie

—Robert Grauer

To Frank, Jessica, and My Parents

—Maryann Barber

PREFACE

We are proud to announce the third edition of the *Exploring Windows* series in conjunction with the release of Microsoft Office 97. There is a separate book for each major application—*Word 97, Excel 97, Access 97,* and *PowerPoint 97*—as well as a book on Windows 95, and eventually, Windows 98. There are also two combined texts, *Exploring Microsoft Office 97 Professional, Volumes I* and *II. Volume I* contains the introductory chapters from each application, supplementary modules on Internet Explorer and Windows 95, and a PC Buying Guide. It is designed for the instructor who seeks to cover the basics of all Office applications in a single course, but who does not need the extensive coverage that is provided in the individual books. *Volume II* consists of the advanced chapters from each application and was developed for the rapidly emerging second course in PC applications. The complete set of titles appears on the back cover.

Each book in the *Exploring Windows* series is accompanied by an Instructor's Resource Manual with solutions to all exercises, PowerPoint lectures, and the printed version of our test bank. (The Instructor's Resource Manual is also available on a CD-ROM, which contains a Windows-based testing program.) Instructors can also use the Prentice Hall Computerized Online Testing System to prepare customized tests for their courses and may obtain Interactive Multimedia courseware as a further supplement.

The *Exploring Windows* series is part of the Prentice Hall custom binding program that enables you to create the ideal text by selecting various modules in *Office Volume I.* One could, for example, create a custom text consisting of the introductory (essential) chapters in Word, Excel, and the Internet Explorer at a substantial saving for the student. One can also take advantage of our ValuePack program to shrink-wrap multiple books together. If, for example, you are teaching a course that covers Excel and Access, and you want substantial coverage of both applications, a ValuePack results in significant saving for the student.

Exploring Microsoft Office 97 Volume II is a revision of our existing book on *Microsoft Office for Windows 95.* In addition to modifying the text to accommodate the new release, we have revised the end-of-chapter material to include a greater number of practice exercises and case studies. The many exercises provide substantial opportunity for students to master the material while simultaneously giving instructors considerable flexibility in student assignments. We have also included a section on Microsoft Outlook, a new application in Office 97.

Our most significant change, however, is the incorporation of the Internet and World Wide Web throughout the text. Students learn Office applications as before, and in addition are sent to the Web as appropriate for supplementary exercises. Students can download the practice files from the *Exploring Windows* home page (***www.prenhall.com/grauer***), which also contains additional practice exercises and case studies. The icon at the left of this paragraph appears throughout the text whenever there is a Web reference.

FEATURES AND BENEFITS

Chapter 3 in Word describes how to create a home page using tools that are built into Office 97. The student learns how to incorporate graphics and tables into a Web page and how to insert hyperlinks to other pages on the Web or on a corporate Intranet.

Chapter 2 in Word presents the basics of desktop publishing and its implementation in Microsoft Word. Students learn how to merge text with graphics to create professional-looking documents without reliance on external sources.

CREATING A HOME PAGE: INTRODUCTION TO HTML

3

OBJECTIVES

After reading this chapter you will be able to:

1. Define HTML and its role on the World Wide Web; describe HTML codes and explain how they control the appearance of a Web document.
2. Use Microsoft Word to create a home page; explain the role of the Save As command in creating an HTML document.
3. Use the Insert Hyperlink command to include hyperlinks in a Web page.
4. Explain how to view the HTML source code of a document from within Microsoft Word; modify the document by changing its source code.
5. Download one or more graphics from the Web, then include those graphics in a Web document.
6. Describe the additional steps needed to place your home page on the Web so that it can be viewed by others.
7. Describe the potential benefits of an Intranet to an organization.

OVERVIEW

Sooner or later anyone who cruises the World Wide Web wants to create a *home page* of their own. That, in turn, requires a basic knowledge of *Hypertext Markup Language (HTML)*, the language in which all Web pages are written. An HTML document consists of text and graphics, together with a set of codes (or tags) that describe how the document is to appear when viewed in a Web browser such as Internet Explorer.

In the early days of the Web, anyone creating a home page had to learn each of these codes and enter it explicitly. Today, however, it's

91

The essence of *desktop publishing* is the merger of text with graphics to produce a professional-looking document without reliance on external services. Desktop publishing will save you time and money because you are doing the work yourself rather than sending it out as you did in traditional publishing. That is the good news. The bad news is that desktop publishing is not as easy as it sounds, precisely because you are doing work that was done previously by skilled professionals. Nevertheless, with a little practice, and a basic knowledge of graphic design, which we include in this chapter, you will be able to create effective and attractive documents.

Our discussion focuses on desktop publishing as it is implemented in Microsoft Word. We show you how to design a multicolumn document, how to import clip art and other objects, and how to position those objects within a document. The chapter also reviews material from earlier chapters on bullets and lists, borders and shading, and section formatting, all of which will be used to create a newsletter.

THE NEWSLETTER

The chapter is built around the newsletter in Figure 2.1. The newsletter itself describes the basics of desktop publishing and provides an overview of the chapter. The material is presented conceptually, after which you implement the design in two hands-on exercises. We provide the text and you do the formatting. The first exercise creates a simple newsletter from copy that we provide. The second exercise uses more sophisticated formatting as described by the various techniques mentioned within the newsletter. Many of the terms are new, and we define them briefly in the next few paragraphs.

A *reverse* (light text on a dark background) is a favorite technique of desktop publishers to emphasize a specific element. It is used in the *masthead* (the identifying information) at the top of the newsletter and provides a distinctive look to the publication. The number of the newsletter and the date of publication also appear in the masthead in smaller letters.

A *pull quote* is a phrase or sentence taken from an article to emphasize a key point. It is typically set in larger type, often in a different typeface and/or italics, and may be offset with parallel lines at the top and bottom.

A *dropped-capital letter* is a large capital letter at the beginning of a paragraph. It, too, catches the reader's eye and calls attention to the associated text.

Clip art, used in moderation, will catch the reader's eye and enhance almost any newsletter. It is available from a variety of sources including the *Microsoft Clip Gallery*, which is included in Office 97. Clip art can also be downloaded from the Web, but be sure you are allowed to reprint the image.

Borders and shading are effective individually, or in combination with one another, to emphasize important stories within the newsletter. Simple vertical and/or horizontal lines are also effective. The techniques are especially useful in the absence of clip art or other graphics and are a favorite of desktop publishers.

Lists, whether bulleted or numbered, help to organize information by emphasizing important topics. A *bulleted list* emphasizes (and separates) the items. A *numbered list* sequences (and prioritizes) the items and is automatically updated to accommodate additions or deletions.

All of these techniques can be implemented with commands you already know, as you will see in the hands-on exercise, which follows shortly.

Creating a Newsletter

Volume I, Number 1   Spring 1997

Desktop publishing is easy, but there are several points to remember. This chapter will take you through the steps in creating a newsletter. The first hands-on exercise creates a simple newsletter with a masthead and three-column design. The second exercise creates a more attractive document by exploring different ways to emphasize the text.

Clip Art and Other Objects
Clip art is available from a variety of sources. You can also use other types of objects such as maps, charts, or organization charts, which are created by other applications, then brought into a document through the Insert Object command. A single dominant graphic is usually more appealing than multiple smaller graphics.

Techniques to Consider
Our finished newsletter contains one or more examples of each of the following desktop publishing techniques. Can you find where each technique is used, and further, implement how to implement that technique in Microsoft Word?
1. Pull Quotes
2. Reverse
3. Drop Caps
4. Tables
5. Styles
6. Bullets and Numbering
7. Borders and Shading

Newspaper-Style Columns
The essence of a newsletter is the implementation of columns in which text flows continuously from the bottom of one column to the top of the next. You specify the number of columns, and optionally, the space between columns. Microsoft Word does the rest. It will compute the width of each column based on the number of columns and the margins.

Beginners often specify margins that are too large and implement too much space between columns. Another way to achieve a more sophisticated look is to avoid the standard two-column design. You can implement columns of varying width and/or insert vertical lines between the columns.

The number of columns will vary in different parts of a document. The masthead is typically a single column, but the body of the newsletter will have two or three. Remember, too, that columns are implemented at the section level and hence, section breaks are required throughout a document.

Typography
Typography is the process of selecting typefaces, type styles, and type sizes, and is a critical element in the success of any document. Type should reinforce the message and should be consistent with the information you want to convey. More is not better, especially in the case of too many typefaces and styles, which produce cluttered documents that impress no one. Try to limit yourself to a maximum of two typefaces per document, but choose multiple sizes and/or styles within those typefaces. Use boldface or italics for emphasis, but do so in moderation, because if you use too many different elements, the effect is lost.

> *A pull quote adds interest to a document while simultaneously emphasizing a key point. It is implemented by increasing the point size, changing to italics, centering the text, and displaying a top and bottom border on the paragraph.*

Use Styles as Appropriate
Styles were covered in the previous chapter, but that does not mean you cannot use them in conjunction with a newsletter. A style stores character and/or paragraph formatting and can be applied to multiple occurrences of the same element within a document. Change the style and you automatically change all text defined by that style. You can also use styles from one edition of your newsletter to the next to ensure consistency.

Borders and Shading
Borders and shading are effective individually or in combination with one another. Use a thin rule (one point or less) and light shading (five or ten percent) for best results. The techniques are especially useful in the absence of clip art or other graphics and are a favorite of desktop publishers.

FIGURE 2.1   The Newsletter

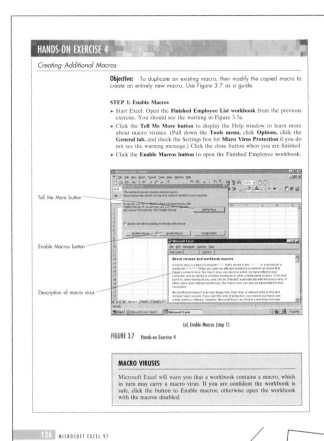

A total of 50 hands-on exercises guide the reader at the computer. The exercises are clearly illustrated with large, full-color screen captures and are accompanied by numerous tips for greater productivity. This exercise is from Chapter 3 in Excel, which introduces macros and Visual Basic for Applications (VBA).

You don't have to be an artist to use the drawing tools in Office 97. Chapter 1 in PowerPoint describes how to modify existing clip art to create new drawings to enliven your presentations.

FIGURE 1.3 What You Can Do with Clip Art

5. The compound document in Figure 1.19 is based on the completed workbook of problem 1. Do the problem (as described on page 46), then sort the list by major (and student name within major), so that you can use the Subtotals command to compute the average GPA for each major. Use OLE to create a compound document similar to the one in Figure 1.19. Enter your name as the academic advisor so that your instructor knows the assignment came from you.

University of Miami

Academic Advisement Office

To: James Foley
Associate Dean

From: Joan Rhyne
Academic Advisor

Subject: Grade Point Averages

Below please find the data that you requested. I have grouped the students by major and determined the average GPA for each major, as well as the average GPA for all students.

Last Name	First Name	Major	Quality Points	Credits	GPA
Flynn	Sean	Business	90	47	1.91
Grauer	Benjamin	Business	190	61	3.11
Moldof	Adam	Business	160	84	1.90
		Business Average			2.31
Fegin	Rick	Communications	193	64	3.02
		Communications Average			3.02
Flynn	Jimmy	Engineering	200	65	3.08
Ford	Judd	Engineering	206	72	2.86
Moldof	Alan	Engineering	60	20	3.00
Stutz	Joel	Engineering	180	75	2.40
		Engineering Average			2.83
Coulter	Maryann	Liberal Arts	135	54	2.50
Grauer	Jessica	Liberal Arts	96	28	3.43
Milgrom	Richard	Liberal Arts	400	117	3.42
Rudolph	Eleanor	Liberal Arts	185	95	1.95
		Liberal Arts Average			2.82
		Grand Average			2.72

I hope that you find this information useful. If you have any questions, please do not hesitate to let me know. It will be easy for me to determine almost any statistic that you may want.

FIGURE 1.19 Document for Practice Exercise 5

CASE STUDIES

The United States of America

What is the total population of the United States? What is its area? Can you name the 13 original states or the last five states admitted to the Union? Do you know the 10 states with the highest population or the five largest states in terms of area? Which states have the highest population density (people per square mile)?

The answers to these and other questions are readily available provided you can analyze the data in the *United States* workbook that is available on the data disk. This assignment is completely open-ended and requires only that you print out the extracted data in a report on the United States database. Format the reports so that they are attractive and informative.

The Super Bowl

How many times has the National Football Conference (NFC) won the Super Bowl? When was the last time the American Football Conference (AFC) won? What was the largest margin of victory? What was the closest game? What is the most points scored by two teams in one game? How many times have the Miami Dolphins appeared? How many times did they win? Use the data in the *Super Bowl* workbook to prepare a trivia sheet on the Super Bowl, then incorporate your analysis into a letter addressed to your instructor. Go to the NFL home page (www.nfl.com) to update our workbook to reflect the most recent game.

Personnel Management

You have been hired as the Personnel Director for a medium-sized firm (500 employees) and are expected to implement a system to track employee compensation. You want to be able to calculate the age of every employee as well as their length of service. You want to know each employee's most recent performance evaluation. You want to calculate the amount of the most recent salary increase, in dollars as well as a percentage of the previous salary. You also want to know how long the employee had to wait for that increase—that is, how much time elapsed between the present and previous salary.

Design a worksheet capable of providing this information. Enter test data for at least five employees to check the accuracy of your formulas. Format the worksheet so that it is attractive and easy to read.

Equal Employment Opportunity

Are you paying your employees fairly? Is there any difference between the salaries paid to men and women? Between minorities and nonminorities? Between minorities of one ethnic background and those of another ethnic background? Use the *Equal Employment* workbook on the data disk to analyze the data for the current employees. Are there any other factors not included in the database that might reasonably be expected to influence an employee's compensation? Write up your findings in the form of a memo to the Vice President for Human Resources.

Every chapter contains an abundant variety of thought-provoking exercises that review and extend the material. There are objective multiple-choice questions, guided computer exercises, and less-structured case studies. OLE and Web-based exercises appear throughout and are accompanied by distinguishing icons for ease of identification.

Microsoft Outlook is included as an additional application in Office 97 and is covered in its own section. Students learn the basic functions in Outlook, with emphasis on its e-mail capabilities.

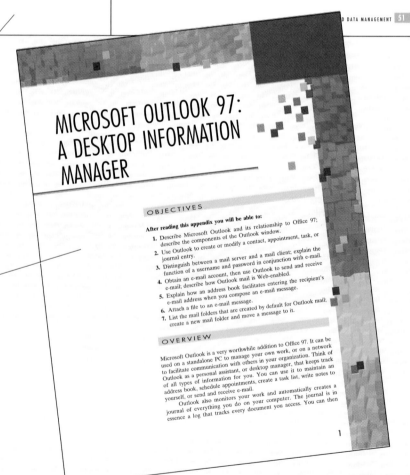

MICROSOFT OUTLOOK 97: A DESKTOP INFORMATION MANAGER

OBJECTIVES

After reading this appendix you will be able to:

1. Describe Microsoft Outlook and its relationship to Office 97; describe the components of the Outlook window.
2. Use Outlook to create or modify a contact, appointment, task, or journal entry.
3. Distinguish between a mail server and a mail client; explain the function of a username and password in conjunction with e-mail.
4. Obtain an e-mail account, then use Outlook to send and receive e-mail; describe how Outlook mail is Web-enabled.
5. Explain how an address book facilitates entering the recipient's e-mail address when you compose an e-mail message.
6. Attach a file to an e-mail message.
7. List the mail folders that are created by default for Outlook mail; create a new mail folder and move a message to it.

OVERVIEW

Microsoft Outlook is a very worthwhile addition to Office 97. It can be used on a standalone PC to manage your own work, or on a network to facilitate communication with others in your organization. Think of Outlook as a personal assistant, or desktop manager, that keeps track of all types of information for you. You can use it to maintain an address book, schedule appointments, create a task list, write notes to yourself, or send and receive e-mail.

Outlook also monitors your work and automatically creates a journal of everything you do on your computer. The journal is in essence a log that tracks every document you access. You can then

1

Chapter 3 in Access shows students how to develop a complete application through macros and prototyping. This "capstone" chapter is the ideal basis for a semester-long project as it enables students to develop realistic applications.

Database design is stressed throughout the Access chapters through a variety of case studies. Full-color illustrations clarify the relationships among tables by highlighting the primary and foreign keys within a database.

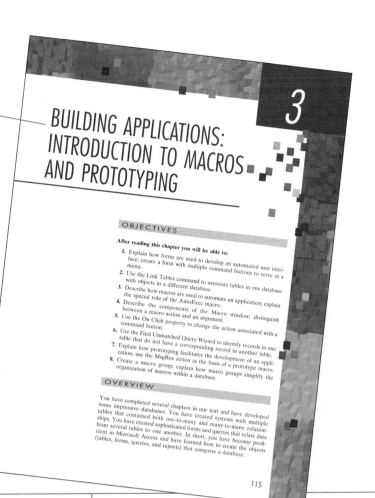

3

BUILDING APPLICATIONS: INTRODUCTION TO MACROS AND PROTOTYPING

OBJECTIVES

After reading this chapter you will be able to:

1. Explain how forms are used to develop an automated user interface; create a form with multiple command buttons to serve as a menu.
2. Use the Link Tables command to associate tables in one database with objects in a different database.
3. Describe how macros are used to automate an application; explain the special role of the AutoExec macro.
4. Describe the components of the Macro window; distinguish between a macro action and an argument.
5. Use the On Click property to change the action associated with a command button.
6. Use the Find Unmatched Query Wizard to identify records in one table that do not have a corresponding record in another table.
7. Explain how prototyping facilitates the development of an application; use the MsgBox action as the basis of a prototype macro.
8. Create a macro group; explain how macro groups simplify the organization of macros within a database.

OVERVIEW

You have completed several chapters in our text and have developed some impressive databases. You have created systems with multiple tables that contained both one-to-many and many-to-many relationships. You have created sophisticated forms and queries that relate data from several tables to one another. In short, you have become proficient in Microsoft Access and have learned how to create the objects (tables, forms, queries, and reports) that comprise a database.

115

---

forms created in this chapter are based on multiple table queries rather than tables. The queries themselves are of a more advanced nature. We show you how to create a parameter query, where the user is prompted to enter the criteria when the query is run. We also show you how to create queries that use the aggregate functions built into Access to perform calculations on groups of records.

The chapter contains four hands-on exercises to implement the case study. We think you will be pleased with what you have accomplished by the end of the chapter, working with a sophisticated system that is typical of real-world applications.

CASE STUDY: THE COMPUTER SUPER STORE

The case study in this chapter is set within the context of a computer store that requires a database for its customers, products, and orders. The store maintains the usual customer data (name, address, phone, etc.). It also keeps data about the products it sells, storing for each product a product ID, description, quantity on hand, quantity on order, and unit price. And finally, the store has to track its orders. It needs to know the date an order was received, the customer who placed it, the products that were ordered, and the quantity of each product ordered.

Think, for a moment, about the tables that are necessary and the relationships between those tables, then compare your thoughts to our solution in Figure 2.1. You probably have no trouble recognizing the need for the Customers, Products, and Orders tables. Initially, you may be puzzled by the Order Details table, but you will soon appreciate why it is there and how powerful it is.

You can use the Customers, Products, and Orders tables individually to obtain information about a specific customer, product, or order, respectively. For example:

Query: What is Jeffrey Muddell's phone number?
Answer: Jeffrey Muddell's phone is (305) 253-3909.

Query: What is the price of a Pentium laptop/133? How many are in stock?
Answer: A Pentium laptop/133 sells for $2,599. Fifteen systems are in stock.

Query: When was order O0003 placed?
Answer: Order O0003 was placed on April 18, 1997.

Other queries require you to relate the tables to one another. There is, for example, a *one-to-many relationship* between customers and orders. One customer can place many orders, but a specific order can be associated with only one customer. The tables are related through the CustomerID, which appears as the *primary key* in the Customers table and as a *foreign key* in the Orders table. Consider:

Query: What is the name of the customer who placed order number O0003?
Answer: Order O0003 was placed by Jeffrey Muddell.

Query: How many orders were placed by Jeffrey Muddell?
Answer: Jeffrey Muddell placed five orders: O0003, O0014, O0016, O0024, and O0025.

These queries require you to use two tables. To answer the first query, you would search the Orders table to find order O0003 and obtain the CustomerID (C0006 in this example). You would then search the Customers table for the customer with this CustomerID and retrieve the customer's name. To answer the

---

Customer ID	First Name	Last Name	Address	City	State	Zip Code	Phone Number
C0001	Benjamin	Lee	1000 Call Street	Tallahassee	FL	33340	(904) 327-4124
C0002	Eleanor	Milgrom	7245 NW 8 Street	Margate	FL	33065	(305) 974-1234
C0003	Neil	Goodman	4215 South 81 Street	Margate	FL	33065	(305) 444-5555
C0004	Nicholas	Colon	9020 N.W. 76 Street	Coral Springs	FL	33065	(305) 753-9987
C0005	Michael	Ware	276 Brickell Avenue	Miami	FL	33131	(305) 444-3980
C0006	Jeffrey	Muddell	9522 S.W. 142 Street	Miami	FL	33176	(305) 253-3909
C0007	Ashley	Geoghegan	7500 Center Lane	Coral Springs	FL	33070	(305) 753-7830
C0008	Serena	Sherard	5000 Jefferson Lane	Gainesville	FL	32601	(904) 375-6442
C0009	Luis	Couto	455 Bargello Avenue	Coral Gables	FL	33146	(305) 666-4801
C0010	Derek	Anderson	6000 Tigertail Avenue	Coconut Grove	FL	33120	(305) 446-8900
C0011	Lauren	Center	12380 S.W. 137 Avenue	Miami	FL	33186	(305) 385-4432
C0012	Robert	Slane	4508 N.W. 7 Street	Miami	FL	33131	(305) 635-3454

(a) Customers Table

Product ID	Product Name	Units In Stock	Units On Order	Unit Price
P0001	Pentium desktop/166 with MMX	50	0	$1,895.00
P0002	Pentium desktop/200 with MMX	25	5	$1,999.00
P0003	Pentium Pro desktop/180	125	15	$2,090.00
P0004	Pentium Pro desktop/200	25	50	$2,299.00
P0005	Pentium laptop/133	15	25	$2,599.00
P0006	15" SVGA Monitor	50	0	$499.00
P0007	17" SVGA Monitor	25	10	$899.00
P0008	20" Multisync Monitor	50	20	$1,599.00
P0009	2.5 Gb SCSI Hard Drive	15	20	$399.00
P0010	2 Gb SCSI Hard Drive	25	15	$799.00
P0011	4 Gb SCSI Hard Drive	10	0	$1,245.00
P0012	CD-ROM 8X	40	0	$249.00
P0013	CD-ROM 12X	50	15	$449.95
P0014	HD Floppy Disks	500	200	$9.99
P0015	1/8 Data Cartridges	100	50	$14.79
P0016	2 Gb Tape Backup	15	8	$179.95
P0017	Serial Mouse	150	50	$69.95
P0018	Trackball	55	0	$59.95
P0019	Joystick	250	100	$39.95
P0020	FaxModem 56 Kbps	36	10	$189.95
P0021	FaxModem 33.6 Kbps	20	0	$65.95
P0022	Laser Printer	100	15	$1,395.00
P0023	Ink Jet Printer	50	50	$249.95
P0024	Color Ink Jet Printer	125	25	$569.95
P0025	Windows 95	400	200	$95.95
P0026	Norton Anti-Virus	150	50	$75.95
P0027	Norton Utilities	150	50	$115.95
P0028	Microsoft Screen Saver	75	25	$29.95
P0029	Microsoft Bookshelf	250	100	$129.95
P0030	Microsoft Cinemania	25	10	$59.95
P0031	Professional Photos on CD-ROM	15	0	$45.95

(b) Products Table

Order ID	Customer ID	Order Date
O0001	C0004	4/15/97
O0002	C0003	4/18/97
O0003	C0006	4/18/97
O0004	C0007	4/18/97
O0005	C0001	4/20/97
O0006	C0001	4/21/97
O0007	C0001	4/21/97
O0008	C0002	4/22/97
O0009	C0003	4/22/97
O0010	C0002	4/23/97
O0011	C0001	4/24/97
O0012	C0007	4/24/97
O0013	C0004	4/24/97
O0014	C0006	4/25/97
O0015	C0009	4/26/97
O0016	C0006	4/26/97
O0017	C0011	4/26/97
O0018	C0011	4/26/97
O0019	C0012	4/27/97
O0020	C0010	4/28/97
O0021	C0010	4/29/97
O0022	C0008	4/30/97
O0023	C0008	4/30/97
O0024	C0006	5/1/97
O0025	C0006	5/1/97

(c) Orders Table

Order ID	Product ID	Quantity
O0001	P0013	1
O0001	P0014	4
O0001	P0027	1
O0002	P0001	1
O0002	P0006	1
O0002	P0020	1
O0002	P0022	1
O0003	P0005	1
O0003	P0020	1
O0003	P0022	1
O0003	P0003	1
O0004	P0010	1
O0004	P0022	2
O0004	P0003	1
O0005	P0016	2
O0005	P0007	1
O0006	P0014	10
O0007	P0028	1
O0007	P0030	3
O0008	P0001	1
O0008	P0004	3
O0008	P0008	4
O0008	P0011	2
O0008	P0012	1
O0009	P0006	1
O0010	P0002	2
O0010	P0022	1
O0011	P0016	2
O0011	P0020	2
O0012	P0021	10
O0012	P0029	10
O0012	P0030	10
O0013	P0009	4
O0013	P0016	10
O0014	P0024	2
O0014	P0019	2
O0015	P0018	1
O0015	P0020	1
O0016	P0029	2
O0017	P0019	2
O0017	P0009	1
O0018	P0025	2
O0019	P0026	1
O0019	P0014	25
O0020	P0024	1
O0021	P0004	1
O0022	P0027	1
O0023	P0021	2
O0023	P0029	1
O0024	P0007	1
O0024	P0013	5
O0024	P0014	3
O0024	P0016	1
O0025	P0012	2
O0025	P0029	2

(d) Order Details Table

FIGURE 2.1 Super Store Database

Acknowledgments

We want to thank the many individuals who helped bring this project to fruition. We are especially grateful to our editor at Prentice Hall, Carolyn Henderson, without whom the series would not have been possible. Cecil Yarbrough and Susan Hoffman did an outstanding job in checking the manuscript and proofs for technical accuracy. Suzanne Behnke developed the innovative and attractive design. John DeLara and David Nusspickel were responsible for our Web site. Carlotta Eaton of Radford University and Karen Vignare of Alfred University wrote the instructor manuals, and Dave Moles produced the CD. Paul Smolenski was manufacturing supervisor. Lynne Breitfeller was project manager. Greg Hubit was in charge of production and kept the project on target from beginning to end. Nancy Evans, our marketing manager at Prentice Hall, developed the innovative campaigns, which made the series a success. Lori Cardillo, editorial assistant at Prentice Hall, helped in ways too numerous to mention. We also want to acknowledge our reviewers who, through their comments and constructive criticism, greatly improved the *Exploring Windows* series.

Lynne Band, Middlesex Community College
Stuart P. Brian, Holy Family College
Carl M. Briggs, Indiana University School of Business
Kimberly Chambers, Scottsdale Community College
Alok Charturvedi, Purdue University
Jerry Chin, Southwest Missouri State University
Dean Combellick, Scottsdale Community College
Cody Copeland, Johnson County Community College
Larry S. Corman, Fort Lewis College
Janis Cox, Tri-County Technical College
Martin Crossland, Southwest Missouri State University
Paul E. Daurelle, Western Piedmont Community College
David Douglas, University of Arkansas
Carlotta Eaton, New River Community College
Raymond Frost, Central Connecticut State University
James Gips, Boston College
Vernon Griffin, Austin Community College
Michael Hassett, Fort Hays State University
Wanda D. Heller, Seminole Community College
Bonnie Homan, San Francisco State University
Ernie Ivey, Polk Community College
Mike Kelly, Community College of Rhode Island
Jane King, Everett Community College
John Lesson, University of Central Florida

David B. Meinert, Southwest Missouri State University
Bill Morse, DeVry Institute of Technology
Alan Moltz, Naugatuck Valley Technical Community College
Kim Montney, Kellogg Community College
Kevin Pauli, University of Nebraska
Mary McKenry Percival, University of Miami
Delores Pusins, Hillsborough Community College
Gale E. Rand, College Misericordia
Judith Rice, Santa Fe Community College
David Rinehard, Lansing Community College
Marilyn Salas, Scottsdale Community College
John Shepherd, Duquesne University
Helen Stoloff, Hudson Valley Community College
Margaret Thomas, Ohio University
Mike Thomas, Indiana University School of Business
Suzanne Tomlinson, Iowa State University
Karen Tracey, Central Connecticut State University
Karen Vignare, Alfred State College
Sally Visci, Lorain County Community College
David Weiner, University of San Francisco
Connie Wells, Georgia State University
Wallace John Whistance-Smith, Ryerson Polytechnic University
Jack Zeller, Kirkwood Community College

A final word of thanks to the unnamed students at the University of Miami, who make it all worthwhile. And most of all, thanks to you, our readers, for choosing this book. Please feel free to contact us with any comments and suggestions.

Robert T. Grauer
rgrauer@umiami.miami.edu
www.bus.miami.edu/~rgrauer
www.prenhall.com/grauer

Maryann Barber
mbarber@homer.bus.miami.edu
www.bus.miami.edu/~mbarber

MICROSOFT OFFICE 97: SIX APPLICATIONS IN ONE

OVERVIEW

Word processing, spreadsheets, and data management have always been significant microcomputer applications. The early days of the PC saw these applications emerge from different vendors with radically different user interfaces. WordPerfect, Lotus, and dBASE, for example, were dominant applications in their respective areas, and each was developed by a different company. The applications were totally dissimilar, and knowledge of one did not help in learning another.

The widespread acceptance of Windows 3.1 promoted the concept of a common user interface, which required all applications to follow a consistent set of conventions. This meant that all applications worked essentially the same way, and it provided a sense of familiarity when you learned a new application, since every application presented the same user interface. The development of a suite of applications from a single vendor extended this concept by imposing additional similarities on all applications within the suite.

This introduction will acquaint you with *Microsoft Office 97* and its four major applications—*Word, Excel, PowerPoint,* and *Access.* The single biggest difference between Office 97 and its predecessor, Office 95, is that the Internet has become an integral part of the Office suite. Thus, we also discuss *Internet Explorer,* the Web browser included in Office 97, and *Microsoft Outlook,* the e-mail and scheduling program that is built into Office 97. The icon at the left of this paragraph appears throughout the text to highlight references to the Internet and enhance your use of Microsoft Office. Our introduction also includes the Clip Gallery, WordArt, and Office Art, three tools built into Microsoft Office that help you to add interest to your documents. And finally, we discuss Object Linking and Embedding, which enables you to combine data from multiple applications into a single document.

Our primary purpose in this introduction is to emphasize the similarities between the applications in Office 97 and to help you transfer your knowledge from one application to the next. You will find the same commands in the same menus. You will also recognize familiar toolbars and will be able to take advantage of similar keyboard shortcuts. You will learn that help can be obtained in a variety of ways, and that it is consistent in every application. Our goal is to show you how much you already know and to get you up and running as quickly as possible.

TRY THE COLLEGE BOOKSTORE

Any machine you buy will come with Windows 95 (or Windows 97), but that is only the beginning since you must also obtain the application software you intend to run. Some hardware vendors will bundle (at no additional cost) Microsoft Office as an inducement to buy from them. If you have already purchased your system and you need software, the best place to buy Microsoft Office is the college bookstore, where it can be obtained at a substantial educational discount.

MICROSOFT OFFICE 97

All Office applications share the ***common Windows interface*** with which you may already be familiar. (If you are new to Windows 95, then read the appendix on the "Essentials of Windows.") Microsoft Office 97 runs equally well under Windows 95, Windows 97, or Windows NT.

Figure 1 displays a screen from each major application in Microsoft Office—Word, Excel, PowerPoint, and Access. Our figure also includes screens from Internet Explorer and Microsoft Outlook, both of which are part of Office 97. Look closely at Figure 1, and realize that each screen contains both an application window and a document window, and that each document window has been maximized within the application window. The title bars of the application and document windows have been merged into a single title bar that appears at the top of the application window. The title bar displays the application (e.g., Microsoft Word in Figure 1a) as well as the name of the document (Web Enabled in Figure 1a) on which you are working.

All six screens in Figure 1 are similar in appearance even though the applications accomplish very different tasks. Each application window has an identifying icon, a menu bar, a title bar, and a minimize, maximize or restore, and a close button. Each document window has its own identifying icon, and its own minimize, maximize or restore, and close button. The Windows taskbar appears at the bottom of each application window and shows the open applications. The status bar appears above the taskbar and displays information relevant to the window or selected object.

Each major application in Microsoft Office uses a consistent command structure in which the same basic menus are found in all applications. The File, Edit, View, Insert, Tools, Window, and Help menus are present in all six applications. The same commands are found in the same menus. The Save, Open, Print, and Exit commands, for example, are contained in the File menu. The Cut, Copy, Paste, and Undo commands are found in the Edit menu.

The means for accessing the pull-down menus are consistent from one application to the next. Click the menu name on the menu bar, or press the Alt key plus the underlined letter of the menu name; for example, press Alt+F to pull down the File menu. If you already know some keyboard shortcuts in one application, there is a good chance that the shortcuts will work in another application. Ctrl+Home and Ctrl+End, for example, move to the beginning and end of a document, respectively. Ctrl+B, Ctrl+I, and Ctrl+U boldface, italicize, and underline text. Ctrl+X (the "X" is supposed to remind you of a pair of scissors), Ctrl+C, and Ctrl+V will cut, copy, and paste, respectively.

Title bar

Identifying icon

Menu bar

Standard toolbar

Formatting toolbar

Minimize button

Restore button

Close button

Status bar

Task bar

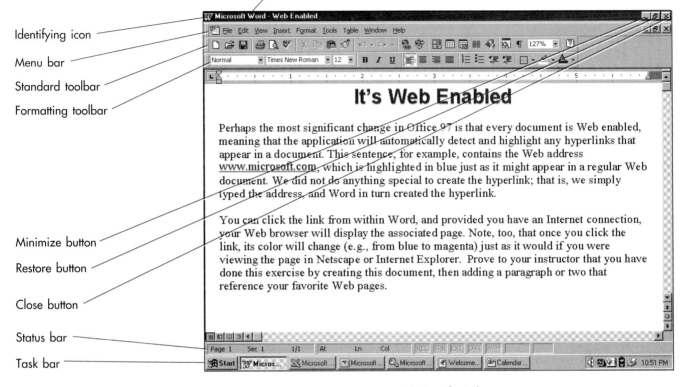

(a) Microsoft Word

Title bar

Identifying icon

Menu bar

Standard toolbar

Formatting toolbar

Minimize button

Restore button

Close button

Status bar

Task bar

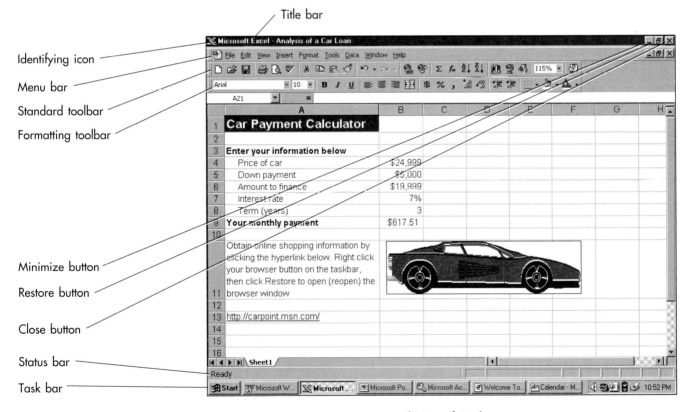

(b) Microsoft Excel

FIGURE 1   The Common User Interface

Title bar

Identifying icon

Menu bar

Standard toolbar

Formatting toolbar

Minimize button

Restore button

Close button

Status bar

Task bar

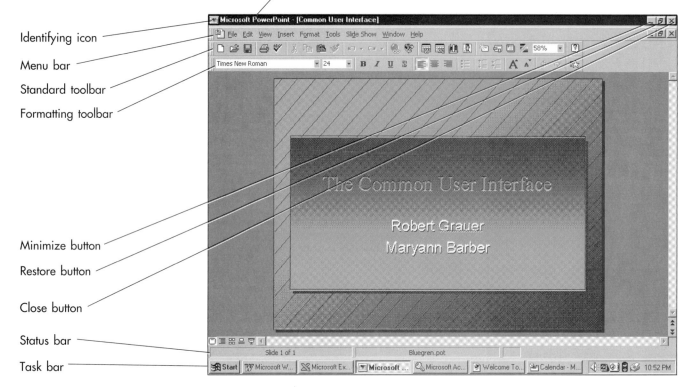

(c) Microsoft PowerPoint

Title bar

Identifying icon

Menu bar

Toolbar

Minimize button

Restore button

Close button

Status bar

Task bar

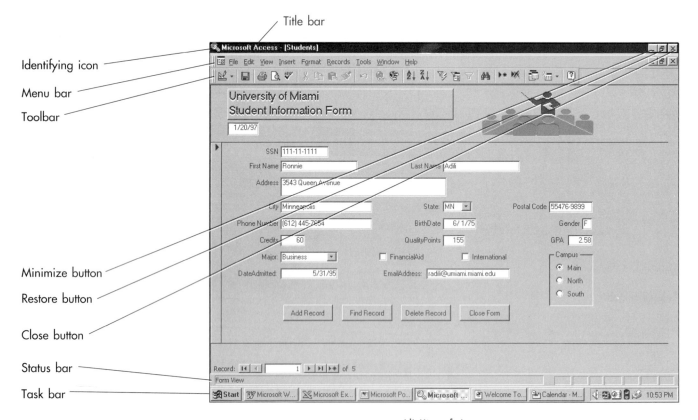

(d) Microsoft Access

FIGURE 1   The Common User Interface (continued)

Title bar

Identifying icon

Menu bar

Toolbar

Minimize button

Restore button

Close button

Status bar

Task bar

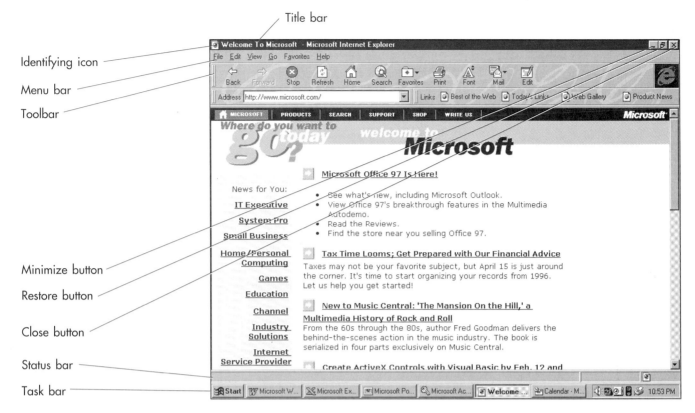

(e) Internet Explorer

Title bar

Identifying icon

Menu bar

Toolbar

Minimize button

Restore button

Close button

Status bar

Task bar

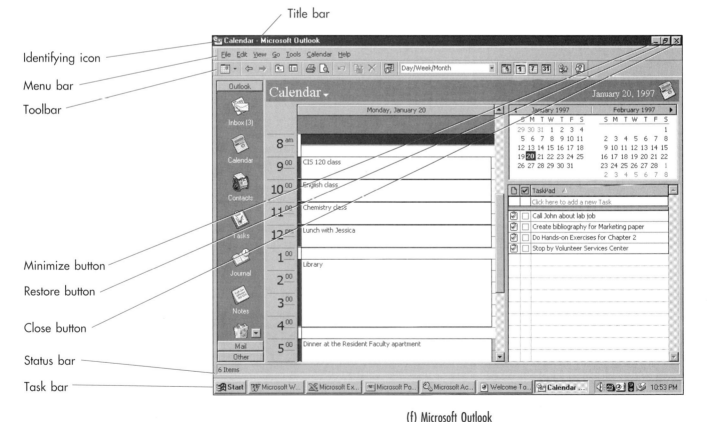

(f) Microsoft Outlook

FIGURE 1   The Common User Interface (continued)

The four major applications use consistent (and often identical) dialog boxes. The dialog boxes to open and close a file, for example, are identical in every application. All four applications also share a common dictionary. The AutoCorrect feature (to correct common spelling mistakes) works identically in all four applications. The help feature also functions identically.

There are, of course, differences between the applications. Each application has unique menus and toolbars. Nevertheless, the Standard and Formatting toolbars in the major applications contain many of the same tools (especially the first several tools on the left of each toolbar). The *Standard toolbar* contains buttons for basic commands such as Open, Save, or Print. It also contains buttons to cut, copy, and paste, and these buttons are identical in all four applications. The *Formatting toolbar* provides access to common operations such as boldface or italics, or changing the font or point size; again, these buttons are identical in all four applications. ScreenTips are present in all applications.

STANDARD OFFICE VERSUS OFFICE PROFESSIONAL

Microsoft distributes both a Standard and a Professional edition of Office 97. Both versions include Word, Excel, PowerPoint, Internet Explorer, and Outlook. Office Professional also has Microsoft Access. The difference is important when you are shopping and you are comparing prices from different sources. Be sure to purchase the version that is appropriate for your needs.

Help for Office 97

Several types of help are available in Office 97. The most basic is accessed by pulling down the Help menu and clicking the Contents and Index command to display the Help Contents window as shown in Figures 2a and 2b. (The Help screens are from Microsoft Word, but similar screens are available for each of the other applications.) The *Contents tab* in Figure 2a is analogous to the table of contents in an ordinary book. It displays the major topics in the application as a series of books that are open or closed. You can click any closed book to open it, which in turn displays additional books and/or help topics. Conversely, you can click any open book to close it and gain additional space on the screen.

The *Index tab* in Figure 2b is similar to the index of an ordinary book. Enter the first several letters of the topic to look up, such as "we" in Figure 2b. Help then returns all of the topics beginning with the letters you entered. Select the topic you want, then display the topic for immediate viewing, or print it for later reference. (The Find tab, not shown in Figure 2, contains a more extensive listing of entries than does the Index tab. It lets you enter a specific word, then it returns every topic that contains that word.)

The *Office Assistant* in Figure 2c is new to Office 97 and is activated by clicking the Office Assistant button on the Standard toolbar or by pressing the F1 function key. The Assistant enables you to ask a question in English, then it returns a series of topics that attempt to answer your question.

Additional help can be obtained from the Microsoft Web site as shown in Figure 2d, provided you have access to the Internet. The easiest way to access the site is to pull down the Help menu from any Office application, click Microsoft on the Web, then click Online Support. This, in turn, will start the Internet Explorer and take you to the appropriate page on the Web, where you will find the most current information available as well as the most detailed support. You can, for example, access the same knowledge base as that used by Microsoft support engineers when you call for technical assistance.

Topic may be viewed or printed by clicking appropriate command button

Double click closed book to open it and display additional help topics

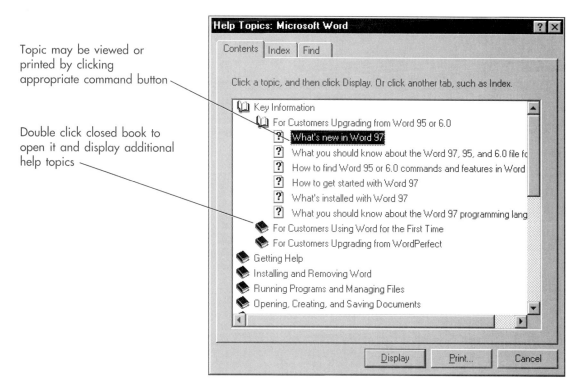

(a) Contents Tab

Type the first few letters in the topic to look up

Select the desired topic

Click Display button to view the information

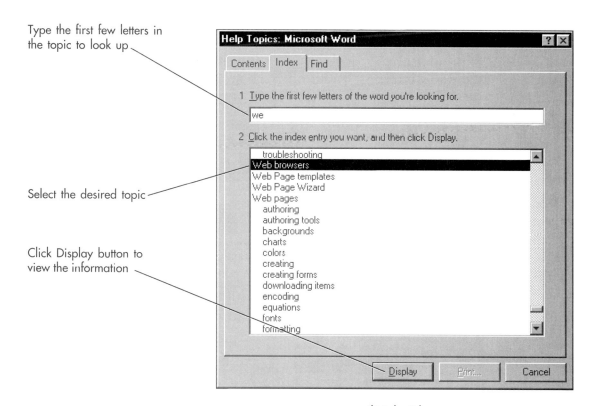

(b) Index Tab

FIGURE 2 Help with Microsoft Office

Help screen contains links
to additional information

Click any topic to display
the help screen

Enter your question, then
click the Search button

Office Assistant (other images
are available)

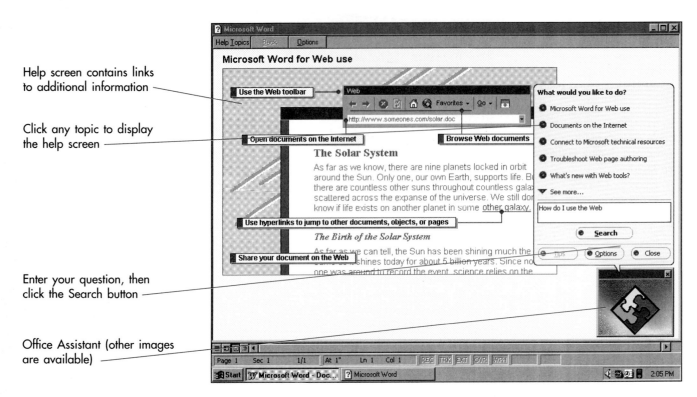

(c) The Office Assistant

Internet Explorer
opens automatically

Web address

Link to Frequently
Asked Questions

Click the link to
desired information

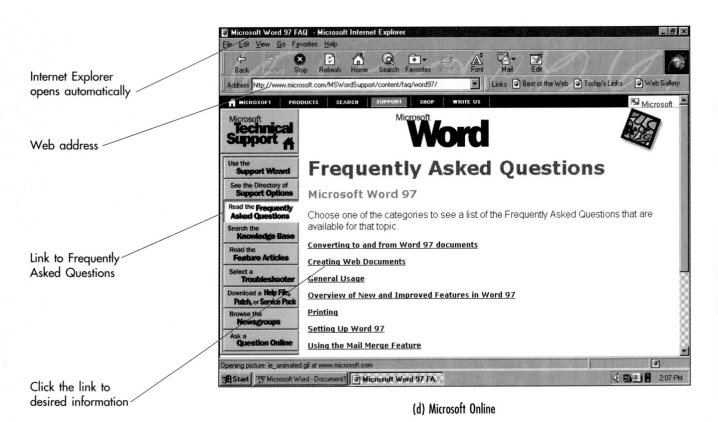

(d) Microsoft Online

FIGURE 2   Help with Microsoft Office (continued)

Office Shortcut Bar

The **Microsoft Office Shortcut Bar** provides immediate access to each application within Microsoft Office. It consists of a row of buttons and can be placed anywhere on the screen. The Shortcut Bar is anchored by default on the right side of the desktop, but you can position it along any edge, or have it "float" in the middle of the desktop. You can even hide it from view when it is not in use.

Figure 3a displays the Shortcut Bar as it appears on our desktop. The buttons that are displayed (and the order in which they appear) are established through the Customize dialog box in Figure 3b. Our Shortcut Bar contains a button for each Office application, a button for the Windows Explorer, and a button for Bookshelf Basics.

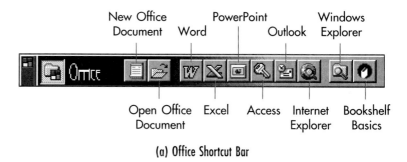

(a) Office Shortcut Bar

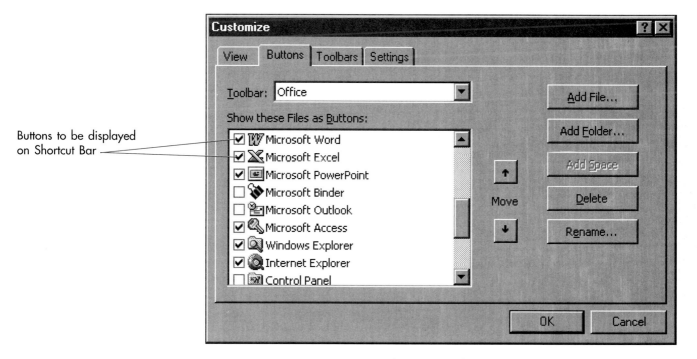

(b) Customize Dialog Box

FIGURE 3   Microsoft Office Shortcut Bar

Docucentric Orientation

Our Shortcut Bar contains two additional buttons: to open an existing document and to start a new document. These buttons are very useful and take advantage of the "docucentric" orientation of Microsoft Office, which lets you think in terms

Selected folder

Double click document name to open it

List of files in the folder

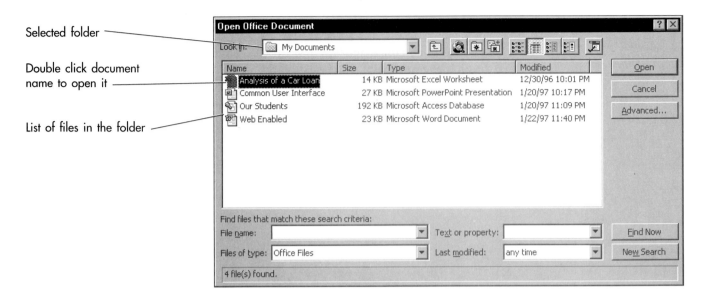

(a) Open an Existing Document

Letters & Faxes tab

Double click template name to open it

Details button

Preview of template

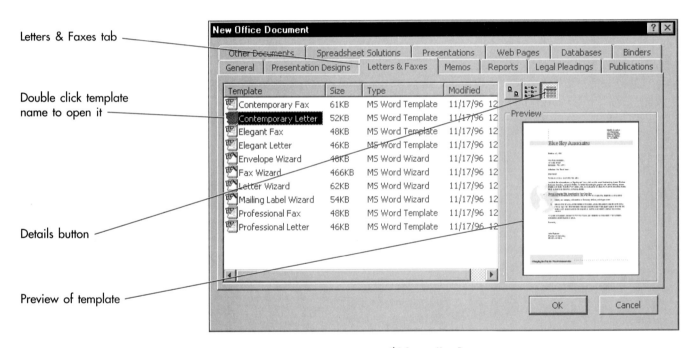

(b) Start a New Document

FIGURE 4   Document Orientation

of a document rather than the associated application. You can still open a document in traditional fashion, by starting the application (e.g., clicking its button on the Shortcut Bar), then using the File Open command to open the document. It's easier, however, to locate the document, then double click its icon, which automatically loads the associated program.

Consider, for example, the Open dialog box in Figure 4a, which is displayed by clicking the Open a Document button on the Shortcut Bar. The Open dialog box is common to the major Office applications, and it works identically in each application. The My Documents folder is selected in Figure 4a, and it contains four documents of various file types. The documents are displayed in the Details view, which shows the document name, size, file type, and date and time the document was last modified. To open any document—for example, "Analysis of a Car Loan"—just double click its name or icon. The associated application (Microsoft Excel in this example) will be started automatically; and it, in turn, will open the selected workbook.

The "docucentric" orientation also applies to new documents. Click the Start a New Document button on the Office Shortcut Bar, and you display the New dialog box in Figure 4b. Click the tab corresponding to the type of document you want to create, such as Letters & Faxes in Figure 4b. Change to the Details view, then click (select) various templates so that you can choose the one most appropriate for your purpose. Double click the desired template to start the application, which opens the template and enables you to create the document.

CHANGE THE VIEW

The toolbar in the Open dialog box contains buttons to display the documents within the selected folder in one of several views. Click the Details button to switch to the Details view and see the date and time the file was last modified, as well as its size and type. Click the List button to display an icon representing the associated application, enabling you to see many more files than in the Details view. The Preview button lets you see a document before you open it. The Properties button displays information about the document, including the number of revisions.

SHARED APPLICATIONS AND UTILITIES

Microsoft Office includes additional applications and shared utilities, several of which are illustrated in Figure 5. The **Microsoft Clip Gallery** in Figure 5a has more than 3,000 clip art images and almost 150 photographs, each in a variety of categories. It also contains a lesser number of sound files and video clips. The Clip Gallery can be accessed from every Office application, most easily through the Insert Picture command, which displays the Clip Gallery dialog box.

The **Microsoft WordArt** utility adds decorative text to a document, and is accessed through the Insert Picture command from Word, Excel, or PowerPoint. WordArt is intuitive and easy to use. In essence, you choose a style for the text from among the selections in the dialog box of Figure 5b, then you enter the specific text in a second dialog box (which is not shown in Figure 5). It's fun, it's easy, and you can create some truly dynamite documents that will add interest to a document.

Office Art consists of a set of drawing tools that is found on the Drawing toolbar in Word, Excel, or PowerPoint. You don't have to be an artist—all it takes is a little imagination and an appreciation for what the individual tools can do. In Figure 5c, for example, we began with a single clip art image, copied it several times within the PowerPoint slide, then rotated and colored the students as shown. We also used the AutoShapes tool to add a callout for our student.

Microsoft Bookshelf Basics contains three of the nine books available in the complete version of Microsoft Bookshelf (which is an additional cost item). The *American Heritage Dictionary,* the *Original Roget's Thesaurus,* and the *Columbia Dictionary of Quotations* are provided at no charge. An excerpt from the *American Heritage Dictionary* is illustrated in Figure 5d. Enter the word you are looking for in the text box on the left, then read the definition on the right. You can click the sound icon and hear the pronunciation of the word.

Choose the type of object

Choose the category

Choose the image

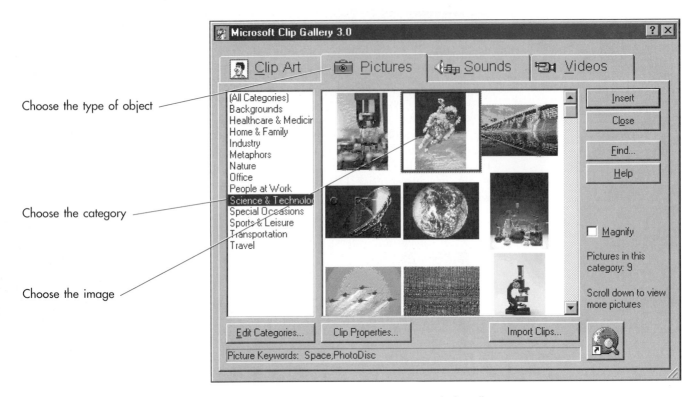

(a) Microsoft Clip Gallery

Select the style to display a second dialog box in which you enter your text

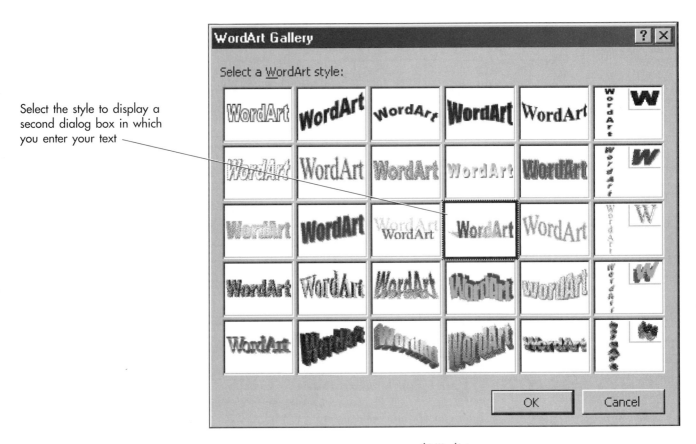

(b) WordArt

FIGURE 5   Shared Applications

Color objects in clip art

Create callout

Callout tool

Drawing toolbar

(c) Office Art

Enter word

Click to
hear pronunciation

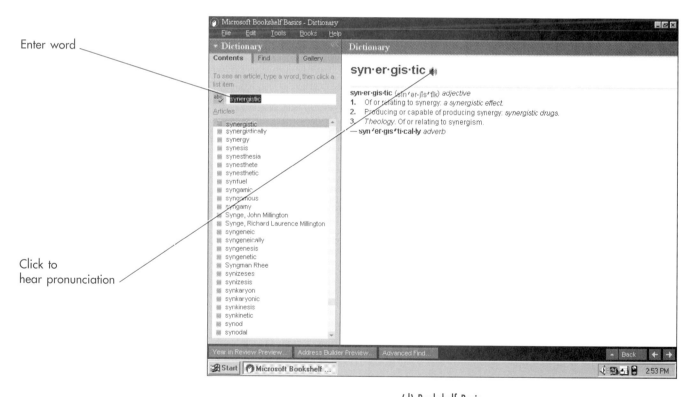

(d) Bookshelf Basics

FIGURE 5   Shared Applications (continued)

OBJECT LINKING AND EMBEDDING

The applications in Microsoft Office are thoroughly integrated with one another. They look alike and they work in consistent fashion. Equally important, they share information through a technology known as ***Object Linking and Embedding (OLE),*** which enables you to create a ***compound document*** containing data (objects) from multiple applications.

The compound document in Figure 6 was created in Word, and it contains objects (a worksheet and a chart) that were created in Excel. The letterhead uses a logo that was taken from the Clip Gallery, while the name and address of the recipient were drawn from an Access database. The various objects were inserted into the compound document through linking or embedding, which are actually two very different techniques. Both operations, however, are much more sophisticated than simply pasting an object, because with either linking or embedding, you can edit the object by using the tools of the original application.

The difference between linking and embedding depends on whether the object is stored within the compound document (***embedding***) or in its own file (***linking***). An *embedded object* is stored in the compound document, which in turn becomes the only user (client) of that object. A *linked object* is stored in its own file, and the compound document is one of many potential clients of that object. The compound document does not contain the linked object per se, but only a representation of the object as well as a pointer (link) to the file containing the object. The advantage of linking is that the document is updated automatically if the object changes.

The choice between linking and embedding depends on how the object will be used. Linking is preferable if the object is likely to change and the compound document requires the latest version. Linking should also be used when the same object is placed in many documents so that any change to the object has to be made in only one place. Embedding should be used if you need to take the object with you (to a different computer) and/or if there is only a single destination document for the object.

Office of Residential Living

University of Miami • P.O. Box 248904 • Coral Gables, FL 33124

January 10, 1998

Mr. Jeffrey Redmond, President
Dynamic Dining Services
4329 Palmetto Lane
Miami, FL 33157

Dear Jeff,

As per our conversation, occupancy is projected to be back up from last year. I have enclosed a spreadsheet and chart that show the total enrollment for the past four school years. Please realize, however, that the 1997–1998 figures are projections, as the Spring 1998 numbers are still incomplete. The final 1997–1998 numbers should be confirmed within the next two weeks. I hope that this helps with your planning. If you need further information, please contact me at the above address.

Dorm Occupancy				
	94-95	95-96	96-97	97-98
Beatty	330	285	270	250
Broward	620	580	620	565
Graham	450	397	352	420
Rawlings	435	470	295	372
Tolbert	550	554	524	635
Totals	2385	2286	2061	2242

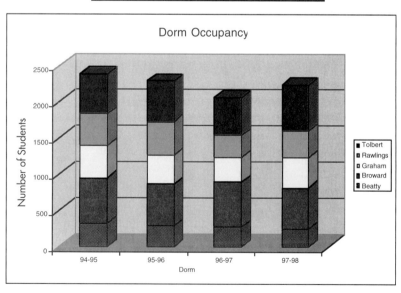

FIGURE 6   A Compound Document

The common user interface requires every Windows application to follow a consistent set of conventions and ensures that all applications work basically the same way. The development of a suite of applications from a single vendor extends this concept by imposing additional similarities on all applications within the suite.

Microsoft distributes both a Standard and a Professional edition of Office 97. Both versions include Word, Excel, PowerPoint, Internet Explorer, and Outlook. Office Professional also has Microsoft Access. The single biggest difference between Office 97 and its predecessor, Office 95, is that the Internet has become an integral part of the Office suite.

Help for all Office applications is available in a variety of formats. The Help Contents window provides access to a Contents and Index tab in which you look up specific topics. The Office Assistant enables you to ask a question in English. Still additional help is available from the Microsoft Web site, provided you have access to the Internet.

Microsoft Office includes several additional applications and shared utilities that can be used to add interest to a document. The Clip Gallery has more than 3,000 clip art images, 150 photographs, and a lesser number of sound files and video clips. WordArt enables you to create decorative text, while Office Art consists of a powerful set of drawing tools.

The Microsoft Office Shortcut Bar provides immediate access to each application in Microsoft Office. The Shortcut Bar is fully customizable with respect to the buttons it displays, its appearance, and its position on the desktop. The Open a Document and Start a New Document buttons enable you to think in terms of a document rather than the associated application.

Object Linking and Embedding (OLE) enables you to create a compound document containing data (objects) from multiple applications. Linking and embedding are different operations. The difference between the two depends on whether the object is stored within the compound document (embedding) or in its own file (linking).

KEY WORDS AND CONCEPTS

Common Windows
   interface
Compound document
Contents tab
Docucentric orientation
Embedding
Formatting toolbar
Index tab
Internet Explorer
Linking
Microsoft Access

Microsoft Bookshelf
   Basics
Microsoft Clip Gallery
Microsoft Excel
Microsoft Office
   Professional
Microsoft Office
   Shortcut Bar
Microsoft Outlook
Microsoft PowerPoint
Microsoft Standard
   Office

Microsoft Word
Microsoft WordArt
Object Linking and
   Embedding (OLE)
Office Art
Office Assistant
Online help
Shared applications
Standard toolbar

ADVANCED FEATURES: OUTLINES, TABLES, STYLES, AND SECTIONS

OBJECTIVES

After reading this chapter you will be able to:

1. Create a bulleted or numbered list; create an outline using a multilevel list.
2. Describe the Outline view; explain how this view facilitates moving text within a document.
3. Describe the tables feature; create a table and insert it into a document.
4. Explain how styles automate the formatting process and provide a consistent appearance to common elements in a document.
5. Use the AutoFormat command to apply styles to an existing document; create, modify, and apply a style to selected elements of a document.
6. Define a section; explain how section formatting differs from character and paragraph formatting.
7. Create a header and/or a footer; establish different headers or footers for the first, odd, or even pages in the same document.
8. Insert page numbers into a document; use the Edit menu's Go To command to move directly to a specific page in a document.
9. Create and update a table of contents.

OVERVIEW

This chapter presents a series of advanced features that will be especially useful the next time you have to write a term paper with specific formatting requirements. We show you how to create a bulleted or numbered list to emphasize important items within a term paper, and how to create an outline for that paper. We also introduce the tables feature, which is one of the most powerful features in Microsoft Word as it provides an easy way to arrange text, numbers, and/or graphics.

The second half of the chapter develops the use of styles, or sets of formatting instructions that provide a consistent appearance to similar elements in a document. We describe the AutoFormat command that assigns styles to an existing document and greatly simplifies the formatting process. We show you how to create a new style, how to modify an existing style, and how to apply those styles to text within a document. We introduce the Outline view, which is used in conjunction with styles to provide a condensed view of a document. We also discuss several items associated with longer documents, such as page numbers, headers and footers, and a table of contents.

The chapter contains four hands-on exercises to apply the material at the computer. This is one more exercise than in our earlier chapters, but we think you will appreciate the practical application of these very important capabilities within Microsoft Word.

BULLETS AND LISTS

A list helps you organize information by highlighting important topics. A *bulleted list* emphasizes (and separates) the items. A *numbered list* sequences (and prioritizes) the items and is automatically updated to accommodate additions or deletions. An *outline* (or multilevel numbered list) extends a numbered list to several levels, and it too is updated automatically when topics are added or deleted. Each of these lists is created through the ***Bullets and Numbering command*** in the Format menu, which displays the Bullets and Numbering dialog box in Figure 1.1.

The tabs within the Bullets and Numbering dialog box are used to choose the type of list and customize its appearance. The Bulleted tab selected in Figure 1.1a enables you to specify one of several predefined symbols for the bullet. Typically, that is all you do, although you can use the Customize button to change the default spacing (of ¼ inch) of the text from the bullet and/or to choose a different symbol for the bullet.

The Numbered tab in Figure 1.1b lets you choose Arabic or Roman numerals, or upper- or lowercase letters, for a Numbered list. As with a bulleted list, the Customize button lets you change the default spacing, the numbering style, and/or the punctuation before or after the number or letter. Note, too, the option buttons to restart or continue numbering, which become important if a list appears in multiple places within a document. In other words, each occurrence of a list can start numbering anew, or it can continue from where the previous list left off.

The Outline Numbered tab in Figure 1.1c enables you to create an outline to organize your thoughts. As with the other types of lists, you can choose one of several default styles, and/or modify a style through the Customize command button. You can also specify whether each outline within a document is to restart its numbering, or whether it is to continue numbering from the previous outline.

CREATING AN OUTLINE

The following exercise explores the Bullets and Numbering command in conjunction with creating an outline for a hypothetical paper on the United States Constitution. The exercise begins by having you create a bulleted list, then asking you to convert it to a numbered list, and finally to an outline. The end result is the type of outline your professor may ask you to create prior to writing a term paper.

As you do the exercise, remember that a conventional outline is created as a multilevel list within the Bullets and Numbering command. Text for the outline is entered in the Page Layout or Normal view, *not* the Outline view. The latter provides a completely different capability—a condensed view of a document that is used in conjunction with styles and is discussed later in the chapter. We mention this to avoid confusion should you stumble into the Outline view.

Choose the type of bullet ──────

Click Customize to choose
additional bullet symbols ──────

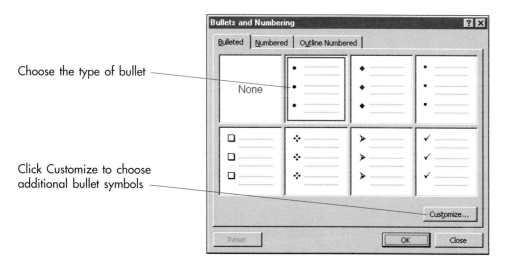

(a) Bulleted List

Click to select numbering style ──────

A numbered list can use letters
rather than numbers ──────

Restarts numbering for each
list within document ──────

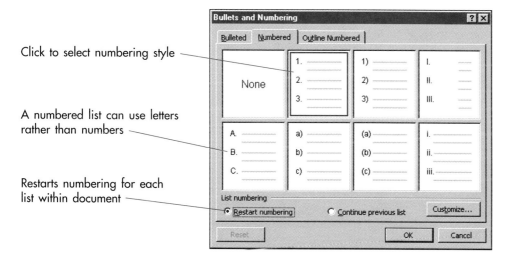

(b) Numbered List

Choose the Outline style ──────

Click Customize to change
the formatting ──────

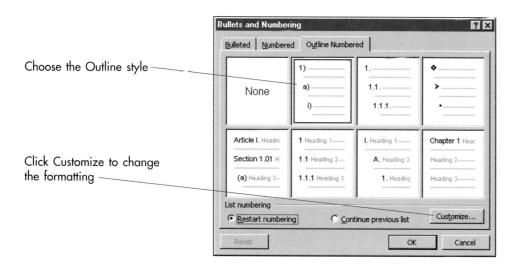

(c) Outline

FIGURE 1.1   Bullets and Numbering

Objective: To use the Bullets and Numbering command to create a bulleted list, a numbered list, and an outline. Use Figure 1.2 as a guide in doing the exercise.

STEP 1: Create a Bulleted List

➤ Start Word and begin a new document. Type **Preamble,** the first topic in our list, and press **enter.**

➤ Type the three remaining topics, **Article I—Legislative Branch, Article II—Executive Branch,** and **Article III—Judicial Branch.** Do not press enter after the last item.

➤ Click and drag to select all four topics as shown in Figure 1.2a. Pull down the **Format menu** and click the **Bullets and Numbering command** to display the Bullets and Numbering dialog box.

➤ If necessary, click the **Bulleted tab,** select the type of bullet you want, then click **OK** to accept this setting and close the dialog box. Bullets have been added to the list.

➤ Click after the words **Judicial Branch** to deselect the list and also to position the insertion point at the end of the list. Press **enter** to begin a new line**.** A bullet appears automatically since Word copies the formatting from one paragraph to the next.

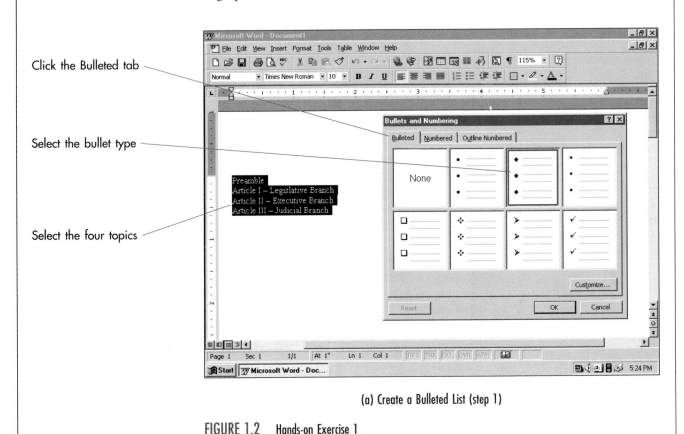

Click the Bulleted tab

Select the bullet type

Select the four topics

(a) Create a Bulleted List (step 1)

FIGURE 1.2   Hands-on Exercise 1

➤ Type **Amendments.** Press **enter** to end this line and begin the next, which already has a bullet. Press **enter** a second time to terminate the bulleted list.
➤ Save the document as **US Constitution** in the **Exploring Word folder.**

THE BULLETS AND NUMBERING BUTTONS

Select the items for which you want to create a list, then click the Numbering or Bullets button on the Formatting toolbar to create a numbered or bulleted list, respectively. The buttons function as toggle switches; that is, click the button once (when the items are selected) and the list formatting is in effect. Click the button a second time and the bullets or numbers disappear. The buttons also enable you to switch from one type of list to another; that is, selecting a bulleted list and clicking the Numbering button changes the list to a numbered list, and vice versa.

STEP 2: Modify a Numbered List
➤ Click and drag to select the five items in the bulleted list, then click the **Numbering button** on the Standard toolbar.
➤ The bulleted list has been converted to a numbered list as shown in Figure 1.2b. (The last two items have not yet been added to the list.)

Numbering button

Drag selected text to the left of first item

Click in selection area to select the sixth item

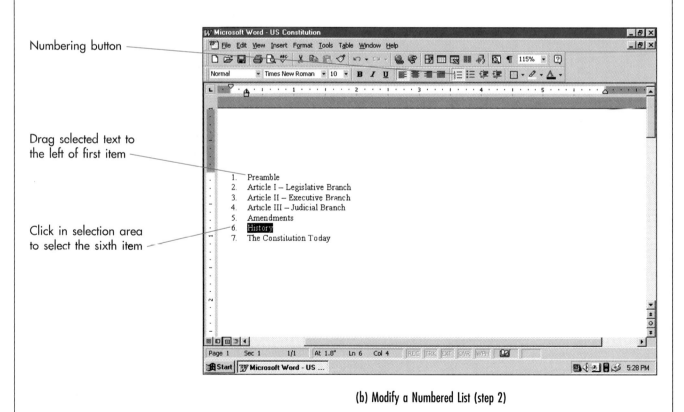

(b) Modify a Numbered List (step 2)

FIGURE 1.2   Hands-on Exercise 1 (continued)

➤ Click immediately after the last item in the list and press **enter** to begin a new line. Word automatically adds the next sequential number to the list. Type **History** and press **enter.** Type **The Constitution Today** as the seventh item.

➤ Click in the selection area to select the sixth item, **History** (only the text is selected). Now drag the selected text to the beginning of the list, in front of *Preamble.* Release the mouse.

➤ The list is automatically renumbered. *History* is now the first item, *Preamble* is the second item, and so on. Save the document.

AUTOMATIC CREATION OF A NUMBERED LIST

Word automatically creates a numbered list whenever you begin a paragraph with a number or letter, followed by a period, tab, or right parenthesis. Once the list is started, press the enter key at the end of a line, and Word generates the next sequential number or letter in the list. To end the list, press the backspace key once, or press the enter key twice. To turn the autonumbering feature on or off, pull down the Tools menu, click AutoCorrect to display the AutoCorrect dialog box, click the AutoFormat as you Type tab, then check (clear) the box for Automatic Numbered lists.

STEP 3: Convert to an Outline

➤ Click and drag to select the entire list, click the **right mouse button** to display a context-sensitive menu, then click the **Bullets and Numbering command** to display the Bullets and Numbering dialog box in Figure 1.2c.

➤ Click the **Outline Numbered tab,** then select the type of outline you want. (Do not be concerned if the selected formatting does not display Roman numerals as we customize the outline later in the exercise.)

➤ Click **OK** to accept the formatting and close the dialog box. The numbered list has been converted to an outline, although that is difficult to see at this point.

➤ Click at the end of the third item, **Article I—Legislative Branch.** Press **enter.** The number 4 is generated automatically for the next item in the list.

➤ Press the **Tab key** to indent this item and automatically move to the next level of numbering (a lowercase *a*). Type **House of Representatives.**

➤ Press **enter.** The next sequential number (a lowercase *b*) is generated automatically. Type **Senate.**

➤ Save the document.

Click the Outline
Numbered tab

Select the entire list

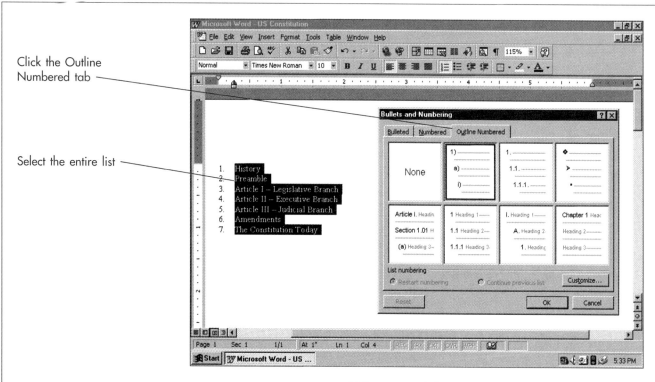

(c) Convert to an Outline (step 3)

FIGURE 1.2 Hands-on Exercise 1 (continued)

THE TAB AND SHIFT+TAB KEYS

The easiest way to enter text into an outline is to type continually from one line to the next, using the Tab and Shift+Tab keys as necessary. Press the enter key after completing an item to move to the next item, which is automatically created at the same level, then continue typing if the item is to remain at this level. To change the level, press the Tab key to demote the item (move it to the next lower level), or the Shift+Tab combination to promote the item (move it to the next higher level).

STEP 4: Complete the Text of the Outline

➤ Your outline should be similar in appearance to Figure 1.2d, except that you have not yet entered most of the text. Click at the end of the line containing *House of Representatives*.

➤ Press **enter** to start a new item (which begins with a lowercase *b*). Press **Tab** to indent one level, changing the number to a lowercase *i*. Type **Length of term.** Press **enter.** Type **Requirements for office.** Enter these two items for the Senate as well.

➤ Enter the remaining text as shown in Figure 1.2.d, using the **Tab** and **Shift+Tab** keys to demote and promote the items. Save the document.

Decrease Indent button

Increase Indent button

Enter text as indicated

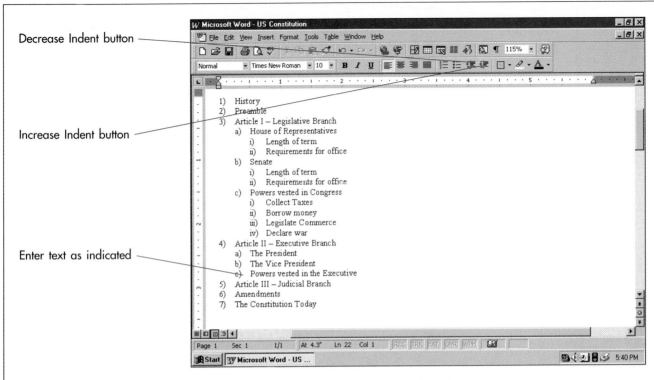

(d) Enter Text into the Outline (step 4)

FIGURE 1.2   Hands-on Exercise 1 (continued)

THE INCREASE AND DECREASE INDENT BUTTONS

The Increase and Decrease Indent buttons on the Standard toolbar are another way to change the level within an outline. Click anywhere within an item, then click the appropriate button to change the level within the outline. Indentation is implemented at the paragraph level, and hence you can click the button without selecting the entire item. You can also click and drag to select multiple item(s), then click the desired button.

STEP 5: Customize the Outline

➤ Select the entire outline, pull down the **Format menu,** then click **Bullets and Numbering** to display the Bullets and Numbering dialog box.

➤ Click **Customize** to display the Customize dialog box as shown in Figure 1.2e. Level **1** should be selected in the Level list box.

- Click the **drop-down arrow** in the Number style list box and select **I, II, III** as the style.

- Click in the Number format text box, which now contains the Roman numeral I followed by a right parenthesis. Click and drag to select the parenthesis and replace it with a period.

- Click the **drop-down arrow** in the Number position list box. Click **right** to right-align the Roman numerals that will appear in your outline.

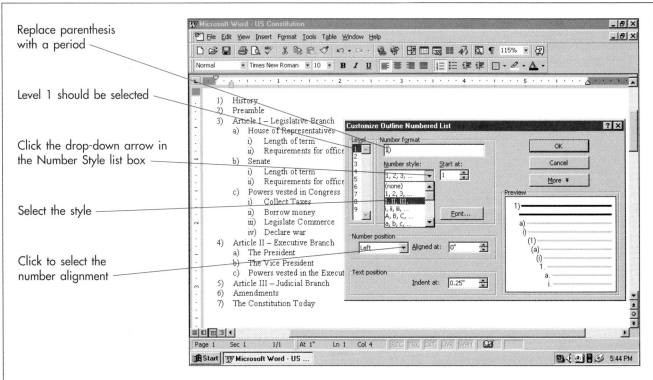

Replace parenthesis with a period

Level 1 should be selected

Click the drop-down arrow in the Number Style list box

Select the style

Click to select the number alignment

(e) Customize the Outline (step 5)

FIGURE 1.2 Hands-on Exercise 1 (continued)

➤ Click the number **2** in the Level list box and select **A, B, C** as the Number style. Click in the Number format text box and replace the right parenthesis with a period.

➤ Click the number **3** in the Level list box and select **1, 2, 3** as the Number style. Click in the Number format text box and replace the right parenthesis with a period.

➤ Click **OK** to accept these settings and close the dialog box. The formatting of your outline has changed to match the customization in this step.

CHANGE THE FORMATTING

Word provides several types of default formatting for an outline. Surprisingly, however, Roman numerals are not provided as the default and hence you may want to change the formatting to meet your exact requirements. The formats are changed one level at a time by selecting the style for a level, then changing the punctuation (e.g., by substituting a period for a right parenthesis). If you make a mistake, you can return to the default format by closing the Custom Outline Numbered List dialog box, then clicking the Reset button from within the Bullets and Numbering dialog box.

STEP 6: The Completed Outline

➤ Your outline should reflect the style in Figure 1.2f. The major headings begin with Roman numerals, the second level headings with uppercase letters, and so on.

➤ Press **Ctrl+Home** to move to the beginning of the outline. The insertion point is after Roman numeral I, in front of the word *History*. Type **The United States Constitution.** Press **enter.**

➤ The new text appears as Roman numeral I and all existing entries have been renumbered appropriately.

➤ The insertion point is immediately before the word *History*. Press **enter** to create a blank line (for your name).

➤ The blank line is now Roman numeral II and *History* has been moved to Roman numeral III.

➤ Press the **Tab** key so that the blank line (which will contain your name) is item A. This also renumbers *History* as Roman numeral II.

➤ Enter your name as shown in Figure 1.2f. Save the document, then print the outline and submit it to your instructor as proof you did this exercise.

➤ Close the document. Exit Word if you do not want to continue with the next exercise at this time.

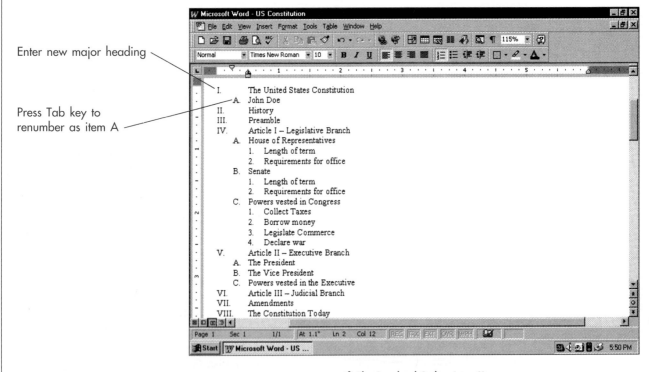

Enter new major heading

Press Tab key to renumber as item A

(f) The Completed Outline (step 6)

FIGURE 1.2   Hands-on Exercise 1 (continued)

The **tables feature** is one of the most powerful in Word and is the basis for an almost limitless variety of documents. The study schedule in Figure 1.3a, for example, is actually a 12 × 8 (12 rows and 8 columns) table as can be seen from the underlying structure in Figure 1.3b. The completed table looks quite impressive, but it is very easy to create once you understand how a table works. (See the practice exercises at the end of the chapter for other examples.)

The rows and columns in a table intersect to form **cells.** Each cell is formatted independently of every other cell and may contain text, numbers and/or graphics. Commands operate on one or more cells. Individual cells can be joined together to form a larger cell as was done in the first and last rows of Figure 1.3a. The rows within a table can be different heights, just as each column can be a different width. You can specify the height or width explicitly, or you can let Word determine it for you.

A cell can contain anything, even clip art as in the bottom right corner of Figure 1.3a. Just click in the cell where you want the clip art to go, then use the Insert Picture command as you have throughout the text. Use the sizing handles once the clip art has been inserted to move and/or position it within the cell.

A table is created through the **Insert Table command** in the **Table menu.** The command produces a dialog box in which you enter the number of rows and columns. Once the table has been defined, you enter text in individual cells. Text wraps as it is entered within a cell, so that you can add or delete text in a cell without affecting the entries in other cells. You can format the contents of an individual cell the same way you format an ordinary paragraph; that is, you can change the font, use boldface or italics, change the alignment, or apply any other formatting command. You can select multiple cells and apply the formatting to all selected cells at once.

You can also modify the structure of a table after it has been created. The Insert and Delete commands in the Table menu enable you to add new rows or columns, or delete existing rows or columns. You can invoke other commands to shade and/or border selected cells or the entire table.

You can work with a table using commands in the Table menu, or you can use the various tools on the Tables and Borders toolbar. (Just point to a button to display a ScreenTip indicative of its function.) Some of the buttons are simply shortcuts for commands within the Table menu. Other buttons offer new and intriguing possibilities, such as the button to Change Text Direction.

It's easy, and as you might have guessed, it's time for another hands-on exercise in which you create the table in Figure 1.3.

LEFT	CENTER	RIGHT

Many documents call for left, centered, and/or right aligned text on the same line, an effect that is achieved through setting tabs, or more easily through a table. To achieve the effect shown in the heading of this box, create a 1 × 3 table (one row and three columns), type the text in the three cells as needed, then use the buttons on the Formatting toolbar to left-align, center, and right-align the respective cells. Select the table, pull down the Format menu, click Borders and Shading, then specify None as the Border setting.

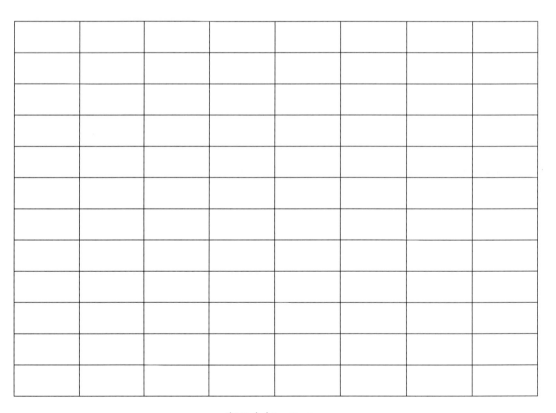

Weekly Class and Study Schedule							
	Monday	Tuesday	Wednesday	Thursday	Friday	Saturday	Sunday
8:00AM							
9:00AM							
10:00AM							
11:00AM							
12:00PM							
1:00PM							
2:00PM							
3:00PM							
4:00PM							
Notes:							

(a) Completed Table

(b) Underlying Structure

FIGURE 1.3 The Tables Feature

Tables

Objective: To create a table; to change row heights and column widths; to join cells together; to apply borders and shading to selected cells. Use Figure 1.4 as a guide in the exercise.

STEP 1: The Page Setup Command

➤ Start Word. Click the **Tables and Borders button** on the Standard toolbar to display the Tables and Borders toolbar as shown in Figure 1.4a. The button functions as a toggle switch—click it once and the toolbar is displayed. Click the button a second time and the toolbar is suppressed.

➤ Pull down the **File menu.** Click **Page Setup.** Click the **Paper Size tab** to display the dialog box in Figure 1.4a. Click the **Landscape option button.**

➤ Click the **Margins tab.** Change the top and bottom margins to **.75** inch. Change the left and right margins to **.5** inch each. Click **OK** to accept the settings and close the dialog box.

➤ Change to the **Page Layout** view. Zoom to **Page Width.**

➤ Save the document as **My Study Schedule** in the Exploring Word folder.

Tables and Borders button

Click Paper Size tab

Click Landscape

Page Layout View

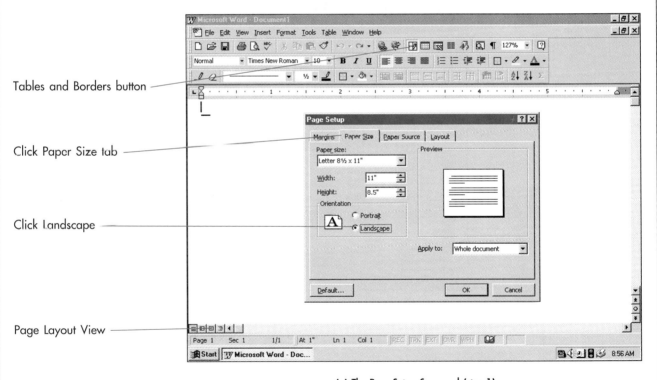

(a) The Page Setup Command (step 1)

FIGURE 1.4   Hands-on Exercise 2

THE TABLES AND BORDERS TOOLBAR

The Tables and Borders toolbar contains a variety of tools for use in creating and/or modifying a table. Some of the buttons are simply shortcuts for commands within the Table menu. Other buttons offer new and intriguing possibilities, such as the button to Change Text Direction. You can point to any button to display a ScreenTip to show the name of the button, which is indicative of its function. You can also use the Help command for additional information.

STEP 2: Create the Table

➤ Pull down the **Table menu.** Click **Insert Table** to display the dialog box in Figure 1.4b.

➤ Enter **8** as the number of columns. Enter **12** as the number of rows. Click **OK** and the table will be inserted into the document.

Insert Table button

Enter 8 for the number of columns

Enter 12 for the number of rows

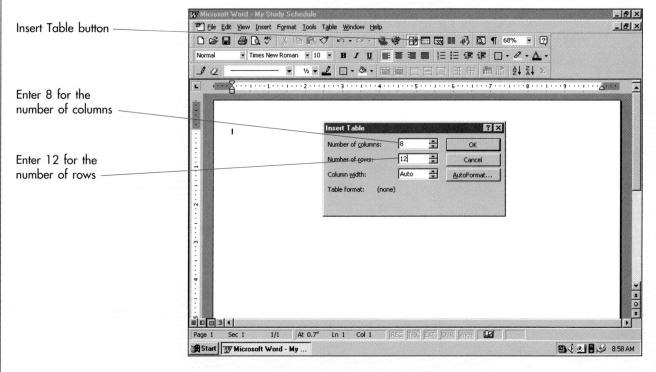

(b) Create the Table (step 2)

FIGURE 1.4   Hands-on Exercise 2 (continued)

THE INSERT TABLE BUTTON

The fastest way to create a table is to use the Insert Table button on the Standard toolbar. Click the Insert Table button to display a grid, then drag the mouse across and down the grid until you have the desired number of rows and columns. Release the mouse to create the table.

STEP 3: Table Basics

➤ Practice moving within the table:

- If the cells in the table are empty (as they are now), press the **left** and **right arrow keys** to move from cell to cell.

➤ If the cells contain text (as they will later in the exercise), you must press **Tab** and **Shift+Tab** to move from cell to cell.

- Press the **up** and **down arrow keys** to move from row to row. This works for both empty cells and cells with text.

➤ Select a cell row, column, or block of contiguous cells:

- To select a single cell, click immediately to the right of the left cell border (the pointer changes to an arrow when you are in the proper position).

- To select an entire row, click outside the table to the left of the first cell in that row.

- To select a column, click just above the top of the column (the pointer changes to a small black arrow).

- To select adjacent cells, drag the mouse over the cells.

- To select the entire table, drag the mouse over the table (or use the **Select Table** command from the Table menu).

TABS AND TABLES

The Tab key functions differently in a table than in a regular document. Press the Tab key to move to the next cell in the current row (or to the first cell in the next row if you are at the end of a row). Press Tab when you are in the last cell of a table to add a new blank row to the bottom of the table. Press Shift+Tab to move to the previous cell in the current row (or to the last cell in the previous row). You must press Ctrl+Tab to insert a regular tab character within a cell.

STEP 4: Merge the Cells

➤ Click outside the table to the left of the first cell in the first row to select the entire first row as shown in Figure 1.4c.

➤ Pull down the **Table menu** and click **Merge Cells** (or click the **Merge Cells button** on the Tables and Borders toolbar).

➤ Type **Weekly Class and Study Schedule** and format the text in 24 point Arial bold. Center the text within the cell.

➤ Click outside the table to the left of the first cell in the last row to select the entire row. Click the **Merge Cells button** to join the cells into a single cell.

➤ Type **Notes:** and format the entry in 12 point Arial bold.

➤ Save the table.

Click Merge Cells

Click here to select the first row of the table

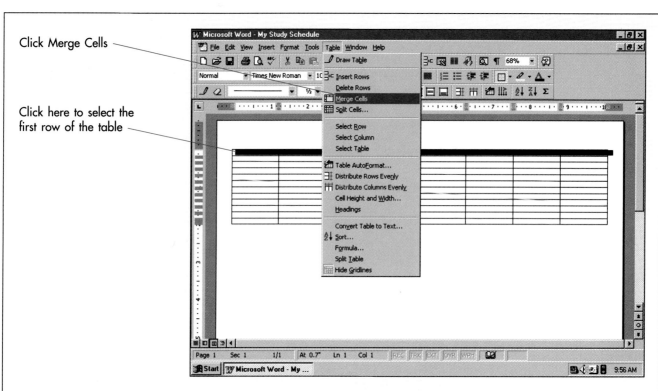

(c) Merge the Cells (step 4)

FIGURE 1.4   Hands-on Exercise 2 (continued)

TABLES AND THE SHOW/HIDE ¶ BUTTON

The Show/Hide ¶ button can be toggled on (off) to display (hide) the non-printing characters associated with a table. The □ symbol indicates the end-of-cell (or end-of-row) marker and is analogous to the ¶ symbol at the end of a paragraph in a regular document.

STEP 5: Enter the Days and Hours

➤ Click the second cell in the second row. Type **Monday.**

➤ Press the **Tab** (or **right arrow) key** to move to the next cell. Type **Tuesday.** Continue until the days of the week have been entered.

➤ Use the Formatting Toolbar to change the font and alignment for the days of the week:

  • Select the entire row. Click the **Bold button.**

  • Click the **Font List box** to choose an appropriate font such as **Arial.**

  • Click the **Font Size List box** to choose an appropriate size such as **10** point.

  • Click the **Center button** on the Formatting toolbar.

➤ Click anywhere in the table to deselect the text and see the effect of the formatting change.

➤ Click the first cell in the third row. Type **8:00AM.** Press the **down arrow key** to move to the first cell in the fourth row. Type **9:00AM.**

➤ Continue in this fashion until you have entered the hourly periods up to **4:00PM.** Format as appropriate. (We right aligned the time periods and changed the font to Arial bold.) Your table should match Figure 1.4d. Save the table.

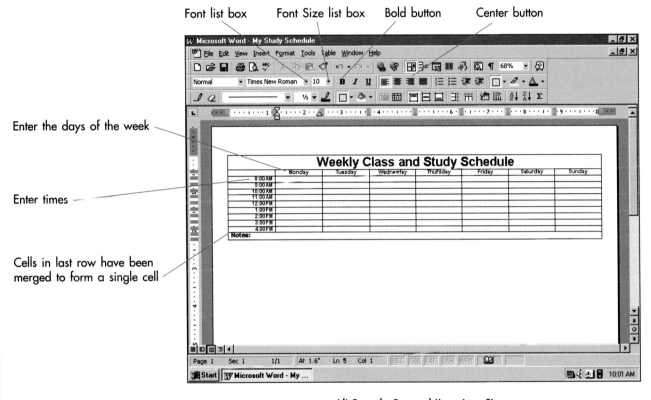

Font list box   Font Size list box   Bold button   Center button

Enter the days of the week

Enter times

Cells in last row have been merged to form a single cell

(d) Enter the Days and Hours (step 5)

FIGURE 1.4   *Hands-on Exercise 2 (continued)*

STEP 6: Change the Row Heights

➤ Click immediately after the word *notes.* Press the **enter key** five times. The height of the cell increases automatically to accommodate the blank lines.

➤ Select the cells containing the hours of the day. Pull down the **Table menu.** Click **Cell Height and Width** to display the dialog box in Figure 1.4e.

➤ If necessary, click the **Row tab.** Click the arrow for the Height of Rows list box. Click **Exactly,** then enter **36** (36 points is equal to ½ inch) in the At text box. Click **OK.**

➤ Click the **Center Vertically button** on the Tables and Borders toolbar to center the times vertically within their respective cells.

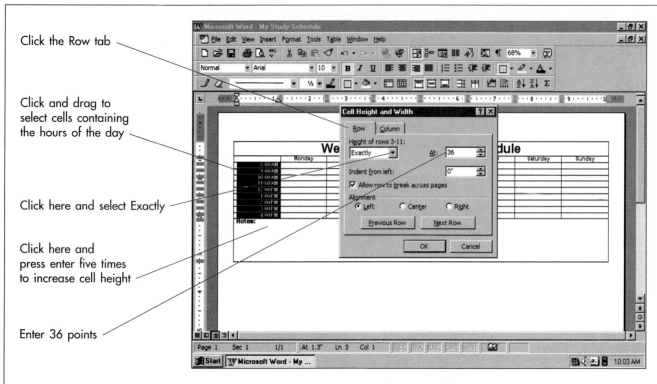

Click the Row tab

Click and drag to select cells containing the hours of the day

Click here and select Exactly

Click here and press enter five times to increase cell height

Enter 36 points

(e) Change the Row Height (step 6)

FIGURE 1.4   Hands-on Exercise 2 (continued)

STEP 7: Borders and Shading

➤ Click outside the first row (the cell containing the title of the table) to select the cell. Pull down the **Format menu,** click the **Borders and Shading** command to display the Borders and Shading dialog box as shown in Figure 1.4f.

➤ Click the **Shading tab.** Click the **drop-down arrow** on the Style list box, then select **100%** as the Style pattern. Click **OK.**

➤ Click outside the cell to see the effect of this command. You should see white letters on a solid black background. Save the document.

USE COLOR REVERSES FOR EMPHASIS

White letters on a solid background (technically called a reverse) is a favorite technique of desktop publishers. It looks even better in color. Select the text, click the Shading button on the Tables and Borders toolbar, then click the desired background color (e.g., red) to create the solid background. Next, click the drop-down arrow on the Font Color list box, click white for the text color, and click the Bold button to emphasize the white text. Click elsewhere in the document to see the result.

Click the Shading tab

Click to left of first row

Click 100%

Click drop-down arrow to
display the style options

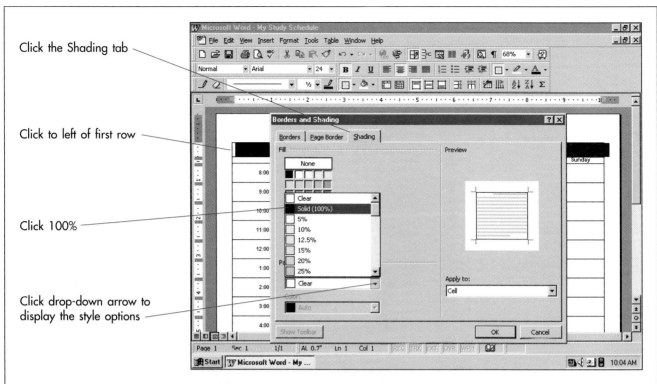

(f) Borders and Shading (step 7)

FIGURE 1.4   Hands-on Exercise 2 (continued)

STEP 8: Insert the Clip Art

➤ Click the **drop-down arrow** on the Zoom list box and zoom to **Whole Page.**
Click in the last cell in the table, the cell for your notes.

➤ Pull down the **Insert menu,** click **Picture,** then click **ClipArt** to display the
Microsoft Clip Gallery as shown in Figure 1.4g. Click **OK** if you see a dialog
box reminding you that additional clip art is available on the Office CD.

➤ If necessary, click the **Clip Art tab** and select (click) the **Academic category.**
Select the Professor lecturing the class (or a different image if you prefer),
then click the **Insert button.**

➤ The Microsoft Clip Gallery dialog box will close and the picture will
be inserted into the table, where it can be moved and sized as described in
step 9. Do not be concerned if the clip art is too large for your table or if it
spills to a second page.

ADDITIONAL CLIP IMAGES

Only a fraction of the more than 3,000 clip art images are installed with
the default installation of Office 97, but you can access the additional
images from the Office CD at any time. You can also install some or all
of the images on your hard disk, provided you have sufficient space. Start
Windows Explorer, then open the ClipArt folder on the Office CD. Double click the Setup icon to start the Setup Wizard, then follow the onscreen
instructions to install the additional components you want.

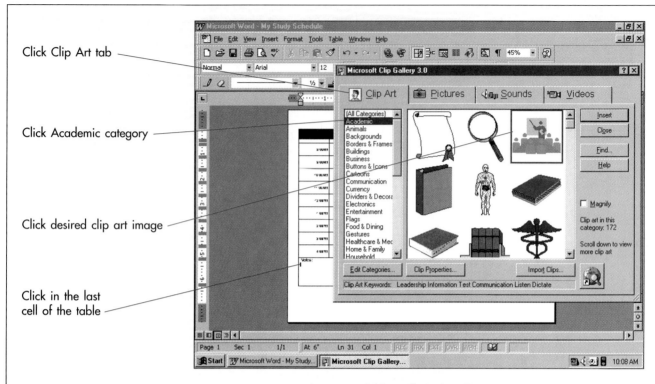

Click Clip Art tab

Click Academic category

Click desired clip art image

Click in the last cell of the table

(g) Insert Clip Art (step 8)

FIGURE 1.4   Hands-on Exercise 2 (continued)

STEP 9: Complete the Table

➤ Point to the clip art, click the **right mouse button** to display a shortcut menu, then click the **Format Picture command** to display the Format Picture dialog box. Click the **Wrapping tab,** select **None** as the Wrapping style, and click **OK** to close the Format Picture dialog box.

➤ The clip art should still be selected as indicated by the sizing handles in Figure 1.4h. Move and size the clip art until you are satisfied with its position within the table.

➤ Add your name somewhere in the table. Add other finishing touches (especially color if you have a color printer) to further personalize your table. Save the document.

➤ Print the completed table and submit it to your instructor as proof you did this exercise.

➤ Close the document. Exit Word if you do not want to continue with the next exercise at this time.

THE PICTURE TOOLBAR

The Picture toolbar is displayed automatically when a picture is selected; otherwise it is suppressed. As with any toolbar, you can point to a button to display a ScreenTip containing the name of the button, which is indicative of its function. You will find buttons for wrapping and formatting a picture, a Line Styles tool to place a border around the picture, and a Cropping tool to crop (erase) part of a picture.

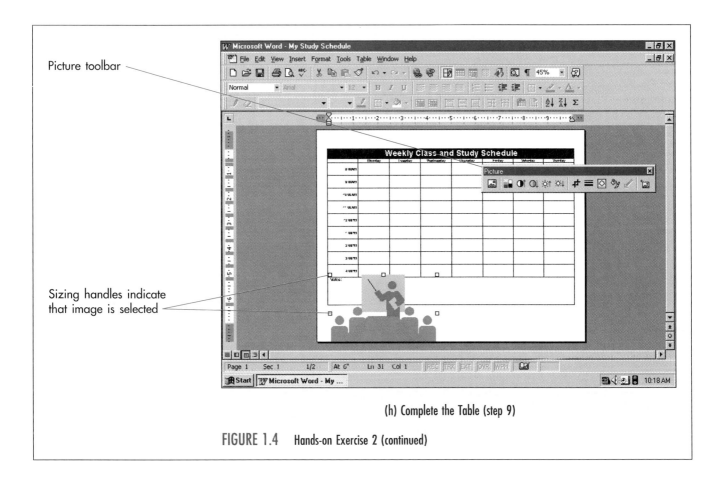

Picture toolbar

Sizing handles indicate
that image is selected

(h) Complete the Table (step 9)

FIGURE 1.4 Hands-on Exercise 2 (continued)

STYLES

A characteristic of professional documents is the use of uniform formatting for each element. Different elements can have different formatting; for example, headings may be set in one font and the text under those headings in a different font. You may want the headings centered and the text fully justified.

If you are like most people, you will change your mind several times before arriving at a satisfactory design, after which you will want consistent formatting for each element in the document. You can use the Format Painter on the Standard toolbar to copy the formatting from one occurrence of an element to another, but it still requires you to select the individual elements and paint each one whenever formatting changes.

A much easier way to achieve uniformity is to store the formatting information as a *style,* then apply that style to multiple occurrences of the same element within the document. Change the style and you automatically change all text defined by that style.

Styles are created on the character or paragraph level. A *character style* stores character formatting (font, size, and style) and affects only the selected text. A *paragraph style* stores paragraph formatting (alignment, line spacing, indents, tabs, text flow, and borders and shading, as well as the font, size, and style of the text in the paragraph). A paragraph style affects the current paragraph or multiple paragraphs if several paragraphs are selected. The *Style command* in the Format menu is used to create and/or modify either type of style, then enables you to apply that style within a document.

Execution of the Style command displays the dialog box shown in Figure 1.5, which lists the styles in use within a document. The *Normal style* contains the

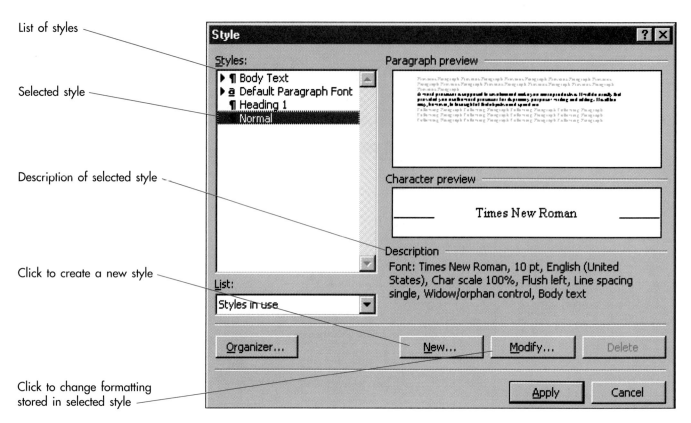

List of styles

Selected style

Description of selected style

Click to create a new style

Click to change formatting stored in selected style

FIGURE 1.5 The Normal Style

default paragraph settings (left aligned, single spacing, and the default font) and is automatically assigned to every paragraph unless a different style is specified. The **Heading 1** and **Body Text** styles are used in conjunction with the AutoFormat command, which applies these styles throughout a document. (The AutoFormat command is illustrated in the next hands-on exercise.) The **Default Paragraph Font** is a character style that specifies the (default) font for new text.

The Description box displays the style definition; for example, Times New Roman, 10 point, flush left, single spacing, and widow/orphan control. The Paragraph Preview box shows how paragraphs formatted in that style will appear. The Modify command button provides access to the Format Paragraph and Format Font commands to change the characteristics of the selected style. The Apply command button applies the style to all selected paragraphs or to the current paragraph. The New command button enables you to define a new style.

Styles automate the formatting process and provide a consistent appearance to a document. Any type of character or paragraph formatting can be stored within a style, and once a style has been defined, it can be applied to multiple occurrences of the same element within a document to produce identical formatting.

STYLES AND PARAGRAPHS

A paragraph style affects the entire paragraph; that is, you cannot apply a paragraph style to only part of a paragraph. To apply a style to an existing paragraph, place the insertion point anywhere within the paragraph, pull down the Style list box on the Formatting toolbar, then click the name of the style you want

THE OUTLINE VIEW

One additional advantage of styles is that they enable you to view a document in the **Outline view.** The Outline view does not display a conventional outline (such as the multilevel list created earlier in the chapter), but rather a structural view of a document that can be collapsed or expanded as necessary. Consider, for example, Figure 1.6, which displays the Outline view of a document that will be the basis of the next hands-on exercise. The document consists of a series of tips for Word 97. The heading for each tip is formatted according to the Heading 1 style. The text of each tip is formatted according to the Body Text style.

The advantage of the Outline view is that you can collapse or expand portions of a document to provide varying amounts of detail. We have, for example, collapsed almost the entire document in Figure 1.6, displaying the headings while suppressing the body text. We also expanded the text for two tips (Download the Practice Files and Moving Within a Document) for purposes of illustration.

Now assume that you want to move the latter tip from its present position to immediately below the first tip. Without the Outline view, the text would stretch over two pages, making it difficult to see the text of both tips at the same time. Using the Outline view, however, you can collapse what you don't need to see, then simply click and drag the headings to rearrange the text within the document.

Outline toolbar appears automatically in the Outline view ——

This text has been expanded ——

The text for these tips has been collapsed ——

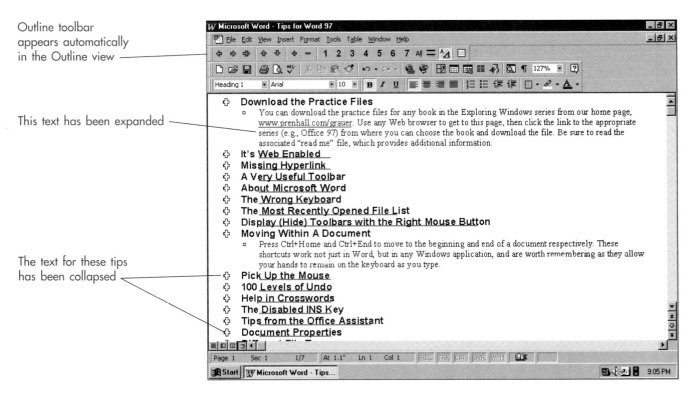

FIGURE 1.6   The Outline View

THE OUTLINE VERSUS THE OUTLINE VIEW

A conventional outline is created as a multilevel list within the Bullets and Numbering command. Text for the outline is entered in the Page Layout or Normal view, *not* the Outline view. The latter provides a condensed view of a document that is used in conjunction with styles.

The AutoFormat Command

Styles are extremely powerful. They enable you to impose uniform formatting within a document and they let you take advantage of the Outline view. What if, however, you have an existing and/or lengthy document that does not contain any styles (other than the default Normal style, which is applied to every paragraph)? Do you have to manually go through every paragraph in order to apply the appropriate style? The AutoFormat command provides a quick solution.

The *AutoFormat command* enables you to format lengthy documents quickly, easily, and in a consistent fashion. In essence, the command analyzes a document and formats it for you. Its most important capability is the application of styles to individual paragraphs; that is, the command goes through an entire document, determines how each paragraph is used, then applies an appropriate style to each paragraph. The formatting process assumes that one-line paragraphs are headings and applies the predefined Heading 1 style to those paragraphs. It applies the Body Text style to ordinary paragraphs and can also detect lists and apply a numbered or bullet style to those lists.

The AutoFormat command will also add special touches to a document if you request those options. It can replace "ordinary quotation marks" with "smart quotation marks" that curl and face each other. It will replace ordinal numbers (1st, 2nd, or 3rd) with the corresponding superscripts (1st, 2nd, or 3rd), or common fractions (1/2 or 1/4) with typographical symbols (½ or ¼).

The AutoFormat command will also replace Internet references (Web addresses and e-mail addresses) with hyperlinks. It will recognize, for example, any entry beginning with http: or www. as a hyperlink and display the entry as underlined blue text (www.microsoft.com). This is not merely a change in formatting, but an actual hyperlink to a document on the Web or corporate Intranet. It also converts entries containing an @ sign, such as rgrauer@umiami.miami.edu to a hyperlink as well. All Office 97 documents are Web-enabled. Thus, clicking on a hyperlink or e-mail address within a Word document opens your Web browser or e-mail program, respectively.

The options for the AutoFormat command are controlled through the Auto-Correct command in the Tools menu as shown in Figure 1.7. Once the options have been set, all formatting is done automatically by selecting the AutoFormat command from the Format menu. The changes are not final, however, as the command gives you the opportunity to review each formatting change individually, then accept the change or reject it as appropriate. (You can also format text automatically as it is entered according to the options specified under the AutoFormat As You Type tab.)

AUTOMATIC BORDERS AND LISTS

The AutoFormat As You Type option applies sophisticated formatting as text is entered. It automatically creates a numbered list any time a number is followed by a period, tab, or right parenthesis (press enter twice in a row to turn off the feature). It will also add a border to a paragraph any time you type three or more hyphens, equal signs, or underscores followed by the enter key. Pull down the Tools menu, click Options, click the AutoFormat tab, then click the AutoFormat As You Type option button to select the desired features.

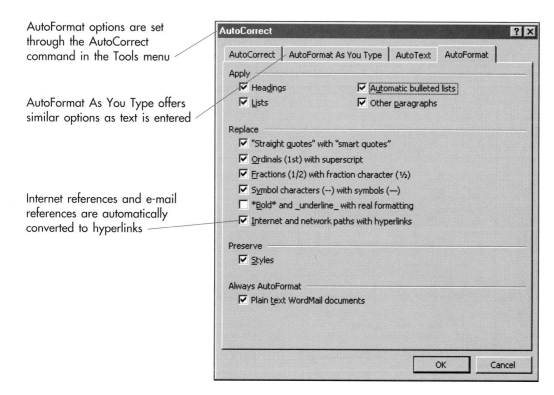

AutoFormat options are set through the AutoCorrect command in the Tools menu

AutoFormat As You Type offers similar options as text is entered

Internet references and e-mail references are automatically converted to hyperlinks

FIGURE 1.7   The AutoFormat Command

HANDS-ON EXERCISE 3

Styles

Objective: To use the AutoFormat command on an existing document; to modify existing styles; to create a new style. Use Figure 1.8 as a guide for the exercise.

STEP 1: Load the Practice Document

➤ Start Word. Pull down the **File menu.** Open the document **Tips for Word 97** from the Exploring Word folder. (This document contains 50 tips that appear throughout the text.)

➤ Pull down the **File menu** a second time. Save the document as **Modified Tips for Word 97** so that you can return to the original if necessary.

➤ If necessary, pull down the **View menu** and click **Normal** (or click the **Normal View button** above the status bar). Pull down the **View menu** a second time, click **Zoom,** click **Page Width,** and click **OK** (or click the **arrow** on the **Zoom Control box** on the Standard toolbar and select **Page Width**).

STEP 2: The AutoFormat Command

➤ Press **Ctrl+Home** to move to the beginning of the document. Pull down the **Format menu.** Click **AutoFormat** to display the AutoFormat dialog box in Figure 1.8a.

➤ Click the **Options command button** to display the AutoCorrect dialog box. Be sure that every check box is selected to implement the maximum amount of automatic formatting. Click **OK.**

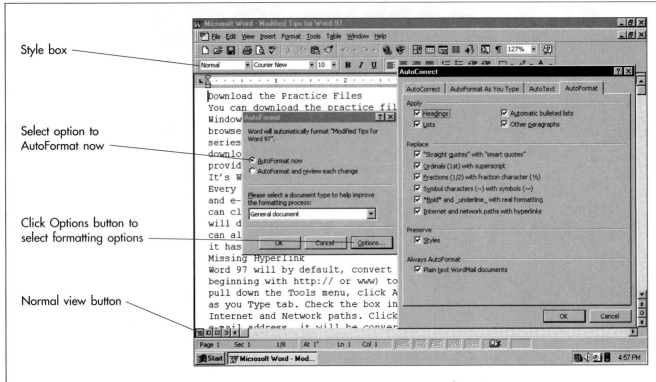

Style box

Select option to
AutoFormat now

Click Options button to
select formatting options

Normal view button

(a) AutoFormat Command (step 2)

FIGURE 1.8   Hands-on Exercise 3

➤ Click the **OK command button** in the AutoFormat dialog box to format the document. You will see a message at the left side of the status bar as the formatting is taking place, then you will see the newly formatted document.

➤ Save the document.

STEP 3: Style Assignments

➤ Click anywhere in the heading of the first tip. The Style box on the Formatting toolbar displays Heading 1 to indicate that this style has been applied to the title of the tip.

➤ Click anywhere in the text of the first tip (except on the hyperlink). The Style box on the Formatting toolbar displays Body Text to indicate that this style has been applied to the current paragraph.

➤ Click the title of any tip and you will see the Heading 1 style in the Style box. Click the text of any tip and you will see the Body Text style in the Style box.

STEP 4: Modify the Body Text Style

➤ Press **Ctrl+Home** to move to the beginning of the document. Click anywhere in the text of the first tip (except within the hyperlink).

➤ Pull down the **Format menu.** Click **Style.** The Body Text style is automatically selected, and its characteristics are displayed within the description box.

➤ Click the **Modify command button** to display the Modify Style dialog box in Figure 1.8b.

Body Text is the
selected style

Click the Modify button

Click Paragraph

Click the Format
command button

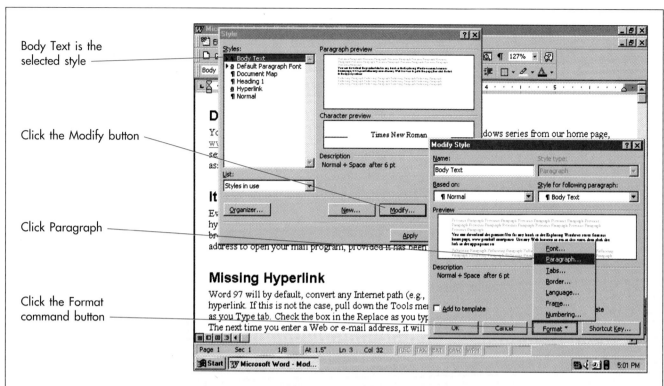

(b) Modify the Body Text Style (step 4)

FIGURE 1.8 Hands-on Exercise 3 (continued)

> ➤ Click the **Format command button.**
>   - Click **Paragraph** to produce the Paragraph dialog box.
>   - Click the **Indents and Spacing** tab.
>   - Click the **arrow** on the **Alignment list box.** Click **Justified.**
>   - Change the **Spacing After** to **12.**
>   - Click the **Line and Page Breaks tab** on the Paragraph dialog box.
>   - Click the **Keep Lines Together** check box so an individual tip will not be broken over two pages. Click **OK** to close the Paragraph dialog box.
> ➤ Click **OK** to close the Modify Style dialog box. Click the **Close command button** to return to the document.
> ➤ All paragraphs in the document change automatically to reflect the new definition of the Body Text style.

SPACE BEFORE AND AFTER

It's common practice to press the enter key twice at the end of a paragraph (once to end the paragraph, and a second time to insert a blank line before the next paragraph). The same effect can be achieved by setting the spacing before or after the paragraph using the Spacing Before or After list boxes in the Format Paragraph command. The latter technique gives you greater flexibility in that you can specify any amount of spacing (e.g., 6 points to leave only half a line) before or after a paragraph. It also enables you to change the spacing between paragraphs more easily because the information is stored within the paragraph style.

STEP 5: Review the Formatting

> Pull down the **Help menu** and click the **What's This command** (or press **Shift+F1**). The mouse pointer changes to a large question mark.

> Click in any paragraph to display the formatting in effect for that paragraph as shown in Figure 1.8c.

> You will see formatting specifications for the Body Text style (Indent: Left 0″, Justified, Space After 12 pt, Keep Lines Together, Font Times New Roman, 10pt, and English (US)).

> Click in any other paragraph to see the formatting in effect for that paragraph. Press **Esc** to return to normal editing.

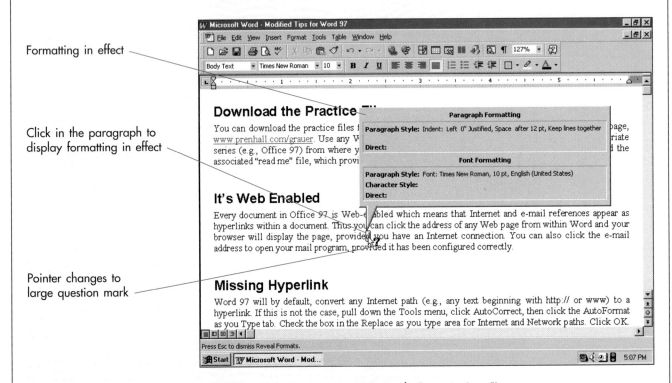

(c) Review the Formatting (step 5)

FIGURE 1.8   Hands-on Exercise 3 (continued)

STEP 6: Modify the Heading 1 Style

> Click anywhere in the title of the first tip. The Style box on the Formatting toolbar contains Heading 1 to indicate that this style has been applied to the current paragraph.

> Pull down the **Format menu.** Click **Style.** The Heading 1 style is automatically selected, and its characteristics are displayed within the description box.

> Click the **Modify command button** to display the Modify Style dialog box.

> Click the **Format command button.**

  • Click **Paragraph** to display the Paragraph dialog box. Click the **Indents and Spacing tab.**

  • Change the **Spacing After** to **0** (there should be no space separating the heading and the paragraph).

- Change the **Spacing Before** to **0** (since there are already 12 points after the Body Text style as per the settings in step 4). Click **OK.**
- Click the **Format command button** a second time.
- Click **Font** to display the Font dialog box.
- Click **10** in the Font size box. Click **OK.**

➤ Click **OK** to close the Modify Style dialog box. Click the **Close command button** to return to the document and view the changes.

➤ Save the document.

MODIFY STYLES BY EXAMPLE

The Modify command button in the Format Style command is one way to change a style, but it prevents the use of the toolbar buttons. Thus it's easier to modify an existing style by example. Select any text that is defined by the style you want to modify, then reformat that text using the Formatting toolbar, shortcut keys, or pull-down menus. Click the Style box on the Formatting toolbar, make sure the selected style is the correct one, press enter, then click OK when asked if you want to update the style to reflect recent changes.

STEP 7: The Outline View

➤ Pull down the **View menu** and click **Outline** (or click the **Outline view button** above the status bar) to display the document in the Outline view.

➤ Pull down the **Edit menu** and click **Select All** (or press **Ctrl+A**) to select the entire document. Click the **Collapse button** on the Outlining toolbar to collapse the entire document so that only the headings are visible.

➤ Click in the heading of the first tip (Download the Practice Files) as shown in Figure 1.7d. Click the **Expand button** on the Outlining toolbar to see the subordinate items under this heading.

➤ Experiment with the Collapse and Expand buttons to display different levels of information in the outline.

HELP WITH THE OUTLINING TOOLBAR

The Outlining toolbar is displayed automatically in the Outline view and suppressed otherwise. Press Shift+F1 to change the mouse pointer to a large arrow next to a question mark, then click any button on the Outlining toolbar to learn its function. You will find buttons to promote and demote items, to display or suppress formatting, and/or to collapse and expand the outline.

Collapse button

Heading was expanded to
display the subordinate items

Click here to change
to the Outline view

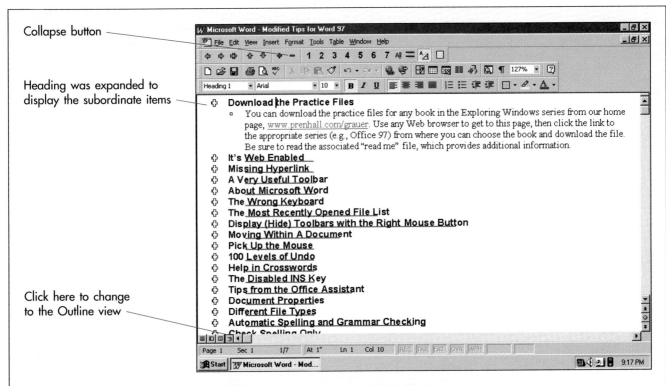

(d) The Outline View (step 7)

FIGURE 1.8   Hands-on Exercise 3 (continued)

STEP 8: Moving Text

➤ The advantage of the Outline view is that it facilitates moving text in a large
document. You can move either an expanded or collapsed item, but the latter is generally easier as you see the overall structure of the document.

➤ Click the **down arrow** on the vertical scroll bar until you see the tip, **Create
Your Own Shorthand.** Click and drag to select the tip as shown in Figure
1.7e.

➤ Point to the **plus sign** next to the selected tip (the mouse pointer changes to
a double arrow), then click and drag to move the tip below the **Different File
Types** as shown in Figure 1.7e. Release the mouse.

➤ Change back to the Page Layout view. Save the document.

THE DOCUMENT MAP

The Document Map is a new feature in Word 97 that helps you to navigate within a large document. Click the Document Map button on the
Standard toolbar to divide the screen into two panes. The headings in a
document are displayed in the left pane and the text of the document is
visible in the right pane. To go to a specific point in a document, click its
heading in the left pane, and the insertion point is moved automatically
to that point in the document, which is visible in the right pane. Click the
Map button a second time to turn the feature off.

Document Map button ——

Release the mouse at the point
where you want the text to go

Click and drag the plus
sign to move the heading
and its subordinate text

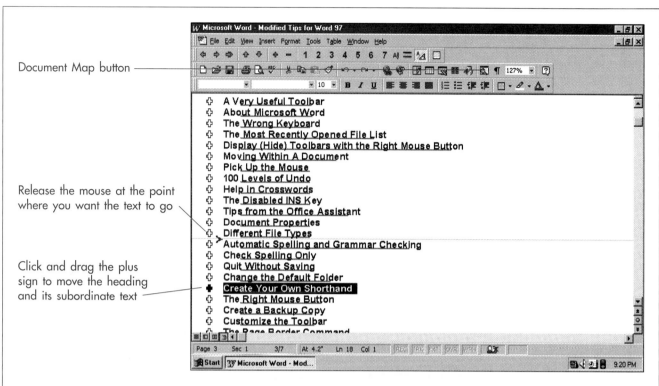

(e) Moving Text (step 8)

FIGURE 1.8 Hands-on Exercise 3 (continued)

STEP 9: Create a New Style

➤ Press **Ctrl+Home** to move to the beginning of the document. Press **Ctrl+enter** to create a page break for a title page.

➤ Move the insertion point on to the page break. Press the **enter key** five to ten times to move to an appropriate position for the title.

➤ Click the **Show/Hide ¶ button** on the Standard toolbar to display the non-printing characters. Select the paragraph marks, pull down the **Style list** on the Formatting toolbar, and click **Normal.**

➤ Deselect the paragraph marks to continue editing.

➤ Place the insertion point immediately to the left of the last hard return above the page break.

➤ Enter the title, **50 Tips in Microsoft Word,** and format it in 28 Point Arial Bold as shown in Figure 1.8f.

➤ Click the **Center button** on the Formatting toolbar.

➤ Check that the title is still selected, then click in the **Styles List box** on the Formatting toolbar. The style name, Normal, is selected.

➤ Type **My Style** (the name of the new style). Press **enter.** You have just created a new style that we will use in the next exercise.

➤ Save the document.

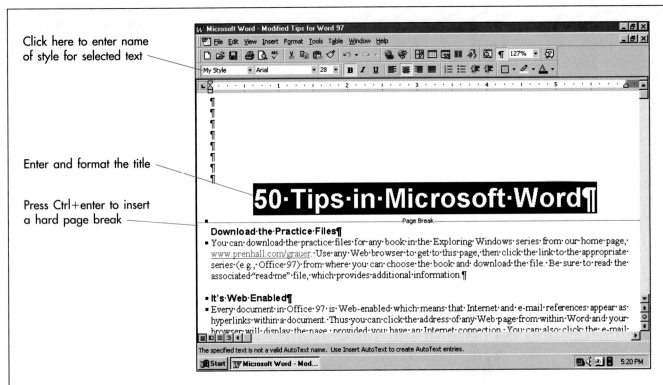

Click here to enter name of style for selected text

Enter and format the title

Press Ctrl+enter to insert a hard page break

(f) Create a New Style (step 9)

FIGURE 1.8   Hands-on Exercise 3 (continued)

STEP 10: Complete the Title Page

➤ Click the **Page Layout View button** above the status bar. Click the **arrow** on the **Zoom box** on the Standard toolbar. Click **Two Pages.**

➤ Scroll through the document to see the effects of your formatting.

➤ Press **Ctrl+Home** to return to the beginning of the document, then change to **Page Width** so that you can read what you are typing. Complete the title page as shown in Figure 1.8g.

➤ Click immediately to the left of the ¶ after the title. Press **enter** once or twice.

➤ Click the **arrow** on the **Font Size box** on the Formatting toolbar. Click **12.** Type **by Robert Grauer and Maryann Barber.** Press **enter.**

➤ Save the document. Exit Word if you do not want to continue with the next exercise at this time.

MORE FONTS

We have restricted our design to the Arial and Times New Roman fonts because they are supplied with Office 97 and hence are always available. In all likelihood, you will have several additional fonts available, in which case you can modify the fonts in the Heading 1 and/or Body Text styles to create a completely different design.

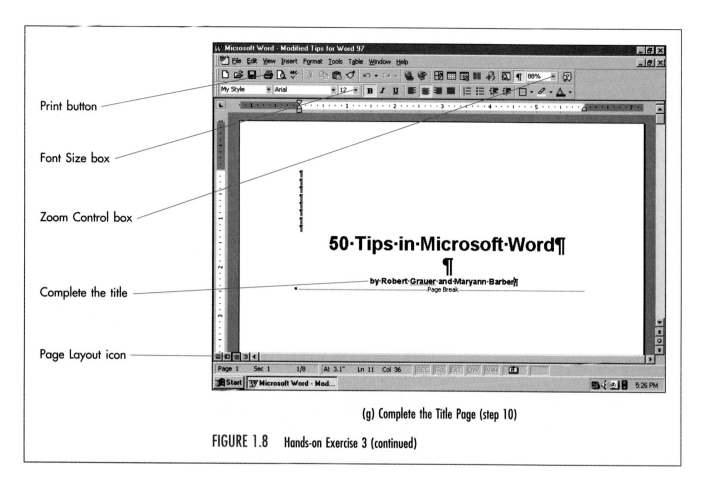

Print button

Font Size box

Zoom Control box

Complete the title

Page Layout icon

50·Tips·in·Microsoft·Word¶
¶
by·Robert·Grauer·and·Maryann·Barber¶
──────Page Break──────

(g) Complete the Title Page (step 10)

FIGURE 1.8   Hands-on Exercise 3 (continued)

WORKING IN LONG DOCUMENTS

Long documents, such as term papers or reports, require additional formatting for better organization. These documents typically contain page numbers, headers and/or footers, and a table of contents. Each of these elements is discussed in turn and will be illustrated in a hands-on exercise.

Page Numbers

The ***Insert Page Numbers command*** is the easiest way to place ***page numbers*** into a document and is illustrated in Figure 1.9a. The page numbers can appear at the top or bottom of a page, and can be left, centered, or right-aligned. Additional flexibility is provided as shown in Figure 1.9b; you can use Roman rather than Arabic numerals, and you need not start at page number one.

The Insert Page Number command is limited in two ways. It does not provide for additional text next to the page number, nor does it allow for alternating left and right placements on the odd and even pages of a document as in a book or newsletter. Both restrictions are overcome by creating a header or footer which contains the page number.

Headers and Footers

Headers and footers give a professional appearance to a document. A ***header*** consists of one or more lines that are printed at the top of every page. A ***footer*** is

Click to display available
positions for the page numbers

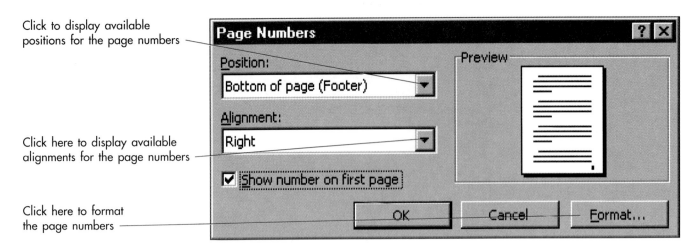

Click here to display available
alignments for the page numbers

Click here to format
the page numbers

(a) Placement

Click to display available
formats for the page numbers

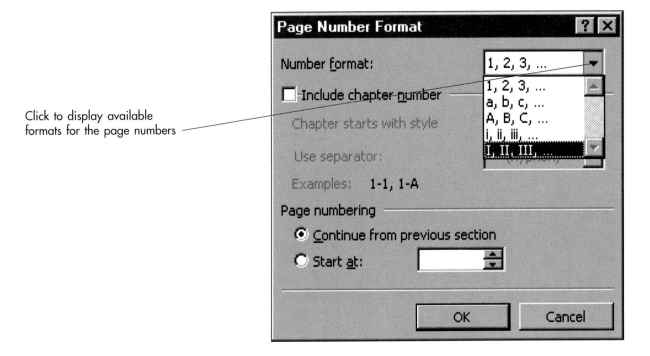

(b) Format

FIGURE 1.9 Page Numbers

printed at the bottom of the page. A document may contain headers but not footers, footers but not headers, or both headers and footers.

Headers and footers are created from the View menu. (A simple header or footer is also created automatically by the Insert Page Number command, depending on whether the page number is at the top or bottom of a page.) Headers and footers are formatted like any other paragraph and can be centered, left- or right-aligned. They can be formatted in any typeface or point size and can include special codes to automatically insert the page number, date, and/or time a document is printed.

The advantage of using a header or footer (over typing the text yourself at the top or bottom of every page) is that you type the text only once, after which it appears automatically according to your specifications. In addition, the placement of the headers and footers is adjusted for changes in page breaks caused by the insertion or deletion of text in the body of the document.

Headers and footers can change continually throughout a document. The Page Setup dialog box (in the File menu) enables you to specify a different header or footer for the first page, and/or different headers and footers for the odd and even pages. If, however, you wanted to change the header (or footer) midway through a document, you would need to insert a section break at the point where the new header (or footer) is to begin.

Sections

Formatting in Word occurs on three levels. You are already familiar with formatting at the character and paragraph levels that have been used throughout the text. Formatting at the section level controls headers and footers, page numbering, page size and orientation, margins, and columns. All of the documents in the text so far have consisted of a single *section,* and thus any section formatting applied to the entire document. You can, however, divide a document into sections and format each section independently.

Formatting at the section level may appear complicated initially, but it gives you the ability to create more sophisticated documents. You can use section formatting to:

> ➤ Change the margins within a multipage letter where the first page (the letterhead) requires a larger top margin than the other pages in the letter.
> ➤ Change the orientation from portrait to landscape to accommodate a wide table at the end of the document. (See practice exercise 2 at the end of the chapter.)
> ➤ Change the page numbering, for example to use Roman numerals at the beginning of the document for a table of contents and Arabic numerals thereafter.
> ➤ Change the number of columns in a newsletter, which may contain a single column at the top of a page for the masthead, then two or three columns in the body of the newsletter.

In all instances, you determine where one section ends and another begins by using the ***Insert menu*** to create a ***section break.*** You also have the option of deciding how the section break will be implemented on the printed page; that is, you can specify that the new section continue on the same page, that it begin on a new page, or that it begin on the next odd or even page even if a blank page has to be inserted.

Word stores the formatting characteristics of each section in the section break at the end of a section. Thus, deleting a section break also deletes the section formatting, causing the text above the break to assume the formatting characteristics of the next section.

Figure 1.10 displays a multipage view of a ten-page document. The document has been divided into two sections, and the insertion point is currently on the fourth page of the document (page four of ten), which is also the first page of the second section. Note the corresponding indications on the status bar and the position of the headers and footers throughout the document.

Figure 1.10 also displays the Headers and Footers toolbar, which contains various icons associated with these elements. As indicated, a header or footer may contain text and/or special codes—for example, the word "page" followed by a code for the page number. The latter is inserted into the header by clicking the appropriate button on the Headers and Footers toolbar.

Insertion point

Header area

Page Numbers button

Footer area

Insertion point is on page 4 of a 10-page document

Insertion point is on page 1 of section 2

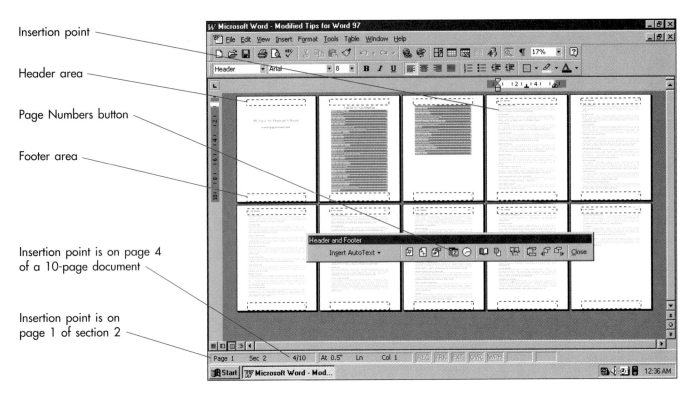

FIGURE 1.10 Headers and Footers

THE SECTION VERSUS THE PARAGRAPH

Line spacing, alignment, tabs, and indents are implemented at the paragraph level. Change any of these parameters anywhere within the current (or selected) paragraph(s) and you change *only* those paragraph(s). Margins, headers and footers, page numbering, page size and orientation, and newspaper columns are implemented at the section level. Change these parameters anywhere within a section, and you change those characteristics for every page within that section.

Table of Contents

A *table of contents* lists headings in the order they appear in a document and the page numbers where the entries begin. Word will create the table of contents automatically, provided you have identified each heading in the document with a built-in heading style (Heading 1 through Heading 9). Word will also update the table automatically to accommodate the addition or deletion of headings and/or changes in page numbers brought about through changes in the document.

The table of contents is created through the *Index and Tables command* from the Insert menu as shown in Figure 1.11. You have your choice of several predefined formats and the number of levels within each format; the latter correspond to the heading styles used within the document. You can also choose the *leader character* and whether or not to right align the page numbers.

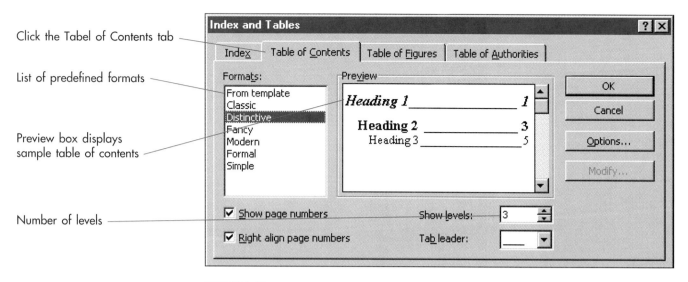

Click the Tabel of Contents tab

List of predefined formats

Preview box displays
sample table of contents

Number of levels

FIGURE 1.11   Index and Tables Command

The Go To Command

The *Go To command* moves the insertion point to the top of a designated page. The command is accessed from the Edit menu, or by pressing the F5 function key, or by double clicking the Page number on the status bar. After the command has been executed, you are presented with a dialog box in which you enter the desired page number. You can also specify a relative page number—for example, P+2 to move forward two pages, or P-1 to move back one page.

HANDS-ON EXERCISE 4

Working in Long Documents

Objective: To create a header (footer) that includes page numbers; to insert and update a table of contents; to insert a section break and demonstrate the Go To command; to view multiple pages of a document. Use Figure 1.12 as a guide for the exercise.

STEP 1: Applying a Style

➤ Open the **Modified Tips for Word 97 document** from the first exercise. Scroll to the top of the second page. Click to the left of the first tip title. (If necessary, click the **Show/Hide ¶ button** on the Standard toolbar to hide the paragraph marks.)

➤ Type **Table of Contents.** Press the **enter key** two times.

➤ Click anywhere within the phrase "Table of Contents". Click the **arrow** on the **Styles list box** to pull down the styles for this document as shown in Figure 1.12a.

➤ Click **My Style** (the style you created at the end of the previous exercise). "Table of Contents" is centered in 28 point Arial bold according to the definition of My Style.

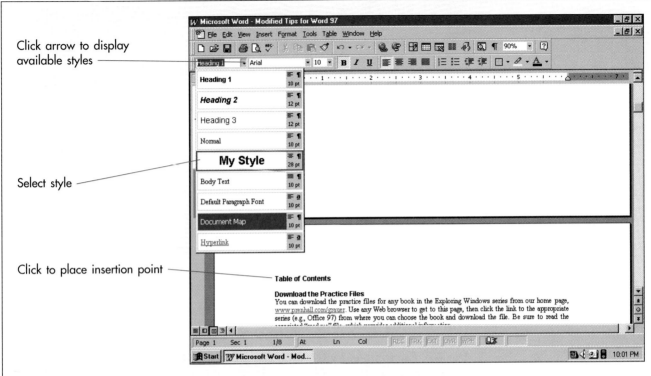

Click arrow to display available styles ——

Select style ——

Click to place insertion point ——

(a) Applying a Style (step 1)

FIGURE 1.12 Hands-on Exercise 4

STEP 2: View Many Pages
➤ Click the line immediately under the heading for the table of contents. Pull down the **View menu.** Click **Zoom** to display the dialog box in Figure 1.12b.
➤ Click the **monitor icon.** Click and drag the **page icons** to display two pages down by five pages across as shown in the figure. Release the mouse.
➤ Click **OK.** The display changes to show all eight pages in the document.

STEP 3: Create the Table of Contents
➤ Pull down the **Insert menu.** Click **Index and Tables.** If necessary, click the **Table of Contents tab** to display the dialog box in Figure 1.12c.
➤ Check the boxes to **Show Page Numbers** and to **Right Align Page Numbers.**
➤ Click **Distinctive** in the **Formats list box.** Click the **arrow** in the **Tab Leader list box.** Choose a dot leader. Click **OK.** Word takes a moment to create the table of contents, which extends to two pages.

AUTOFORMAT AND THE TABLE OF CONTENTS

Word will create a table of contents automatically, provided you use the built-in heading styles to define the items for inclusion. If you have not applied the heading styles to the document, the AutoFormat command will do it for you. Once the heading styles are in the document, pull down the Insert command, click Index and Tables, then click the Table of Contents command.

Click the monitor icon to
display the page grid

Drag across a 2 × 5 grid

Text is formatted according to
the My Style specifications

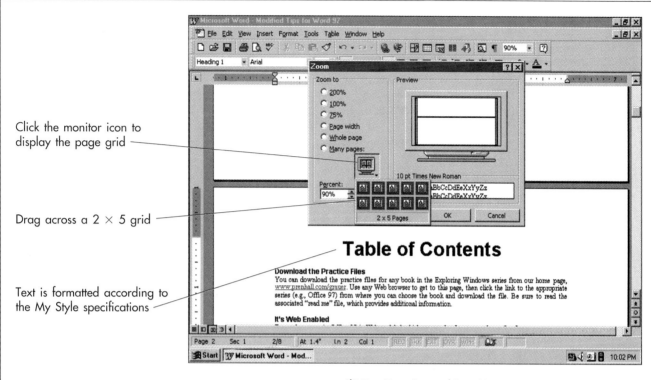

(b) View Zoom Command (step 2)

Click the Table of
Contents tab

Select the format for
the table of contents

Select both check boxes

Click to select a dot leader

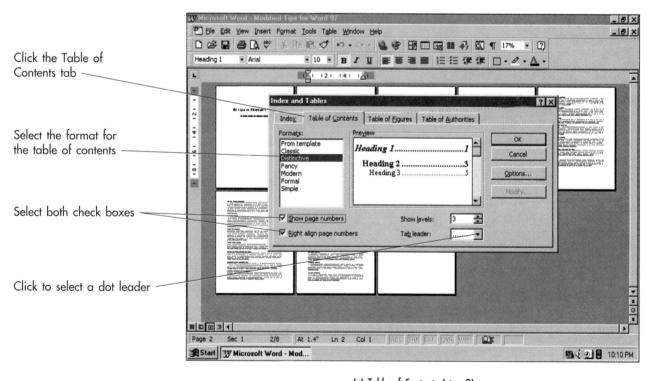

(c) Table of Contents (step 3)

FIGURE 1.12   Hands-on Exercise 4 (continued)

STEP 4: Field Codes versus Field Text

➤ Click the **arrow** on the **Zoom Control box** on the Standard toolbar. Click **Page Width** in order to read the table of contents as in Figure 1.12d.

➤ Use the **up arrow key** to scroll to the beginning of the table of contents. Click in the first entry in the table of contents, then press **Shift+F9.** The entire table of contents is replaced by an entry similar to {TOC \o "1-3"} to indicate a field code; the exact code depends on your selections in step 4.

➤ Press **Shift+F9** a second time. The field code for the table of contents is replaced by text.

➤ Pull down the **Edit menu.** Click **Go To** to display the dialog box in Figure 1.12d.

➤ Type **3** and press the **enter key** to go to page 3, which contains the bottom portion of the table of contents. Click **Close.**

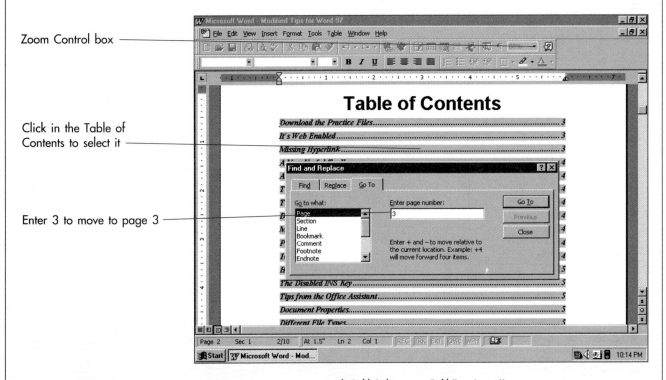

Zoom Control box

Click in the Table of Contents to select it

Enter 3 to move to page 3

(d) Field Codes versus Field Text (step 4)

FIGURE 1.12   Hands-on Exercise 4 (continued)

THE GO TO AND GO BACK COMMANDS

The F5 key is the shortcut equivalent of the Edit Go To command and produces a dialog box to move to a specific location (a page or section) within a document. The Shift+F5 combination executes the Go Back command and returns to a previous location of the insertion point; press Shift+F5 repeatedly to cycle through the last three locations of the insertion point.

STEP 5: Insert a Section Break

➤ Scroll down page three until you are at the end of the table of contents. Click to the left of the first tip heading as shown in Figure 1.12e.

➤ Pull down the **Insert menu.** Click **Break** to display the Break dialog box. Click the **Next Page button** under Section Breaks. Click **OK** to create a section break, simultaneously forcing the first tip to begin on a new page.

➤ The status bar displays Page 1 Sec 2 to indicate you are on page one in the second section. (See the boxed tip on page numbering if the status bar indicates Page 4 Sec 2.) The entry 4/10 indicates that you are physically on the fourth page of a ten-page document.

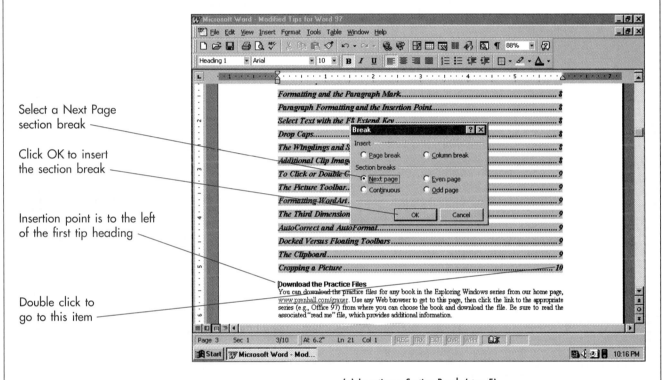

Select a Next Page section break

Click OK to insert the section break

Insertion point is to the left of the first tip heading

Double click to go to this item

(e) Inserting a Section Break (step 5)

FIGURE 1.12 Hands-on Exercise 4 (continued)

SECTIONS AND PAGE NUMBERING

Word gives you the option of numbering pages consecutively from one section to the next, or alternatively, of starting each section from page one. To view (change) the page numbering options in effect, pull down the Insert menu, click Page Numbers, click the Format command button, then click the option button for the page numbering you want. To start each section at page one, click the Start At option button, type 1 as the beginning page number, then click OK.

MOVING WITHIN LONG DOCUMENTS

Double click the page indicator on the status bar to display the dialog box for the ***Edit Go To command.*** You can also double click a page number in the table of contents (created through the Index and Tables command in the Insert menu) to go directly to the associated entry.

STEP 6: Create the Header

➤ Pull down the **File menu.** Click **Page Setup.** If necessary, click the **Layout tab** to display the dialog box in Figure 1.12f.

➤ If necessary, clear the box for Different Odd and Even Pages and for Different First Page, as all pages in this section (section two) are to have the same header. Click **OK.**

Click the Layout tab

Clear these check boxes

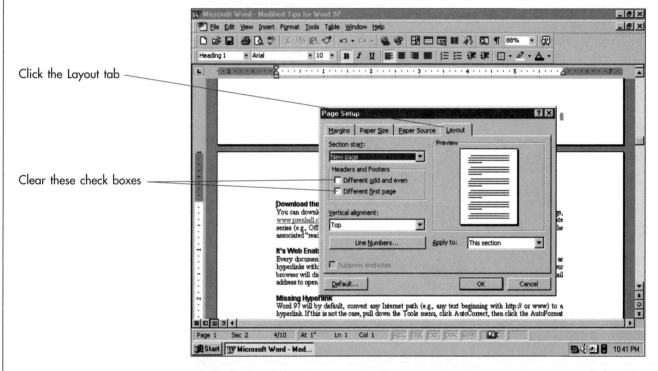

(f) Page Setup Command (step 6)

FIGURE 1.12   Hands-on Exercise 4 (continued)

HEADERS AND FOOTERS

If you do not see a header or footer, it is most likely because you are in the wrong view. Headers and footers are displayed in the Page Layout view but not in the Normal view. (Click the Page Layout button on the status bar to change the view.) Even in the Page Layout view the header (footer) is faded, indicating that it cannot be edited unless it is selected (opened) by double clicking.

STEP 7: Create the Header (continued)

➤ Pull down the **View menu.** Click **Header and Footer** to produce the screen in Figure 1.12g. The text in the document is faded to indicate that you are editing the header, as opposed to the document.

➤ The "Same as Previous" indicator is on since Word automatically uses the header from the previous section. Click the **Same as Previous button** on the Header and Footer toolbar to toggle the indicator off and to create a different header for this section. The indicator disappears from the header.

➤ If necessary, click in the header. Click the **arrow** on the **Font list box** on the Formatting toolbar. Click **Arial.** Click the **arrow** on the Font size box. Click **8.** Type **50 Tips In Microsoft Word.**

➤ Press the **Tab key** twice. Type **PAGE.** Press the **space bar.** Click the **Insert Page Number button** on the Header and Footer toolbar to insert a code for the page number.

➤ Click the **Close button.** The header is faded, and the document text is available for editing.

➤ Save the document.

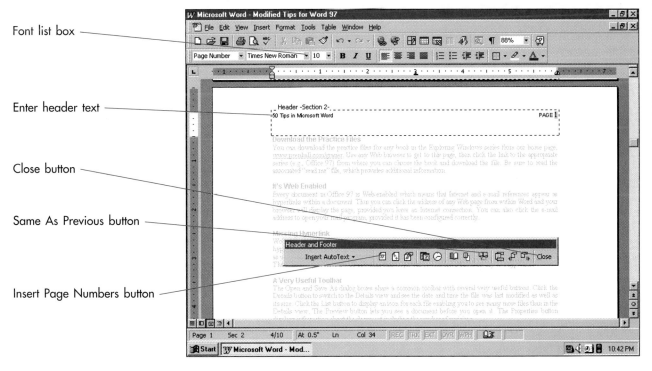

Font list box

Enter header text

Close button

Same As Previous button

Insert Page Numbers button

(g) Create the Header (step 7)

FIGURE 1.12   Hands-on Exercise 4 (continued)

STEP 8: Update the Table of Contents

➤ Press **Ctrl+Home** to move to the beginning of the document. The status bar indicates Page 1, Sec 1.

➤ Click the **Select Browse Object button** on the Vertical scroll bar, then click the **Browse by Page** icon.

➤ Click the **Next button** on the vertical scroll bar (or press **Ctrl+PgDn**) to move to the page containing the table of contents.

➤ Click in the table of contents. Press the **F9 key** to update the table of contents. If necessary, click the **Update Entire Table** button as shown in Figure 1.12h, then click **OK.**

➤ The pages are renumbered to reflect the actual page numbers in the second section.

Page numbers will change

Select Update entire table

Click the Select Browse Object button

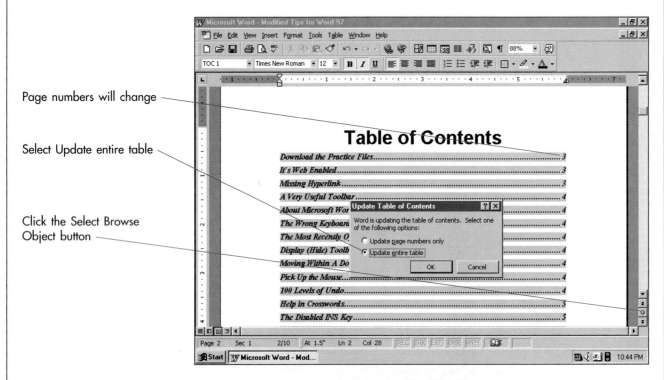

(h) Update the Table of Contents (step 8)

FIGURE 1.12   Hands-on Exercise 4 (continued)

SELECT BROWSE OBJECT

Click the Select Browse Object button toward the bottom of the vertical scroll bar to display a menu in which you specify how to browse through a document. Typically you browse from one page to the next, but you can browse by footnote, section, graphic, table, or any of the other objects listed. Once you select the object, click the Next or Previous buttons on the vertical scroll bar (or press Ctrl+PgDn or Ctrl+PgUp) to move to the next or previous occurrence of the selected object.

STEP 9: The Completed Document

➤ Pull down the **View menu.** Click **Zoom.** Click **Many Pages.** Click the **monitor icon.**

➤ Click and drag across the **page icons** to display two pages down by five pages. Release the mouse. Click **OK.**

➤ The completed document is shown in Figure 1.12i.

➤ Press **Ctrl+End** to move to the last page in the document.

➤ The status bar displays Page 7, Sec 2, 10/10 to indicate the seventh page in the second section, which is also the tenth page in the ten-page document.

➤ Save the document. Print the entire document. Exit Word.

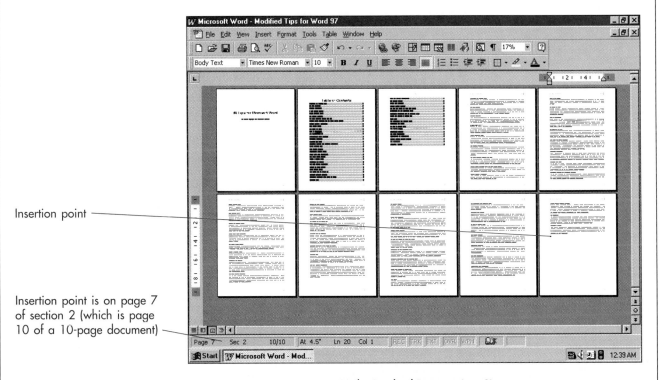

Insertion point

Insertion point is on page 7 of section 2 (which is page 10 of a 10-page document)

(i) The Completed Document (step 9)

FIGURE 1.12   Hands-on Exercise 4 (continued)

UPDATING THE TABLE OF CONTENTS

Use a shortcut menu to update the table of contents. Point anywhere in the table of contents, then press the right mouse button, to display a shortcut menu. Click Update Field, click the Update Entire Table command button, and click OK. The table of contents will be adjusted automatically to reflect page number changes as well as the addition or deletion of any items defined by any built-in heading style.

A list helps to organize information by emphasizing important topics. A bulleted or numbered list can be created by clicking the appropriate button on the Formatting toolbar or by executing the Bullets and Numbering command in the Format menu. An outline extends a numbered list to several levels.

Tables represent a very powerful capability within Word and are created through the Insert Table command in the Table menu or by using the Insert Table button on the Standard toolbar. Each cell in a table is formatted independently and may contain text, numbers, and/or graphics.

A style is a set of formatting instructions that has been saved under a distinct name. Styles are created at the character or paragraph level and provide a consistent appearance to similar elements throughout a document. Existing styles can be modified to change the formatting of all text defined by that style.

The Outline view displays a condensed view of a document based on styles within the document. Text may be collapsed or expanded as necessary to facilitate moving text within long documents.

The AutoFormat command analyzes a document and formats it for you. The command goes through an entire document, determines how each paragraph is used, then applies an appropriate style to each paragraph.

Formatting occurs at the character, paragraph, or section level. Section formatting controls margins, columns, page orientation and size, page numbering, and headers and footers. A header consists of one or more lines that are printed at the top of every (designated) page in a document. A footer is text that is printed at the bottom of designated pages. Page numbers may be added to either a header or footer.

A table of contents lists headings in the order they appear in a document with their respective page numbers. It can be created automatically, provided the built-in heading styles were previously applied to the items for inclusion. The Edit Go To command enables you to move directly to a specific page, section, or bookmark within a document.

KEY WORDS AND CONCEPTS

AutoFormat command
Body Text style
Bookmark
Bulleted list
Bullets and Numbering command
Cell
Character style
Default Paragraph Font style
Footer
Format Style command
Go To command

Header
Heading 1 style
Index and Tables command
Insert menu
Insert Page Numbers command
Insert Table command
Leader character
Multilevel numbered list
Normal style
Numbered list

Outline
Outline view
Page numbers
Paragraph style
Section
Section break
Style
Style command
Table menu
Table of contents
Tables feature

MULTIPLE CHOICE

1. Which of the following can be stored within a paragraph style?
   (a) Tabs and indents
   (b) Line spacing and alignment
   (c) Shading and borders
   (d) All of the above

2. What is the easiest way to change the alignment of five paragraphs scattered throughout a document, each of which has been formatted with the same style?
   (a) Select the paragraphs individually, then click the appropriate alignment button on the Formatting toolbar
   (b) Select the paragraphs at the same time, then click the appropriate alignment button on the Formatting toolbar
   (c) Change the format of the existing style, which changes the paragraphs
   (d) Retype the paragraphs according to the new specifications

3. The AutoFormat command will do all of the following except:
   (a) Apply styles to individual paragraphs
   (b) Apply boldface italics to terms that require additional emphasis
   (c) Replace ordinary quotes with smart quotes
   (d) Substitute typographic symbols for ordinary letters—such as © for (C)

4. Which of the following is used to create a conventional outline?
   (a) The Bullets and Numbering command
   (b) The Outline view
   (c) Both (a) and (b)
   (d) Neither (a) nor (b)

5. In which view do you see headers and/or footers?
   (a) Page Layout view
   (b) Normal view
   (c) Both (a) and (b)
   (d) Neither (a) nor (b)

6. Which of the following numbering schemes can be used with page numbers?
   (a) Roman numerals (I, II, III . . . or i, ii, iii)
   (b) Regular numbers (1, 2, 3, . . .)
   (c) Letters (A, B, C . . . or a, b, c)
   (d) All of the above

7. Which of the following is true regarding headers and footers?
   (a) Every document must have at least one header
   (b) Every document must have at least one footer
   (c) Both (a) and (b)
   (d) Neither (a) nor (b)

8. Which of the following is a *false* statement regarding lists?
   (a) A bulleted list can be changed to a numbered list and vice versa
   (b) The symbol for the bulleted list can be changed to a different character
   (c) The numbers in a numbered list can be changed to letters or roman numerals
   (d) The bullets or numbers cannot be removed

9. Page numbers can be specified in:
   (a) A header but not a footer
   (b) A footer but not a header
   (c) A header or a footer
   (d) Neither a header nor a footer

10. Which of the following is true regarding the formatting within a document?
    (a) Line spacing and alignment are implemented at the section level
    (b) Margins, headers, and footers are implemented at the paragraph level
    (c) Both (a) and (b)
    (d) Neither (a) nor (b)

11. What happens when you press the Tab key from within a table?
    (a) A Tab character is inserted just as it would be for ordinary text
    (b) The insertion point moves to the next column in the same row or the first column in the next row if you are at the end of the row
    (c) Both (a) and (b)
    (d) Neither (a) nor (b)

12. Which of the following is true, given that the status bar displays Page 1, Section 3, followed by 7/9?
    (a) The document has a maximum of three sections
    (b) The third section begins on page 7
    (c) The insertion point is on the very first page of the document
    (d) All of the above

13. The Edit Go To command enables you to move the insertion point to:
    (a) A specific page
    (b) A relative page forward or backward from the current page
    (c) A specific section
    (d) Any of the above

14. Once a table of contents has been created and inserted into a document:
    (a) Any subsequent page changes arising from the insertion or deletion of text to existing paragraphs must be entered manually
    (b) Any additions to the entries in the table arising due to the insertion of new paragraphs defined by a heading style must be entered manually
    (c) Both (a) and (b)
    (d) Neither (a) nor (b)

15. Which of the following is *false* about the Outline view?
    (a) It can be collapsed to display only headings
    (b) It can be expanded to show the entire document
    (c) It requires the application of styles
    (d) It is used to create a conventional outline

PRACTICE WITH MICROSOFT WORD

1. Use your favorite search engine to locate the text of the United States Constitution. There are many available sites and associated documents, one of which is displayed in Figure 1.13. We erased the address, however; otherwise the problem would be too easy. Once you locate the text of the Constitution, expand the outline created in the first hands-on exercise to include information about the other provisions of the Constitution (Articles IV through VII, the Bill of Rights, and the other amendments). Submit the completed outline to your professor as proof you did this exercise.

2. Sections and Page Orientation: Formatting in Word takes place at the character, paragraph, or section level. The latter controls the margins and page orientation within a document and is illustrated in Figure 1.14. Create the study schedule as described in the second hands-on exercise, then insert a title page in front of the table. Note, however, that the title page and table must appear in different sections so that you can use the portrait and landscape orientations, respectively. Print the two-page document, consisting of the title page and table, and submit it to your instructor.

3. For the health conscious: Figure 1.15 displays the first five tips in a document describing tips for healthier living. Retrieve the document *Volume II Chapter 1 Practice 3* from the Exploring Word folder, then modify it as follows:

    a. Use the AutoFormat command to apply the Heading 1 and Body Text styles throughout the document.

    b. Change the specifications for the Body Text and Heading 1 styles so that your document matches the document in the figure. The Heading 1 style calls for 12 point Arial bold with a blue top border (which requires a color printer). The Body Text style is 12 point Times New Roman, justified, with a ¼ inch left indent.

    c. Create a title page for the document consisting of the title, *Tips for Healthy Living,* the author, *Marion B. Grauer,* and an additional line, indicating that the document was prepared for you.

    d. Create a header for the document consisting of the title, *Tips for Healthy Living,* and a page number. The header is not to appear on the title page.

4. Sports fans: The tables feature is perfect to display the standings of any league, be it amateur or professional. Figure 1.16, for example, shows standings in baseball and was a breeze. Pick any sport or league that you like and create a table with the standings as of today. You can use a newspaper, but it's more fun to use the Web.

    Use Figure 1.16 as a guide, but feel free to improve on our design, perhaps through the inclusion of clip art. Color is a nice touch, but it is definitely not required. White text on a black background is also very effective. Experiment freely, but set a time limit for yourself.

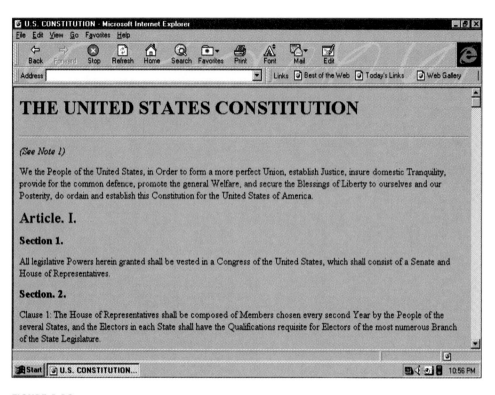

FIGURE 1.13   Screen for Practice Exercise 1

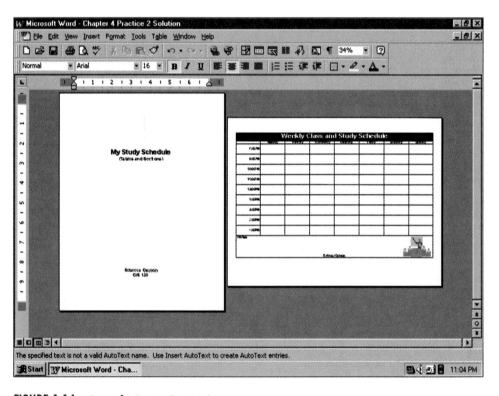

FIGURE 1.14   Screen for Practice Exercise 2

Start a Diet Journal

Keep a daily record of your weight and the foods you've eaten. Study your journal to become aware of your eating behavior. It will tell you when you're eating too much or if you're eating the wrong foods.

Why Do You Want to Lose Weight?

Write a list of reasons in your diet journal and refer to it often to sustain your motivation. Good health, good looks, more self-confidence, and new romantic possibilities are only the beginning.

Fighting Fatigue

Paradoxically, the more you do, the less tired you'll feel. Regular balanced exercise will speed up your metabolism, burn calories more efficiently, raise your energy level, and lift your spirits.

You Are What You Eat

Foods laden with fat, salt, and sugar leave you feeling lethargic and depressed. They set you up for more overeating. A nutritious low-fat diet has the opposite effect. You feel energized, revitalized, and happier.

"Water is the only drink for a wise man." —Thoreau

Water is the perfect weight-loss beverage. It fills your stomach, curbs your appetite, and cleanses your entire system. Add a twist of lemon or lime to improve the taste, and drink eight glasses every day.

FIGURE 1.15   Document for Practice Exercise 3

American League
Standings as of May 2, 1997

East	Wins	Losses	Percent
Baltimore Orioles	17	7	.708
Boston Red Sox	13	12	.520
New York Yankees	14	13	.519
Toronto Blue Jays	11	13	.458
Detroit Tigers	11	16	.407
Central	**Wins**	**Losses**	**Percent**
Milwaukee Brewers	12	11	.522
Cleveland Indians	13	13	.500
Kansas City Royals	12	12	.500
Minnesota Twins	11	16	.407
Chicago White Sox	8	17	.320
West	**Wins**	**Losses**	**Percent**
Seattle Mariners	16	11	.593
Texas Rangers	14	10	.583
California Angels	12	12	.500
Oakland A's	13	14	.481

FIGURE 1.16   Document for Practice Exercise 4

5. Form design: The tables feature is ideal to create forms as shown by the document in Figure 1.17, which displays an employment application. Reproduce the document shown in the figure or design your own application. Submit the completed document to your instructor.

Computer Consultants, Inc.
Employee Application Form

Last Name:		First Name:		Middle Name:

Address:

City:	State:	Zip Code:	Telephone:

Date of Birth:	Place of Birth:	Citizenship:

Highest Degree Attained:
   High School Diploma
   Bachelor's Degree
   Master's Degree
   Ph.D.
	List Schools Attended (include years attended):

List Specific Computer Skills:

List Relevant Computer Experience:

References (list name, title, and current mailing address):

1.

2.

3.

FIGURE 1.17   Document for Practice Exercise 5

6. Graphics: A table may contain anything—text, graphics, or numbers as shown by the document in Figure 1.18, which displays a hypothetical computer advertisement. It's not complicated; in fact, it was really very easy; just follow the steps below:

a. Create a 7 × 4 table.

b. Merge all of the cells in row one and enter the heading. Merge all of the cells in row two and type the text describing the sale.

c. Use the Clip Gallery to insert a picture into the table. (Various computer graphics are available in the Business and Technology categories.)

d. Enter the sales data in rows three through seven of the table; all entries are centered within the respective cells.

e. Change the font, colors, and formatting, then print the completed document. Use any format you think is appropriate.

Of course, it isn't quite as simple as it sounds, but we think you get the idea. Good luck and feel free to improve on our design. Color is a nice touch, but it is definitely not required. You might also make your table more realistic by going to the Web and searching for current prices and configurations. Go to the Exploring Windows home page (www.prenhall.com/grauer), click on Additional Resources, then click the link to PC Buying Guide as one source of information.

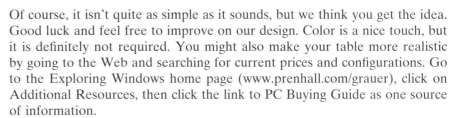

Computers To Go

Our tremendous sales volume enables us to offer the fastest, most powerful series of Pentium and Pentium Pro computers at prices almost too good to be true. Each microprocessor is offered in a variety of configurations so that you get exactly what you need. All configurations include a local bus video, a 17-inch monitor, a mouse, and Windows 95.

Capacity	Configuration 1 16 Mb RAM 1.6 Gb Hard Drive	Configuration 2 32 Mb RAM 2.5 Gb Hard Drive	Configuration 3 64 Mb RAM 4 Gb Hard Drive
Pentium w/MMX – 166 MHz	$1,599	$2,199	$3,099
Pentium w/MMX – 200 MHz	$1,799	$2,399	$3,299
Pentium Pro – 180 MHz	$1,999	$2,599	$3,499
Pentium Pro – 200 MHz	$2,199	$2,799	$3,699

FIGURE 1.18   Document for Practice Exercise 6

Milestones in Communications

We take for granted immediate news of everything that is going on in the world, but it was not always that way. Did you know, for example, that it took five months for Queen Isabella to hear of Columbus' discovery, or that it took two weeks for Europe to learn of Lincoln's assassination? We've done some research on milestones in communications and left the file for you (Milestones in Communications). It runs for two, three, or four pages, depending on the formatting, which we leave to you. We would like you to include a header, and we think you should box the quotations that appear at the end of the document (it's your call as to whether to separate the quotations or group them together). Please be sure to number the completed document and don't forget a title page.

The Term Paper

Go to your most demanding professor and obtain the formatting requirements for the submission of a term paper. Be as precise as possible; for example, ask about margins, type size, and so on. What are the requirements for a title page? Is there a table of contents? Are there footnotes or endnotes, headers or footers? What is the format for the bibliography? Summarize the requirements, then indicate the precise means of implementation within Microsoft Word.

Tips for Windows 95

Open the *Tips for Windows 95* document that can be found in the Exploring Windows folder. The tips are not formatted so we would like you to use the Auto-Format command to create an attractive document. There are lots of tips so a table of contents is also appropriate. Add a cover page with your name and date, then submit the completed document to your instructor.

Word Outlines and PowerPoint Presentations

A Word document can be the basis of a PowerPoint presentation, provided the document has been formatted to include styles. Each paragraph formatted according to the Heading 1 style becomes the title of a slide, each paragraph formatted with the Heading 2 style becomes the first level of text, and so on.

Use the *Milestones in Communications* document in the Exploring Word folder as the basis of a PowerPoint presentation (see the first case study). Use the AutoFormat command to apply the necessary styles, pull down the File menu, select the Send To command, then choose Microsoft PowerPoint. Your system will start PowerPoint, then convert the styles in the Word document to a PowerPoint outline. Complete the presentation based on facts in the Word document, then submit the completed presentation to your instructor.

DESKTOP PUBLISHING: CREATING A NEWSLETTER

OBJECTIVES

After reading this chapter you will be able to:

1. Design and implement a multicolumn newsletter; explain how sections are used to vary the number of columns in a document.
2. Describe one advantage and one disadvantage of using the Newsletter Wizard as opposed to creating a newsletter from scratch.
3. Define a pull quote and a reverse; explain how to implement these features using Microsoft Word.
4. Use the Borders and Shading command to emphasize a selected article.
5. Define typography; explain how styles can be used to implement changes in typography throughout a document.
6. Use the Insert Picture command to insert clip art into a document; explain how the Format Picture command is used to move and size a graphic.
7. Discuss the importance of a grid in the design of a document; describe the use of white space as a design element.

OVERVIEW

Desktop publishing evolved through a combination of technologies including faster computers, laser printers, and sophisticated page composition software to manipulate text and graphics. Desktop publishing was initially considered a separate application, but today's generation of word processors has matured to such a degree, that it is difficult to tell where word processing ends and desktop publishing begins. Microsoft Word is, for all practical purposes, a desktop publishing program that can be used to create all types of documents.

The essence of *desktop publishing* is the merger of text with graphics to produce a professional-looking document without reliance on external services. Desktop publishing will save you time and money because you are doing the work yourself rather than sending it out as you did in traditional publishing. That is the good news. The bad news is that desktop publishing is not as easy as it sounds, precisely because you are doing work that was done previously by skilled professionals. Nevertheless, with a little practice, and a basic knowledge of graphic design, which we include in this chapter, you will be able to create effective and attractive documents.

Our discussion focuses on desktop publishing as it is implemented in Microsoft Word. We show you how to design a multicolumn document, how to import clip art and other objects, and how to position those objects within a document. The chapter also reviews material from earlier chapters on bullets and lists, borders and shading, and section formatting, all of which will be used to create a newsletter.

THE NEWSLETTER

The chapter is built around the newsletter in Figure 2.1. The newsletter itself describes the basics of desktop publishing and provides an overview of the chapter. The material is presented conceptually, after which you implement the design in two hands-on exercises. We provide the text and you do the formatting. The first exercise creates a simple newsletter from copy that we provide. The second exercise uses more sophisticated formatting as described by the various techniques mentioned within the newsletter. Many of the terms are new, and we define them briefly in the next few paragraphs.

A *reverse* (light text on a dark background) is a favorite technique of desktop publishers to emphasize a specific element. It is used in the *masthead* (the identifying information) at the top of the newsletter and provides a distinctive look to the publication. The number of the newsletter and the date of publication also appear in the masthead in smaller letters.

A *pull quote* is a phrase or sentence taken from an article to emphasize a key point. It is typically set in larger type, often in a different typeface and/or italics, and may be offset with parallel lines at the top and bottom.

A *dropped-capital letter* is a large capital letter at the beginning of a paragraph. It, too, catches the reader's eye and calls attention to the associated text.

Clip art, used in moderation, will catch the reader's eye and enhance almost any newsletter. It is available from a variety of sources including the *Microsoft Clip Gallery,* which is included in Office 97. Clip art can also be downloaded from the Web, but be sure you are allowed to reprint the image.

Borders and shading are effective individually, or in combination with one another, to emphasize important stories within the newsletter. Simple vertical and/or horizontal lines are also effective. The techniques are especially useful in the absence of clip art or other graphics and are a favorite of desktop publishers.

Lists, whether bulleted or numbered, help to organize information by emphasizing important topics. A *bulleted list* emphasizes (and separates) the items. A *numbered list* sequences (and prioritizes) the items and is automatically updated to accommodate additions or deletions.

All of these techniques can be implemented with commands you already know, as you will see in the hands-on exercise, which follows shortly.

Creating a Newsletter

Volume I, Number 1   Spring 1997

Desktop publishing is easy, but there are several points to remember. This chapter will take you through the steps in creating a newsletter. The first hands-on exercise creates a simple newsletter with a masthead and three-column design. The second exercise creates a more attractive document by exploring different ways to emphasize the text.

Clip Art and Other Objects

Clip art is available from a variety of sources. You can also use other types of objects such as maps, charts, or organization charts, which are created by other applications, then brought into a document through the Insert Object command. A single dominant graphic is usually more appealing than multiple smaller graphics.

Techniques to Consider

Our finished newsletter contains one or more examples of each of the following desktop publishing techniques. Can you find where each technique is used, and further, explain, how to implement that technique in Microsoft Word?
1. Pull Quotes
2. Reverse
3. Drop Caps
4. Tables
5. Styles
6. Bullets and Numbering
7. Borders and Shading

Newspaper-Style Columns

The essence of a newsletter is the implementation of columns in which text flows continuously from the bottom of one column to the top of the next. You specify the number of columns, and optionally, the space between columns. Microsoft Word does the rest. It will compute the width of each column based on the number of columns and the margins.

Beginners often specify margins that are too large and implement too much space between the columns. Another way to achieve a more sophisticated look is to avoid the standard two-column design. You can implement columns of varying width and/or insert vertical lines between the columns.

The number of columns will vary in different parts of a document. The masthead is typically a single column, but the body of the newsletter will have two or three. Remember, too, that columns are implemented at the section level and hence, section breaks are required throughout a document.

Typography

Typography is the process of selecting typefaces, type styles, and type sizes, and is a critical element in the success of any document. Type should reinforce the message and should be consistent with the information you want to convey. More is not better, especially in the case of too many typefaces and styles, which produce cluttered documents that impress no one. Try to limit yourself to a maximum of two typefaces per document, but choose multiple sizes and/or styles within those typefaces. Use boldface or italics for emphasis, but do so in moderation, because if you use too many different elements, the effect is lost.

A pull quote adds interest to a document while simultaneously emphasizing a key point. It is implemented by increasing the point size, changing to italics, centering the text, and displaying a top and bottom border on the paragraph.

Use Styles as Appropriate

Styles were covered in the previous chapter, but that does not mean you cannot use them in conjunction with a newsletter. A style stores character and/or paragraph formatting and can be applied to multiple occurrences of the same element within a document. Change the style and you automatically change all text defined by that style. You can also use styles from one edition of your newsletter to the next to ensure consistency.

Borders and Shading

Borders and shading are effective individually or in combination with one another. Use a thin rule (one point or less) and light shading (five or ten percent) for best results. The techniques are especially useful in the absence of clip art or other graphics and are a favorite of desktop publishers.

FIGURE 2.1   The Newsletter

Typography

Typography is the process of selecting typefaces, type styles, and type sizes, and it is a critical, often subtle, element in the success of a document. Good typography goes almost unnoticed, whereas poor typography calls attention to itself and detracts from a document. Our discussion uses basic terminology, which we review below.

A *typeface* (or *font*) is a complete set of characters (upper- and lowercase letters, numbers, punctuation marks, and special symbols). Typefaces are divided into two general categories, serif and sans serif. A *serif typeface* has tiny cross lines at the ends of the characters to help the eye connect one letter with the next. A *sans serif typeface* (sans from the French for *without*) does not have these lines. A commonly accepted practice is to use serif typefaces with large amounts of text and sans serif typefaces for smaller amounts. The newsletter in Figure 2.1, for example, uses *Times New Roman* (a serif typeface) for the text and *Arial* (a sans serif typeface) for the headings.

Type size is a vertical measurement and is specified in points. One *point* is equal to ¹⁄₇₂ of an inch. The text in most documents is set in 10- or 12-point type. (The book you are reading is set in 10-point.) Different elements in the same document are often set in different type sizes to provide suitable emphasis. A variation of at least two points, however, is necessary for the difference to be noticeable. The headings in the newsletter, for example, were set in 12-point type, whereas the text of the articles is in 10-point type.

The introduction of columns into a document poses another concern in that the type size should be consistent with the width of a column. Nine-point type, for example, is appropriate in columns that are two inches wide, but much too small in a single-column term paper. In other words, longer lines or wider columns require larger type sizes. Conversely, the shorter the line or narrower the column, the smaller the point size. A related rule is to avoid very narrow columns (less than two inches) because narrow columns are choppy and difficult to read. Overly wide columns or very long lines are just as bad because the reader can easily get lost.

We reiterate that there are no hard and fast rules for the selection of type, only guidelines and common sense. You will find that the design that worked so well in one document may not work at all in a different document. Indeed, good typography is often the result of trial and error, and we encourage you to experiment freely.

TYPOGRAPHY TIP: USE RESTRAINT

More is not better, especially in the case of too many typefaces and styles, which produce cluttered documents that impress no one. Try to limit yourself to a maximum of two typefaces per document, but choose multiple sizes and/or styles within those typefaces. Use boldface or italics for emphasis, but do so in moderation, because if you emphasize too many elements the effect is lost.

The Columns Command

The columnar formatting in a newsletter is implemented through the *Columns command* as shown in Figure 2.2. Start by selecting one of the preset designs and Microsoft Word takes care of everything else. It calculates the width of each col-

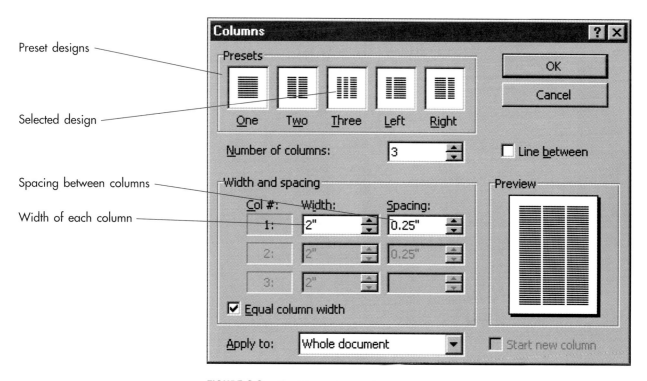

Preset designs

Selected design

Spacing between columns

Width of each column

FIGURE 2.2 The Columns Command

umn based on the number of columns, the left and right margins on the page, and the specified (default) space between columns.

Consider, for example, the dialog box in Figure 2.2 in which the preset design of three equal columns is selected with a spacing of ¼ inch between each column. The 2-inch width of each column is computed automatically based on left and right margins of 1 inch each and the ¼-inch spacing between columns. The width of each column is computed by subtracting the sum of the margins and the space between the columns (a total of 2½ inches in this example) from the page width of 8½ inches. The result of the subtraction is 6 inches, which is divided by 3, resulting in a column width of 2 inches.

You can change any of the settings in the Columns dialog box and Word will automatically make the necessary adjustments. The newsletter in Figure 2.1, for example, uses a two-column layout with wide and narrow columns. We prefer this design to columns of uniform width, as we think it adds interest to our document. Note, too, that once columns have been defined, text will flow continuously from the bottom of one column to the top of the next

Return for a minute to the newsletter in Figure 2.1, and notice that the number of columns varies from one part of the newsletter to another. The masthead is displayed over a single column at the top of the page, whereas the remainder of the newsletter is formatted in two columns of different widths. The number of columns is specified at the section level, and thus a *section break* is required whenever the column specification changes. (Section formatting was described in the previous chapter in conjunction with changing margins, headers and footers, page numbering, size, and orientation.)

THE NEWSLETTER WIZARD

At first glance the *Newsletter Wizard* appears to answer the prayers of the would-be desktop publisher. The Newsletter Wizard asks you a series of questions as shown in Figure 2.3, then creates a template for you on which to base a document.

(a) The Newsletter Wizard

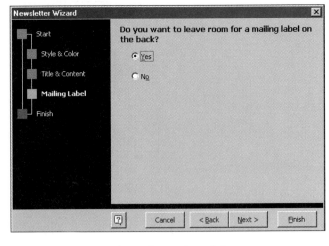

(d) Specify a Mailing Label

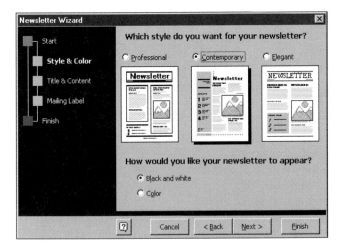

(b) Choose the Style and Color

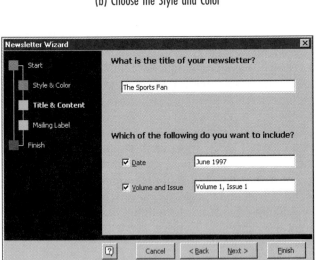

(c) Choose the Title

(e) The Completed Template

FIGURE 2.3   The Newsletter Wizard

The Newsletter Wizard provides a considerable amount of flexibility, as can be inferred from the screens in Figure 2.3a, b, c, and d, which let you specify the style, number of columns, title, and elements to include. The resulting template in Figure 2.3e is based on your answers, and further, incorporates good typography and other elements of graphic design.

What, then, is the drawback, and why would you not use the Newsletter Wizard for every newsletter you create? The problem is one of adaptability in that the wizard may not be suitable for the newsletter you wish to create. What if you wanted to include two graphics rather than one, or you wanted the graphics in a different position? What if you needed a newsletter with columns of varying width or you wanted to include a pull quote or a reverse?

You could, of course, use the template created by the wizard as the starting point for the newsletter, then execute the necessary commands in Word to modify the document according to your specifications. You will find, however, that it is just as easy to create the newsletter from the beginning and bypass the wizard entirely. You will wind up with a superior document that is exactly what you need, not what the wizard thinks you need. Creating a newsletter is a lot easier than you might imagine, as you will see in the following hands-on exercise.

HANDS-ON EXERCISE 1

Newspaper Columns

Objective: To create a basic newsletter through the Format columns command; to use section breaks to change the number of columns within a document. Use Figure 2.4 as a guide in the exercise.

STEP 1: The Page Setup Command

➤ Start Word. Open the **Text for Newsletter document** in the Exploring Word folder. Save the document as **Modified Newsletter** so that you can return to the original document if necessary.

➤ Pull down the **File menu.** Click **Page Setup** to display the Page Setup dialog box in Figure 2.4a. Change the top, bottom, left, and right margins to .75 as shown in the figure. (Press the **Tab key** to move from one text box to another.)

➤ Click **OK** to accept these settings and close the Page Setup dialog box. If necessary, click the **Page Layout View button** above the status bar. Set the magnification (zoom) to **Page Width.**

CHANGE THE MARGINS

The default margins of 1 inch at the top and bottom of a page, and 1¼ inches on the sides, are fine for a typical document. A multicolumn newsletter, however, looks better with smaller margins, which in turn enables you to create wider columns. Margins are defined at the section level, and hence it's easiest to change the margins at the very beginning, when a document consists of only a single section.

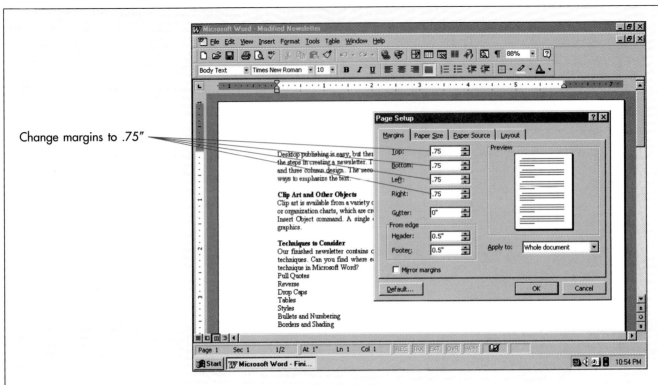

Change margins to .75"

(a) The Page Setup Command (step 1)

FIGURE 2.4   Hands-on Exercise 1

STEP 2: Check the Document

➤ Pull down the **Tools menu,** click **Options,** click the **Spelling and Grammar tab,** and select the option for **Standard writing style.** Click **OK** to close the Options dialog box.

➤ Click the **Spelling and Grammar button** on the Standard toolbar to check the document for errors.

➤ The first error detected by the spelling and grammar check is the omitted hyphen between the words *three* and *column* as shown in Figure 2.4b. (This is a subtle mistake and emphasizes the need to check a document using the tools provided by Word.) Click **Change** to accept the indicated suggestion.

➤ Continue checking the document, accepting (or rejecting) the suggested corrections as you see fit.

➤ Save the document.

USE THE SPELLING AND GRAMMAR CHECK

Our eyes are less discriminating than we would like to believe, allowing misspellings and simple typos to go unnoticed. To prove the point, count the number of times the letter f appears in this sentence, *"Finished files are the result of years of scientific study combined with the experience of years."* The correct answer is six, but most people find only four or five. Checking your document takes only a few minutes. Do it!

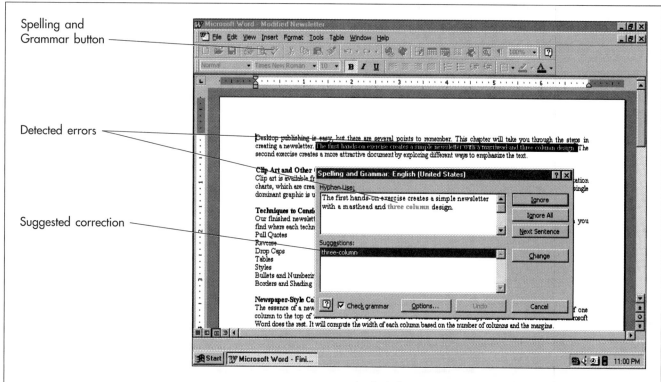

Spelling and Grammar button

Detected errors

Suggested correction

(b) Check the Document (step 2)

FIGURE 2.4   Hands-on Exercise 1 (continued)

STEP 3: Implement Newspaper Columns

➤ Pull down the **Format menu.** Click **Columns** to display the dialog box in Figure 2.4c. Click the **Presets icon** for **Two.** The column width for each column and the spacing between columns will be determined automatically from the existing margins.

➤ If necessary, clear the **Line Between box.** Click **OK** to accept the settings and close the Columns dialog box.

➤ The text of the newsletter should be displayed in two columns. If you do not see the columns, it is probably because you are in the wrong view. Click the **Page Layout View button** above the status bar to change to this view.

THE COLUMNS BUTTON

The Columns button on the Standard toolbar is the fastest way to create columns in a document. Click the button, drag the mouse to choose the number of columns, then release the mouse to create the columns. The toolbar lets you change the number of columns, but not the spacing between columns. The toolbar is also limited in that you cannot create columns of different widths or select a line between columns.

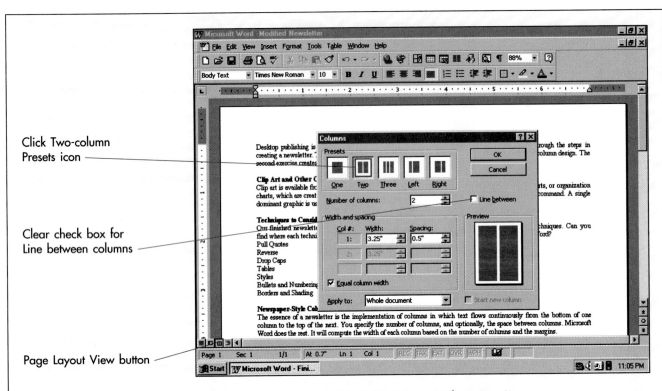

Click Two-column
Presets icon

Clear check box for
Line between columns

Page Layout View button

(c) Implement Newspaper Columns (step 3)

FIGURE 2.4   Hands-on Exercise 1 (continued)

STEP 4: Balance the Columns

➤ Use the **Zoom box** on the Standard toolbar to zoom to **Whole Page** to see the entire newsletter as shown in Figure 2.4d. Do not be concerned if the columns are of different lengths.

➤ Press **Ctrl+End** to move the insertion point to the end of the document. Pull down the **Insert menu.** Click **Break** to display the Break dialog box in Figure 2.4d. Select the **Continuous option button** under Section breaks.

➤ Click **OK** to accept the settings and close the dialog box. The columns should be balanced, although one column may be one line longer than the other.

USE THE RULER TO CHANGE COLUMN WIDTH

Click anywhere within the column whose width you want to change, then point to the ruler and click and drag the right margin (the mouse pointer changes to a double arrow) to change the column width. Changing the width of one column in a document with equal-sized columns changes the width of all other columns so that they remain equal. Changing the width in a document with unequal columns changes only that column. You can also double click the top of the ruler to display the Page Setup dialog box, then click the Margins tab to change the left and right margins, which in turn will change the column width.

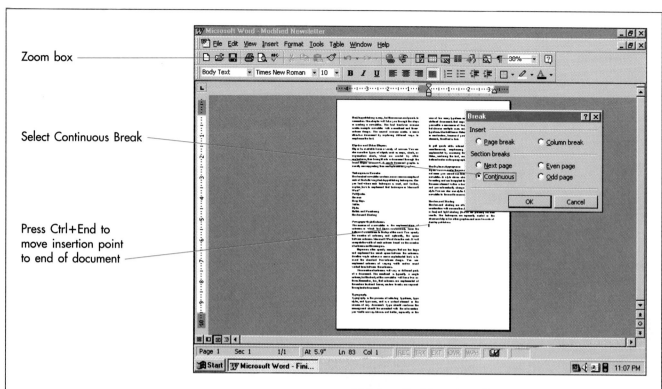

Zoom box

Select Continuous Break

Press Ctrl+End to
move insertion point
to end of document

(d) Balance the Columns (step 4)

FIGURE 2.4   Hands-on Exercise 1 (continued)

STEP 5: Create the Masthead

➤ Use the Zoom box on the Standard toolbar to change to **Page Width.** Click the **Show/Hide ¶ button** to display the paragraph and section marks.

➤ Press **Ctrl+Home** to move the insertion point to the beginning of the document. Pull down the **Insert menu,** click **Break,** select the **Continuous option button,** and click **OK.** You should see a double dotted line indicating a section break as shown in Figure 2.4e.

➤ Click immediately to the left of the dotted line, which will place the insertion point to the left of the line. Check the status bar to be sure you are in section one.

➤ Change the format for this section to a single column by clicking the **Columns button** on the Standard toolbar and selecting one column. (Alternatively, you can pull down the **Format menu,** click **Columns,** and choose **One** from the Presets column formats.)

➤ Type **Creating a Newsletter** and press the **enter key** twice. Select the newly entered text, click the **Center button** on the Formatting toolbar. Change the font to **48 point Arial Bold.**

➤ Save the newsletter.

Align Right button   Columns button   Show/Hide ¶ button   Zoom box

Center button

Enter title for newsletter and
format in 48-point Arial bold

Insert table (2 columns
× 1 row)

Section break

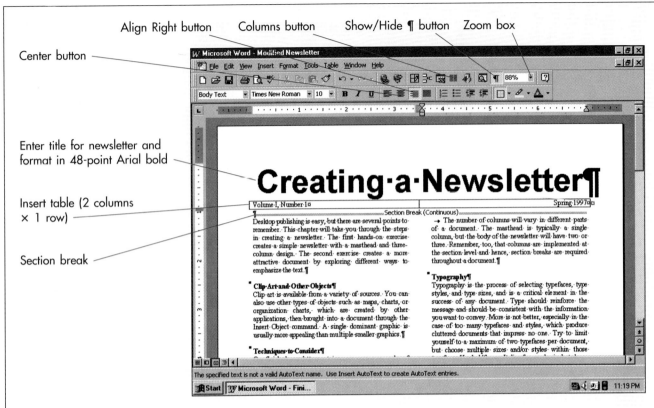

(e) Create the Masthead (steps 5 and 6)

FIGURE 2.4 Hands-on Exercise 1 (continued)

COLUMNS AND SECTIONS

Columns are implemented at the section level and thus a new section is
required whenever the number of columns changes within a document.
Select the text that is to be formatted in columns, click the Columns button on the Standard toolbar, then drag the mouse to set the desired number of columns. Microsoft Word will automatically insert the section
breaks before and after the selected text.

STEP 6: Create the Masthead (Continued)

➤ Click underneath the masthead (to the left of the section break). Pull down
the **Table menu,** click **Insert Table,** and insert a table with one row and two
columns as shown in Figure 2.4e.

➤ Click in the left cell of the table. Type **Volume I, Number 1.** Click in the right
cell (or press the **Tab key** to move to this cell and type the current semester
(for example, **Spring 1997**). Click the **Align Right button** on the Standard
toolbar to realign the text.

➤ Save the newsletter.

| LEFT ALIGNED | CENTERED | RIGHT ALIGNED |

Many documents call for left, centered, and/or right aligned text on the same line, an effect that is achieved through setting tabs, or more easily through a table. To achieve the effect shown at the top of this box, create a 1 × 3 table (one row and three columns), type the text in the three cells as needed, then use the buttons on the Formatting toolbar to left-align, center, and right-align the respective cells. Select the table, pull down the Format menu, click Borders and Shading, then specify None as the Border setting.

STEP 7: Create a Reverse

➤ Press **Ctrl+Home** to move the insertion point to the beginning of the newsletter. Click anywhere within the title of the newsletter.

➤ Pull down the **Format menu,** click **Borders and Shading** to display the Borders and Shading dialog box, then click the **Shading tab** as shown in Figure 2.4f.

➤ Click the **drop-down arrow** in the Style list box (in the Patterns area) and select **Solid (100%)** shading. Click **OK** to accept the setting and close the dialog box. Click elsewhere in the document to see the results.

Show/Hide ¶ button

Click Shading tab

Click anywhere in title

Click drop-down arrow in Style list box

Select Solid

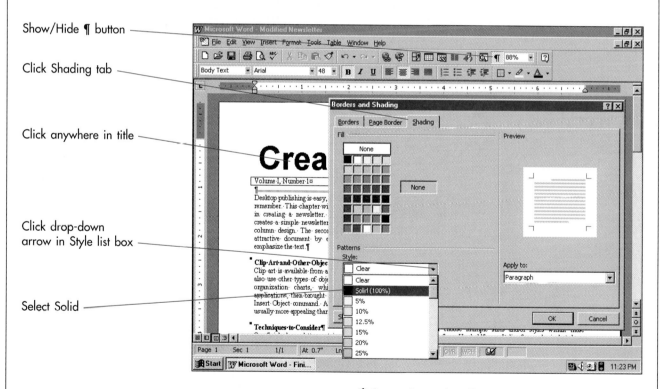

(f) Create a Reverse (step 7)

FIGURE 2.4   Hands-on Exercise 1 (continued)

➤ The final step is to remove the default border that appears around the table. Click in the selection area to the left of the table to select the entire table.

➤ Pull down the **Format menu,** click **Borders and Shading,** and if necessary click the **Borders tab.** Click the **None icon** in the Presets area. Click **OK.** Click elsewhere in the document to see the result.

USE COLOR REVERSES FOR EMPHASIS

White letters on a solid background (technically called a reverse) is a favorite technique of desktop publishers. It looks even better in color—if you have a color printer. Select the text, pull down the Format menu, click the Borders and Shading command, and click the Shading tab. Click the drop-down arrow in the Style list box and choose solid (100%) shading to create the reverse. Click the drop-down arrow in the Color list box and choose the background color (e.g., blue), then click OK to close the dialog box. Click and drag to select the text, click the down arrow on the Font color button on the Formatting toolbar, and select white. Click the Bold button on the Formatting toolbar, then click elsewhere in the document to see the results.

STEP 8: Modify the Heading Style

➤ Two styles have been implemented for you in the newsletter. Click in any text paragraph and you see the Body Text style name displayed in the Style box on the Formatting toolbar. Click in any heading and you see the Heading 1 style.

➤ Click and drag to select the heading **Clip Art and Other Objects.** Click the **drop-down arrow** on the Font list box and change the font to **Arial.** Change the **Font Size** to **12** point.

➤ Click the **Heading 1** style name within the Style list box on the Formatting toolbar. Press enter to select this style and display the Modify Style dialog box as shown in Figure 2.4g.

➤ The option button to update the style according to the current formatting is selected. Click **OK** to change the style, which automatically reformats every element defined by this style.

➤ Save the newsletter.

USE STYLES AS APPROPRIATE

Styles were covered in the previous chapter, but that does not mean you cannot use them in conjunction with a newsletter. A style stores character and/or paragraph formatting and can be applied to multiple occurrences of the same element within a document. Change the style and you automatically change all text defined by that style. You can also use the same styles from one edition of your newsletter to the next to ensure consistency.

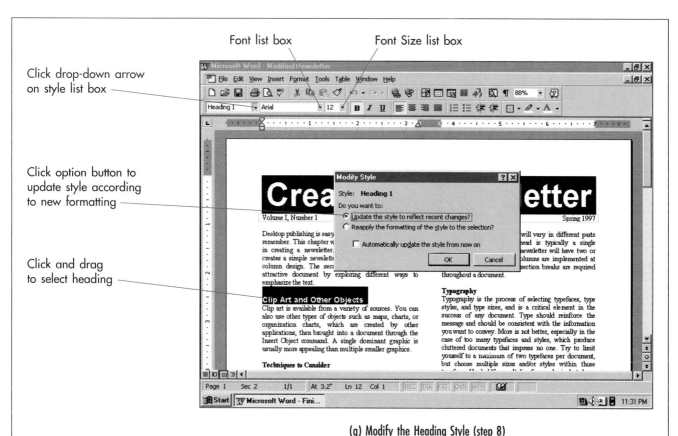

Font list box   Font Size list box

Click drop-down arrow on style list box

Click option button to update style according to new formatting

Click and drag to select heading

(g) Modify the Heading Style (step 8)

FIGURE 2.4   Hands-on Exercise 1 (continued)

STEP 9: The Print Preview Command

➤ Pull down the **File menu** and click **Print Preview** (or click the **Print Preview button** on the Standard toolbar) to view the newsletter as in Figure 2.4h. This is a basic two-column newsletter with the masthead appearing as a reverse and stretching over a single column.

➤ Click the **Print button** to print the newsletter at this stage so that you can compare this version with the finished newsletter at the end of the next exercise. Click the **Close button** on the Print Preview toolbar to close the Preview view and return to the Page Layout view.

➤ Exit Word if you do not want to continue with the next exercise at this time.

THE PRINT PREVIEW TOOLBAR

Click the Context Sensitive Help button on the extreme right of the Print Preview toolbar (the mouse pointer changes to an arrow and a question mark), then click any other button for an explanation of its function. The Shrink to Fit button is especially useful if a small portion of the newsletter spills over to a second page—click the button and it uniformly reduces the fonts throughout the document to eliminate the second page.

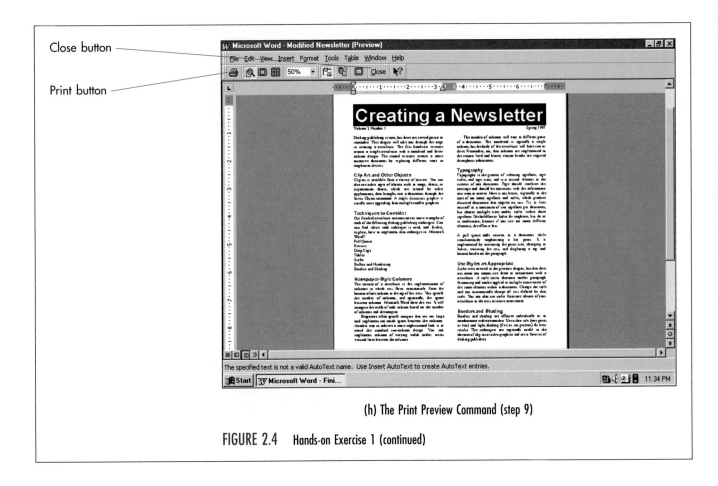

Close button

Print button

Creating a Newsletter

(h) The Print Preview Command (step 9)

FIGURE 2.4 Hands-on Exercise 1 (continued)

ELEMENTS OF GRAPHIC DESIGN

We trust you have completed the first hands-on exercise without difficulty and that you were able to duplicate the initial version of the newsletter. That, however, is the easy part of desktop publishing. The more difficult aspect is to develop the design in the first place because the mere availability of a desktop publishing program does not guarantee an effective document, any more than a word processor will turn its author into another Shakespeare. Other skills are necessary, and so we continue with a brief introduction to graphic design.

Much of what we say is subjective, and what works in one situation will not necessarily work in another. Your eye is the best judge of all, and you should follow your own instincts. Experiment freely and realize that successful design is the result of trial and error. Seek inspiration from others by collecting samples of real documents that you find attractive, then use those documents as the basis for your own designs.

The Grid

The design of a document is developed on a ***grid,*** an underlying, but *invisible,* set of horizontal and vertical lines that determine the placement of the major elements. A grid establishes the overall structure of a document by indicating the number of columns, the space between columns, the size of the margins, the placement of headlines, art, and so on. The grid does *not* appear in the printed document or on the screen.

A grid may be simple or complex, but is always distinguished by the number of columns it contains. The three-column grid of Figures 2.5a and 2.5b is one

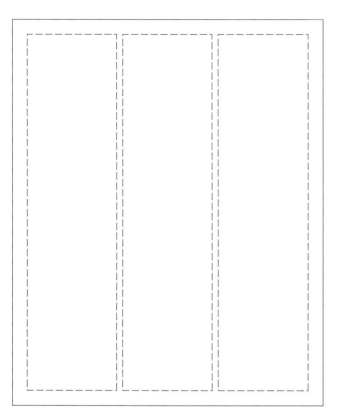

(a) Empty Three-column Grid

No Can Do

He felt more and more pressure to play the game of not playing. Maybe that's why he stepped in front of that truck.

People wonder why people do things like this, but all you have to do is look around and see all the stress and insanity each person in responsibility is required to put up with. There is no help or end in sight. It seems that managers are managing less and shoveling the workloads on to their underlings. This seems to be the overall response to the absence of raises or benefit packages they feel are their entitlement. Something must be done now!

People wonder why people do things like this, but all you have to do is look around and see all the stress and insanity each person in responsibility is required to put up with. There is no help or end in sight. It seems that managers are managing less and shoveling the workloads on to their underlings. This seems to be the overall response to the absence of raises or benefit packag es they feel are their entitlement. Something must be done now!

People wonder why people do things like this, but all you have

to do is look around and see all the stress and insanity each person in responsibility is required to put up with. There is no help or end in sight. It seems that managers are managing less and shoveling the workloads on to their underlings. This seems to be the overall response to the absence of raises or benefit packag es they feel are their entitlement.

People wonder why people do things like this, but all y o u have to do is look

around and see all the stress and insanity each person in responsibility is required to put up with. There is no help or end in sight. It seems that managers are managing less and shoveling the workloads on to their underlings. This seems to be the overall response to the absence of raises or benefit packages they feel are their entitlement. Something must be done now!

People wonder why people do things like this, but all you have to do is look around and see all the stress and insanity each person in responsibility is required to put up with. There is no help or end in sight. It seems that managers are managing less. Something must be done now!

People wonder why people do things like this, but all you have to do is look around and see all the stress and insanity each person in ▼

(b) Three-column Grid

No Can Do

He felt more and more pressure to play the game of not playing. Maybe that's why he stepped in front of that truck.

People wonder why people do things like this, but all you have to do is look around and see all the stress and insanity each person in responsibility is required to put up with. There is no help or end in sight. It seems that managers are managing less and shoveling the workloads on to their underlings. This seems to be the overall response to the absence of raises or benefit packages they feel are their entitlement. Something must be done now!

People wonder why people do things like this, but all you have to do is look around and see all the

look around and see all the stress and insanity each person in responsibility is required to put up with. There is no help or end in sight. It seems that managers are managing less and shoveling the workloads on to their underlings. This seems to be the overall response to the absence of raises or benefit packages they feel are their entitlement.

People wonder why people do things like this, but all you have to do is look around and see all the stress and insanity each person in re

sponsibility is required to put up with. There is no help or end in sight. It seems that managers are managing less and shoveling the workloads on to their underlings. This seems to be the overall response to the absence of raises or benefit packages they feel are their entitlement.

People wonder why people do things like this, but all you have to do is look around and see all the stress and insanity each person in responsibility is required to put up with. There is no help or end in sight. It seems that

managers are managing less and shoveling the workloads on to their underlings. This seems to be the overall response to the absence of raises or benefit packages they feel are their entitlement. Something must be done now!

People wonder why people do things like this, but all you have to do is look around and see all the stress and insanity each person in responsibility is required to put up with. There is no help or end in sight. It seems that managers are managing less. Something must be done now!

People wonder why people do things like this, but all you have to do is look around and see all the stress and insanity each person in responsibility is required to put up with. There is no help or end in sight. It seems that managers are managing less and shoveling the workloads on to their underlings. This seems to be the overall response to the ▼

(c) Four-column Grid

People wonder why people do things like this, but all you have to do is look around and see all the stress and insanity each person in responsibility is required to put up with. There is no help or end in sight. It seems that managers are managing less and shoveling the workloads on to their underlings. This seems to be the overall response to the absence of raises or benefit packages they feel are their entitlement. Something must be done!

People wonder why people do things like this, but all you have to do is look around and see all the stress and insanity each person in responsibility is required to put up with. There is no help or end in sight. It seems that managers are managing less and shoveling the workloads on to their underlings. This seems to be the overall response to the absence of raises or benefit packages they feel are their entitlement. Something must be done!

People wonder why people do things like this, but all you have to do is look around and see all the stress and insanity each person in responsibility is required to put up with. There is no help or end in sight. It seems that manag

He felt more and more pressure to play the game of not playing. Maybe that's why he stepped in front of that truck.

ers are managing less and shoveling the workloads on to their underlings. This seems to be the overall response to the absence of raises or benefit packages they feel are their

things like this, but all you have to do is look around and see all the stress and insanity each person in responsibility is required to put up with. There is no help or end in sight. It seems that managers are managing less and shoveling the workloads on to their underlings. This seems to be the overall response to the absence of raises or

benefit packages they feel are their entitlement. Something must be done now!

People wonder why people do things like this, but all you have to do is look around and see all the stress and insanity each person in responsibility is required to put up with. There is no help or end in sight. It seems that managers are managing less and shoveling the workloads on to their underlings. This seems to be the overall response to the absence of raises or benefit packages they feel are their

entitlement. Something must be done!

People wonder why people do things like this, but all you have to do is look around and see all the stress and insanity each person in responsibility is required to put up with. There is no help or end in sight. It seems that managers are managing less and shoveling the workloads on to their underlings. This seems to be the overall response to the absence of raises or benefit packages they feel are their entitlement. Something must be done!

People wonder why people do things like this, but all you have to do is look around and see all the stress and insanity each person in responsibility is required to put up with. There is no help or end in sight. It seems that managers are managing less and shoveling the workloads on to their underlings. Something must be done now!

People wonder why people do things like this, but all you have to do ▼

(d) Five-column Grid

FIGURE 2.5   The Grid System of Design

of the most common and utilitarian designs. Figure 2.5c shows a four-column design for the same document, with unequal column widths to provide interest. Figure 2.5d illustrates a five-column grid that is often used with large amounts of text. Many other designs are possible as well. A one-column grid is used for term papers and letters. A two-column, wide and narrow format is appropriate for textbooks and manuals. Two- and three-column formats are used for newsletters and magazines.

The simple concept of a grid should make the underlying design of any document obvious, which in turn gives you an immediate understanding of page composition. Moreover, the conscious use of a grid will help you organize your material and result in a more polished and professional-looking publication. It will also help you to achieve consistency from page to page within a document (or from issue to issue of a newsletter). Indeed, much of what goes wrong in desktop publishing stems from failing to follow or use the underlying grid.

Clip Art

Clip art is available from a variety of sources including the Microsoft Clip Gallery. The complete gallery, contained on the Office 97 CD, is a wonderful resource with more than 3,000 clip art images and almost 150 photographs. The Clip Gallery can be accessed in a variety of ways, most easily through the ***Insert Picture command.*** Once clip art has been inserted into a document, it can be moved and sized just like any other Windows object, as will be illustrated in our next hands-on exercise.

The ***Format Picture command*** provides additional flexibility in the placement of clip art. The Wrapping tab, in the Format Picture dialog box, determines the way text is positioned around a picture. The Top and Bottom option (no wrapping) is selected in Figure 2.6a and the resulting document is shown in Figure 2.6b. The sizing handles around the clip art indicate that it is currently selected, enabling you to move and/or resize the clip art using the mouse. (You can also use the Size and Position tabs in the Format Picture dialog box for more precision with either setting.) Changing the size or position of the object, however, does not affect the way in which text wraps around the clip art.

The document in Figure 2.6c illustrates a different wrapping selection in which text is wrapped on both sides. Figure 2.6c also uses an option on the Colors and Lines tab to draw a blue border around the clip art. The document in Figure 2.6d eliminates the border and chooses the tight wrapping style so that the text is positioned as closely as possible to the figure in a free-form design. Choosing among the various documents in Figure 2.6 is one of personal preference. Our point is simply that Word provides multiple options, and it is up to you, the desktop publisher, to choose the design that best suits your requirements.

Emphasis

Good design makes it easy for the reader to determine what is important. As indicated earlier, emphasis can be achieved in several ways, the easiest being variations in type size and/or type style. Headings should be set in type sizes (at least two points) larger than body copy. The use of **boldface** is effective as are *italics,* but both should be done in moderation. (UPPERCASE LETTERS and underlining are alternative techniques that we believe are less effective.)

Boxes and/or shading call attention to selected articles. Horizontal lines are effective to separate one topic from another or to call attention to a pull quote. A reverse can be striking for a small amount of text. Clip art, used in moderation, will catch the reader's eye and enhance almost any newsletter.

Top and Bottom Wrapping Style is selected

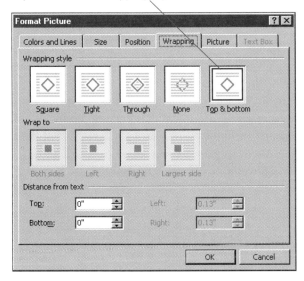

(a) Wrapping Tab

(b) Top and Bottom Wrapping

(c) Square Wrapping (both sides)

(d) Tight Wrapping (both sides)

FIGURE 2.6   The Format Picture Command

Objective: To insert clip art into a newsletter; to format a newsletter using styles, borders and shading, pull quotes, and lists. Use Figure 2.7.

STEP 1: Change the Column Layout

➤ Open the **Modified Newsletter** from the previous exercise. Click in the masthead and change the number of this edition from 1 to **2.**

➤ Click anywhere in the body of the newsletter. The status bar should indicate that you are in the second section. Pull down the **Format menu.** Click **Columns** to display the dialog box in Figure 2.7a. Click the **Left Preset icon.**

➤ Change the width of the first column to **2.25** and the space between columns to **.25.** Check (click) the **Line Between box.** Click **OK.** Save the newsletter.

Click Left Presets icon

Click check box to create a Line Between the columns

Change column width to 2.25"

Change space between columns to .25"

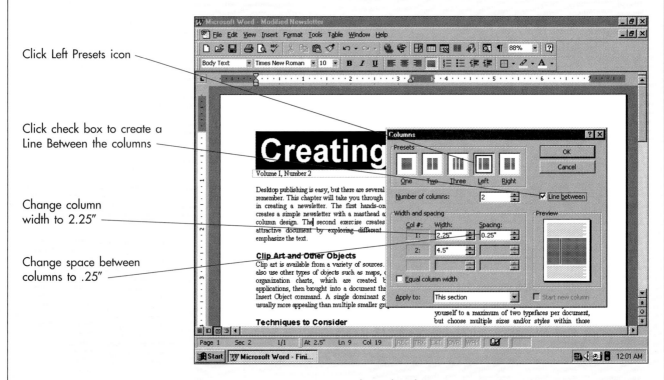

(a) Change the Column Layout (step 1)

FIGURE 2.7 Hands-on Exercise 2

EXPERIMENT WITH THE DESIGN

The number and width of the columns in a newsletter is the single most important element in its design. Experiment freely. Good design is often the result of trial and error.

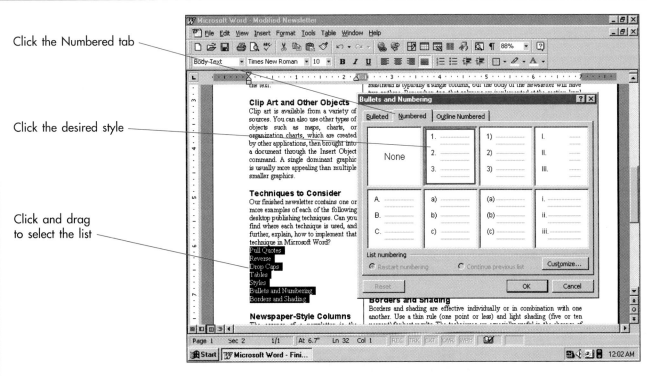

Click the Numbered tab

Click the desired style

Click and drag
to select the list

(b) Bullets and Numbering (step 2)

FIGURE 2.7   Hands-on Exercise 2 (continued)

STEP 2: Bullets and Numbering

➤ Scroll in the document until you come to the list within the **Techniques to Consider** paragraph. Select the entire list as shown in Figure 2.7b.

➤ Pull down the **Format menu** and click **Bullets and Numbering** to display the Bullets and Numbering dialog box. If necessary, click the **Numbered tab** and choose the numbering style with Arabic numbers followed by periods. Click **OK** to accept these settings and close the Bullets and Numbering dialog box.

➤ Click anywhere in the newsletter to deselect the text. Save the newsletter.

LISTS AND THE FORMATTING TOOLBAR

The Formatting toolbar contains four buttons for use with bulleted and numbered lists. The Increase Indent and Decrease Indent buttons move the selected items one tab stop to the right and left, respectively. The Bullets button creates a bulleted list from unnumbered items or converts a numbered list to a bulleted list. The Numbering button creates a numbered list or converts a bulleted list to numbers. The Bullets and Numbering buttons also function as toggle switches; for example, clicking the Bullets button when a bulleted list is already in effect will remove the bullets.

STEP 3: Insert the Clip Art

➤ Click immediately to the left of the article beginning **Clip Art and Other Objects.** Pull down the **Insert menu,** click **Picture,** then click **Clip Art** to display the Microsoft Clip Gallery. (Click **OK** if you see a dialog box reminding you that additional clip art is available on a CD-ROM.)

➤ If necessary, click the **Clip Art tab** and select (click) the **Cartoons category** as shown in Figure 2.7c. Select the **man with many hats** (or a different image if you prefer), then click the **Insert button** to place the clip art into the newsletter.

➤ The Microsoft Clip Gallery dialog box will close and the picture will appear in the newsletter. Do not be concerned about the size or position of the clip art.

Click the Clip Art tab

Click to position
the insertion point

Click the Cartoons category

Click the desired
clip art image

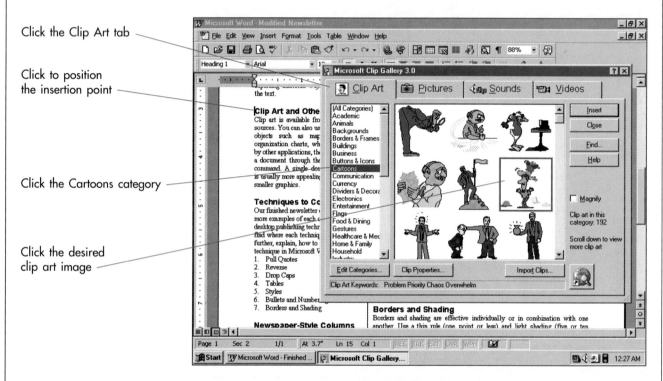

(c) Insert the Clip Art (step 3)

FIGURE 2.7 Hands-on Exercise 2 (continued)

ADDITIONAL CLIP IMAGES

The Microsoft Clip Gallery contains over 100MB of data consisting of more than 3,000 clip art images, 144 photographs, 28 sounds, and 20 video clips. Only a fraction of these are installed with Microsoft Office, but you can access the additional objects from the Office CD at any time. You can also install some or all of the objects on your hard disk, provided you have sufficient space. Start the Windows Explorer, then open the ClipArt folder on the Office CD. Double click the Setup icon to start the Setup Wizard, then follow the on-screen instructions to install the additional components you want.

STEP 4: Move and Size the Clip Art

➤ The clip art is initially too large and forces the newsletter to spill over to a second page. Click the **drop-down arrow** on the Zoom list box and select **Two Pages.** You can move and size the clip art just as you can any Windows object.

➤ To size the clip art, click anywhere within the clip art to select it and display the sizing handles. Drag a corner handle (the mouse pointer changes to a double arrow) to change the length and width of the picture simultaneously and keep the object in proportion.

➤ To move the clip art, click the object to select it and display the sizing handles. Point to any part of the object except a sizing handle (the mouse pointer changes to a four-sided arrow), then click and drag to move the clip art elsewhere in the document.

➤ It's faster, however, to use the Format Picture command. Select (click) the clip art, then pull down the **Format menu** and select the **Picture command** to display the Format Picture dialog box in Figure 2.7d.

➤ Click the **Size tab,** click in the **Width list box,** enter **1.5″,** then click **OK** to accept the settings and close the Format Picture dialog box. The newsletter should fit on one page, and all of the items in the numbered list should fit in the first column. (Change the width if the figure does not fit.)

➤ Save the document.

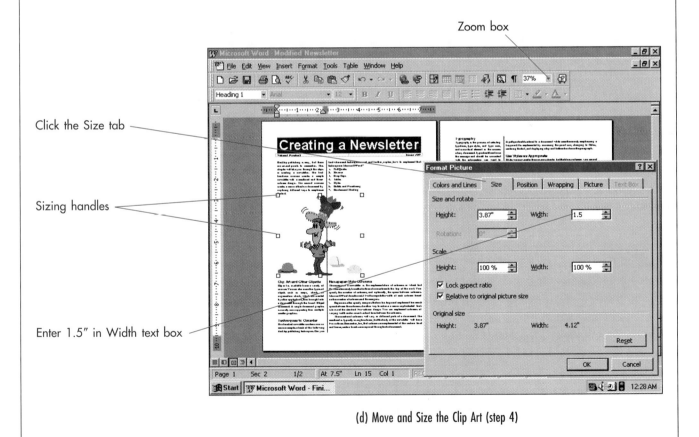

(d) Move and Size the Clip Art (step 4)

FIGURE 2.7   Hands-on Exercise 2 (continued)

THE PICTURE TOOLBAR

The Picture toolbar offers the easiest way to execute the various commands associated with a picture or clip art image. As with any toolbar, you can point to a button to display a ScreenTip containing the name of the button, which is indicative of its function. You will find buttons for wrapping and formatting a picture, a Line Styles button to place a border around a picture, and a cropping button to crop (erase) part of a picture. (If you do not see the Picture toolbar when clip art is selected, right click any visible toolbar, then toggle the Picture toolbar on.)

STEP 5: Borders and Shading

➤ Change to **Page Width** and click the **Show/Hide ¶ button** to display the paragraph marks. Press **Ctrl+End** to move to the end of the document, then select the heading and associated paragraph for Borders and Shading. (Do not select the ending paragraph mark or else the shading will continue below the section break.)

➤ Pull down the **Format menu.** Click **Borders and Shading.** If necessary click the **Borders tab** to display the dialog box in Figure 2.4e. Click the **Box icon** in the Setting area. Click the **drop-down arrow** in the Width list box and select the **1 point** line style.

Click Borders tab

Click Box icon

Click drop-down arrow to display available line widths

Click and drag to select heading and text

Do not select paragraph mark

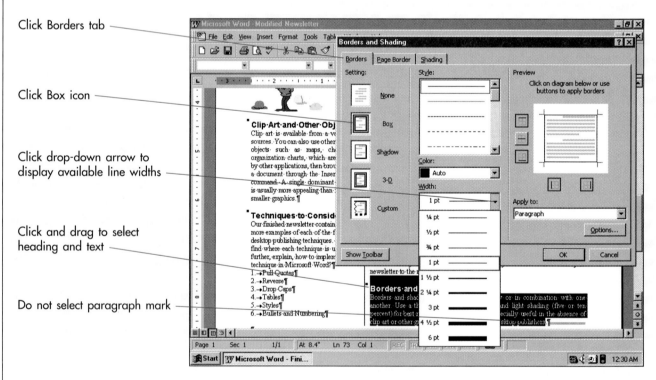

(e) Borders and Shading (step 5)

FIGURE 2.7   Hands-on Exercise 2 (continued)

- Click the **Shading tab.** Click the **drop-down arrow** in the Style list box (in the Patterns area) and select 5% shading. Click **OK** to accept the setting and close the dialog box.
- Click elsewhere in the document to see the results. The heading and paragraph should be enclosed in a border with light shading.
- Save the newsletter.

BORDERS AND SHADING

The Borders and Shading command takes practice, but once you get used to it you will love it. To place a border around multiple paragraphs (the paragraphs should have the same indents or else a different border will be placed around each paragraph), select the paragraphs prior to execution of the Borders and Shading command. Select (click) the line style you like, then click the Box or Shadow Preset button to place the border around the selected paragraphs. To change the border on one side, click the desired style and then click the side within the Preview area. Click OK to accept the settings and close the dialog box.

STEP 6: Create a Pull Quote

- Scroll to the bottom of the document until you find the paragraph describing a pull quote. Select the entire paragraph and change the text to 14-point Arial italic.
- Click in the paragraph to deselect the text, then click the **Center button** to center the paragraph.
- Click the **drop-down arrow** on the **Border button** to display the different border styles as shown in Figure 2.7f.
- Click the **Top Border button** to add a top border to the paragraph.
- Click the **Bottom border button** to create a bottom border and complete the pull quote.

EMPHASIZE WHAT'S IMPORTANT

Good design makes it easy for the reader to determine what is important. A pull quote (a phrase or sentence taken from an article) adds interest to a document while simultaneously emphasizing a key point. Boxes and shading are also effective in catching the reader's attention. A simple change in typography, such as increasing the point size, changing the typeface, and/or the use of boldface or italics, calls attention to a heading and visually separates it from the associated text.

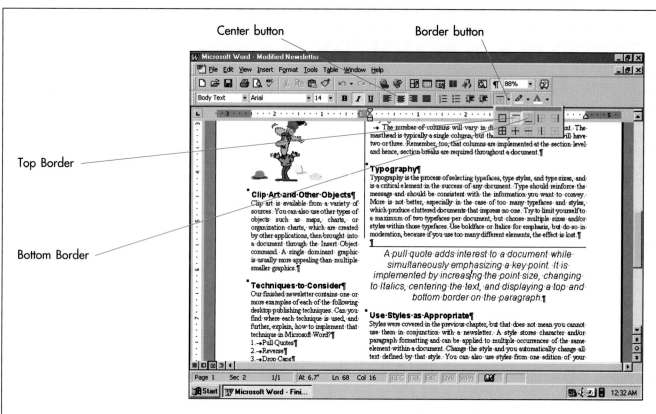

Center button   Border button

Top Border

Bottom Border

(f) Create a Pull Quote (step 6)

FIGURE 2.7 Hands-on Exercise 2 (continued)

STEP 7: Create a Drop Cap

➤ Scroll to the beginning of the newsletter. Click immediately before the D in *Desktop publishing*.

➤ Pull down the **Format menu.** Click **Drop Cap** to display the dialog box in Figure 2.7g. Click the **Position icon** for **Dropped** as shown in the figure. We used the default settings, but you can change the font, size (lines to drop), or distance from the text by clicking the arrow on the appropriate list box.

➤ Click **OK** to create the Drop Cap dialog box. Click outside the frame around the drop cap. Save the newsletter.

MODIFYING A DROP CAP

Select (click) a dropped capital letter to display a thatched border known as a frame, then click the border or frame to display its sizing handles. You can move and size a frame just as you can any Windows object; for example, click and drag a corner sizing handle to change the size of the frame (and the drop cap it contains). To delete the frame (and remove the drop cap) press the delete key.

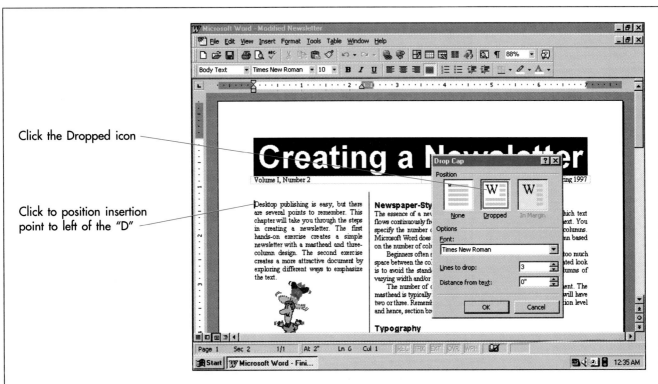

Click the Dropped icon

Click to position insertion
point to left of the "D"

(g) Create a Drop Cap (step 7)

FIGURE 2.7   Hands-on Exercise 2 (continued)

STEP 8: The Completed Newsletter

➤ Zoom to **Whole Page** to view the completed newsletter as shown in Figure 2.7h. The newsletter should fit on a single page, but if not, there are several techniques that you can use:

- Pull down the **File menu,** click the **Page Setup command,** click the **Margins tab,** then reduce the top and/or bottom margins to .5 inch. Be sure to apply this change to the **Whole document** within the Page Setup dialog box.

- Change the **Heading 1 style** to reduce the point size to **10 points** and/or the space before the heading to **6 points.**

- Click the **Print Preview button** on the Standard toolbar, then click the **Shrink to Fit button** on the Print Preview toolbar.

- Save the document a final time. Print the completed newsletter and submit it to your instructor as proof you did this exercise. Congratulations on a job well done.

A FINAL WORD OF ADVICE

Desktop publishing is not a carefree operation. It is time-consuming to implement and you will be amazed at the effort required for even a simple document. Computers are supposed to save time, not waste it, and while desktop publishing is clearly justified for some documents, the extensive formatting it requires is not necessary for most documents. And finally, remember that the content of a document is its most important element.

Print Preview button

Zoom box

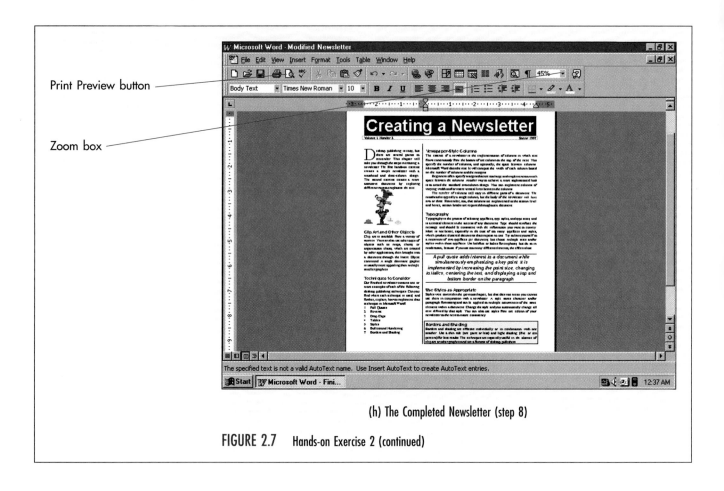

(h) The Completed Newsletter (step 8)

FIGURE 2.7   Hands-on Exercise 2 (continued)

The essence of desktop publishing is the merger of text with graphics to produce a professional-looking document. Proficiency in desktop publishing requires knowledge of the associated commands in Microsoft Word, as well as familiarity with the basics of graphic design.

Typography is the process of selecting typefaces, type styles, and type sizes. A typeface (or font) is a complete set of characters (upper- and lowercase letters, numbers, punctuation marks, and special symbols). Type size is a vertical measurement and is specified in points. One point is equal to $\frac{1}{72}$ of an inch.

The design of a document is developed on a grid, an underlying but invisible set of horizontal and vertical lines that determine the placement of the major elements. A newsletter can be divided into any number of newspaper-style columns in which text flows from the bottom of one column to the top of the next. Columns are implemented by clicking the Columns button on the Standard toolbar or by selecting the Columns command from the Format menu. Sections are required if different column arrangements are present in the same document. The Page Layout view is required to see the columns displayed side by side.

Emphasis can be achieved in several ways, the easiest being variations in type size and/or type style. Boxes and/or shading call attention to selected articles in a document. Horizontal lines are effective in separating one topic from another or calling attention to a pull quote (a phrase or sentence taken from an article to emphasize a key point). A reverse (light text on a solid background) is striking for a small amount of text. Clip art, used in moderation, will catch the reader's eye and enhance almost any newsletter.

Clip art is available from a variety of sources including the Microsoft Clip Gallery, which is accessed most easily through the Insert Picture command. Once clip art has been inserted into a document, it can be moved and sized just like any other Windows object. The Format Picture command provides additional flexibility and precision in the placement of an object.

Graphic design does not have hard and fast rules, only guidelines and common sense. Creating an effective document is an iterative process and reflects the result of trial and error. We encourage you to experiment freely with different designs.

KEY WORDS AND CONCEPTS

Arial	Grid	Sans serif typeface
Borders and Shading command	Insert Picture command	Section break
Bulleted list	Masthead	Serif typeface
Clip art	Microsoft Clip Gallery	Times New Roman
Columns command	Newsletter Wizard	Type size
Desktop publishing	Newspaper-style columns	Typeface
Drop cap	Numbered list	Typography
Emphasis	Point size	
Font	Pull quote	
Format Picture command	Reverse	

MULTIPLE CHOICE

1. Which of the following is a commonly accepted guideline in typography?
   (a) Use a serif typeface for headings and a sans serif typeface for text
   (b) Use a sans serif typeface for headings and a serif typeface for text
   (c) Use a sans serif typeface for both headings and text
   (d) Use a serif typeface for both headings and text

2. Which of the following best enables you to see a multicolumn document as it will appear on the printed page?
   (a) Normal view at 100% magnification
   (b) Normal view at whole page magnification
   (c) Page Layout view at 100% magnification
   (d) Page Layout view at whole page magnification

3. What is the width of each column in a document with two uniform columns, given 1¼-inch margins and ½-inch spacing between the columns?
   (a) 2½ inches
   (b) 2¾ inches
   (c) 3 inches
   (d) Impossible to determine

4. What is the minimum number of sections in a three-column newsletter whose masthead extends across all three columns?
   (a) One
   (b) Two
   (c) Three
   (d) Four

5. Which of the following describes the Arial and Times New Roman fonts?
   (a) Arial is a sans serif font, Times New Roman is a serif font
   (b) Arial is a serif font, Times New Roman is a sans serif font
   (c) Both are serif fonts
   (d) Both are sans serif fonts

6. How do you balance the columns in a newsletter so that each column contains the same amount of text?
   (a) Check the Balance Columns box in the Format Columns command
   (b) Visually determine where the break should go, then insert a column break at the appropriate place
   (c) Insert a continuous section break at the end of the last column
   (d) All of the above

7. What is the effect of dragging one of the four corner handles on a selected object?
   (a) The length of the object is changed but the width remains constant
   (b) The width of the object is changed but the length remains constant
   (c) The length and width of the object are changed in proportion to one another
   (d) Neither the length nor width of the object is changed

8. Which type size is the most reasonable for columns of text, such as those appearing in the newsletter created in the chapter?
   (a) 6 point
   (b) 10 point
   (c) 14 point
   (d) 18 point

9. A grid is applicable to the design of:
   (a) Documents with one, two, or three columns and moderate clip art
   (b) Documents with four or more columns and no clip art
   (c) Both (a) and (b)
   (d) Neither (a) nor (b)

10. Which of the following can be used to add emphasis to a document?
    (a) Borders and shading
    (b) Pull quotes and reverses
    (c) Both (a) and (b)
    (d) Neither (a) nor (b)

11. Which of the following is a recommended guideline in the design of a document?
    (a) Use at least three different clip art images in every newsletter
    (b) Use at least three different typefaces in a document to maintain interest
    (c) Use the same type size for the heading and text of an article
    (d) None of the above

12. Which of the following is implemented at the section level?
    (a) Columns
    (b) Margins
    (c) Both (a) and (b)
    (d) Neither (a) nor (b)

13. What is the easiest way to change the type size of various headings scattered throughout a document, each of which has been formatted with the same style?
    (a) Select the headings individually, then choose the new type size
    (b) Select the headings at the same time, then choose the new type size
    (c) Change the point size in the style, which automatically changes the headings
    (d) Retype the headings according to the new specifications

14. A reverse is implemented:
    (a) By selecting 100% shading in the Borders and Shading command
    (b) By changing the Font color to black
    (c) Both (a) and (b)
    (d) Neither (a) nor (b)

15. The Format Picture command enables you to:
    (a) Change the way in which text is wrapped around a figure
    (b) Change the size of a figure
    (c) Place a border around a figure
    (d) All of the above

ANSWERS

1. b	**6.** c	**11.** d
2. d	**6.** c	**12.** c
3. b	**8.** b	**13.** c
4. b	**9.** c	**14.** a
5. a	**10.** c	**15.** d

PRACTICE WITH MICROSOFT WORD

1. The flyers in Figure 2.8 were created using clip art from the Microsoft Clip Gallery. (We used the complete selection, which is found on the Office 97 CD, but you can use different images if ours are not available to you.) Once the clip art was brought into the document, it was moved and sized as necessary to create the documents in the figure.

   Recreate either or both of our flyers, or better yet, design your own with our text but your own layout. Alternatively, you can create a flyer for a hypothetical intramural sporting event or a fraternity or sorority rushing function. (Use the Insert Symbol command to select Greek letters from the Symbols font.) The flyers are simpler to create than a newsletter. Submit your flyers and a cover sheet to your instructor as proof you did this exercise.

UM Jazz Band
Plays Dixieland

Where: Gusman Hall

When: Friday
November 10

Time: 8:00 PM

(a)

CIS 120 Study Sessions

For those who don't know a bit from a byte
Come to Stanford College this Tuesday night
We'll study the concepts that aren't always clear
And memorize terms that hackers hold dear

We'll hit the books from 7 to 10
And then Thursday night, we'll do it again
It can't hurt to try us - so come on by
And give the CIS tutors that old college try!

(b)

FIGURE 2.8 Screens for Practice Exercise 1

2. Figure 2.9 displays three additional mastheads suitable for the newsletter that was developed in the chapter. Each masthead was created as follows:

   a. A two-by-two table was used in Figure 2.9a in order to right justify the date of the newsletter.

   b. Microsoft WordArt was used to create the masthead in Figure 2.9b. (Use the pull-down Help menu to learn more about this application if you have not used it before.)

   c. A different font was used for the masthead in Figure 2.9c.

   Choose the masthead you like best, then modify the newsletter as it existed at the end of the second hands-on exercise to include the new masthead. Submit the modified newsletter to your instructor as proof that you did the hands-on exercises in this chapter as well as this problem.

Creating a Newsletter
Volume 1, Number 1   Spring 1997

(a)

Creating a Newsletter

(b)

Creating a Newsletter

(c)

FIGURE 2.9   Mastheads for Practice Exercise 2

3. Create a newsletter containing at least one graphic image from the Microsoft Clip Gallery. The intent of this problem is simply to provide practice in graphic design. There is no requirement to write meaningful text, but the headings in the newsletter should follow the theme of the graphic.

   a. Select a graphic, then write one or two sentences in support of that graphic. If, for example, you choose a clip art image of a dog or cat, write a sentence about your pet.

   b. As indicated, there is no requirement to write meaningful text for the newsletter; just copy the sentences from part (a) once or twice to create a paragraph, then copy the paragraph several times to create the newsletter. You should, however, create meaningful headings to add interest to the document.

   c. Develop an overall design away from the computer—that is, with pencil and paper. Use a grid to indicate the placement of the articles, headings, clip art, and masthead. You may be surprised to find that it is easier to master commands in Word than it is to design the newsletter; do not, however, underestimate the importance of graphic design in the ultimate success of your document.

4. A Guide to Smart Shopping: This problem is more challenging than the previous exercises in that you are asked to consider content as well as design. The objective is to develop a one- (or two-) page document with helpful tips to the novice on buying a computer. We have, however, written the copy for you and put the file on the data disk.

  a. Open and print the *Volume II Chapter 2 Practice 4* document on the data disk, which takes approximately a page and a half as presently formatted. Read our text and determine the tips you want to retain and those you want to delete. Add other tips as you see fit.

  b. Examine the available clip art through the Insert Picture command or through the Microsoft Clip Gallery. There is no requirement, however, to include a graphic; that is, use clip art only if you think it will enhance the document.

  c. Consult a current computer magazine (or another source) to determine actual prices for one or more configurations, then include this information prominently in your document.

  d. Create the masthead for the document, then develop with pencil and paper a rough sketch of the completed document showing the masthead, the placement of the text, clip art, and the special of the month (the configuration in part c).

  e. Return to the computer and implement the design of part d. Try to create a balanced publication that completely fills the space allotted; that is, your document should take exactly one or two pages (rather than the page and a half in the original document on the data disk).

5. What You Can Do with Clip Art: We are not artistic by nature, and there is no way that we could have created an original clip art image of the man with his many hats. We did, however, create the variation shown in Figure 2.10 using various tools on the Drawing toolbar. All it took was a little imagination and a sense of what can be done.

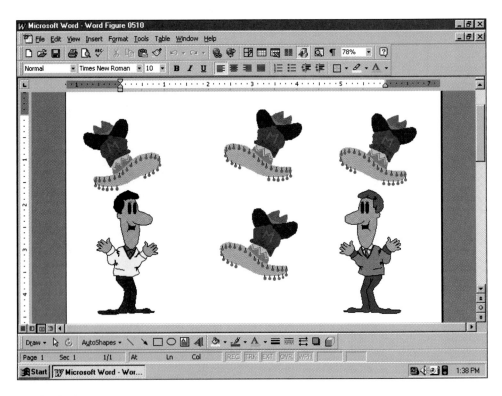

FIGURE 2.10   Screen for Practice Exercise 5

Start by inserting the clip art image into a new document and displaying the Drawing toolbar. Select the clip art image, click the drop-down arrow on the Draw button on the Drawing toolbar, and click the Ungroup command one or more times as necessary until the man and his hats are separate objects, each of which can be selected and manipulated separately. The rest is up to you. Use the ScreenTips and online help to learn about the different tools on the Drawing toolbar.

Prove to your instructor that you have done this exercise by developing a one-page document containing the original clip art and its final form. Include a brief description of what you did to create the modified image.

6. The Equation Editor: Create a simple newsletter such as the two-column design in Figure 2.11. There is no requirement to write meaningful text, as the intent of this exercise is to illustrate the Equation Editor. Thus all you need to do is write a sentence or two, then copy that sentence so that it fills the newsletter.

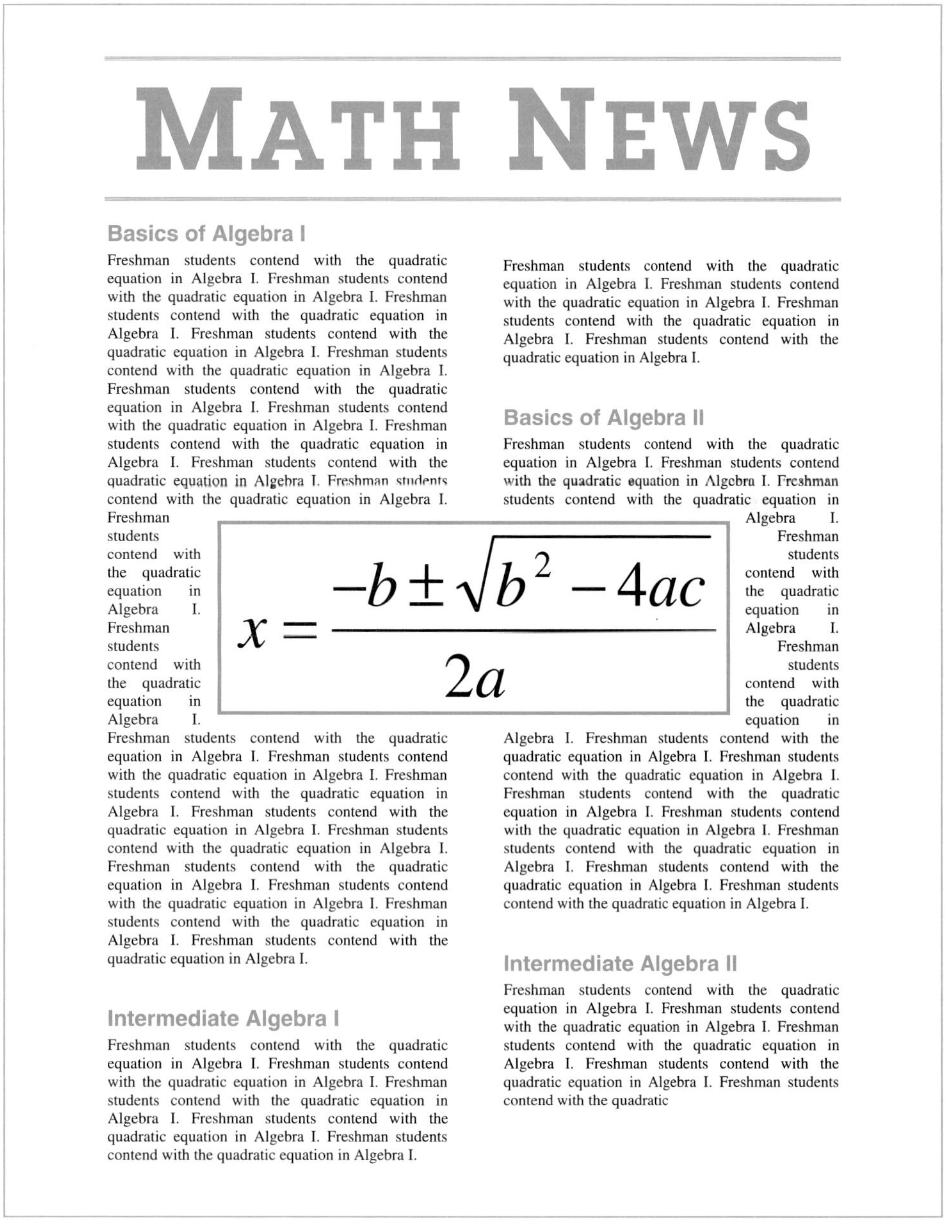

MATH NEWS

Basics of Algebra I

Freshman students contend with the quadratic equation in Algebra I. Freshman students contend with the quadratic equation in Algebra I. Freshman students contend with the quadratic equation in Algebra I. Freshman students contend with the quadratic equation in Algebra I. Freshman students contend with the quadratic equation in Algebra I. Freshman students contend with the quadratic equation in Algebra I. Freshman students contend with the quadratic equation in Algebra I. Freshman students contend with the quadratic equation in Algebra I. Freshman students contend with the quadratic equation in Algebra I. Freshman students contend with the quadratic equation in Algebra I. Freshman students contend with the quadratic equation in Algebra I.

$$x = \frac{-b \pm \sqrt{b^2 - 4ac}}{2a}$$

Freshman students contend with the quadratic equation in Algebra I. Freshman students contend with the quadratic equation in Algebra I. Freshman students contend with the quadratic equation in Algebra I. Freshman students contend with the quadratic equation in Algebra I. Freshman students contend with the quadratic equation in Algebra I. Freshman students contend with the quadratic equation in Algebra I. Freshman students contend with the quadratic equation in Algebra I. Freshman students contend with the quadratic equation in Algebra I.

Intermediate Algebra I

Freshman students contend with the quadratic equation in Algebra I. Freshman students contend with the quadratic equation in Algebra I. Freshman students contend with the quadratic equation in Algebra I. Freshman students contend with the quadratic equation in Algebra I. Freshman students contend with the quadratic equation in Algebra I.

Freshman students contend with the quadratic equation in Algebra I. Freshman students contend with the quadratic equation in Algebra I. Freshman students contend with the quadratic equation in Algebra I. Freshman students contend with the quadratic equation in Algebra I.

Basics of Algebra II

Freshman students contend with the quadratic equation in Algebra I. Freshman students contend with the quadratic equation in Algebra I. Freshman students contend with the quadratic equation in Algebra I. Freshman students contend with the quadratic equation in Algebra I. Freshman students contend with the quadratic equation in Algebra I. Freshman students contend with the quadratic equation in Algebra I. Freshman students contend with the quadratic equation in Algebra I. Freshman students contend with the quadratic equation in Algebra I. Freshman students contend with the quadratic equation in Algebra I. Freshman students contend with the quadratic equation in Algebra I. Freshman students contend with the quadratic equation in Algebra I. Freshman students contend with the quadratic equation in Algebra I. Freshman students contend with the quadratic equation in Algebra I. Freshman students contend with the quadratic equation in Algebra I. Freshman students contend with the quadratic equation in Algebra I.

Intermediate Algebra II

Freshman students contend with the quadratic equation in Algebra I. Freshman students contend with the quadratic equation in Algebra I. Freshman students contend with the quadratic equation in Algebra I. Freshman students contend with the quadratic equation in Algebra I. Freshman students contend with the quadratic equation in Algebra I. Freshman students contend with the quadratic

FIGURE 2.11   Screen for Practice Exercise 6

To create the equation, pull down the Insert menu, click the Object command, click the Create New tab, then select Microsoft Equation to start the Equation Editor. This is a new application and we do not provide instruction in its use. It does, however, follow the conventions of other Office applications, and through trial and error, and reference to the Help menu, you should be able to duplicate our equation.

Once the equation (object) has been created, you can move and size it within the document. Clicking an object selects the object and displays the sizing handles to move, size, or delete the object. Double clicking an object loads the application that created it, and enables you to modify the object using the tools of the original application.

CASE STUDIES

Before and After

The best way to learn about the do's and don'ts of desktop publishing is to study the work of others. Choose a particular type of document—for example, a newsletter, résumé, or advertising flyer, then collect samples of that document. Choose one sample that is particularly bad and redesign the document. You need not enter the actual text, but you should keep all of the major headings so that the document retains its identity. Add or delete clip art as appropriate. Bring the before and after samples to class for your professor.

Clip Art

Clip art—you see it all the time, but where do you get it, and how much does it cost? Scan the computer magazines and find at least two sources for additional clip art. Better yet, use your favorite search engine to locate additional sources of clip art on the Web. Return to class with specific information on prices and types of the clip art.

Color Separations

It's difficult to tell where word processing stops and desktop publishing begins. One distinguishing characteristic of a desktop publishing program, however, is the ability to create color separations, which in turn enable you to print a document in full color. Use your favorite search engine to learn more about the process of color separations. Summarize the results of your research in a short paper to your instructor.

Subscribe to a Newsletter

There are literally thousands of regularly published newsletters that are distributed in printed and/or electronic form. Some charge a subscription fee, but many are available just for the asking. Use your favorite search engine to locate a free newsletter in an area of interest to you. Download an issue, then summarize the results of your research in a brief note to your instructor.

CREATING A HOME PAGE: INTRODUCTION TO HTML

3

OBJECTIVES

After reading this chapter you will be able to:

1. Define HTML and its role on the World Wide Web; describe HTML codes and explain how they control the appearance of a Web document.

2. Use Microsoft Word to create a home page; explain the role of the Save As command in creating an HTML document.

3. Use the Insert Hyperlink command to include hyperlinks in a Web page.

4. Explain how to view the HTML source code of a document from within Microsoft Word; modify the document by changing its source code.

5. Download one or more graphics from the Web, then include those graphics in a Web document.

6. Describe the additional steps needed to place your home page on the Web so that it can be viewed by others.

7. Describe the potential benefits of an Intranet to an organization.

OVERVIEW

Sooner or later anyone who cruises the World Wide Web wants to create a *home page* of their own. That, in turn, requires a basic knowledge of *Hypertext Markup Language* (*HTML*), the language in which all Web pages are written. An HTML document consists of text and graphics, together with a set of codes (or tags), that describe how the document is to appear when viewed in a Web browser such as Internet Explorer.

In the early days of the Web, anyone creating a home page had to learn each of these codes and enter it explicitly. Today, however, it's much easier as you can use an HTML editor to generate the codes for you. Office 97 goes one step further as it enables you to create an HTML document directly in Microsoft Word. In essence, you enter the text of a document, apply basic formatting such as boldface or italics, then simply save the file as an HTML document. There are, of course, additional commands that you will need to learn, but all commands are executed from within Word, through pull-down menus, toolbars, or keyboard shortcuts.

This chapter shows you how to create a home page in Word 97, how to include graphics and other formatting effects, and how to include links to other pages. As always, the hands-on exercises are essential to our learn-by-doing philosophy, as they enable you to apply the conceptual material at the computer. The exercises are structured in such a way that you can view the Web pages you create, even if you don't have access to the Internet.

LEARN MORE ABOUT THE INTERNET

Use your favorite Web search engine to look for additional information about the Internet. One excellent place to begin is the resource page maintained by the Library of Congress at http://lcweb.loc.gov/global. This site contains links to several HTML tutorials and also provides you with information about the latest HTML standard.

INTRODUCTION TO HTML

Figure 3.1 displays a home page similar to the one you will create in the hands-on exercises, which follow shortly. Our page has the look and feel of Web pages you see when you access the World Wide Web. It includes different types of formatting, a bulleted list, underlined links, horizontal lines (rules) that separate elements on the page, and a heading displayed in a larger font. All of these elements are created by inserting codes, called *HTML tags,* into a document to identify the formatting that should be applied at that location. Figure 3.1a displays the document as it would appear when viewed using Internet Explorer. Figure 3.1b shows the underlying HTML codes (tags) that are necessary to format the page.

HTML source codes become less intimidating when you realize that the tags are enclosed in angle brackets and are used consistently from document to document. Most tags occur in pairs, at the beginning and end of the text to be formatted, with the ending code preceded by a slash. In Figure 3.1b, for example, the text *John Doe's Home Page* is enclosed within the <TITLE> and </TITLE> tags. (The function of the Title tag is to indicate the text that will be displayed in the title bar of the browser's application window when that page is accessed. Look at the title and other tags in Figure 3.1b, then observe the effect of these tags as they are read and displayed by the browser in Figure 3.1a.)

Tags can also be nested within one another. The welcome message that John has chosen to place at the top of his page is nested within codes to center (<CENTER>) and boldface (<B>) the text, as well as display it in a larger font size (<FONT SIZE=5>). Links to other pages (which are known as *hyperlinks*) are enclosed within a pair of anchor tags <A> and </A> in which you specify the URL address of the document through the HREF parameter. Note, too, that some tags, such as <P> or <HR>, appear individually to indicate a new paragraph or horizontal rule, respectively.

Text for title bar

Text is boldfaced, centered, and set in a larger font size

Links to other pages

Horizontal rule

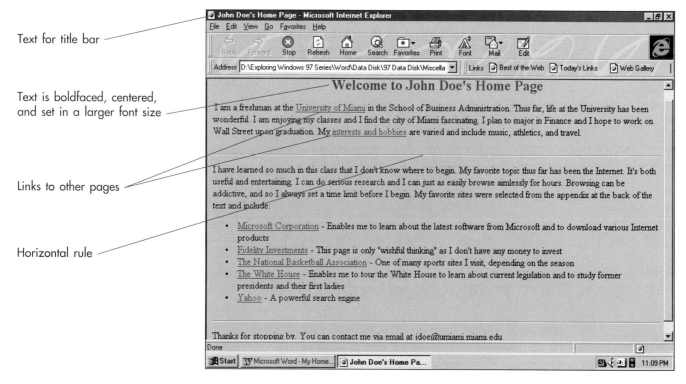

(a) Internet Explorer

Text that will appear in the title bar is enclosed in <TITLE> tags

HTML tags to boldface, establish the font size, and center the text

Ending tags

<A HREF> tag is used to specify a URL address for a hyperlink

<HR> tag specifies a horizontal rule

Ending tags

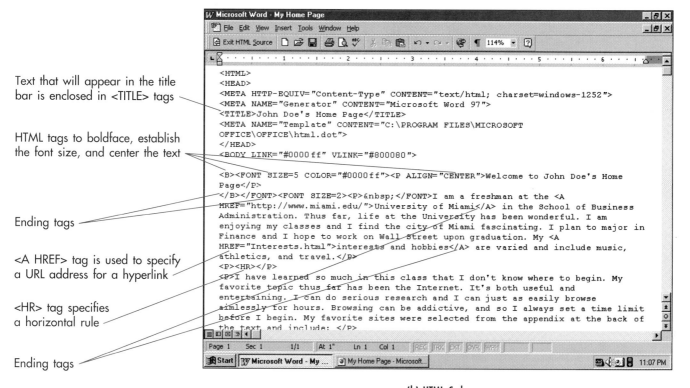

(b) HTML Codes

FIGURE 3.1   A Home Page

Fortunately, however, it is not necessary to memorize HTML tags since you can usually determine their meaning from the codes themselves. Nor is it even necessary for you to enter the tags, as Word will create an HTML document for you based on commands executed from its pull-down menus or toolbars.

THE HEAD AND THE BODY

An HTML document is composed of two parts—a head and a body. The heading contains the text that will be displayed on the browser's title bar and is found between the <HEAD> and </HEAD> tags. The main portion (body) of the document is entered between the <BODY> AND </BODY> tags, which contain the necessary codes to format the document for display on a Web browser.

Microsoft Word 97

As indicated, there are two ways to create an HTML document. The original (and more difficult) method was to enter the codes explicitly in a text editor such as Notepad. The easier technique (and the only one you need to consider) is to use Microsoft Word 97 to create the document for you without having to enter or reference the HTML tags at all.

Figure 3.2 displays the Word 97 screen used to create John Doe's home page. Look carefully and you will see that the toolbars are subtly different from those you are used to seeing. The Standard toolbar, for example, contains an additional tool, the Web Page Preview button, that enables you to see your document as it will appear in the default browser (Internet Explorer). The Formatting toolbar contains tools to increase and decrease font size, in lieu of the drop-down list box to specify a specific point size. (This is because Web documents specify a relative type size rather than an absolute type size.) The Formatting toolbar in Figure 3.2 also has tools to create a horizontal line and change the background, two techniques that are used frequently in creating Web documents.

To create a Web document, start Word in the usual fashion and enter the text of the document with basic formatting. However, instead of saving the document in the default format (as a Word 97 document), you use the ***Save As command*** to specify an HTML document. Microsoft Word does the rest, generating the HTML tags needed to create the document. You can continue to enter text and/or change the formatting for existing text just as you can with an ordinary Word document. You can also enter any additional HTML tags as appropriate— for example, click the Insert Hyperlink button to insert a hyperlink into a document.

Going on the Web

Once you've completed your home page, you'll want to place your page on the Web so that other people will be able to access it. This requires that you obtain an account on a Web server (typically a UNIX-based machine) with adequate disk space to hold the various pages you create. To do so, you need to check with your system administrator at school or work, or with your local Internet provider, to determine how to submit your page when it is complete.

Realize, however, that even if you do not place your page on the Web, you can still view it locally on your PC. This is the approach we follow in the next hands-on exercise, which enables you to create an HTML document and see the

Web Page Preview button

Insert Hyperlink button

Increase Font Size button

Decrease Font Size button

Horizontal Line button

Background button

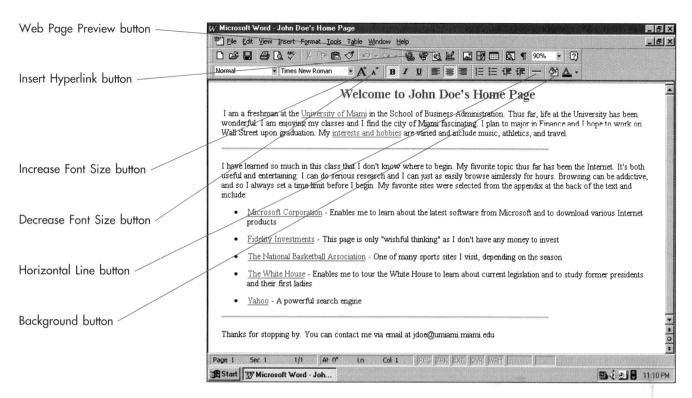

FIGURE 3.2   Microsoft Word 97

results of your effort. Your document is stored on a local drive (e.g., on drive A or drive C) rather than on an Internet server, but it can still be viewed through Internet Explorer (or any other browser). After you have completed the exercise, you (and/or your instructor) can decide whether it is worthwhile to place your page on your school or university's server, where it can be accessed by anyone.

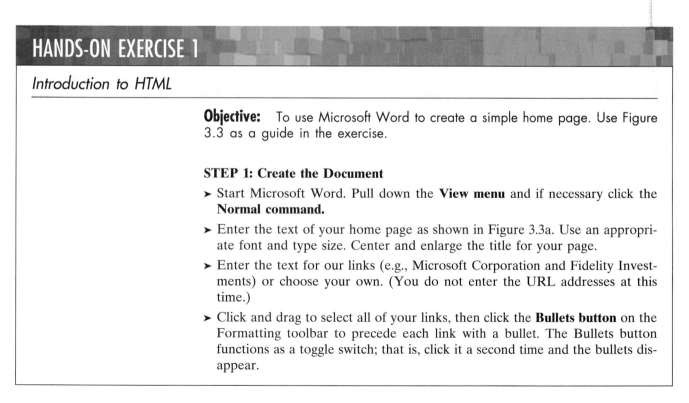

HANDS-ON EXERCISE 1

Introduction to HTML

Objective: To use Microsoft Word to create a simple home page. Use Figure 3.3 as a guide in the exercise.

STEP 1: Create the Document

➤ Start Microsoft Word. Pull down the **View menu** and if necessary click the **Normal command.**

➤ Enter the text of your home page as shown in Figure 3.3a. Use an appropriate font and type size. Center and enlarge the title for your page.

➤ Enter the text for our links (e.g., Microsoft Corporation and Fidelity Investments) or choose your own. (You do not enter the URL addresses at this time.)

➤ Click and drag to select all of your links, then click the **Bullets button** on the Formatting toolbar to precede each link with a bullet. The Bullets button functions as a toggle switch; that is, click it a second time and the bullets disappear.

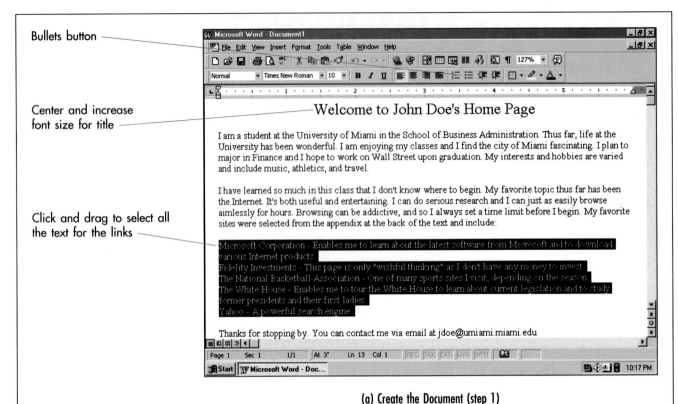

Bullets button

Center and increase font size for title

Click and drag to select all the text for the links

(a) Create the Document (step 1)

FIGURE 3.3   Hands-on Exercise 1

SELECT THEN DO

All formatting operations in Word take place within the context of select-then-do; that is, you select a block of text, then you execute the command to operate on that text. You may select the text in many different ways, the most basic of which is to click and drag over the desired characters. You may also take one of many shortcuts, which include double clicking on a word, pressing Ctrl as you click a sentence, and triple clicking on a paragraph.

STEP 2: Save the Document

➤ Pull down the **File menu.** Click the **Save as HTML command** to display the Save As HTML dialog box in Figure 3.3b.

- Select the appropriate drive (and optionally the folder) where you want to save your document—for example, the **Exploring Word folder** on drive A or C.

- Enter **My Home Page** as the name of the document.

- Click the **Save button** in the Save As HTML dialog box to save the document. Click **Yes** in response to the warning that indicates some formatting may be lost in converting to an HTML document.

➤ The display changes ever so slightly (the Standard and Formatting toolbars include additional buttons for use with an HTML document), but otherwise you continue to work in Word as usual.

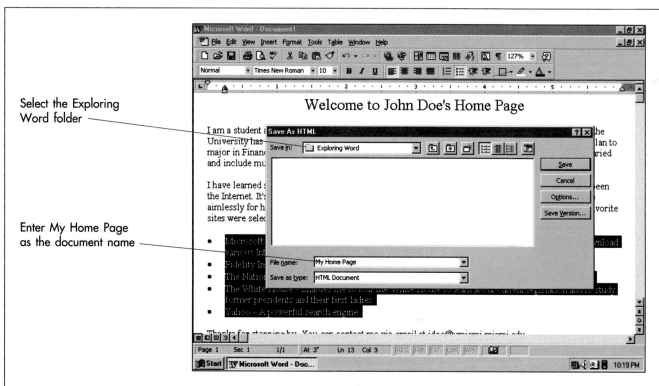

Select the Exploring
Word folder

Welcome to John Doe's Home Page

Enter My Home Page
as the document name

(b) Save the Document (step 2)

FIGURE 3.3   Hands-on Exercise 1 (continued)

MISSING TOOLBARS

The Standard and Formatting toolbars are displayed by default, but either or both can be hidden from view. To display (or hide) a toolbar, point to any toolbar, click the right mouse button to display the Toolbar shortcut menu, then click the individual toolbars on or off as appropriate. If you do not see any toolbars at all, pull down the View menu, click Toolbars to display a dialog box listing the available toolbars, check the toolbars you want displayed, and click OK.

STEP 3: Complete the Formatting

➤ Click and drag to select the title of your document. Pull down the **Format menu,** then click **Font** to display the Font dialog box shown in Figure 3.3c.

➤ Click the **drop-down arrow** on the Font Color list box, then click **Blue** to change the color of the selected text. Click **OK** to close the dialog box.

➤ Click at the end of the first paragraph, then click the **Horizontal Line button** to insert a horizontal rule at the end of the paragraph. Click to the left of the paragraph that begins *Thanks for stopping by,* then click the **Horizontal Line button** a second time.

➤ Enter additional formatting as you see fit. Delete (or enter) blank lines before (after) the rules as necessary.

➤ Click the **Spelling and Grammar button** to check your document for spelling. Save the document.

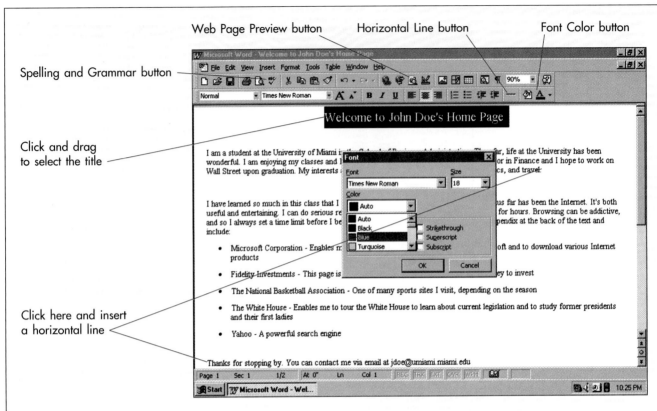

Web Page Preview button   Horizontal Line button   Font Color button

Spelling and Grammar button

Click and drag
to select the title

Click here and insert
a horizontal line

(c) Complete the Formatting (step 3)

FIGURE 3.3 Hands-on Exercise 1 (continued)

STEP 4: View the Completed Page

➤ Click the **Web Page Preview button** on the Standard toolbar to open the default browser (e.g., Internet Explorer) to see how the finished document will appear when viewed on the Web or a corporate Intranet. Click **OK** if asked to save the document.

➤ You should see your home page as shown in Figure 3.3d. The URL address (C:\Exploring Word\My Home Page.html) indicates that you are viewing the home page on a local drive (drive C) as opposed to an actual Web server.

➤ View your home page and write down any changes you want to make. Click the **Microsoft Word button** on the Windows 95 taskbar to return to Word in order to modify your page.

MULTITASKING

Multitasking, the ability to run multiple programs at the same time, is one of the primary advantages of the Windows environment. Each open application is represented as a button on the Windows 95 taskbar. The easiest way to switch from one open application to another is to click the appropriate button on the taskbar. You can also use the Alt+Tab shortcut that worked in Windows 3.1.

Click Refresh button

URL indicates that current
page is on a local drive

Click to return to Word

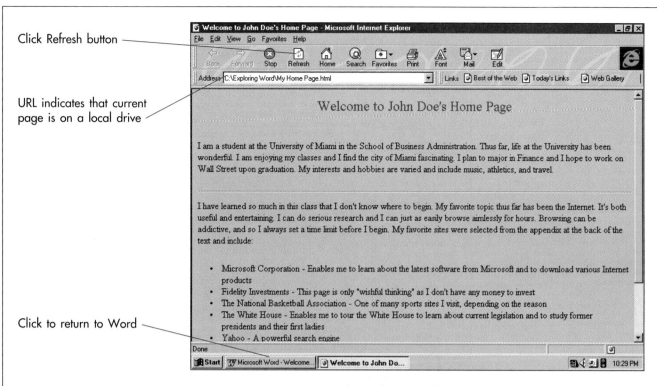

(d) View the Completed Page (step 4)

FIGURE 3.3 Hands-on Exercise 1 (continued)

STEP 5: View the HTML Tags

➤ Pull down the **View menu** and click **HTML Source** to display the HTML source code as shown in Figure 3.3e. Word has created all of the necessary HTML tags for you.

➤ Delete the words **Welcome to** that appear after the <TITLE> tag. Change the word **student** to **freshman** within the body of the document. Make any other changes you want to the text of your page.

➤ Click the **Exit HTML source button** on the Standard toolbar (or pull down the **View menu** and click **Exit HTML source**), then click **Yes** when asked whether to save the changes. The HTML tags are no longer visible.

➤ Click the **Web Page Preview button** on the Standard toolbar to return to Internet Explorer. Click the **Refresh button.**

➤ The entry in the title bar has changed, as has the text in the document, corresponding to the changes you just made.

➤ Close Internet Explorer. Exit Word if you do not want to continue with the next exercise at this time.

MODIFY THE SOURCE DOCUMENT

Don't be intimidated by the HTML tags, which are quite understandable after you study them for a few minutes. You can modify an HTML document in the Source view by inserting and deleting text and/or codes. Any changes that you make are reflected automatically in the Word document.

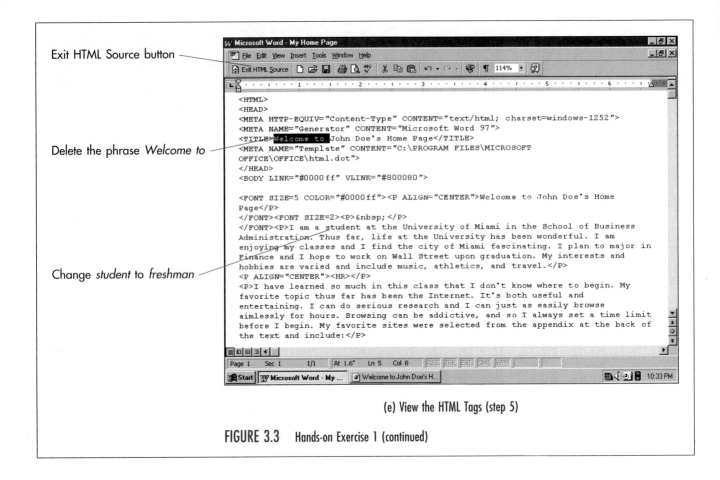

Exit HTML Source button

Delete the phrase *Welcome to*

Change *student* to *freshman*

(e) View the HTML Tags (step 5)

FIGURE 3.3   Hands-on Exercise 1 (continued)

HYPERLINKS

The hands-on exercise just completed had you create a Web page without links of any kind. What makes the Web so fascinating, however, is the ability to jump from one page to the next. Think, for a minute, of the time you have spent in exploring the Web as you clicked on one hyperlink after another. It didn't matter if the linked documents were on the same server (computer) or if they were on an entirely different computer. Either way you were able to go from one document to another simply by clicking on the links of interest to you. It's apparent, therefore, that if you are to develop a meaningful home page, you must learn how to include hyperlinks of your own.

Figure 3.4a displays your home page as it will appear at the end of the next hands-on exercise. It looks very similar to the page you just created except that it contains links to other Web documents. The links appear as underlined text, such as University of Miami or National Basketball Association. Click on a desired link and the browser (e.g., Internet Explorer) displays the associated document. Note, too, that the links (underlined text) appear in two colors, blue and magenta. A blue link indicates that the associated page has not been previously displayed. Magenta, on the other hand, indicates that the page has been viewed.

The *Insert Hyperlink* command enables you to create a link within your document. You need to know the URL address of the associated page, such as www.nba.com to display the home page for the National Basketball Association. You need not, however, concern yourself with the syntax of the HTML tags, as Word will prompt you for the necessary information, via the Hyperlink dialog box in Figure 3.4b.

Link appears as underlined text

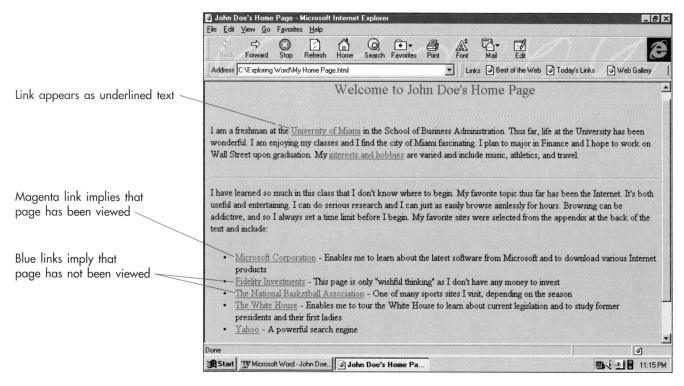

Magenta link implies that page has been viewed

Blue links imply that page has not been viewed

(a) The Completed Web Page

URL address of associated page

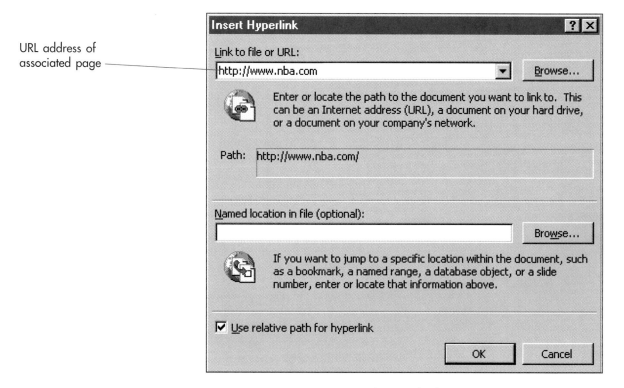

(b) External Link

FIGURE 3.4 Hyperlinks

Filename rather than URL
address indicates that link
is to a local document

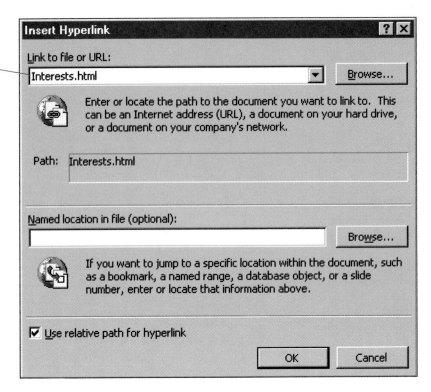

(c) Local Link

FIGURE 3.4 Hyperlinks (continued)

Figure 3.4c displays a second hyperlink dialog box but this time the link is to a local document (a document on your PC or on the LAN to which your PC is connected) rather than to an external Web page. The dialog box in Figure 3.4c contains a file name (interests.html) rather than a URL address. This enables you to link one document, such as your home page, to a second document that describes your hobbies and interests in detail, which in turn can be linked to another document and so on.

The following exercise has you modify the home page you created earlier to include links to other documents. We will show you how to create two types of links—one to a local document on your PC and another to an external document anywhere on the Web.

THE INTRANET

The ability to create links to local documents and to view those pages through a Web browser has created an entirely new way to disseminate information. Indeed, many organizations are taking advantage of this capability to develop a corporate Intranet, in which Web pages are placed on a local area network for use within the organization. The documents on an Intranet are available only to individuals with access to the LAN on which the documents are stored. This is in contrast to loading the pages onto a Web server where they can be viewed by anyone with access to the Web.

Hyperlinks

Objective: To create a Web page with both local and external hyperlinks. Use Figure 3.5 as a guide in the exercise.

STEP 1: Create a Second Web Document

➤ Start Word. Create a document describing your interests such as the document in Figure 3.5a. Your document does not have to be long, as its purpose is to demonstrate how you can link one Web document to another.

➤ Pull down the **File menu.** Click the **Save As HTML command** to display the Save As HTML dialog box. Save the document in the same drive and folder (e.g., the Exploring Word folder on drive C) you used in the previous exercise.

  • Enter **Interests** as the name of the document.

  • Click the **Save button** to save the document. Click **Yes** in response to the warning that indicates some formatting may be lost in conversion to an HTML document.

➤ Close the document.

Format the title (center it and enlarge the font size)

Select the Exploring Word folder

Enter Interests as the document name

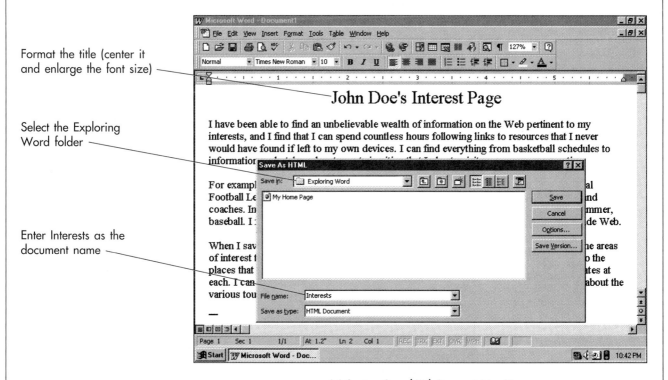

(a) Create a Second Web Document (step 1)

FIGURE 3.5   Hands-on Exercise 2

SOME FORMATTING IS LOST

The Save As command converts an existing Word document to its HTML equivalent. Some formatting (e.g., spacing before and after paragraphs) is lost in the process, but most is retained. To learn the limitations of the conversion process, pull down the Help menu, click the Contents and Index command, click the Index tab, type *formatting*, select the Web page entry under formatting, then select the topic *Word features that are different or unavailable during Web authoring*. To obtain a hard copy of the information, point anywhere in the Help window, click the right mouse button to display a shortcut menu, then click the Print Topic command.

STEP 2: Open Your Home Page

➤ Pull down the **File menu,** click **Open** (or click the **Open button** on the Standard toolbar). If necessary, change to the appropriate drive and folder (e.g., the Exploring Word folder on drive C).

➤ Click the **drop-down arrow** on the Files of type list box, then select **All Files** as shown in Figure 3.5b.

➤ Scroll until you can select **My Home Page** (the HTML document created in the first exercise), then click **Open** to open the document.

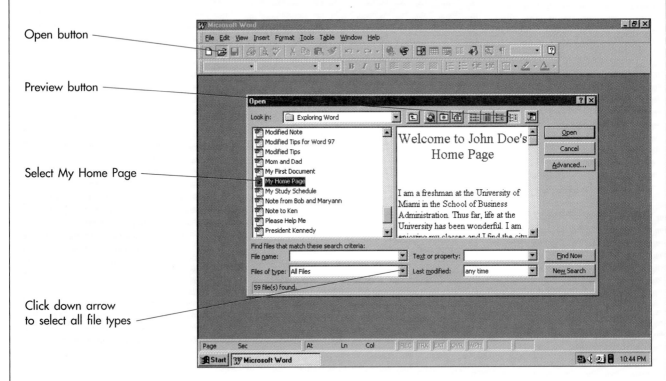

(b) Open Your Home Page (step 2)

FIGURE 3.5 Hands-on Exercise 2 (continued)

A VERY USEFUL TOOLBAR

The Open and Save As dialog boxes share a common toolbar with several very useful buttons, three of which display different views. The Details button enables you to see the date and time the file was last modified as well as its size. The List button displays an icon for each file (omitting the details), which lets you see many more files at one time than in the Details view. Note, too, the different icons for the various file types (e.g., there are different icons for Word and HTML documents). The Preview button enables you to see the contents of a document before you open it.

STEP 3: Create the Link

➤ Read through your home page until you come to the phrase describing your interests and hobbies at the end of the first paragraph. Click and drag to select the text **interests and hobbies.**

➤ Pull down the **Insert menu** and click **Hyperlink** (or click the **Insert Hyperlink button** on the Standard toolbar) to display the Hyperlink dialog box in Figure 3.5c.

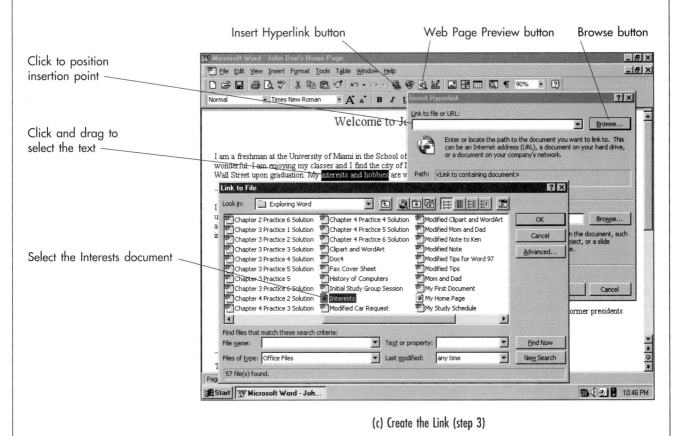

(c) Create the Link (step 3)

FIGURE 3.5   Hands-on Exercise 2 (continued)

➤ Check that the insertion point is positioned in the **Link to File** or **URL text box,** then click the **Browse button** to display the **Link to File dialog box** shown in the figure. Select (click) the **Interests** document you created earlier, then click **OK** to select the file and close the Link to File dialog box.

➤ Click **OK** to close the Hyperlink dialog box. If necessary, add a space between the link and the next word. Save the document.

HYPERLINKS BEFORE AND AFTER

Hyperlinks are displayed in different colors, depending on whether (or not) the associated page has been displayed. Pull down the Format menu and click Text Colors to display the associated dialog box. Click the drop-down arrow next to the appropriate list box to change the color associated with hyperlinks before and after they are viewed. Click OK to accept your changes and close the dialog box.

STEP 4: Test the Link

➤ Click the **Web Page Preview button** on the Standard toolbar to view your home page in Internet Explorer as shown in Figure 3.5d.

➤ The URL address (C:\Exploring Word\My Home Page.html) in the Address bar indicates that you are viewing the home page from a local drive (drive C) as opposed to an actual Web server.

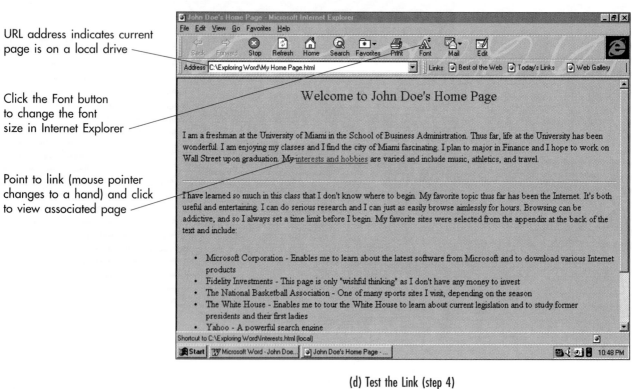

(d) Test the Link (step 4)

FIGURE 3.5   Hands-on Exercise 2 (continued)

➤ Point to the link (the mouse pointer changes to a hand to indicate a hyperlink, and the status bar displays the associated address), then click the **hobbies and interests** hyperlink you just created to view this page.

CHANGE THE FONT SIZE

Internet Explorer enables you to view and/or print a page in one of five font settings (smallest, small, medium, large, and largest). Click the Font button on the toolbar to cycle through the various settings, or alternatively, pull down the View menu, click Fonts, then click the desired font size. The setting pertains to both the displayed page as well as the printed page.

STEP 5: View Your Interests Page

➤ You should see your hobbies and interests as shown in Figure 3.5e. The URL address in Figure 3.5e (C:\Exploring Word\Interests.html) indicates that you are viewing this page from a local drive (drive C) as opposed to an actual server.

➤ Click the **Back button** on the Internet Explorer toolbar to return to your home page. Click the **Close button** to close the browser and return to Word, where you can make additional changes.

Back button

URL address indicates
that current page is
on a local drive

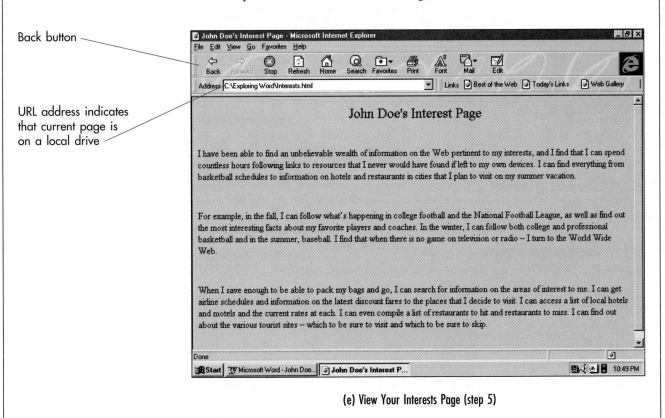

(e) View Your Interests Page (step 5)

FIGURE 3.5 Hands-on Exercise 2 (continued)

MICROSOFT ON THE WEB

Microsoft's home page (www.microsoft.com) is well worth including in any list of Web links. Not only are you able to download free clip art and other Web resources, but you also have access to the latest developments from the software giant. You can also search the Microsoft Knowledge Base for specific information on Windows or any Microsoft application.

STEP 6: Create an External Link

➤ You should see your home page displayed within Word as shown in Figure 3.5f. Click and drag to select the phrase **Microsoft Corporation.**

➤ Pull down the **Insert menu** and click **Hyperlink** (or click the **Insert Hyperlink button** on the Standard toolbar) to display the Insert Hyperlink dialog box in Figure 3.5f.

➤ Check that the insertion point is positioned in the **Link to file** or **URL text box,** then enter the URL of a specific site such as **www.microsoft.com** (the http:// is assumed).

➤ Click **OK** to close the Hyperlink dialog box. Add spaces as necessary to separate the link from the adjacent text.

➤ Add the additional links for your other interests, then save the document. The addresses in our document are: www.cbs.com, www.fidelity.com, www.nba.com, www.whitehouse.gov, and www.yahoo.com.

Web Page Preview button

Insert Hyperlink button

Enter URL of associated page

Click and drag to select text

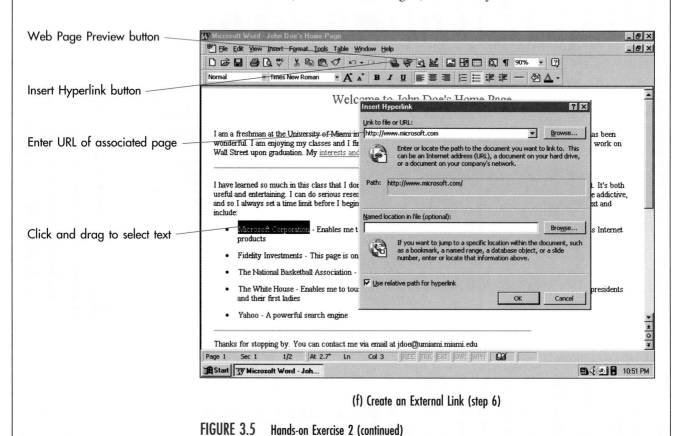

(f) Create an External Link (step 6)

FIGURE 3.5   Hands-on Exercise 2 (continued)

GUESS THE URL

You can often guess the address of a site according to a consistent addressing scheme—for example, www.company.com. The addresses of the Lycos and Yahoo search engines (www.lycos.com and www.yahoo.com) both follow this pattern. So do the home pages of many companies—for example, www.netscape.com and www.microsoft.com for Netscape and Microsoft, respectively. And if you are in the mood for sports, try www.nfl.com or www.nba.com to go to the home pages of the National Football League or National Basketball Association.

STEP 7: Test the External Link

➤ Click the **Web Page Preview button** on the Standard toolbar to view the document in your default browser. You should see your home page with the newly added links.

➤ Click the link to **Microsoft.** Realize, however, that unlike the link to a local document in step 5, you need access to the Internet in order for this step to work.

➤ You should see the Microsoft home page as shown in Figure 3.5g. The URL address displayed by Internet Explorer corresponds to the address you entered in the Insert Hyperlink dialog box in step 6.

➤ If you are unable to connect, it is most likely because you entered the URL incorrectly or because you are not connected to the Internet. To correct the

Back button

URL of associated
page (corresponds to
address entered in Insert
Hyperlink dialog box)

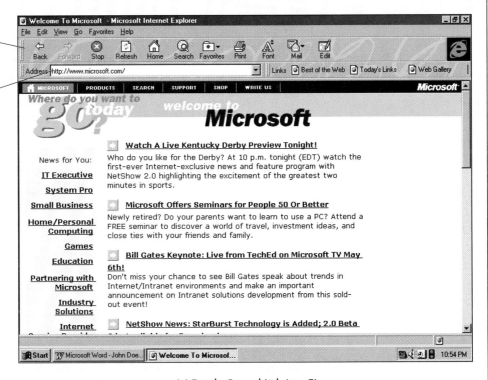

(g) Test the External Link (step 7)

FIGURE 3.5 Hands-on Exercise 2 (continued)

problem, you need to close the browser and return to Word, where you should delete the invalid link, repeat step 6, then be sure you are connected to the Internet.

➤ If you link successfully, click the **Back button** in your browser to return to your home page, then test the various other links to be sure that they are working.

➤ Exit Word and Internet Explorer if you do not want to continue with the next exercise at this time.

ADD YOUR HOME PAGE TO THE LYCOS CATALOG

After you have completed your home page and your LAN administrator has placed it on a server, you want others to be able to find it. You can add your page to various catalogs such as the Lycos Search Engine, which claims to index more than 90% of the Web. Go to www.lycos.com/addasite.html and fill out the form. Wait a week or two, then try a search on your name. You should be cataloged on the Web!

TOWARD MORE SOPHISTICATED PAGES

You have completed two exercises and have gained valuable experience in HTML. The first exercise had you create a simple home page using commands in Microsoft Word. The second exercise showed you how to link Web pages to one another. We continue with another exercise, which reviews the earlier material and, in addition, shows you how to incorporate graphic elements into a Web page.

The document in Figure 3.6 represents the home page of a hypothetical travel agency, *World Wide Travel*. It contains hyperlinks to four additional pages, each of which describes a specific vacation. The document also contains a link (Return to Top of Page) that references a hidden *bookmark* at the top of the page. Bookmarks are a valuable addition to long documents that extend beyond a single screen, as they enable you to jump from one place to another within a document without having to manually scroll through the document.

The document in Figure 3.6 also contains three graphic images to enhance the page and make it more interesting. Graphics may come from a variety of sources such as commercial clip art and/or photographs, either of which may be scanned or downloaded from the Internet. (The graphics in our figure were downloaded from Microsoft's Multimedia Gallery, as will be described in the following hands-on exercise.) Remember, too, that graphics increase the time necessary to display a page, especially over a modem. Be careful, therefore, about including too many graphics or graphics with large file sizes—you don't want your user to lose interest as he or she waits for the page to load.

The ease with which you create the document in Figure 3.6 depends (in part) on your proficiency in Microsoft Word. We use the Tables feature, for example, to position the graphics within the document. We also use the Bullets and Numbering command to accentuate the different vacations. Even if you have only limited experience with Microsoft Word, however, our instructions are sufficiently detailed that you should be able to complete the exercise with little difficulty.

Hidden bookmark

World Wide Travel

(800) 123- 4567

We are a full service travel agency with trips all over the world. We cater to individuals and groups, especially campus organizations. We offer the lowest air fares and hotel accommodations and always provide the ultimate in service. We run specials all the time and urge you to consider the following:

- Honeymoon to the Bahamas
- Spring Break

- Summer Special to Europe
- See the West

Graphic images

You need identification when you travel outside the United States. Passports are not required in North America, but are for most other destinations. They take time to get, so be sure you apply for the passport well in advance of your trip.

Film and other equipment are always cheaper in the United States, so be sure to purchase all of your equipment before you leave. It's always a good idea to bring spare batteries for your camera. You can also bring postage paid envelopes to mail your film home so it will be developed and waiting for you when you return.

Hyperlink to a bookmark

Return to Top of Page

FIGURE 3.6 World Wide Web Travel Page

RESPECT THE COPYRIGHT

A copyright provides legal protection to written and artistic work, and gives the author exclusive rights to its use and reproduction. There are exceptions, however, such as the fair use exclusion, which permits you to use a portion of a work for educational, nonprofit purposes, or for the purpose of critical review or commentary. It is a complicated issue to say the least, and our advice is when in doubt, assume that you do not have permission. Go to the Copyright Web Site at http://www.benedict.com to learn more about copyright law.

Toward More Sophisticated Pages

Objective: To create a more sophisticated HTML document containing graphics, links, and bookmarks. This step requires access to the Internet in order to download material from the Web for inclusion in your document. Use Figure 3.7 as a guide in the exercise.

STEP 1: Download Web Resources

➤ Start Word, then click the **New button** on the Standard toolbar to begin a new document. Use the **Save As HTML** command to save the document as **World Wide Travel** in the same drive and folder you have used throughout the chapter.

➤ Pull down the **Insert menu,** click **Picture,** then click the **Browse Web Art Page command.** (If you do not see the Browse Web Art Page command it is because you did not save the document as an HTML file.) Click **Yes** if asked whether you want to browse the Microsoft Web site. (You must have an Internet connection to do this step.)

➤ Click the link to **IE MMGallery Themes** to display the page in Figure 3.7a. (If do not see this page try entering its address **(www.microsoft.com/ workshop/design/mmgallry)** directly in the address box.

➤ Scroll down in the page until you can click the link to **Travel** to display the images for this category.

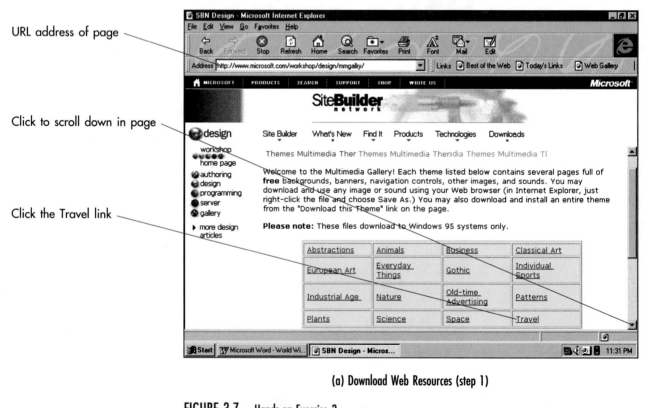

URL address of page

Click to scroll down in page

Click the Travel link

(a) Download Web Resources (step 1)

FIGURE 3.7   Hands-on Exercise 3

THE MICROSOFT SEARCH ENGINE

Microsoft is continually changing its home page and you may not find the exact links we describe. You can, however, find the equivalent information by using Microsoft's internal search engine. Go to Microsoft's home page and click the Search icon to display a search form. Enter the scope of the search (a full site search) and the key words (*Multimedia gallery*), then click the Search button. You should see one or more articles that will take you to the multimedia gallery.

STEP 2: Download the Travel Images

➤ Scroll down in the Travel page until you come to the **General Images section.** Be patient, especially if you are on a modem connection, as it takes time for the images to be displayed.

➤ Point to the image of the **Two Globes,** then click the **right mouse button** to display a shortcut menu. Click the **Save Image as** command to display the Save As dialog box in Figure 3.7b.

- Click the **drop-down arrow** in the Save in list box to select the same folder you have been using throughout the chapter.

- Change the default name *images01* to **Two Globes** (a more meaningful name). This will facilitate selecting the appropriate image later in the exercise.

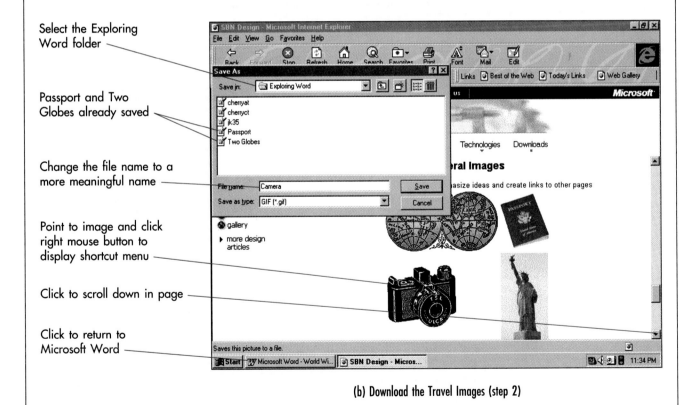

Select the Exploring Word folder

Passport and Two Globes already saved

Change the file name to a more meaningful name

Point to image and click right mouse button to display shortcut menu

Click to scroll down in page

Click to return to Microsoft Word

(b) Download the Travel Images (step 2)

FIGURE 3.7 Hands-on Exercise 3 (continued)

- Click the **Save button** to download the figure and save it on your local drive.

➤ Repeat the process to save the other two images (**Passport** and **Camera**) as shown in the figure. Now that you have the necessary resources, you are ready to create the HTML document.

DOWNLOADING A THEME

You can download an entire theme with a single command as opposed to downloading each of the objects individually. Go to the Multimedia Gallery page, click the link to the desired theme (e.g., travel), then click the link to Download this Theme, which appears at the top of the Web page. You should see the Save As dialog box. Choose the folder in which to save the file, then click the Save button to begin downloading. After downloading is complete (the process takes a few minutes), start the Windows Explorer, open the folder in which you saved the file, then double click the file to install the theme on your PC. The installation program places the objects in the Mmgallry (Multimedia Gallery) folder in the Program Files folder on drive C. See problem 4 at the end of the chapter.

STEP 3: Create the Travel Document

➤ Click the **Word button** on the Windows 95 taskbar. Pull down the **Table menu** and click the **Insert Table command** to display a table grid. Click and drag to select a one-by-two grid, then release the mouse to create a table consisting of one row and two columns.

➤ Pull down the **Tables menu** and toggle the **Show Gridlines command** on if you do not see the table.

➤ Click in the leftmost cell of the table. Type **World Wide Travel** and press the **enter key.** Enter the phone number **(800) 123-4567.**

➤ Click and drag to select **World Wide Travel,** then pull down the **Format menu.** Click **Font** and choose a larger font size (e.g., 24 points). Click **OK.** Select both lines of text and click the **Center button** on the Formatting toolbar.

➤ Pull down the **File menu** and click **Save** (or click the **Save button** on the Standard toolbar).

➤ Click below the table and click the **Horizontal Line button** on the Formatting toolbar. Enter the additional text shown in Figure 3.7c.

➤ Click the **Horizontal Line button** a second time. Your document should approximate the one in our figure.

STEP 4: Insert the Picture

➤ Click in the rightmost cell of the table. Pull down the **Insert menu** and click (or point to) **Picture,** then click **From file** to display the Insert Picture dialog box in Figure 3.7d.

➤ Click the **drop-down arrow** in the Look in list box, then select the folder containing the clip art images. (This is the folder where you saved the images in step 2.)

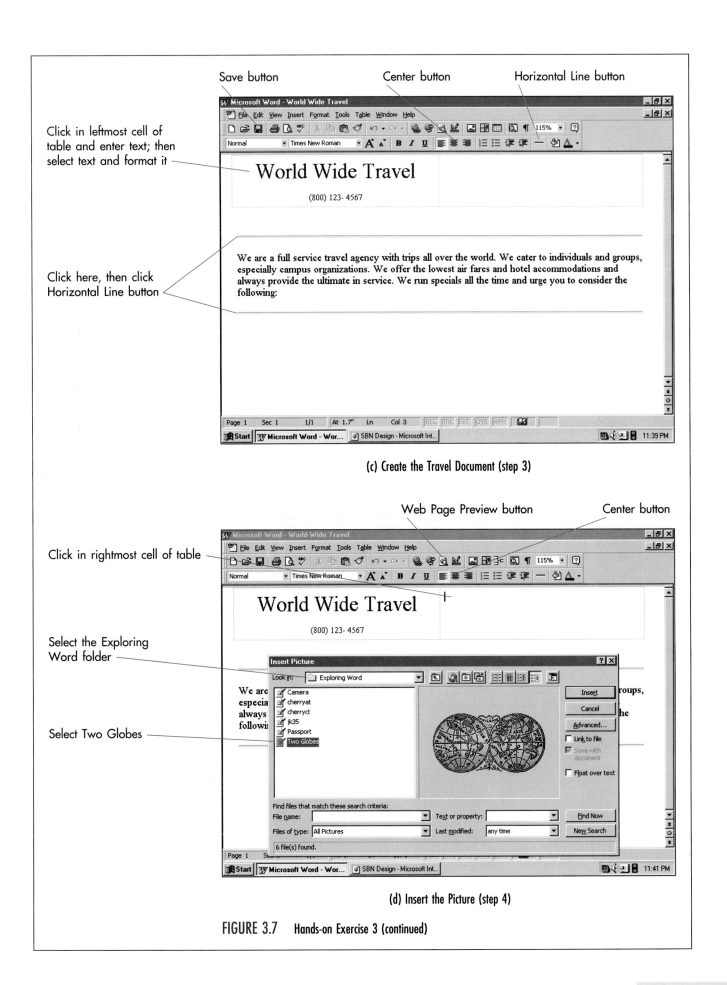

Save button   Center button   Horizontal Line button

Click in leftmost cell of table and enter text; then select text and format it

Click here, then click Horizontal Line button

(c) Create the Travel Document (step 3)

Web Page Preview button   Center button

Click in rightmost cell of table

Select the Exploring Word folder

Select Two Globes

(d) Insert the Picture (step 4)

FIGURE 3.7   Hands-on Exercise 3 (continued)

➤ Select the **Two Globes** graphic as shown in Figure 3.7d. Click **Insert** to insert the image and close the Insert Picture dialog box.

➤ Click the **Center button** on the Formatting toolbar to center the image in the cell. Save the document.

STEP 5: Change the Background

➤ Click the **Web Page Preview button** on the Standard toolbar to see how your page will appear in the default browser that is installed on your system. Click **Yes** if asked to save the document.

➤ You should see the document in Internet Explorer. The document has a gray background by default. Click the **Word button** on the Windows 95 taskbar to return to Word to change the background.

➤ Pull down the **Format menu.** Click **Background** to display the Background color palette in Figure 3.7e. Click **Fill Effects.** Click **Parchment.** Click **OK.**

Save button

Select Parchment

Word button on Taskbar

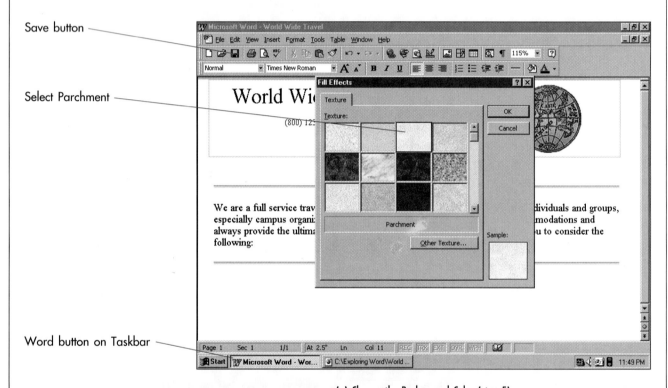

(e) Change the Background Color (step 5)

FIGURE 3.7 Hands-on Exercise 3 (continued)

KEEP IT SIMPLE

Too many would-be designers clutter a page unnecessarily by importing a complex background, which tends to obscure the text. The best design is a simple design—either no background or a very simple pattern. We also prefer light backgrounds with dark text (e.g., black or dark blue text on a white background) as opposed to the other way around. Design, however, is subjective and there is no consensus as to what makes an attractive page. Variety is indeed the spice of life.

➤ Save the document. Click the **Web Page Preview button** on the Standard toolbar to reactivate the browser, then click the **Refresh button** to obtain the most recent copy of the document. You should see the same document as before, except that the background has changed.

STEP 6: Create the Second Document

➤ Click the **Word button** on the Windows taskbar to return to Word. Click the **New button** on the Standard toolbar to start a new document, then double click the **Blank document icon** in the New dialog box.

➤ Enter the text of the document as shown in Figure 3.7f. (This is the document that will be associated with the various travel links in the main document.)

➤ Save the document as an **HTML document** called **Dream Vacation** as shown in Figure 3.7f. Be sure to save the document in the same drive and folder you have been using throughout the chapter.

➤ Click the **Background button** on the Formatting toolbar and select the same background as in the previous step.

➤ Pull down the **File menu** and click **Close** to close this document but remain in Word. Answer **Yes** if prompted to save your changes.

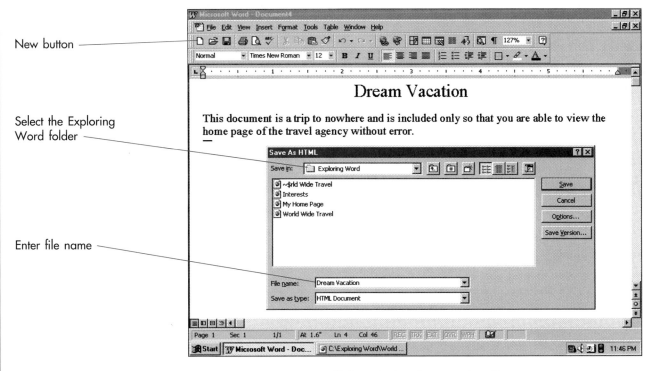

(f) Create the Second Document (step 6)

FIGURE 3.7   Hands-on Exercise 3 (continued)

STEP 7: Add the Links

➤ You should see the World Wide Travel document as before. Scroll through the document until you come to the point where you want to insert a hyperlink (above the last horizontal rule).

➤ If necessary, add a blank line, then type **Honeymoon to the Bahamas.** Click and drag to select this text as shown in Figure 3.7g.

➤ Pull down the **Insert menu** and click **Hyperlink** (or click the **Insert Hyperlink button** on the Standard toolbar) to display the Insert Hyperlink dialog box.

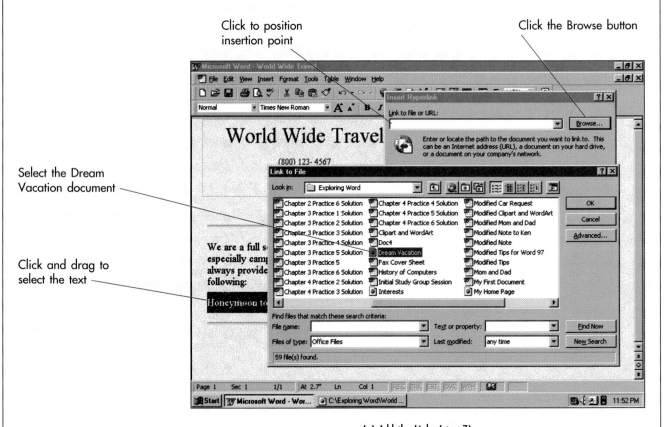

(g) Add the Links (step 7)

FIGURE 3.7   Hands-on Exercise 3 (continued)

➤ Check that the insertion point is positioned in the **Link to File** or **URL text box,** then click the **Browse button** to display the **Link to File dialog box** shown in the figure.

➤ Select (click) the **Dream Vacation document** you created earlier, then click **OK** to select the file and close the Link to File dialog box.

➤ Click **OK** to close the Insert Hyperlink dialog box. You should see the underlined link Honeymoon to the Bahamas in the document.

➤ Click the **Bullets button** on the Formatting toolbar to place a bullet in front of the link. Press the **enter key** to move to the next line, then add additional links for **Spring Break, Summer Special to Europe,** and **See the West.**

➤ All of your links should reference the same Dream Vacation document. (Eventually, however, you will have to create separate documents, one for each vacation. See practice exercise 1 at the end of the chapter.)

➤ Save the document after the links have been added.

PROTOTYPING

Prototyping is a widely used technique that enables an end user to experience the look and feel of a system before the system has been completed. The user is shown the highest level screen (e.g., the travel agency's home page) and provided with a set of links to partially completed documents. The user gets the sense of the eventual system even though the latter is far from finished. Prototyping also provides valuable feedback to the developer, who is able to make the necessary adjustments before any extensive work has been done.

STEP 8: Test the Links

➤ Click the **Web Page Preview button** on the Standard toolbar to view the document in your browser. Click **Yes** if prompted to save the document.

➤ You should see the travel document in your Web browser as shown in Figure 3.7h. The URL address (C:\Exploring Word\World Wide Travel.html) that is displayed in the Location text box indicates that you are viewing the page from a local drive (drive C) as opposed to an actual Web server.

➤ Point to the first link (the mouse pointer changes to a hand to indicate a link), then click the **Honeymoon to the Bahamas** hyperlink you just created to change to view the Dream Vacation page.

➤ Click the **Back button** on the Internet Explorer toolbar to return to the home page for the travel agency. Select (click) a different link to once again display the Dream Vacation page. Click the **Back button** to return to the home page.

➤ Continue testing in this fashion until you are satisfied your links are working. Click the **Word button** on the Windows 95 taskbar to return to Word in order to complete the home page for the travel agency.

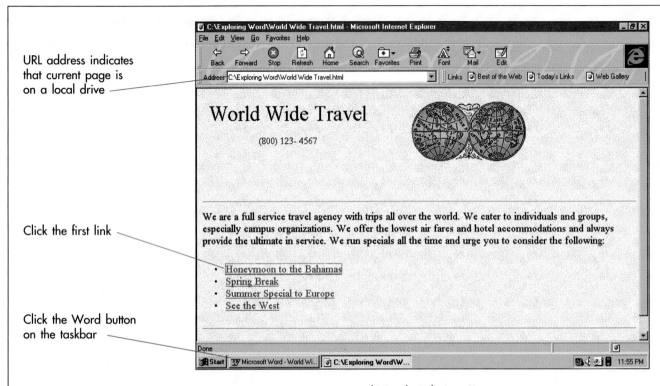

URL address indicates that current page is on a local drive

Click the first link

Click the Word button on the taskbar

(h) Test the Links (step 8)

FIGURE 3.7   Hands-on Exercise 3 (continued)

EXPLORING WWW

OBTAINING A PASSPORT

You can't obtain a passport online, but you can get all of the information you need. Go to travel.state.gov, the home page of the Bureau of Consular Affairs in the U. S. Department of State, then click the link to Passport Information to learn how to apply for a passport. You will be able to download an actual passport application with detailed instructions including a list of the documents you need to supply. You can also access a nationwide list of places where you can apply.

STEP 9: Complete the Document

➤ You should be back in Word as shown in Figure 3.7i. Click below the second horizontal rule.

➤ Pull down the **Table menu** and click the **Insert Table command** to display a grid. Click and drag to select a two-by-two grid, then release the mouse to create the table.

➤ Click in the left cell of the first row and insert the Passport graphic you downloaded earlier.

➤ Press the **Tab** or **right arrow key** to move to the next cell in that row and enter the text shown in Figure 3.7i.

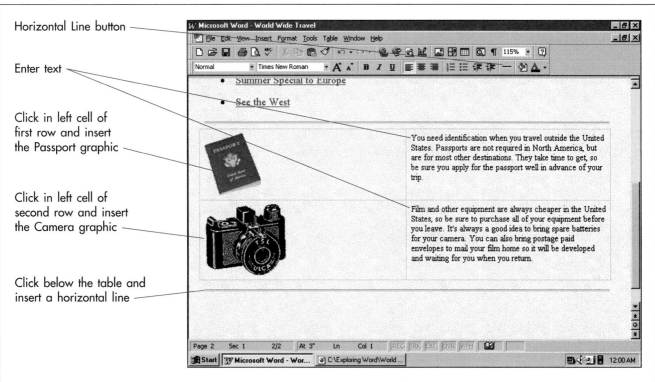

Horizontal Line button

Enter text

Click in left cell of
first row and insert
the Passport graphic

Click in left cell of
second row and insert
the Camera graphic

Click below the table and
insert a horizontal line

(i) Complete the Document (step 9)

FIGURE 3.7   Hands-on Exercise 3 (continued)

➤ Complete the second row of the table by entering the camera graphic and associated text.

➤ Click below the table, then click the **Horizontal Line button** to insert the horizontal line at the bottom of the document. Save the document.

THE UNDO COMMAND

The Undo command enables you to undo the last 100 changes to a document. Click the drop-down arrow next to the Undo button to produce a list of your previous actions, then click the action you want to undo, which also undoes all of the preceding commands. Undoing the fifth command in the list, for example, will also undo the preceding four commands.

STEP 10: Add a Bookmark

➤ Creating a bookmark and a link that points to it is a two-step process (the second step is shown in Figure 3.7j). You start by creating the bookmark itself (which in our example is hidden at the top of the page), then you create the link(s) to the bookmark elsewhere in the document.

➤ To create the bookmark:
  • Press **Ctrl+Home** to move to the top of the page. Pull down the **Insert menu** and click **Bookmark** to display the Bookmark dialog box.

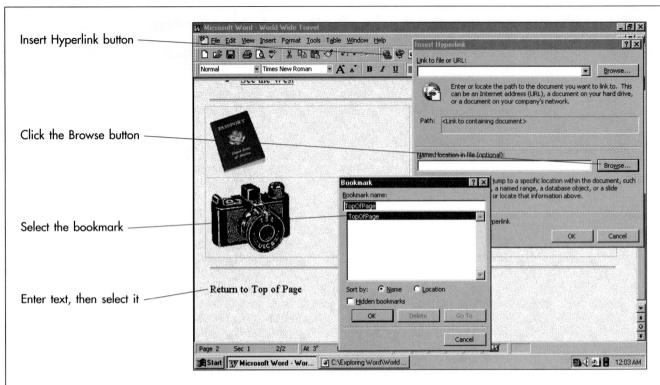

Insert Hyperlink button

Click the Browse button

Select the bookmark

Enter text, then select it

(j) Add a Bookmark (step 10)

FIGURE 3.7   Hands-on Exercise 3 (continued)

- Enter **TopOfPage** (spaces are not allowed) as the name of the bookmark, then click the **Add button** to add the bookmark and close the dialog box. (The bookmark is visible in the HTML source but not in the document.)
- ➤ To create the link to the bookmark:
  - Press **Ctrl+End** to move to the end of the document (the place where you want the reference to the bookmark). Type **Return to Top of Page,** then select the text.

LEARN FROM OTHERS

You can incorporate elements from existing Web pages into your own documents. Once you find a Web page of interest to you, pull down the View menu in your browser, then select the Source command to view the underlying HTML codes. Click and drag to select the codes you need, press Ctrl+C to copy the code to the Windows clipboard, then return to Word and the document on which you are working. Pull down the View menu from within Word, select HTML Source to view the source code for your page, then press Ctrl+V to paste the codes into your document. *Do not, however, incorporate copyrighted material into your document.*

- Click the **Insert Hyperlink button** to display the Insert Hyperlink dialog box, then click the **Browse button** next to the Named Location in File text box. Select the bookmark you just created (TopOfPage). Click **OK.**
- Click **OK** to close the Insert Hyperlink dialog box.

➤ You now have a link to jump from the bottom of your page to the top. Save the completed document.

STEP 11: Preview in the Browser

➤ Click the **Web Page Preview button** to preview the document. Check each of the links to be sure they work.

➤ Proofread the document, making note of any changes, then close the browser and return to Word to make corrections as necessary. Return to the browser to verify that the corrections have taken effect.

➤ Return to Word. Pull down the **File menu** and click the **Print Preview command** to see the entire document as shown in Figure 3.7k.

➤ Click the **Magnifier button** to turn the magnifier on, then click the page to increase (decrease) the magnification of the document.

➤ Click the **Print button** to print the document and submit it to your instructor. Congratulations on a job well done. Bon Voyage!

Zoom box

Magnifier button

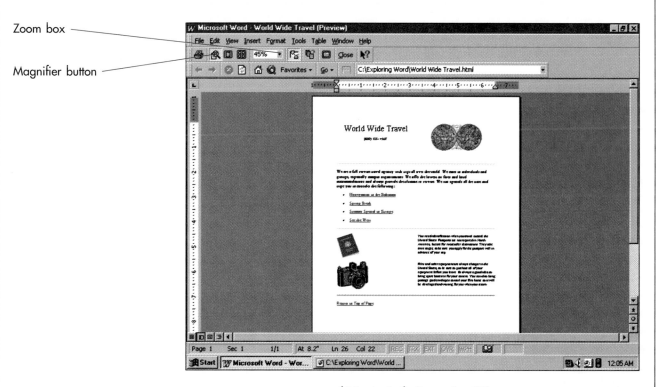

(k) Preview in the Browser (step 11)

FIGURE 3.7 Hands-on Exercise 3 (continued)

Hypertext Markup Language (HTML) is the language used to create a Web page. In essence, HTML consists of a set of codes that format a document for display on the World Wide Web. There are two ways to create a document containing HTML tags. The original (and more difficult) method was to explicitly enter the text and codes in a text editor such as Notepad. The easier technique (and the only one you need to consider) is to use Microsoft Word and have it create the HTML tags for you.

To create a Web document, start Word in the usual fashion and enter the text of the document with basic formatting. Pull down the File menu and click the Save As command, then specify HTML document as the file type. Microsoft Word does the rest, generating the HTML tags needed to create the document. You can continue to enter text and/or change the formatting for existing text just as you can with an ordinary Word document.

Tables facilitate the creation of more complex documents. The Insert Hyperlink command is used to link a document to other pages. Clip art and other graphics are inserted into a document through the Insert Picture command.

After a home page is created, it has to be placed on a Web server or local area network so that other people will be able to access it. This, in turn, requires you to check with your system administrator if, in fact, your page is to become part of the World Wide Web or a corporate Intranet. Even if your page is not placed on the Web, you can still view it locally on your PC through a Web browser.

KEY WORDS AND CONCEPTS

Bookmark

Browser

Graphics

Home page

HTML tags

Hyperlink

Hypertext Markup
    Language (HTML)

Insert Hyperlink
    Command

Insert Picture
    Command

Internet Explorer

Intranet

Microsoft Multimedia
    Gallery

Save As command

Tables command

Tag

MULTIPLE CHOICE

1. Which of the following requires you to enter HTML tags explicitly in order to create a Web document?
   (a) A text editor such as the Notepad accessory
   (b) Word 97
   (c) Both (a) and (b) above
   (d) Neither (a) nor (b) above

2. Which of the following is true about the Formatting toolbar in Word 97?
   (a) It is displayed with Word documents but not with HTML documents
   (b) It is displayed with HTML documents but not with Word documents
   (c) It is displayed with both types of documents, and further it displays the identical buttons regardless of the type of document
   (d) It is displayed with both types of documents, but displays different buttons depending on the type of document

3. Which of the following is true about the Standard toolbar in Word 97?
   (a) It is displayed with Word documents but not with HTML documents
   (b) It is displayed with HTML documents but not with Word documents
   (c) It is displayed with both types of documents, and further it displays the identical buttons regardless of the type of document
   (d) It is displayed with both types of documents, but displays different buttons depending on the type of document

4. What is the easiest way to switch back and forth between Word and Internet Explorer, given that both are open?
   (a) Click the appropriate button on the Windows 95 taskbar
   (b) Click the Start button, click Programs, then choose the appropriate program
   (c) Minimize all applications to display the Windows 95 desktop, then double click the icon for the appropriate application
   (d) All of the above are equally convenient

5. The Format Background command:
   (a) Enables you to change the background color of a Web document
   (b) Enables you to change the texture of a Web document
   (c) Both (a) and (b)
   (d) Neither (a) nor (b)

6. All of the following tags require a matching code except:
   (a) <HR>
   (b) <TITLE>
   (c) <CENTER>
   (d) <A>

7. When should you click the Refresh button on the Internet Explorer toolbar?
   (a) Whenever you visit a new Web site
   (b) Whenever you return to a Web site within a session
   (c) Whenever you view a document on a corporate Intranet
   (d) Whenever you return to a document within a session and the document has changed during the session

8. Which of the following codes creates a horizontal rule across a page in an HTML document?
   (a) <HR>
   (b) <HL>
   (c) <P>
   (d) <UL>

9. How do you view the HTML tags for a Web document from within Word?
   (a) Pull down the View menu and select the HTML Source command
   (b) Pull down the File menu, click the Save As command, and specify HTML as the file type
   (c) Click the Web Page Preview button on the Standard toolbar
   (d) All of the above

10. Which of the following was the source of the clip art used to create the travel document in the chapter?
    (a) The Microsoft Clip Gallery that is included with Office 97
    (b) The Multimedia Gallery on the Microsoft Web site
    (c) The clip art home page at www.clipart.com
    (d) The clip art collection of the Smithsonian Institution

11. Which of the following is required to jump to another section of the same HTML document?
    (a) A bookmark
    (b) An ordered list of the document's contents
    (c) An anchored graphic image
    (d) All of the above

12. Where will the text enclosed in the <TITLE> </TITLE> tags appear when an HTML document is displayed using a Web browser?
    (a) In the title bar
    (b) At the top of the document
    (c) Both (a) and (b) above
    (d) Neither (a) nor (b) above

13. Which of the following statements regarding HTML tags is true?
    (a) They cannot be created in Word 97
    (b) They cannot be viewed in Word 97
    (c) They cannot be viewed in Internet Explorer
    (d) None of the above

14. Internet Explorer can display an HTML page that is stored on:
    (a) A local area network as part of a company's Intranet
    (b) A web server as part of the World Wide Web
    (c) Drive A or drive C of a standalone PC
    (d) All of the above

15. How do you convert an existing Word document to its HTML equivalent?
    (a) Click the Save button on the Standard toolbar
    (b) Pull down the File menu, click the Save As command, then specify an HTML file type
    (c) Both (a) and (b)
    (d) Neither (a) nor (b)

ANSWERS

1. a	**6.** a	**11.** a
2. d	**7.** d	**12.** a
3. d	**8.** a	**13.** d
4. a	**9.** a	**14.** d
5. c	**10.** b	**15.** b

126   MICROSOFT WORD 97

Practice with Microsoft Word

1. The Travel Agent: Create a page for at least two additional excursions for use with the travel page(s) created in the chapter. Figure 3.8, for example, creates the page for the *Honeymoon to the Bahamas* link and incorporates a graphic from the Microsoft Clip Gallery. You might also consult the Virtual Tourist Web site (www.vtourist.com/vt) for information about other destinations.

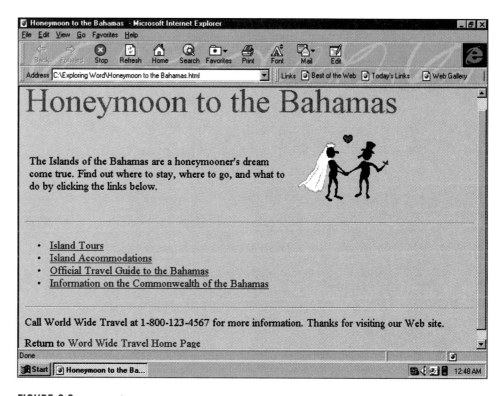

FIGURE 3.8 Screen for Practice Exercise 1

2. The Multimedia Gallery: Figure 3.9 displays a banner from three different themes within the Microsoft Multimedia Gallery. Use one of these banners (or select another banner of your own choosing) as the basis for a Web page. Design is important, so make the page as attractive as you can. Submit a copy of the completed page to your instructor for inclusion in a class contest to determine the most attractive banner.

3. Milestones in Communications: The availability of HTML facilitates the creation of interactive documents such as the document in Figure 3.10. The author used Microsoft Word to create *Milestones in Communications*, then used the Save As command to convert the Word document to its HTML equivalent. Next he bookmarked each of the nine events and created a table of bookmarks at the beginning of the document. And finally, he created a common *Return to Milestones* bookmark (not shown in the figure), which appears at the end of each event. The result is an interactive document that lets the user browse through it.

(a) Travel Banner

(b) European Art Banner

(c) Science Banner

FIGURE 3.9   Banners for Practice Exercise 2

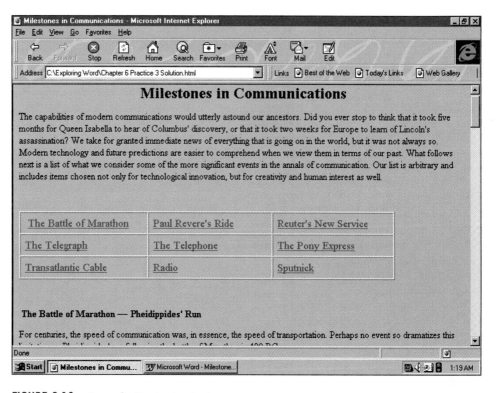

FIGURE 3.10   Screen for Practice Exercise 3

Create your own interactive document containing at least four book-marks, or alternatively, duplicate the document in Figure 3.10. You can find the text for the document in the file *Milestones in Communications,* which is found in the *Exploring Word* folder.

4. Downloading a theme: The chapter described how to download individual images from the Microsoft Multimedia Gallery for inclusion in a Web document. It's often easier, however, to download an entire theme as shown in Figure 3.11. Go to the Multimedia Gallery as described in the third hands-on exercise, select a theme that interests you, then create a Web document based on that theme.

5. The Web Page Wizard: Figure 3.12 displays one of several templates that can be selected using the Web Page Wizard in Word 97. Pull down the File menu, click New to display the New dialog box, click the Web Pages tab, then double click the icon for the Web Page Wizard. Create a Web page based on one of the existing templates and submit it to your instructor as proof you did the exercise. Include a reference on your page to the specific Wizard, together with a sentence or two describing your impression of the Wizard.

6. Update the Wizard: Microsoft is continually updating its Web site with new templates, styles, and so on. Pull down the Help menu, click Microsoft on the Web, then click Free Stuff to connect to the Microsoft Web site. Scroll down the page until you can click the link to Word Web Page Wizard Accessories to display a page similar to Figure 3.13. Download the latest offering, then incorporate that material into the document created in the previous exercise.

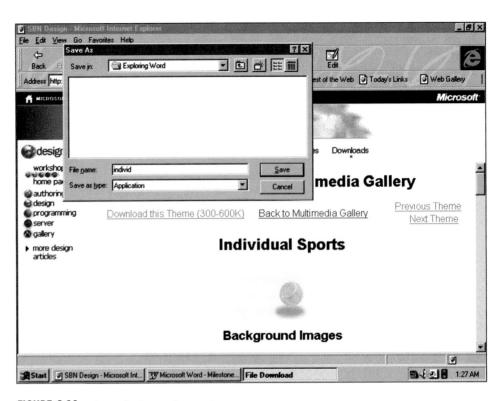

FIGURE 3.11 Screen for Practice Exercise 4

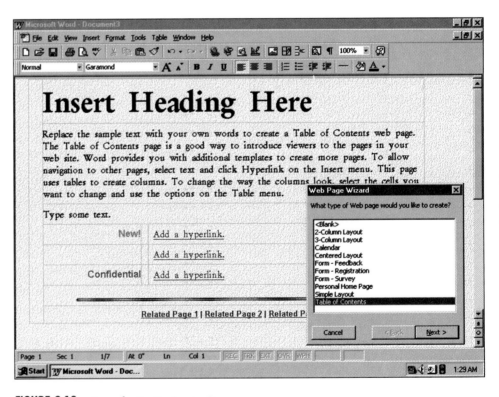

FIGURE 3.12 Screen for Practice Exercise 5

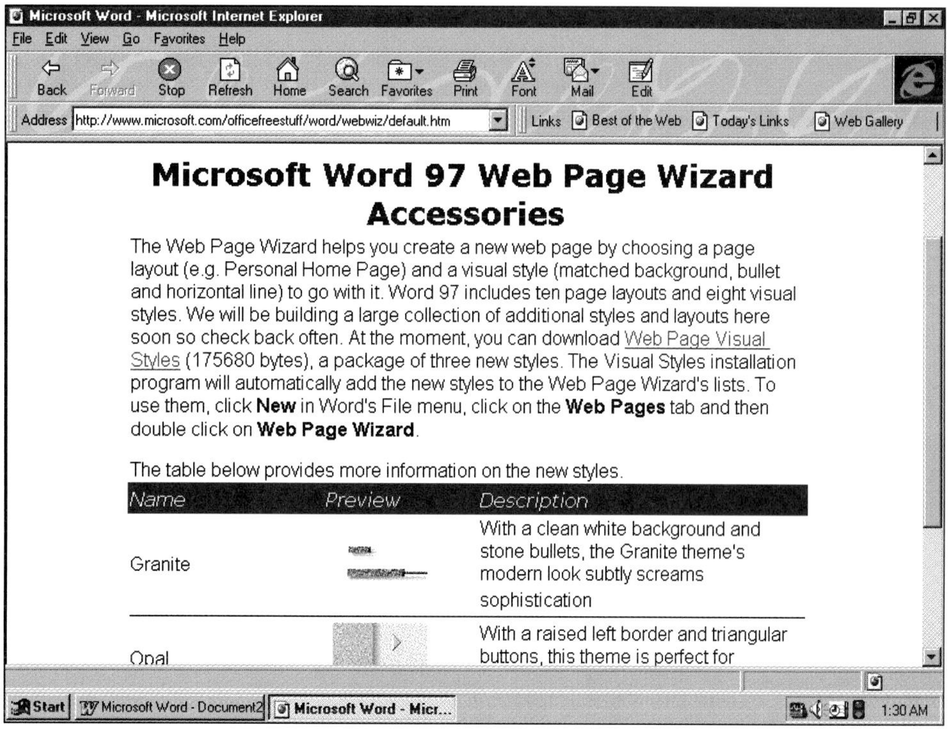

FIGURE 3.13 Screen for Practice Exercise 6

Case Studies

Designer Home Pages

Everyone has a personal list of favorite Web sites, but have you ever thought seriously about what makes an attractive Web page? Is an attractive page the same as a useful page? Try to develop a set of guidelines for a designer to follow as he or she creates a Web site, then incorporate these guidelines into a brief report for your instructor. Support your suggestions by referring to specific Web pages that you think qualify for your personal "Best (Worst) of the Web" award.

Employment Opportunities

The Internet abounds with employment opportunities, help-wanted listings, and places to post your résumé. Your home page reflects your skills and experience to the entire world, and represents an incredible opportunity never before available to college students. You can encourage prospective employers to visit your home page, and make contact with hundreds more companies than would otherwise be possible. Update your home page to include a link to your résumé, and then surf the Net to find places to register it.

Forms in HTML Documents

Many Web pages require you to enter information into a text box, then submit that information to a Web server. Every time you use a search engine, for example, you enter key words into a form, which transmits your request to the search engine. Other common forms include a guest book where you register as having visited the site. Including a form on a page is not difficult but it does require additional knowledge of HTML. Use an appropriate search engine to see what you can find about forms, then summarize your results in a note to your instructor.

The Contest

Almost everyone enjoys some form of competition. Ask your instructor to choose a theme for a Web site such as a school club, and to declare a contest in the class to produce the "best" document. Submit your entry, but write your name on the back of the document so that it can be judged anonymously. Your instructor may want to select a set of semi-finalists, then distribute copies of those documents so that the class can vote on the winner.

Front Page 97

Microsoft Word 97 is an excellent way to begin creating Web documents. It is only a beginning, however, and there are many specialty programs that offer significantly more capability. One such product is Front Page 97, a product aimed at creating a Web site as opposed to isolated documents. Search the Web for information on Front Page 97, then summarize your findings in a short note to your instructor. Be sure to include information on capabilities that are included in Front Page that are not found in Word.

APPENDIX A: OBJECT LINKING AND EMBEDDING

OVERVIEW

The ability to create a document containing data (objects) from multiple applications is one of the primary advantages of the Windows environment. The memo in Figure A.1, for example, was created in Microsoft Word, and it contains a worksheet from Microsoft Excel. **Object Linking and Embedding** (abbreviated OLE and pronounced "OH-lay") is the means by which you insert an object from a source file (e.g., an Excel workbook) into a destination file (e.g., a Word document).

The essential difference between linking and embedding is whether the object in the destination file maintains a connection to the source file. A **linked** object maintains the connection. An **embedded object** does not. A linked object can be associated with many different destination files that do not contain the object per se, but only a representation of the object as well as a pointer (link) to the source file containing the object. Any change to the object in the source file is reflected automatically in every destination file that is linked to that object. An embedded object, however, is contained entirely within the destination file. Changes to the object in the destination file are *not* reflected in the source file.

The choice between linking and embedding depends on how the object will be used. Linking is preferable if the object is likely to change and the destination file requires the latest version. Linking should also be used when the same object is placed in many documents, so that any change to the object has to be made in only one place. Embedding is preferable if you intend to edit the destination file on a computer other than the one on which it was created.

The exercise that follows shows you how to create the compound document in Figure A.1. The exercise uses the **Insert Object command** to embed a copy of the Excel worksheet into a Word document. Once an object has been embedded into a document, it can be modified

Lionel Douglas

402 Mahoney Hall • Coral Gables, Florida 33124

June 25, 1997

Dear Folks,

I heard from Mr. Black, the manager at University Commons, and the apartment is a definite for the Fall. Ken and I are very excited, and can't wait to get out of the dorm. The food is poison, not that either of us are cooks, but anything will be better than this! I have been checking into car prices (we are definitely too far away from campus to walk!), and have done some estimating on what it will cost. The figures below are for a Jeep Wrangler, the car of my dreams:

Price of car	$11,995			
Manufacturer's rebate	$1,000			
Down payment	$3,000		**My assumptions**	
Amount to be financed	$7,995		Interest rate	7.90%
Monthly payment	$195		Term (years)	4
Gas	$40			
Maintenance	$50			
Insurance	$100			
Total per month	$385			

My initial estimate was $471 based on a $2,000 down payment and a three year loan at 7.9%. I know this is too much so I plan on earning an additional $1,000 and extending the loan to four years. That will bring the total cost down to a more manageable level (see the above calculations). If that won't do it, I'll look at other cars.

Lionel

FIGURE A.1   A Compound Document

through *in-place editing.* In-place editing enables you to double click an embedded object (the worksheet) and change it, using the tools of the source application (Excel). In other words, you remain in Microsoft Word, but you have access to the Excel toolbar and pull-down menus. In-place editing modifies the copy of the embedded object in the destination file. It does *not* change the original object because there is no connection (or link) between the source file (if indeed there is a source file) and the destination file.

Embedding

Objective: To embed an Excel worksheet into a Word document; to use in-place editing to modify the worksheet within Word. Use Figure A.2 as a guide in the exercise.

STEP 1: Open the Word Document

➤ Start Word. Open the **Car Request document** in the **Exploring Word folder.** Zoom to **Page Width** so that the display on your monitor matches ours.

➤ Save the document as **Modified Car Request** so that you can return to the original document if you edit the duplicated file beyond redemption.

➤ Point to the date field, click the **right mouse button** to display the shortcut menu in Figure A.2a, then click the **Update Field command.**

THE DATE FIELD

The Insert Date and Time command enables you to insert the date as a specific value (the date on which a document is created) or as a field. The latter will be updated automatically whenever the document is printed or when the document is opened in Page Layout view. Opening the document in the Normal view requires the date field to be updated manually.

Point to the date and click the right mouse button to produce the shortcut menu

Click Update Field to change the date to the current date

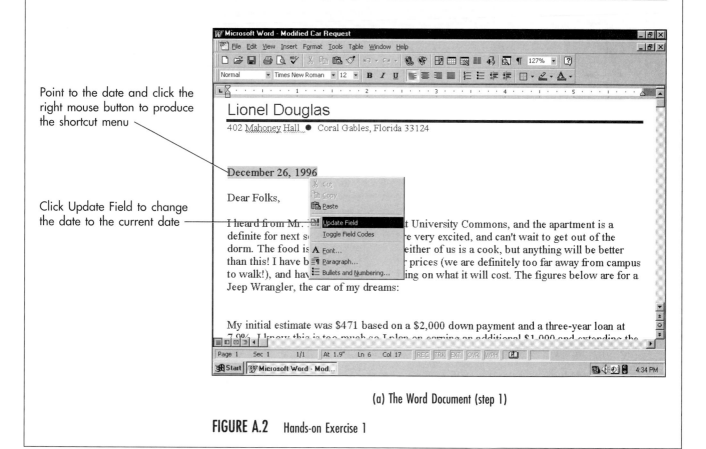

(a) The Word Document (step 1)

FIGURE A.2 Hands-on Exercise 1

STEP 2: Insert an Object

➤ Click the blank line above paragraph two as shown in Figure A.2b. This is the place in the document where the worksheet is to go.

➤ Pull down the **Insert menu**, and click the **Object command** to display the Object dialog box in Figure A.2b.

➤ Click the **Create from File tab,** then click the **Browse command button** in order to open the Browse dialog box and select the object.

➤ Click (select) the **Car Budget workbook** (note the Excel icon), which is in the Exploring Word folder.

➤ Click **OK** to select the workbook and close the Browse dialog box.

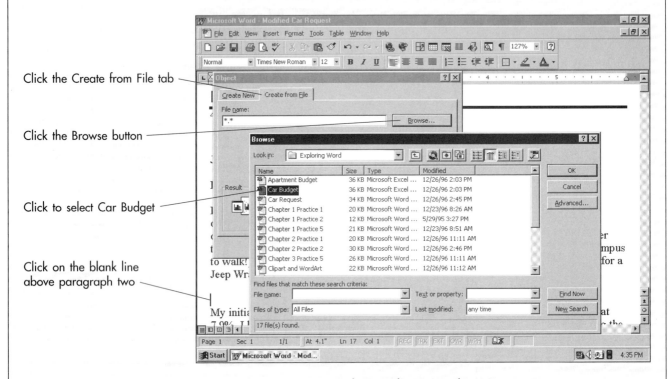

Click the Create from File tab

Click the Browse button

Click to select Car Budget

Click on the blank line above paragraph two

(b) Insert Object Command (step 2)

FIGURE A.2   Hands-on Exercise 1 (continued)

STEP 3: Insert an Object (continued)

➤ The file name of the object (Car Budget.xls) has been placed into the File Name text box, as shown in Figure A.2c.

➤ Verify that the Link to File and Display as Icon check boxes are clear and that the Float over text box is checked.

➤ Note the description at the bottom of the Object dialog box, which indicates that you will be able to edit the object using the application that created the source file.

➤ Click **OK** to insert the Excel worksheet into the Word document. Save the document.

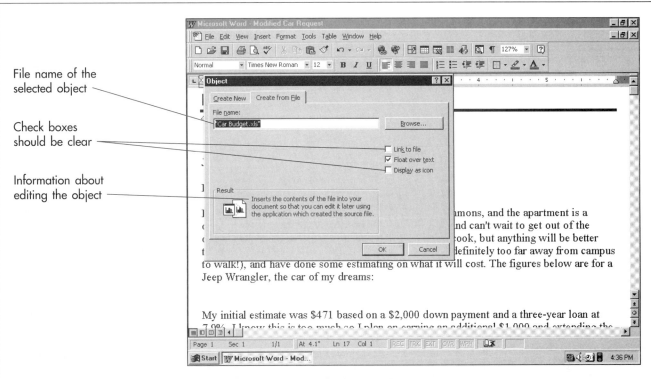

File name of the selected object

Check boxes should be clear

Information about editing the object

(c) Insert Object Command, continued (step 3)

FIGURE A.2   Hands-on Exercise 1 (continued)

STEP 4: Position the Worksheet

➤ The worksheet should appear within the Word document. If necessary, click (select) the worksheet to display the sizing handles as shown in Figure A.2d.

➤ To move the worksheet:

  • Point to any part of the worksheet except a sizing handle (the mouse pointer changes to a four-sided arrow), then click and drag to move the worksheet.

➤ To size the worksheet:

  • Drag a corner handle (the mouse pointer changes to a double arrow) to change the length and width simultaneously and keep the worksheet in proportion.

  • Drag a handle on the horizontal or vertical border to change one dimension only (which distorts the worksheet).

➤ Click anywhere in the document, except for the worksheet. The sizing handles disappear and the worksheet is no longer selected.

➤ If necessary, click above and/or below the worksheet, then press the **enter key** to insert a blank line(s) for better spacing.

➤ Save the document.

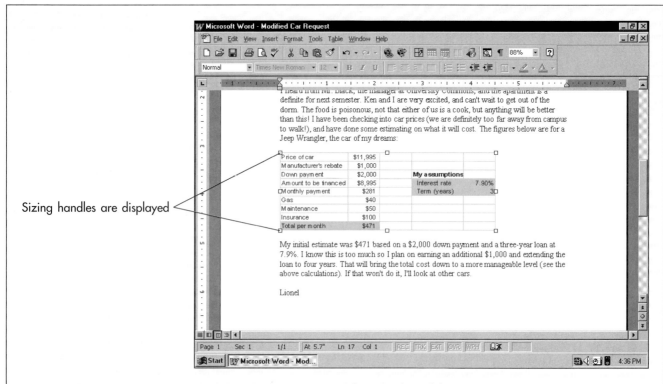

Sizing handles are displayed

(d) Position the Worksheet (step 4)

FIGURE A.2 Hands-on Exercise 1 (continued)

TO CLICK OR DOUBLE CLICK

Clicking an object selects the object and displays the sizing handles, which let you move and/or size the object. Double clicking an object starts the application that created the object and enables you to modify the object using that application. Double click a worksheet, for example, and you start Microsoft Excel from where you can modify the worksheet without exiting from Microsoft Word.

STEP 5: In-place Editing

➤ We will change the worksheet to reflect Lionel's additional $1,000 for the down payment. Double click the worksheet object to edit the worksheet in place.

➤ Be patient as this step takes a while, even on a fast machine. The Excel grid, consisting of the row and column labels, will appear around the worksheet, as shown in Figure A.2e.

➤ You are still in Word, as indicated by the title bar (Microsoft Word - Modified Car Request), but the Excel toolbars are displayed.

➤ Click in cell **B3,** type the new down payment of **$3,000,** and press **enter.**

➤ Click in cell **E5,** type **4,** and press **enter.** The Monthly payment (cell B5) and Total per month (cell B9) drop to $195 and $385, respectively.

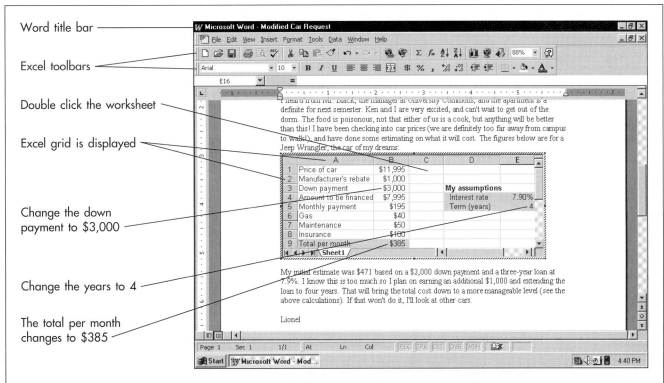

Word title bar

Excel toolbars

Double click the worksheet

Excel grid is displayed

Change the down payment to $3,000

Change the years to 4

The total per month changes to $385

(e) In-place Editing (step 5)

FIGURE A.2   Hands-on Exercise 1 (continued)

IN-PLACE EDITING

In-place editing enables you to edit an embedded object using the toolbar and pull-down menus of the original application. Thus, when editing an Excel worksheet embedded into a Word document, the title bar is that of Microsoft Word, but the toolbars and pull-down menus are from Excel. There are, however, two exceptions; the File and Window menus are from Microsoft Word, so that you can save the compound document and/or arrange multiple documents.

STEP 6: The Completed Document

➤ Click anywhere outside the worksheet to deselect it. Press **Ctrl+Home** to move to the beginning of the document, then scroll as necessary to view the completed Word document as shown in Figure A.2f.

➤ Pull down the **File menu** and click **Save** (or click the **Save button** on the Standard toolbar).

➤ Pull down the **File menu** a second time. Click **Exit** if you do not want to continue with the next hands-on exercise once this exercise is completed. Otherwise click **Close** to remove the document from memory but leave Word open.

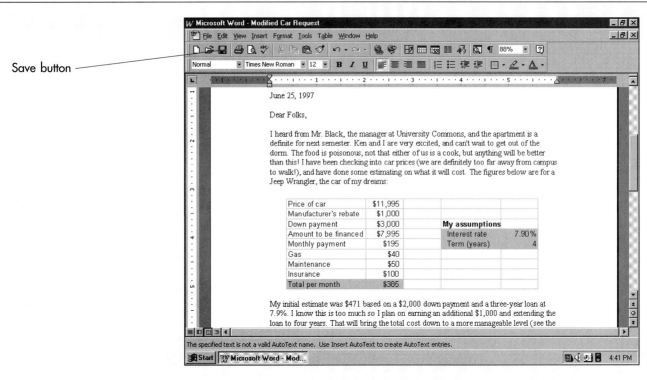

Save button

(f) The Completed Word Document (step 6)

FIGURE A.2   Hands-on Exercise 1 (continued)

STEP 7: View the Original Object

➤ Click the **Start Button,** click (or point to) the **Programs menu,** then click **Microsoft Excel** to open the program.

➤ If necessary, click the **Maximize button** in the application window so that Excel takes the entire desktop, as shown in Figure A.2g.

➤ Pull down the **File menu** and click **Open** (or click the **Open button** on the Standard toolbar) to display the Open dialog box.

• Click the **drop-down arrow** on the Look In list box. Click the appropriate drive, drive C or drive A, depending on the location of your data.

• Double click the **Exploring Word folder** to make it the active folder.

• Click (select) **Car Budget** to select the workbook that we have used throughout the exercise.

• Click the **Open command button** to open the workbook, as shown in Figure A.2g.

• Click the **Maximize button** in the document window (if necessary) so that the document window is as large as possible.

➤ You should see the original (unmodified) worksheet, with a down payment of $2,000, a three-year loan, a monthly car payment of $281, and total expenses per month of $471. The changes that were made in step 6 were made to the compound document and are *not* reflected in the source file.

➤ Pull down the **File menu.** Click **Exit** to exit Microsoft Excel.

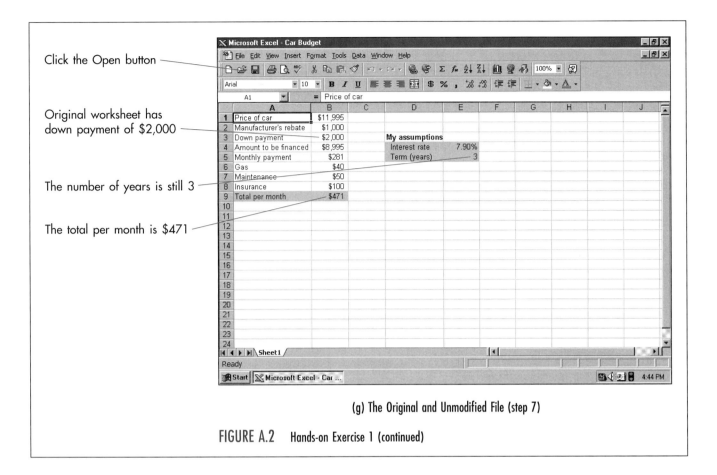

Click the Open button

Original worksheet has
down payment of $2,000

The number of years is still 3

The total per month is $471

(g) The Original and Unmodified File (step 7)

FIGURE A.2 Hands-on Exercise 1 (continued)

LINKING

The exercise just completed used embedding rather than linking to place a copy of the Excel worksheet into the Word document. The last step in the exercise demonstrated that the original worksheet was unaffected by changes made to the embedded copy within the compound document (destination file).

Linking is very different from embedding as you shall see in the next exercise. Linking maintains a dynamic connection between the source and destination files. Embedding does not. With linking, the object created by the source application (e.g., an Excel worksheet) is tied to the destination file (e.g., a Word document) in such a way that any changes in the Excel worksheet are automatically reflected in the Word document. The Word document does not contain the worksheet per se, but only a representation of the worksheet, as well as a pointer (or link) to the Excel workbook.

Linking requires that an object be saved in its own file because the object does not actually exist within the destination file. Embedding, on the other hand, lets you place the object directly in a destination file without having to save it as a separate file. (The embedded object simply becomes part of the destination file.)

Consider now Figure A.3, in which the same worksheet is linked to two different documents. Both documents contain a pointer to the worksheet, which may be edited by double clicking the object in either document. Alternatively, you may open the source application and edit the object directly. In either case, changes to the Excel workbook are reflected in every destination file that is linked to the workbook.

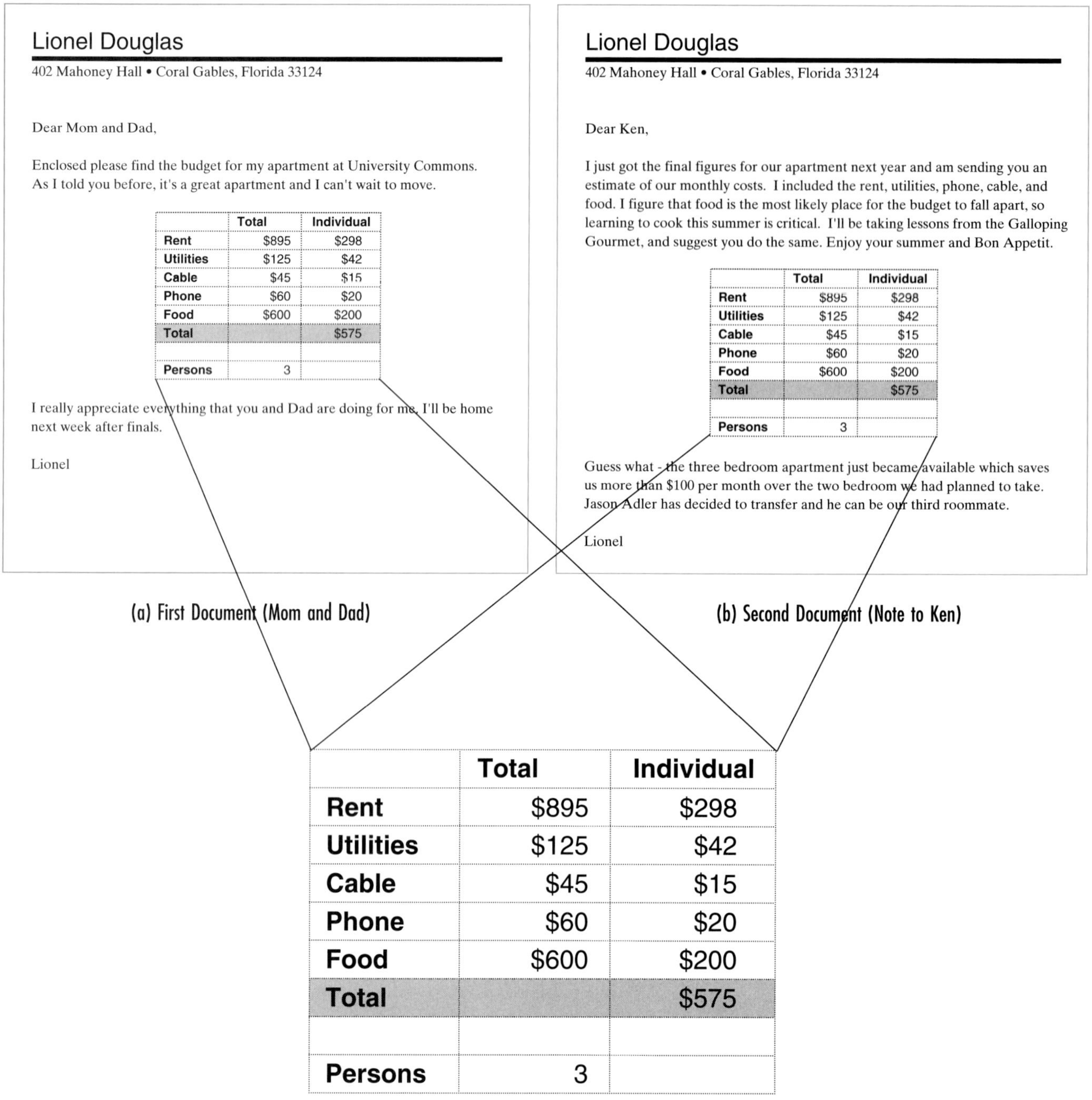

Lionel Douglas

402 Mahoney Hall • Coral Gables, Florida 33124

Dear Mom and Dad,

Enclosed please find the budget for my apartment at University Commons. As I told you before, it's a great apartment and I can't wait to move.

	Total	Individual
Rent	$895	$298
Utilities	$125	$42
Cable	$45	$15
Phone	$60	$20
Food	$600	$200
Total		$575
Persons	3	

I really appreciate everything that you and Dad are doing for me. I'll be home next week after finals.

Lionel

(a) First Document (Mom and Dad)

Lionel Douglas

402 Mahoney Hall • Coral Gables, Florida 33124

Dear Ken,

I just got the final figures for our apartment next year and am sending you an estimate of our monthly costs. I included the rent, utilities, phone, cable, and food. I figure that food is the most likely place for the budget to fall apart, so learning to cook this summer is critical. I'll be taking lessons from the Galloping Gourmet, and suggest you do the same. Enjoy your summer and Bon Appetit.

	Total	Individual
Rent	$895	$298
Utilities	$125	$42
Cable	$45	$15
Phone	$60	$20
Food	$600	$200
Total		$575
Persons	3	

Guess what - the three bedroom apartment just became available which saves us more than $100 per month over the two bedroom we had planned to take. Jason Adler has decided to transfer and he can be our third roommate.

Lionel

(b) Second Document (Note to Ken)

	Total	Individual
Rent	$895	$298
Utilities	$125	$42
Cable	$45	$15
Phone	$60	$20
Food	$600	$200
Total		$575
Persons	3	

(c) Worksheet (Apartment Budget)

FIGURE A.3   Linking

The next exercise links a single Excel worksheet to two different Word documents. During the course of the exercise both applications (Word and Excel) will be explicitly open, and it will be necessary to switch back and forth between the two. Thus, the exercise also demonstrates the multitasking capability within Windows and the use of the taskbar to switch between the open applications.

Linking

Objective: To demonstrate multitasking and the ability to switch between applications; to link an Excel worksheet to multiple Word documents. Use Figure A.4 as a guide in the exercise.

STEP 1: Open the Word Document

➤ Check the taskbar to see whether there is a button for Microsoft Word indicating that the application is already active in memory. Start Word if you do not see its button on the taskbar.

➤ Open the **Mom and Dad document** in the **Exploring Word folder** as shown in Figure A.4a. The document opens in the Normal view (the view in which it was last saved). If necessary, zoom to **Page Width** so that the display on your monitor matches ours.

➤ Save the document as **Modified Mom and Dad.**

Click here to zoom to Page Width

Lionel is a proper name and is flagged as a misspelling

Click the start button

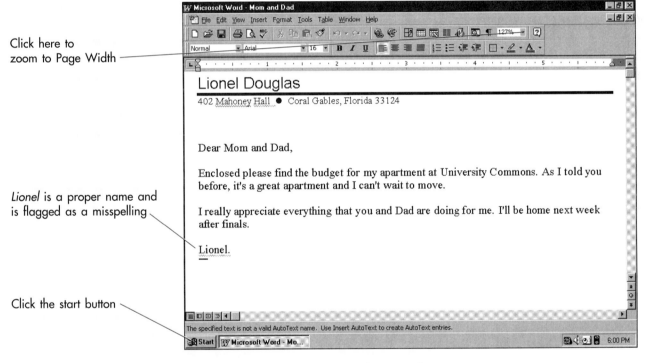

(a) Open the First Word Document (step 1)

FIGURE A.4   Hands-on Exercise 2

STEP 2: Open the Excel Worksheet

➤ Click the **Start button,** click (or point to) the **Programs menu,** then click **Microsoft Excel** to open the program.

➤ If necessary, click the **Maximize button** in the application window so that Excel takes the entire desktop. Click the **Maximize button** in the document window (if necessary) so that the document window is as large as possible.

➤ The taskbar should now contain buttons for both Microsoft Word and Microsoft Excel. Click either button to move back and forth between the open applications. End by clicking the Microsoft Excel button, since you want to work in that application.

➤ Pull down the **File menu** and click **Open** (or click the **Open button** on the Standard toolbar) to display the Open dialog box in Figure A.4b.

➤ Click the **drop-down arrow** on the Look In list box. Click the appropriate drive, drive C or drive A, depending on the location of your data. Double click the **Exploring Word folder** to make it the active folder. Double click **Apartment Budget** to open the workbook.

Click the Open button

Select the Exploring
Word folder

Double click Apartment
Budget to open it

Taskbar has buttons
for Word and Excel

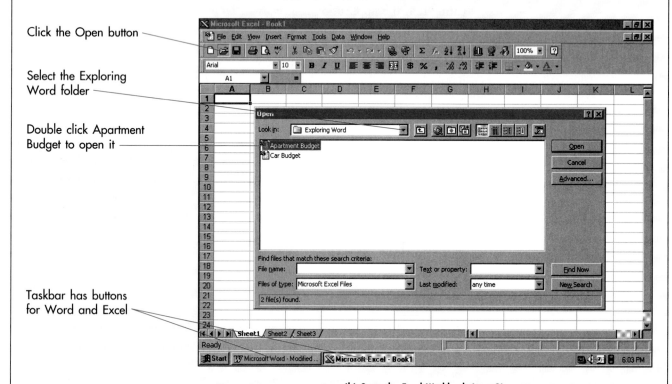

(b) Open the Excel Workbook (step 2)

FIGURE A.4   Hands-on Exercise 2 (continued)

THE COMMON USER INTERFACE

The *common user interface* provides a sense of familiarity from one Windows application to the next. Even if you have never used Excel, you will recognize many of the elements present in Word. Both applications share a common menu structure with consistent ways to execute commands from those menus. The Standard and Formatting toolbars are present in both applications. Many keyboard shortcuts are also common—for example Ctrl+Home and Ctrl+End to move to the beginning and end of a document.

STEP 3: Copy the Worksheet to the Clipboard

➤ **Click in cell A1.** Drag the mouse over cells **A1 through C9** so that the entire worksheet is selected as shown in Figure A.4c.

➤ Point to the selected cells, then click the **right mouse button** to display the shortcut menu shown in the figure. Click **Copy.** A moving border appears around the selected area in the worksheet, indicating that it has been copied to the clipboard.

➤ Click the **Microsoft Word button** on the Windows taskbar to return to the Word document.

Click in A1 and drag to C9 to select the entire spreadsheet

Point to the selected cells and click the right mouse button

Click Copy

Click to return to Microsoft Word

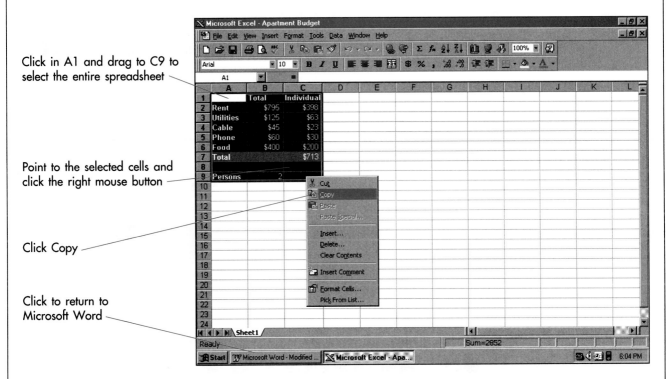

(c) Copy the Worksheet to the Clipboard (step 3)

FIGURE A.4   Hands-on Exercise 2 (continued)

THE WINDOWS TASKBAR

Multitasking, the ability to run multiple applications at the same time, is one of the primary advantages of the Windows environment. Each button on the taskbar appears automatically when its application or folder is opened and disappears upon closing. (The buttons on are resized automatically according to the number of open windows.) You can customize the taskbar by right clicking an empty area to display a shortcut menu, then clicking the Properties command. You can resize the taskbar by pointing to its inside edge, then dragging when you see a double-headed arrow. You can also move the taskbar to the left or right edge of the desktop, or to the top of the desktop, by dragging a blank area of the taskbar to the desired position.

STEP 4: Create the Link

➤ Click in the document between the two paragraphs. Press **enter** to enter an additional blank line.

➤ Pull down the **Edit menu.** Click **Paste Special** to produce the dialog box in Figure A.4d.

➤ Click the **Paste Link option button.** Click **Microsoft Excel Worksheet Object.** Click **OK** to insert the worksheet into the document. You may want to insert a blank line before and/or after the worksheet to make it easier to read.

➤ Save the document containing the letter to Mom and Dad.

Click Microsoft Excel
Worksheet Object

Click the Paste Link
option button

Click between paragraphs
and press the enter key

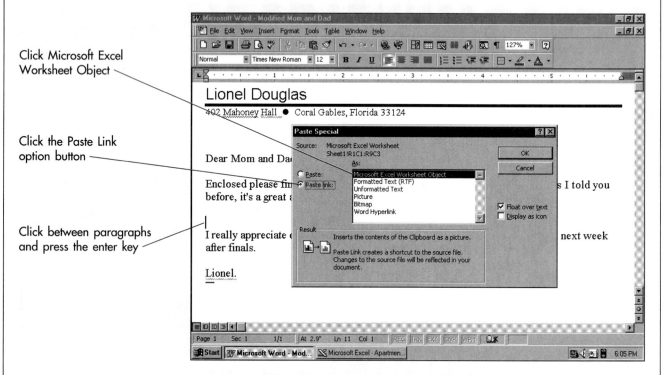

(d) Create the Link (step 4)

FIGURE A.4   Hands-on Exercise 2 (continued)

LINKING VERSUS EMBEDDING

The *Paste Special command* will link or embed an object, depending on whether the Paste Link or Paste Option button is checked. Linking stores a pointer to the source file containing the object together with a reference to the source application. Changes to the object are automatically reflected in all destination files that are linked to the object. Embedding stores a copy of the object with a reference to the source application. Changes to the object within the destination file, however, are not reflected in the original object. Linking and embedding both allow you to double click the object in the destination file to edit the object by using the tools of the source application.

STEP 5: Open the Second Word Document

➤ Open the **Note to Ken document** in the **Exploring Word folder.** Save the document as **Modified Note to Ken** so that you can always return to the original document.

➤ The Apartment Budget worksheet is still in the clipboard since the contents of the clipboard have not been changed. Click at the end of the first paragraph (after the words Bon Appetit). Press the **enter key** to insert a blank line after the paragraph.

➤ Pull down the **Edit menu.** Click **Paste Special.** Click the **Paste Link option button.** Click **Microsoft Excel Worksheet Object.** Click **OK** to insert the worksheet into the document, as shown in Figure A.4e.

➤ If necessary, enter a blank line before or after the object to improve the appearance of the document. Save the document.

➤ Click anywhere on the worksheet to select the worksheet, as shown in Figure A.4e. The message on the status bar indicates you can double click the worksheet to edit the object.

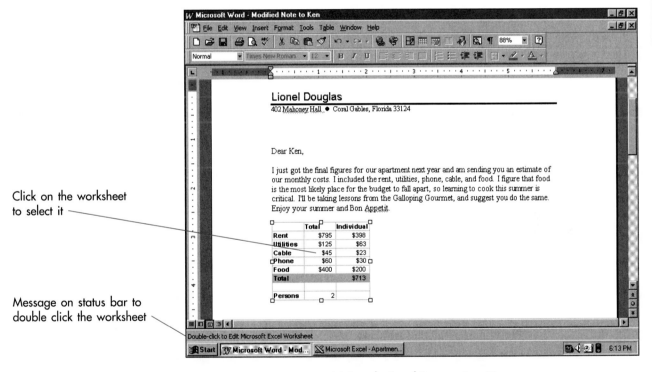

Click on the worksheet to select it

Message on status bar to double click the worksheet

(e) Open the Second Document (step 5)

FIGURE A.4   Hands-on Exercise 2 (continued)

STEP 6: Modify the Worksheet

➤ The existing spreadsheet indicates the cost of a two-bedroom apartment, but you want to show the cost of a three-bedroom apartment. Double click the worksheet in order to change it.

➤ The system pauses (the faster your computer, the better) as it switches back to Excel. Maximize the document window.

➤ Cells **A1 through C9** are still selected from step 3. Click outside the selected range to deselect the worksheet. Press **Esc** to remove the moving border.

➤ Click in cell **B2.** Type **$895** (the rent for a three-bedroom apartment).

➤ Click in cell **B6.** Type **$600** (the increased amount for food).

➤ Click in cell **B9.** Type **3** to change the number of people sharing the apartment. Press **enter.** The total expenses (in cell C9) change to $575, as shown in Figure A.4f.

➤ Save the worksheet.

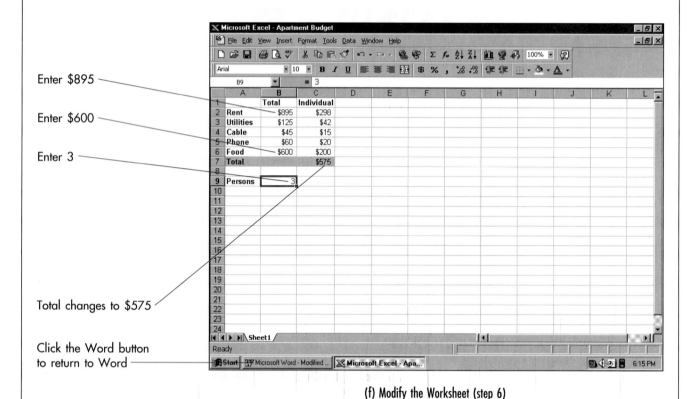

Enter $895

Enter $600

Enter 3

Total changes to $575

Click the Word button to return to Word

(f) Modify the Worksheet (step 6)

FIGURE A.4   Hands-on Exercise 2 (continued)

STEP 7: View the Modified Document

➤ Click the **Microsoft Word button** on the taskbar to return to Microsoft Word and the note to Ken, as shown in Figure A.4g.

➤ The note to Ken displays the modified worksheet because of the link established earlier.

➤ Click below the worksheet and add the additional text shown in Figure A.4g to let Ken know about the new apartment.

➤ Save the document.

STEP 8: View the Completed Note to Mom and Dad

➤ Pull down the **Window menu.** Click **Modified Mom and Dad** to switch to this document as shown in Figure A.4h.

➤ The note to your parents also contains the updated worksheet (with three roommates) because of the link established earlier.

➤ Save the completed document.

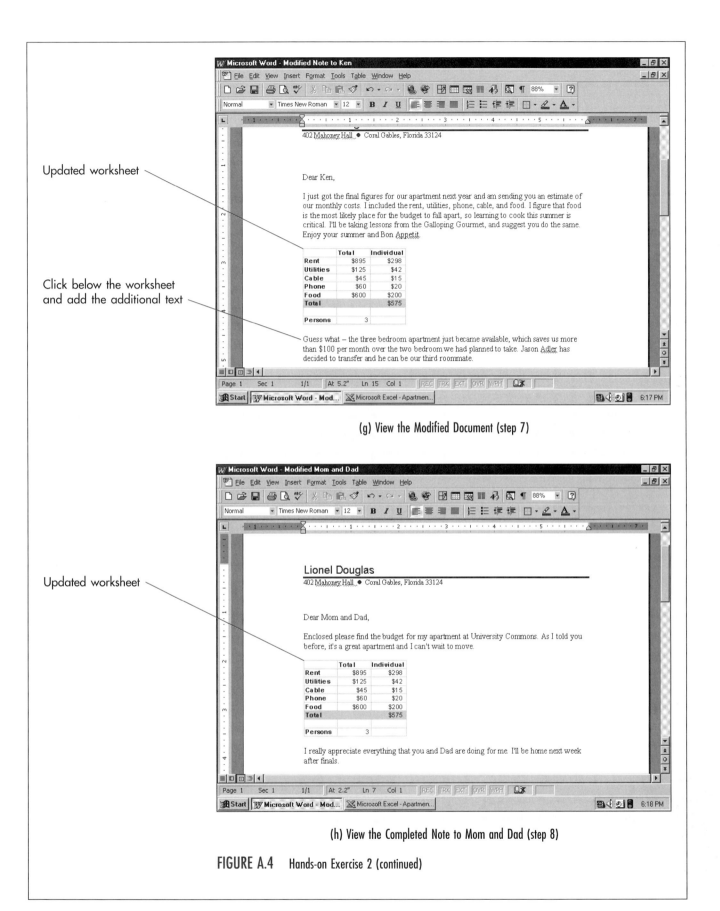

Updated worksheet

Click below the worksheet and add the additional text

(g) View the Modified Document (step 7)

Updated worksheet

(h) View the Completed Note to Mom and Dad (step 8)

FIGURE A.4   Hands-on Exercise 2 (continued)

ALT+TAB STILL WORKS

Alt+Tab was a treasured shortcut in Windows 3.1 that enabled users to switch back and forth between open applications. The shortcut also works in Windows 95. Press and hold the Alt key while you press and release the Tab key repeatedly to cycle through the open applications. Note that each time you release the Tab key, the icon of a different application is selected in the small rectangular window that is displayed in the middle of the screen. Release the Alt key when you have selected the icon for the application you want.

STEP 9: Exit Word

➤ Exit Word. Save the files if you are requested to do so. The button for Microsoft Word disappears from the taskbar.

➤ Exit Excel. Save the files if you are requested to do so. The button for Microsoft Excel disappears from the taskbar.

SUMMARY

The essential difference between linking and embedding is that linking does not place an object into the destination file (compound document), but only a pointer (link) to that object. Embedding, on the other hand, places (a copy of) the object into the destination file. Linking is dynamic whereas embedding is not.

Linking requires that an object be saved in its own (source) file, and further that the link between the source file and the destination file be maintained. Linking is especially useful when the same object is present in multiple documents, because any subsequent change to the object is made in only one place (the source file), but will be automatically reflected in the multiple destination files.

Embedding does not require an object to be saved in its own file because the object is contained entirely within the destination file. Thus, embedding lets you distribute a copy of the destination file, without including a copy of the source file, and indeed, there need not be a separate source file. You would not, however, want to embed the same object into multiple documents because any subsequent change to the object would have to be made in every document.

KEY WORDS AND CONCEPTS

Common user interface
Compound document
Embedding
In-place editing

Insert Object command
Linking
Multitasking

Object linking and
  embedding (OLE)
Paste Special command

APPENDIX B:
TOOLBAR SUMMARY

OVERVIEW

Microsoft Word has 16 predefined toolbars that provide access to commonly used commands. The toolbars are displayed in Figure B.1 and are listed here for convenience. They are the Standard, Formatting, AutoText, Control toolbox, Database, Drawing, Forms, Microsoft, Picture, Reviewing, Shadow Settings, Tables and Borders, Visual Basic, Web, WordArt, and 3-D Settings toolbars.

The Standard and Formatting toolbars are displayed by default immediately below the menu bar. The other predefined toolbars are displayed (hidden) at the discretion of the user. Six additional toolbars are displayed automatically when their corresponding features are in use. These toolbars appear (and disappear) automatically and are shown in Figure B.2. They are the Equation Editor, Header/Footer, Macro, Mail Merge, Master Document, and Outlining toolbars.

The buttons on the toolbars are intended to indicate their functions. Clicking the Printer button, for example, executes the Print command. If you are unsure of the purpose of any toolbar button, point to it, and a ScreenTip will appear that displays its name.

You can display multiple toolbars at one time, move them to new locations on the screen, or customize their appearance. To display or hide a toolbar, pull down the View menu and click the Toolbars command. Select (deselect) the toolbar(s) that you want to display (hide). The selected toolbar(s) will be displayed in the same position as when last displayed. You may also point to any toolbar and click with the right mouse button to bring up a shortcut menu.

Toolbars are either docked (along the edge of the window) or floating (in their own window). A toolbar moved to the edge of the window will dock along that edge. A toolbar moved anywhere else in the window will float in its own window. Docked toolbars are one tool wide (high), whereas floating toolbars can be resized by clicking and dragging a border or corner as you would with any window. To move a docked toolbar, click and drag the move handle (the pair of parallel lines) at the left of the toolbar. To move a floating toolbar, drag its title bar to its new location.

Standard Toolbar

New   Save   Print Preview   Cut   Paste   Undo   Insert Hyperlink   Tables and Borders   Insert Excel Worksheet   Drawing   Show Hide   Office Assistant

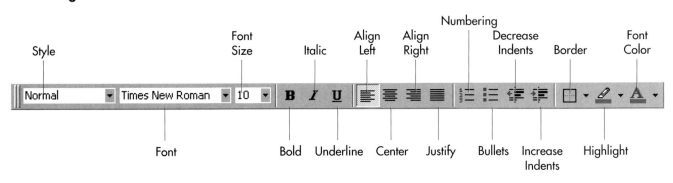

Open   Print   Spelling and Grammar   Copy   Format Painter   Redo   Web Toolbar   Insert Table   Columns   Document Map   Zoom

Formatting Toolbar

Style   Font Size   Italic   Align Left   Align Right   Numbering   Decrease Indents   Border   Font Color

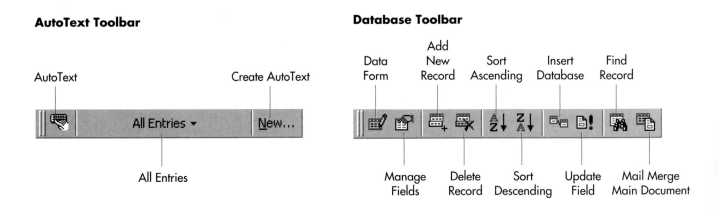

Font   Bold   Underline   Center   Justify   Bullets   Increase Indents   Highlight

AutoText Toolbar

AutoText   Create AutoText

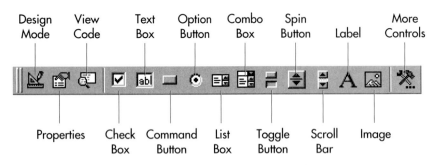

All Entries

Database Toolbar

Data Form   Add New Record   Sort Ascending   Insert Database   Find Record

Manage Fields   Delete Record   Sort Descending   Update Field   Mail Merge Main Document

Control Toolbox

Design Mode   View Code   Text Box   Option Button   Combo Box   Spin Button   Label   More Controls

Properties   Check Box   Command Button   List Box   Toggle Button   Scroll Bar   Image

FIGURE B.1

Drawing Toolbar

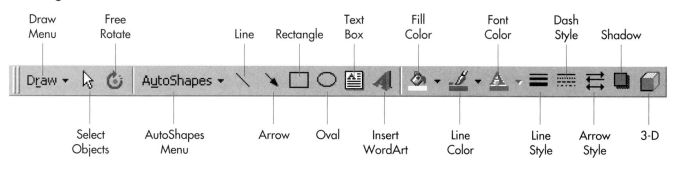

Draw Menu · Free Rotate · Line · Rectangle · Text Box · Fill Color · Font Color · Dash Style · Shadow

Select Objects · AutoShapes Menu · Arrow · Oval · Insert WordArt · Line Color · Line Style · Arrow Style · 3-D

Forms Toolbar

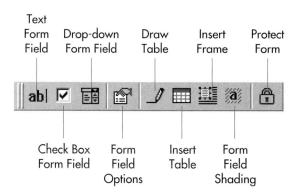

Text Form Field · Drop-down Form Field · Draw Table · Insert Frame · Protect Form

Check Box Form Field · Form Field Options · Insert Table · Form Field Shading

Microsoft Toolbar

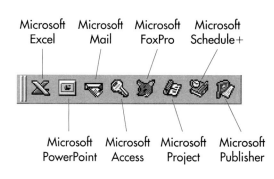

Microsoft Excel · Microsoft Mail · Microsoft FoxPro · Microsoft Schedule+

Microsoft PowerPoint · Microsoft Access · Microsoft Project · Microsoft Publisher

Picture Toolbar

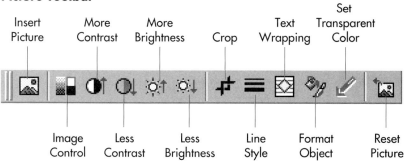

Insert Picture · More Contrast · More Brightness · Crop · Text Wrapping · Set Transparent Color

Image Control · Less Contrast · Less Brightness · Line Style · Format Object · Reset Picture

Reviewing Toolbar

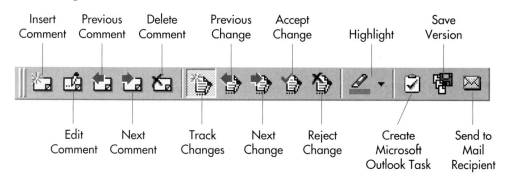

Insert Comment · Previous Comment · Delete Comment · Previous Change · Accept Change · Highlight · Save Version

Edit Comment · Next Comment · Track Changes · Next Change · Reject Change · Create Microsoft Outlook Task · Send to Mail Recipient

FIGURE B.1   (continued)

Shadow Settings Toolbar

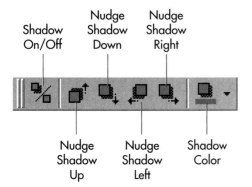

Shadow On/Off

Nudge Shadow Down

Nudge Shadow Right

Nudge Shadow Up

Nudge Shadow Left

Shadow Color

Visual Basic Toolbar

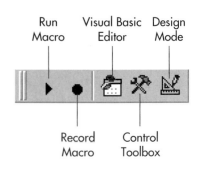

Run Macro

Visual Basic Editor

Design Mode

Record Macro

Control Toolbox

Tables and Borders Toolbar

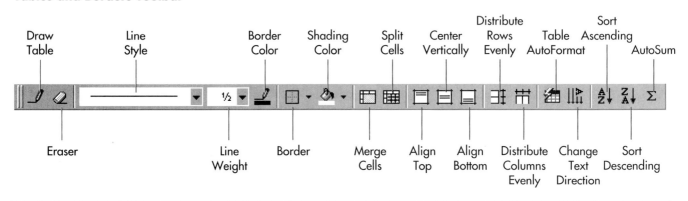

Draw Table

Line Style

Border Color

Shading Color

Split Cells

Center Vertically

Distribute Rows Evenly

Table AutoFormat

Sort Ascending

AutoSum

Eraser

Line Weight

Border

Merge Cells

Align Top

Align Bottom

Distribute Columns Evenly

Change Text Direction

Sort Descending

Web Toolbar

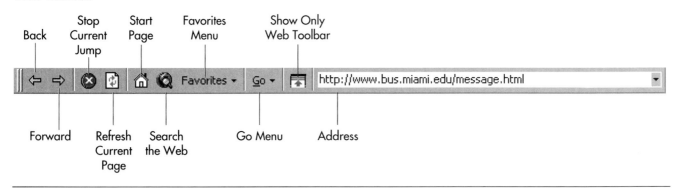

Back

Stop Current Jump

Start Page

Favorites Menu

Show Only Web Toolbar

Forward

Refresh Current Page

Search the Web

Go Menu

Address

WordArt Toolbar

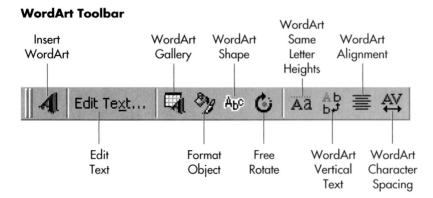

Insert WordArt

WordArt Gallery

WordArt Shape

WordArt Same Letter Heights

WordArt Alignment

Edit Text

Format Object

Free Rotate

WordArt Vertical Text

WordArt Character Spacing

FIGURE B.1 (continued)

3-D Settings Toolbar

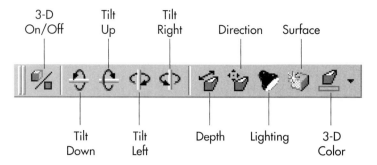

FIGURE B.1 (continued)

Equation Editor Toolbar

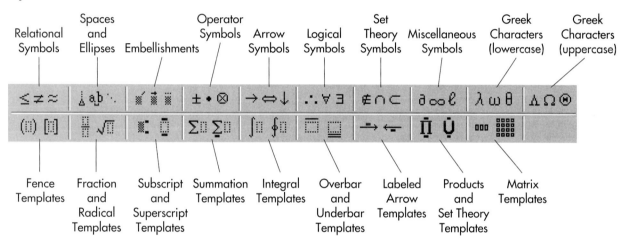

Header/Footer Toolbar

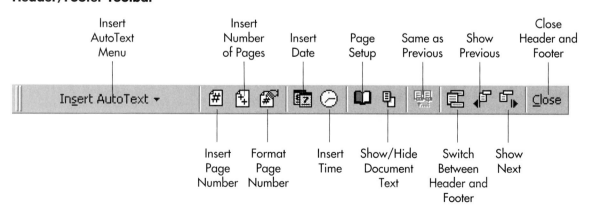

FIGURE B.2

Macro Toolbar

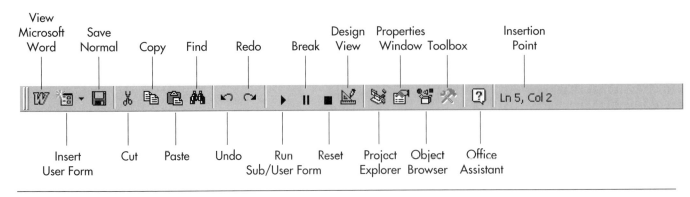

Mail Merge Toolbar

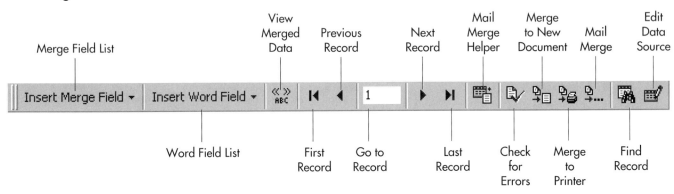

Master Document Toolbar

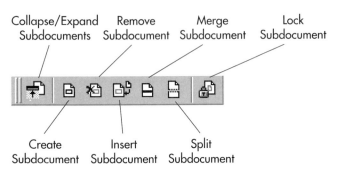

Outlining Toolbar

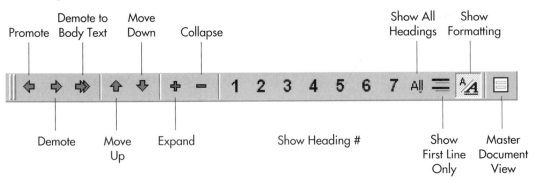

FIGURE B.2 (continued)

APPENDIX C: MAIL MERGE

OVERVIEW

A *mail merge* takes the tedium out of sending *form letters,* as it creates the same letter many times, changing the name, address, and other information as appropriate from letter to letter. You might use a mail merge to look for a job upon graduation, when you send essentially the same letter to many different companies. The concept is illustrated in Figure C.1, in which John Smith drafts a letter describing his qualifications, then merges that letter with a set of names and addresses, to produce the individual letters.

The mail merge process uses two files as input, a main document and a data source. A set of form letters is created as output. The *main document* (e.g., the cover letter in Figure C.1a) contains standardized text together with one or more *merge fields* that indicate where variable information is to be inserted into the individual letters. The *data source* (the set of names and addresses in Figure C.1b) contains the information that varies from letter to letter.

The first row in the data source is called the header row and identifies the fields in the remaining rows. Each additional row contains the data to create one letter and is called a *data record.* Every data record contains the same fields in the same order—for example, Title, First-Name, LastName, and so on.

The main document and the data source work in conjunction with one another, with the merge fields in the main document referencing the corresponding fields in the data source. The first line in the address of Figure C.1a, for example, contains the entries in angled brackets, *<<Title>> <<FirstName>> <<LastName>>*. (These entries are not typed explicitly but are entered through special commands as described in the hands-on exercise that follows shortly.) The merge process examines each record in the data source and substitutes the appropriate field values for the corresponding merge fields as it creates the individual form letters. For example, the first three fields in the first record will

John H. Smith

426 Jenny Lake Drive • Coral Gables, FL 33146 • (305) 666-4801

May 11, 1997

«Title» «FirstName» «LastName»
«JobTitle»
«Company»
«Address1»
«City», «State» «PostalCode»

Dear «Title» «LastName»:

I am writing to inquire about a position with «Company» as an entry level computer programmer. I have just graduated from the University of Miami with a Bachelor's Degree in Computer Information Systems (May, 1997) and I am very interested in working for you. I have a background in both microcomputer applications (Windows 95, Word, Excel, PowerPoint, and Access) as well as extensive experience with programming languages (Visual Basic, C++ and COBOL). I feel that I am well qualified to join your staff as over the past two years I have had a great deal of experience designing and implementing computer programs, both as a part of my educational program and during my internship with Personalized Computer Designs, Inc.

I am eager to put my skills to work and would like to talk with you at your earliest convenience. I have enclosed a copy of my résumé and will be happy to furnish the names and addresses of my references, if you so desire. You may reach me at the above address and phone number. I look forward to hearing from you.

Sincerely,

John Smith

(a) The Main Document

FIGURE C.1   **The Mail Merge**

produce *Mr. Jason Frasher.* The same fields in the second record will produce *Ms. Elizabeth Schery,* and so on.

In similar fashion, the second line in the address of the main document contains the *<<JobTitle>>* field. The third line contains the *<<Company>>* field. The fourth line references the *<<Address1>>* field, and the last line contains the *<<City>>, <<State>,* and *<<PostalCode>>* fields. The salutation repeats the *<<Title>>* and *<<LastName>>* fields. The first sentence uses the *<<Company>>* field a second time. The mail merge prepares the letters one at a time, with one letter created for every record in the data source until the file of names and addresses is exhausted. The individual form letters are shown in Figure C.1c. Each letter begins automatically on a new page.

Title	FirstName	LastName	JobTitle	Company	Address1	City	State	PostalCode
Mr.	Jason	Frasher	President	Frasher Systems	100 S. Miami Avenue	Miami	FL	33103
Ms.	Elizabeth	Schery	Director of Personnel	Custom Computing	8180 Kendall Drive	Miami	FL	33156
Ms.	Lauren	Howard	President	Unique Systems	475 LeJeune Road	Coral Gables	FL	33146

(b) The Data Source

John H. Smith

426 Jenny Lake Drive • Coral Gables, FL 33146 • (305) 666-4801

May 11, 1997

Mr. Jason Frasher
President
Frasher Systems
100 S. Miami Avenue
Miami, FL 33103

Dear Mr. Frasher:

I am writing to inquire about a position
programmer. I have just graduated from
Computer Information Systems (May,
have a background in both microcomput
PowerPoint, and Access) as well as ex
(Visual Basic, C++ and COBOL). I fe
past two years I have had a great deal o
programs, both as a part of my educatio
Personalized Computer Designs, Inc.

I am eager to put my skills to work and
convenience. I have enclosed a copy o
and addresses of my references, if you
and phone number. I look forward to he

Sincerely,

John Smith

John H. Smith

426 Jenny Lake Drive • Coral Gables, FL 33146 • (305) 666-4801

May 11, 1997

Ms. Elizabeth Schery
Director of Personnel
Custom Computing
8180 Kendall Drive
Miami, FL 33156

Dear Ms. Schery:

I am writing to inquire about a position with Custom Computing as an entry level computer
programmer. I have just graduated from
Computer Information Systems (May, 19
have a background in both microcomputer
PowerPoint, and Access) as well as exte
(Visual Basic, C++ and COBOL). I feel
past two years I have had a great deal of
programs, both as a part of my education
Personalized Computer Designs, Inc.

I am eager to put my skills to work and
convenience. I have enclosed a copy of
and addresses of my references, if you s
and phone number. I look forward to hea

Sincerely,

John Smith

John H. Smith

426 Jenny Lake Drive • Coral Gables, FL 33146 • (305) 666-4801

May 11, 1997

Ms. Lauren Howard
President
Unique Systems
475 LeJeune Road
Coral Gables, FL 33146

Dear Ms. Howard:

I am writing to inquire about a position with Unique Systems as an entry level computer
programmer. I have just graduated from the University of Miami with a Bachelor's Degree in
Computer Information Systems (May, 1997) and I am very interested in working for you. I
have a background in both microcomputer applications (Windows 95, Word, Excel,
PowerPoint, and Access) as well as extensive experience with programming languages
(Visual Basic, C++ and COBOL). I feel that I am well qualified to join your staff as over the
past two years I have had a great deal of experience designing and implementing computer
programs, both as a part of my educational program and during my internship with
Personalized Computer Designs, Inc.

I am eager to put my skills to work and would like to talk with you at your earliest
convenience. I have enclosed a copy of my résumé and will be happy to furnish the names
and addresses of my references, if you so desire. You may reach me at the above address
and phone number. I look forward to hearing from you.

Sincerely,

John Smith

(c) The Printed Letters

FIGURE C.1 The Mail Merge (continued)

FILE DESIGN

The zip code should be defined as a separate field in the data source in order to sort on zip code and take advantage of bulk mail. A person's first and last name should also be defined separately, so that you have access to either field, perhaps to create a friendly salutation such as Dear Joe or to sort on last name.

MAIL MERGE HELPER

The implementation of a mail merge in Microsoft Word is easy, provided you understand the basic concept. In essence, there are three things you must do:

1. Create and save the main document
2. Create and save the data source
3. Merge the main document and data source to create the individual letters

The Mail Merge command is located in the Tools menu. Execution of the command displays the **Mail Merge Helper,** which lists the steps in the mail merge process and guides you every step of the way.

The screen in Figure C.2 shows the Mail Merge Helper as it appears after steps 1 and 2 have been completed. The main document is the file *Modified Form Letter.doc.* The data source is the file *Names and Addresses.doc.* All that remains is to merge the files and create the individual form letters. The options in effect

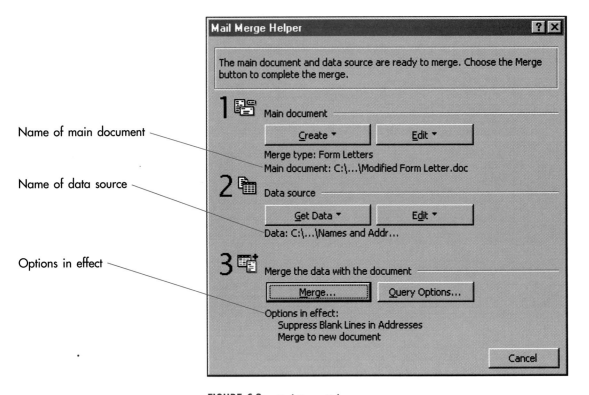

FIGURE C.2 Mail Merge Helper

indicate that the letters will be created in a new document and that blank lines, if any, in addresses (e.g., a missing company or title) will be suppressed. The Query Options command button lets you select and/or *sort* the records in the data source prior to the merge. These options are discussed after the hands-on exercise.

PAPER MAKES A DIFFERENCE

Most of us take paper for granted, but the right paper can make a significant difference in the effectiveness of a document. Reports and formal correspondence are usually printed on white paper, but you would be surprised how many different shades of white there are. Other types of documents lend themselves to colored paper for additional impact. In short, the choice of paper you use is far from an automatic decision. Our favorite source for paper is a company called PAPER DIRECT (1-800-APAPERS). Ask for a catalog, then consider the use of a specialty paper the next time you have an important project, such as the cover letter for your résumé.

HANDS-ON EXERCISE 1

Mail Merge

Objective: To create a main document and associated data source; to implement a mail merge and produce a set of form letters. Use Figure C.3 as a guide in the exercise.

STEP 1: Open the Cover Letter

➤ Open the **Form Letter document** in the **Exploring Word Folder** as shown in Figure C.3a. (The dialog box will not yet be displayed.)

- If necessary, pull down the **View menu** and click **Page Layout** (or click the **Page Layout button** above the status bar).
- If necessary, click the **Zoom Control arrow** to change to **Page Width.**

➤ Save the document as **Modified Form Letter** so that you can return to the original document if necessary.

THE LETTER WIZARD

It is the rare individual who has never been confronted by writer's block and the frustration of a blank screen and a flashing cursor. The Letter Wizard is Microsoft's attempt to get you started. Pull down the File menu, click New, click the Letters & Faxes tab in the New dialog box, then double click the Letter Wizard. The Wizard asks you a series of questions about the type of letter you want to write, then supplies a template for you to complete. It will even let you choose one of several prewritten letters, including a résumé cover letter. It's not perfect, but it is a starting point, and that may be all you need.

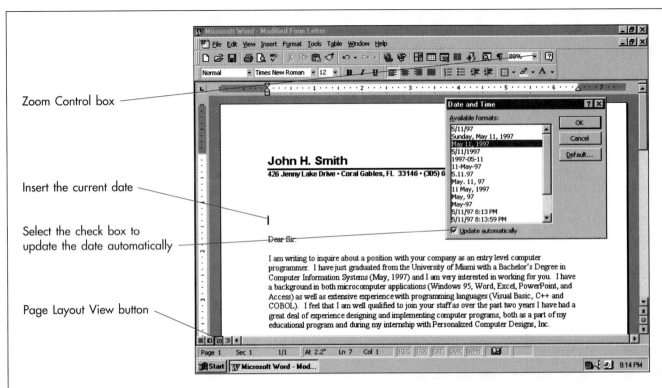

Zoom Control box

Insert the current date

Select the check box to
update the date automatically

Page Layout View button

(a) Insert Today's Date (step 2)

FIGURE C.3   Hands-on Exercise 1

STEP 2: Insert Today's Date

➤ Click to the left of the "D" in Dear Sir, then press **enter** twice to insert two
lines. Press the **up arrow** two times to return to the first line you inserted.

➤ Pull down the **Insert menu** and click the **Date and Time command** to display
the dialog box in Figure C.3a.

➤ Select (click) the date format you prefer and, if necessary, check the box to
update the date automatically. Click **OK** to close the dialog box.

FIELD CODES VERSUS FIELD RESULTS

All fields are displayed in a document in one of two formats, as a *field
code* or as a *field result.* A field code appears in braces and indicates
instructions to insert variable data when the document is printed; a field
result displays the information as it will appear in the printed document.
You can toggle the display between the field code and field result by
selecting the field and pressing Shift+F9 during editing.

STEP 3: Create the Main Document

➤ Pull down the **Tools menu.** Click **Mail Merge.** Click the **Create command button** under step 1 to create the main document as shown in Figure C.3b.

➤ Click **Form Letters,** then click **Active Window** to indicate that you will use
the Modified Form Letter document (in the active window) as the main document.

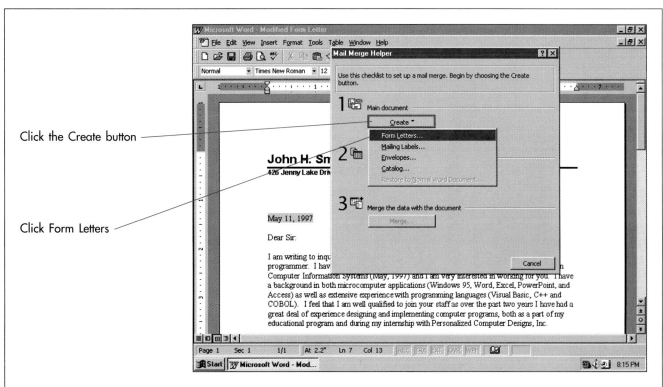

Click the Create button

Click Form Letters

(b) Create the Main Document (step 3)

FIGURE C.3   Hands-on Exercise 1 (continued)

STEP 4: Create the Data Source

➤ Click **Get Data** under step 2, then click **Create Data Source** to display the dialog box in Figure C.3c.

➤ Word provides commonly used field names for the data source, but not all of the data fields are necessary. Click **Address2,** then click the **Remove Field Name command button.** Delete the Country, HomePhone, and WorkPhone fields in similar fashion.

➤ Click **OK** to complete the definition of the data source. You will then be presented with the Save As dialog box as you need to save the data source.

➤ Type **Names and Addresses** in the File Name text box as the name of the data source. Click **Save** to save the file.

➤ You will see a message indicating that the data source does not contain any data records. Click **Edit Data Source** in order to add records at this time.

STEP 5: Add the Data

➤ Enter data for the first record. Type **Mr.** in the Title field. Press **Tab** to move to the next (FirstName) field, and type **Jason.** Continue in this fashion until you have completed the first record as shown in Figure C.3d.

➤ Click **Add New** to enter the data for the next person to receive the letter:

• Ms. Elizabeth Schery
• Director of Personnel
• Custom Computing
• 8180 Kendall Drive
• Miami, FL 33156

Click Get Data

Click Remove
Field Name button

Click Address2

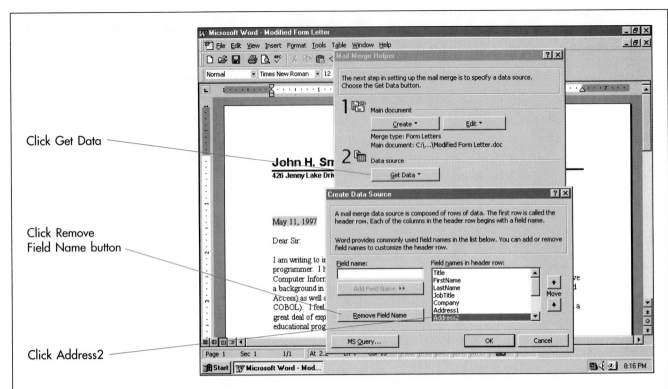

(c) Create the Data Source (step 4)

Enter the data for the first
record, pressing Tab to
move from field to field

Click Add New to
add a new record

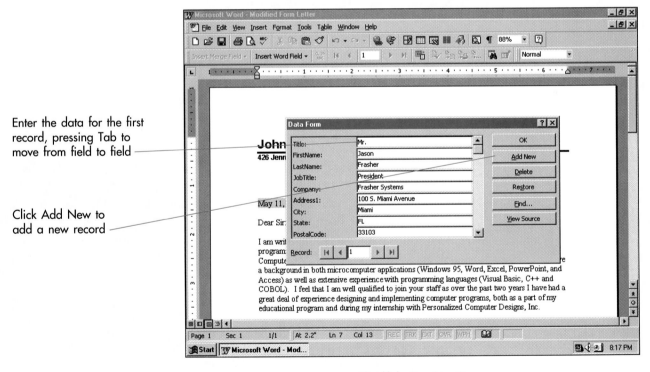

(d) Add the Data (step 5)

FIGURE C.3   Hands-on Exercise 1 (continued)

➤ Click **Add New** to enter the data for the third and last recipient:
- Ms. Lauren Howard
- President
- Unique Systems
- 475 LeJeune Road
- Coral Gables, FL 33146

➤ Click **OK** to end the data entry and return to the main document. The Mail Merge toolbar is displayed immediately below the Formatting toolbar.

STEP 6: Add the Data Fields

➤ Click in the main document immediately below the date. Press **enter** to leave a blank line between the date and the first line of the address.

➤ Click the **Insert Merge Field button** on the Merge toolbar. Click **Title** from the list of fields within the data source. The title field is inserted into the main document and enclosed in angled brackets as shown in Figure C.3e.

➤ Press the **space bar** to add a space between the words. Click the **Insert Merge Field button** a second time. Click **FirstName.** Press the **space bar.**

➤ Click the **Insert Merge Field button** again. Click **LastName.**

➤ Press **enter** to move to the next line. Enter the remaining fields in the address as shown in Figure C.3e. Be sure to add a comma after the **City field** as well as a space.

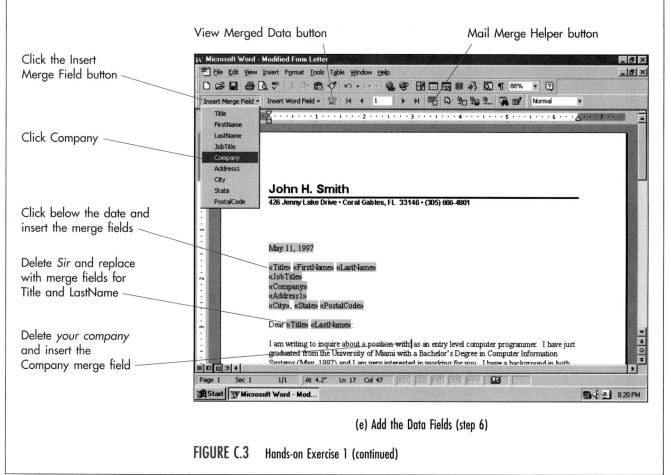

(e) Add the Data Fields (step 6)

FIGURE C.3   Hands-on Exercise 1 (continued)

> Delete the word "Sir" in the salutation and replace it with the **Title** and **Last-Name fields.**

> Delete the words "your company" in the first sentence and replace them with the **Company field.**

> Save the main document.

STEP 7: The Mail Merge Toolbar

> The Mail Merge toolbar enables you to preview the form letters before they are created.

> Click the **<<abc>> button** on the Merge toolbar to display field values rather than field codes; you will see Mr. Jason Frasher instead of <<Title>> <<First-Name>> <<LastName>>, etc.

> The **<<abc>> button** functions as a toggle switch. Click it once and you switch from field codes to field values; click it a second time and you go from field values back to field codes. End with the field values displayed.

> Look at the text box on the Mail Merge toolbar, which displays the number 1 to indicate that the first record is displayed. Click the ▶ **button** to display the form letter for the next record (Ms. Elizabeth Schery in our example).

> Click the ▶ **button** again to display the form letter for the next record (Ms. Lauren Howard). The toolbar indicates you are on the third record. Click the ◀ **button** to return to the previous (second) record.

> Click the |◀ **button** to move directly to the first record (Jason Frasher). Click the ▶| **button** to display the form letter for the last record (Lauren Howard).

> Toggle the **<<abc>> button** to display the field codes.

STEP 8: The Mail Merge Helper

> Click the **Mail Merge Helper button** on the Merge toolbar to display the dialog box in Figure C.3f.

> The Mail Merge Helper shows your progress thus far:
> • The main document has been created and saved as Modified Form Letter.
> • The data source has been created and saved as Names and Addresses.

> Click the **Merge command button** to display the dialog box in Figure C.3g.

EDIT THE DATA SOURCE

Click the Mail Merge Helper button to display a dialog box with information about the mail merge, click the Edit command button under Data Source, then click the file containing the data source. Click the View Source command button to see multiple records in the data source displayed within a table; the first row contains the field names, and each succeeding row contains a data record. Edit the data source, then pull down the Window menu and click the name of the file containing the main document to continue working on the mail merge.

STEP 9: The Merge

> The selected options in Figure C.3g should already be set:
> • If necessary, click the **arrow** in the Merge To list box and select New document.

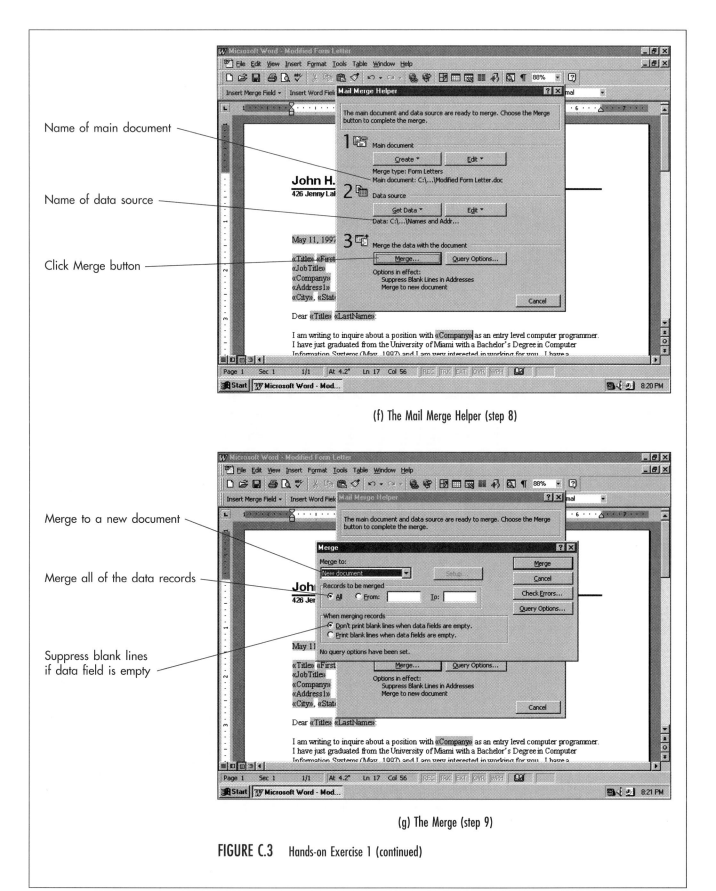

Name of main document

Name of data source

Click Merge button

(f) The Mail Merge Helper (step 8)

Merge to a new document

Merge all of the data records

Suppress blank lines
if data field is empty

(g) The Merge (step 9)

FIGURE C.3   Hands-on Exercise 1 (continued)

- If necessary, click the **All options button** to include all records in the data source.
  - If necessary, click the **option button** to suppress blank lines if data fields are empty.
➤ Click the **Merge command button.** Word pauses momentarily, then generates the three form letters in a new document.

STEP 10: The Individual Form Letters

➤ The title bar of the active window changes to Form Letters1. Scroll through the letters to review them individually.

➤ Pull down the **View menu.** Click **Zoom.** Click **Many Pages.** Click the **monitor icon,** then click and drag within the resulting dialog box to display three pages side by side. Click **OK.** You should see the three form letters as shown in Figure C.3h.

➤ Print the letters.

➤ Pull down the **File menu** and click **Exit** to exit Word. Pay close attention to the informational messages that ask whether to save the modified file(s):

  - There is no need to save the merged document (Form Letters1) because you can always re-create the merged letters, provided you have saved the main document and data source.

  - Save the Modified Form Letter and Names and Addresses documents if you are asked to do so.

➤ Congratulations on a job well done. Good luck in your job hunting!

Title bar indicates
FormLetters1

Print button

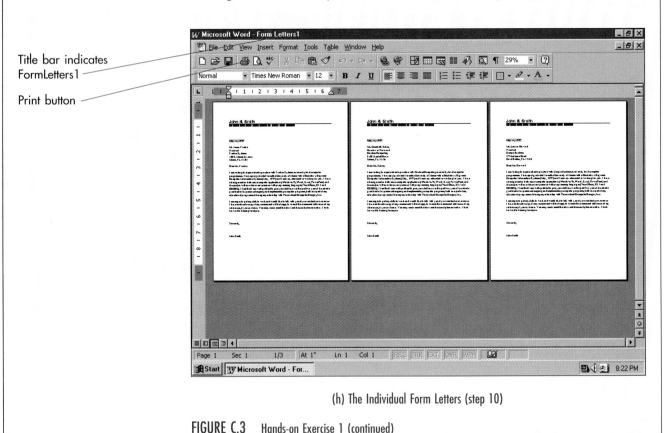

(h) The Individual Form Letters (step 10)

FIGURE C.3   Hands-on Exercise 1 (continued)

LIST AND DATA MANAGEMENT: CONVERTING DATA TO INFORMATION

OBJECTIVES

After reading this chapter you will be able to:

1. Create a list within Excel; explain the importance of proper planning and design prior to creating the list.
2. Add, edit, and delete records in an existing list; explain the significance of data validation.
3. Distinguish between data and information; describe how one is converted to the other.
4. Describe the TODAY function and explain the use of date arithmetic.
5. Use the Sort command; distinguish between an ascending and a descending sort, and among primary, secondary, and tertiary keys.
6. Use the DSUM, DAVERAGE, DMAX, DMIN, and DCOUNT functions.
7. Use the AutoFilter and Advanced Filter commands to display a subset of a list.
8. Use the Subtotals command to summarize data in a list.
9. Create a pivot table and explain how it provides flexibility in data analysis.

OVERVIEW

All businesses maintain data in the form of lists. Companies have lists of their employees. Magazines and newspapers keep lists of their subscribers. Political candidates monitor voter lists, and so on. This chapter presents the fundamentals of list management as it is implemented in Excel. We begin with the definition of basic terms, such as field and record, then cover the commands to create a list, to add a new record, and to modify or delete an existing record.

The second half of the chapter distinguishes between data and information and describes how one is converted to the other. We introduce the AutoFilter and Advanced Filter commands that display selected records in a list. We use the Sort command to rearrange the list. We discuss database functions and the associated criteria range. We also introduce date functions and date arithmetic. The chapter ends with a discussion of subtotals and pivot tables, two powerful capabilities associated with lists.

All of this is accomplished using Excel, and although it may eventually be necessary for you to use a dedicated database program (e.g., Microsoft Access), you will be pleased with what you can do. The chapter contains three hands-on exercises, each of which focuses on a different aspect of data management.

LIST AND DATA MANAGEMENT

Imagine that you are the personnel director of a medium-sized company with offices in several cities, and that you manually maintain employee data for the company. Accordingly, you have recorded the specifics of every individual's employment (name, salary, location, title, and so on) in a manila folder, and you have stored the entire set of folders in a file cabinet. You have written the name of each employee on the label of his or her folder and have arranged the folders alphabetically in the filing cabinet.

The manual system just described illustrates the basics of data management terminology. The set of manila folders corresponds to a *file.* Each individual folder is known as a *record.* Each data item (fact) within a folder is called a *field.* The folders are arranged alphabetically in the file cabinet (according to the employee name on the label) to simplify the retrieval of any given folder. Likewise, the records in a computer-based system are also in sequence according to a specific field known as a *key.*

Excel maintains data in the form of a list. A *list* is an area in the worksheet that contains rows of similar data. A list can be used as a simple *database,* where the rows correspond to records and the columns correspond to fields. The first row contains the column labels or *field names,* which identify the data that will be entered in that column (field). Each additional row in the list contains a record. Each column represents a field. Each cell in the list area (other than the field names) contains a value for a specific field in a specific record. Every record (row) contains the same fields (columns) in the same order as every other record.

Figure 1.1 contains an employee list with 13 records. There are four fields in every record—name, location, title, and salary. The field names should be meaningful and must be unique. (A field name may contain up to 255 characters, but you should keep them as short as possible so that a column does not become too wide and thus difficult to work with.) The arrangement of the fields within a record is consistent from record to record. The employee name was chosen as the key, and thus the records are in alphabetical order.

Normal business operations require that you make repeated trips to the filing cabinet to maintain the accuracy of the data. You will have to add a folder whenever a new employee is hired. In similar fashion, you will have to remove the folder of any employee who leaves the company, or modify the data in the folder of any employee who receives a raise, changes location, and so on.

Changes of this nature (additions, deletions, and modifications) are known as file maintenance and constitute a critical activity within any system. Indeed, without adequate file maintenance, the data in a system quickly becomes obsolete and the information useless. Imagine the consequences of producing a payroll based on data that is six months old.

	A	B	C	D
1	Name	Location	Title	Salary
2	Adams	Atlanta	Trainee	$19,500
3	Adamson	Chicago	Manager	$52,000
4	Brown	Atlanta	Trainee	$18,500
5	Charles	Boston	Account Rep	$40,000
6	Coulter	Atlanta	Manager	$100,000
7	Frank	Miami	Manager	$75,000
8	James	Chicago	Account Rep	$42,500
9	Johnson	Chicag	Account Rep	$47,500
10	Manin	Boston	Accout Rep	$49,500
11	Marder	Chicago	Account Rep	$38,500
12	Milgrom	Boston	Manager	$57,500
13	Rubin	Boston	Account Rep	$45,000
14	Smith	Atlanta	Account Rep	$65,000

FIGURE 1.1   The Employee List

Nor is it sufficient simply to add (edit or delete) a record without adequate checks on the validity of the data. Look carefully at the entries in Figure 1.1 and ask yourself if a computer-generated report listing employees in the Chicago office will include Johnson. Will a report listing account reps include Manin? The answer to both questions is *no* because the data for these employees was entered incorrectly. Chicago is misspelled in Johnson's record (the "o" was omitted). Account rep is misspelled in Manin's title. *You* know that Johnson works in Chicago, but the computer does not, because it searches for the correct spelling. It also will omit Manin from a listing of account reps because of the misspelled title.

GARBAGE IN, GARBAGE OUT (GIGO)

A computer does exactly what you tell it to do, which is not necessarily what you want it to do. It is absolutely critical, therefore, that you validate the data that goes into a system, or else the associated information will not be correct. No system, no matter how sophisticated, can produce valid output from invalid input. In other words, garbage in—garbage out.

IMPLEMENTATION IN EXCEL

Creating a list is easy because there is little to do other than enter the data. You choose the area in the worksheet that will contain the list, then you enter the field names in the first row of the designated area. Each field name should be a unique text entry. The data for the individual records should be entered in the rows immediately below the row of field names.

Once a list has been created, you can edit any field, in any record, just as you would change the entries in an ordinary worksheet. The ***Insert Rows command*** lets you add new rows (records) to the list. The ***Insert Columns command*** lets you add additional columns (fields). The ***Delete command*** in the Edit menu enables you to delete a row or column. You can also use shortcut menus to execute commands more quickly. And finally, you can also format the entries within a list, just as you format the entries in any other worksheet.

Data Form Command

A *data form* provides an easy way to add, edit, and delete records in a list. The *Form command* in the Data menu displays a dialog box based on the fields in the list and contains the command buttons shown in Figure 1.2. Every record in the list contains the same fields in the same order (e.g., Name, Location, Title, and Salary in Figure 1.2), and the fields are displayed in this order within the dialog box. You do not have to enter a value for every field; that is, you may leave a field blank if the data is unknown.

Next to each field name is a text box into which data can be entered for a new record, or edited for an existing record. The scroll bar to the right of the data is used to scroll through the records in the list. The functions of the various command buttons are explained briefly:

New — Adds a record to the end of a list, then lets you enter data in that record. The formulas for computed fields, if any, are automatically copied to the new record.

Delete — Permanently removes the currently displayed record. The remaining records move up one row.

Fields

Scroll bar to scroll
through records in the list

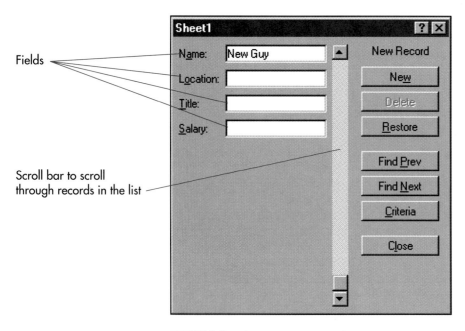

FIGURE 1.2 The Data Form Command

Restore — Cancels any changes made to the current record. (You must press the Restore button before pressing the enter key or scrolling to a new record.)

Find Prev — Displays the previous record (or the previous record that matches the existing criteria when criteria are defined).

Find Next — Displays the next record (or the next record that matches the existing criteria when criteria are defined).

Criteria — Displays a dialog box in which you specify the criteria for the Find Prev and/or Find Next command buttons to limit the displayed records to those that match the criteria.

Close — Closes the data form and returns to the worksheet.

Note, too, the What's This button (the question mark) on the title bar of the Data Form, which provides access to online help. Click the What's This button, then click any of the command buttons for an explanation. As indicated, the Data Form command provides an easy way to add, edit, and delete records in a list. It is not required, however, and you can use the Insert and Delete commands within the Edit menu as an alternate means of data entry.

Sort Command

The *Sort command* arranges the records in a list according to the value of one or more fields within that list. You can sort the list in *ascending* (low-to-high) or *descending* (high-to-low) *sequence.* (Putting a list in alphabetical order is considered an ascending sort.) You can also sort on more than one field at a time—for example, by location and then alphabetically by last name within each location. The field(s) on which you sort the list is (are) known as the key(s).

The records in Figure 1.3a are listed alphabetically (in ascending sequence according to employee name). Adams comes before Adamson, who comes before Brown, and so on. Figure 1.3b displays the identical records but in descending sequence by employee salary. The employee with the highest salary is listed first, and the employee with the lowest salary is last.

Figure 1.3c sorts the employees on two keys—by location, and by descending salary within location. Location is the more important, or *primary key.* Salary is the less important, or *secondary key.* The Sort command groups employees according to like values of the primary key (location), then within the like values of the primary key arranges them in descending sequence (ascending could have been chosen just as easily) according to the secondary key (salary). Excel provides a maximum of three keys—primary, secondary, and *tertiary.*

CHOOSE A CUSTOM SORT SEQUENCE

Alphabetic fields are normally arranged in strict alphabetical order. You can, however, choose a custom sort sequence such as the days of the week or the months of the year. Pull down the Data menu, click Sort, click the Options command button, then click the arrow on the drop-down list box to choose a sequence other than the alphabetic. You can also create your own sequence. Pull down the Tools menu, click Options, click the Custom Lists tab, select NewList, then enter the items in desired sequence in the List Entries Box. Click Add to create the sequence, then close the dialog box.

Records are listed in ascending sequence by employee name

	A	B	C	D
1	Name	Location	Title	Salary
2	Adams	Atlanta	Trainee	$19,500
3	Adamson	Chicago	Manager	$52,000
4	Brown	Atlanta	Trainee	$18,500
5	Charles	Boston	Account Rep	$40,000
6	Coulter	Atlanta	Manager	$100,000
7	Frank	Miami	Manager	$75,000
8	James	Chicago	Account Rep	$42,500
9	Johnson	Chicago	Account Rep	$47,500
10	Manin	Boston	Account Rep	$49,500
11	Marder	Chicago	Account Rep	$38,500
12	Milgrom	Boston	Manager	$57,500
13	Rubin	Boston	Account Rep	$45,000
14	Smith	Atlanta	Account Rep	$65,000
15				

(a) Ascending Sequence (by name)

Records are listed in descending sequence by salary

	A	B	C	D
1	Name	Location	Title	Salary
2	Coulter	Atlanta	Manager	$100,000
3	Frank	Miami	Manager	$75,000
4	Smith	Atlanta	Account Rep	$65,000
5	Milgrom	Boston	Manager	$57,500
6	Adamson	Chicago	Manager	$52,000
7	Manin	Boston	Account Rep	$49,500
8	Johnson	Chicago	Account Rep	$47,500
9	Rubin	Boston	Account Rep	$45,000
10	James	Chicago	Account Rep	$42,500
11	Charles	Boston	Account Rep	$40,000
12	Marder	Chicago	Account Rep	$38,500
13	Adams	Atlanta	Trainee	$19,500
14	Brown	Atlanta	Trainee	$18,500
15				

(b) Descending Sequence (by salary)

Location is the primary key (ascending sequence)

Salary is the secondary key (descending sequence)

	A	B	C	D
1	Name	Location	Title	Salary
2	Coulter	Atlanta	Manager	$100,000
3	Smith	Atlanta	Account Rep	$65,000
4	Adams	Atlanta	Trainee	$19,500
5	Brown	Atlanta	Trainee	$18,500
6	Milgrom	Boston	Manager	$57,500
7	Manin	Boston	Account Rep	$49,500
8	Rubin	Boston	Account Rep	$45,000
9	Charles	Boston	Account Rep	$40,000
10	Adamson	Chicago	Manager	$52,000
11	Johnson	Chicago	Account Rep	$47,500
12	James	Chicago	Account Rep	$42,500
13	Marder	Chicago	Account Rep	$38,500
14	Frank	Miami	Manager	$75,000
15				

(c) Primary and Secondary Keys

FIGURE 1.3   The Sort Command

DATE ARITHMETIC

Microsoft Excel stores a date as the integer (serial number) equivalent to the elapsed number of days since the turn of the century. Thus January 1, 1900 is stored as the number 1, January 2, 1900 as the number 2, and so on. March 16, 1977 corresponds to the number 28,200 as can be seen in Figure 1.4.

The fact that dates are stored as numbers enables you to add and subtract two different dates and/or to use a date in any type of arithmetic computation. A person's age, for example, can be computed by subtracting the date of birth from today's date, and dividing the result by 365 (or more accurately by 365¼ to adjust for leap years). In similar fashion, you could add a constant (e.g., the number 30) to the date of purchase, to determine when payment is due (assuming, in this example, that payment is due 30 days after the item was purchased).

A date can be entered into a spreadsheet in various ways, most easily by typing the date in conventional fashion—for example, 1/21/97, to enter the date January 21, 1997. There is, however, one subtlety in anticipation of the turn of the century. Any entry containing a year from 00 to 29 is assumed to be a date in the 21st century; for example, 1/21/00, will be stored as January 21, 2000. Any year between 30 and 99, however, is stored as a date in this (the 20th) century. Thus, 3/23/48 would be stored as March 23, 1948. (To avoid confusion and be sure of the date, you can enter all four digits of the year—e.g., 10/31/2001 for October 31, 2001.)

The *TODAY( ) function* is used in conjunction with date arithmetic and always returns the current date (i.e., the date on which the spreadsheet is opened). If, for example, you entered the Today( ) function into a spreadsheet created on March 21 and you opened the spreadsheet a month later, the value of the function would be automatically updated to April 21. The Today( ) function is illustrated in Figure 1.4 to calculate a person's age. Note, too, the IF function in Figure 1.4, which examines the computed age, then displays an appropriate message indicating whether the individual is of legal age or still under the age of 21.

BIRTH DATE VERSUS AGE

An individual's age and birth date provide equivalent information, as one is calculated from the other. It might seem easier, therefore, to enter the age directly into the list and avoid the calculation, but this would be a mistake. A person's age changes continually, whereas the birth date remains constant. Thus, the date, not the age, should be stored, so that the data in the list remains current. Similar reasoning applies to an employee's hire date and length of service.

Displays the current date —

Always displays same date —

Age is calculated —

	A	B	C	D
1		Cell Formulas	Date Format	Number Format
2	Today's Date	=TODAY()	7/29/97	35640
3	Birth Date	3/16/77	3/16/77	28200
4				
5	Elapsed Time (days)	=B2-B3		7440
6	Age (years)	=B5/365		20.4
7				
8		=IF(B6>=21,"You're Legal","Still a Minor")		Still a Minor

FIGURE 1.4 Date Arithmetic

Creating and Maintaining a List

Objective: To add, edit, and delete records in an employee list; to introduce the Data Form and Data Sort commands; to use the spell check to validate data. Use Figure 1.5 as a guide in the exercise.

STEP 1: Open the Employee Workbook

➤ Start Excel. Open the **Employee List** workbook in the **Exploring Excel folder** as shown in Figure 1.5a.

➤ Save the workbook as **Finished Employee List.**

Select a cell within the list

Enter data for a new record

Click Close to return to worksheet

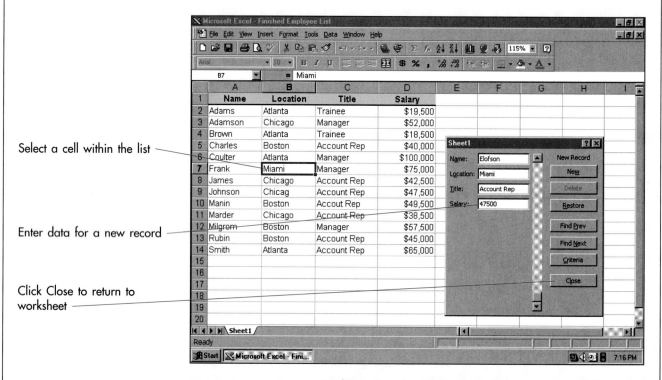

(a) The Data Form Command (steps 1 and 2)

FIGURE 1.5   Hands-on Exercise 1

EMPHASIZE THE COLUMN LABELS (FIELD NAMES)

Use a different font, alignment, style (boldface and/or italics), pattern, or border to distinguish the first row containing the field names from the remaining rows (records) in a list. This ensures that Excel will recognize the first row as a header row, enabling you to sort the list simply by selecting a cell in the list, then clicking the Ascending or Descending sort buttons on the Standard toolbar.

STEP 2: Add a Record (The Data Form Command)

➤ Click a single cell anywhere within the employee list (**cells A1** through **D14**).

➤ Pull down the **Data menu.** Click **Form** to display a dialog box with data for the first record in the list (Adams). Click the **New command button** to clear the text boxes and begin entering a new record.

➤ Enter the data for **Elofson** as shown in Figure 1.5a. Click the **Close command button** after entering the salary. Elofson has been added to the list and appears in row 15. Save the workbook.

PRESS TAB, NOT ENTER

Press the Tab key to move to the next field within a data form. Press Shift+Tab to move to the previous field. Press the enter key only after the last field has been entered to move to the first field in the next record.

STEP 3: Add a Record (The Insert Rows Command)

➤ Click the **row heading** for **row 8.** Pull down the **Insert menu.** Click **Rows** as shown in Figure 1.5b.

➤ Add the data for **Gillenson,** who works in **Miami** as an **Account Rep** with a salary of **$55,000.** Save the workbook.

Click row heading to select row 8

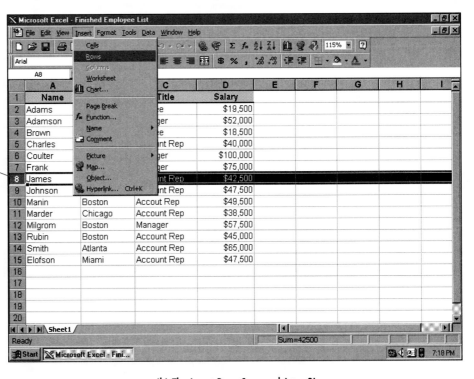

(b) The Insert Rows Command (step 3)

FIGURE 1.5   Hands-on Exercise 1 (continued)

THE FREEZE PANES COMMAND

The Freeze Panes command is useful with large lists as it prevents the column labels (field names) from scrolling off the screen. Click in the first column (field) of the first record. Pull down the Window menu, then click the Freeze Panes command. A horizontal line will appear under the field names to indicate that the command is in effect.

STEP 4: The Spell Check

➤ Select **cells B2:C16** as in Figure 1.5c. Pull down the **Tools menu** and click **Spelling** (or click the **Spelling button** on the Standard toolbar).

➤ Chicago is misspelled in cell B10 and flagged accordingly. Click the **Change command button** to accept the suggested correction and continue checking the document.

➤ Account is misspelled in cell C11 and flagged accordingly. Click **Account** in the Suggestions list box, then click the **Change command button** to correct the misspelling.

➤ Excel will indicate that it has finished checking the selected cells. Click **OK** to return to the worksheet.

➤ Save the workbook.

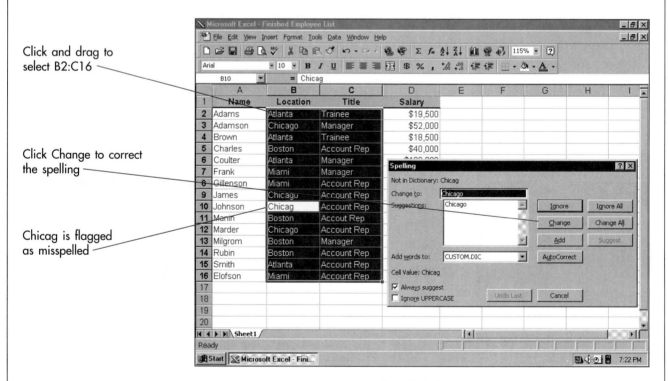

Click and drag to select B2:C16

Click Change to correct the spelling

Chicag is flagged as misspelled

(c) The Spell Check (step 4)

FIGURE 1.5   Hands-on Exercise 1 (continued)

CREATE YOUR OWN SHORTHAND

The AutoCorrect feature is common to all Office applications and corrects mistakes as they are made according to entries in a predefined list. Type *teh,* for example, and it is corrected automatically to *the* as soon as you press the space bar. You can use the feature to create your own shorthand by having it expand abbreviations such as *cis* for *Computer Information Systems.* Pull down the Tools menu, click AutoCorrect, type the abbreviation in the Replace text box and the expanded entry in the With text box. Click the Add command button, then click OK to exit the dialog box and return to the document. The next time you type *cis* in a spreadsheet, it will automatically be expanded to *Computer Information Systems.*

STEP 5: Sort the List

➤ Click a single cell anywhere in the employee list (**cells A1** through **D16**). Pull down the **Data menu.** Click **Sort** to display the dialog box in Figure 1.5d.

- Click the **drop-down arrow** in the Sort By list box. Select **Location** as the primary key.

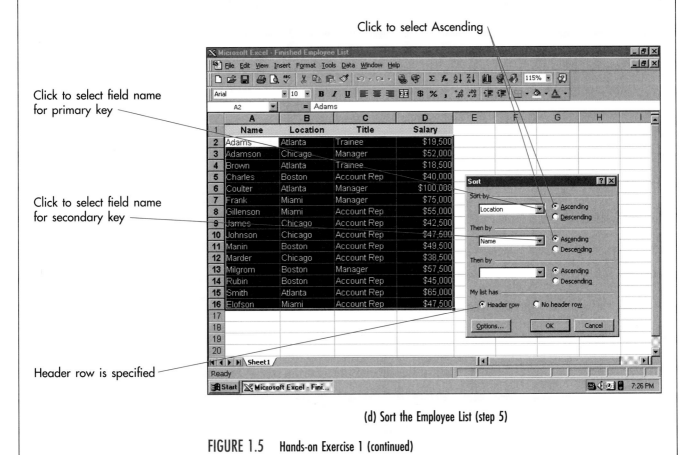

Click to select Ascending

Click to select field name for primary key

Click to select field name for secondary key

Header row is specified

(d) Sort the Employee List (step 5)

FIGURE 1.5   Hands-on Exercise 1 (continued)

- Click the **drop-down arrow** in the first Then By list box. Select **Name** as the secondary key.
- Be sure the **Header Row option button** is selected (so that the field names are not mixed in with the records in the list).
- Check that the **Ascending option button** is selected for both the primary and secondary keys.
- Click **OK** to sort the list and return to the worksheet.

➤ The employees are listed by location and alphabetically within location.

➤ Save the workbook.

USE THE SORT BUTTONS

Use the Sort Ascending or Sort Descending buttons on the Standard toolbar to sort on one or more keys. To sort on a single key, click any cell in the column containing the key, then click the appropriate button, depending on whether you want an ascending or a descending sort. You can also sort on multiple keys, by clicking either button multiple times, but the trick is to do it in the right sequence. Sort on the least significant field first, then work your way up to the most significant. For example, to sort a list by location, and name within location, sort by name first (the secondary key), then sort by location (the primary key).

STEP 6: Delete a Record

➤ A record may be deleted by using the Edit Delete command or the Data Form command; both methods will be illustrated to delete the record for Frank, which is currently in row 15.

➤ To delete a record by using the Edit Delete command:
- Click the **row heading** in **row 15** (containing the record for Frank, which is slated for deletion).
- Pull down the **Edit menu.** Click **Delete.** Frank has been deleted.

➤ Click the **Undo button** on the Standard toolbar. The record for Frank has been restored.

➤ To delete a record by using the Data Form command:
- Click a single cell within the employee list.
- Pull down the **Data menu.** Click **Form** to display the data form.
- Click the **down arrow** in the scroll bar until you come to the record for Frank.
- Click the **Delete command button.**
- Click **OK** in response to the warning message shown in Figure 1.5e. (The record cannot be undeleted as it could with the Edit Delete command.)
- Click **Close** to close the Data Form.

➤ Save the workbook.

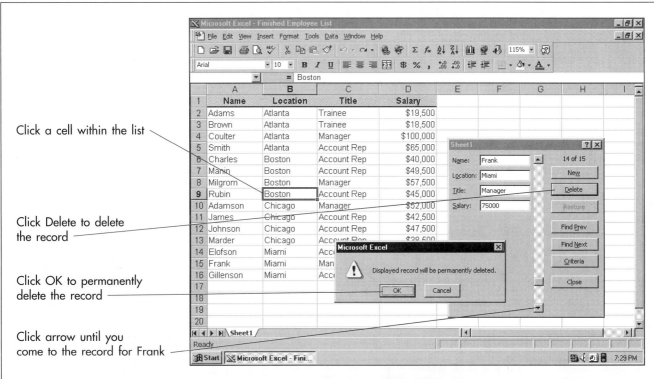

Click a cell within the list

Click Delete to delete the record

Click OK to permanently delete the record

Click arrow until you come to the record for Frank

(e) Delete a Record (step 6)

FIGURE 1.5   Hands-on Exercise 1 (continued)

STEP 7: Insert a Field

➤ Click the **column heading** in **column D.** Click the **right mouse button** to display a shortcut menu. Click **Insert.** The employee salaries have been moved to column E.

➤ Click **cell D1.** Type **Hire Date** and press **enter.** Adjust the column width if necessary.

STEP 8: Enter the Hire Dates

➤ Dates may be entered in several different formats. Do not be concerned if Excel displays the date in a different format from the way you entered it.

- Type **11/24/93** in cell D2. Press the **down arrow key.**
- Type **Nov 24, 1993** in cell D3. Type a **comma** after the day, but do not type a period after the month. Press the **down arrow key** to move to cell D4.
- Type **=Date(93,11,24)** in cell D4. Press the **down arrow key.**
- Type **11-24-93** in cell D5.

➤ For ease of data entry, assume that the next several employees were hired on the same day, 3/16/92.

- Click in **cell D6.** Type **3/16/92.** Press **enter.**
- Click in **cell D6.** Click the **Copy button** on the Standard toolbar, which produces a moving border around cell D6. Drag the mouse over **cells D7** through **D10.** Click the **Paste button** on the Standard toolbar to complete the copy operation.
- Press **Esc** to remove the moving border around cell D6.

➤ The last five employees were hired one year apart, beginning October 31, 1989.
  - Click in **cell D11** and type **10/31/89.**
  - Click in **cell D12** and type **10/31/90.**
  - Select **cells D11** and **D12.**
  - Drag the **fill handle** at the bottom of cell D12 over **cells D13, D14,** and **D15.** Release the mouse to complete the AutoFill operation.
➤ Save the workbook.

DATES AND THE FILL HANDLE

The AutoFill facility is the fastest way to create a series of dates. Enter the first two dates in the series, then select both cells and drag the fill handle over the remaining cells. Excel will create a series based on the increment between the first two cells; for example, if the first two dates are one month apart, the remaining dates will also be one month apart.

STEP 9: Format the Date

➤ Click in the **column heading** for **column D** to select the column of dates as in Figure 1.5f.

➤ Click the **right mouse button** to display a shortcut menu. Click **Format Cells.**

➤ Click the **Number tab** in the Format Cells dialog box. Click **Date** in the Category list box. Select (click) the date format shown in Figure 1.5f. Click **OK.**

➤ Click elsewhere in the workbook to deselect the dates. Reduce the width of column D as appropriate. Save the workbook.

DATES VERSUS FRACTIONS

A fraction is entered into a cell by preceding the fraction with an equal sign—for example, =1/4. The fraction is displayed as its decimal equivalent (.25) unless the cell is formatted to display fractions. Select the cell, pull down the Format menu, and click the Cells command. Click the Numbers tab, then choose Fraction from the Category list box. Omission of the equal sign, when entering a fraction, treats the entry as a date; that is, typing 1/4 (without the equal sign) will store the entry as a date and display it as January 4th (of the current year).

STEP 10: Exit Excel

➤ Click the **Office Assistant button** to open the Office Assistant. Click the **Tips button** to review the tips (if any) suggested by the Assistant. Click the **Close button** to close the Office Assistant.

➤ Close the workbook. Exit Excel if you do not want to continue with the next exercise at this time.

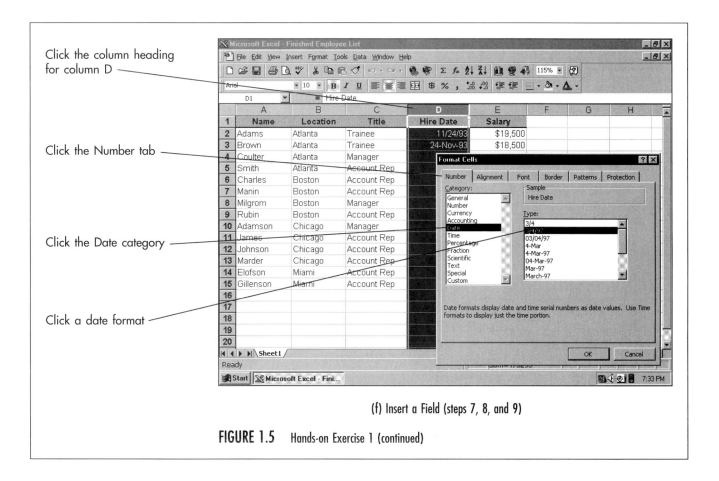

Click the column heading for column D

Click the Number tab

Click the Date category

Click a date format

(f) Insert a Field (steps 7, 8, and 9)

FIGURE 1.5 Hands-on Exercise 1 (continued)

DATA VERSUS INFORMATION

Data and information are not synonymous. **Data** refers to a fact or facts about a specific record, such as an employee's name, title, or salary. **Information,** on the other hand, is data that has been rearranged into a form perceived as useful by the recipient. A list of employees earning more than $35,000 or a total of all employee salaries are examples of information produced from data about individual employees. Put another way, data is the raw material, and information is the finished product.

Decisions in an organization are based on information rather than raw data; for example, in assessing the effects of a proposed across-the-board salary increase, management needs to know the total payroll rather than individual salary amounts. In similar fashion, decisions about next year's hiring will be influenced, at least in part, by knowing how many individuals are currently employed in each job category.

Data is converted to information through a combination of database commands and functions whose capabilities are illustrated by the reports in Figure 1.6. The reports are based on the employee list as it existed at the end of the first hands-on exercise. Each report presents the data in a different way, according to the information requirements of the end-user. As you view each report, ask yourself how it was produced; that is, what was done to the data in order to produce the information?

Figure 1.6a contains a master list of all employees, listing employees by location, and alphabetically by last name within location. The report was created by sorting the list on two keys, location and name. Location is the more important or primary key. Name is the less important or secondary key. The sorted report

Location Report

Name	Location	Title	Hire Date	Salary
Adams	Atlanta	Trainee	11/24/93	$19,500
Brown	Atlanta	Trainee	11/24/93	$18,500
Coulter	Atlanta	Manager	11/24/93	$100,000
Smith	Atlanta	Account Rep	11/24/93	$65,000
Charles	Boston	Account Rep	3/16/92	$40,000
Manin	Boston	Account Rep	3/16/92	$49,500
Milgrom	Boston	Manager	3/16/92	$57,500
Rubin	Boston	Account Rep	3/16/92	$45,000
Adamson	Chicago	Manager	3/16/92	$52,000
James	Chicago	Account Rep	10/31/89	$42,500
Johnson	Chicago	Account Rep	10/31/90	$47,500
Marder	Chicago	Account Rep	10/31/91	$38,500
Elofson	Miami	Account Rep	10/31/92	$47,500
Gillenson	Miami	Account Rep	10/31/93	$55,000

(a) Employees by Location and Name within Location

Employees Earning Between $40,000 and $60,000

Name	Location	Title	Hire Date	Salary
Milgrom	Boston	Manager	3/16/92	$57,500
Gillenson	Miami	Account Rep	10/31/93	$55,000
Adamson	Chicago	Manager	3/16/92	$52,000
Manin	Boston	Account Rep	3/16/92	$49,500
Johnson	Chicago	Account Rep	10/31/90	$47,500
Elofson	Miami	Account Rep	10/31/92	$47,500
Rubin	Boston	Account Rep	3/16/92	$45,000
James	Chicago	Account Rep	10/31/89	$42,500
Charles	Boston	Account Rep	3/16/92	$40,000

(b) Employees Earning between $40,000 and $60,000

Summary Statistics

Total Salary for Account Reps:	$430,500
Average Salary for Account Reps:	$47,833
Maximum Salary for Account Reps:	$65,000
Minimum Salary for Account Reps:	$38,500
Number of Account Reps:	9

(c) Account Rep Summary Data

FIGURE 1.6   Data versus Information

groups employees according to like values of the primary key (location), then within the primary key, groups the records according to the secondary key (name).

The report in Figure 1.6b displays a subset of the records in the list, which includes only those employees who meet specific criteria. The criteria can be based on any field or combination of fields—in this case, employees whose salaries are between $40,000 and $60,000 (inclusive). The employees are shown in descending order of salary so that the employee with the highest salary is listed first.

The report in Figure 1.6c displays summary statistics for the selected employees—in this example, the salaries for the account reps within the company. Reports of this nature omit the salaries of individual employees (known as detail lines), in order to present an aggregate view of the organization.

CITY, STATE, AND ZIP CODE—ONE FIELD OR THREE?

The answer depends on whether the fields are referenced as a unit or individually. However, given the almost universal need to sort or select on zip code, it is almost invariably defined as a separate field. An individual's last name, first name, and middle initial are defined as individual fields for the same reason.

AutoFilter Command

A *filtered list* displays a subset of records that meet a specific criterion or set of criteria. It is created by the *AutoFilter command* (or the Advanced Filter command discussed in the next section). Both commands temporarily hide those records (rows) that do not meet the criteria. The hidden records are *not* deleted; they are simply not displayed.

Figure 1.7a displays the employee list in alphabetical order. Figure 1.7b displays a filtered version of the list in which only the Atlanta employees (in rows 2, 4, 6, and 15) are visible. The remaining employees are still in the worksheet but are not shown as their rows are hidden.

Execution of the AutoFilter command places drop-down arrows next to each column label (field name). Clicking a drop-down arrow produces a list of the

Drop-down arrows appear next to each field name

Click here to display only The Atlanta employees

	A	B	C	D	E
1	Name ▾	Location ▾	Title ▾	Hire Dat ▾	Salary ▾
2	Adams	(All)	Trainee	11/24/93	$19,500
3	Brown	(Top 10...)	Trainee	11/24/93	$18,500
4	Coulter	(Custom...)	Manager	11/24/93	$100,000
5	Smith	Atlanta	Account Rep	11/24/93	$65,000
6	Charles	Boston	Account Rep	3/16/92	$40,000
		Chicago			
7	Manin	Miami	Account Rep	3/16/92	$49,500
8	Milgrom	Boston	Manager	3/16/92	$57,500
9	Rubin	Boston	Account Rep	3/16/92	$45,000
10	Adamson	Chicago	Manager	3/16/92	$52,000
11	James	Chicago	Account Rep	10/31/89	$42,500
12	Johnson	Chicago	Account Rep	10/31/90	$47,500
13	Marder	Chicago	Account Rep	10/31/91	$38,500
14	Elofson	Miami	Account Rep	10/31/92	$47,500
15	Gillenson	Miami	Account Rep	10/31/93	$55,000

(a) Unfiltered List

Only Atlanta employees are displayed

	A	B	C	D	E
1	Name ▾	Location ▾	Title ▾	Hire Date ▾	Salary ▾
2	Adams	Atlanta	Trainee	11/24/93	$19,500
4	Brown	Atlanta	Trainee	11/24/93	$18,500
6	Coulter	Atlanta	Manager	11/24/93	$100,000
15	Smith	Atlanta	Account Rep	11/24/93	$65,000

(b) Filtered List (Atlanta employees)

FIGURE 1.7   Filter Command

Click drop-down arrow to
further filter the list to
Atlanta Managers

	A	B	C	D	E
1	Name ▾	Location ▾	Title ▾	Hire Date ▾	Salary ▾
2	Adams	Atlanta	(All)	11/24/93	$19,500
4	Brown	Atlanta	(Top 10...)	11/24/93	$18,500
6	Coulter	Atlanta	(Custom...)	11/24/93	$100,000
15	Smith	Atlanta	Account Rep	11/24/93	$65,000
			Manager		
			Trainee		

(c) Imposing a Second Condition

Blue arrows indicate fields for which
a filter condition is in effect

	A	B	C	D	E
1	Name ▾	Location ▾	Title ▾	Hire Date ▾	Salary ▾
6	Coulter	Atlanta	Manager	11/24/93	$100,000

(d) Filtered List (Atlanta managers)

FIGURE 1.7   Filter Command (continued)

unique values for that field, enabling you to establish the criteria for the filtered list. Thus, to display the Atlanta employees, click the drop-down arrow for Location, then click Atlanta.

A filter condition can be imposed on multiple columns as shown in Figure 1.7c. The filtered list in Figure 1.7c contains just the Atlanta employees. Clicking the arrow next to Title, then clicking Manager, will filter the list further to display the employees who both work in Atlanta *and* have Manager as a title. Only one employee meets both conditions, as shown in Figure 1.7d. The drop-down arrows next to Location and Title are displayed in blue to indicate that a filter is in effect for these columns.

The AutoFilter command has additional options as can be seen from the drop-down list box in Figure 1.7c. (All) removes existing criteria in the column and effectively "unfilters" the list. (Custom...) enables you to use the relational operators (=, >, <, >=, <=, or <>) within a criterion. (Top 10...) displays the records with the top (or bottom) values in the field, and makes most sense if you sort the list to see the entries in sequence.

Advanced Filter Command

The *Advanced Filter command* extends the capabilities of the AutoFilter command in two important ways. It enables you to develop more complex criteria than are possible with the AutoFilter Command. It also enables you to copy the selected records to a separate area in the worksheet. The Advanced Filter command is illustrated in detail in the hands-on exercise that follows shortly.

Criteria Range

A *criteria range* is used with both the Advanced Filter command and the database functions that are discussed in the next section. It is defined independently of the list on which it operates and exists as a separate area in the worksheet. A criteria range must be at least two rows deep and one column wide as illustrated in Figure 1.8.

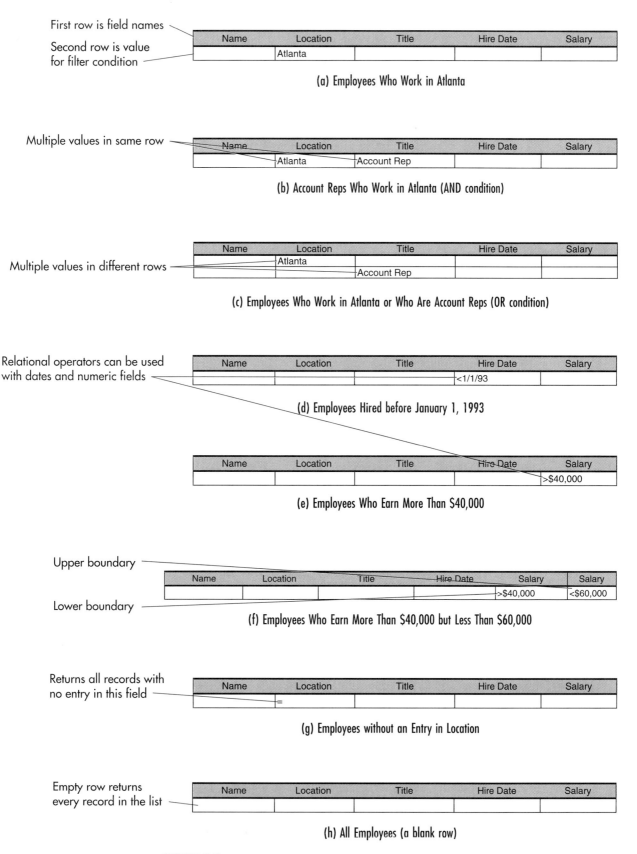

First row is field names

Second row is value for filter condition

Name	Location	Title	Hire Date	Salary
	Atlanta			

(a) Employees Who Work in Atlanta

Multiple values in same row

Name	Location	Title	Hire Date	Salary
	Atlanta	Account Rep		

(b) Account Reps Who Work in Atlanta (AND condition)

Multiple values in different rows

Name	Location	Title	Hire Date	Salary
	Atlanta			
		Account Rep		

(c) Employees Who Work in Atlanta or Who Are Account Reps (OR condition)

Relational operators can be used with dates and numeric fields

Name	Location	Title	Hire Date	Salary
			<1/1/93	

(d) Employees Hired before January 1, 1993

Name	Location	Title	Hire Date	Salary
				>$40,000

(e) Employees Who Earn More Than $40,000

Upper boundary

Lower boundary

Name	Location	Title	Hire Date	Salary	Salary
				>$40,000	<$60,000

(f) Employees Who Earn More Than $40,000 but Less Than $60,000

Returns all records with no entry in this field

Name	Location	Title	Hire Date	Salary
	=			

(g) Employees without an Entry in Location

Empty row returns every record in the list

Name	Location	Title	Hire Date	Salary

(h) All Employees (a blank row)

FIGURE 1.8   The Criteria Range

The simplest criteria range consists of two rows and as many columns as there are fields in the list. The first row contains the field names as they appear in the list. The second row holds the value(s) you are looking for. The criteria range in Figure 1.8a selects the employees who work in Atlanta.

Multiple values in the same row are connected by an AND and require that the selected records meet *all* of the specified criteria. The criteria range in Figure 1.8b identifies the account reps in Atlanta; that is, it selects any record in which the Location field is Atlanta *and* the Title field is Account Rep.

Values entered in multiple rows are connected by an OR in which the selected records satisfy *any* of the indicated criteria. The criteria range in Figure 1.8c will identify employees who work in Atlanta *or* whose title is Account Rep.

Relational operators may be used with date or numeric fields to return records within a designated range. The criteria range in Figure 1.8d selects the employees hired before January 1, 1993. The criteria range in Figure 1.8e returns employees whose salary is more than $40,000.

An upper and lower boundary may be established for the same field by repeating the field within the criteria range. This was done in Figure 1.8f, which returns all records in which the salary is more than $40,000 but less than $60,000.

The equal and unequal signs select records with empty and nonempty fields, respectively. An equal sign with nothing after it will return all records without an entry in the designated field; for example, the criteria range in Figure 1.8g selects any record that is missing a value for the Location field. An unequal sign (<>) with nothing after it will select all records with an entry in the field.

An empty row in the criteria range returns *every* record in the list, as shown in Figure 1.8h. All criteria are *case-insensitive* and return records with any combination of upper- and lowercase letters that match the entry.

THE IMPLIED WILD CARD

Any text entry within a criteria range is treated as though it were followed by the asterisk **wild card;** that is, *New* is the same as *New**. Both entries will return New York and New Jersey. To match a text entry exactly, begin with an equal sign, enter a quotation mark followed by another equal sign, the entry you are looking for, and the closing quotation mark—for example, ="=New" to return only the entries that say New.

Database Functions

The *database functions* DSUM, DAVERAGE, DMAX, DMIN, and DCOUNT operate on *selected* records in a list. These functions parallel the statistical functions (SUM, AVERAGE, MAX, MIN, and COUNT) except that they affect only records that satisfy the established criteria.

The summary statistics in Figure 1.9 are based on the salaries of the managers in the list, rather than all employees. Each database function includes the criteria range in cells A17:E18 as one of its arguments, and thus limits the employees that are included to managers. The **DAVERAGE function** returns the average salary for just the managers. The **DMAX** and **DMIN functions** display the maximum and minimum salaries for the managers. The **DSUM function** computes the total salary for all the managers. The **DCOUNT function** indicates the number of managers.

	A	B	C	D	E
1	Name	Location	Title	Hire Date	Salary
2	Adams	Atlanta	Trainee	11/24/93	$19,500
3	Adamson	Chicago	Manager	3/16/92	$52,000
4	Brown	Atlanta	Trainee	11/24/93	$18,500
5	Charles	Boston	Account Rep	3/16/92	$40,000
6	Coulter	Atlanta	Manager	11/24/93	$100,000
7	Elofson	Miami	Account Rep	10/31/92	$47,500
8	Gillenson	Miami	Account Rep	10/31/93	$55,000
9	James	Chicago	Account Rep	10/31/89	$42,500
10	Johnson	Chicago	Account Rep	10/31/90	$47,500
11	Manin	Boston	Account Rep	3/16/92	$49,500
12	Marder	Chicago	Account Rep	10/31/91	$38,500
13	Milgrom	Boston	Manager	3/16/92	$57,500
14	Rubin	Boston	Account Rep	3/16/92	$45,000
15	Smith	Atlanta	Account Rep	11/24/93	$65,000
16					
17	Name	Location	Title	Hire Date	Salary
18			Manager		
19					
20					
21			Summary Statistics		
22	Average Salary:				$69,833
23	Maximum Salary:				$100,000
24	Minimum Salary:				$52,000
25	Total Salary:				$209,500
26	Number of Employees:				3

Criteria range is A17:E18 (filters list to Managers)

Summary statistics for Managers

FIGURE 1.9   Database Functions and the Data Extract Command

Each database function has three arguments: the range for the list on which it is to operate, the field to be processed, and the criteria range. Consider, for example, the DAVERAGE function as shown below:

=DAVERAGE(list,"field",criteria)

The criteria range can be entered as a cell range (such as A17:E18) or as a name assigned to a cell range (e.g., Criteria)

The name of the field to be processed is enclosed in quotation marks

The list can be entered as a cell range (such as A1:E15) or as a name assigned to a cell range (e.g., Database).

FORMAT THE DATABASE

Formatting has no effect on the success or failure of database commands, so you can format the entries in a list to any extent you like. Select the currency format where appropriate, change fonts, use borders or shading, or any other formatting option. Be sure to format the row containing the column names differently from the rest of the list, so that it can be recognized as the header row in conjunction with the Ascending and Descending Sort buttons on the Standard toolbar.

The entries in the criteria range may be changed at any time, in which case the values of the database functions are automatically recalculated. The other database functions have arguments identical to those used in the DAVERAGE example.

Name Command

The *Name command* in the Insert menu equates a mnemonic name such as *employee_list* to a cell or cell range such as *A1:E15,* then enables you to use that name to reference the cell(s) in all subsequent commands. A name can be up to 255 characters in length, but must begin with a letter or an underscore. It can include upper- or lowercase letters, numbers, periods, and underscore characters.

Once defined, names adjust automatically for insertions and/or deletions within the range. If, in the previous example, you were to delete row 4, the definition of *employee_list* would change to A1:E14. And, in similar fashion, if you were to add a new column between columns B and C, the range would change to A1:F14.

A name can be used in any formula or function instead of a cell address; for example, =SALES−EXPENSES instead of =C1−C10, where Sales and Expenses have been defined as the names for cells C1 and C10, respectively. A name can also be entered into any dialog box where a cell range is required.

THE GO TO COMMAND

Names are frequently used in conjunction with the Go To command. Pull down the Edit menu and click Go To (or click the F5 key) to display a dialog box containing the names that have been defined within the workbook. Double click a name to move directly to the first cell in the associated range and simultaneously select the entire range.

HANDS-ON EXERCISE 2

Data versus Information

Objective: To sort a list on multiple keys; to demonstrate the AutoFilter and Advanced Filter commands; to define a named range; to use the DSUM, DAVERAGE, DMAX, DMIN, and DCOUNT functions. Use Figure 1.10 as a guide in the exercise.

STEP 1: Calculate the Years of Service

➤ Start Excel. Open the **Finished Employee List** workbook created in the previous exercise.

➤ Click the **column heading** in **column D.** Click the **right mouse button** to display a shortcut menu. Click **Insert.** The column of hire dates has been moved to column E.

➤ Click in **cell D1.** Type **Service** and press **enter.**

➤ Click in **cell D2** and enter the formula to compute the years of service **=(Today( )-E2)/365** as shown in Figure 1.10a. Press **enter;** the years of service for the first employee are displayed in cell D2.

➤ Click in **cell D2,** then click the **Decrease Decimal button** on the Formatting toolbar several times to display the length of service with only one decimal place. Reduce the column width as appropriate.

➤ Drag the **fill handle** in cell D2 to the remaining cells in that column (**cells D3** through **D15**) to compute the service for the remaining employees.

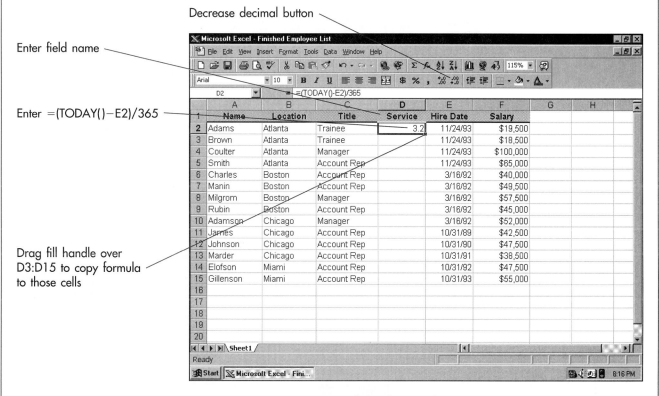

(a) Calculate the Years of Service (step 1)

FIGURE 1.10 Hands-on Exercise 2

THE COLUMN HIDE (UNHIDE) COMMAND

As its name implies, the Column Hide command hides a column from view. Point to the column heading, then click the right mouse button to select the column and display a shortcut menu. Click the Hide command, and the column is no longer visible (although it remains in the worksheet). The column headings will reflect a hidden column in that the letter for the hidden column is not seen. To display (unhide) a hidden column, select (click) the column headings of the adjacent columns on either side, click the right mouse button to display a shortcut menu, then click the Unhide command.

STEP 2: The AutoFilter Command

➤ Click a single cell anywhere within the list. Pull down the **Data menu.** Click the **Filter** command.

➤ Click **AutoFilter** from the resulting cascade menu to display the down arrows to the right of each field name.

➤ Click the **down arrow** next to **Title** to display the list of titles in Figure 1.10b. Click **Account Rep.**

- The display changes to show only those employees who meet the filter condition.

- The worksheet is unchanged, but only those rows containing account reps are visible.

- The row numbers for the visible records are blue.

- The drop-down arrow for Title is also blue, indicating that it is part of the filter condition.

➤ Click the **down arrow** next to **Location.** Click **Boston** to display only the employees in this city. The combination of the two filter conditions shows only the account reps in Boston.

➤ Click the **down arrow** next to **Location** a second time. Click **(All)** to remove the filter condition on location. Only the account reps are displayed since the filter on Title is still in effect.

➤ Save the workbook.

Click to display the list of titles

Click a single cell within the list

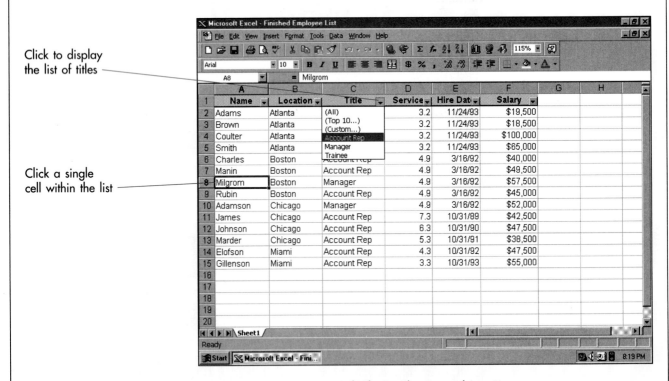

(b) The AutoFilter Command (step 2)

FIGURE 1.10   Hands-on Exercise 2 (continued)

THE TOP 10 AUTOFILTER

To see the records containing the top 10 values in a specific field, turn the AutoFilter condition on, then click the drop-down arrow next to the column heading. Click Top 10 from the list of AutoFilter options, then choose the options you want. You can see any number of the top (or bottom) records by entering the desired values in the Top 10 AutoFilter dialog box. You can also see a desired (top or bottom) percentage rather than a specified number of records. Click the Sort Ascending or Sort Descending button to display the selected records in order.

STEP 3: The Custom AutoFilter Command

➤ Click the **arrow** next to **Salary** to display the list of salaries. Click **Custom** to display the dialog box in Figure 1.10c.

➤ Click the **arrow** in the leftmost drop-down list box for **Salary,** then click the **is greater than** as the relational operator.

➤ Click in the text box for the salary amount. Type **45000.** Click **OK.**

➤ The list changes to display only those employees whose title is account rep *and* who earn more than $45,000.

➤ Pull down the **Data menu.** Click **Filter.** Click **AutoFilter** to toggle the Auto-Filter command off, which removes the arrows next to the field names and cancels all filter conditions. All of the records in the list are visible.

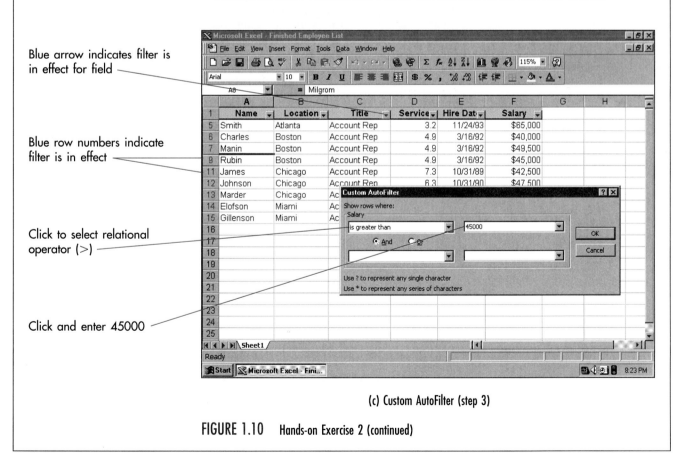

Blue arrow indicates filter is in effect for field

Blue row numbers indicate filter is in effect

Click to select relational operator (>)

Click and enter 45000

(c) Custom AutoFilter (step 3)

FIGURE 1.10   Hands-on Exercise 2 (continued)

STEP 4: The Advanced Filter Command

➤ The field names in the criteria range must be spelled exactly the same way as in the associated list. The best way to ensure that the names are identical is to copy the entries from the list to the criteria range.

➤ Click and drag to select **cells A1** through **F1.** Click the **Copy button** on the Standard toolbar. A moving border appears around the selected cells. Click in **cell A17.** Click the **Paste button** on the Standard toolbar to complete the copy operation. Press **Esc** to cancel the moving border.

➤ Click in **cell C18.** Enter **Manager.** (Be sure you spell it correctly.)

➤ Click a single cell anywhere within the employee list. Pull down the **Data menu.** Click **Filter.** Click **Advanced Filter** from the resulting cascade menu to display the dialog box in Figure 1.10d. (The range is already entered because you had selected a cell in the list prior to executing the command.)

➤ Click in the **Criteria Range** text box. Click in **cell A17** in the worksheet and drag the mouse to cell F18. Release the mouse. A moving border appears around these cells in the worksheet, and the corresponding cell reference is entered in the dialog box.

➤ Check that the **option button** to Filter the List in-place is selected. Click **OK.** The display changes to show just the managers; that is, only rows 4, 8, and 10 are visible.

➤ Click in **cell B18.** Type **Atlanta.** Press **enter.**

➤ Pull down the **Data menu.** Click **Filter.** Click **Advanced Filter.** The Advanced Filter dialog box already has the cell references for the List and Criteria ranges (which were the last entries made).

➤ Click **OK.** The display changes to show just the manager in Atlanta; that is, only row 4 is visible.

➤ Pull down the **Data menu.** Click **Filter.** Click **Show All** to remove the filter condition. The entire list is visible.

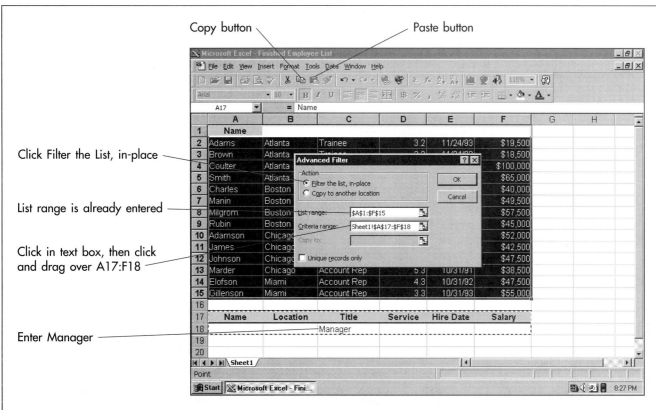

Copy button   Paste button

Click Filter the List, in-place

List range is already entered

Click in text box, then click
and drag over A17:F18

Enter Manager

(d) Advanced Filter Command (step 4)

FIGURE 1.10 Hands-on Exercise 2 (continued)

STEP 5: The Insert Name Command

➤ Click and drag to select **cells A1** through **F15** as shown in Figure 1.10e.

➤ Pull down the **Insert menu.** Click **Name.** Click **Define.** Type **Database** in the Define Name dialog box. Click **OK.**

➤ Pull down the **Edit menu** and click **Go To** (or press the **F5 key**) to display the Go To dialog box. There are two names in the box: Database, which you just defined, and Criteria, which was defined automatically when you specified the criteria range in step 4.

➤ Double click **Criteria** to select the criteria range (**cells A17** through **F18**). Click elsewhere in the worksheet to deselect the cells.

➤ Save the workbook.

THE NAME BOX

Use the *Name box* on the formula bar to select a cell or named range by clicking in the box and then typing the appropriate cell reference or name. You can also click the down arrow next to the Name box to select a named range from a drop-down list. And, finally, you can use the Name box to define a named range, by first selecting the cell(s) in the worksheet to which the name is to apply, clicking in the Name box in order to enter the range name, and then pressing the enter key.

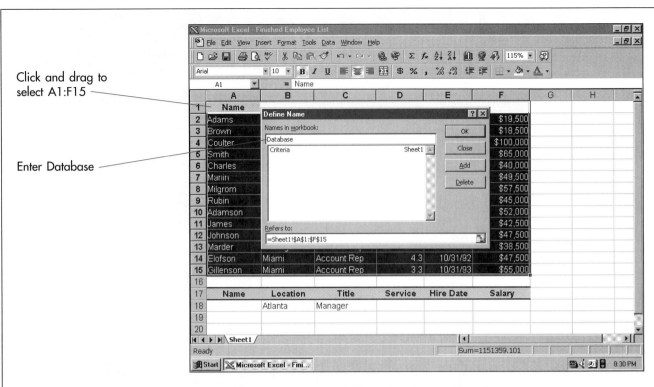

Click and drag to
select A1:F15

Enter Database

(e) Insert Name Command (step 5)

FIGURE 1.10   Hands-on Exercise 2 (continued)

STEP 6: Database Functions

➤ Click in cell **A21,** type **Summary Statistics,** press the **enter key,** then click and drag to select cells **A21** through **F21.**

➤ Pull down the **Format menu,** click **Cells,** click the **Alignment tab,** then select **Center Across Selection** as the Horizontal alignment. Click **OK.** (You cannot use the Merge and Center button.)

➤ Enter the labels for **cells A22** through **A26** as shown in Figure 1.10f.

➤ Click in **cell B18.** Press the **Del key.** The criteria range is now set to select only managers.

➤ Click in **cell F22.** Click the **Paste Function button** on the Standard toolbar to display the dialog box in Figure 1.10f.

➤ Select **Database** in the Function Category list box, select **DAVERAGE** as the function name, then click **OK.**

THE MERGE AND CENTER BUTTON

The Merge and Center button on the Formatting toolbar merges the selected cells into a single cell (similar to the Table Merge Cells command in Microsoft Word). (This is very different from the effect of the Center Alignment button in Excel 7.0.) Merging cells seems harmless enough, but it precludes the subsequent execution of certain commands; e.g., you could not insert a column between cells A through F if the cells in any given row have been merged.

Click DAVERAGE ———

Click Database ———

Enter labels in A22:A26 ———

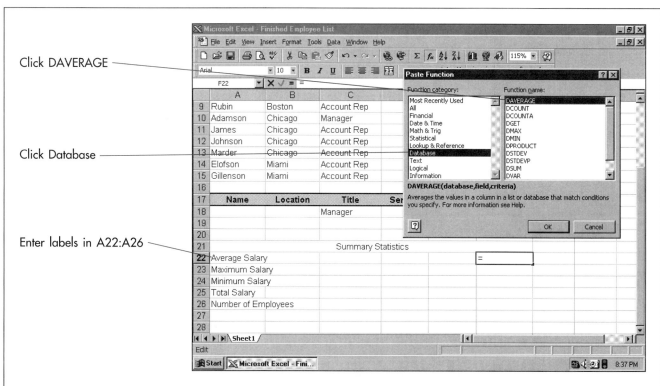

(f) Database Functions (step 6)

FIGURE 1.10 Hands-on Exercise 2 (continued)

STEP 7: The DAVERAGE Function

➤ Click the **database** text box in the Paste Function dialog box of Figure 1.10g. Type **Database** (the range name defined in step 5), which references the employee list.

➤ Click the **field** text box. Type **"Salary"** (you must include the quotation marks), which is the name of the field within the list that you want to average.

➤ Click the **criteria** text box. Type **Criteria** (the range name assigned to the criteria range during the Advanced Filter operation). The Paste Function dialog box displays the computed value of 69833.33333.

➤ Click **OK** to enter the DAVERAGE function into the worksheet. Save the workbook.

THE COLLAPSE DIALOG BUTTON

It's usually easier to enter a cell reference in the Formula Palette by clicking the underlying cell(s) within the worksheet, rather than explicitly typing the entry. The Formula Palette, however, often hides the cell(s). Should this occur, just click the Collapse Dialog button (which appears to the right of any parameter within the dialog box) to collapse (hide) the Formula Palette, enabling you to click the underlying cell(s), which is (are) now visible. Click the Collapse Dialog button a second time to display the entire dialog box.

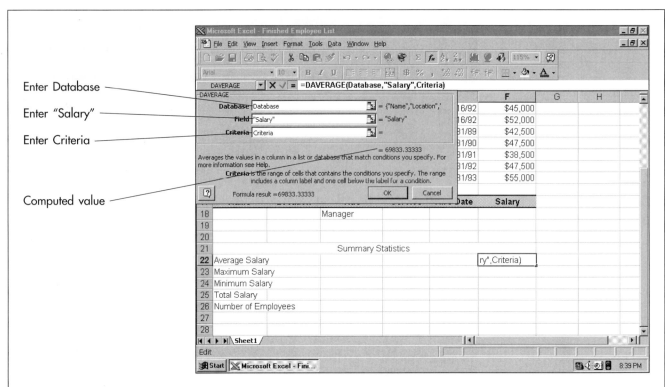

Enter Database
Enter "Salary"
Enter Criteria

Computed value

(g) DAVERAGE Function (step 7)

FIGURE 1.10   Hands-on Exercise 2 (continued)

STEP 8: The DMAX, DMIN, DSUM, and DCOUNT Functions

➤ Enter the DMAX, DMIN, DSUM, and DCOUNT functions in cells F23 through F26, respectively. You can use the **Paste Function button** to enter each function individually, *or* you can copy the DAVERAGE function and edit appropriately:

- Click in **cell F22.** Drag the **fill handle** to **cells F23** through **F26** to copy the DAVERAGE function to these cells.

- Double click in **cell F23** to edit the contents of this cell, then click within the displayed formula to substitute **DMAX** for DAVERAGE. Press **enter** when you have completed the change.

- **Double click** in the remaining cells and edit them appropriately. Figure 1.10h shows how double clicking a cell displays the cell contents, enabling you to edit within the cell itself rather than on the formula bar.

➤ The computed values (except for the DCOUNT function, which has a computed value of 3) are shown in Figure 1.10h.

➤ Select **cells F22** through **F25,** then format these cells to currency with no decimals. Widen the column if necessary.

➤ Save the workbook.

STEP 9: Change the Criteria

➤ Click in the **Name box.** Type **B18** and press **enter** to make cell B18 the active cell. Type **Chicago** to change the criteria to Chicago managers. Press **enter.**

Print button

Name box

Database functions
entered in F22:F26

Double click to
edit in the cell

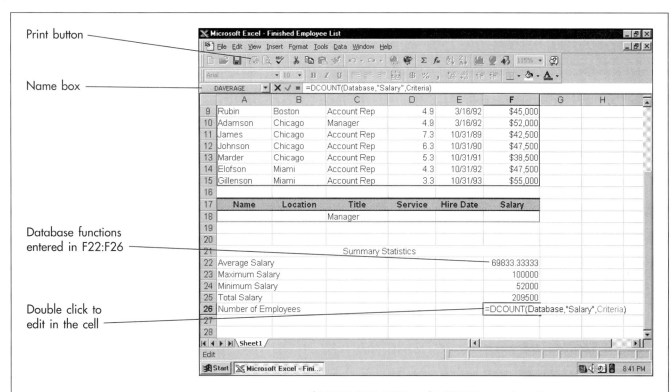

	A	B	C	D	E	F	G	H
9	Rubin	Boston	Account Rep	4.9	3/16/92	$45,000		
10	Adamson	Chicago	Manager	4.9	3/16/92	$52,000		
11	James	Chicago	Account Rep	7.3	10/31/89	$42,500		
12	Johnson	Chicago	Account Rep	6.3	10/31/90	$47,500		
13	Marder	Chicago	Account Rep	5.3	10/31/91	$38,500		
14	Elofson	Miami	Account Rep	4.3	10/31/92	$47,500		
15	Gillenson	Miami	Account Rep	3.3	10/31/93	$55,000		
16								
17	**Name**	**Location**	**Title**	**Service**	**Hire Date**	**Salary**		
18			Manager					
19								
20								
21			Summary Statistics					
22	Average Salary					69833.33333		
23	Maximum Salary					100000		
24	Minimum Salary					52000		
25	Total Salary					209500		
26	Number of Employees					=DCOUNT(Database,"Salary",Criteria)		
27								
28								

(h) DMAX, DMIN, DSUM, and DCOUNT Functions (step 8)

FIGURE 1.10   Hands-on Exercise 2 (continued)

➤ The values displayed by the DAVERAGE, DMIN, DMAX, and DSUM functions change to $52,000, reflecting the one employee (Adamson) who meets the current criteria (a manager in Chicago). The value displayed by the DCOUNT function changes to 1 to indicate one employee.

➤ Click in **cell C18.** Press the **Del key.**

➤ The average salary changes to $45,125, reflecting all employees in Chicago.

➤ Click in **cell B18.** Press the **Del key.**

➤ The criteria range is now empty. The DAVERAGE function displays $48,429, which is the average salary of all employees in the database.

➤ Click in **cell C18.** Type **Manager** and press the **enter key.** The average salary is $69,833, the average salary for all managers.

STEP 10: Print the Worksheet

➤ Save the worksheet. To print the entire worksheet, click the **Print button** on the Standard toolbar.

➤ To print only a portion of the worksheet (e.g., just the summary statistics), select the cells you wish to print, pull down the **File menu,** and click **Print.** Click the **Selection option button.** Click **OK** to print the selected cells.

➤ Close the workbook. Exit Excel if you do not want to continue with the next exercise at this time.

SUBTOTALS

The **Subtotals command** computes subtotals based on data groups in a selected field. It also computes a grand total. The totals may be displayed with or without the detail lines as shown in Figures 1.11a and 1.11b, respectively.

Execution of the Subtotals command inserts a subtotal row into the list whenever the value of the selected field (Location in this example) changes from row to row. In Figure 1.11a the subtotal for the Atlanta employees is inserted into the list as we go from the last employee in Atlanta to the first employee in Boston. In similar fashion, the subtotal for Boston is inserted into the list as we go from

Atlanta subtotal ⟶

Boston subtotal ⟶

	A	B	C	D	E	F
1	Name	Location	Title	Service	Hire Date	Salary
2	Adams	Atlanta	Trainee	3.2	11/24/93	$19,500
3	Brown	Atlanta	Trainee	3.2	11/24/93	$18,500
4	Coulter	Atlanta	Manager	3.2	11/24/93	$100,000
5	Smith	Atlanta	Account Rep	3.2	11/24/93	$65,000
6		Atlanta Total				$203,000
7	Charles	Boston	Account Rep	4.9	3/16/92	$40,000
8	Manin	Boston	Account Rep	4.9	3/16/92	$49,500
9	Milgrom	Boston	Manager	4.9	3/16/92	$57,500
10	Rubin	Boston	Account Rep	4.9	3/16/92	$45,000
11		Boston Total				$192,000
12	Adamson	Chicago	Manager	4.9	3/16/92	$52,000
13	James	Chicago	Account Rep	7.3	10/31/89	$42,500
14	Johnson	Chicago	Account Rep	6.3	10/31/90	$47,500
15	Marder	Chicago	Account Rep	5.3	10/31/91	$38,500
16		Chicago Total				$180,500
17	Elofson	Miami	Account Rep	4.3	10/31/92	$47,500
18	Gillenson	Miami	Account Rep	3.3	10/31/93	$55,000
19		Miami Total				$102,500
20		Grand Total				$678,000

(a) Detail Lines

Only totals are displayed ⟶

	A	B	C	D	E	F
1	Name	Location	Title	Service	Hire Date	Salary
6		Atlanta Total				$203,000
11		Boston Total				$192,000
16		Chicago Total				$180,500
19		Miami Total				$102,500
20		Grand Total				$678,000

(b) Summary Lines (SUM function)

Displays number of employees ⟶

	A	B	C	D	E	F
1	Name	Location	Title	Service	Hire Date	Salary
6		Atlanta Count				4
11		Boston Count				4
16		Chicago Count				4
19		Miami Count				2
20		Grand Count				14

(c) Summary Lines (Count function)

FIGURE 1.11   The Subtotals Command

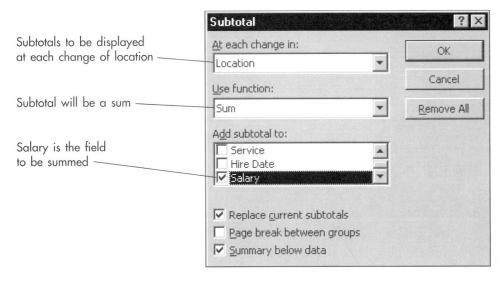

Subtotals to be displayed
at each change of location —

Subtotal will be a sum —

Salary is the field
to be summed —

(d) Subtotals Dialog Box

FIGURE 1.11   The Subtotals Command (continued)

the last employee in Boston to the first employee in Chicago. It is critical, therefore, that the list be in sequence according to the field on which the subtotals will be based, *prior* to executing the Subtotals command.

Figure 1.11d displays the Subtotal dialog box to compute the subtotals in Figure 1.11a. The various list boxes within the dialog box show the flexibility within the command. You can specify when the subtotals will be computed (in this example, at each change in the Location field). You can specify different functions (such as Sum in Figure 1.11b and Count in Figure 1.11c). Finally, you can specify the field(s) for which the computation is to take place (Salary). Subtotals are removed from a worksheet by clicking the Remove All command button.

PIVOT TABLES

A **pivot table** extends the capability of individual database functions by presenting the data in summary form. It divides the records in a list into categories, then computes summary statistics for those categories. The pivot tables in Figure 1.12, for example, compute statistics based on salary and location.

The pivot table in Figure 1.12a displays the number of employees in each location according to job title. The column labels are the unique values within the list for the Location field. The row labels are the unique values within the list for the Title field. The values in the table show the number of employees in each

	A	B	C	D	E	F
1	Count of Name	Location				
2	Title	Atlanta	Boston	Chicago	Miami	Grand Total
3	Account Rep	1	3	3	2	9
4	Manager	1	1	1	0	3
5	Trainee	2	0	0	0	2
6	Grand Total	4	4	4	2	14

Number of Account
Reps in Atlanta —

(a) Number of Employees in Each Job Title at Each Location

FIGURE 1.12   Pivot Tables

	A	B	C	D	E	F
1	Sum of Salary	Location				
2	Title	Atlanta	Boston	Chicago	Miami	Grand Total
3	Account Rep	$65,000	$134,500	$128,500	$102,500	$430,500
4	Manager	$100,000	$57,500	$52,000	$0	$209,500
5	Trainee	$38,000	$0	$0	$0	$38,000
6	Grand Total	$203,000	$192,000	$180,500	$102,500	$678,000

Total salaries for Account Reps in Atlanta

(b Total Salaries for Each Job Title and at Each Location

FIGURE 1.12 Pivot Tables (continued)

Title–Location combination. Figure 1.12b uses the identical categories (Title and Location) but computes the total salaries instead of the number of employees. Both pivot tables are based on the employee list we have been using.

A pivot table is created by using the **PivotTable Wizard,** which prompts you for the information to develop the pivot table. You indicate the field names for the row and column labels (Title and Location in Figures 1.12a and 1.12b). You also indicate the field on which the computation is to be based and the means of computation (a count of names in Figure 1.12a and a summation of Salary in Figure 1.12b). The PivotTable Wizard does the rest.

Pivot tables provide the utmost in flexibility, in that you can vary the row or column categories and/or the way the statistics are computed. Figure 1.13a illustrates a different pivot table, in which we analyze by gender rather than location. This table computes two statistics rather than one, and displays the number of employees as well as the average salary for each combination of title and gender.

The PivotTable dialog box in Figure 1.13b shows just how easy it is to create a pivot table. The field names within the associated list appear at the right of the dialog box. To create the pivot table, you simply drag a field name(s) to the row, column, or data areas of the table. Click the Next command button to supply the finishing touches to the pivot table, after which the pivot table will appear in its own worksheet.

Once a pivot table has been created, you can easily add or remove categories by dragging the field names on or off the table within the PivotTable Wizard. You can also switch the orientation (pivot the table) by dragging a field to or from the row or column area. And finally, you can modify the worksheet on which the pivot table is based (by adding, editing, or deleting employee records), then refresh the pivot table to reflect the changes made to the worksheet.

	A	B	C	D	E
1			Gender		
2	Title	Data	F	M	Grand Total
3	Account Rep	Count of Name	5	4	9
4		Average of Salary	$45,600	$50,625	$47,833
5	Manager	Count of Name	1	2	3
6		Average of Salary	$52,000	$78,750	$69,833
7	Trainee	Count of Name	1	1	2
8		Average of Salary	$18,500	$19,500	$19,000
9	Total Count of Name		7	7	14
10	Total Average of Salary		$42,643	$54,214	$48,429

Two statistics computed (count and average salary)

(a) The Pivot Table

FIGURE 1.13 The PivotTable Wizard

Field names within associated list

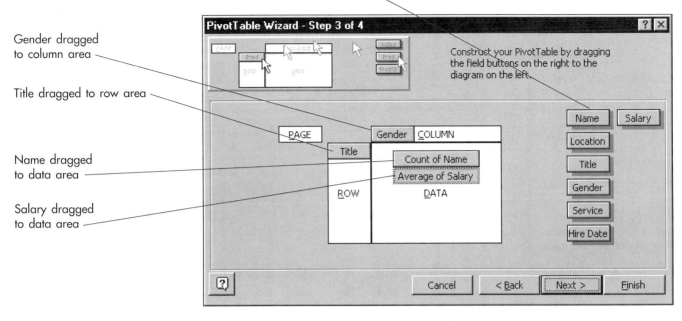

Gender dragged
to column area

Title dragged to row area

Name dragged
to data area

Salary dragged
to data area

(b) The PivotTable Wizard

FIGURE 1.13   The PivotTable Wizard (continued)

HANDS-ON EXERCISE 3

Subtotals and Pivot Tables

Objective: To display and modify subtotals within a list; to use the PivotTable Wizard to create and modify a pivot table. Use Figure 1.14 as a guide in the exercise.

STEP 1: Insert a Field

➤ Open the **Finished Employee List** workbook from the previous exercise. Clear the criteria range in row 18 so that the summary statistics pertain to all employees.

➤ Click any cell in **column C,** the column containing the employee titles. Click the **Sort Ascending button** on the Standard toolbar. The employees should be arranged according to title within the worksheet, as shown in Figure 1.14a. (This is the field on which the subtotals will be grouped.)

➤ Point to the **column heading** in **column D,** which presently contains the length of service. Press the **right mouse button** to display a shortcut menu. Click **Insert** to insert a new column.

➤ Click in **cell D1.** Type **Gender** (the field name). Press the **down arrow key** to move to **cell D2.** Type **M.**

➤ Add the remaining entries in column D to match those in Figure 1.14a.

➤ Drag the border between the column headings for columns D and E to the left to make column D narrower.

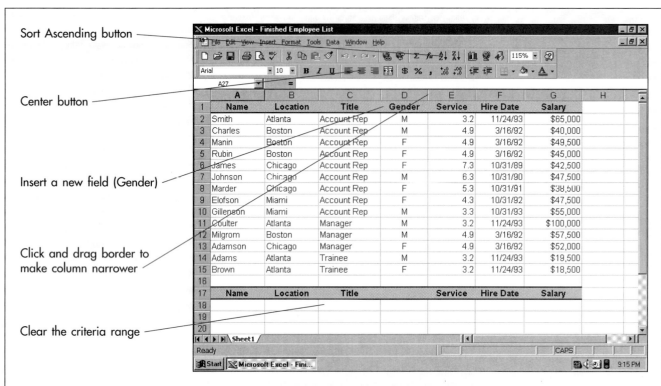

Sort Ascending button

Center button

Insert a new field (Gender)

Click and drag border to make column narrower

Clear the criteria range

	A	B	C	D	E	F	G	H
1	Name	Location	Title	Gender	Service	Hire Date	Salary	
2	Smith	Atlanta	Account Rep	M	3.2	11/24/93	$65,000	
3	Charles	Boston	Account Rep	M	4.9	3/16/92	$40,000	
4	Manin	Boston	Account Rep	F	4.9	3/16/92	$49,500	
5	Rubin	Boston	Account Rep	F	4.9	3/16/92	$45,000	
6	James	Chicago	Account Rep	F	7.3	10/31/89	$42,500	
7	Johnson	Chicago	Account Rep	M	6.3	10/31/90	$47,500	
8	Marder	Chicago	Account Rep	F	5.3	10/31/91	$38,500	
9	Elofson	Miami	Account Rep	F	4.3	10/31/92	$47,500	
10	Gillenson	Miami	Account Rep	M	3.3	10/31/93	$55,000	
11	Coulter	Atlanta	Manager	M	3.2	11/24/93	$100,000	
12	Milgrom	Boston	Manager	M	4.9	3/16/92	$57,500	
13	Adamson	Chicago	Manager	F	4.9	3/16/92	$52,000	
14	Adams	Atlanta	Trainee	M	3.2	11/24/93	$19,500	
15	Brown	Atlanta	Trainee	F	3.2	11/24/93	$18,500	
16								
17	Name	Location	Title		Service	Hire Date	Salary	
18								
19								
20								

(a) Insert a Field (step 1)

FIGURE 1.14   Hands-on Exercise 3

➤ Click and drag to select **cells D2** through **D15.** Click the **Center button** on the Formatting toolbar.

➤ Click outside the selected cells to deselect the range. Save the workbook.

THE DOCUMENTS SUBMENU

One of the fastest ways to get to a recently used document, regardless of the application, is through the Windows 95 Start menu, which includes a Documents submenu containing the last 15 documents that were opened. Click the Start button, click (or point to) the Documents submenu, then click the document you wish to open (e.g., Finished Employee List), assuming that it appears on the submenu.

STEP 2: Create the Subtotals

➤ Click anywhere in the employee list. Pull down the **Data menu.** Click **Sub-totals** to display the Subtotal dialog box in Figure 1.14b.

➤ Click the **arrow** in the At Each Change in list box. Click **Title** to create a subtotal whenever there is a change in title.

➤ Set the other options to match the dialog box in Figure 1.14b. Click **OK** to create the subtotals.

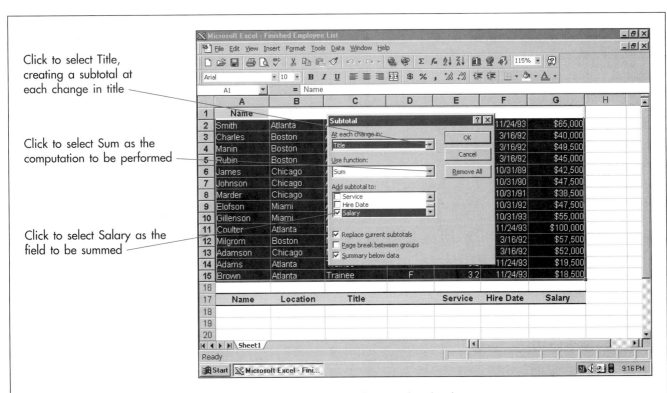

Click to select Title, creating a subtotal at each change in title

Click to select Sum as the computation to be performed

Click to select Salary as the field to be summed

(b) Create the Subtotals (step 2)

FIGURE 1.14 Hands-on Exercise 3 (continued)

STEP 3: Examine the Subtotals

➤ Your worksheet should display subtotals as shown in Figure 1.14c.

➤ Click in **cell G11,** the cell containing the Account Rep subtotal. The formula bar displays =SUBTOTAL(9,G2:G10), which computes the sum for cells G2 through G10. (The number 9 within the argument of the function indicates a sum.)

➤ Click in **cell G15,** the cell containing the Manager subtotal. The formula bar displays =SUBTOTAL(9,G12:G14), which computes the sum for cells G12 through G14.

➤ Click the **level 2 button** (under the Name box) to suppress the detail lines. The list collapses to display the subtotals and grand total.

THE SUBTOTAL FUNCTION

The SUBTOTAL function can be entered explicitly into a worksheet or implicitly (and more easily) through the Subtotal command in the Data menu. The function has two arguments: a function number to indicate the type of computation, and the associated cell range. A function number of 9 indicates a sum; thus, the entry =SUBTOTAL(9,E2:E10) computes the sum for cells E2 through E10. Pull down the Help menu and search on the SUBTOTAL function for additional information.

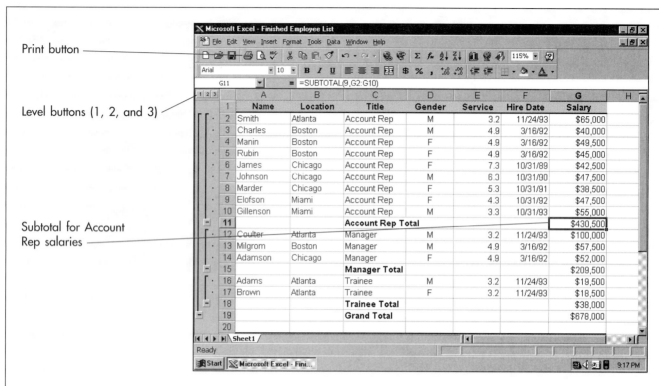

Print button ——

Level buttons (1, 2, and 3) ——

Subtotal for Account
Rep salaries ——

(c) Examine the Subtotals (step 3)

FIGURE 1.14 Hands-on Exercise 3 (continued)

➤ Click the **level 1 button** to suppress the subtotals. The list collapses further to display only the grand total.

➤ Click the **level 3 button** to restore the detail lines and subtotals. The list expands to display the employee records, subtotals, and grand total.

➤ Save the workbook. Click the **Print button** on the Standard toolbar if you wish to print the list with the subtotals.

STEP 4: The PivotTable Wizard

➤ The subtotals must be cleared in order to create a pivot table. Click anywhere within the employee list or subtotals. Pull down the **Data menu.** Click **Subtotals.** Click the **Remove All command button.**

➤ Pull down the **Data menu.** Click **PivotTable Report** to produce step 1 of the PivotTable Wizard. The option button indicates the pivot table will be created from data in a Microsoft Excel List or Database.

➤ Click the **Next command button** to move to step 2 of the PivotTable Wizard. You will see a dialog box where **Database** (the name assigned to the employee list in Hands-on Exercise 2) has already been entered in the Range text box.

➤ Click the **Next command button** to move to step 3 as shown in Figure 1.14d:
  • Click the **Title field button** and drag it to the row area.
  • Click the **Location field button** and drag it to the column area.
  • Click the **Salary field button** and drag it to the data area. (Sum is the default computation for a numeric field, such as Salary. Count is the default computation for a text field, such as Name.)

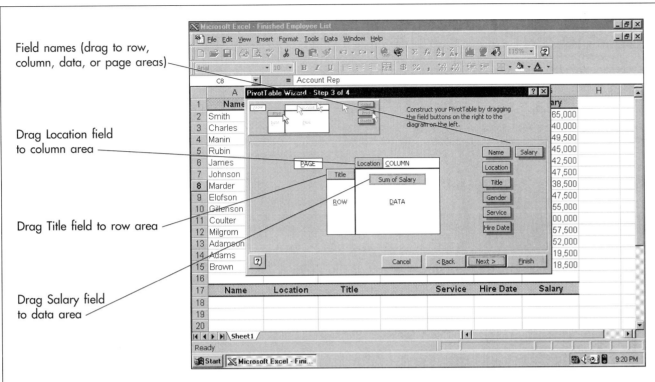

Field names (drag to row, column, data, or page areas)

Drag Location field to column area

Drag Title field to row area

Drag Salary field to data area

(d) The PivotTable Wizard (step 4)

FIGURE 1.14   Hands-on Exercise 3 (continued)

➤ Click the **Next command button** to move to step 4, the final step in the Pivot-Table Wizard. The option button to put the pivot table in a **New Worksheet** should be selected.

➤ Click the **Finish command button** to create the pivot table and exit the Pivot-Table Wizard. Save the workbook.

STEP 5: Modify the Pivot Table

➤ You should see the pivot table in its own worksheet as shown in Figure 1.14e.

➤ Rename the worksheets within the workbook:

• Point to the **Sheet2 tab** and click the **right mouse button** to display a short-cut menu. Click **Rename** to select the current name (Sheet 2). Type **Pivot Table** as the new name and press **enter.**

• Point to the **Sheet1 tab** and click the **right mouse button** to display a short-cut menu. Click **Rename.** Type **Employee List** as the new name. Press **enter.**

➤ Click the **PivotTable tab** to return to this worksheet, then click anywhere within the pivot table.

➤ Click the **PivotTable Wizard button** on the Pivot Table toolbar to reopen the PivotTable wizard as shown in Figure 1.14e. (If you are not on step 3 of the PivotTable Wizard, it is because you did not click in the pivot table prior to invoking the Wizard. Click Cancel, click in the pivot table, then click the PivotTable Wizard button.)

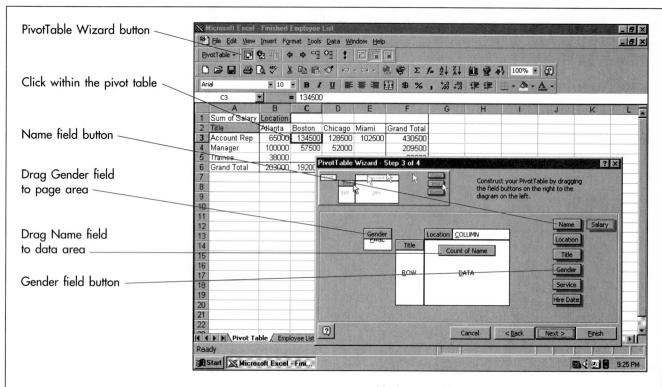

PivotTable Wizard button

Click within the pivot table

Name field button

Drag Gender field
to page area

Drag Name field
to data area

Gender field button

(e) Modify the Pivot Table (step 5)

FIGURE 1.14   Hands-on Exercise 3 (continued)

- Click and drag the **Name field button** to the data area. The button displays "Count of Name" (the default function for a text field).
- Click and drag the **Gender field** to the page area.
- Click and drag the **Sum of Salary field button** out of the data area.
- Click the **Next command button.** The option button to put the pivot table in the **Existing Worksheet** is selected. Click the **Finish command button.**

➤ The pivot table changes to display the number of employees for each location–title combination. Note that there are two account reps and no managers or trainees in Miami.

THE PAGE FIELD

A page field adds a third dimension to a pivot table. Unlike items in the row and column fields, however, the items in a page field are displayed one at a time. Creating a page field on gender, for example, enables you to view the data for each gender separately, by clicking the drop-down arrow on the page field list box, then clicking the appropriate value of gender. You can see the statistics for all male employees, for all female employees, or for all employees (both male and female).

STEP 6: Modify the Employee List

➤ Click the **Employee List tab** to return to the employee worksheet.

➤ Click in **cell C10.** Type **Manager.** Press **enter** to change Gillenson's title from account rep to manager. Note that Gillenson works in Miami.

➤ Click the **PivotTable tab** to return to the pivot table. There are still two account reps and no managers or trainees in Miami because Gillenson's change in title is not yet reflected in the pivot table.

➤ Click within the pivot table, then click the **Refresh Data button** on the Pivot Table toolbar to update the pivot table.

➤ Miami now has one manager and one account rep, which reflects the change made to the employee list with respect to Gillenson's change of title. Save the workbook.

REFRESH THE PIVOT TABLE

The data in a pivot table is tied to an underlying list and cannot be edited directly. Thus, to change the data in a pivot table, you must edit the underlying list. Any changes in the list, however, are not reflected in the pivot table until the pivot table is refreshed. Click anywhere in the pivot table, then click the Refresh Data button on the Pivot Table toolbar to update the pivot table.

STEP 7: Pivot the Table

➤ The pivot table on your monitor should match Figure 1.14f with Gender, Title, and Location as the page, row, and column fields, respectively.

➤ Click and drag the **Gender button** next to the Location button. The page field disappears, and there are now two column fields, Gender and Location.

➤ Click and drag the **Location button** to the previous location of the Gender field to make Location a page field. You have changed the orientation of the table and have a completely different analysis.

STEP 8: The Completed Pivot Table

➤ The pivot table has been modified as shown in Figure 1.14g. Location is now the page field and Gender is the column field. This arrangement of the table makes it easy to see the number of male and female employees in each job classification in each location.

➤ Click the **down arrow** for the Location page field. Click **Atlanta** to display the job descriptions for just the Atlanta employees.

➤ Click the **down arrow** on the Location page field. Click **All** to view the data for all employees.

➤ Save the workbook. Print the completed workbook and submit it to your instructor. Exit Excel.

Refresh Data button

Change reflects 1 Account Rep and 1 Manager in Miami

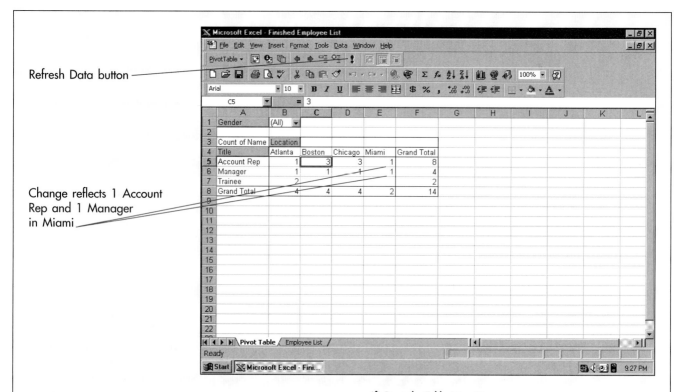

(f) Pivot the Table (step 7)

Drag Location to page area

Drag Gender to column area

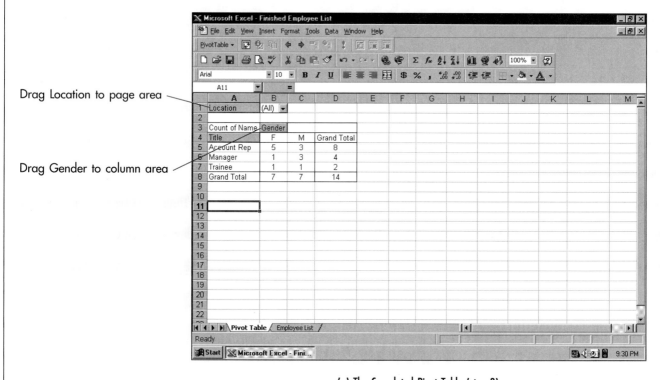

(g) The Completed Pivot Table (step 8)

FIGURE 1.14   Hands-on Exercise 3 (continued)

A list is an area in a worksheet that contains rows of similar data. The first row in the list contains the column labels (field names). Each additional row contains data for a specific record. A data form provides an easy way to add, edit, and delete records in a list.

A date is stored internally as an integer number corresponding to the number of days in this century. (January 1, 1900 is stored as the number 1.) The number of elapsed days between two dates can be determined by simple subtraction. The TODAY function always returns the current date (the date on which a worksheet is created or retrieved).

Data and information are not synonymous. Data refers to a fact or facts about a specific record, such as an employee's name, title, or salary. Information is data that has been rearranged into a form perceived as useful by the recipient.

A filtered list displays only those records that meet specific criteria. Filtering is implemented through AutoFilter or the Advanced Filter command. The latter enables you to specify a criteria range and to copy the selected records elsewhere in the worksheet.

The Sort command arranges a list according to the value of one or more keys (known as the primary, secondary, and tertiary keys). Each key may be in ascending or descending sequence.

The database functions (DSUM, DAVERAGE, DMAX, DMIN, and DCOUNT) have three arguments: the associated list, the field name, and the criteria range. The simplest criteria range consists of two rows and as many fields as there are in the list.

The Subtotals command inserts subtotals (based on a variety of functions) into a list. A list should be sorted prior to execution of the Subtotals command.

A pivot table extends the capability of individual database functions by presenting the data in summary form. It divides the records in a list into categories, then computes summary statistics for those categories. Pivot tables provide the utmost flexibility in that you can vary the row or column categories and/or the way that the statistics are computed.

KEY WORDS AND CONCEPTS

Advanced Filter command	DSUM function	Name command
Ascending sequence	Field	Pivot table
AutoFilter command	Field name	PivotTable Wizard
Criteria range	File	Primary key
Data	File maintenance	Record
Data form	Filtered list	Secondary key
Database functions	Form command	Sort command
DAVERAGE function	Information	Subtotals command
DCOUNT function	Insert Columns command	SUBTOTAL function
Delete command	Insert Rows command	Tertiary key
Descending sequence	Key	TODAY( ) function
DMAX function	List	Wild card
DMIN function	Name box	

MULTIPLE CHOICE

1. Which of the following describes the implementation of data management in Excel?
   (a) The rows in a list correspond to records in a file
   (b) The columns in a list correspond to fields in a record
   (c) Both (a) and (b)
   (d) Neither (a) nor (b)

2. Which of the following is suggested for the placement of a list within a worksheet?
   (a) There should be at least one blank row between the list and the other entries in the worksheet
   (b) There should be at least one blank column between the list and the other entries in the worksheet
   (c) Both (a) and (b)
   (d) Neither (a) nor (b)

3. Which of the following is suggested for the placement of database functions within a worksheet?
   (a) Above or below the list with at least one blank row separating the database functions from the list to which they refer
   (b) To the left or right of the list with at least one blank column separating the database functions from the list to which they refer
   (c) Both (a) and (b)
   (d) Neither (a) nor (b)

4. Assume that cells A21:B22 have been defined as the criteria range, that cells A21 and B21 contain the field names City and Title, respectively, and that cells A22 and B22 contain New York and Manager. The selected records will consist of:
   (a) All employees in New York, regardless of title
   (b) All managers, regardless of the city
   (c) Only the managers in New York
   (d) All employees in New York (regardless of title) or all managers (regardless of city)

5. Assume that cells A21:B23 have been defined as the criteria range, that cells A21 and B21 contain the field names City and Title, respectively, and that cells A22 and B23 contain New York and Manager, respectively. The selected records will consist of:
   (a) All employees in New York regardless of title
   (b) All managers regardless of the city
   (c) Only the managers in New York
   (d) All employees in New York (regardless of title) or all managers (regardless of city)

6. If employees are to be listed so that all employees in the same city appear together in alphabetical order by the employee's last name:
   (a) City and last name are both considered to be the primary key
   (b) City and last name are both considered to be the secondary key
   (c) City is the primary key and last name is the secondary key
   (d) Last name is the primary key and city is the secondary key

7. Which of the following can be used to delete a record from a database?
   (a) The Edit Delete command
   (b) The Data Form command
   (c) Both (a) and (b)
   (d) Neither (a) nor (b)

8. Which of the following is true about the DAVERAGE function?
   (a) It has a single argument
   (b) It can be entered into a worksheet using the Function Wizard
   (c) Both (a) and (b)
   (d) Neither (a) nor (b)

9. The Name box can be used to:
   (a) Define a range name
   (b) Select the range
   (c) Both (a) and (b)
   (d) Neither (a) nor (b)

10. Which of the following is recommended to distinguish the first row in a list (the field names) from the remaining entries (the data)?
    (a) Insert a blank row between the first row and the remaining rows
    (b) Insert a row of dashes between the first row and the remaining rows
    (c) Either (a) or (b)
    (d) Neither (a) nor (b)

11. The AutoFilter command:
    (a) Permanently deletes records from the associated list
    (b) Requires the specification of a criteria range elsewhere in the worksheet
    (c) Either (a) or (b)
    (d) Neither (a) nor (b)

12. Which of the following is true of the Sort command?
    (a) The primary key must be in ascending sequence
    (b) The secondary key must be in descending sequence
    (c) Both (a) and (b)
    (d) Neither (a) nor (b)

13. What is the best way to enter January 21, 1996 into a worksheet, given that you create the worksheet on that date, and further, that you always want to display that specific date?
    (a) =TODAY()
    (b) 1/21/96
    (c) Both (b) and (b) are equally acceptable
    (d) Neither (a) nor (b)

14. Which of the following best describes the relationship between the Sort and Subtotals commands?
    (a) The Sort command should be executed before the Subtotals command
    (b) The Subtotals command should be executed before the Sort command
    (c) The commands can be executed in either sequence
    (d) There is no relationship because the commands have nothing to do with one another

15. Which of the following changes may be implemented in an existing pivot table?

(a) A row field may be added or deleted
(b) A column field may be added or deleted
(c) Both (a) and (b)
(d) Neither (a) nor (b)

ANSWERS

1. c	**6.** c	**11.** d
2. c	**7.** c	**12.** d
3. a	**8.** b	**13.** b
4. c	**9.** c	**14.** a
5. d	**10.** d	**15.** c

PRACTICE WITH EXCEL 97

1. Figure 1.15 displays the *Volume II Chapter 1 Practice 1* workbook as it exists on the data disk. Open the workbook, then implement the following changes:
   a. Delete the record for Julie Rubin, who has dropped out of school.
   b. Change the data in Rick Fegin's record to show 193 quality points.
   c. Use the Data Form command to add a transfer student, Jimmy Flynn, majoring in Engineering. Jimmy has completed 65 credits and has 200 quality points. Use the Tab key to move from one field to the next within the data form; be sure to enter the data in the appropriate text boxes. You cannot enter Jimmy's GPA as it will be computed automatically.
   d. Sort the list so that the students are listed in alphabetical order. Specify last name and first name as the primary and secondary keys, respectively.
   e. Create the Dean's List by using the Advanced Filter command to copy the qualified students (those with a GPA > 3.20) to cells A22 through F27. Use A19:F20 as the criteria range.
   f. Create the list of students on academic probation by using the Advanced Filter command to copy the selected students (those with a GPA < 2.00) to cells A33 through F40. Use A30:F31 as the criteria range for this Advanced Filter command.
   g. Add your name as the academic advisor in cell C1. Print the worksheet two ways, with displayed values and cell formulas, and submit both to your instructor.

2. A partially completed version of the worksheet in Figure 1.16 can be found in the *Volume II Chapter 1 Practice 2* workbook on the data disk. Open the workbook, then develop the necessary formulas so that your workbook matches the completed version.

   Realize, however, that the displayed values on your worksheet will be different from those displayed in the figure in that you are making the calculations on a different day. Thus, when you retrieve the workbook, the entry in cell B1 will reflect the current date, rather than the date in the figure. Other numbers, such as the days to maturity and the indication of whether a CD has matured, will change as well.

	A	B	C	D	E	F
1	Academic Advisor:					
2						
3	Last Name	First Name	Major	Quality Points	Credits	GPA
4	Moldof	Alan	Engineering	60	20	3.00
5	Stutz	Joel	Engineering	180	75	2.40
6	Rubin	Julie	Liberal Arts	140	65	2.15
7	Milgrom	Richard	Liberal Arts	400	117	3.42
8	Grauer	Jessica	Liberal Arts	96	28	3.43
9	Moldof	Adam	Business	160	84	1.90
10	Grauer	Benjamin	Business	190	61	3.11
11	Rudolph	Eleanor	Liberal Arts	185	95	1.95
12	Ford	Judd	Engineering	206	72	2.86
13	Fegin	Rick	Communications	190	64	2.97
14	Flynn	Sean	Business	90	47	1.91
15	Coulter	Maryann	Liberal Arts	135	54	2.50
16						
17						
18	The Dean's List					
19	Last Name	First Name	Major	Quality Points	Credits	GPA
20						
21						
22	Last Name	First Name	Major	Quality Points	Credits	GPA
23						
24						
25						
26						
27						
28						
29	Academic Probation					
30	Last Name	First Name	Major	Quality Points	Credits	GPA
31						
32						
33	Last Name	First Name	Major	Quality Points	Credits	GPA
34						
35						
36						
37						
38						
39						
40						

FIGURE 1.15   Spreadsheet for Practice Exercise 1

	A	B	C	D	E	F
1	Date:	7/30/97				
2						
3			Certificates of Deposit			
4			First National Bank of Miami			
5						
6	Customer	Amount of CD	Date Purchased	Duration	Maturity Date	# Days Remaining Til Mature
7	Harris	$500,000	4/15/97	180	10/12/97	74
8	Bodden	$50,000	1/5/97	180	7/4/97	Mature
9	Dorsey	$25,000	7/18/97	180	1/14/98	168
10	Rosell	$10,000	8/1/96	365	8/1/97	2
11	Klinger	$10,000	5/31/97	365	5/31/98	305

FIGURE 1.16   Spreadsheet for Practice Exercise 2

Completion of the workbook reviews material from earlier chapters, specifically the use of relative and absolute addressing, and the IF function to determine the maturity status. The determination of whether or not the CD has matured can be made by comparing the Maturity date to the current date; that is, if the Maturity date is greater than the current date, the CD has not yet matured.

The workbook on the data disk is unformatted, so you will have to add formatting. Be sure to add your name to the worksheet as a bank officer. Print the worksheet two ways, with displayed values and cell formulas, and submit both to your instructor.

3. Figure 1.17 is a revised version of the employee list that was used throughout the chapter. A field has been added for an employee's previous salary as well as two additional fields for computations based on the previous salary. A partially completed version of this worksheet can be found on the data disk as *Volume II Chapter 1 Practice 3*.

   The employees in the workbook on the data disk appear in a different sequence from the list in Figure 1.17. Hence, when you open the workbook, you must first determine the proper sequence in which to sort the employees. Note, too, that the recently hired employees do not have a previous salary, and thus the formulas to compute the amount of the salary increase and the associated percent salary increase must first determine if the employee actually had an increase. (You can suppress zero values in a spreadsheet through the View tab in the Options command of the Tools menu.) The summary statistics at the bottom of the worksheet reflect only those employees who actually had an increase.

   Complete the workbook on the data disk so that it matches Figure 1.17. Add your name somewhere in the workbook as compensation analyst. Print the cell formulas as well as the displayed values and submit both to your instructor.

	A	B	C	D	E	F	G	Previous H	I	J
	Name	Location	Title	Gender	Service	Hire Date	Salary	Previous Salary	Increase	Percentage
1	Johnson	Chicago	Account Rep	M	4.7	10/31/90	$47,500	$40,000	$7,500	18.75%
2	Rubin	Boston	Account Rep	F	3.4	3/16/92	$45,000	$40,000	$5,000	12.50%
3	Coulter	Atlanta	Manager	M	1.7	11/24/93	$100,000	$90,000	$10,000	11.11%
4	Manin	Boston	Account Rep	F	3.4	3/16/92	$49,500	$45,000	$4,500	10.00%
5	Marder	Chicago	Account Rep	F	3.7	10/31/91	$38,500	$35,000	$3,500	10.00%
6	Elofson	Miami	Account Rep	F	2.7	10/31/92	$47,500	$45,000	$2,500	5.56%
7	Gillenson	Miami	Account Rep	M	1.7	10/31/93	$55,000	$52,500	$2,500	4.76%
8	Milgrom	Boston	Manager	M	3.4	3/16/92	$57,500	$55,000	$2,500	4.55%
9	James	Chicago	Account Rep	F	5.7	10/31/89	$42,500	$41,000	$1,500	3.66%
10	Adams	Atlanta	Trainee	M	1.7	11/24/93	$19,500			
11	Brown	Atlanta	Trainee	F	1.7	11/24/93	$18,500			
12	Smith	Atlanta	Account Rep	M	1.7	11/24/93	$65,000			
13	Charles	Boston	Account Rep	M	3.4	3/16/92	$40,000			
14	Adamson	Chicago	Manager	F	3.4	3/16/92	$52,000			
15										
16	Name	Location	Title	Gender	Service	Hire Date	Salary	Previous Salary	Increase	Percentage
17								>0		
18										
19										
20										
21						Evaluation of Salary Increase				
22						Average Increase		$4,389	8.99%	
23						Maximum Increase		$10,000	18.75%	
24						Minimum Increase		$1,500	3.66%	
25						Number of Employees		9	9	

FIGURE 1.17   Spreadsheet for Practice Exercise 3

4. The compound document in Figure 1.18 consists of a memo created in Microsoft Word and a modified version of the pivot table created in the third hands-on exercise. The document was created in such a way that any change in the worksheet will be automatically reflected in the memo.

We want you to create the compound document and submit it to your instructor. You will have to return to the pivot table at the end of the third hands-on exercise in order to modify the table so that it matches Figure 1.18. (Don't forget to format the table.) Then you will have to open Microsoft Word in order to create the memo, and finally you will have to link the worksheet to the memo. *Print this version of the memo and submit it to your instructor.*

Prove to yourself that Object Linking and Embedding really works by returning to the Excel worksheet *after* you have created the document in Figure 1.18. Change Milgrom's salary in cell G12 to $75,000, then refresh the pivot table in the Excel workbook. Switch back to the Word memo, and the pivot table should reflect the adjusted salary (the total of all salaries should be $695,500). Add a postscript to the memo indicating that this reflects Milgrom's revised salary, then print the revised memo and submit it to your instructor with the earlier version.

Soleil Shoes

Italy, London, Madrid

Dear John,

Enclosed please find the salary analysis you requested last Friday. I have broken down the salaries by title and location.

Sum of Salary	Location				
Title	Atlanta	Boston	Chicago	Miami	Grand Total
Account Rep	$65,000	$134,500	$128,500	$47,500	$375,500
Manager	$100,000	$57,500	$52,000	$55,000	$264,500
Trainee	$38,000	$0	$0	$0	$38,000
Grand Total	$203,000	$192,000	$180,500	$102,500	$678,000

I noticed that the manager in Atlanta is paid disproportionately well compared to his counterparts in the other cities. Let me know if you need any other information.

Bob

FIGURE 1.18 Compound Document for Practice Exercise 4

5. The compound document in Figure 1.19 is based on the completed workbook of problem 1. Do the problem (as described on page 46), then sort the list by major (and student name within major), so that you can use the Subtotals command to compute the average GPA for each major. Use OLE to create a compound document similar to the one in Figure 1.19. Enter your name as the academic advisor so that your instructor knows the assignment came from you.

University of Miami

Academic Advisement Office

To: James Foley
        Associate Dean

From: Joan Rhyne
        Academic Advisor

Subject: Grade Point Averages

Below please find the data that you requested. I have grouped the students by major and determined the average GPA for each major, as well as the average GPA for all students.

Last Name	First Name	Major	Quality Points	Credits	GPA
Flynn	Sean	Business	90	47	1.91
Grauer	Benjamin	Business	190	61	3.11
Moldof	Adam	Business	160	84	1.90
		Business Average			2.31
Fegin	Rick	Communications	193	64	3.02
		Communications Average			3.02
Flynn	Jimmy	Engineering	200	65	3.08
Ford	Judd	Engineering	206	72	2.86
Moldof	Alan	Engineering	60	20	3.00
Stutz	Joel	Engineering	180	75	2.40
		Engineering Average			2.83
Coulter	Maryann	Liberal Arts	135	54	2.50
Grauer	Jessica	Liberal Arts	96	28	3.43
Milgrom	Richard	Liberal Arts	400	117	3.42
Rudolph	Eleanor	Liberal Arts	185	95	1.95
		Liberal Arts Average			2.82
		Grand Average			2.72

I hope that you find this information useful. If you have any questions, please do not hesitate to let me know. It will be easy for me to determine almost any statistic that you may want.

FIGURE 1.19   Document for Practice Exercise 5

CASE STUDIES

The United States of America

What is the total population of the United States? What is its area? Can you name the 13 original states or the last five states admitted to the Union? Do you know the 10 states with the highest population or the five largest states in terms of area? Which states have the highest population density (people per square mile)?

The answers to these and other questions are readily available provided you can analyze the data in the *United States* workbook that is available on the data disk. This assignment is completely open-ended and requires only that you print out the extracted data in a report on the United States database. Format the reports so that they are attractive and informative.

The Super Bowl

How many times has the National Football Conference (NFC) won the Super Bowl? When was the last time the American Football Conference (AFC) won? What was the largest margin of victory? What was the closest game? What is the most points scored by two teams in one game? How many times have the Miami Dolphins appeared? How many times did they win? Use the data in the *Super Bowl* workbook to prepare a trivia sheet on the Super Bowl, then incorporate your analysis into a letter addressed to your instructor. Go to the NFL home page (www.nfl.com) to update our workbook to reflect the most recent game.

Personnel Management

You have been hired as the Personnel Director for a medium-sized firm (500 employees) and are expected to implement a system to track employee compensation. You want to be able to calculate the age of every employee as well as their length of service. You want to know each employee's most recent performance evaluation. You want to calculate the amount of the most recent salary increase, in dollars as well as a percentage of the previous salary. You also want to know how long the employee had to wait for that increase—that is, how much time elapsed between the present and previous salary.

Design a worksheet capable of providing this information. Enter test data for at least five employees to check the accuracy of your formulas. Format the worksheet so that it is attractive and easy to read.

Equal Employment Opportunity

Are you paying your employees fairly? Is there any difference between the salaries paid to men and women? Between minorities and nonminorities? Between minorities of one ethnic background and those of another ethnic background? Use the *Equal Employment* workbook on the data disk to analyze the data for the current employees. Are there any other factors not included in the database that might reasonably be expected to influence an employee's compensation? Write up your findings in the form of a memo to the Vice President for Human Resources.

The Year 2000 Problem

Some forecasts estimate that American business will spend hundreds of millions (perhaps billions) of dollars to modify existing computer systems to accommodate the year 2000. Is this a realistic estimate, and if so, does it affect spreadsheets that run on PCs, or is it restricted to systems running on mainframe computers? Use your favorite search engine to see what you can learn about this very timely topic. Summarize your findings in a report to your instructor, with emphasis on the effects on the PC.

Data Validation

The best way to ensure that a workbook contains only valid data is to check the data as it is entered and reject any inappropriate values. Use the Excel Help menu to search for data validation to determine what (if any) capability is built into Excel. Is it possible, for example, to prevent a user from entering an invalid location or title in the Employee workbook that was used throughout the chapter? Summarize your findings in a brief note to your instructor. Better yet, take the final version of the Employee workbook (as it existed at the end of the last hands-on exercise) and incorporate any data validation you deem appropriate.

CONSOLIDATING DATA: 3-D WORKBOOKS AND FILE LINKING

2

OBJECTIVES

After reading this chapter you will be able to:

1. Distinguish between a cell reference, a worksheet reference, and a 3-D reference; use appropriate references to consolidate data from multiple worksheets within a workbook.

2. Select and group multiple worksheets in order to enter common formulas and/or formats.

3. Explain the advantage of using a function rather than a formula when consolidating data from multiple worksheets.

4. Explain the importance of properly organizing and documenting a workbook.

5. Use the Copy and Paste commands to copy selected data to a second workbook; copy an entire worksheet by dragging its tab from one workbook to another.

6. Distinguish between a source workbook and a dependent workbook; create external references to link workbooks to one another.

OVERVIEW

This chapter considers the problem of combining data from different sources into a summary report. Assume, for example, that you are the marketing manager for a national corporation with offices in several cities. Each branch manager reports to you on a quarterly basis, providing information about each product sold in his or her office. Your job is to consolidate the data from the individual offices into a single report.

The situation is depicted graphically in Figure 2.1. Figures 2.1a, 2.1b, and 2.1c show reports for the Atlanta, Boston, and Chicago offices, respectively. Figure 2.1d shows the summary report for the corporation.

Atlanta Office

	Qtr 1	Qtr 2	Qtr 3	Qtr 4
Product 1	$10	$20	$30	$40
Product 2	$1,100	$1,200	$1,300	$1,400
Product 3	$200	$200	$300	$400

(a)

Boston Office

	Qtr 1	Qtr 2	Qtr 3	Qtr 4
Product 1	$55	$25	$35	$45
Product 2	$150	$250	$350	$450
Product 3	$1,150	$1,250	$1,350	$1,400

(b)

Chicago Office

	Qtr 1	Qtr 2	Qtr 3	Qtr 4
Product 1	$850	$950	$1,050	$1,150
Product 2	$100	$0	$300	$400
Product 3	$75	$150	$100	$200

(c)

Corporate Totals

	Qtr 1	Qtr 2	Qtr 3	Qtr 4
Product 1	$915	$995	$1,115	$1,235
Product 2	$1,350	$1,450	$1,950	$2,250
Product 3	$1,425	$1,600	$1,750	$2,000

(d)

FIGURE 2.1   Consolidating Data

You should be able to reconcile the corporate totals for each product in each quarter with the detail amounts in the individual offices. Consider, for example, the sales of Product 1 in the first quarter. The Atlanta office has sold $10, the Boston office $55, and the Chicago office $850; thus, the corporation as a whole has sold $915 ($10+$55+$850). In similar fashion, the Atlanta, Boston, and Chicago offices have sold $1,100, $150, and $100, respectively, of Product 2 in the first quarter, for a corporate total of $1,350.

The chapter presents two approaches to computing the corporate totals in Figure 2.1. One approach is to use the three-dimensional capability within Excel, in which one workbook contains multiple worksheets. The workbook contains a separate worksheet for each of the three branch offices, and a fourth worksheet to hold the corporate data. An alternate technique is to keep the data for each branch office in its own workbook, then create a summary workbook that uses file linking to reference cells in the other workbooks.

There are advantages and disadvantages to each technique, as will be discussed in the chapter. As always, the hands-on exercises are essential to mastering the conceptual material.

THE THREE-DIMENSIONAL WORKBOOK

An Excel workbook is the electronic equivalent of the three-ring binder. It contains one or more worksheets, each of which is identified by a tab at the bottom of the document window. The workbook in Figure 2.2, for example, contains four worksheets. The title bar displays the name of the workbook (Corporate Sales).

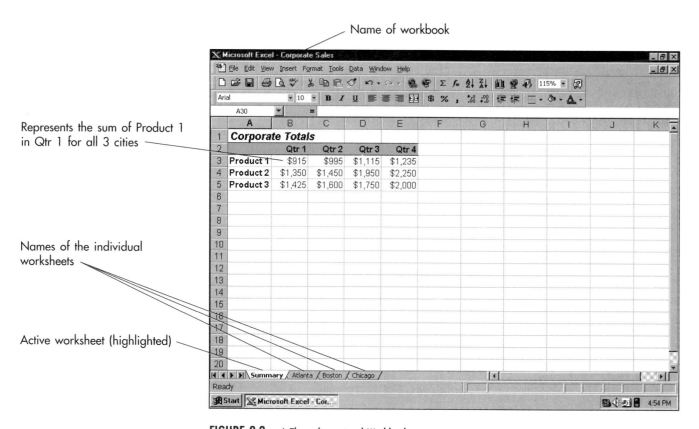

FIGURE 2.2 A Three-dimensional Workbook

The tabs at the bottom of the workbook window display the names of the individual worksheets (Summary, Atlanta, Boston, and Chicago). The highlighted tab indicates the name of the active worksheet (Summary). To display a different worksheet, click on a different tab; for example, click the Atlanta tab to display the Atlanta worksheet.

The Summary worksheet shows the total amount for each product in each quarter. The data in the worksheet reflects the amounts shown earlier in Figure 2.1; that is, each entry in the Summary worksheet represents the sum of the corresponding entries in the worksheets for the individual cities. The amounts in the individual cities, however, are not visible in Figure 2.2. It is convenient, therefore, to open multiple windows in order to view the individual city worksheets at the same time you view the summary sheet.

Figure 2.3 displays the four worksheets in the Corporate Sales workbook, with a different sheet displayed in each window. The individual windows are smaller than the single view in Figure 2.2, but you can see at a glance how the Summary worksheet consolidates the data from the individual worksheets. The *New Window command* (in the Window menu) is used to open each additional window. Once the windows have been opened, the *Arrange command* (in the Window menu) is used to tile or cascade the open windows.

Only one window can be active at a time, and all commands apply to just the active window. In Figure 2.3, for example, the window in the upper left is active, as can be seen by the highlighted title bar. (To activate a different window, just click in that window.)

Copying Worksheets

The workbook in Figure 2.3 summarizes the data in the individual worksheets, but how was the data placed in the workbook? You could, of course, manually type

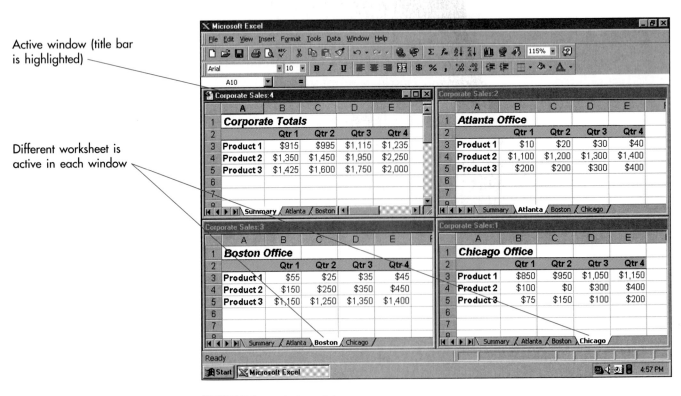

Active window (title bar is highlighted)

Different worksheet is active in each window

FIGURE 2.3   Multiple Worksheets

in the entries, but there is an easier way, given that each branch manager sends you a workbook with the data for his or her office. All you have to do is copy the data from the individual workbooks into the appropriate worksheets in a new corporate workbook. (The specifics for how this is done are explained in detail in a hands-on exercise.)

Consider now Figure 2.4, which at first glance appears almost identical to Figure 2.3. The two figures are very different, however. Figure 2.3 displayed four different worksheets from the same workbook. Figure 2.4, on the other hand, displays four different workbooks. There is one workbook for each city (Atlanta, Boston, and Chicago) and each of these workbooks contains only a single worksheet. The fourth workbook, Corporate Sales, contains four worksheets (Atlanta, Boston, Chicago, and Summary) and is the workbook displayed in Figure 2.3.

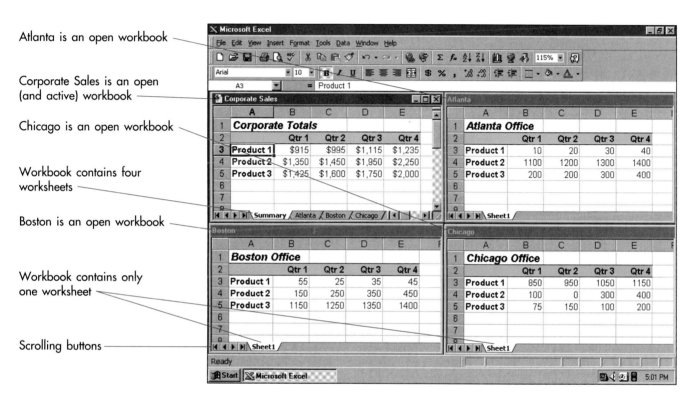

FIGURE 2.4   Multiple Workbooks

THE HORIZONTAL SCROLL BAR

The horizontal scroll bar contains four scrolling buttons to scroll through the worksheet tabs in a workbook. (The default workbook has three worksheets.) Click ◄ or ► to scroll one tab to the left or right. Click I◄ or ►I to scroll to the first or last tab in the workbook. Once the desired tab is visible, click the tab to select it. The number of tabs that are visible simultaneously depends on the setting of the horizontal scroll bar; that is, you can drag the tab split bar to change the number of tabs that can be seen at one time.

Objective: To open multiple workbooks; to use the Windows Arrange command to tile the open workbooks; to copy a worksheet from one workbook to another. Use Figure 2.5 as a guide in the exercise.

STEP 1: Open a New Workbook

➤ Start Excel. If necessary, click the **New button** on the Standard toolbar to open a new workbook.

➤ Delete all worksheets except for Sheet1:

- Click the tab for **Sheet2.** Press the **Shift key** as you click the tab for **Sheet3.** (Sheets 2 and 3 should be selected and their worksheet tabs appear in white.)

- Point to the tab for **Sheet3** and click the **right mouse button** to display a shortcut menu. Click **Delete.** Click **OK** in response to the warning that the selected sheets will be permanently deleted.

➤ The workbook should contain only Sheet1 as shown in Figure 2.5a. Save the workbook as **Corporate Sales** in the **Exploring Excel folder.**

THE DEFAULT WORKBOOK

A new workbook contains three worksheets, but you can change the default value to any number. Pull down the Tools menu, click Options, then click the General tab. Click the up (down) arrow in the Sheets in New Workbook text box to enter a new default value, then click OK to exit the Options dialog box and continue working. The next time you open a new workbook, it will contain the new number of worksheets.

STEP 2: Open the Individual Workbooks

➤ Pull down the **File menu.** Click **Open** to display the Open dialog box as shown in Figure 2.5a. (If necessary, open the Exploring Excel folder.)

➤ Click the **Atlanta workbook,** then press and hold the **Ctrl key** as you click the **Boston** and **Chicago workbooks** to select all three workbooks at the same time.

➤ Click **Open** to open the selected workbooks. The workbooks will be opened one after another with a brief message appearing on the status bar as each workbook is opened.

➤ Pull down the **Window menu,** which should indicate the four open workbooks at the bottom of the menu. Only the Chicago workbook is visible at this time.

➤ Click **Arrange** to display the Arrange Windows dialog box. If necessary, select the Tiled option, then click **OK.** You should see four open workbooks as shown in Figure 2.5b. (Do not be concerned if your workbooks are arranged differently from ours.)

Click to select Atlanta
workbook

Press Ctrl as you click
to select Boston and
Chicago workbooks

Sheets 2 and 3
have been deleted

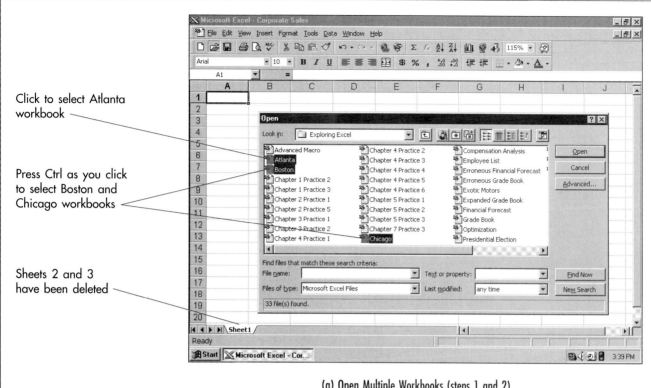

(a) Open Multiple Workbooks (steps 1 and 2)

A different workbook is
open in each window

Scrolling buttons

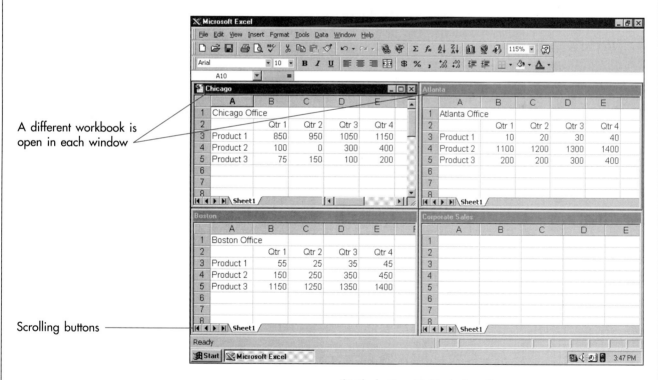

(b) Tile the Open Workbooks (step 2)

FIGURE 2.5 Hands-on Exercise 1

THE XLS EXTENSION—NOW YOU SEE IT, NOW YOU DON'T

Long-time DOS users will recognize a three-character extension at the end of a filename to indicate the file type. XLS, for example, indicates an Excel workbook. The extension is displayed or hidden in the application's title bar (and in the Open and Save dialog boxes) according to an option in the View menu of My Computer or the Windows Explorer. We suggest you hide the extension if it is currently visible. Open either My Computer or the Explorer, pull down the View menu, click the Options command, click the View tab, then check the box to hide MS-DOS file extensions. Click OK to accept the setting and exit the dialog box. The next time you open a workbook, the title bar will display the name of the workbook, but not the XLS extension.

STEP 3: Copy the Atlanta Data

➤ Click in the **Atlanta workbook** to make it the active workbook. Reduce the column widths (if necessary) so that you can see the entire worksheet in the window.

➤ Click and drag to select **cells A1** through **E5** as shown in Figure 2.5c. Pull down the **Edit menu** and click **Copy** (or click the **Copy button** on the Standard toolbar).

➤ Click the **Corporate Sales** workbook to activate it, then click in cell **A1**.

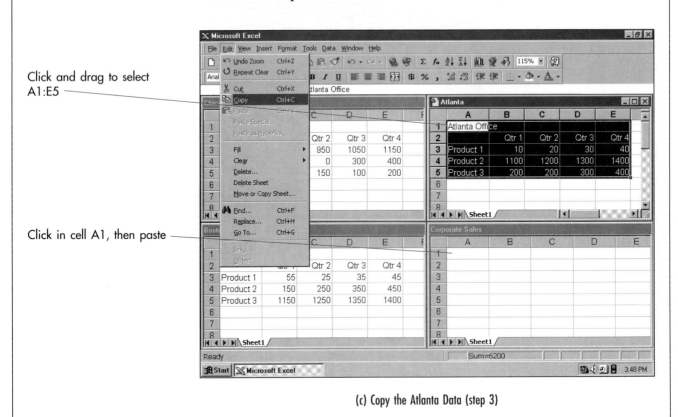

(c) Copy the Atlanta Data (step 3)

FIGURE 2.5   Hands-on Exercise 1 (continued)

➤ Click the **Paste button** on the Standard toolbar to copy the Atlanta data into this workbook. Press **Esc** to remove the moving border from the copy range.

➤ Point to the **Sheet1 tab** at the bottom of the Corporate Sales worksheet window, then click the **right mouse button** to produce a shortcut menu. Click **Rename,** which selects the worksheet name.

➤ Type **Atlanta** to replace the existing name and press **enter.** The worksheet tab has been changed from Sheet1 to Atlanta.

➤ Click the **Save button** to save the active workbook (Corporate Sales).

RENAMING A WORKSHEET

The fastest way to rename a worksheet is to double click the worksheet tab, which automatically selects the current worksheet name. Type the new name for the worksheet, then press the enter key.

STEP 4: Copy the Boston and Chicago Data (a Shortcut)

➤ Click in the **Boston workbook** to make it the active workbook as shown in Figure 2.5d.

➤ Click the **Sheet1 tab,** then press and hold the **Ctrl key** as you drag the tab to the right of the Atlanta tab in the Corporate Sales workbook. You will see a tiny spreadsheet with a plus sign as you drag the tab. The plus sign indicates

Click in window to make Boston the active workbook

Click the Sheet1 tab, press Ctrl as you drag the tab to the right of the Atlanta tab in the Corporate Sales workbook

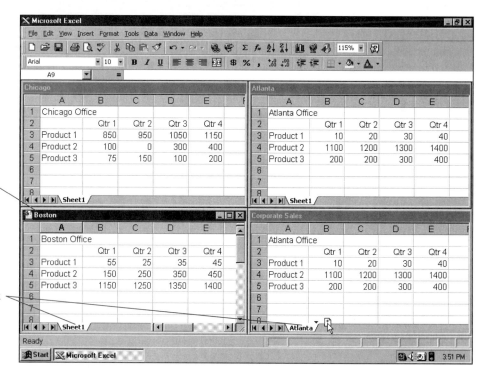

(d) A Shortcut (step 4)

FIGURE 2.5   Hands-on Exercise 1 (continued)

that the worksheet is being copied; the ▼ symbol indicates where the worksheet will be placed.

➤ Release the mouse, then release the Ctrl key. The worksheet from the Boston workbook should have been copied to the Corporate Sales workbook and appears as Sheet1 in that workbook.

➤ The Boston workbook should still be open; if it isn't, it means that you did not press the Ctrl key as you were dragging the tab to copy the worksheet. If this is the case, pull down the **File menu,** reopen the Boston workbook, and if necessary, tile the open windows.

➤ Double click the **Sheet1 tab** in the Corporate Sales workbook in order to rename the tab. Type **Boston** as the new name, then press the **enter key.**

➤ The Boston worksheet should appear to the right of the Atlanta worksheet; if the worksheet appears to the left of Atlanta, click and drag the tab to its desired position. (The ▼ symbol indicates where the worksheet will be placed.)

➤ Repeat the previous steps to copy the Chicago data to the Corporate Sales workbook, placing the new sheet to the right of the Boston sheet. Rename the copied worksheet **Chicago.** Remember, you must click in the window containing the Chicago workbook to activate the window before you can copy the worksheet.

➤ Save the Corporate Sales workbook. (The Summary worksheet will be built in the next exercise.)

MOVING AND COPYING WORKSHEETS

You can move or copy a worksheet within a workbook by dragging its tab. To move a worksheet, click its tab, then drag the tab to the new location (a black triangle shows where the new sheet will go). To copy a worksheet, click its tab, then press and hold the Ctrl key as you drag the tab to its new location. The copied worksheet will have the same name as the original worksheet, followed by a number in parentheses indicating the copy number.

STEP 5: Print the Corporate Sales Workbook

➤ Check that the Corporate Sales workbook is the active workbook. Click the **Maximize button** so that this workbook takes the entire screen.

➤ The Corporate Sales workbook contains three worksheets. Click the **Atlanta tab** to display the worksheet for Atlanta. Click the **Boston tab** to display the worksheet for Boston. Click the **Chicago tab** to display the worksheet for Chicago.

➤ Pull down the **File menu.** Click **Print.** Click the **Entire Workbook option button** as shown in Figure 2.5e. Click **OK** to print the workbook.

➤ Close the open workbooks, saving changes if requested to do so. Exit Excel if you do not want to continue with the next exercise at this time.

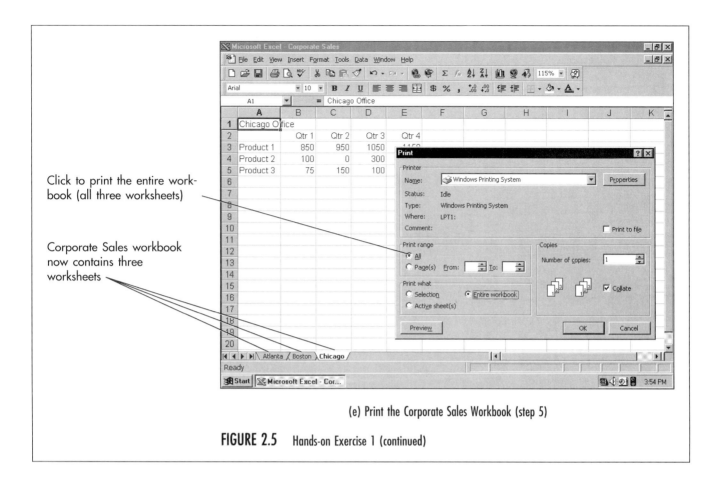

Click to print the entire work-book (all three worksheets)

Corporate Sales workbook now contains three worksheets

(e) Print the Corporate Sales Workbook (step 5)

FIGURE 2.5   Hands-on Exercise 1 (continued)

WORKSHEET REFERENCES

The presence of multiple worksheets in a workbook creates an additional require-ment for cell references. You continue to use the same row and column conven-tion when you reference a cell on the current worksheet; that is, cell A1 is still A1. What if, however, you want to reference a cell on another worksheet within the same workbook? It is no longer sufficient to refer to cell A1 because every worksheet has its own cell A1.

To reference a cell (or cell range) in a worksheet other than the current (active) worksheet, you need to preface the cell address with a ***worksheet refer-ence;*** for example, Atlanta!A1 references cell A1 in the Atlanta worksheet. A worksheet reference may also be used in conjunction with a cell range—for exam-ple, Summary!B2:E5 to reference cells B2 through E5 on the Summary worksheet. Omission of the worksheet reference in either example defaults to the cell refer-ence in the active worksheet.

An exclamation point separates the worksheet reference from the cell reference. The worksheet reference (e.g., Atlanta or Summary) remains constant (i.e., it is an absolute reference). The cell reference can be either relative (e.g., Atlanta!A1 or Summary!B2:E5) or absolute (e.g., Atlanta!$A$1 or Summary!$B$2:$E$5).

Consider how worksheet references are used in the Summary worksheet in Figure 2.6. Each entry in the Summary worksheet computes the sum of the corresponding cells in the Atlanta, Boston, and Chicago worksheets. The cell for-mula in cell B3, for example, would be entered as follows:

Worksheet reference

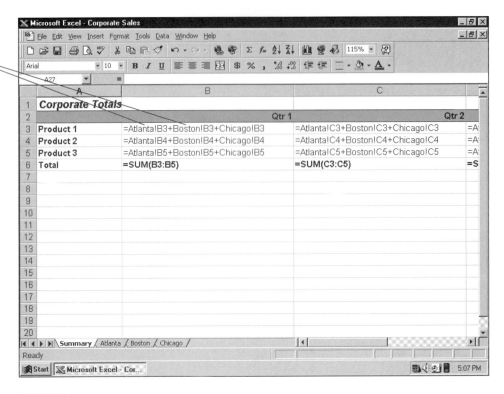

FIGURE 2.6   Worksheet References

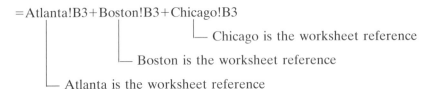

=Atlanta!B3+Boston!B3+Chicago!B3
└─ Chicago is the worksheet reference
└─ Boston is the worksheet reference
└─ Atlanta is the worksheet reference

The combination of relative cell references and constant worksheet references enables you to enter the formula once (in cell B3), then copy it to the remaining cells in the worksheet. In other words, you enter the formula in cell B3 to compute the total sales for Product 1 in Quarter 1, then you copy that formula to the other cells in row three (C3 through E3) to obtain the totals for Product 1 in Quarters 2, 3, and 4. You then copy the entire row (B3 through E3) to rows four and five (cells B4 through E5) to obtain the totals for Products 2 and 3 in all four quarters.

The proper use of relative and absolute references in the original formula in cell B3 is what makes it possible to copy the cell formulas. Consider, for example, the formula in cell C3 (which was copied from cell B3):

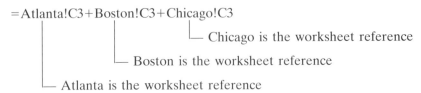

=Atlanta!C3+Boston!C3+Chicago!C3
└─ Chicago is the worksheet reference
└─ Boston is the worksheet reference
└─ Atlanta is the worksheet reference

The worksheet references remain absolute (e.g., Atlanta!) while the cell references adjust for the new location of the formula (cell C3). Similar adjustments are made in all of the other copied formulas.

3-D Reference

A *3-D reference* is a range that spans two or more worksheets in a workbook—for example, =SUM(Atlanta:Chicago!B3) to sum cell B3 in the Atlanta, Boston, and Chicago worksheets. The sheet range is specified with a colon between the beginning and ending sheets. An exclamation point follows the ending sheet, followed by the cell reference. The worksheet references are constant and will not change if the formula is copied. The cell reference may be relative or absolute.

Three-dimensional references can be used in the Summary worksheet as an alternative way to compute the corporate total for each product–quarter combination. To compute the corporate sales for Product 1 in Quarter 1 (which appears in cell B3 of the Summary worksheet), you would use the function:

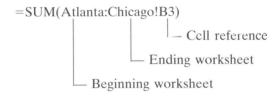

=SUM(Atlanta:Chicago!B3)
— Cell reference
— Ending worksheet
— Beginning worksheet

The 3-D reference includes all worksheets between the Atlanta and Chicago worksheets. (Only one additional worksheet, Boston, is present in the example, but the reference would automatically include any additional worksheets that were inserted between Atlanta and Chicago. In similar fashion, it would also adjust for the deletion of worksheets between Atlanta and Chicago.) Note, too, that the cell reference is relative and thus the formula can be copied from cell B3 in the Summary worksheet to the remaining cells in row 3 (C3 through E3). Those formulas can then be copied to the appropriate cells in rows 4 and 5.

A 3-D reference can be typed directly into a cell formula, but it is easier to enter the reference by pointing. Click in the cell that is to contain the 3-D reference, then enter an equal sign to begin the formula. To reference a cell in another worksheet, click the tab for the worksheet you want to reference, then click the cell or cell range you want to include in the formula.

FORMULAS VERSUS FUNCTIONS

Many worksheet calculations, such as an average or a sum, can be performed in one of two ways. You can either enter a formula—for example, =Atlanta!B3+Boston!B3+Chicago!B3—or you can use the equivalent function, =SUM(Atlanta:Chicago!B3). Functions are preferable in that they will adjust automatically for the deletion of existing worksheets or the insertion of new worksheets (within the existing range).

Grouping Worksheets

The worksheets in a workbook are often similar to one another in terms of content and/or formatting. In Figure 2.3, for example, the formatting is identical in all four worksheets of the workbook. You can format the worksheets individually or more easily through grouping.

Excel provides the capability for *grouping worksheets* in order to enter or format data in multiple worksheets at the same time. Once the worksheets are grouped, anything you do in one of the worksheets is automatically done to the other sheets in the group. You could, for example, group all of the worksheets together when you enter row and column labels, when you format data, or when you enter formulas to compute row and column totals. You must, however, ungroup the worksheets when you enter data in a specific worksheet. Grouping and ungrouping is illustrated in the following hands-on exercise.

HANDS-ON EXERCISE 2

3-D References

Objective: To use 3-D references to summarize data from multiple worksheets within a workbook; to group worksheets to enter common formatting and formulas; to open multiple windows to view several worksheets at the same time. Use Figure 2.7 as a guide in the exercise.

STEP 1: Insert a Worksheet

➤ Start Excel. Open the **Corporate Sales workbook** created in the previous exercise. The workbook contains three worksheets: Atlanta, Boston, and Chicago.

➤ Click the **Atlanta tab** to select this worksheet. Pull down the **Insert menu,** and click the **Worksheet command.** You should see a new worksheet, Sheet1, which is displayed on the screen and whose tab is to the left of the Atlanta tab.

➤ Double click the **tab** of the newly inserted worksheet to select the name. Type **Summary** and press **enter.** The name of the new worksheet has been changed to Summary.

➤ Save the workbook.

SHORTCUT MENUS

Shortcut menus provide an alternate (and generally faster) way to execute common commands. Point to a tab, then click the right mouse button to display a shortcut menu with commands to insert, delete, rename, move, or copy, or select all worksheets. Point to the desired command, then click the left mouse button to execute the command from the shortcut menu. Press the Esc key or click outside the menu to close the menu without executing the command.

STEP 2: The AutoFill Command

➤ Click in **cell A1** of the Summary worksheet. Type **Corporate Totals** as shown in Figure 2.7a.

➤ Click in **cell B2.** Enter **Qtr 1.** Click in **cell B2,** then point to the fill handle in the lower-right corner of cell B2. The mouse pointer changes to a thin crosshair.

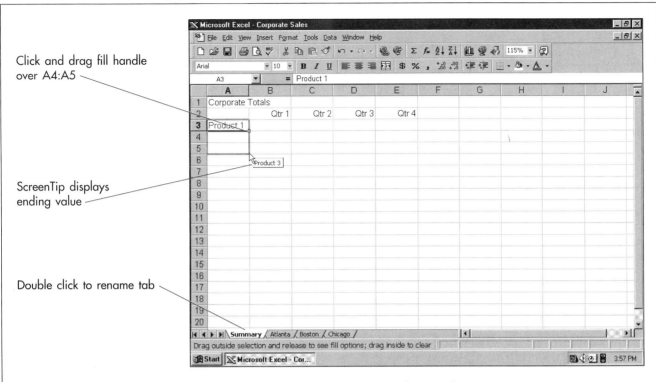

Click and drag fill handle over A4:A5

ScreenTip displays ending value

Double click to rename tab

(a) The AutoFill Command (step 2)

FIGURE 2.7 Hands-on Exercise 2

➤ Click and drag the fill handle over **cells C2, D2,** and **E2.** A border appears to indicate the destination range. Release the mouse. Cells C2 through E2 contain the labels Qtr 2, Qtr 3, and Qtr 4, respectively. Right align the column labels.

➤ Click in **cell A3.** Enter **Product 1.** Use the AutoFill capability to enter the labels **Product 2** and **Product 3** in cells A4 and A5.

THE AUTOFILL COMMAND

The AutoFill command is the fastest way to enter any type of series in adjacent cells. If, for example, you needed the months of the year in 12 successive cells, you would enter January (or Jan) in the first cell, then drag the fill handle over the next 11 cells in the direction you want to fill. If you need the days of the week, enter Monday (or Mon) and drag over the appropriate number of cells. You can also create a numeric series by entering the first two numbers in that series; for example, to enter the years 1990 through 1999, enter 1990 and 1991 in the first two cells, then select both cells and drag the fill handle.

STEP 3: Sum the Worksheets

➤ Click in **cell B3** of the Summary worksheet as shown in Figure 2.7b. Enter **=SUM(Atlanta:Chicago!B3),** then press the **enter key.** You should see 915

Undo button ——

Function entered in B3 ——

Click and drag fill handle
over C3:E3 to copy formula

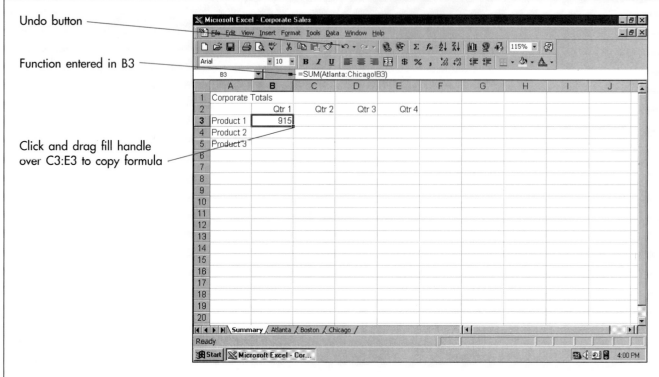

(b) Sum the Worksheets (step 3)

FIGURE 2.7 Hands-on Exercise 2 (continued)

as the sum of the sales for Product 1 in Quarter 1 for the three cities (Atlanta, Boston, and Chicago).

➤ Click the **Undo button** on the Standard toolbar to erase the function so that you can re-enter the function by using pointing.

➤ Check that you are in cell B3 of the Summary worksheet. Enter **=SUM(.**

• Click the **Atlanta tab** to begin the pointing operation.

• Press and hold the **Shift key,** click the **Chicago tab** (scrolling if necessary), then release the Shift key and click **cell B3.** The formula bar should now contain =SUM(Atlanta:Chicago!B3).

• Press the **enter key** to complete the function (which automatically enters the closing right parenthesis) and return to the Summary worksheet.

➤ You should see once again the displayed value of 915 in cell B3 of the Summary worksheet.

➤ If necessary, click in **cell B3,** then drag the fill handle over cells **C3** through **E3** to copy this formula and obtain the total sales for Product 1 in quarters two, three, and four.

➤ Be sure that cells B3 through E3 are still selected, then drag the fill handle to **cell E5.** You should see the total sales for all products in all quarters as shown in Figure 2.7c.

➤ Click **cell E5** to examine the formula in this cell and note that the worksheet references are constant (i.e., they remained the same), whereas the cell references are relative (they were adjusted). Click in other cells to review their formulas in similar fashion.

➤ Save the workbook.

POINTING TO CELLS IN OTHER WORKSHEETS

A worksheet reference can be typed directly into a cell formula, but it is easier to enter the reference by pointing. Click in the cell that is to contain the reference, then enter an equal sign to begin the formula. To reference a cell in another worksheet, click the tab for the worksheet you want to reference, then click the cell or cell range you want to include in the formula. Complete the formula as usual, continuing to first click the tab whenever you want to reference a cell in another worksheet.

STEP 4: The Arrange Windows Command

➤ Pull down the **Window menu,** which displays the names of the open windows. (If the list of open windows includes Book1, close that workbook.)

➤ Click **New Window** to open a second window. Note, however, that your display will not change at this time, because the windows are maximized and only one window is displayed at a time.

➤ Pull down the **Window menu** a second time. Click **New Window** to open a third window. Open a fourth window in similar fashion.

➤ Pull down the **Window menu** once again. You should see the names of the four open windows as shown in Figure 2.7c.

➤ Click **Arrange** to display the Arrange Windows dialog box. If necessary, select the **Tile** option, then click **OK.** You should see four tiled windows.

➤ Change the column widths in the Summary worksheet so that they are approximately the same as in the other windows.

Names of open windows (all four reference the same workbook)

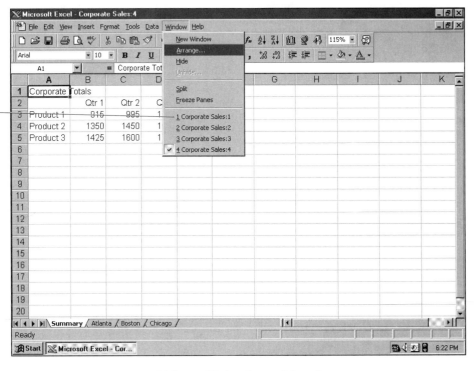

(c) Arrange Windows Command (step 4)

FIGURE 2.7   Hands-on Exercise 2 (continued)

STEP 5: Changing Data

➤ Click in the **upper-right window** in Figure 2.7d. Click the **Atlanta tab** to display the Atlanta worksheet in this window.

➤ Click the **lower-left window.** Click the **Boston tab** to display the Boston worksheet in this window.

➤ Click in the **lower-right window.** Click the **Tab scrolling button** until you can see the Chicago tab, then click the **Chicago tab** to display the Chicago worksheet.

➤ Note that cell B3 in the Summary worksheet displays the value 915, which reflects the total sales for Product 1 in Quarter 1 for Atlanta, Boston, and Chicago (10, 55, and 850, respectively).

➤ Click in **cell B3** of the Chicago worksheet. Enter **250.** Press **enter.** The value of cell B3 in the Summary worksheet changes to 315 to reflect the decreased sales in Chicago.

➤ Click the **Undo button** on the Standard toolbar. The sales for Chicago revert to 850 and the Corporate total is again 915.

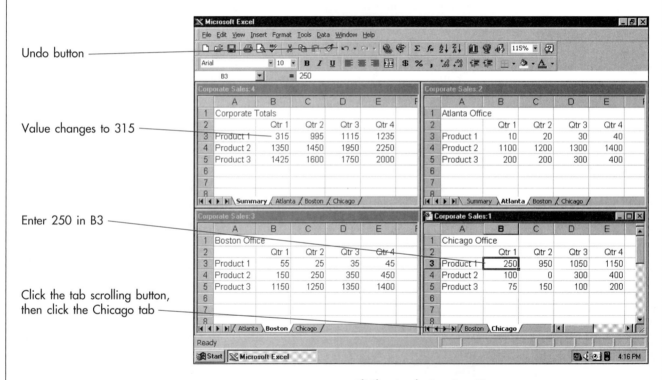

(d) Changing the Data (step 5)

FIGURE 2.7   Hands-on Exercise 2 (continued)

STEP 6: Group Editing

➤ Click in the **upper-left window,** which displays the Summary worksheet. Point to the tab split bar separating the tab scrolling buttons from the horizontal scroll bar. (The pointer becomes a two-headed arrow.) Click and drag to the right until you can see all four tabs at the same time.

➤ If necessary, click the **Summary tab.** Press and hold the **Shift key** as you click the tab for the **Chicago worksheet.** All four tabs should be selected (and are displayed in white) as in Figure 2.7e, and you see [Group] in the title bar.

Font Size list box

Click the Summary tab, then press Shift as you click the Chicago tab to select all four tabs

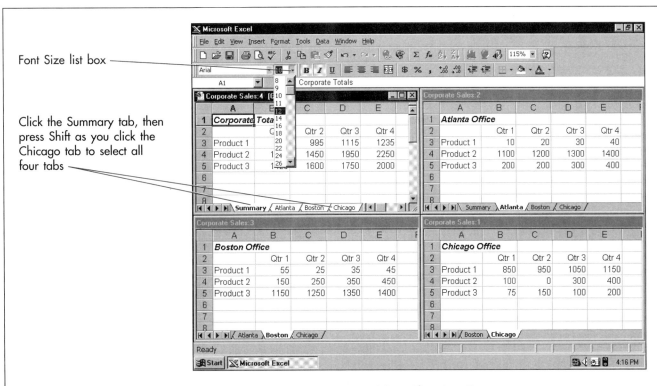

(e) Group Editing (step 6)

FIGURE 2.7   Hands-on Exercise 2 (continued)

> Click in **cell A1,** then click the **Bold** and **Italic buttons** to boldface and italicize the title of each worksheet. Click the **drop-down arrow** for the Font Size list box and change the font to 12.

> Boldface the quarterly and product labels. Note that all four sheets are being formatted simultaneously because of group editing.

> Click and drag to select **cells B3** through **E5,** the cells containing the numerical values. Format these cells in the currency format with zero decimals. Add borders and color as desired.

> Save the workbook.

SELECTING MULTIPLE SHEETS

You can group (select) multiple worksheets simultaneously, then perform the same operation on the selected sheets. To select adjacent sheets, select (click) the first sheet in the range, then press and hold the Shift key as you click the last sheet in the group. If the worksheets are not adjacent to one another, click the first tab, then press and hold the Ctrl key as you click the tab of each additional sheet you want to include in the group. To select all of the sheets at one time, right click the active tab, then choose Select All from the shortcut menu. Once multiple sheets have been selected, Excel indicates that grouping is in effect by appending [Group] to the workbook name in the title bar. Click any tab within the selected group to deselect the group.

STEP 7: Sum the Rows and Columns

➤ Be sure that all four tabs are still selected so that group editing is still in effect.

➤ Scroll until you can click in **cell F3** in the Summary worksheet. Enter the function **=SUM(B3:E3).** Copy this formula to **cells F4** through **F6.**

➤ Click in **cell B6** as shown in Figure 2.7f. Enter the function **=SUM(B3:B5).** Copy this formula to **cells C6** through **E6.** Note that the formula is being entered in all four sheets simultaneously since group editing is still in effect.

➤ Enter **Total** in cell F2, then copy the formatting in cells E2 to F2 using the **Format Painter** on the Standard toolbar. Enter **Total** in cell A6 and boldface it. Boldface the row and column totals.

➤ Click any tab other than the Summary tab to ungroup the worksheets. Save the workbook.

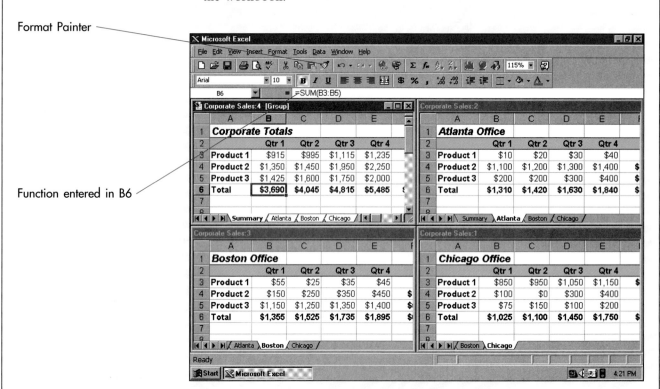

(f) Sum the Rows and Columns (step 7)

FIGURE 2.7   Hands-on Exercise 2 (continued)

THE AUTOSUM BUTTON

The *AutoSum* button on the Standard toolbar invokes the Sum function over a suggested range of cells. To sum a single row or column, click in the blank cell at the end of the row or column, click the AutoSum button to see the suggested function, then click the button a second time to enter the function into the worksheet. To sum multiple rows or columns, select all of the cells that are to contain the Sum function prior to clicking the AutoSum button.

STEP 8: Print the Workbook

➤ Pull down the **File menu** and click the **Page Setup command.**

➤ Click the **Margins tab,** then click the check box to center the worksheet horizontally.

➤ Click the **Sheet tab.** Check the boxes to include row and column headings and gridlines.

➤ Click the **Print button** to display the Print dialog box. Click the option button to print the **Entire Workbook.**

➤ Click **OK** to print the workbook, which will print on four separate pages, one worksheet per page.

STEP 9: Exit Excel

➤ Close all four windows, clicking **Yes** to save the workbook as you close the last window.

➤ Exit Excel if you do not want to continue with the next exercise at this time.

THE DOCUMENTATION WORKSHEET

Throughout the text we have emphasized the importance of properly designing a worksheet and of isolating the assumptions and initial conditions on which the worksheet is based. A workbook can contain up to 255 worksheets, and it, too, should be well designed so that the purpose of every worksheet is evident. Documenting a workbook, and the various worksheets within it, is important because spreadsheets are frequently used by individuals other than the author. You are familiar with every aspect of your workbook because you created it. Your colleague down the hall (or across the country) is not, however, and that person needs to know at a glance the purpose of the workbook and its underlying structure. Even if you don't share your worksheet with others, you will appreciate the documentation six months from now, when you have forgotten some of the nuances you once knew so well.

One way of documenting a workbook is through the creation of a ***documentation worksheet*** that describes the contents of each worksheet within the workbook as shown in Figure 2.8. The worksheet in Figure 2.8 has been added to the Corporate Sales workbook that was created in the first two exercises. (The Insert menu contains the command to add a worksheet.)

The documentation worksheet shows the author and date the spreadsheet was last modified. It contains a description of the overall workbook, a list of all the sheets within the workbook, and the contents of each. The information in the documentation worksheet may seem obvious to you, but it will be greatly appreciated by someone seeing the workbook for the first time.

The documentation worksheet is attractively formatted and takes advantage of the ability to wrap text within a cell. The description in cell B6, for example, wraps over several lines (just as in a word processor). The worksheet also takes advantage of color and larger fonts to call attention to the title of the worksheet. The grid lines have been suppressed through the View tab in the Options command of the Tools menu. The documentation worksheet is an important addition to any workbook.

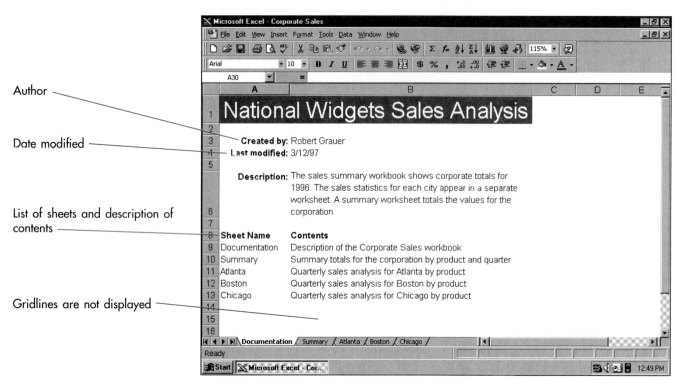

Author

Date modified

List of sheets and description of contents

Gridlines are not displayed

FIGURE 2.8 The Documentation Worksheet

HANDS-ON EXERCISE 3

The Documentation Worksheet

Objective: To improve the design of a workbook through the inclusion of a documentation worksheet. To illustrate sophisticated formatting. Use Figure 2.9 as a guide in the exercise.

STEP 1: Insert a Worksheet

➤ Start Excel. Open the **Corporate Sales workbook** created in the previous exercise. The workbook contains four worksheets—Summary, Atlanta, Boston, and Chicago—each in its own window. Close all but one of the windows, then maximize that window.

➤ Click the **Summary tab** to select this worksheet. Pull down the **Insert menu,** and click the **Worksheet command.** You should see a new worksheet, Sheet1, whose tab is to the left of the Summary worksheet. Do not be concerned if the worksheet is other than Sheet1.

➤ Double click the **tab** of the newly inserted worksheet. Enter **Documentation** as the new name and press **enter.** The name of the new worksheet has been changed to Documentation as shown in Figure 2.9a.

➤ Save the workbook.

STEP 2: Enter the Documentation Information

➤ Enter the descriptive entries in cells A3, A4, and A6 as shown in Figure 2.9a.

➤ Click and drag to select **cells A3** through **A6** so that you can format these cells at the same time. Click the **Bold button.** Click the **Align Right button.**

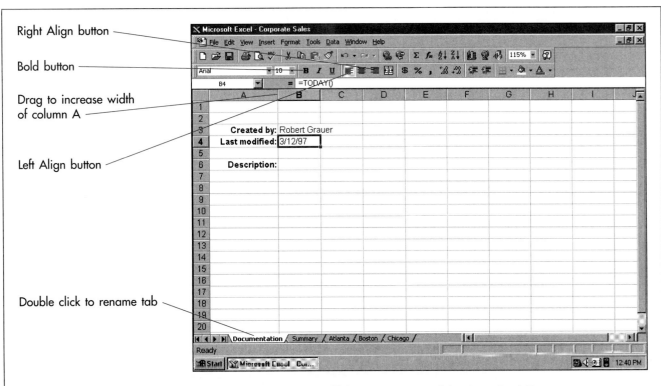

Right Align button

Bold button

Drag to increase width of column A

Left Align button

Double click to rename tab

(a) Add the Documentation Worksheet (steps 1 and 2)

FIGURE 2.9 Hands-on Exercise 3

➤ Increase the width of column A so that its contents are completely visible.

➤ Enter your name in cell B3. Enter **=Today( )** in cell B4. Press **enter.** Click the **Left Align button** to align the date as shown in Figure 2.9a.

STEP 3: The Format Cells Command

➤ Increase the width of column B as shown in Figure 2.9b, then click in **cell B6** and enter the descriptive entry shown in the formula bar.

➤ Type the entire entry *without* pressing the enter key as you will be able to wrap the text within the cell. (You are limited to a maximum of 256 characters in the entry.) Do not be concerned when the text in cell B6 appears to spill into the other cells in row six.

➤ Press the **enter key** when you have completed the entry. Click in **cell B6,** then pull down the **Format menu** and click **Cells** (or right click **cell B6** and click **Format Cells**) to display the dialog box in Figure 2.9b.

➤ Click the **Alignment tab.** Click the box to **Wrap Text** as shown in the figure. Click **OK** to close the dialog box. The text in cell B6 wraps to the width of column B. (You can change the width of the column, and the text will wrap automatically.)

➤ Point to **cell A6,** then click the **right mouse button** to display a shortcut menu. Click **Format Cells** to display the Format Cells dialog box. If necessary, click the **Alignment tab,** click the **drop-down arrow** on the Vertical list box, and click **Top.** Click **OK.**

➤ The entry in cell A6 (the word *Description*) now aligns with the top of the description in cell B6.

➤ Save the workbook.

Entry in B6

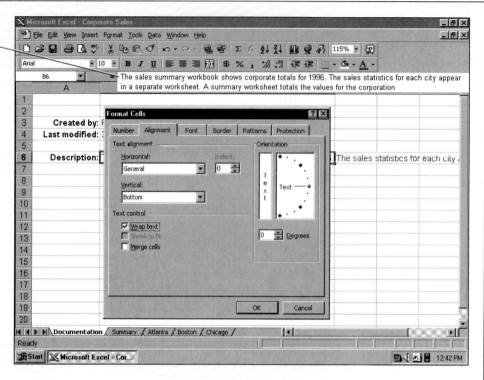

(b) The Format Cells Command (step 3)

FIGURE 2.9 Hands-on Exercise 3 (continued)

EDIT WITHIN A CELL

Double click within the cell whose contents you want to change, then make the changes directly in the cell itself rather than on the formula bar. Use the mouse or arrow keys to position the insertion point at the point of correction. Press the Ins key to toggle between the insertion and over-type modes and/or use the Del key to delete a character. Press the Home and End keys to move to the first and last characters, respectively.

STEP 4: Complete the Descriptive Entries

➤ Complete the text entries in cells A8 through B13 as shown in Figure 2.9c. Click and drag to select cells **A8** and **B8.** Click the **Bold button** to match the formatting in the figure.

➤ Save the workbook.

STEP 5: Add the Worksheet Title

➤ Click in **cell A1.** Enter **National Widgets Sales Analysis.** Change the font size to **24.**

➤ Click and drag to select **cells A1** and **B1.** Pull down the **Format menu,** click the **Alignment tab,** click the **drop-down arrow** on the Horizontal list box, and click **Center Across Selection.** Click **OK.**

➤ Check that cells A1 and B1 are still selected. Pull down the **Format menu.** Click **Cells** to display the Format Cells dialog box as shown in Figure 2.9d.

Bold button

Center Align button

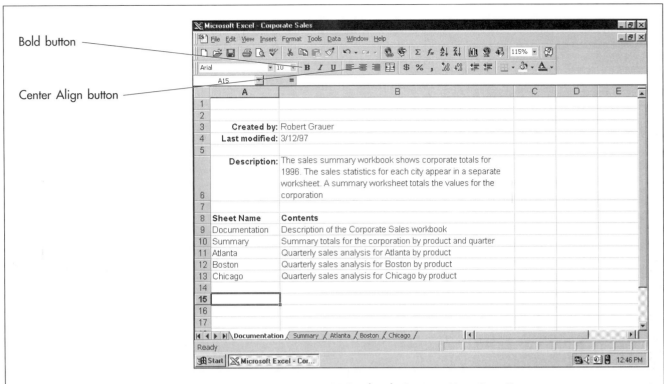

(c) Complete the Descriptive Entries (step 4)

Click and drag to select A1:B1

Click Patterns tab

Click Red

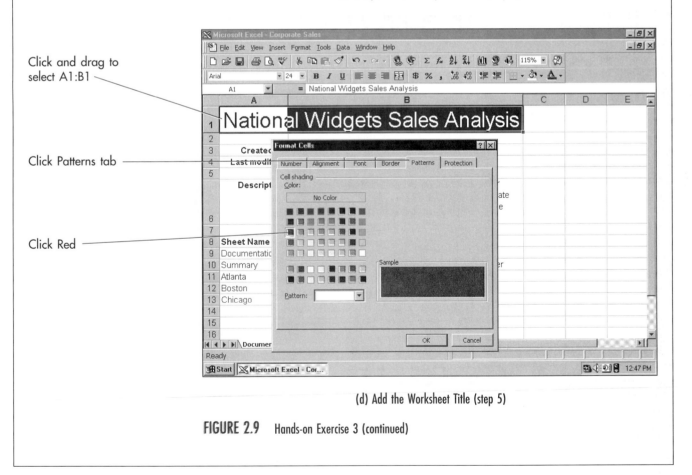

(d) Add the Worksheet Title (step 5)

FIGURE 2.9   Hands-on Exercise 3 (continued)

- Click the **Patterns tab.** Click the **Red** color to shade the selected cells.
- Click the **Font tab.** Click the **drop-down arrow** in the Color list box. Click the **White** color.
- Click **OK** to accept the settings and close the Format Cells dialog box.

➤ Click outside the selected cells to see the effects of the formatting change. You should see white letters on a red background.

➤ Remove the gridlines. Pull down the **Tools menu.** Click **Options.** Click the **View tab** and clear the check box for Gridlines in the Window options area. Click **OK.**

➤ Save the workbook.

THE FORMATTING TOOLBAR

Use the Fill Color and Font Color buttons on the Formatting toolbar to change the shading (pattern color) and font color, respectively. Select the cell(s) you wish to format, click the down arrow of the appropriate button to display the palette, then click the desired color.

STEP 6: Exit Excel

➤ Click the **Spelling button** on the Standard toolbar to initiate the spell check. Make corrections as necessary. Save the workbook.

➤ You have completed the descriptive worksheet shown earlier in Figure 2.8. Close the workbook. Exit Excel if you do not want to continue with the next exercise at this time.

THE SPELL CHECK

Anyone familiar with a word processor takes the spell check for granted, but did you know the same capability exists within Excel? Click the Spelling button on the Standard toolbar to initiate the spell check, then implement corrections just as you do in Microsoft Word. All of the applications in Microsoft Office share the same custom dictionary, so that any words you add to the custom dictionary in one application are automatically recognized in other applications.

LINKING WORKBOOKS

As indicated at the beginning of the chapter, there are two approaches to combining data from multiple sources. You can store all of the data on separate sheets in a single workbook, then create a summary worksheet within that workbook that references values in the other worksheets. Alternatively, you can retain the source data in separate workbooks, and create a summary workbook that references those workbooks.

The two approaches are equally valid, and the choice depends on where you want to keep the source data. In general, it's easier to keep all of the data in a single workbook as has been done throughout the chapter. Occasionally, however, it may be impractical to keep all of the data in a single workbook, in which case it becomes necessary to link the individual workbooks to one another.

Linking is established through the creation of ***external references*** that specify a cell (or range of cells) in another workbook. The ***dependent workbook*** (the Corporate Links workbook in our next example) contains the external references and thus reflects (is dependent on) data in the source workbook(s). The ***source workbooks*** (the Atlanta, Boston, and Chicago workbooks in our example) contain the data referenced by the dependent workbook.

Figure 2.10 illustrates the use of linking within the context of the example we have been using. The figure resembles figures that have appeared earlier in the chapter, but with subtle differences.

Four different workbooks are open, each with one worksheet. The Corporate Links workbook is the dependent workbook and contains external references to obtain the summary totals. The Atlanta, Boston, and Chicago workbooks are the source workbooks.

Cell B3 is the active cell, and its contents are displayed in the formula bar. The corporate sales for Product 1 in the first quarter are calculated by summing the corresponding values in the source workbooks. Note how the workbook names are enclosed in square brackets to indicate the external references to the Atlanta, Boston, and Chicago workbooks. The precise format of an external reference is as follows:

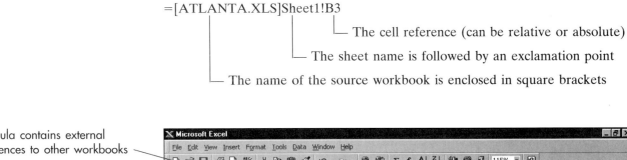

=[ATLANTA.XLS]Sheet1!B3

                          └ The cell reference (can be relative or absolute)

               └ The sheet name is followed by an exclamation point

      └ The name of the source workbook is enclosed in square brackets

Formula contains external references to other workbooks

Different workbooks are open in each window

Corporate Links is the dependent workbook

Active cell whose formula is displayed in formula bar

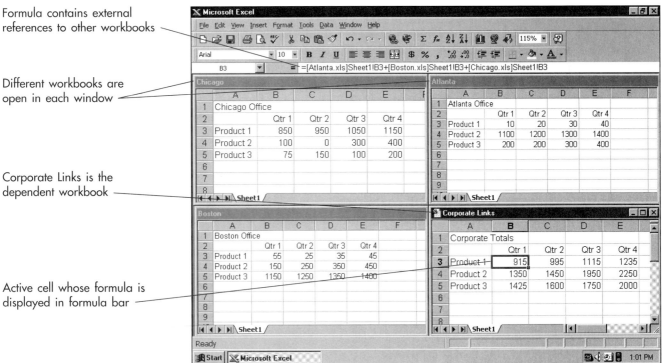

FIGURE 2.10   File Linking

The formulas to compute the corporate totals for Product 1 in the second, third, and fourth quarters contain external references similar to those shown in the formula bar of Figure 2.10. The *workbook references* and sheet references remain constant, whereas the cell reference may be relative (as in this example) or absolute. Once the formula has been entered in cell B3, it may be copied to the remaining cells in this row to compute the totals for Product 1 in the remaining quarters. Cells B3 through E3 may then be copied to rows 4 and 5 to obtain the totals for the other products.

HANDS-ON EXERCISE 4

Linked Workbooks

Objective: To create a dependent workbook with external references to multiple source workbooks; to use pointing to create the external reference rather than entering the formula explicitly. Use Figure 2.11 as a guide in the exercise.

STEP 1: Open the Workbooks

➤ Start Excel. If necessary, click the **New Workbook button** on the Standard toolbar to open a new workbook.

➤ Delete all worksheets except for Sheet1 as you did in step 1 of the first hands-on exercise. Save the workbook as **Corporate Links** in the **Exploring Excel folder.**

➤ Pull down the **File menu.** Click **Open** to display the Open dialog box. Click the **Atlanta workbook.** Press and hold the **Ctrl key** as you click the **Boston** and **Chicago workbooks** to select all three workbooks at the same time.

➤ Click **Open** to open the selected workbooks. The workbooks will be opened one after another, with a brief message appearing on the status bar as each workbook is opened.

➤ Pull down the **Window menu,** which should indicate four open workbooks at the bottom of the menu. Click **Arrange** to display the Arrange Windows dialog box. If necessary, select the **Tile** option, then click **OK.**

➤ You should see four open workbooks as shown in Figure 2.11a, although the row and column labels have not yet been entered in the Corporate Links workbook. (Do not be concerned if your workbooks are arranged differently.)

STEP 2: The AutoFill Command

➤ Click in **cell A1** in the **Corporate Links workbook** to make this the active cell in the active workbook. Enter **Corporate Totals** as shown in Figure 2.11a.

➤ Click **cell B2.** Enter **Qtr 1.** Click in **cell B2,** then point to the fill handle in the lower-right corner. The mouse pointer changes to a thin crosshair.

➤ Drag the fill handle over **cells C2, D2,** and **E2.** A border appears, to indicate the destination range. Release the mouse. Cells C2 through E2 contain the labels Qtr 2, Qtr 3, and Qtr 4, respectively.

➤ Right-align the entries in **cells B2** through **E2,** then reduce the column widths so that you can see the entire worksheet in the window.

➤ Click **cell A3.** Enter **Product 1.** Use the AutoFill capability to enter the labels **Product 2** and **Product 3** in cells A4 and A5.

New button

Different workbook open
in each window

Complete the text entries in
Corporate Links workbook

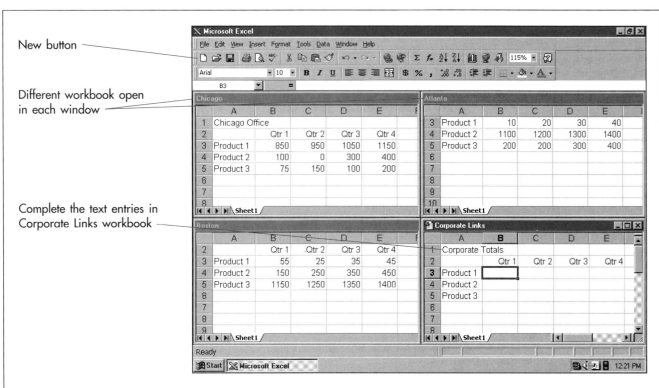

(a) Open the Workbooks (steps 1 and 2)

FIGURE 2.11   Hands-on Exercise 4

STEP 3: File Linking

➤ Click **cell B3** of the **Corporate Links workbook.** Enter an **equal sign** so that
you can create the formula by pointing:

- Click in the window for the **Atlanta workbook.** Click **cell B3.** The formula
bar should display =[ATLANTA.XLS]Sheet1!$B$3. Press the **F4 key** continually until the cell reference changes to B3.

- Enter a **plus sign.** Click in the window for the **Boston workbook.** Click **cell
B3.** The formula expands to include +[BOSTON.XLS]Sheet1!$B$3. Press
the **F4 key** continually until the cell reference changes to B3.

- Enter a **plus sign.** Click in the window for the **Chicago workbook.** Click
cell B3. The formula expands to include +[CHICAGO.XLS]Sheet1!$B$3.
Press the **F4 key** continually until the cell reference changes to B3.

THE F4 KEY

The F4 key cycles through relative, absolute, and mixed addresses. Click
on any reference within the formula bar; for example, click on A1 in the
formula =A1+A2. Press the F4 key once, and it changes to an absolute
reference, $A$1. Press the F4 key a second time, and it becomes a mixed
reference, A$1; press it again, and it is a different mixed reference, $A1.
Press the F4 key a fourth time, and it returns to the original relative
address, A1.

- Press **enter.** The formula is complete, and you should see 915 in cell B3 of the Corporate Links workbook. Click in **cell B3.** The entry on the formula bar should match the entry in Figure 2.11b. Save the workbook.

Formula with external references entered in B3

Click in B3

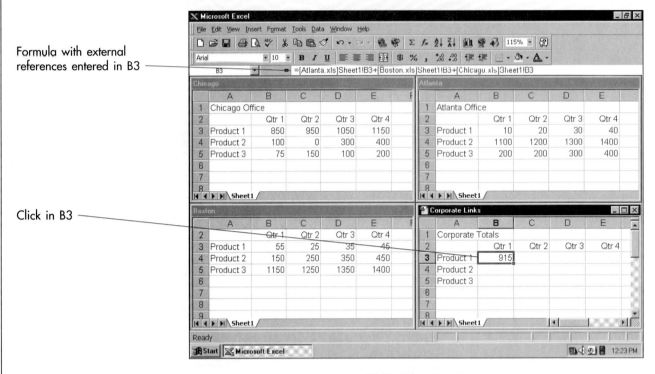

(b) File Linking (step 3)

FIGURE 2.11   Hands-on Exercise 4 (continued)

STEP 4: Copy the Formulas

➤ If necessary, click **cell B3** in the **Corporate Links workbook,** then drag the fill handle over **cells C3** through **E3** to copy this formula to the remaining cells in row 3.

➤ Be sure that cells B3 through E3 are still selected, then drag the fill handle to **cell E5.** You should see the total sales for all products in all quarters as shown in Figure 2.11c.

➤ Click **cell E5** to view the copied formula as shown in the figure. Note that the workbook and sheet references are the same but that the cell references have adjusted. Save the workbook.

DRIVE AND FOLDER REFERENCE

An external reference is updated regardless of whether or not the source workbook is open. The reference is displayed differently, however, depending on whether or not the source workbook is open. The references include the path (the drive and folder) if the source workbook is closed; the path is not shown if the source workbook is open.

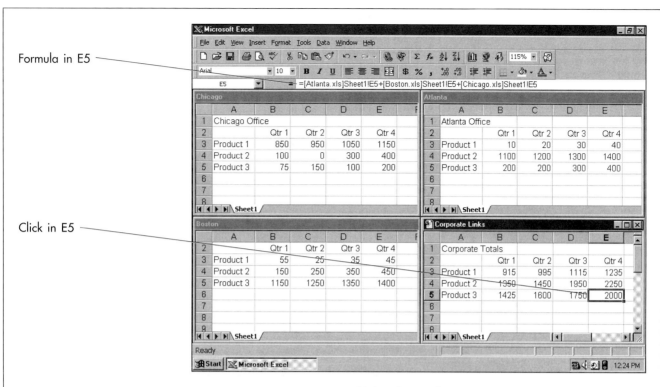

Formula in E5

Click in E5

(c) Copy the Formulas (step 4)

FIGURE 2.11   Hands-on Exercise 4 (continued)

STEP 5: Change the Data

➤ Click **cell B3** to make it the active cell. Note that the value displayed in the cell is 915.

➤ Pull down the **File menu.** Click **Close.** Answer **Yes** if asked whether to save the changes.

➤ Click in the window containing the **Chicago workbook,** click **cell B3,** enter **250,** and press **enter.** Pull down the **File menu.** Click **Close.** Answer **Yes** if asked whether to save the changes. Only two workbooks, Atlanta and Boston, are now open.

➤ Pull down the **File menu** and open the **Corporate Links workbook.** You should see the dialog box in Figure 2.11d, asking whether to re-establish the links. (Note that cell B3 still displays 915). Click **Yes** to re-establish the links.

➤ The value in cell B3 of the Corporate Links workbook changes to 315 to reflect the change in the Chicago workbook, even though the latter is closed.

➤ If necessary, click in **cell B3.** The formula bar displays the contents of this cell, which include the drive and folder reference for the Chicago workbook, because the workbook is closed.

STEP 6: Close the Workbooks

➤ Close the Atlanta and Boston workbooks. Close the Corporate Links workbook. Click **Yes** if asked whether to save the changes.

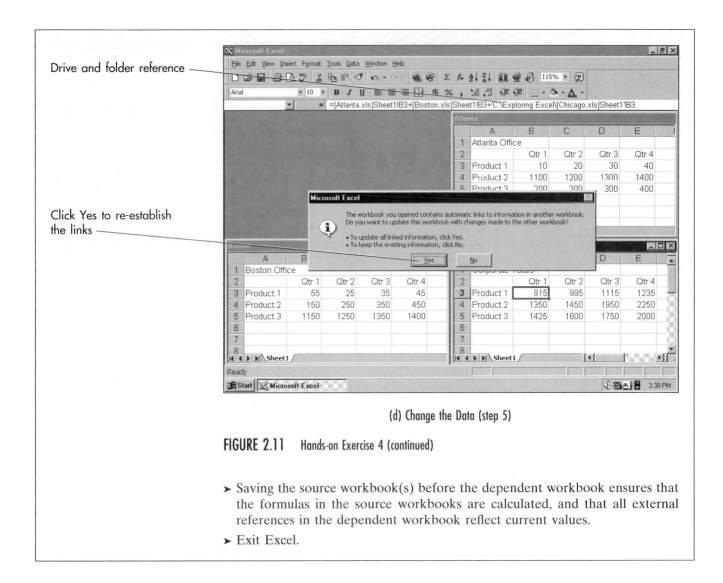

Drive and folder reference

Click Yes to re-establish the links

(d) Change the Data (step 5)

FIGURE 2.11   Hands-on Exercise 4 (continued)

➤ Saving the source workbook(s) before the dependent workbook ensures that the formulas in the source workbooks are calculated, and that all external references in the dependent workbook reflect current values.

➤ Exit Excel.

SUMMARY

The chapter showed how to combine data from different sources into a summary report. The example is quite common and applicable to any business scenario requiring both detail and summary reports. One approach is to store all of the data in separate sheets of a single workbook, then summarize the data in a summary worksheet within that workbook. Alternatively, the source data can be kept in separate workbooks and consolidated through linking to a summary workbook. Both approaches are valid, and the choice depends on where you want to keep the source data.

An Excel workbook may contain up to 255 worksheets, each of which is identified by a tab at the bottom of the window. Worksheets may be added, deleted, moved, copied, or renamed through a shortcut menu. The highlighted tab indicates the active worksheet.

A worksheet reference is required to indicate a cell in another worksheet of the same workbook. An exclamation point separates the worksheet reference from the cell reference. The worksheet reference is absolute and remains the same when the formula is copied. The cell reference may be relative or absolute. A 3-D reference is a range that spans two or more worksheets in a workbook.

A workbook should be clearly organized so that the purpose of every worksheet is evident. One way of documenting a workbook is through the creation of a documentation worksheet that describes the purpose of each worksheet within the workbook.

Linking is used when it is impractical to keep all of the data in the same workbook. Linking is established through an external reference that specifies a cell (or range of cells) in a source workbook. The dependent workbook contains the external references and uses (is dependent on) the data in the source workbook(s).

KEY WORDS AND CONCEPTS

3-D reference	External reference	Tab split bar
Arrange command	Grouping worksheets	Workbook reference
AutoSum	Linking	Worksheet reference
Dependent workbook	New Window command	
Documentation worksheet	Source workbook	

MULTIPLE CHOICE

1. Which of the following is true regarding workbooks and worksheets?
   (a) A workbook contains one or more worksheets
   (b) Only one worksheet can be selected at a time within a workbook
   (c) Every workbook contains the same number of worksheets
   (d) All of the above

2. Assume that a workbook contains three worksheets. How many cells are included in the function =SUM(Sheet1:Sheet3!A1)?
   (a) Three
   (b) Four
   (c) Twelve
   (d) Twenty-four

3. Assume that a workbook contains three worksheets. How many cells are included in the function =SUM(Sheet1:Sheet3!A1:B4)?
   (a) Three
   (b) Four
   (c) Twelve
   (d) Twenty-four

4. Which of the following is the preferred way to sum the value of cell A1 from three different worksheets?
   (a) =Sheet1!A1+Sheet2!A1+Sheet3!A1
   (b) =SUM(Sheet1:Sheet3!A1)
   (c) Both (a) and (b) are equally good
   (d) Neither (a) nor (b)

5. The reference CIS120!$A$2:
   (a) Is an absolute reference to cell A2 in the CIS120 workbook
   (b) Is a relative reference to cell A2 in the CIS120 workbook
   (c) Is an absolute reference to cell A2 in the CIS120 worksheet
   (d) Is a relative reference to cell A2 in the CIS120 worksheet

6. Assume that Sheet1 is the active worksheet and that cells A2 through A4 are currently selected. What happens if you press and hold the Shift key as you click the tab for Sheet3, then press the Del key?
   (a) Only Sheet1 will be deleted from the workbook
   (b) Only Sheet3 will be deleted from the workbook
   (c) Sheet1, Sheet2, and Sheet3 will be deleted from the workbook
   (d) The contents of cells A2 through A4 will be erased from Sheet1, Sheet2, and Sheet3

7. Which of the following is true about the reference Sheet1:Sheet3!A1:B2?
   (a) The worksheet reference is relative, the cell reference is absolute
   (b) The worksheet reference is absolute, the cell reference is relative
   (c) The worksheet and cell references are both absolute
   (d) The worksheet and cell references are both relative

8. You are in the Ready mode and are positioned in cell B2 of Sheet1. You enter an equal sign, click the worksheet tab for Sheet2, click cell B1, and press enter.
   (a) The content of cell B2 in Sheet1 is =Sheet2!B1
   (b) The content of cell B1 in Sheet2 is = Sheet1!B2
   (c) Both (a) and (b)
   (d) Neither (a) nor (b)

9. You are in the Ready mode and are positioned in cell A10 of Sheet1. You enter an equal sign, click the worksheet tab for the worksheet called This Year, and click cell C10. You then enter a minus sign, click the worksheet tab for the worksheet called LastYear, click cell C10, and press enter. What are the contents of cell A10?
   (a) =ThisYear:LastYear!C10
   (b) =(ThisYear−LastYear)!C10
   (c) =ThisYear!C10-LastYear!C10
   (d) =ThisYear:C10-LastYear:C10

10. Which of the following can be accessed from a shortcut menu?
    (a) Inserting or deleting a worksheet
    (b) Moving or copying a worksheet
    (c) Renaming a worksheet
    (d) All of the above

11. You are in the Ready mode and are positioned in cell A1 of Sheet1 of Book1. You enter an equal sign, click in the open window for Book2, click the tab for Sheet1, click cell A1, then press the F4 key continually until you have a relative cell reference. What reference appears in the formula bar?
    (a) =[BOOK1.XLS]Sheet1!$A$1
    (b) =[BOOK1.XLS]Sheet1!A1
    (c) =[BOOK2.XLS]Sheet1!$A$1
    (d) =[BOOK2.XLS]Sheet1!A1

12. The Arrange Windows command can display:
(a) Multiple worksheets from one workbook
(b) One worksheet from multiple workbooks
(c) Both (a) and (b)
(d) Neither (a) nor (b)

13. Pointing can be used to reference a cell in:
(a) A different worksheet
(b) A different workbook
(c) Both (a) and (b)
(d) Neither (a) nor (b)

14. The appearance of [Group] within the title bar indicates that:
(a) Multiple workbooks are open and are all active
(b) Multiple worksheets are selected within the same workbook
(c) Both (a) and (b)
(d) Neither (a) nor (b)

15. Which of the following is true regarding the example on file linking that was developed in the chapter?
(a) The Atlanta, Boston, and Chicago workbooks were dependent workbooks
(b) The Linked workbook was a source workbook
(c) Both (a) and (b)
(d) Neither (a) nor (b)

ANSWERS

1. a	**6.** d	**11.** d
2. a	**7.** b	**12.** c
3. d	**8.** a	**13.** c
4. b	**9.** c	**14.** b
5. c	**10.** d	**15.** d

PRACTICE WITH EXCEL 97

1. A partially completed version of the workbook in Figure 2.12 can be found on the data disk as *Volume II Chapter 2 Practice 1*. This workbook contains worksheets for the individual sections but does not contain the summary worksheet.

   a. Retrieve the Chapter 2 Practice 1 workbook from the data disk, then open multiple windows so that the display on your monitor matches Figure 2.12.

   b. Complete the individual worksheets by adding the appropriate formulas (functions) to compute the class average on each test.

   c. Add a summary worksheet that includes the test averages from each of the sections as shown in the figure.

   d. Add a documentation worksheet that includes your name as the grading assistant, shows the date of modification, and lists all of the worksheets in the workbook.

   e. Print the entire workbook and submit it to your instructor.

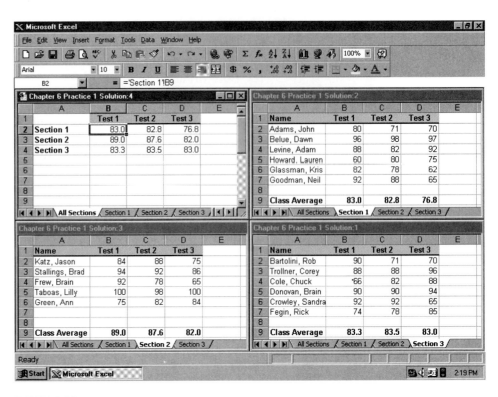

FIGURE 2.12   Screen for Practice Exercise 1

2. A partially completed version of the workbook in Figure 2.13 can be found on the data disk as *Volume II Chapter 2 Practice 2*. The workbook contains a separate worksheet for each month of the year as well as a summary worksheet for the entire year. Thus far, only the months of January, February, and

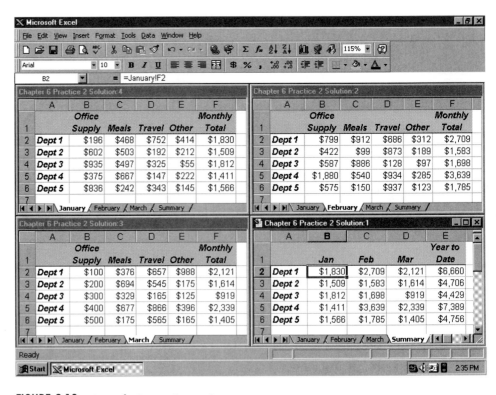

FIGURE 2.13   Screen for Practice Exercise 2

March are complete. Each monthly worksheet tallies the expenses for five departments in each of four categories to compute a monthly total for each department. The summary worksheet displays the total expense for each department.

a. Retrieve the Chapter 2 Practice 2 workbook from the data disk, then open multiple windows so that the display on your monitor matches Figure 2.13.

b. Use the Group Editing feature to select the worksheets for January, February, and March simultaneously. Enter the formula to compute the monthly total for each department in each month.

c. Use the Group Editing feature to format the worksheets.

d. Enter the appropriate formulas in the summary worksheet to compute the year-to-date totals for each department.

e. Add an additional worksheet for the month of April. Assume that department 1 spends $100 in each category, department 2 spends $200 in each category, and so on. Update the summary worksheet to include the expenses for April.

f. Add a documentation worksheet that includes your name, the date of modification, plus a description of each worksheet within the workbook.

g. Print the entire workbook (all five worksheets), then print the cell formulas for the summary worksheet only.

3. Object Linking and Embedding: Create the compound document in Figure 2.14, which consists of a memo, summary worksheet, and three-dimensional chart. The chart is to be created in its own chart sheet within the Corporate Sales workbook, then incorporated into the memo using Object Linking and Embedding. Address the memo to your instructor, sign your name, then print the memo as it appears in Figure 2.14.

Prove to yourself that Object Linking and Embedding really works by returning to the Atlanta worksheet *after* you have created the document in Figure 2.14. Change the sales for Product 2 in Quarter 4 to $3,000. Switch back to the Word memo, and the chart should reflect the increase in the sales for Product 2. Add a postscript to the memo, indicating that the corrected chart reflects the last-minute sale of Product 2 in Atlanta. Print the revised memo and submit it to your instructor with the earlier version.

4. Figure 2.15 contains a pivot table that was created from the Corporate Sales workbook used throughout the chapter. The pivot table was created *without* the benefit of a list (as was done in Chapter 1) by specifying multiple consolidation ranges. Do Hands-on Exercises 1, 2, and 3 as they appear in this chapter. Review the material on pivot tables, then follow the steps below to create the pivot table in its own worksheet within the Corporate Sales workbook.

a. Pull down the Data menu and click the Pivot Table Report command. Click the option button to select Multiple Consolidation Ranges in step 1 of the Pivot Table Wizard. Click Next.

b. Click the option button that says *I will create the page fields* in step 2a. Click Next.

c. Specify the range in step 2b of the PivotTable wizard through pointing. Click the Sheet tab for Atlanta, select cells A2 through E5, then click the Add command button. You should see Atlanta!$A$2:$E$5 in the All Ranges list box. Repeat this step for the other two cities. You should see the same range for Atlanta, Boston, and Chicago.

d. Remain in step 2b of the PivotTable Wizard. Click the option button for 1 page field. Select (click) the Atlanta range within the All ranges list box, then click in the Field one list box and type Atlanta. Do not press the

National Widgets, Inc.

Atlanta • Boston • Chicago

To: John Graves, President
           National Widgets, Inc

From: Susan Powers
           Vice President, Marketing

Subject: Sales Analysis Data

Our overall fourth quarter sales have improved considerably over those in the first quarter. Please note, however, that Product 1, despite a growth in sales, is still trailing the other products, and discontinuing its production should be considered. I will await your reply on this matter.

Corporate Totals	Qtr 1	Qtr 2	Qtr 3	Qtr 4	Totals
Product 1	$915	$995	$1,115	$1,235	$4,260
Product 2	$1,350	$1,450	$1,950	$2,250	$7,000
Product 3	$1,425	$1,600	$1,750	$2,000	$6,775
Totals	$3,690	$4,045	$4,815	$5,485	$18,035

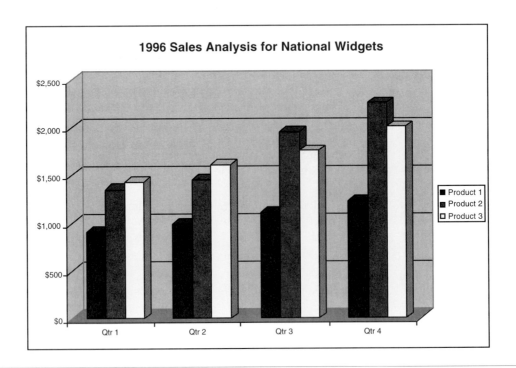

FIGURE 2.14   Memo for Practice Exercise 3

Sum of Value		Product			
Quarter	City	Product 1	Product 2	Product 3	Grand Total
Qtr 1	Atlanta	$10	$1,100	$200	$1,310
	Boston	$55	$150	$1,150	$1,355
	Chicago	$850	$100	$75	$1,025
Qtr 1 Total		$915	$1,350	$1,425	$3,690
Qtr 2	Atlanta	$20	$1,200	$200	$1,420
	Boston	$25	$250	$1,250	$1,525
	Chicago	$950	$0	$150	$1,100
Qtr 2 Total		$995	$1,450	$1,600	$4,045
Qtr 3	Atlanta	$30	$1,300	$300	$1,630
	Boston	$35	$350	$1,350	$1,735
	Chicago	$1,050	$300	$100	$1,450
Qtr 3 Total		$1,115	$1,950	$1,750	$4,815
Qtr 4	Atlanta	$40	$1,400	$400	$1,840
	Boston	$45	$450	$1,400	$1,895
	Chicago	$1,150	$400	$200	$1,750
Qtr 4 Total		$1,235	$2,250	$2,000	$5,485
Grand Total		$4,260	$7,000	$6,775	$18,035

FIGURE 2.15   Pivot Table for Practice Exercise 4

enter key. Select (click) the Boston range within the All Ranges list box, then click in the Field one list box and type Boston. Do not press enter. Repeat this step for Chicago.

e. Click Next, then click Next again to bypass step 3. Click the option button to create the pivot table on a New Worksheet. Click Finish.

f. Edit the pivot table so that it matches Figure 2.15. Click in cell B3 (the field name is Column), then click the formula bar and enter Quarter. Change the entry in cell A4 from Row to Product in similar fashion. Change the entry in cell A1 from Page1 to City.

g. Pivot the table by dragging Quarter to the row position, Product to the column position, and City to the row position below and to the right of Quarter.

h. Format the pivot table so that it matches Figure 2.15. Save the workbook.

The process seems long, but with practice it's done rather easily, and the flexibility inherent in the resulting pivot table is worth the effort. Modify the description on the Documentation worksheet to include the pivot table, then print the entire workbook and submit it to your instructor.

CASE STUDIES

Urban Sophisticates

The *Urban Sophisticates* workbook on the data disk is only partially complete as it contains worksheets for individual stores, but does not yet have a summary worksheet. Your job is to retrieve the workbook and create a summary worksheet, then use the summary worksheet as the basis of a three-dimensional column chart reflecting the sales for the past year. Add a documentation worksheet containing your name as financial analyst, then print the entire workbook.

External References

As marketing manager you are responsible for consolidating the sales information for all of the branch offices within the corporation. Each branch manager creates an identically formatted workbook with the sales information for his or her branch office. Your job is to consolidate the information into a single table, then graph the results appropriately. The branch data is to remain in the individual workbooks; that is, the formulas in your workbook are to contain external references to the *Eastern, Western,* and *Foreign workbooks* on the data disk. Your workbook is to be developed in such a way that any change in the individual workbooks should be automatically reflected in the consolidated workbook.

Pivot Tables

What advantages, if any, does a pivot table have over a conventional worksheet with respect to analyzing and consolidating data from multiple sources? What are the disadvantages? Does the underlying data have to be entered in the form of a list, or can it be taken directly from a worksheet? Use what you learn to extend the analysis of the Atlanta, Boston, and Chicago data that appeared throughout the chapter. (See practice exercise 4 for one example of a pivot table.)

The Spreadsheet Audit

Which tools are found on the Auditing toolbar? What is the difference between precedent and dependent cells? Can the Auditing toolbar detect precedent cells that are located in a different worksheet? In a different workbook? The answers to these and other questions can be found by studying Appendix B, then experimenting on your own. A spreadsheet audit is an important concept and one with which you should become familiar.

Kid Stuff

Create a new workbook based on data from the Uptown, Midtown, and Downtown workbooks in the Exploring Excel folder. The completed workbook should contain a summary worksheet as well as a documentation worksheet with your name, date, and a list of all worksheets in the workbook. Print the completed workbook, along with the cell formulas from the summary worksheet, then submit the printouts to your instructor as proof you did this exercise.

AUTOMATING REPETITIVE TASKS: MACROS AND VISUAL BASIC

OBJECTIVES

After reading this chapter you will be able to:

1. Define a macro; explain how macros facilitate the execution of repetitive tasks.
2. Record and run a macro; view and edit the statements in a simple macro.
3. Use the InputBox statement to obtain input for a macro as it is running.
4. Use a keyboard shortcut and/or a customized toolbar to run a macro; create a custom button to execute a macro.
5. Describe the function of the Personal Macro workbook.
6. Use the Step Into command to execute a macro one statement at a time.
7. Use the Copy and Paste commands to duplicate an existing macro; modify the copied macro to create an entirely new macro.
8. Use the Visual Basic If and Do statements to implement decision making and looping within an Excel macro.

OVERVIEW

Have you ever pulled down the same menus and clicked the same sequence of commands over and over? Easy as the commands may be to execute, it is still burdensome to have to continually repeat the same mouse clicks or keystrokes. If you can think of any task that you do repeatedly, whether in one workbook or in a series of workbooks, you are a perfect candidate to use macros.

A *macro* is a set of instructions that tells Excel which commands to execute. It is in essence a program, and its instructions are written in Visual Basic, a programming language. Fortunately, however, you don't have to be a programmer to write macros. Instead, you use the macro recorder within Excel to record your commands, and let Excel write the macros for you.

This chapter introduces you to the power of Excel macros. We begin by creating a simple macro to insert your name and class into a worksheet. We show you how to modify the macro once it has been created and how to execute the macro one statement at a time. We also show you how to store the macro in the Personal Macro workbook, so that it will be available automatically whenever you start Excel.

The second half of the chapter describes how to create more powerful macros that automate commands associated with list management, as presented in Chapter 1. We show you how to copy and edit a macro, and how to create customized buttons with which to execute a macro. We also show you how the power of an Excel macro can be extended through the inclusion of additional Visual Basic statements that implement loops and decision making.

VISUAL BASIC FOR APPLICATIONS

Visual Basic is a powerful programming language that can be used to develop all types of applications. Visual Basic for Applications (VBA) is a subset of Visual Basic that is built into Office 97. The best introduction to VBA is to use the macro recorder in Excel to create simple macros, which are in fact complete programs in Visual Basic. You get results that are immediately usable and can learn a good deal about Visual Basic through observation and intuition.

INTRODUCTION TO MACROS

The *macro recorder* stores Excel commands, in the form of *Visual Basic* instructions, within a workbook. To use the recorder, you pull down the Tools menu and click the Record New Macro command. From that point on (until you stop recording), every command you execute will be stored by the recorder. It doesn't matter whether you execute commands from pull-down menus via the mouse, or whether you use the toolbar or keyboard shortcuts. The macro recorder captures every action you take and stores the equivalent Visual Basic statements as a macro within the workbook.

Figure 3.1 illustrates a simple macro to enter your name and class in cells A1 and A2 of the active worksheet. The macro is displayed in the *Visual Basic Editor (VBE),* which is used to create, edit, execute, and debug Excel macros. The Visual Basic Editor is a separate application (as can be determined from its button on the taskbar in Figure 3.1), and it is accessible from any application in Office 97.

The left side of the VBE window in Figure 3.1 contains the *Project Explorer,* which is similar in concept and appearance to the Windows Explorer, except that it displays only open workbooks and/or other Visual Basic projects. The Visual Basic statements for the selected module (Module1 in Figure 3.1) appear in the *Code window* in the right pane. As you shall see, a Visual Basic module consists of one or more procedures, each of which corresponds to an Excel macro. Thus, in this example, Module1 contains the NameAndCourse procedure corresponding to the Excel macro of the same name. Module1 itself is stored in the My Macros.XLS workbook.

As indicated, a macro consists of Visual Basic statements that were created through the macro recorder. We don't expect you to be able to write the Visual

Project Explorer Window

Begins with a Sub statement

Comments begin
with an apostrophe

Module1 is the selected module

Ends with an End Sub statement

Visual Basic Editor is
an open application

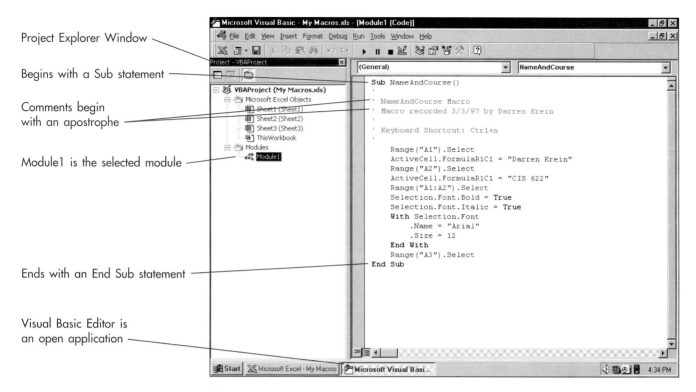

FIGURE 3.1 A Simple Macro

Basic procedure yourself, and you don't have to. You just invoke the recorder and let it capture the Excel commands for you. We do think it is important, however, to understand the macro and so we proceed to explain its statements. As you read our discussion, do not be concerned with the precise syntax of every statement, but try to get an overall appreciation for what the statements do.

A macro always begins and ends with the Sub and End Sub statements, respectively. The ***Sub statement*** contains the name of the macro—for example, NameAndCourse in Figure 3.1. (Spaces are not allowed in a macro name.) The ***End Sub statement*** is physically the last statement and indicates the end of the macro. Sub and End Sub are Visual Basic key words and appear in blue.

The next several statements begin with an apostrophe, appear in green, and are known as ***comments.*** They provide information about the macro, but do not affect its execution. In other words, the results of a macro are the same, whether or not the comments are included. Comments are inserted automatically by the recorder to document the macro name, its author, and shortcut key (if any). You can add comments (a comment line must begin with an apostrophe), or delete or modify existing comments, as you see fit.

Every other statement is a Visual Basic instruction that was created as a result of an action taken in Excel. For example, the statements:

       Range ("A1").Select
and   ActiveCell.FormulaR1C1 = "Darren Krein"

select cell A1 as the active cell, then enter the text "Darren Krein" into the active cell. These statements are equivalent to clicking in cell A1 of a worksheet, typing the indicated entry into the active cell, then pressing the enter key (or an arrow key) to complete the entry. In similar fashion, the statements

       Range ("A2").Select
and   ActiveCell.FormulaR1C1 = "CIS622"

select cell A2 as the active cell, then enter the text entry "CIS622" into that cell. The concept of select-then-do applies equally well to statements within a macro. Thus, the statements

```
Range ("A1:A2").Select
Selection.Font.Bold = True
Selection.Font.Italic = True
```

select cells A1 through A2, then change the font for the selected cells to bold italic. The *With statement* enables you to perform multiple actions on the same object. All commands between the With and corresponding *End With statements* are executed collectively; for example, the statements

```
With Selection.Font
    .Name = "Arial"
    .Size = 12
End With
```

change the formatting of the selected cells (A1:A2) to 12-point Arial. The statements are equivalent to selecting cells A1 and A2, selecting Arial as the typeface, then specifying 12-point type. The last statement in the macro, Range ("A3").Select, deselects all other cells, a practice we use throughout the chapter.

As we have already indicated, you are not expected to be able to write the Visual Basic statements from scratch, but you should be able to understand the statements once they have been recorded. Moreover, you can edit the macro (after it has been recorded) to change the selected cells and/or their values. You can also change the typeface, point size, or style, simply by changing the appropriate statement in the macro.

HANDS-ON EXERCISE 1

Introduction to Macros

Objective: To record, run, view, and edit a simple macro; to establish a keyboard shortcut to run a macro. Use Figure 3.2 as a guide in the exercise.

PLAN AHEAD

The macro recorder records everything you do, including entries that are made by mistake or commands that are executed incorrectly. Plan the macro in advance, before you begin recording. Write down what you intend to do, then try out the commands with the recorder off. Be sure you go all the way through the intended sequence of operations prior to turning the macro recorder on.

STEP 1: Create a Macro

➤ Start Excel. Open a new workbook if one is not already open. Save the workbook as **My Macros** in the **Exploring Excel folder.**

➤ Pull down the **Tools menu,** click (or point to) the **Macro command,** then click **Record New Macro** to display the Record Macro dialog box in Figure 3.2a.

➤ Enter **NameAndCourse** as the name of the macro. Do not leave any spaces in the macro name.

➤ The description is entered automatically and contains today's date and the name of the person in whose name this copy of Excel is registered. If necessary, change the description to include your name.

➤ Click in the **Shortcut Key** check box and enter a **lowercase n.** Ctrl+n should appear as the shortcut as shown in Figure 3.2a. (If you see Ctrl+Shift+N it means you typed an uppercase N rather than a lowercase letter. Correct the entry to a lowercase n.)

➤ Check that the option to Store macro in **This Workbook** is selected. Click **OK** to begin recording the macro, which displays the Stop Recording toolbar.

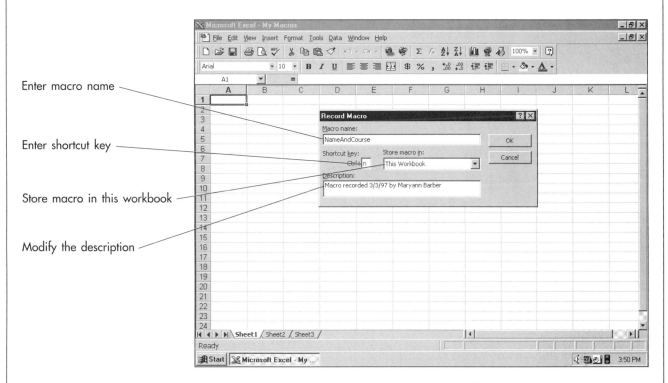

Enter macro name

Enter shortcut key

Store macro in this workbook

Modify the description

(a) Create a Macro (step 1)

FIGURE 3.2   Hands-on Exercise 1

MACRO NAMES

Macro names are not allowed to contain spaces or punctuation except for the underscore character. To create a macro name containing more than one word, capitalize the first letter of each word to make the words stand out and/or use the underscore character; for example, NameAndCourse or Name_And_Course.

STEP 2: Record the Macro

➤ Look carefully at the Relative References button on the Stop Recording button to be sure it is flush with the other buttons; that is, the button should *not* be pushed in. (See boxed tip on "Is the Button In or Out?")

➤ You should be in Sheet1, ready to record the macro, as shown in Figure 3.2b. The status bar indicates that you are in the Recording mode:

• Click in cell **A1** even if it is already selected. Enter your name.

• Click in cell **A2.** Enter the course you are taking.

• Click and drag to select cells **A1** through **A2.**

• Click the **Bold button.**

• Click the **Italic button.**

• Click the arrow on the **Font Size list box.** Click **12** to change the point size.

• Click in cell **A3** to deselect all other cells prior to ending the macro.

➤ Click the **Stop Recording button** to end the macro.

➤ Save the workbook.

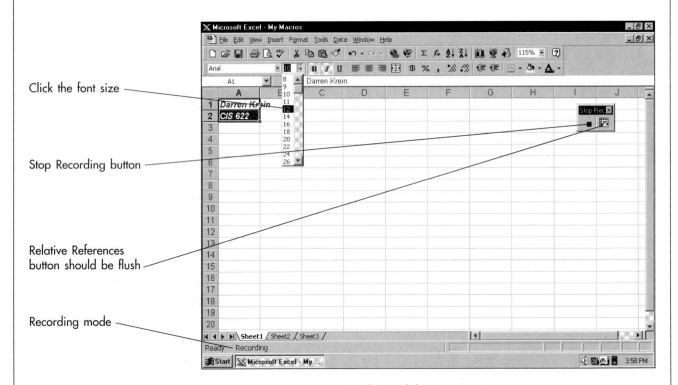

(b) Record the Macro (step 2)

FIGURE 3.2   Hands-on Exercise 1 (continued)

IS THE BUTTON IN OR OUT?

The distinction between relative and absolute references within a macro is critical and is described in detail at the end of this exercise. The Relative References button on the Stop Recording toolbar toggles between the two—absolute references when the button is out, relative references when the button is in. The ScreenTip, however, displays Relative References regardless of whether the button is in or out. We wish that Microsoft had made it easier to tell which type of reference you are recording, but they didn't.

STEP 3: Test the Macro

➤ To run (test) the macro you have to remove the contents and formatting from cells A1 and A2. Click and drag to select cells **A1** through **A2.**

➤ Pull down the **Edit menu.** Click **Clear.** Click **All** from the cascaded menu to erase both the contents and formatting from the selected cells. Cells A1 through A2 are empty as shown in Figure 3.2c.

➤ Pull down the **Tools menu.** Click **Macro,** then click the **Macros . . . command** to display the dialog box in Figure 3.2c.

➤ Click **NameAndCourse,** which is the macro you just recorded. Click **Run.** Your name and class are entered in cells A1 and A2, then formatted according to the instructions in the macro.

Clear cells A1 and A2
to test the macro

Click to select
NameAndCourse macro

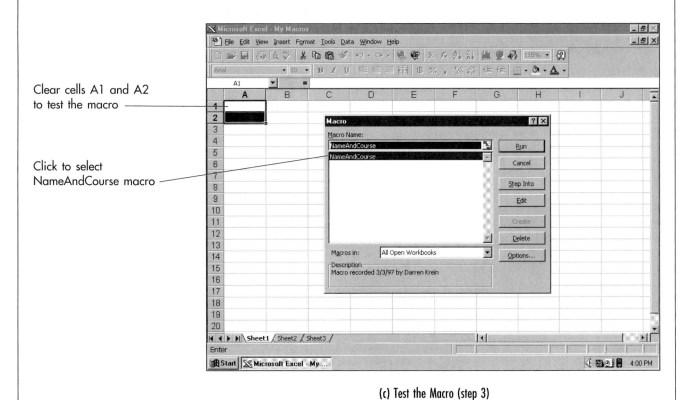

(c) Test the Macro (step 3)

FIGURE 3.2   Hands-on Exercise 1 (continued)

THE EDIT CLEAR COMMAND

The Edit Clear erases the contents of a cell, its formatting, and/or its comments. Select the cell or cells to erase, pull down the Edit menu, click the Clear command, then click All, Formats, Contents, or Comments from the cascaded menu. Pressing the Del key is equivalent to executing the Edit Clear Contents command as it clears the contents of a cell, but retains the formatting and comments.

STEP 4: Start the Visual Basic Editor

➤ Pull down the **Tools menu,** click the **Macro command,** then click **Visual Basic Editor** (or press **Alt+F11**) to open the Visual Basic Editor. Maximize the VBE window.

➤ If necessary, pull down the **View menu.** Click **Project Explorer** to open the Project window in the left pane. There is currently one open VBA project, My Macros.XLS, which is the name of the open workbook in Excel.

➤ If necessary, click the **plus sign** next to the Modules folder to expand that folder, click (select) **Module1,** pull down the **View menu,** and click **Code** to open the Code window in the right pane. Click the maximize button in the Code window.

➤ Your screen should match the one in Figure 3.2d. The first statement below the comments should be *Range("A1").Select,* which indicates that the macro was correctly recorded with absolute references.

➤ If you see a very different statement, *ActiveCell.FormulaR1C1,* it means that you incorrectly recorded the macro with relative references. Right click the module, select the **Remove Module command,** then return to step 1 and rerecord the macro.

THE END RESULT

The macro recorder records only the result of the selection process, with no indication of how the selection was arrived at. It doesn't matter how you get to a particular cell. You can click in the cell directly, use the Go To command in the Edit menu, or use the mouse or arrow keys. The end result is the same and the macro indicates only the selected cell(s).

STEP 5: Simplify the Macro

➤ Click in the Code window, immediately after the number **12,** then click and drag to select the highlighted statements as shown in Figure 3.2d.

➤ Press the **Del key** to delete these statements from the macro. (These statements contain default values and are unnecessary.)

➤ Press **Alt+F11** to toggle back to the Excel workbook (or click the Excel button on the taskbar). Clear the entries and formatting in cells A1 and A2 as you did earlier, then rerun the **NameAndCourse** macro.

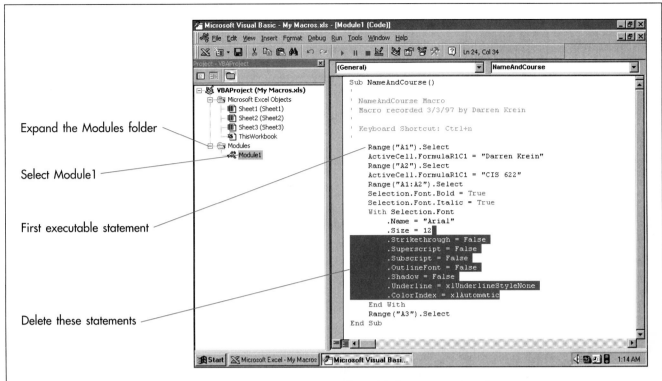

Expand the Modules folder

Select Module1

First executable statement

Delete these statements

(d) Simplify the Macro (steps 4 and 5)

FIGURE 3.2   Hands-on Exercise 1 (continued)

➤ Your name and class should once again be entered in cells A1 and A2. (If the macro does not execute correctly, press **Alt+F11** to toggle back to the Visual Basic Editor in order to correct your macro.)

➤ Save the workbook.

SIMPLIFY THE MACRO

The macro recorder usually sets all possible options for an Excel command or dialog box even if you do not change those options. We suggest, therefore, that you make a macro easier to read by deleting the unnecessary statements.

STEP 6: Create the Erase Macro

➤ Pull down the **Tools menu.** Click the **Macro command,** then click **Record New Macro** from the cascaded menu. You will see the Record Macro dialog box as described earlier.

➤ Enter **EraseNameAndCourse** as the name of the macro. Do not leave any spaces in the macro name. If necessary, change the description to include your name.

➤ Click in the **Shortcut Key** check box and enter a **lowercase e.** (Ctrl+e should appear as the shortcut.) Check that the option to Store macro in **This Workbook** is selected.

➤ Click **OK** to begin recording the macro, which displays the Stop Recording toolbar. Be sure you are recording absolute references (i.e., the Relative References button should be flush on the toolbar).

 • Click and drag to select cells **A1** through **A2** as shown in Figure 3.2e, even if they are already selected.

 • Pull down the **Edit menu.** Click **Clear.** Click **All** from the cascaded menu to erase both the contents and formatting from the selected cells. Cells A1 through A2 should now be empty.

 • Click in cell **A3** to deselect all other cells prior to ending the macro.

➤ Click the **Stop Recording button** to end the macro.

➤ Save the workbook.

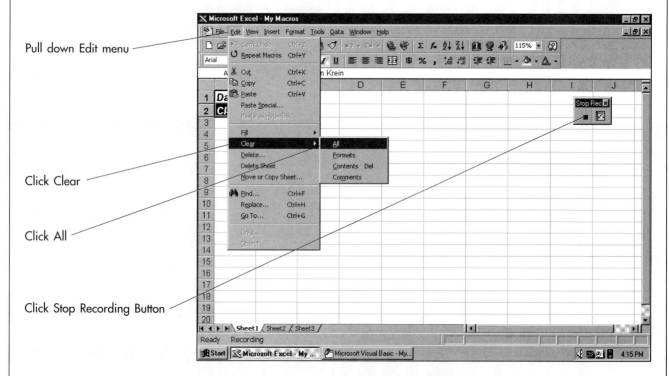

Pull down Edit menu

Click Clear

Click All

Click Stop Recording Button

(e) Create the Erase Macro (step 6)

FIGURE 3.2   Hands-on Exercise 1 (continued)

TO SELECT OR NOT SELECT

If you start recording, then select a cell(s) within the macro, the selection becomes part of the macro, and the macro will always operate on the same cell. If, however, you select the cell(s) prior to recording, the macro is more general and operates on the selected cells, which may differ every time the macro is executed. Both techniques are valid, and the decision depends on what you want the macro to do.

STEP 7: Shortcut Keys

➤ Press **Ctrl+n** to execute the NameAndCourse macro. (You need to reenter your name and course in order to test the newly created EraseNameAnd-Course macro.) Your name and course should again appear in cells A1 and A2.

➤ Press **Ctrl+e** to execute the EraseNameAndCourse macro. Cells A1 and A2 should again be empty.

➤ You can press **Ctrl+n** and **Ctrl+e** repeatedly, to enter and then erase your name and course. End this step after having erased the data.

TROUBLESHOOTING

If the shortcut keys do not work, it is probably because they were not defined properly. Pull down the Tools menu, click Macro, click the Macros . . . command, then select the desired macro in the Macro Name list box. Click the Options button, then check the entry in the Shortcut Key text box. A lowercase letter creates a shortcut with just the Ctrl key, whereas an uppercase letter uses Ctrl+Shift with the shortcut. Thus, "n" and "N" will establish shortcuts of Ctrl+n and Ctrl+Shift+N, respectively.

STEP 8: Edit the Macro

➤ Press **Alt+F11** to switch to the Visual Basic Editor. Click the down (up) arrow on the vertical scroll bar to view both macros as shown in Figure 3.2f.

➤ Edit the NameAndCourse macro as follows:

• Change the Font Name to **Times New Roman.**

• Change the Font Size to **16 point.**

• Click and drag to select the statement **Selection.Font.Bold = True,** then press the **Del key** to delete the statement from the macro.

➤ Press **Alt+F11** to toggle back to the Excel workbook. Press **Ctrl+n** to run the revised NameAndCourse macro. Your name and course should appear in 16-point Times New Roman Italic.

➤ Press **Ctrl+e** to run the Erase macro before testing the NameAndCourse macro.

USE WHAT YOU KNOW

The Cut, Copy, and Paste commands are the mainstays of editing regardless of the application. Select the statements to cut or copy to the clipboard, then paste them elsewhere in the macro, as necessary. If the results are different from what you expected or intended, click the Undo command immediately to reverse the effects of the previous command.

Delete statement

Change typeface

Change point size

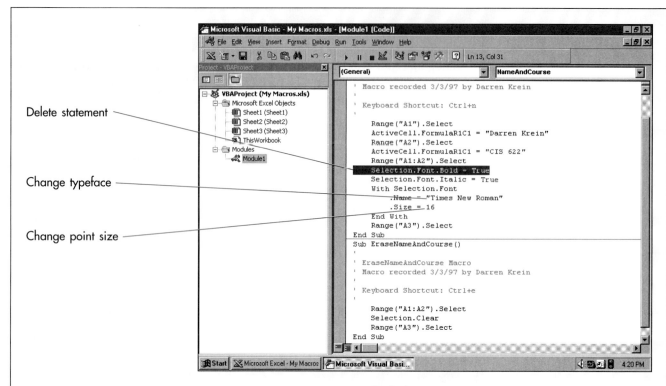

(f) Edit the Macro (step 8)

FIGURE 3.2   Hands-on Exercise 1 (continued)

STEP 9: Step through the Macro

➤ Press **Alt+F11** to switch back to the VBE window. Click the **Close button** to close the **Project window** within the Visual Basic Editor. The Code window expands to take the entire Visual Basic Editor window.

➤ Point to an empty area on the Windows taskbar, then click the **right mouse button** to display a shortcut menu. Click **Tile Vertically** to tile the open windows (Excel and the Visual Basic Editor).

➤ Your desktop should be similar to Figure 3.2g. It doesn't matter if the workbook is in the left or right window. (If additional windows are open on the desktop, minimize the other windows, then repeat the previous step to tile the open windows.)

➤ Click in the Visual Basic Editor window, then click anywhere within the NameAndCourse macro. Pull down the **Debug menu** and click the **Step Into command** (or press the **F8 key**) to enter the macro. The Sub statement is highlighted.

➤ Press the **F8 key** a second time to move to the first executable statement (the comments are skipped). The statement is selected (highlighted), but it has not yet been executed.

➤ Press the **F8 key** again to execute this statement (which selects cell A1 and moves to the next statement). Continue to press the **F8 key** to execute the statements in the macro one at a time. You can see the effect of each statement as it is executed in the Excel window.

View the effects of
the statements as they
are executed

This statement is about
to be executed

Right click an empty space
on the taskbar

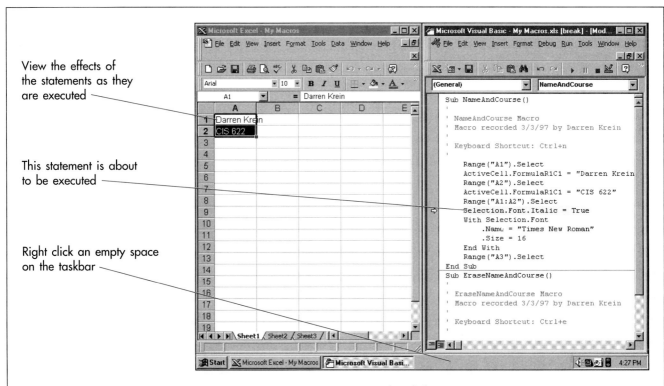

(g) Step through the Macro (step 9)

FIGURE 3.2   Hands-on Exercise 1 (continued)

THE STEP INTO COMMAND

The Step Into command is useful to slow down the execution of a macro
in the event the macro does not perform as intended. In essence, you execute the macro one statement at a time, while viewing the results of each
statement in the associated worksheet. If a statement does not do what
you want it to do, just change the statement in the Visual Basic window,
then continue to press the F8 key to step through the procedure and see
the results of your change.

STEP 10: Print the Module

➤ Click in the Visual Basic window. Pull down the **File menu.** Click **Print** to
display the Print VBA Project dialog box in Figure 3.2h.

➤ Click the option button to print the current module. Click **OK.** Submit the
listing of the current module, which contains the procedures for both macros,
to your instructor as proof you did this exercise.

➤ Close the My Macros workbook, which automatically closes the Visual Basic
Editor. Click **Yes** if asked to save the workbook.

➤ Exit Excel if you do not wish to continue with the next exercise at this time.

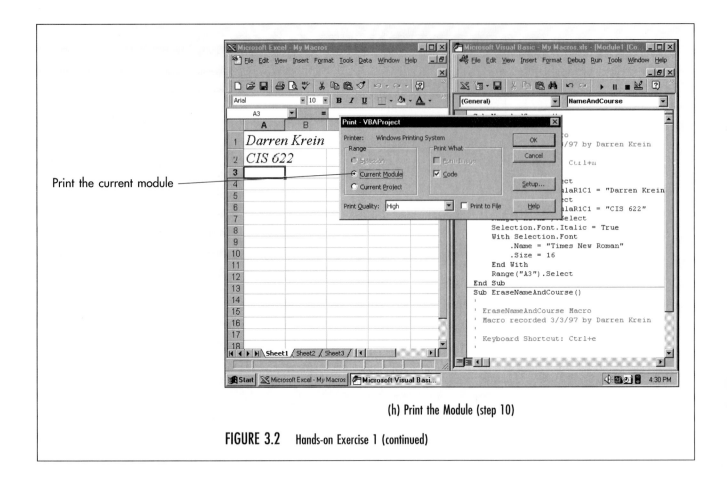

Print the current module

(h) Print the Module (step 10)

FIGURE 3.2   Hands-on Exercise 1 (continued)

RELATIVE VERSUS ABSOLUTE REFERENCES

One of the most important options to specify when recording a macro is whether the references are to be relative or absolute. A reference is a cell address. An *absolute reference* is a constant address that always refers to the same cell. A *relative reference* is variable in that the reference will change from one execution of the macro to the next, depending on the location of the active cell when the macro is executed.

To appreciate the difference, consider Figure 3.3, which displays a modified version of the NameAndCourse macro from the previous exercise with absolute and relative references. Figure 3.3a uses absolute references to place your name, course, and date in cells A1, A2, and A3. The data will always be entered in these cells regardless of which cell is selected when you execute the macro.

Figure 3.3b enters the same data, but with relative references, so that the cells in which the data is entered depend on which cell is selected when the macro is executed. If cell A1 is selected, your name, course, and date will be entered in cells A1, A2, and A3. If, however, cell E4 is the active cell when you execute the macro, then your name, course, and date will be entered in cells E4, E5, and E6.

A relative reference is specified by an *offset* that indicates the number of rows and columns from the active cell. An offset of (1,0) indicates a cell one row below the active cell. An offset of (0,1) indicates a cell one column to the right of the active cell. In similar fashion, an offset of (1,1) indicates a cell one row below and one column to the right of the active cell. Negative offsets are used for cells above or to the left of the current selection.

Absolute reference
to specified cell

```
Range("A1").Select
ActiveCell.FormulaR1C1 = "Darren Krein"
Range("A2").Select
ActiveCell.FormulaR1C1 = "CIS 622"
Range("A3").Select
ActiveCell.FormulaR1C1 = "TODAY()"
Range("A1:A3").Select
Selection.Font.Italic = True
With Selection.Font
    .Name = "Arial"
    .Size = 12
End With
Range("A3").Select
End Sub
```

(a) Absolute References

Relative reference to the cell
one row below the active cell

Indicates a column of three
cells, not cells A1 to A3

```
ActiveCell.FormulaR1C1 = "Darren Krein"
ActiveCell.Offset(1, 0).Range("A1").Select
ActiveCell.FormulaR1C1 = "CIS 622"
ActiveCell.Offset(1, 0).Range("A1").Select
ActiveCell.FormulaR1C1 = "=TODAY()"
ActiveCell.Offset(-2, 0).Range("A1:A3").Select
Selection.Font.Italic = True
With Selection.Font
    .Name = "Arial"
    .Size = 12
End With
ActiveCell.Offset(3, 0).Range("A1").Select
End Sub
```

(b) Relative References

FIGURE 3.3   Absolute versus Relative References

Relative references may appear confusing at first, but they extend the power of a macro by making it more general. You will appreciate this capability as you learn more about macros. Let us begin by recognizing that the statement:

ActiveCell.Offset (1,0).Range ("A1").Select

means select the cell one row below the active cell. It has nothing to do with cell A1, and you might wonder why the entry Range ("A1") is included. The answer is that the offset specifies the location of the new range (one row below the current cell), and the A1 indicates that the size of that range is a single cell (A1).

In similar fashion, the statement:

ActiveCell.Offset (-2,0).Range ("A1:A3").Select

selects a range, starting two rows above the current cell, that is one column by three rows in size. Again, it has nothing to do with cells A1 through A3. The offset specifies the location of a new range (two rows above the current cell) and the shape of that range (a column of three cells). If you are in cell D11 when the statement is executed, the selected range will be cells D9 through D11. The selection starts with the cell two rows above the active cell (cell D9), then it continues from that point to select a range consisting of one column by three rows (cells D9:D11).

The hands-on exercise at the beginning of the chapter created the NameAnd-Course macro in the My Macros workbook, where it is available to that workbook or to any other workbook that is in memory when the My Macros workbook is open. What if, however, you want the macro to be available at all times, not just when the My Macros workbook is open? This is easily accomplished by storing the macro in the Personal Macro workbook when it is first recorded.

The *Personal Macro workbook* is a special workbook that opens automatically whenever Excel is loaded. The macros within the Personal Macro workbook are available to any workbook as long as the Personal Macro workbook is open. The following hands-on exercise modifies the NameAndCourse macro to include relative references, then stores that macro in the Personal Macro workbook.

The exercise also expands the original macro to enter the date of execution, and further generalizes the macro to accept the name of the course as input. The latter is accomplished through the *InputBox command* that prompts the user for a specific response, then stores that response within the macro.

NETWORK PRIVILEGES

If you are on a network, as opposed to a stand-alone machine, you will not be able to save the Personal Macro workbook in the XLStart folder, as only the network supervisor has rights to that folder. Ask your instructor or the network administrator how to establish your own Personal Macro workbook.

HANDS-ON EXERCISE 2

The Personal Macro Workbook

Objective: To create and store a macro in the Personal Macro workbook; to assign a toolbar button to a macro; to use the Visual Basic InputBox statement. Use Figure 3.4 as a guide in the exercise.

STEP 1: Record with Relative References

➤ Start Excel. Open a new workbook if one is not already open. Pull down the **Tools menu,** click (or point to) the **Macro command,** then click **Record New Macro** to display the Record Macro dialog box

➤ Enter **NameAndCourse** as the name of the macro. Do not leave any spaces in the macro name. Click in the **Shortcut Key** check box and enter a **lower-case n.** Ctrl+n should appear as the shortcut.

➤ Click the **drop-down arrow** in the Store macro in list box and select the Personal Macro workbook. Click **OK** to begin recording the macro, which displays the Stop Recording toolbar.

➤ Click the **Relative References** button on the Stop Recording toolbar so that the button is **pushed in** as shown in Figure 3.4a.

➤ The Relative References button functions as a toggle switch—click it and the button is pushed in to record relative references. Click it again and you record absolute references. Be sure to record relative references.

Click to select font size ——

Stop Recording button ——

Relative References button ——

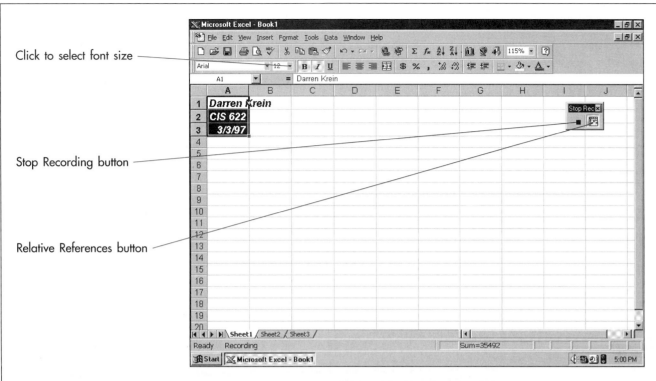

(a) Record the Macro (steps 1 and 2)

FIGURE 3.4   Hands-on Exercise 2

RELATIVE VERSUS ABSOLUTE REFERENCES

Relative references appear confusing at first but they extend the power of a macro by making it more general. Macro statements that have been recorded with relative references include an offset to indicate the number of rows and columns the selection is to be from the active cell. An offset of (1,0) indicates a cell one row below the active cell, whereas an offset of (0,1) indicates a cell one column to the right of the active cell. Negative offsets are used for cells above or to the left of the current selection.

STEP 2: Record the Macro

➤ Enter your name in the active cell (e.g., cell A1 in Figure 3.4a).

➤ Press the **down arrow key** to move to the cell immediately underneath the current cell. Enter the course you are taking.

➤ Press the **down arrow key** to move to the next cell. Enter **=TODAY()** to enter today's date.

➤ Click and drag to select the three cells containing the data values you just entered (cells A1 through A3 in Figure 3.4a).

• Click the **Bold button.**

• Click the **Italic button.**

• Click the arrow on the **Font Size list box.** Click **12** to change the point size.

- If necessary, click and drag the border between the column headings for Columns A and B to increase the width of column A if you see a series of number signs in cell A3.
- Click in cell **A4** to deselect all other cells prior to ending the macro.
➤ Click the **Stop Recording button** to end the macro.

STEP 3: The Personal Workbook

➤ Pull down the **Tools menu,** click the **Macro command,** then click **Visual Basic Editor** (or press **Alt+F11**) to open the Visual Basic Editor as shown in Figure 3.4b. Maximize the VBE window. Do not be concerned if your screen is different from ours.

➤ If necessary, pull down the **View menu.** Click **Project Explorer** to open the Project window in the left pane.

➤ There are currently two open VBA projects (Book1, the name of the workbook on which you are working, and Personal.XLS, the Personal Macro workbook in which you saved the macro).

➤ Click the **plus sign** to expand the Personal Workbook folder, then click the **plus sign** to expand the **Modules folder** within this project.

➤ Click (select) **Module1,** pull down the **View menu,** and click **Code** to open the Code window in the right pane. Maximize the Code window.

➤ Close any other open windows within the Visual Basic Editor. Your screen should match the one in Figure 3.2b. The first executable statement in your module should begin with *ActiveCell.FormulaR1C1,* which indicates that the macro was correctly recorded with relative references.

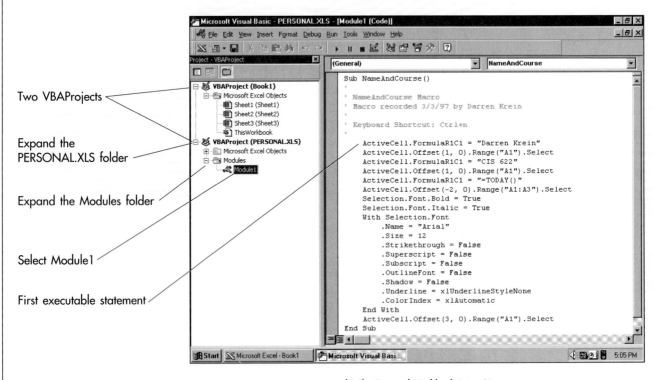

Two VBAProjects

Expand the PERSONAL.XLS folder

Expand the Modules folder

Select Module1

First executable statement

(b) The Personal Workbook (step 3)

FIGURE 3.4   Hands-on Exercise 2 (continued)

➤ If you see a very different statement, *Range("A1").Select,* it means that you incorrectly recorded the macro with absolute references. Right click the module, select the **Remove Module command,** then return to step 1 and rerecord the macro.

WHAT DOES RANGE ("A1:A3") REALLY MEAN?

The statement ActiveCell.Offset(−2,0).Range ("A1:A3").Select has nothing to do with cells A1 through A3, so why is the entry Range ("A1:A3") included? The effect of the statement is to select three cells (one cell under the other) starting with the cell two rows above the current cell. The offset (−2,0) specifies the starting point of the selected range (two rows above the current cell). The range ("A1:A3") indicates the size and shape of the selected range (a vertical column of three cells) from the starting cell.

STEP 4: Edit the Macro

➤ Click and drag to select the name of the course, which is found in the third executable statement of the macro. Be sure to include the quotation marks (e.g., "CIS622" in our example) in your selection.

➤ Enter **InputBox("Enter the Course You Are Taking")** to replace the selected text. Note that as you enter the Visual Basic key word, *InputBox,* a prompt (containing the correct syntax for this statement) is displayed on the screen as shown in Figure 3.4c.

➤ Just ignore the prompt and keep typing to complete the entry. Press the **Home key** as you complete the entry to scroll back to the beginning of the line.

➤ Click immediately after the number **12,** then click and drag to select the next seven statements. Press the **Del key** to delete the highlighted statements from the macro.

➤ Delete the **Selection.Font.Bold = True** statement. Click the **Save button** to save the modified macro.

THE INPUT BOX STATEMENT

The InputBox statement adds flexibility to a macro by obtaining input from the user when the macro is executed. It is used in this example to generalize the NameAndCourse macro by asking the user for the name of the course as opposed to storing the name within the macro. The InputBox statement, coupled with storing the macro in the Personal Macro workbook, enables the user to personalize any workbook by executing the associated macro.

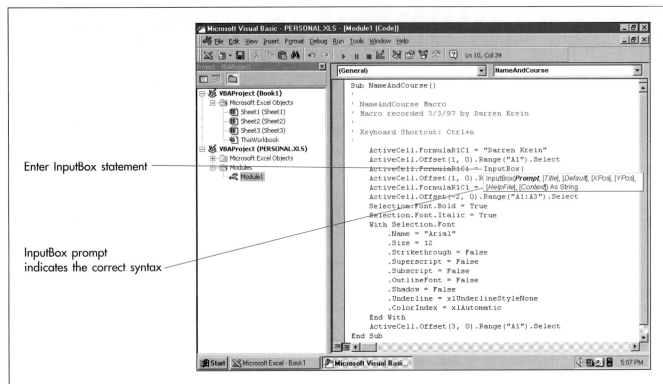

Enter InputBox statement

InputBox prompt
indicates the correct syntax

(c) Edit the Macro (step 4)

FIGURE 3.4   Hands-on Exercise 2 (continued)

STEP 5: Test the Revised Macro

➤ Press **Alt+F11** to view the Excel workbook. Click in any cell—for example cell C5 as shown in Figure 3.4d.

➤ Pull down the **Tools menu.** Click **Macro,** click the **Macros . . . command,** select **PERSONAL.XLS!NameAndCourse,** then click the **Run command button** to run the macro. (Alternatively you can use the Ctrl+n shortcut.)

➤ The macro enters your name in cell C5 (the active cell), then displays the input dialog box shown in Figure 3.4d.

➤ Enter any appropriate course and press the **enter key.** You should see the course you entered followed by the date. All three entries will be formatted according to the commands you specified in the macro.

➤ Click in a different cell, then press **Ctrl+n** to rerun the macro. The macro will enter your name, the course you specify, and the date in the selected location.

RED, GREEN, AND BLUE

Visual Basic automatically assigns different colors to different types of statements (or a portion of those statements). Any statement containing a syntax error appears in red. Comments appear in green. Key words—such as Sub and End Sub, With and End With, and True and False—appear in blue.

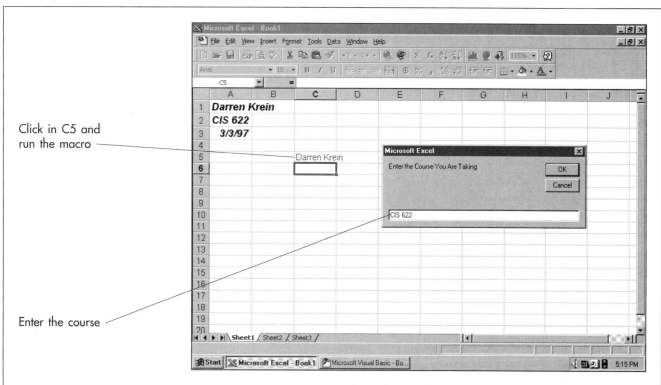

Click in C5 and
run the macro

Enter the course

(d) Test the Revised Macro (step 5)

FIGURE 3.4   Hands-on Exercise 2 (continued)

STEP 6: Add a Custom Button

➤ Point to any toolbar, then click the **right mouse button** to display a shortcut menu. Click **Customize** to display the Customize dialog box in Figure 3.4e.

➤ Click the **Commands tab.** Click the **down arrow** to scroll through the Categories list box until you can select the **Macros category.**

➤ Click and drag the **Custom (Happy Face) button** to an available space at the right of the Standard toolbar. Release the mouse. (You must drag the button *within* the toolbar.)

➤ Click the **Modify Selection button** within the Customize dialog box to display the cascaded menu in Figure 3.4e. Click and drag to select the name of the button (&Custom Button) and replace it with **NameAndCourse,** to create a ScreenTip for that button. Do not press the enter key.

➤ Click the **Assign Macro command** at the end of the cascaded menu to display the Assign Macro dialog box. Select **PERSONAL.XLS!NameAnd-Course** and click **OK.** Click **Close** to exit the Custom dialog box.

CUSTOMIZE THE TOOLBAR

You can customize any toolbar to display additional buttons as appropriate. Pull down the View menu, click Toolbars, click Customize to display the Customize dialog box, then click the Commands tab. Choose the category containing the button you want, then click and drag that button to an existing toolbar.

Drag custom button to toolbar

Select Macros category

Enter NameAndCourse

Click the Assign Macro command

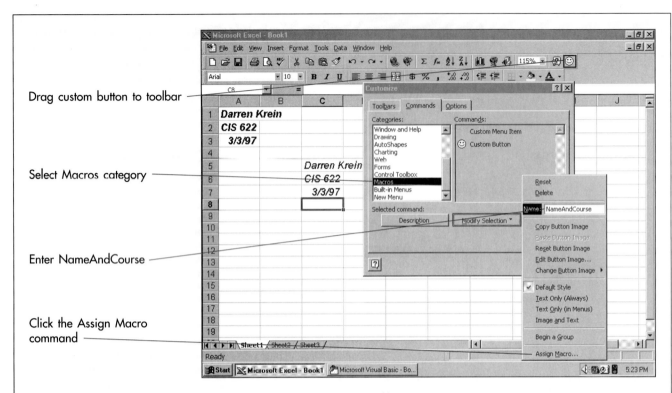

(e) Add a Custom Button (step 6)

FIGURE 3.4   Hands-on Exercise 2 (continued)

STEP 7: Test the Custom Button

➤ Click the **New Workbook button** on the Standard toolbar to open a new workbook (Book2 in Figure 3.4f; the book number is not important). Click cell **B2** as the active cell from which to execute the macro.

➤ Point to the **Happy Face button** to display the ScreenTip you just created. The ScreenTip will be useful in future sessions should you forget the function of this button.

➤ Click the **Happy Face button** to execute the NameAndCourse macro. Enter the name of a course you are taking. The macro inserts your name, course, and today's date in cells B2 through B4.

CHANGE THE CUSTOM BUTTON ICON

The Happy Face icon is automatically associated with the Custom Macro button. You can, however, change the image after the button has been added to a toolbar. Right click the button to display the Customize dialog box, which must remain open in order to change the image. Right click the button a second time to display a different shortcut menu with commands pertaining to the specific button. Click the command to Change the Button Image, select a new image, then close the Customize dialog box.

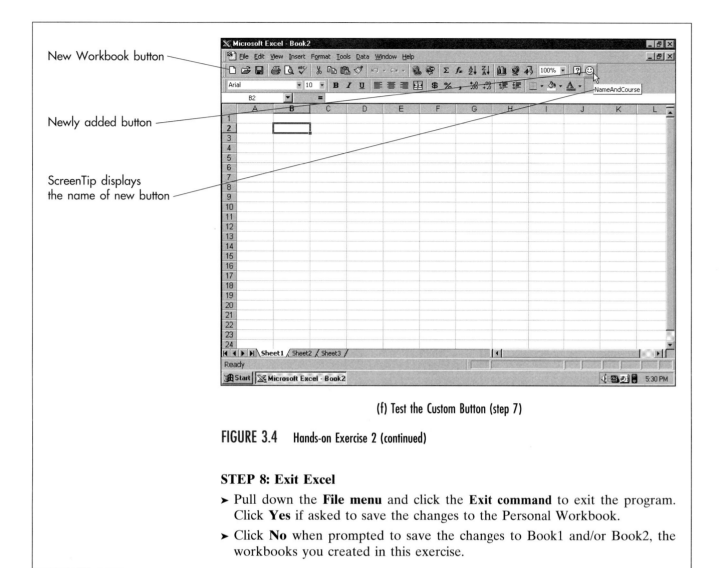

New Workbook button

Newly added button

ScreenTip displays
the name of new button

(f) Test the Custom Button (step 7)

FIGURE 3.4   Hands-on Exercise 2 (continued)

STEP 8: Exit Excel

➤ Pull down the **File menu** and click the **Exit command** to exit the program.
Click **Yes** if asked to save the changes to the Personal Workbook.

➤ Click **No** when prompted to save the changes to Book1 and/or Book2, the
workbooks you created in this exercise.

DATA MANAGEMENT MACROS

Thus far we have covered the basics of macros in the context of entering your
name, course, and today's date in a worksheet. As you might expect, macros are
capable of much more and can be used to automate any repetitive task. The next
several pages illustrate the use of macros in conjunction with the list (data) management examples that were presented in an earlier chapter.

The worksheet in Figure 3.5a displays an employee list and the associated
summary statistics. As you already know, a list is an area in a worksheet that contains rows of similar data. The first row in the list contains the column labels or
field names. Each additional row contains a record. Every record contains the
same fields in the same order. The list in Figure 3.5a has 14 records. Each record
has seven fields: name, location, title, gender, service, hire date, and salary.

A criteria range has been established in cells A17 through G18 for use with
the database functions in cells G22 through G26. Criteria values have not been
entered in Figure 3.5a, and so the database functions reflect the values of the entire
list (all 14 employees).

The worksheet in Figure 3.5b displays selected employees, those who work
in Chicago. Look carefully at the worksheet and you will see that only rows 3, 9,

Field names ———

Data records ———

	A	B	C	D	E	F	G
1	Name	Location	Title	Gender	Service	Hire Date	Salary
2	Adams	Atlanta	Trainee	M	1.8	11/24/93	$19,500
3	Adamson	Chicago	Manager	F	3.5	3/16/92	$52,000
4	Brown	Atlanta	Trainee	F	1.8	11/24/93	$18,500
5	Charles	Boston	Account Rep	M	3.5	3/16/92	$40,000
6	Coulter	Atlanta	Manager	M	1.8	11/24/93	$100,000
7	Elofson	Miami	Account Rep	F	2.9	10/31/92	$47,500
8	Gillenson	Miami	Manager	M	1.9	10/31/93	$55,000
9	James	Chicago	Account Rep	F	5.9	10/31/89	$42,500
10	Johnson	Chicago	Account Rep	M	4.9	10/31/90	$47,500
11	Manin	Boston	Account Rep	F	3.5	3/16/92	$49,500
12	Marder	Chicago	Account Rep	F	3.9	10/31/91	$38,500
13	Milgrom	Boston	Manager	M	3.5	3/16/92	$57,500
14	Rubin	Boston	Account Rep	F	3.5	3/16/92	$45,000
15	Smith	Atlanta	Account Rep	M	1.8	11/24/93	$65,000
16							

Criteria range (A17:G18) ———

	A	B	C	D	E	F	G
17	Name	Location	Title	Gender	Service	Hire Date	Salary
18							
19							
20							

Database functions (G22:G26)
compute summary statistics ———

	Summary Statistics	
21	Summary Statistics	
22	Average Salary	$48,429
23	Maximum Salary	$100,000
24	Minimum Salary	$18,500
25	Total Salary	$678,000
26	Number of Employees	14

(a) All Employees

List is filtered to employees
who work in Chicago ———

	A	B	C	D	E	F	G
1	Name	Location	Title	Gender	Service	Hire Date	Salary
3	Adamson	Chicago	Manager	F	3.5	3/16/92	$52,000
9	James	Chicago	Account Rep	F	5.9	10/31/89	$42,500
10	Johnson	Chicago	Account Rep	M	4.9	10/31/90	$47,500
12	Marder	Chicago	Account Rep	F	3.9	10/31/91	$38,500
16							
17	Name	Location	Title	Gender	Service	Hire Date	Salary
18		Chicago					
19							
20							

Summary statistics reflect only
the Chicago employees ———

	Summary Statistics	
21	Summary Statistics	
22	Average Salary	$45,125
23	Maximum Salary	$52,000
24	Minimum Salary	$38,500
25	Total Salary	$180,500
26	Number of Employees	4

(b) Chicago Employees

Figure 3.5 Data Management Macros

10, and 12 are visible. The other rows within the list have been hidden by the Advanced Filter command, which displays only those employees who satisfy the specified criteria. The summary statistics reflect only the Chicago employees; for example, the DCOUNT function in cell G26 shows four employees (as opposed to the 14 employees in Figure 3.5a).

You already know how to execute the list management commands to enter criteria and filter a list accordingly. The process is not difficult, but it does require the execution of several commands. Consider, for example, the steps that would be necessary to modify the worksheet in Figure 3.5b if you wanted to display managers rather than Chicago employees.

You would have to clear the existing criterion (Chicago) in cell B18, then enter the new criterion (Manager) in cell C18. You would then execute the Advanced Filter command, which requires the specification of the list (cells A1 through G15), the location of the criteria range (cells A17 through G18), and the option to filter the list in place.

And what if you wanted to see the Chicago employees after you executed the commands to display the managers? You would have to repeat all of the previous commands to change the criterion back to what it was, then filter the list accordingly. Suffice it to say that the entire process can be simplified through creation of the appropriate macros.

The following exercise develops the macro to select the Chicago employees from the worksheet in Figure 3.5a. A subsequent exercise, later in the chapter, develops two additional macros, one to select the managers and another to select the managers who work in Chicago.

HANDS-ON EXERCISE 3

Data Management Macros

Objective: To create a data management macro in conjunction with an employee list; to create a custom button to execute a macro. Use Figure 3.6 as a guide in the exercise.

PLAN AHEAD

Plan a macro ahead of time by testing its commands prior to turning on the macro recorder. Go through every command to make sure you produce the desired results. Determine the cells you will need to select so that you can assign names to these cells prior to recording the macro.

STEP 1: Data Management Functions

➤ Start Excel. Open the **Finished Employee List** workbook that was created in Chapter 1.

➤ Click any cell between A2 and A15, then click the **Ascending Sort button** on the Standard toolbar. The employees should be listed in alphabetical order as shown in Figure 3.6a.

➤ Click in **cell D17.** Type **Gender** to complete the field names in the criteria range. Clear all entries in the range **A18** through **G18.**

➤ Click in **cell G22,** which contains the DAVERAGE function, to compute the average salary of all employees who satisfy the specified criteria. No criteria have been entered, however, so the displayed value of $48,429 represents the average salary of all 14 employees.

➤ Click **cell B18.** Enter **Chicago.** Press **enter.** The average salary changes to $45,125 to indicate the average salary of the four Chicago employees.

➤ Click **cell C18.** Enter **Manager.** Press **enter.** The average salary changes to $52,000 to indicate the average salary of the one Chicago manager.

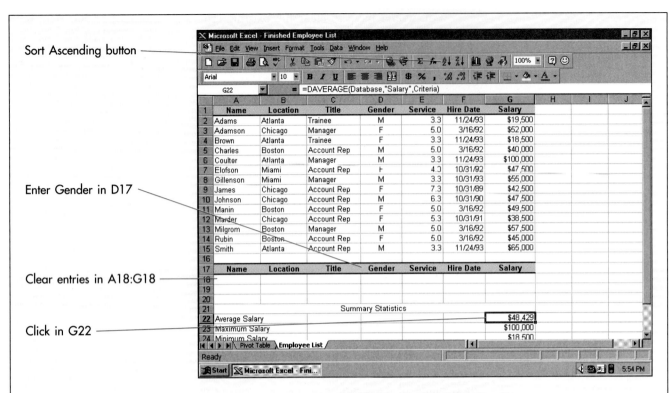

Sort Ascending button

Enter Gender in D17

Clear entries in A18:G18

Click in G22

(a) Data Management Functions (step 1)

FIGURE 3.6   Hands-on Exercise 3

NAMED RANGES

Use the Name command in the Insert menu to establish a mnemonic name (e.g., Database) for a cell range (e.g., A1:G15). Once defined, names adjust automatically for insertions and/or deletions within the range or a movement of the range within the worksheet. A name can be used in any command or function that requires a cell reference, and its use is highly recommended. This is especially true in macros, both to make the macro easier to read and to make it immune from changes to the worksheet.

STEP 2: The Create Name Command

➤ Click and drag to select **cells A17** through **G18** as shown in Figure 3.6b. Pull down the **Insert menu,** click **Name,** then click **Create** to display the Create Names dialog box.

➤ The box to **Create Names in Top Row** is already checked. Click **OK.** This command assigns the text in each cell in row 17 to the corresponding cell in row 18; for example, cells B18 and C18 will be assigned the names Location and Title, respectively.

➤ Click and drag to select only **cells A18** through **G18.** (You need to assign a name to these seven cells collectively as you will have to clear the criteria values in row 18 later in the chapter.)

➤ Pull down the **Insert menu.** Click **Name.** Click **Define.** Enter **Criteria Values** in the Define Name dialog box. Click **OK.**

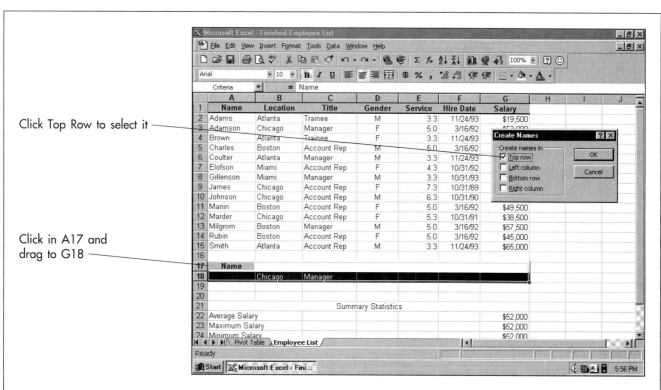

Click Top Row to select it

Click in A17 and drag to G18

(b) The Create Name Command (step 2)

FIGURE 3.6 Hands-on Exercise 3 (continued)

THE NAME BOX

Use the Name box to define a range by selecting the cell(s) in the worksheet to which the name is to apply, clicking the Name box, then entering the name. For example, to assign the name CriteriaValues to cells A18:G18, select the range, click in the Name box, type CriteriaValues, and press enter. The Name box can also be used to select a previously defined range by clicking the drop-down arrow next to the box and choosing the desired name from the drop-down list.

STEP 3: The Go To Command

➤ Pull down the **Edit menu.** Click **Go To** to produce the Go To dialog box in Figure 3.6c. You should see the names you defined (CriteriaValues, Gender, Hire_Date, Location, Name, Salary, Service, and Title) as well as the two names defined previously by the authors (Criteria and Database).

➤ Click **Database.** Click **OK.** Cells A1 through G5 should be selected, corresponding to cells assigned to the name *Database*.

➤ Press the **F5 key** (a shortcut for the Edit Go To command), which again produces the Go To dialog box. Click **Criteria.** Click **OK.** Cells A17 through G18 should be selected.

Click to see a list
of defined names

List of defined names
produced with Edit Go To
command or by pressing F5

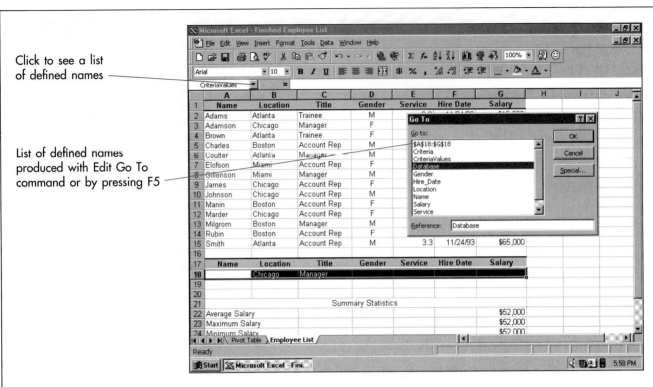

(c) The Go To Command (step 3)

FIGURE 3.6 Hands-on Exercise 3 (continued)

➤ Click the **drop-down arrow** next to the Name box. Click **Location.** Cell B18 should be selected.

➤ You are now ready to record the macro.

STEP 4: Record a Macro

➤ Pull down the **View menu,** click **Toolbars,** then check **Visual Basic** to display the Visual Basic Toolbar. Click the **Record Macro** button on the Visual Basic toolbar to display the Record Macro dialog box.

➤ Enter **Chicago** in the Macro Name text box. Verify that the macro will be stored in **This Workbook** and that the shortcut key check box is empty.

➤ Click **OK** to begin recording the macro. If necessary, click the **Relative References button** on the Stop Recording toolbar to record Absolute references (the button should be out).

THE VISUAL BASIC TOOLBAR

The Visual Basic Toolbar consists of six buttons associated with macros and Visual Basic. You will find a button to run an existing macro, to record (or stop recording) a new macro, and to open (toggle to) the Visual Basic Editor. The toolbar can be displayed (or hidden) by right clicking any visible toolbar, then checking (or clearing) Visual Basic from the list of toolbars.

STEP 5: Record the Macro (Edit Clear Command)

➤ Pull down the **Edit menu,** click **Go To,** select **CriteriaValues** from the Go To dialog box, and click **OK.** Cells A18 through G18 should be selected as shown in Figure 3.6d. (Alternatively, you can also use the **F5 key** or the Name box to select CriteriaValues.)

➤ Pull down the **Edit menu.** Click **Clear,** then click **All** from the cascaded menu as shown in Figure 3.6d. Cells A18 through G18 (the criteria range) should be empty, and a new criterion can be entered in the macro.

Click All to clear entries and formats in selected range (A18:G18)

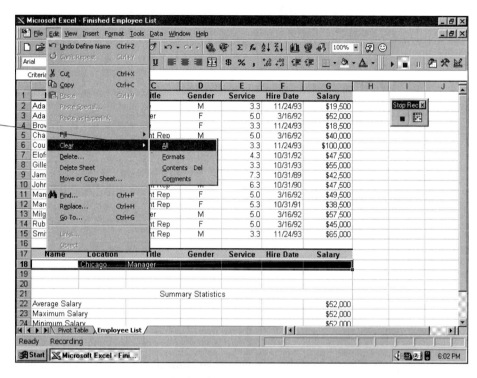

(d) The Edit Clear Command (step 5)

FIGURE 3.6   Hands-on Exercise 3 (continued)

STEP 6: Record the Macro (Advanced Filter Command)

➤ Pull down the **Edit menu,** click **Go To,** select **Location** from the Go To dialog box, and click **OK.**

➤ Cell B18 should be selected. Enter **Chicago** to establish the criterion for both the database functions and the Advanced Filter command.

➤ Click in **cell A2** to position the active cell within the employee list. Pull down the **Data menu.** Click **Filter,** then click **Advanced Filter** from the cascaded menu to display the dialog box in Figure 3.6e.

➤ Enter **Database** as the List Range. Press the **tab key.** Enter **Criteria** as the Criteria Range.

➤ Check that the option to **Filter the List in-place** is checked.

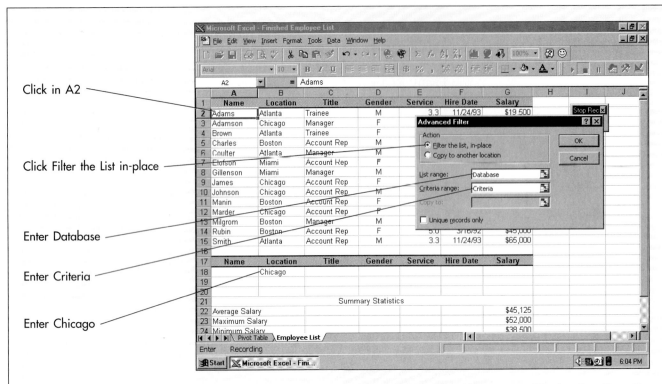

Click in A2

Click Filter the List in-place

Enter Database

Enter Criteria

Enter Chicago

(e) Advanced Filter Command (step 6)

FIGURE 3.6   Hands-on Exercise 3 (continued)

➤ Click **OK.** You should see only those employees who satisfy the current criteria (i.e., Adamson, James, Johnson, and Marder, who are the employees who work in Chicago).

➤ Click the **Stop Record button** to stop recording.

➤ Click the **Save button** to save the workbook with the macro.

STEP 7: View the Macro

➤ Click the **Visual Basic Editor** button on the Visual Basic toolbar to open the editor as shown in Figure 3.6f. If necessary, pull down the **View menu.** Click **Project Explorer** to open the Project window in the left pane.

➤ If necessary, expand the **Modules folder,** click (select) **Module1,** pull down the **View menu,** and click **Code** to open the Code window in the right pane.

➤ Close any other open windows within the Visual Basic Editor. Your screen should match the one in Figure 3.6f. If necessary, correct your macro so that it matches ours.

➤ If the correction is minor, it is easiest to edit the macro directly; otherwise delete the macro, then return to step 4 and rerecord the macro from the beginning. (To delete a macro, pull down the Tools menu, click Macro, select the macro you wish to delete, then click the Delete button.)

➤ Click the **View Microsoft Excel button** at the left of the toolbar or press **Alt+F11** to return to the Employee worksheet.

View Microsoft Excel button

Expand the Modules folder

Select Module1

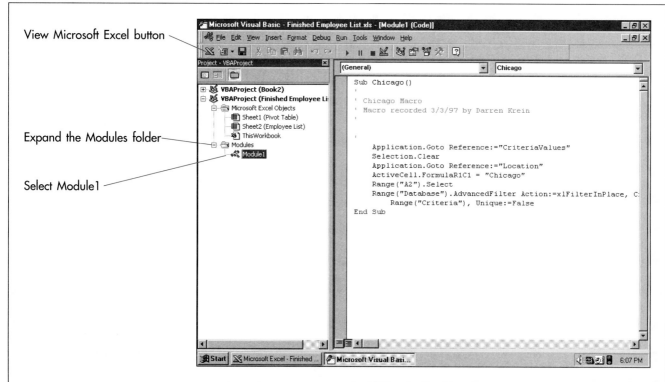

```
Sub Chicago()

' Chicago Macro
' Macro recorded 3/3/97 by Darren Krein
'


    Application.Goto Reference:="CriteriaValues"
    Selection.Clear
    Application.Goto Reference:="Location"
    ActiveCell.FormulaR1C1 = "Chicago"
    Range("A2").Select
    Range("Database").AdvancedFilter Action:=xlFilterInPlace, C:
        Range("Criteria"), Unique:=False
End Sub
```

(f) View the Macro (step 7)

FIGURE 3.6   Hands-on Exercise 3 (continued)

STEP 8: Assign the Macro

➤ Pull down the **View menu,** click **Toolbars,** then click **Forms** to display the Forms toolbar as shown in Figure 3.6g.

➤ Click the **Button tool** (the mouse pointer changes to a tiny crosshair). Click and drag in the worksheet as shown in Figure 3.6g to draw a button on the worksheet. Be sure to draw the button *below* the employee list, or the button may be hidden when a subsequent Data Filter command is executed.

➤ Release the mouse, and the Assign Macro dialog box will appear. Choose **Chicago** (the macro you just created) from the list of macro names. Click **OK**.

➤ The button should still be selected. Click and drag to select the name of the button, **Button 1.**

➤ Type **Chicago** as the new name. Do *not* press the enter key. Click outside the button to deselect it.

SELECTING A BUTTON

You cannot select a Macro button by clicking it, because that executes the associated macro. Thus, to select a macro button, you must press and hold the Ctrl key as you click the mouse. (You can also select a button by clicking the right mouse button to produce a shortcut menu.) Once the button has been selected, you can edit its name, and/or move or size the button just as you can any other Windows object.

Button tool

Forms toolbar

Chicago macro will be
assigned to selected button

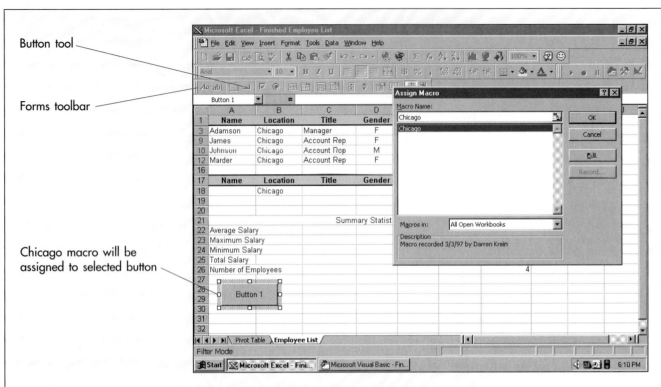

(g) Assign the Macro (step 8)

FIGURE 3.6 Hands-on Exercise 3 (continued)

STEP 9: Test the Macro

➤ Pull down the **Data menu,** click **Filter,** then click **Show All.**

➤ Click **cell B12.** Enter Miami to change the location for Marder. Press **enter.** The number of employees changes in the summary statistics area, as do the results of the other summary statistics.

➤ Click the **Chicago button** as shown in Figure 3.6h to execute the macro. Marder is *not* listed this time because she is no longer in Chicago.

➤ Pull down the **Data menu.** Click **Filter.** Click **Show All** to display the entire employee list.

EXECUTING A MACRO

There are several different ways to execute a macro. The most basic way is to pull down the Tools menu, click Macro, click Macros to display the Macros dialog box, then double click the desired macro to run it. You can assign a macro to a button within a worksheet or to a custom button on a toolbar, then click the button to run the macro. The fastest way is to use a keyboard shortcut, provided that a shortcut has been defined for the macro. All techniques are equally acceptable.

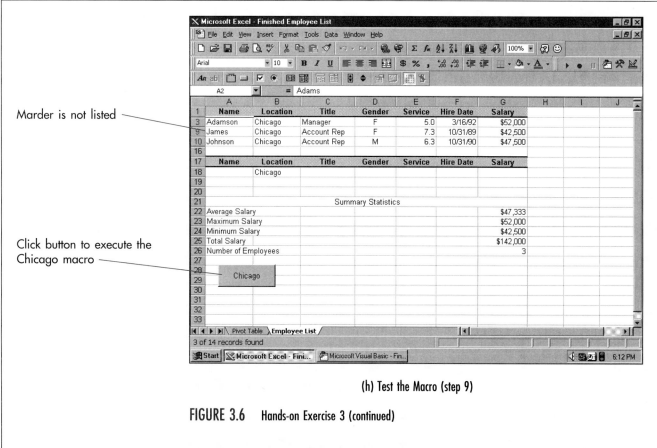

Marder is not listed

Click button to execute the
Chicago macro

(h) Test the Macro (step 9)

FIGURE 3.6   Hands-on Exercise 3 (continued)

> Click **cell B12.** Enter **Chicago** to change the location for this employee back
  to Chicago. Press **enter.** Click the **Chicago button** to execute the macro a second time. Marder is once again displayed with the Chicago employees.

> Pull down the **Data menu.** Click **Filter.** Click **Show All.**

> Save the workbook. Close the workbook. Exit Excel if you do not want to
  continue with the next exercise at this time.

CREATING ADDITIONAL MACROS

The macro to filter the Chicago employees is only one of several macros that could
be developed in conjunction with the employee list with which we have been working. It's reasonable to assume that you might want additional macros to select
other groups of employees, such as employees in another city or employees with
a particular job title.

You could develop the additional macros by recording them from scratch as
you did the Chicago macro. Alternatively, you could copy the Chicago macro, give
it a different name, then edit the copied macro so that it performs the desired
function. This is the approach we follow in the next hands-on exercise.

Visual Basic statements are edited the same way text is cditcd in a word processing program. Thus, you toggle back and forth between the insertion or over-
type modes to insert or type over text. You can also use the Cut, Copy, and Paste
commands just as you would with a word processor. Text (Visual Basic commands)
is cut or copied from one location to the clipboard, from where it can be pasted
to another location.

Creating Additional Macros

Objective: To duplicate an existing macro, then modify the copied macro to create an entirely new macro. Use Figure 3.7 as a guide.

STEP 1: Enable Macros

➤ Start Excel. Open the **Finished Employee List workbook** from the previous exercise. You should see the warning in Figure 3.7a.

➤ Click the **Tell Me More button** to display the Help window to learn more about macro viruses. (Pull down the **Tools menu,** click **Options,** click the **General tab,** and check the Settings box for **Micro Virus Protection** if you do not see the warning message.) Click the close button when you are finished.

➤ Click the **Enable Macros button** to open the Finished Employee workbook.

Tell Me More button

Enable Macros button

Description of macro virus

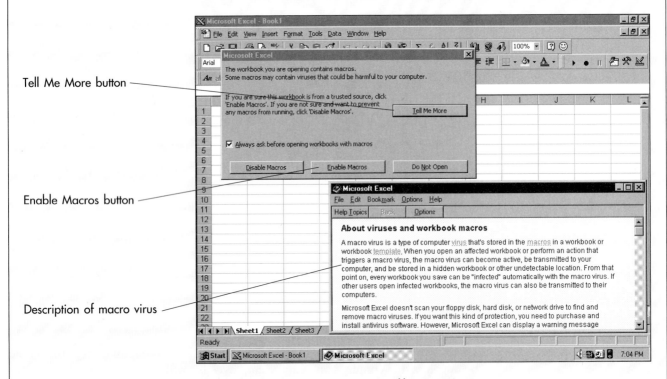

(a) Enable Macros (step 1)

FIGURE 3.7   Hands-on Exercise 4

MACRO VIRUSES

Microsoft Excel will warn you that a workbook contains a macro, which in turn may carry a macro virus. If you are confident the workbook is safe, click the button to Enable macros; otherwise open the workbook with the macros disabled.

STEP 2: Copy the Chicago Macro

➤ Pull down the **Tools menu,** click the **Macro command,** then click **Visual Basic Editor** (or press **Alt+F11**) to open the Visual Basic Editor.

➤ Click and drag to select the entire Chicago macro as shown in Figure 3.7b.

➤ Pull down the **Edit menu** and click **Copy** (or click the **Copy button** on the Standard toolbar).

➤ Click below the End Sub statement to deselect the macro and simultaneously establish the position of the insertion point. Press **enter** to insert a blank line below the End Sub statement.

➤ Pull down the **Edit menu** and click **Paste** (or click the **Paste button** on the Standard toolbar). The Chicago macro has been copied and now appears twice in Module1.

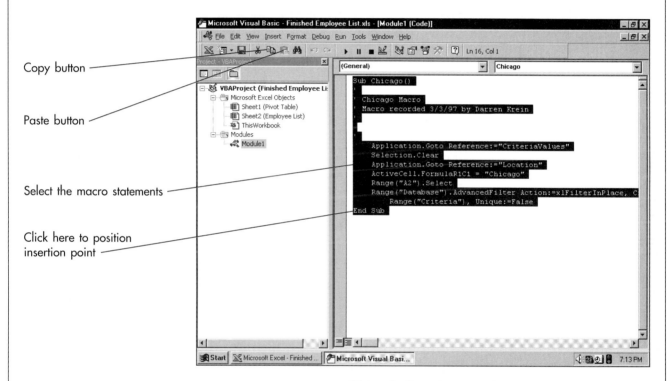

(b) Copy the Chicago Macro (step 2)

FIGURE 3.7 Hands-on Exercise 4 (continued)

THE SHIFT KEY

You can select text for editing (or replacement) with the mouse, or alternatively, you can select by using the cursor keys on the keyboard. Set the insertion point where you want the selection to begin, then press and hold the Shift key as you use the cursor keys to move the insertion point to the end of the selection.

STEP 3: Create the Manager Macro

➤ Click in front of the second (i.e., the copied) Chicago macro to set the insertion point. Pull down the **Edit menu.** Click **Replace** to display the Replace dialog box as shown in Figure 3.7c.

➤ Enter **Chicago** in the Find What text box. Press the **tab key.** Enter **Manager** in the Replace With text box. Select the option button to search in the *current* procedure. Click the **Find Next command button.**

➤ Excel searches for the first occurrence of Chicago, which should be in the Sub statement of the copied macro. (If this is not the case, click the **Find Next command button** until your screen matches Figure 3.7c.)

➤ Click the **Replace command button.** Excel substitutes Manager for Chicago, then looks for the next occurrence of Chicago. Click **Replace.** Click **Replace** a third time to make another substitution.

➤ You should see a dialog box indicating the specified region has been searched. Click **OK.** Close the Replace dialog box.

➤ Click and drag to select **Location** within the Application.Goto.Reference statement in the Manager macro. Enter **Title.** (The criteria within the macro have been changed from employees who work in Chicago to those whose title is Manager.)

➤ Save the module.

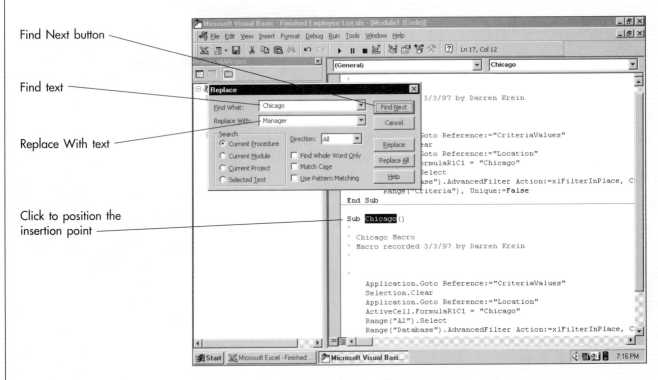

Find Next button

Find text

Replace With text

Click to position the insertion point

(c) Create the Manager Macro (step 3)

FIGURE 3.7   Hands-on Exercise 4 (continued)

THE FIND AND REPLACE COMMANDS

Anyone familiar with a word processor takes the Find and Replace commands for granted, but did you know the same capabilities exist in Excel? Pull down the Edit menu and choose either command. You have the same options as in the parallel command in Word, such as a case-sensitive (or insensitive) search or a limitation to a whole word search.

STEP 4: Run the Manager Macro

➤ Click the **Excel button** on the Windows taskbar or press **Alt+F11** to return to the Employee List worksheet.

➤ Pull down the **Tools menu.** Click **Macro,** then click the **Macros . . . command** to display the Macro dialog box as shown in Figure 3.7d.

➤ You should see two macros: Chicago, which was created in the previous exercise, and Manager, which you just created. (If the Manager macro does not appear, return to the Visual Basic Editor and correct the appropriate Sub statement to include Manager() as the name of the macro.)

➤ Select the **Manager macro,** then click **Run** to run the macro, after which you should see four employees (Adamson, Coulter, Gillenson, and Milgrom). If the macro does not execute correctly, return to the Visual Basic Editor to make the necessary corrections, then rerun the macro.

Click Run to execute the macro

Click the Manager macro

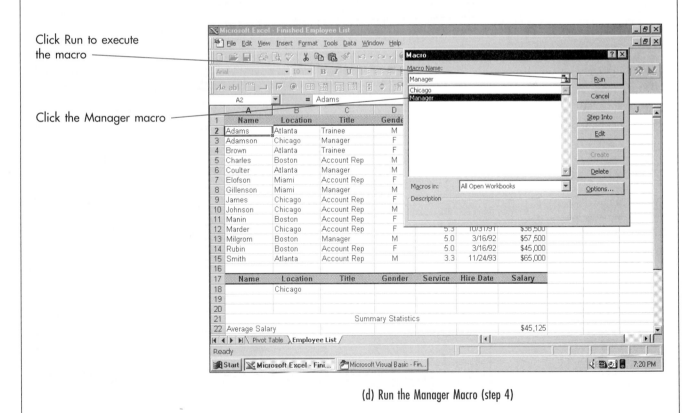

(d) Run the Manager Macro (step 4)

FIGURE 3.7   Hands-on Exercise 4 (continued)

THE STEP INTO COMMAND

The Step Into command helps to debug a macro, as it executes the statements one at a time. Pull down the Tools menu, click Macro, click Macros, select the macro to debug, then click the Step Into command button. Move and/or size the Visual Basic Editor window so that you can see both the worksheet and the macro. Pull down the *Debug menu* and click the *Step Into* command (or press the *F8* function key) to execute the first statement in the macro and view its results. Continue to press the *F8* function key to execute the statements one at a time until the macro has completed execution.

STEP 5: Assign a Button

➤ Click the **Button tool** on the Forms toolbar (the mouse pointer changes to a tiny crosshair), then click and drag in the worksheet to draw a button on the worksheet. Release the mouse.

➤ Choose **Manager** (the macro you just created) from the list of macro names as shown in Figure 3.7e. Click **OK** to close the Assign Macro dialog box.

➤ The button should still be selected. Click and drag to select the name of the button, **Button 2,** then type **Manager** as the new name. Do *not* press the enter key. Click outside the button to deselect it.

➤ There should be two buttons on your worksheet, one each for the Chicago and Manager macros.

Click Manager to assign it to the selected macro button

Click and drag to draw the button

Click and drag to select Button 2 and type Manager as the new name

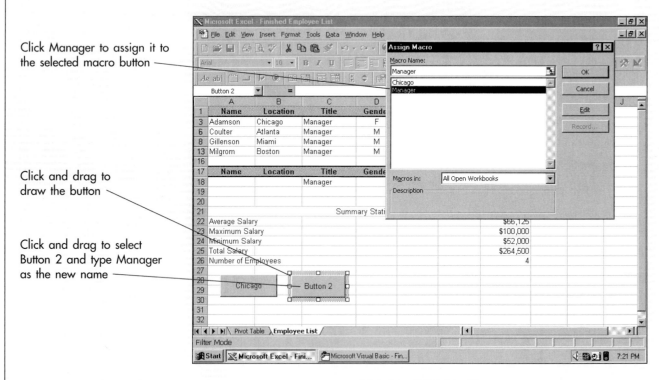

(e) Assign a Button (step 5)

FIGURE 3.7 Hands-on Exercise 4 (continued)

STEP 6: Test the Buttons

➤ Click the **Chicago button** to execute the Chicago macro. You should see four employees with an average salary of $45,125.

➤ Click the **Manager button** to execute the Manager macro. You should see four employees with an average salary of $66,125.

STEP 7: Create the ChicagoManager Macro

➤ Return to the Visual Basic Editor. Press **Ctrl+Home** to move to the beginning of Module1. Click and drag to select the entire Chicago macro. Be sure to include the End Sub statement in your selection.

➤ Click the **Copy button** on the Standard toolbar to copy the Chicago macro to the clipboard.

➤ Press **Ctrl+End** to move to the end of the module sheet. Click the **Paste button** on the Standard toolbar to complete the copy operation.

➤ Change **Chicago** to **ChicagoManager** in both the comment statement and the Sub statement as shown in Figure 3.7f.

➤ Click and drag to select the two statements in the **Manager macro** as shown in Figure 3.7f. Click the **Copy button** to copy these statements to the clipboard.

➤ Click in the **ChicagoManager macro** at the end of the line ActiveCell.FormulaR1C1 = "Chicago". Press **enter** to begin a new line. Click the **Paste button** to complete the copy operation.

➤ Delete any unnecessary blank lines or spaces that may remain.

➤ Save the module.

Copy button

Paste button

Copy selected statements to clipboard

Chicago macro has been copied and renamed

Insert a blank line, then paste the copied statements here

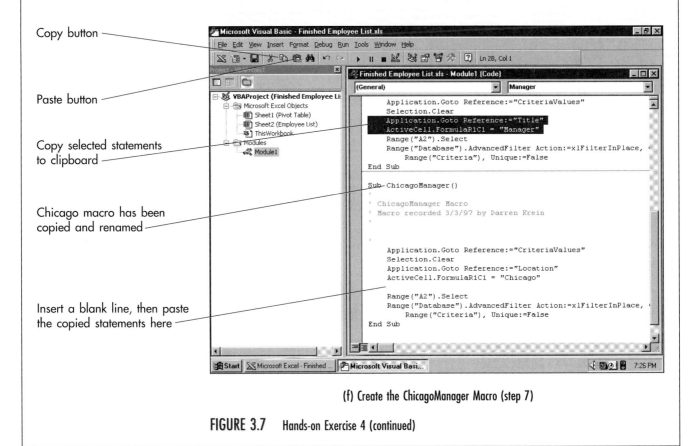

(f) Create the ChicagoManager Macro (step 7)

FIGURE 3.7   Hands-on Exercise 4 (continued)

STEP 8: Assign a Button

➤ Return to the workbook. Click the **button tool** on the Forms toolbar, then click and drag to draw a new button on the worksheet. Assign the **Chicago-Manager macro** to this button.

➤ Click and drag to select the name of the Button, **Button 3.** Enter **Chicago Manager** as the new name. Do not press enter.

➤ Click outside the button to deselect it. Point to the **ChicagoManager button,** then press and hold the **Ctrl key** as you click the mouse to select the button.

➤ Drag a sizing handle to size the button appropriately. Click outside the button to deselect it.

➤ Click the **ChicagoManager button** to execute the macro. You should see one employee, Adamson, who is the only Chicago manager.

➤ Click the **Chicago button** to execute the Chicago macro. You should see an average salary of $45,125.

➤ Click the **Manager button** to execute the Manager macro. You should see an average salary of $66,125.

CREATE UNIFORM BUTTONS

One way to create buttons of a uniform same size is to create the first button, then copy that button to create the others. To copy a button, press the Ctrl key as you select (click) the button, then click the Copy button on the Standard toolbar. Click in the worksheet where you want the new button to appear, then click the Paste button. Click and drag over the name of the button and enter a new name. Right click the new button, then click Assign Macro from the shortcut menu. Select the name of the new macro, then click OK.

STEP 9: Change the Button Properties

➤ Point to the **ChicagoManager button,** then press and hold the **Ctrl key** to select this button.

➤ Press the **Ctrl key,** then press and hold the **Shift key** as you click the **Chicago button.** The ChicagoManager and Chicago buttons are both selected.

➤ Press and hold both the **Shift** and **Ctrl keys** as you click the **Manager button** to add it to the selection.

➤ All three buttons should be selected as shown in Figure 3.7g. Pull down the **Format menu.** Click **Control** to display the Format control dialog box in Figure 3.7g.

➤ Click the **Properties tab** in the Format Object dialog box:
  • Check the **Print Object box** so that the macro buttons are included on the printed output.
  • Click the **Move but Don't Size with Cells** option button.
  • Click **OK** to exit the dialog box and return to the worksheet.

➤ Click anywhere in the worksheet to deselect the buttons.

Properties tab

Select Move but Don't
Size with Cells

Click the Print
Object check box

Select all three buttons

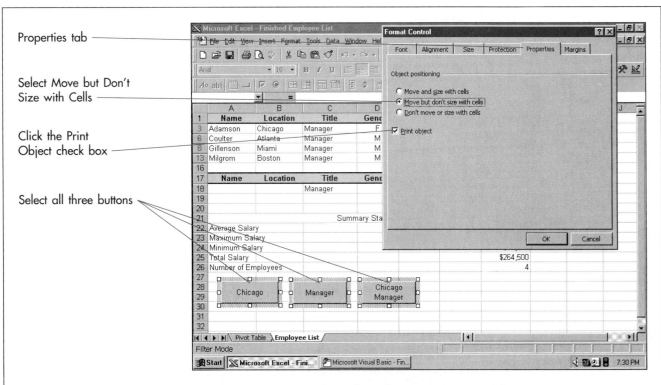

(g) Change the Button Properties (step 9)

FIGURE 3.7   Hands-on Exercise 4 (continued)

STEP 10: Print the Workbook

➤ Click the **Print button** on the Standard toolbar to print the worksheet. The buttons should appear on the printed output.

➤ Return to the VBE window. Pull down the **File menu,** click **Print,** and click **OK.** Click the **Print button** to print the macros.

➤ Close the workbook. Exit Excel if you don't want to continue with the next exercise at this time.

THE SIZE PROPERTY

Change the size property of existing buttons to a consistent setting. Press and hold the Ctrl and Shift keys to select the buttons, then pull down the Format menu and click the Control command to display the Format Control dialog box. Click the Size tab, enter the width and height for the selected buttons, then click OK to accept the settings and close the dialog box. The buttons are uniform but may overlap because the dimensions have changed. Click anywhere in the worksheet to deselect the buttons, then press the Ctrl key and click to select a single button. Click and drag the selected button to a new position in the worksheet.

Thus far, all of the macros in the chapter have consisted entirely of Excel commands that were captured by the macro recorder as they were executed. Excel macros can be made significantly more powerful by incorporating additional Visual Basic statements that enable true programming. These include the If statement for decision making, and the Do statement to implement a *loop* (one or more commands that are executed repeatedly until a condition is met).

Consider, for example, the worksheet and associated macro in Figure 3.8. The worksheet is similar to those used in the preceding exercises, except that the font color of the data for managers is red. Think for a minute how you would do this manually. You would look at the first employee in the list, examine the employee's title to determine if that employee is a manager, and if so, change the font color for that employee. You would then repeat these steps for all of the other employees on the list. It sounds tedious, but that is exactly what you would do if asked to change the font color for the managers.

Now ask yourself whether you could implement the entire process with the macro recorder. You could use the recorder to capture the commands to select a specific row within the list and change the font color. You could not, however, use the recorder to determine whether or not to select a particular row (i.e., whether the employee is a manager) because you make that decision by comparing the cell contents to a specific criterion. Nor is there a way to tell the recorder to repeat the process for every employee. In other words, you need to go beyond merely capturing Excel commands. You need to include additional Visual Basic statements to enable true programming.

The HighlightManager macro in Figure 3.8 uses the If statement to implement a decision (to determine whether the selected employee is a manager) and the Do statement to implement a loop (to repeat the commands until all employees in the list have been processed). To understand how the macro works, you need to know the basic syntax of each statement.

If Statement

The *If statement* conditionally executes a statement (or group of statements), depending on the value of an expression (condition). The If statement determines whether an expression is true, and if so, executes the commands between the If and End If. For example:

```
If ActiveCell.Offset(0, 2) = "Manager" Then
    Selection.Font.ColorIndex = 3
End If
```

IF-THEN-ELSE

The If statement includes an optional Else clause whose statements are executed if the condition is false. Consider:

If condition Then statements [Else statements] End If

The condition is evaluated as either true or false. If the condition is true, the statements following Then are executed; otherwise the statements following Else are executed. Either way, execution continues with the statement following End If. Use the Help command for additional information and examples.

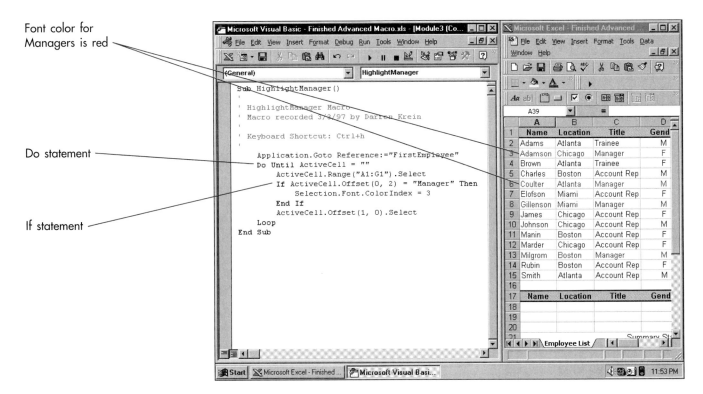

Font color for
Managers is red

Do statement

If statement

FIGURE 3.8   Loops and Decision Making

This If statement determines whether the cell two columns to the right of
the active cell (the offset indicates a relative reference) contains the text *Manager,*
and if so, changes the font color of the (previously) selected text. The number
three corresponds to the color red. No action is taken if the condition is false.
Either way, execution continues with the command below the End If.

Do Statement

The ***Do statement*** repeats a block of statements until a condition becomes true.
For example:

```
Do Until ActiveCell = ""
    ActiveCell.Range("A1:G1").Select
    If ActiveCell.Offset(0, 2) = "Manager" Then
        Selection.Font.ColorIndex = 3
    End If
    ActiveCell.Offset(1, 0).Select
Loop
```

The statements within the loop are executed repeatedly until the active cell
is empty (i.e., ActiveCell = ""). The first statement in the loop selects the cells in
columns A through G of the current row. (Relative references are used, and you
may want to refer to the earlier discussion that indicated that A1:G1 specifies the
shape of a range rather than a specific cell address.) The If statement determines
whether the current employee is a manager and, if so, changes the font color for
the selected cells. The last statement selects the cell one row below the active cell
to process the next employee. (Omission of this statement would process the same
row indefinitely, creating what is known as an infinite loop.)

The macro in Figure 3.8 is a nontrivial macro that illustrates the potential of Visual Basic. Try to gain a conceptual understanding of how the macro works, but do not be concerned if you are confused initially. Do the hands-on exercise, and you'll be pleased at how much clearer it will be when you have created the macro yourself.

A SENSE OF FAMILIARITY

Visual Basic has the basic capabilities found in any other programming language. If you have programmed before, whether in Pascal, C, or even COBOL, you will find all of the logic structures you are used to. These include the Do While and Do Until statements, the If-Then-Else statement for decision making, nested If statements, a Case statement, and/or calls to subprograms.

HANDS-ON EXERCISE 5

Loops and Decision Making

Objective: To implement loops and decision making in a macro through the Do Until and If statements. Use Figure 3.9 as a guide in doing the exercise.

STEP 1: The ClearColor Macro

➤ Open the **Advanced Macro workbook** in the **Exploring Excel folder.** Click the button to **Enable Macros.**

➤ Save the workbook as **Finished Advanced Macro** workbook. The data for the employees in rows 3, 6, 8, and 13 appears in red to indicate these employees are managers.

➤ Pull down the **Tools menu.** Click the **Macro command** and click **Macros** to display the dialog box in Figure 3.9a.

➤ Select **ClearColor,** then click **Run** to execute this macro and clear the red color from the managerial employees. It is important to know that the Clear-Color macro works, as you will use it throughout the exercise.

STEP 2: Record the HighlightManager Macro

➤ You must choose the active cell before recording the macro. Click **cell A3,** the cell containing the name of the first manager.

➤ Pull down the **Tools menu,** click (or point to) the **Macro command,** then click **Record New Macro** (or click the **Record macro button** on the Visual Basic toolbar) to display the Record Macro dialog box

➤ Enter **HighlightManager** as the name of the macro. Do not leave any spaces in the macro name. Click in the **Shortcut Key** check box and enter a **lower-case h.** Check that **This Workbook** is selected. Click **OK.**

➤ The Stop Recording toolbar appears and the status bar indicates that you are recording the macro. Click the **Relative References button** so that the button is pushed in as shown in Figure 3.9b.

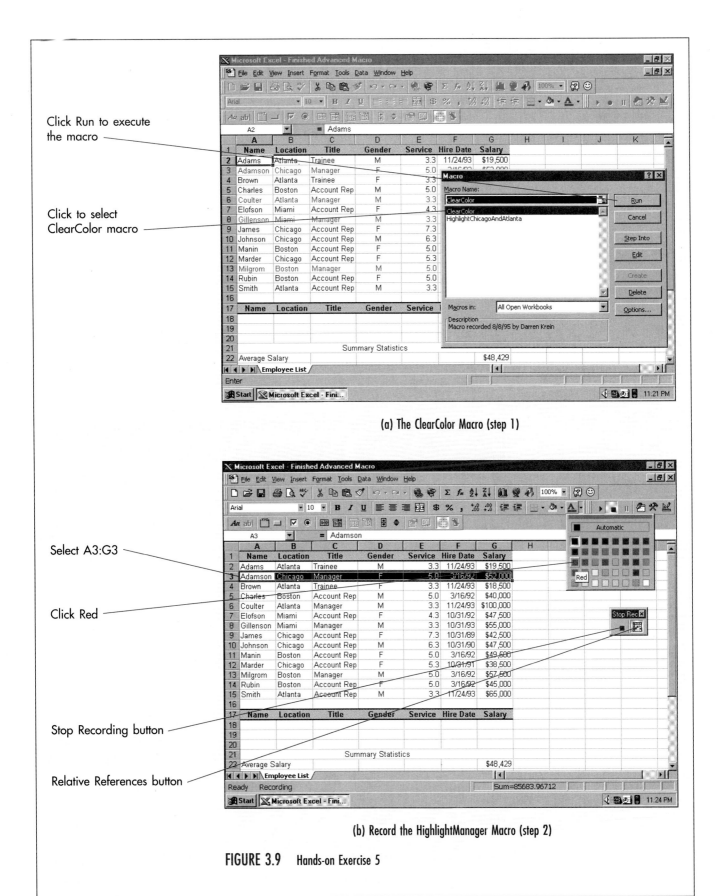

Click Run to execute the macro

Click to select ClearColor macro

(a) The ClearColor Macro (step 1)

Select A3:G3

Click Red

Stop Recording button

Relative References button

(b) Record the HighlightManager Macro (step 2)

FIGURE 3.9   Hands-on Exercise 5

➤ Click and drag to select cells **A3** through **G3** as shown in Figure 3.9b. Click the arrow in the **Font color list box.** Click **Red.** Click the **Stop Recording button.**

➤ Click anywhere in the worksheet to deselect cells A3 through G3 so you can see the effect of the macro; cells A3 through G3 should be displayed in red.

➤ Save the workbook.

Step 3: View the Macro

➤ Press **Alt+F11** to open the Visual Basic Editor. If necessary, double click the **Modules folder** within the Project window to display the three modules within the workbook.

➤ Select (click) **Module3.** Pull down the **View menu** and click **Code** (or press the **F7 key**) to display the Visual Basic code for the HighlightManager macro you just created as shown in Figure 3.9c.

➤ Be sure that your code is identical to ours (except for the comments). If you see the absolute reference, Range("A3:G3"), rather than the relative reference in our figure, you need to correct your macro to match ours.

➤ Click the **close button** (the X on the Project Window title bar) to close the **Projects window.** The Code window expands to occupy the entire Visual Basic Editor window.

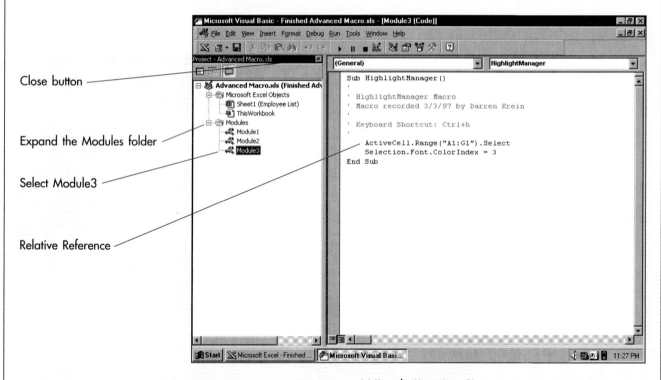

Close button

Expand the Modules folder

Select Module3

Relative Reference

(c) View the Macro (step 3)

FIGURE 3.9 Hands-on Exercise 5 (continued)

STEP 4: Test the Macro

➤ Point to an empty area on the Windows taskbar, then click the **right mouse button** to display a shortcut menu. Click **Tile Vertically** to tile the open windows (Excel and the Visual Basic Editor).

➤ Your desktop should be similar to Figure 3.9d except that the additional employees will not yet appear in red. It doesn't matter if the workbook is in the same window as ours. (If additional windows are open on the desktop, minimize each open window, then repeat the previous step to tile the open windows.)

➤ Click the **Excel window.** Click **cell A6** (the cell containing the name of the next manager). Press **Ctrl+h** to execute the HighlightManager macro. The font in cells A6 to G6 changes to red. (If not, modify your macro to match ours.)

➤ Click **cell A7.** Press **Ctrl+h** to execute the HighlightManager macro. The font for this employee is also in red, although the employee is not a manager.

➤ Save the workbook.

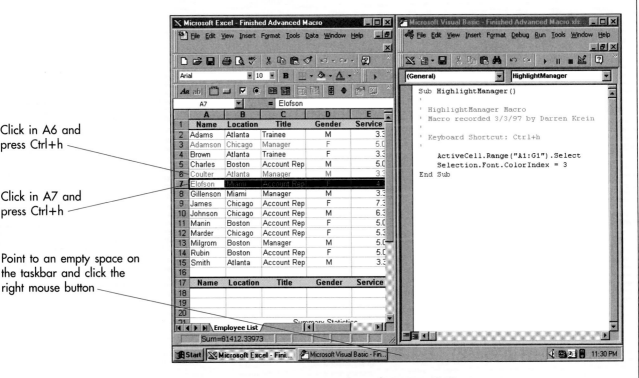

(d) Test the Macro (step 4)

FIGURE 3.9   Hands-on Exercise 5 (continued)

THE FIRST BUG

A bug is a mistake in a computer program; hence debugging refers to the process of correcting program errors. According to legend, the first bug was an unlucky moth crushed to death on one of the relays of the electro-mechanical Mark II computer, bringing the machine's operation to a halt. The cause of the failure was discovered by Grace Hopper, who promptly taped the moth to her logbook, noting, *"First actual case of bug being found."*

STEP 5: Add the If Statement

➤ Press **Ctrl+c** to execute the ClearColor macro. The data for all employees is again displayed in black.

➤ Click in the window containing the **HighlightManager** macro. Add the **If** and **End If** statements exactly as they are shown in Figure 3.9e. Use the **Tab key** (or press the **space bar**) to indent the Selection statement within the If and End If statements.

➤ Click in the window containing the worksheet, then click **cell A3.** Press **Ctrl+h** to execute the modified HighlightManager macro. Cells A3 through G3 are highlighted since this employee is a manager.

➤ Click **cell A4.** Press **Ctrl+h.** The row is selected, but the color of the font remains unchanged. The If statement prevents these cells from being highlighted because the employee is not a manager. Press **Ctrl+c** to remove all highlighting.

➤ Save the workbook.

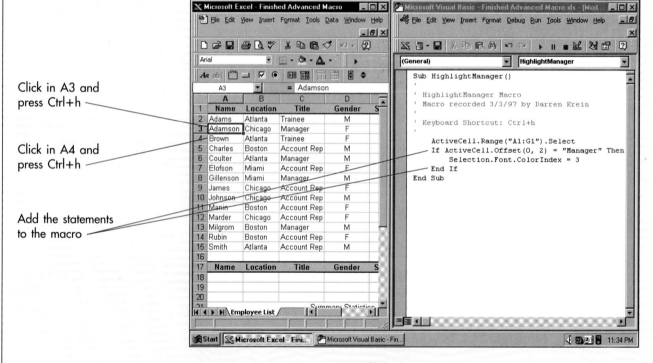

Click in A3 and press Ctrl+h

Click in A4 and press Ctrl+h

Add the statements to the macro

(e) Add the If Statement (step 5)

FIGURE 3.9   Hands-on Exercise 5 (continued)

INDENT

Indentation does not affect the execution of a macro. It, does, however, make the macro easier to read, and we suggest you follow common conventions in developing your macros. Indent the conditional statements associated with an If statement by a consistent amount. Place the End If statement on a line by itself, directly under the associated If.

STEP 6: An Endless Loop

➤ Click in the window containing the **HighlightManager** macro. Add the **Do Until** and **Loop** statements exactly as they appear in Figure 3.9f. Indent the other statements as shown in the figure.

➤ Click **cell A3** of the worksheet. Press **Ctrl+h** to execute the macro. Cells A3 through G3 will be displayed in red, but the macro continues to execute indefinitely as it applies color to the same record over and over. The macro is in an infinite loop (as can be seen by the hourglass that remains on your monitor).

➤ Press **Ctrl+Break** to cease execution of the macro. You will see the dialog box in Figure 3.9f, indicating that an error has been encountered during the execution of the macro. Click the **End button.**

➤ Pull down the **Debug menu** and click the **Step Into command** (or press the **F8 key**) to enter the macro. The first statement is highlighted in yellow.

➤ Press the **F8 key** several times to view the execution of the next several steps. You will see that the macro is stuck in a loop as the If statement is executed indefinitely.

➤ Click the **Reset button** in the Visual Basic window to terminate the debugging process.

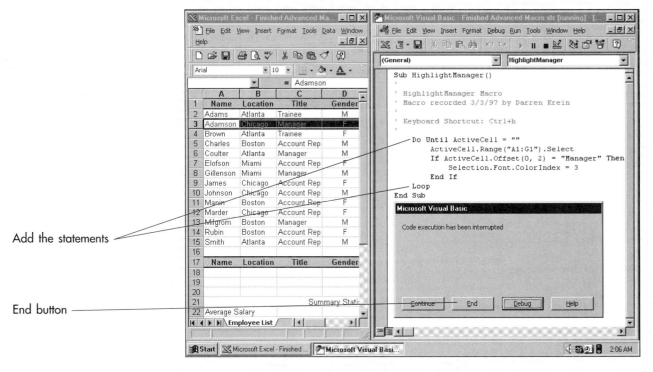

Add the statements

End button

(f) An Endless Loop (step 6)

FIGURE 3.9   Hands-on Exercise 5 (continued)

STEP 7: Complete the Macro

➤ Click in **cell A2** of the worksheet. Click in the **Name Box.** Enter **FirstEmployee** to name this cell. Press **enter.**

➤ Click in the window containing the macro. Click after the last comment and press **enter** to insert a blank line.

➤ Add the statement to select the cell named FirstEmployee as shown in Figure 3.9g. This ensures that the macro always begins in row two by selecting the cell named FirstEmployee.

Add this statement to select the first employee

Add this statement to prevent the endless loop

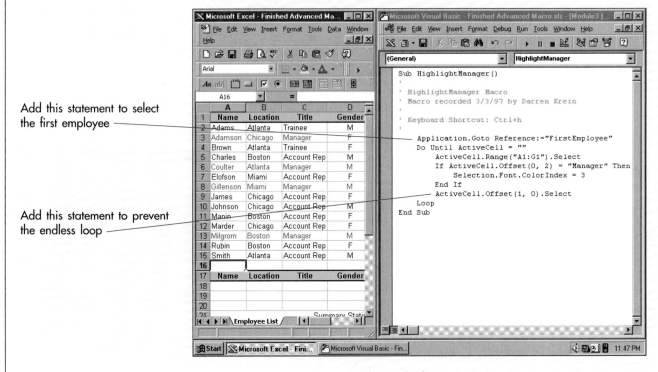

(g) The Completed Macro (step 7)

FIGURE 3.9   Hands-on Exercise 5 (continued)

- ➤ Click immediately after the End If statement. Press **enter.** Add the statement containing the offset (1,0) as shown in Figure 3.9g, which selects the cell one row below the current row.
- ➤ Click anywhere in the worksheet except cell A2. Press **Ctrl+c** to clear the color. Press **Ctrl+h** to execute the HighlightManager macro.
- ➤ The macro begins by selecting cell A2, then proceeds to highlight all managers in red. Save the workbook a final time.
- ➤ Print the workbook and its macro for your instructor. Exit Excel.

HELP FOR VISUAL BASIC

Click within any Visual Basic key word, then press the F1 key for context-sensitive help. You will see a help screen containing a description of the statement, its syntax, key elements, and several examples. You can print the help screen by clicking the Options command button and selecting Print Topic. (If you do not see the help screens, ask your instructor to install Visual Basic Help.)

SUMMARY

A macro is a set of instructions that automates a repetitive task. It is, in essence, a program, and its instructions are written in Visual Basic, a programming language. The macro recorder in Excel records your commands and writes the macro for you. Once a macro has been created, it can be edited by manually inserting, deleting, or changing its statements.

Macros are stored in one of two places, either in the current workbook or in a Personal Macro workbook. Macros that are specific to a particular workbook should be stored in that workbook. Generic macros that can be used with any workbook should be stored in the Personal Macro workbook.

A macro is run (executed) by pulling down the Tools menu and selecting the Run Macro command. A macro can also be executed through a keyboard shortcut, by placing a button on the worksheet, or by customizing a toolbar to include an additional button to run the macro.

A comment is a nonexecutable statement that begins with an apostrophe. Comments are inserted automatically at the beginning of a macro by the macro recorder to remind you of what the macro does. Comments may be added, deleted, or modified, just as any other statement.

A macro begins and ends with the Sub and End Sub statements, respectively. The Sub statement contains the name of the macro.

The With statement enables you to perform multiple actions on the same object. All commands between the With and corresponding End With statements are executed collectively.

A macro records either absolute or relative references. An absolute reference is constant; that is, Excel keeps track of the exact cell address and selects that specific cell. A relative reference depends on the previously selected cell, and is entered as an offset, or number of rows and columns from the current cell.

An Excel macro can be made more powerful through inclusion of Visual Basic statements that enable true programming. These include the If statement to implement decision making and the Do statement to implement a loop.

Absolute reference	Find command	Personal Macro
Button tool	If statement	workbook
Code window	InputBox command	Project Explorer
Comment statement	Keyboard shortcut	Relative reference
Copy command	Loop	Replace command
Cut command	Macro	Shortcut key
Debugging	Macro recorder	Step Into command
Do statement	Name box	Sub statement
End If statement	Name command	Visual Basic
End Sub statement	Offset	Visual Basic Editor
End With statement	Paste command	With statement

MULTIPLE CHOICE

1. Which of the following best describes the recording and execution of a macro?
   - (a) A macro is recorded once and executed once
   - (b) A macro is recorded once and executed many times
   - (c) A macro is recorded many times and executed once
   - (d) A macro is recorded many times and executed many times

2. Which of the following can be used to execute a macro?
   - (a) A keyboard shortcut
   - (b) A customized toolbar button
   - (c) Both (a) and (b)
   - (d) Neither (a) nor (b)

3. A macro can be stored:
   - (a) In any Excel workbook
   - (b) In the Personal Macro workbook
   - (c) Both (a) and (b)
   - (d) Neither (a) nor (b)

4. Which of the following is true regarding comments in Visual Basic?
   - (a) A comment is executable; that is, its inclusion or omission affects the outcome of a macro
   - (b) A comment begins with an apostrophe
   - (c) Both (a) and (b)
   - (d) Neither (a) nor (b)

5. Which statement must contain the name of the macro?
   - (a) The Sub statement at the beginning of the macro
   - (b) The first comment statement
   - (c) Both (a) and (b)
   - (d) Neither (a) nor (b)

6. Which of the following indicates an absolute reference within a macro?
   (a) ActiveCell.Offset(1,1).Range("A1")
   (b) $A$1
   (c) Range("A1")
   (d) All of the above

7. The statement Selection.Offset (1,0).Range ("A1").Select will select the cell:
   (a) In the same column as the active cell but one row below
   (b) In the same row as the active cell but one column to the right
   (c) In the same column as the active cell but one row above
   (d) In the same row as the active cell but one column to the left

8. The statement Selection.Offset (1,1).Range ("A1").Select will select the cell:
   (a) One cell below and one cell to the left of the active cell
   (b) One cell below and one cell to the right of the active cell
   (c) One cell above and one cell to the right of the active cell
   (d) One cell above and one cell to the left of the active cell

9. The statement Selection.Offset (1,1).Range ("A1:A2").Select will select:
   (a) Cell A1
   (b) Cell A2
   (c) Both (a) and (b)
   (d) Neither (a) nor (b)

10. Which commands are used to duplicate an existing macro so that it can become the basis of a new macro?
    (a) Copy command
    (b) Paste command
    (c) Both (a) and (b)
    (d) Neither (a) nor (b)

11. Which of the following is used to protect a macro from the subsequent insertion or deletion of rows or columns in the associated worksheet?
    (a) Range names
    (b) Absolute references
    (c) Both (a) and (b)
    (d) Neither (a) nor (b)

12. Which of the following is true regarding a customized button that has been inserted as an object onto a worksheet and assigned to an Excel macro?
    (a) Point to the customized button, then click the left mouse button to execute the associated macro
    (b) Point to the customized button, then click the right mouse button to select the macro button and simultaneously display a shortcut menu
    (c) Point to the customized button, then press and hold the Ctrl key as you click the left mouse to select the button
    (d) All of the above

13. The InputBox statement:
    (a) Displays a message (prompt) requesting input from the user
    (b) Stores the user's response in a designated cell
    (c) Both (a) and (b)
    (d) Neither (a) nor (b)

14. You want to create a macro to enter your name in a specific cell. The best way to do this is to:
   (a) Select the cell for your name, turn on the macro recorder with absolute references, then type your name
   (b) Turn on the macro recorder with absolute references, select the cell for your name, then type your name
   (c) Either (a) or (b)
   (d) Neither (a) nor (b)

15. You want to create a macro to enter your name in the active cell (which will vary whenever the macro is used) and the course you are taking in the cell immediately below. The best way to do this is to:
   (a) Select the cell for your name, turn on the macro recorder with absolute references, type your name, press the down arrow, and type the course
   (b) Turn on the macro recorder with absolute references, select the cell for your name, type your name, press the down arrow, and type the course
   (c) Select the cell for your name, turn on the macro recorder with relative references, type your name, press the down arrow, and type the course
   (d) Turn on the macro recorder with relative references, select the cell for your name, type your name, press the down arrow, and type the course

ANSWERS

1. b	**6.** c	**11.** a
2. c	**7.** a	**12.** d
3. c	**8.** b	**13.** c
4. b	**9.** d	**14.** b
5. a	**10.** c	**15.** c

PRACTICE WITH EXCEL 97

1. Figure 3.10 displays a modified version of the Finished Employee List workbook that was developed in Hands-on Exercises 3 and 4. The worksheet contains the three command buttons (Chicago, Manager, and Chicago/Manager) that correspond to the macros that were developed in the chapter. It also contains a fourth command button (Any City, Any Title) that is the focus of this problem.
   a. Do Hands-on Exercises 3 and 4 as they are described in the chapter in order to create the first three macros and associated command buttons.
   b. Create a fourth macro that prompts the user to enter a city, prompts the user a second time to enter a title, then displays all employees with that city–title combination.
   c. Create a command button corresponding to the macro in part b as shown in the figure.
   d. Add a documentation worksheet that describes all of the macros in the workbook. Be sure your name and date are on this worksheet.
   e. Submit a disk containing the completed workbook to your instructor.

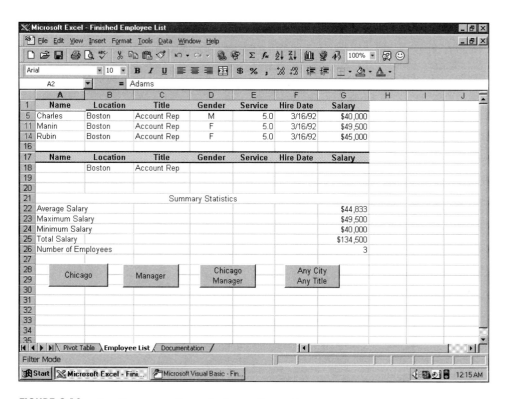

FIGURE 3.10 Data Management Macros for Practice Exercise 1

2. Figure 3.11 displays a partially completed macro that can be found in Module2 in the Finished Advanced Macro workbook used in the fifth hands-on exercise. The macro is intended to highlight the Chicago employees in red and the Atlanta employees in blue.

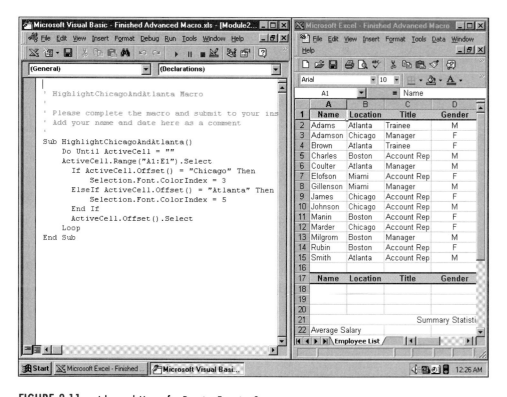

FIGURE 3.11 Advanced Macro for Practice Exercise 2

a. Do Hands-on Exercise 5 as it is described in the chapter, which introduced loops and decision making within a macro.

b. Complete the HighlightChicagoAndAtlanta macro by entering the appropriate offsets in three different statements within the macro. Completion of the macro also requires you to enter a statement at the beginning of the macro that positions you at the first employee within the list.

c. Test the completed macro to be sure that it works properly. You can use the existing ClearColor macro within the workbook (press Ctrl+c as a shortcut) to clear the color within the employee list.

d. Assign Ctrl+a as the shortcut for the macro. The workbook should now have three shortcuts. Ctrl+c and Ctrl+h to clear color and highlight the managers are shortcuts for the ClearColor and HighlightManager macros from the existing hands-on exercise.

e. Add a documentation worksheet that describes all of the macros in the workbook. Be sure your name and date are on this worksheet.

f. Submit a disk containing the completed workbook to your instructor.

3. The workbook in Figure 3.12 is based on the three-dimensional example from Chapter 2. Open the *Volume II Chapter 3 Practice 3* workbook as it exists on the data disk and save it as *Finished Chapter 3 Practice 3*. Do the following:

a. Run Macro1, Macro2, and Macro 3. What does each macro do?

b. Run the StartOver macro. What does this macro do?

c. Run Macro4. What does it do? How many statements does the macro contain? Explain why the macro is so powerful even though it contains a limited number of statements.

d. A branch office has been opened in a fourth city, and its sales are found in the New York workbook. Determine which macro(s) have to be modified so that the sales of the New York office are included in the corporate totals, then modify those macros appropriately.

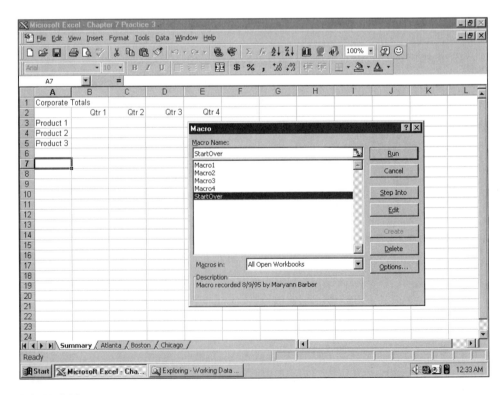

FIGURE 3.12   Screen for Practice Exercise 3

e. Modify Macro4 and the StartOver macro so that they can be run with the keyboard shortcuts Ctrl+a and Ctrl+b, respectively.

f. Submit a disk containing the finished workbook to your instructor. (The disk should also contain the Atlanta, Boston, Chicago, and New York workbooks.)

4. The Power of Macros: Microsoft Excel includes several templates to help run a business or plan your personal finances. A template is a partially completed workbook that contains formatting, text, formulas, and macros, and it is the latter that makes the template so valuable. One of those templates, the Loan Manager, is the basis of the workbook in Figure 3.13.

To create the workbook in Figure 3.13, pull down the File menu, click New, click the Spreadsheet Solutions tab, open the Loan Manager template, then save it as *Chapter 3 Practice 4 Solution*. If you do not see the Loan template, you need to obtain it from the Office 97 CD. Open the ValuPack folder on the CD, open the Templates folder, then open the Excel folder to display the available templates, which include the Loan Manager. The template can be opened on the CD or it can be copied to the Program Files folder on drive C (Program Files/Microsoft Office/Templates/Spreadsheet Solutions).

Once you find the template, click the Customize Your Loan Manager tab and enter your personal information. Enter the parameters for a real (or imaginary) loan, then explore the workbook by examining its worksheets. Enter a beginning date at least two years prior to today's date so that the workbook will record several loan payments. Print the Loan Data, Loan Amortization Table, and Summary worksheets, then submit all three pages as proof that you did the exercise. Do you have a better appreciation for what can be accomplished with macros?

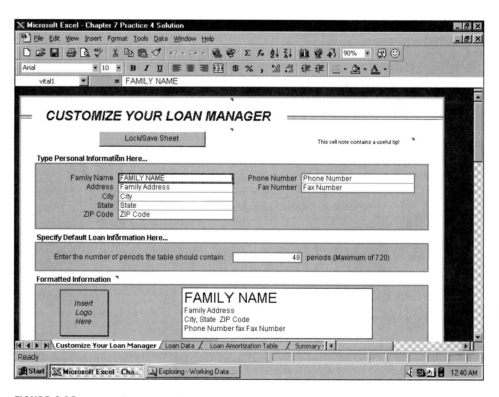

FIGURE 3.13   Screen for Practice Exercise 4

CASE STUDIES

Spreadsheet Solutions

The Loan Manager is one of several templates that are supplied with Microsoft Excel. The other templates include a Sales Invoice, Purchase Order, Expense Statement, Business Planner, and Personal Budget. Choose any template that seems of interest to you, then enter real or hypothetical data. Print one or more worksheets from the workbook and submit the output to your instructor.

Microsoft Word

Do you use Microsoft Word on a regular basis? Are there certain tasks that you do repeatedly, whether in the same document or in a series of different documents? If so, you would do well to explore the macro capabilities within Microsoft Word. How are these capabilities similar to Excel's? How do they differ?

Starting Up

Your instructor is very impressed with the Excel workbook and associated macros that you have created. He would like you to take the automation process one step further and simplify the way in which Excel is started and the workbook is loaded. Use your knowledge of Windows 95 to implement your instructor's request. The problem is open ended, and there are many different approaches. You might, for example, create a shortcut on the desktop to open the workbook. You might also explore the use of the Startup folder.

Dade County Metro Zoo

The Dade County Metro Zoo workbook is similar in concept to the Employee List workbook that was used throughout the chapter. Open the workbook and run the three existing macros. Create two additional macros of your own that you think are appropriate, then submit a disk containing the completed workbook to your instructor.

Antivirus Programs

What is an antivirus program and how do you get one? How do these programs supplement the macro virus protection that is built into Microsoft Excel? Use your favorite search engine to find two such programs, then summarize their capability and cost in a short note to your instructor. You can also visit the National Computer Security Association (www.ncsa.com) and the Computer Emergency Response Team (www.cert.org) to learn more about computer security.

APPENDIX A: TOOLBARS

OVERVIEW

Microsoft Excel has 20 predefined toolbars that provide access to commonly used commands. The toolbars are displayed in Figure A.1 and are listed here for convenience. They are the Standard, Formatting, Auditing, Chart, Circular Reference, Control Toolbox, Drawing, Exit Design Mode, External Data, Forms, Full Screen, Picture, Pivot Table, Reviewing, Shadow Settings, Stop Recording, Visual Basic, Web, WordArt, and 3-D Settings toolbars.

The Standard and Formatting toolbars are displayed by default and appear immediately below the menu bar. The other predefined toolbars are displayed (hidden) at the discretion of the user, and in some cases are displayed automatically when their corresponding features are in use (e.g., the Chart toolbar and the Pivot Table toolbar).

The buttons on the toolbars are intended to indicate their functions. Clicking the Printer button (the fourth button from the left on the Standard toolbar), for example, executes the Print command. If you are unsure of the purpose of any toolbar button, point to it, and a ScreenTip will appear that displays its name.

You can display multiple toolbars at one time, move them to new locations on the screen, customize their appearance.

- To display or hide a toolbar, pull down the View menu and click the Toolbars command. Select (deselect) the toolbar(s) that you want to display (hide). The selected toolbar(s) will be displayed in the same position as when last displayed. You may also point to any toolbar and click with the right mouse button to bring up a shortcut menu, after which you can select the toolbar to be displayed (hidden).
- To change the size of the buttons or suppress the display of the ScreenTips, pull down the View menu, click Toolbars, and click Customize to display the Customize dialog box. If necessary, click the Options tab, then select (deselect) the appropriate check box.

- Toolbars are either docked (along the edge of the window) or floating (in their own window). A toolbar moved to the edge of the window will dock along that edge. A toolbar moved anywhere else in the window will float in its own window. Docked toolbars are one tool wide (high), whereas floating toolbars can be resized by clicking and dragging a border or corner as you would with any window.
  - To move a docked toolbar, click anywhere in the gray background area and drag the toolbar to its new location. You can also click and drag the move handle (the pair of parallel lines) at the left of the toolbar.
  - To move a floating toolbar, drag its title bar to its new location.
- To customize one or more toolbars, display the toolbar(s) on the screen. Then pull down the View menu, click Toolbars, click Customize to display the Customize dialog box, then select the Toolbars tab. Alternatively, you can click on any toolbar with the right mouse button, select Customize from the shortcut menu, and then click the Toolbars tab.
  - To move a button, drag the button to its new location on that toolbar or any other displayed toolbar.
  - To copy a button, press the Ctrl key as you drag the button to its new location on that toolbar or any other displayed toolbar.
  - To delete a button, drag the button off the toolbar and release the mouse button.
  - To add a button, click the Commands tab in the Customize dialog box, select the category from the Categories list box that contains the button you want to add, then drag the button to the desired location on the toolbar. (To see a description of a tool's function before adding it to a toolbar, select the tool, then click the Description command button.)
  - To restore a predefined toolbar to its default appearance, pull down the View menu, click Toolbars, click Customize, click the Toolbars tab, select (highlight) the desired toolbar, and click the Reset command button.
- Buttons can also be moved, copied, or deleted without displaying the Customize dialog box.
  - To move a button, press the Alt key as you drag the button to the new location.
  - To copy a button, press the Alt and Ctrl keys as you drag the button to the new location.
  - To delete a button, press the Alt key as you drag the button off the toolbar.
- To create your own toolbar, pull down the View menu, click Toolbars, click Customize, click the Toolbars tab, then click the New command button. Alternatively, you can click on any toolbar with the right mouse button, select Customize from the shortcut menu, click the Toolbars tab, and then click the New command button.
  - Enter a name for the toolbar in the dialog box that follows. The name can be any length and can contain spaces.
  - The new toolbar will appear on the screen. Initially it will be big enough to hold only one button. Add, move, and delete buttons following the same procedures as outlined above. The toolbar will automatically size itself as new buttons are added and deleted.
  - To delete a custom toolbar, pull down the View menu, click Toolbars, click Customize, and click the Toolbars tab. *Verify that the custom toolbar to be deleted is the only one selected (highlighted).* Click the Delete command button. Click Yes to confirm the deletion. (Note that a predefined toolbar cannot be deleted.)

MICROSOFT EXCEL 97 TOOLBARS

Standard Toolbar

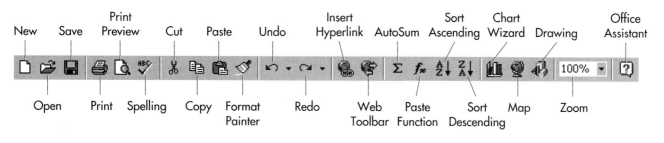

Formatting Toolbar

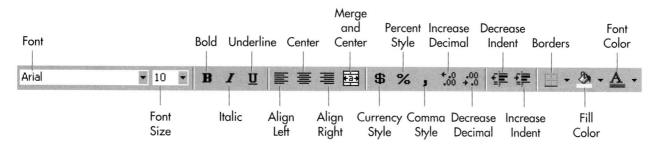

Auditing Toolbar

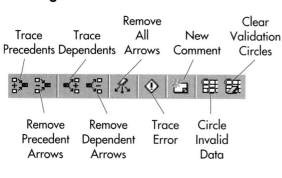

Chart Toolbar

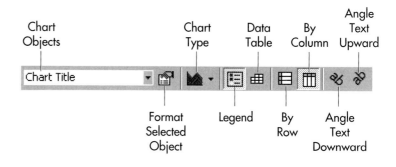

Circular Reference

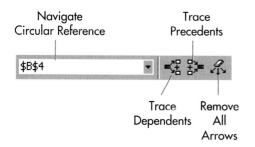

Control Toolbox Toolbar

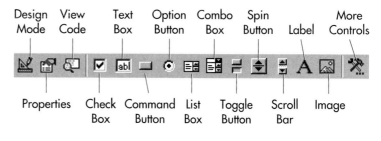

FIGURE A.1   Toolbars

Drawing Toolbar

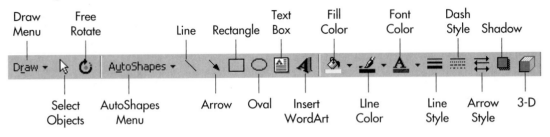

Draw Menu · Free Rotate · Line · Rectangle · Text Box · Fill Color · Font Color · Dash Style · Shadow

Select Objects · AutoShapes Menu · Arrow · Oval · Insert WordArt · LIne Color · Line Style · Arrow Style · 3-D

Exit Design Mode Toolbar

Design Mode

External Data Toolbar

Edit Query · Query Parameters · Cancel Refresh · Refresh Status

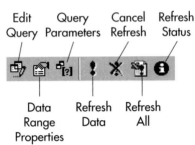

Data Range Properties · Refresh Data · Refresh All

Forms Toolbar

Label · Group Box · Check Box · List Box · Combination List-Edit · Scroll Bar · Control Properties · Toggle Grid

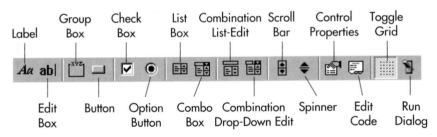

Edit Box · Button · Option Button · Combo Box · Combination Drop-Down Edit · Spinner · Edit Code · Run Dialog

Full Screen Toolbar

Toggle Full-Screen View

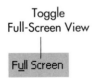

Picture Toolbar

Insert Picture From File · More Contrast · More Brightness · Crop · Format Object · Reset Picture

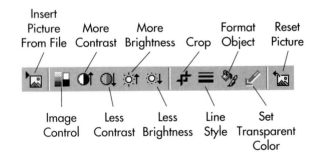

Image Control · Less Contrast · Less Brightness · Line Style · Set Transparent Color

FIGURE A.1 Toolbars (continued)

Pivot Table Toolbar

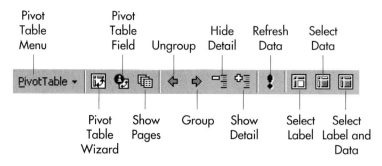

Pivot Table Menu · Pivot Table Field · Ungroup · Hide Detail · Refresh Data · Select Data

Pivot Table Wizard · Show Pages · Group · Show Detail · Select Label · Select Label and Data

Shadow Settings Toolbar

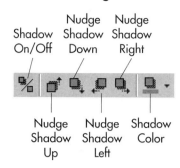

Shadow On/Off · Nudge Shadow Down · Nudge Shadow Right

Nudge Shadow Up · Nudge Shadow Left · Shadow Color

Reviewing Toolbar

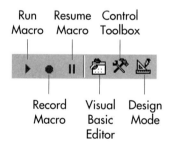

New Comment · Next Comment · Hide All Comments · Create Microsoft Outlook Task · Send to Mail Recipient

Previous Comment · Show Comment · Delete Comment · Update File

Stop Recording Toolbar

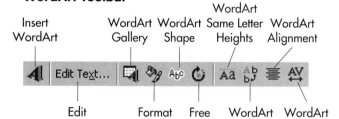

Stop Macro

Relative Reference

Visual Basic Toolbar

Run Macro · Resume Macro · Control Toolbox

Record Macro · Visual Basic Editor · Design Mode

WordArt Toolbar

Insert WordArt · WordArt Gallery · WordArt Shape · WordArt Same Letter Heights · WordArt Alignment

Edit Text · Format Object · Free Rotate · WordArt Vertical Text · WordArt Character Spacing

Web Toolbar

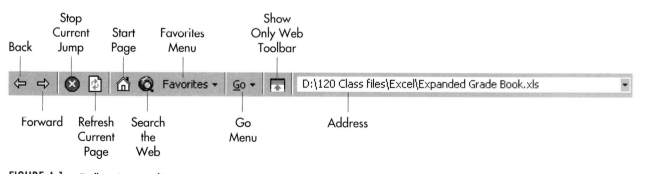

Back · Stop Current Jump · Start Page · Favorites Menu · Show Only Web Toolbar

Forward · Refresh Current Page · Search the Web · Go Menu · Address

FIGURE A.1   Toolbars (continued)

3-D Settings Toolbar

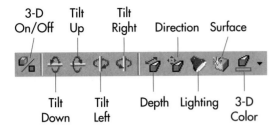

FIGURE A.1   Toolbars (continued)

APPENDIX B: THE SPREADSHEET AUDIT

OVERVIEW

In one of the most celebrated spreadsheet errors of all time, the comptroller of James A. Cummings, Inc, a Florida construction company, used a spreadsheet to develop a bid on a multi-million dollar office complex. At the last minute, he realized that he had forgotten to include $254,000 for overhead, and so he inserted this number at the top of a column of numbers. Unfortunately for both the comptroller and the company, the $254,000 was not included in the final total, and the contract was underbid by that amount. The company was awarded the contract and forced to make good on its unrealistically low estimate.

Seeking to recover its losses, the construction company brought suit against the spreadsheet vendor, claiming that a latent defect within the spreadsheet failed to add the entry in question. The vendor contended that the mistake was in fact a *user error* and the court agreed, citing the vendor's licensing agreement:

> *". . . Because software is inherently complex and may not be completely free of errors, you are advised to verify your work. In no event will the vendor be liable for direct, indirect, special, incidental, or consequential damages arising out of the use of or inability to use the software or documentation, even if advised of the possibility of such damages. In particular, said vendor is not responsible for any costs including, but not limited to, those incurred as a result of lost profits or revenue."*

The purpose of this appendix is to remind you that the spreadsheet is only a tool, and like all other tools it must be used properly, or there can be serious consequences. Think, for a moment, how business has become totally dependent on the spreadsheet, and how little validity checking is actually done. Ask yourself if any of your spreadsheets contained an error, and if so, what the consequences would have been if those spreadsheets represented real applications rather than academic exercises.

USE FUNCTIONS RATHER THAN FORMULAS

The entries =A1+A2+A3+A4 and =SUM(A1:A4) may appear equivalent, but the function is inherently superior and should be used whenever possible. A function adjusts automatically for the insertion (deletion) of rows within the designated range, whereas a formula does not. Including a blank row at the beginning and end of the function's range ensures that any value added to the top or bottom of a column of numbers will automatically be included in the sum. Had this technique been followed by the Cummings company, the error would not have occurred.

A WORD OF CAUTION

The formatting capabilities within Excel make it all too easy to get caught up in the appearance of a worksheet without paying attention to its accuracy. Consider, for example, the grade book in Figure B.1, which is used by a hypothetical professor to assign final grades in a class. The grade book is nicely formatted, *but its calculations are wrong*, and no amount of fancy formatting can compensate for the erroneous results. Consider:

- Baker should have received an A rather than a B. He has an 87 average on his quizzes, he received an 87 on the final exam, and with two bonus points for each of his two homeworks, he should have had an overall final average of 91.
- Charles should have received a B rather than a C. True, he did not do any homework and he did do poorly on the final, but, with the semester quizzes and final exam counting equally, his semester average should have been 80.

	Name	HW 1	HW 2	HW 3	Quiz 1	Quiz 2	Quiz 3	Quiz Average	Final Exam	HW Bonus	Semester Average	Grade
1	Name	HW 1	HW 2	HW 3	Quiz 1	Quiz 2	Quiz 3	Quiz Average	Final Exam	HW Bonus	Semester Average	Grade
2	Baker		OK	OK	77	89	95	87	87	2	89	B
3	Charles				84	76	86	82	78	0	79	C
4	Goodman	OK	OK			95	94	63	95	4	89	B
5	Johnson	OK	OK		90	86	70	82	90	4	92	A
6	Jones		OK	OK	75	85	71	77	86	2	85	B
7	Irving	OK		OK	65	85	75	75	78	2	79	C
8	Lang				84	88	83	85	94	0	91	A
9	London		OK		72	69	75	72	82	2	81	B
10	Milgrom	OK	OK		100	65	90	85	100	4	100	A
11	Mills	OK	OK		75	85	80	80	65	4	74	C
12	Nelson	OK	OK		65	60	61	62	60	4	65	D
13												
14		Grading Criteria									Grading Scale	
15		Bonus for each homework					2				Average	Grade
16		Weight of semester quizzes					50%				0	F
17		Weight of final exam					50%				60	D
18											70	C
19											80	B
20											90	A

Baker should have received an A

Charles should have received a B

Goodman should have received an A

FIGURE B.1   The Professor's Grade Book

- Goodman should have received an A rather than a B. She aced both quizzes (she was excused from the first quiz) as well as the final, and in addition, she received a four-point bonus for homework.

The errors in our example are contrived, but they could occur. Consider:

- At the class's urging, the professor decided at the last minute to assign a third homework but neglected to modify the formulas to include the additional column containing the extra homework.
- The professor changed the grading scheme at the last minute and decided to count the semester quizzes and final exam evenly. (The original weights were 30% and 70%, respectively.) Unfortunately, however, the formulas to compute each student's semester average specify constants (.30 and .70) rather than absolute references to the cells containing the exam weights. Hence the new grading scheme is not reflected in the student averages.
- The professor forgot that he had excused Goodman from the first quiz and hence did not adjust the formula to compute Goodman's average on the basis of two quizzes rather than three.

Our professor is only human, but he would have done well to print the cell formulas in order to audit the mechanics of the worksheet and double check its calculations. Suffice it to say that the accuracy of a worksheet is far more important than its appearance, and you are well advised to remember this thought as you create and/or use a spreadsheet.

THE SPREADSHEET AUDIT

The *Auditing toolbar* helps you understand the relationships between the various cells in a worksheet. It enables you to trace the *precedents* for a formula and identify the cells in the worksheet that are referenced by that formula. It also enables you to trace the *dependents* of a cell and identify the formulas in the worksheet that reference that cell.

Precedent and/or dependent cells are identified graphically by displaying tracers on the worksheet. You simply click in the cell for which you want the information, then you click the appropriate button on the Auditing toolbar. The blue arrows (tracers) appear on the worksheet, and will remain on the worksheet until you click the appropriate removal button. The tracers always point forward, from the precedent cells to the dependent formula.

To see how valuable the tracers can be, consider Figure B.2, which contrasts the professor's original worksheet (Figure B.2a) with the corrected worksheet (Figure B.2b). Consider first the precedents for cell J2, which contains the formula to compute Baker's homework bonus. The tracers (the blue lines) in the invalid worksheet identify homeworks 1 and 2 (note the box around cells B2 and C2) as precedents. The corrected worksheet, however, shows that all three homeworks (cells B2, C2, and D2) are used to determine the bonus. (Both worksheets show that cell G15, which contains the homework bonus, is also a precedent for cell J2.)

The analysis of dependent cells is equally telling. There are no dependent cells for cell G16 in the invalid spreadsheet because the formulas to compute the students' semester averages do not reference this cell. The valid worksheet, however, corrects the error, and hence each cell in column K is dependent on cell G16.

The Auditing toolbar is displayed through the View menu and is shown in both Figures B.2a and B.2b. You can point to any button on the Auditing toolbar to display a ScreenTip to indicate the purpose of that button.

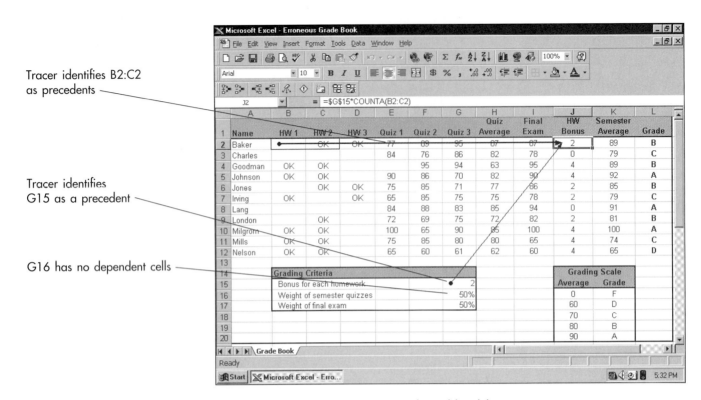

Tracer identifies B2:C2 as precedents

Tracer identifies G15 as a precedent

G16 has no dependent cells

(a) The Invalid Worksheet

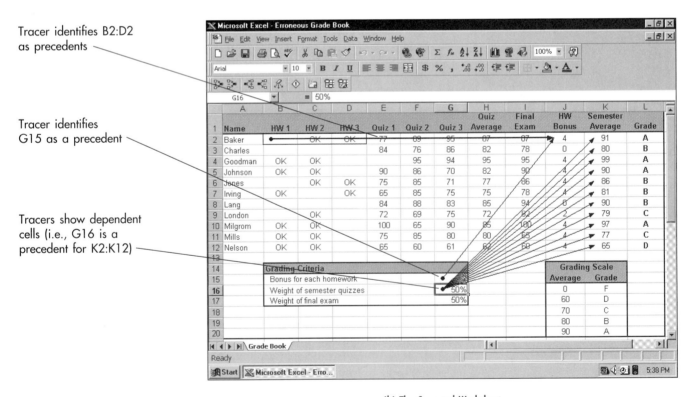

Tracer identifies B2:D2 as precedents

Tracer identifies G15 as a precedent

Tracers show dependent cells (i.e., G16 is a precedent for K2:K12)

(b) The Corrected Worksheet

FIGURE B.2   The Spreadsheet Audit

A SECOND EXAMPLE

Financial planning and budgeting is one of the most common business applications of spreadsheets. Figure B.3 contains an *invalid* version of a financial forecast. The worksheet calculates projected revenues, expenses, and earnings before taxes for a five-year horizon. As in the professor's grade book, the spreadsheet is nicely formatted, but its calculations are wrong, as will be explained shortly. Any decisions based on the spreadsheet will also be in error.

How do you know when a spreadsheet displays invalid results? One way is to "eyeball" the spreadsheet and try to approximate its results. Look for any calculations that are obviously incorrect. Look at the financial forecast, for example, and see whether all the values are growing at the projected rates of change. The number of units sold and the unit price increase every year as expected, but the cost of the production facility remains constant after 1997. This is an obvious error because the production facility is supposed to increase at eight percent annually, according to the assumptions at the bottom of the spreadsheet. The consequence of this error is that the production costs (after 1997) are too low and hence the projected earnings are too high. The error was easy to find, even without the use of a calculator.

Cost of the production facility is not increasing as expected after 1997

Earnings should be $0 ($225,000 − $225,000)

Isolate assumptions and initial conditions

	A	B	C	D	E	F
1	Get Rich Quick - Financial Forecast					
2		1996	1997	1998	1999	2000
3	Income					
4	Units sold	100,000	110,000	121,000	133,100	146,410
5	Unit price	$2.25	$2.36	$2.48	$2.60	$2.73
6	Gross revenue	$225,000	$259,875	$300,156	$346,680	$400,415
7						
8	Fixed costs					
9	Production facility	$50,000	$54,000	$54,000	$54,000	$54,000
10	Administration	$25,000	$26,250	$27,563	$28,941	$30,388
11	Variable cost					
12	Unit mfg cost	$1.50	$1.65	$1.82	$2.00	$2.20
13	Variable mft cost	$150,000	$181,500	$219,615	$265,734	$321,538
14						
15	Earnings before taxes	$25,000	$24,375	$26,541	$26,946	$24,877
16						
17	Initial conditions		Annual increase			
18	First year sales	100,000	10%			
19	Selling price	$2.25	5%			
20	Unit mfg cost	$1.50	10%			
21	Production facility	$50,000	8%			
22	Administration	$25,000	5%			
23	First year of forecast	1996				

FIGURE B.3 The Erroneous Financial Forecast

CHANGE THE YEAR

A well-designed spreadsheet facilitates change by isolating the assumptions and initial conditions. 1996 has come and gone, but all you have to do to update the forecast is to click in cell B23, and enter 1997 as the initial year. The entries in cells B2 through F2 (containing years of the forecast) are changed automatically as they contain formulas (rather than specific values) that depend on the initial year in cell B23.

A more subtle error occurs in the computation of the earnings before taxes. Look at the numbers for 1996. The gross revenue is $225,000. The total cost is also $225,000 ($50,000 for the production facility, $25,000 for administration, and $150,000 for the manufacturing cost). The projected earnings should be zero, but are shown incorrectly as $25,000, because the administration cost was not subtracted from the gross revenue in determining the profit.

The errors in the financial forecast are easy to discover if only you take the time to look. Unfortunately, however, too many people are prone to accept the results of a spreadsheet, simply because it is nicely formatted on a laser printer. We urge you, therefore, to "eyeball" every spreadsheet for obvious errors, and if a mistake is found, a spreadsheet audit is called for.

TEST WITH SIMPLE AND PREDICTABLE DATA

Test a spreadsheet initially with simple and predictable data that you create yourself so that you can manually verify that the spreadsheet is performing as expected. Once you are confident that the spreadsheet works with data you can control, test it again with real data to further check its validity. Adequate testing is time-consuming, but it can save you from embarrassing, not to mention costly, mistakes.

DATA VALIDATION

GIGO (Garbage In, Garbage Out) implies that a spreadsheet model is only as good as the data on which it is based. Entering invalid or unreasonable data into a spreadsheet will invalidate even the most sophisticated spreadsheet model. The best way to stop such errors from occurring is to prevent their entry in the first place. Excel 97 introduces the **Data Validation command,** which enables you to restrict the values that will be accepted into a cell. If, for example, a cell is to contain a text entry, you can limit the values to those that appear in a list, such as Atlanta, Boston, or Chicago. In similar fashion, you can specify a quantitative relationship for numeric values such as > 0 or > 100.

Figure B.4a displays the Settings tab in the Data Validation dialog box in which the developer requires the value in cell D18 (the annual sales increase) to be less than 15%. Figure B.4b shows the type of error alert (a **Warning**) and the associated message that is to appear if the user does not enter a valid value. Figure B.4c displays the dialog box the user sees if the criteria are violated, together with the indicated choice of actions. *Yes* accepts the invalid data into the cell despite the warning, *No* returns the user to the cell for further editing, and *Cancel* restores the previous value to the cell. (Other types of error messages include *Stop* and *Information*.)

ANNOTATE YOUR SPREADSHEETS

The New Comment button on the Auditing Toolbar enables you to create the equivalent of your own ScreenTip for any cell in a spreadsheet. It is an excellent way to annotate a spreadsheet and attach an explanation to any cell containing a complex formula. See step 5 in the hands-on exercise for details on inserting a comment.

Contents of cell D18 must
be less than .15

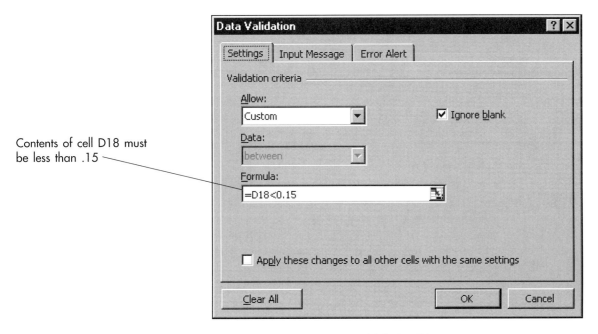

(a) Settings Tab

Title will appear in title bar of
displayed message

Choose Warning, Stop,
or Informational message

Message to be displayed
on entry of invalid data

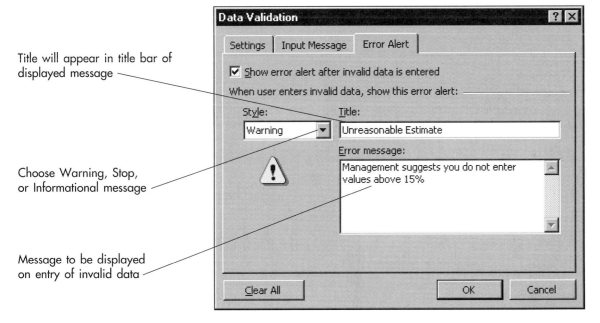

(b) Error Alert Tab

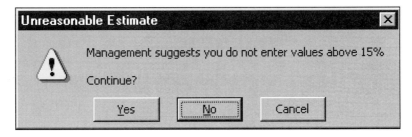

(c) Displayed Error Message

FIGURE B.4   The Data Validation Command

Objective: To illustrate the tools on the Auditing toolbar; to trace errors in spreadsheet formulas; to identify precedent and dependent cells; to attach a note to a cell. Use Figure B.5 as a guide in the exercise.

STEP 1: Display the Auditing Toolbar

➤ Start Excel. Open the **Erroneous Financial Forecast** workbook in the **Exploring Excel folder** as shown in Figure B.5a. Save the workbook as **Finished Erroneous Financial Forecast.**

➤ Point to any toolbar, click the **right mouse button** to display the shortcut menu in Figure B.5a. Click **Customize,** check the box for the Auditing toolbar, then close the Customize dialog box to display the Auditing toolbar.

➤ If necessary, click and drag the move handle of the Auditing toolbar to dock the toolbar under the Formatting toolbar.

THE #VALUE ERROR

The #VALUE error occurs when the wrong type of entry is used in a formula or as an argument in a function. It typically occurs when a formula references a text rather than a numeric entry. The easiest way to resolve the error is to display the Auditing toolbar, select the cell in question, then click the Trace Error button.

STEP 2: The Trace Error Command

➤ Click in **cell C4,** the first cell that displays the #VALUE error. Click the **Trace Error button** on the Auditing toolbar to display the tracers in Figure B.5b.

➤ The tracers identify the error in graphic fashion and show that cell C4 is dependent on cells A4 and D18 (i.e., cells A4 and D18 are precedents of cell C4). Cell A4 contains a text entry and is obviously incorrect.

➤ Click in the formula bar to edit the formula for cell C4 so that it references cell B4 rather than cell A4. (The correct formula is =B4+B4*$D$18). Press **enter** when you have corrected the formula.

➤ The tracer arrows disappear (they disappear automatically whenever you edit a formula to which they refer). The #VALUE errors are also gone because the formula has been corrected and all dependent formulas have been automatically recalculated.

THE RANGE FINDER

Double-click a cell whose formula you want to change. The Range Finder feature displays the formula in the cell and, further, highlights each cell reference in a different color, corresponding to the border color of the referenced cells. To change a cell reference (e.g., from A4 to B4), drag the color-coded border surrounding A4 (the reference you want to change) to cell B4 (the new reference).

Point to a toolbar and click right mouse button to display shortcut menu

Select Customize to display additional toolbars

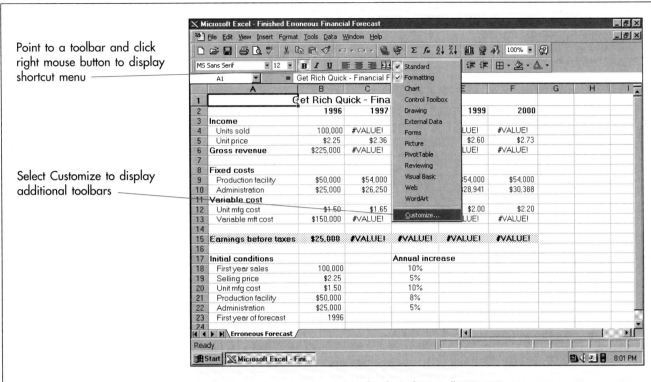

(a) Display the Auditing Toolbar (step 1)

Trace Error tool

Auditing toolbar

Cell A4 should not be a precedent

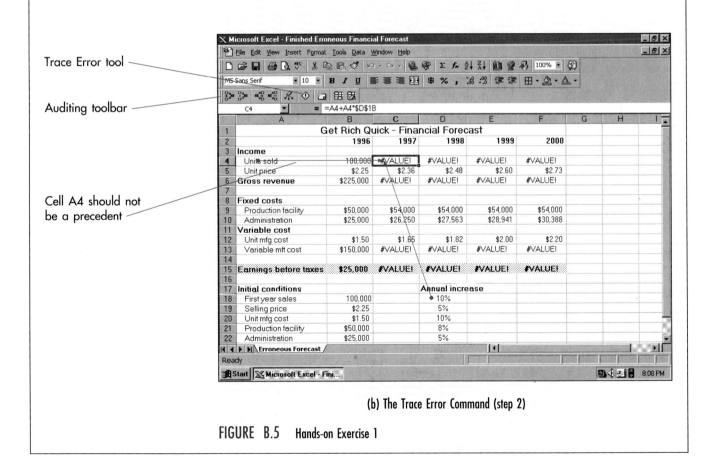

(b) The Trace Error Command (step 2)

FIGURE B.5   Hands-on Exercise 1

STEP 3: Trace Dependents

➤ The worksheet is still in error because the production costs do not increase after 1997. Click in **cell D21** (the cell containing the projected increase in the cost of the production facility).

➤ Click the **Trace Dependents button** to display the dependent cells as shown in Figure B.5c. Only one dependent cell (cell C9) is shown. This is clearly an error because cells D9 through F9 should also depend on cell D1.

➤ Click in **cell C9** to examine its formula (=B9+B9*D21). The production costs for the second year are based on the first-year costs (cell B9) and the rate of increase (cell D21). The latter, however, was entered as a relative rather than an absolute address.

➤ Change the formula in cell C9 to include an absolute reference to cell D21 (i.e., the correct formula is =B9+B9*$D$21). The tracer arrow disappears due to the correction.

➤ Drag the fill handle in **cell C9** to copy the corrected formula to **cells D9, E9, and F9.** (The displayed value for cell F9 should be $68,024.)

➤ Click in **cell D21.** Click the **Trace Dependents button,** and this time it points to the production costs for years 2 through 5 in the forecast. Click the **Remove Dependent Arrows button** to remove the arrows.

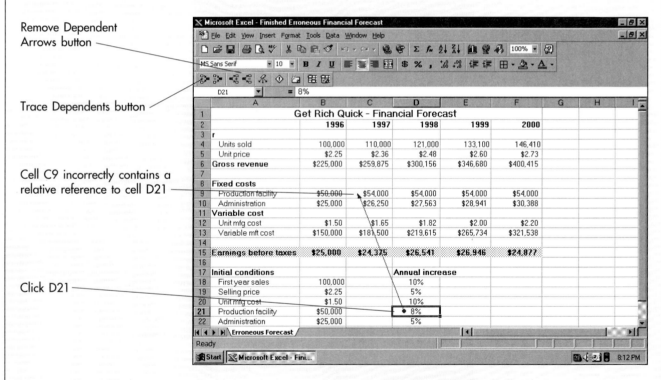

(c) The Trace Dependents Command (step 3)

FIGURE B.5   Hands-on Exercise 1 (continued)

STEP 4: Trace Precedents

➤ The earnings before taxes in cell B15 should be zero, not $25,000. (The gross revenue is $225,000, as are the total expenses, which consist of production, administration, and manufacturing costs of $50,000, $25,000, and $150,000, respectively.) Click in **cell B15.**

➤ Click the **Trace Precedents button** to display the precedent cells as shown in Figure B.5d. The projected earnings depend on the revenue (cell B6) and various expenses (cells B9 and B13). The problem is that the administration expense (cell B10) is omitted, and hence the earnings are too high.

➤ Change the formula in cell B15 to **=B6−(B9+B10+B13)** so that the administration expense is included in the expenses that are deducted from the gross revenue. The tracer arrow disappears.

➤ Drag the fill handle in **cell B15** to copy the corrected formula to **cells C15** through **F15.** (The displayed value in cell F15 should be a *negative* $19,535.)

➤ The formulas in the worksheet are now correct. Save the workbook.

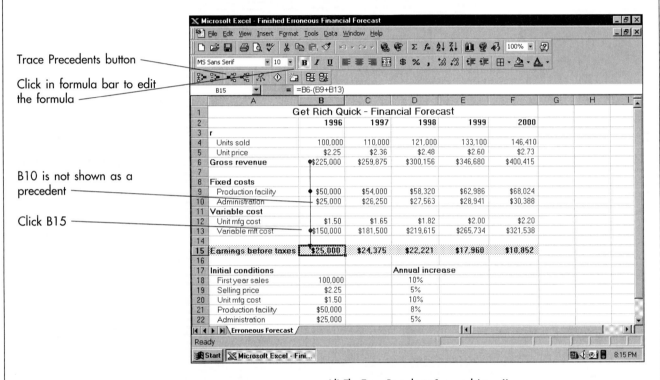

(d) The Trace Precedents Command (step 4)

FIGURE B.5   Hands-on Exercise 1 (continued)

STEP 5: Insert a Comment

➤ Click in **cell B19** (the cell containing the selling price for the first year). Pull down the **Insert menu** and click the **Comment command** (or click the **New Comment button** on the Auditing toolbar).

➤ A comment box opens as shown in Figure B.5e. Enter the text of your comment as shown in the figure, then click outside the comment when you are finished.

➤ The comment box closes, but a tiny red triangle appears in the upper corner of cell B19. (If you do not see the triangle, pull down the **Tools menu,** click **Options,** click the **View tab,** then click the option button in the Comments area to show **Comment Indicator only.**)

➤ Point to cell **B19** and the text of your comment appears as a ScreenTip. Point to a different cell and the comment disappears.

➤ Save the workbook.

New Comment button

Enter the text of your comment in the Comment box

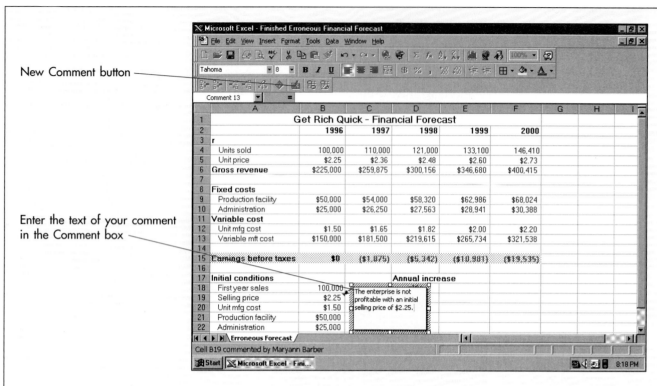

(e) Insert a Comment (step 5)

FIGURE B.5   Hands-on Exercise 1 (continued)

EDITING OR DELETING COMMENTS

The easiest way to edit or delete an existing comment is to point to the cell containing the comment, then click the right mouse button to display a context-sensitive menu in which you select the appropriate command. You can use the right mouse button to insert a comment, by right clicking in the cell, then choosing the Insert Comment command.

STEP 6: Data Validation

➤ Click in cell **D18.** Type **.20.** Excel displays the error message in Figure B.5f because of data validation we built into the worksheet. Press **Esc** to cancel and try another entry.

➤ Enter **.25.** Excel displays the same error message. No matter how many times you try, you will not be able to enter a value above .15 in cell D18 because the error type was specified as *Stop* rather than a warning.

➤ Pull down the **Data menu.** Click the **Validation command** to display the Data Validation dialog box, and if necessary, click the **Error Alert tab.**

➤ Click the **drop-down arrow** on the Style list box, click **Warning,** then click **OK** to accept the new setting and close the dialog box.

➤ Reenter **.20** in cell **D18.** This time you see a Warning message, rather than a Stop message. Click **Yes** to accept the new value. Save the spreadsheet.

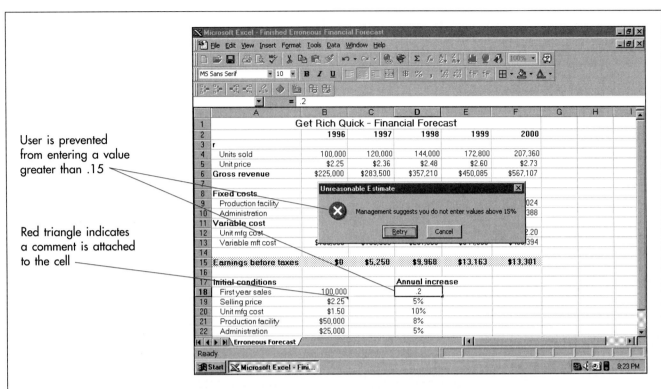

User is prevented from entering a value greater than .15

Red triangle indicates a comment is attached to the cell

(f) Data Validation (step 6)

FIGURE B.5   Hands-on Exercise 1 (continued)

CIRCLE INVALID DATA

The Circle Invalid Data button on the Auditing Toolbar will identify all cells containing invalid data. Pull down the View menu, click Toolbars, click Customize, then check the box to display the Auditing toolbar. Click the tool to Circle Invalid Data (second from the end). Click the adjacent tool to clear the validation circles.

STEP 7: Conduct Your Own Audit

➤ The erroneous grade book that was described earlier is available so that you can continue to practice.

➤ Open the **Erroneous Grade Book** workbook in the **Exploring Excel folder.** You should see the professor's grade book that was described at the beginning of the appendix.

➤ Conduct your own audit of the professor's grade book, using the techniques in the exercise.

➤ Exit Excel when you have completed the exercise.

A spreadsheet is only a tool, and like all other tools, it must be used properly, or else there can be serious consequences. The essential point in the grade book and financial forecast examples is that the potential for spreadsheet error does exist, and that you cannot blindly accept the results of a spreadsheet. Every spreadsheet should be checked for obvious errors, and if any are found, a spreadsheet audit is called for.

The Auditing toolbar helps you understand the relationships between the various cells in a worksheet. It enables you to trace the precedents for a formula and identify the cells in the worksheet that are referenced by that formula. It also enables you to trace the dependents of a cell and identify the formulas in the worksheet that reference that cell.

The Data Validation command enables you to specify the values that will be accepted into a cell. You can restrict the values to a list for text entries (e.g., Atlanta, Boston, or Chicago) or you can specify a quantitative relationship for numeric values.

KEY WORDS AND CONCEPTS

Audit

Auditing toolbar

Data Validation
   command

Dependents

GIGO (Garbage In,
   Garbage Out)

Information alert

Insert Comment
   command

Precedents

Range Finder

Stop alert

Trace Error command

Warning alert

APPENDIX C: SOLVER

OVERVIEW

The use of a spreadsheet in decision making has been emphasized throughout the text. We showed you how to design a spreadsheet based on a set of initial conditions and assumptions, then see at a glance the effect of changing one or more of those values. We introduced the Scenario Manager to store sets of assumptions so that they could be easily recalled and reevaluated. We discussed the Goal Seek command, which enables you to set the value of a target cell, then determine the input needed to arrive at that target value. However, the Goal Seek command, as useful as it is, is limited to a *single* input variable. This appendix discusses *Solver,* a powerful add-in that is designed for problems involving *multiple* variables.

Solver is an optimization and resource allocation tool that helps you achieve a desired goal. You specify a goal, such as maximizing profit or minimizing cost. You indicate the constraints (conditions) that must be satisfied for the solution to be valid, and you specify the cells whose values can change in order to reach that goal. Solver will then determine the values for the adjustable cells (i.e., it will tell you how to allocate your resources) in order to reach the desired goal.

This appendix provides an introduction to Solver through two different examples. The first example shows how to maximize profit. The second example illustrates how to minimize cost. Both examples are accompanied by a hands-on exercise.

EXAMPLE 1—MAXIMIZE PROFIT

Assume that you are the production manager for a company that manufactures computers. Your company divides its product line into two basic categories—desktop computers and laptops. Each product is sold under two labels, a discount line and a premium line. As production manager you are to determine how many computers of each type, and of each product line, to make each week.

Your decision is subject to various constraints that must be satisfied during the production process. Each computer requires a specified number of hours for assembly. Discount and premium-brand desktops require two and three hours, respectively. Discount and premium-brand laptops use three and five hours, respectively. The factory is working at full capacity, and you have only 4,500 hours of labor to allocate among the various products.

Your production decision is also constrained by demand. The marketing department has determined that you cannot sell more than 800 desktop units, nor more than 900 laptops, per week. The total demand for the discount and premium lines is 700 and 1,000 computers, respectively, per week.

Your goal (objective) is to maximize the total profit, which is based on a different profit margin for each type of computer. A desktop and a laptop computer from the discount line have unit profits of $600 and $800, respectively. The premium desktop and laptop computers have unit profits of $1,000 and $1,300, respectively. How many computers of each type do you manufacture each week in order to maximize the total profit?

This is a complex problem, but one that can be easily solved provided you can design the spreadsheet to display all of the information. Figure C.1 illustrates one way to set up the problem. In essence, you need to determine the values of cells B2 through B5, which represent the quantity of each computer to produce. You might be able to solve the problem manually through trial and error, by substituting different values and seeing the impact on profit. That is exactly what Solver will do for you, only it will do it much more quickly. (Solver uses various optimization techniques that are beyond the scope of this discussion.)

Once Solver arrives at a solution, assuming that it can find one, it creates a report such as the one shown in Figure C.2. The solution shows the value of the target cell (the profit in this example), based on the values of the adjustable cells (the quantity of each type of computer). The solution that will maximize profit is to manufacture 700 discount laptops and 800 premium desktops for a profit of $1,270,000.

The report in Figure C.2 also examines each constraint and determines whether it is binding or not binding. A *binding constraint* is one in which the resource is fully utilized (i.e., the slack is zero). The number of available hours, for example, is a binding constraint because every available hour is used, and hence the value of the target cell (profit) is limited by the amount of this resource (the number of hours). Or stated another way, any increase in the number of available hours (above 4,500) will also increase the profit.

A *nonbinding constraint* is just the opposite. It has a nonzero slack (i.e., the resource is not fully utilized), and hence it does not limit the value of the target cell. The laptop demand, for example, is not binding because a total of only 700 laptops were produced, yet the allowable demand was 900 (the value in cell E13). In other words, there is a slack value of 200 for this constraint, and increasing the allowable demand will have no effect on the profit. (The demand could actually be decreased by up to 200 units with no effect on profit.)

SOLVER

The information required by Solver is entered through the *Solver Parameters dialog box* as shown in Figure C.3. The dialog box is divided into three sections: the target cell, the adjustable cells, and the constraints. The dialog box in Figure C.3 corresponds to the spreadsheet shown earlier in Figure C.1.

Need to determine the values of cells B2:B5

	A	B	C	D	E
1		Quantity	Hours	Unit Profit	
2	Discount desktop		2	$600	
3	Discount laptop		3	$800	
4	Premium desktop		3	$1,000	
5	Premium laptop		5	$1,300	
6					
7	Constraints				
8	Total number of hours used				
9	Labor hours available				4,500
10	Number of desktops produced				
11	Total demand for desktop computers				800
12	Number of laptops produced				
13	Total demand for laptop computers				900
14	Number of discount computers produced				
15	Total demand for discount computers				700
16	Number of premium computers produced				
17	Total demand for premium computers				1,000
18	Hourly cost of labor				$20
19	Profit				

FIGURE C.1   The Initial Worksheet

Value of target cell (profit)

Target Cell (Max)

Cell	Name	Original Value	Final Value
$E$19	Profit	$0	$1,270,000

Quantity of each type of computer to be produced

Adjustable Cells

Cell	Name	Original Value	Final Value
$B$2	Discount desktop Quantity	0	0
$B$3	Discount laptop Quantity	0	700
$B$4	Premium desktop Quantity	0	800
$B$5	Premium laptop Quantity	0	0

Indicates whether constraint is binding or nonbinding

Constraints

Cell	Name	Cell Value	Formula	Status	Slack
$E$8	Total number of hours used	4500	$E$8<=$E$9	Binding	0
$E$10	Number of desktops produced	800	$E$10<=$E$11	Binding	0
$E$12	Number of laptops produced	700	$E$12<=$E$13	Not Binding	200
$E$16	Number of premium computers produced	800	$E$16<=$E$17	Not Binding	200
$E$14	Number of discount computers produced	700	$E$14<=$E$15	Binding	0
$B$2	Discount desktop Quantity	0	$B$2>=0	Binding	0
$B$3	Discount laptop Quantity	700	$B$3>=0	Not Binding	700
$B$4	Premium desktop Quantity	800	$B$4>=0	Not Binding	800
$B$5	Premium laptop Quantity	0	$B$5>=0	Binding	0

FIGURE C.2   The Solution

The *target cell* identifies the goal (or objective function)—that is, the cell whose value you want to maximize, minimize, or set to a specific value. Our problem seeks to maximize profit, the formula for which is found in cell E19 (the target cell) of the underlying spreadsheet.

The *adjustable cells* (or decision variables) are the cells whose values are adjusted until the constraints are satisfied and the target cell reaches its optimum value. The changing cells in this example contain the quantity of each computer to be produced and are found in cells B2 through B5.

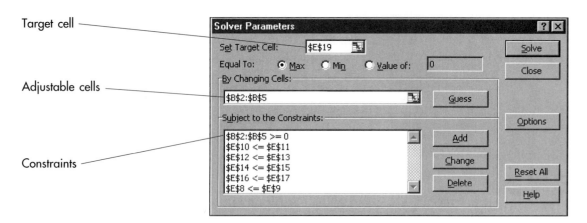

Target cell

Adjustable cells

Constraints

FIGURE C.3   Solver Parameters Dialog Box

The *constraints* specify the restrictions. Each constraint consists of a cell or cell range on the left, a relational operator, and a numeric value or cell reference on the right. (The constraints can be entered in any order, but they always appear in alphabetical order.) The first constraint references a cell range, cells B2 through B5, and indicates that each of these cells must be greater than or equal to zero. The remaining constraints reference a single cell rather than a cell range.

The functions of the various command buttons are apparent from their names. The Add, Change, and Delete buttons, are used to add, change, or delete a constraint. The Options button enables you to set various parameters that determine how Solver attempts to find a solution. The Reset All button clears all settings and resets all options to their defaults. The Solve button begins the search for a solution.

THE GREATER-THAN-ZERO CONSTRAINT

One constraint that is often overlooked is the requirement that the value of each adjustable cell be greater than or equal to zero. Physically, it makes no sense to produce a negative number of computers in any category. Mathematically, however, a negative value in an adjustable cell may produce a higher value for the target cell. Hence the nonnegativity (greater than or equal to zero) constraint should always be included for the adjustable cells.

HANDS-ON EXERCISE 1

Maximize Profit

Objective: To use Solver to maximize profit; to create a report containing binding and nonbinding constraints. Use Figure C.4 as a guide in the exercise.

STEP 1: Enter the Cell Formulas

➤ Start Excel. Open the **Optimization** workbook in the **Exploring Excel folder.** Save the workbook as **Finished Optimization** so that you can return to the original workbook if necessary.

➤ If necessary, click the tab for the **Production Mix** worksheet, then click **cell E8** as shown in Figure C.4a. Enter the formula shown in Figure C.4a to compute the total number of hours used in production.

➤ Enter the remaining cell formulas as shown below:
- Cell E10 (Number of desktops produced) **=B2+B4**
- Cell E12 (Number of laptops produced) **=B3+B5**
- Cell E14 (Number of discount computers produced) **=B2+B3**
- Cell E16 (Number of premium computers produced) **=B4+B5**
- Cell E19 (Profit) **=B2*D2+B3*D3+B4*D4+B5*D5−E18*E8**

➤ Save the workbook.

Click E8 and enter formula to compute total hours used

Click Production Mix tab

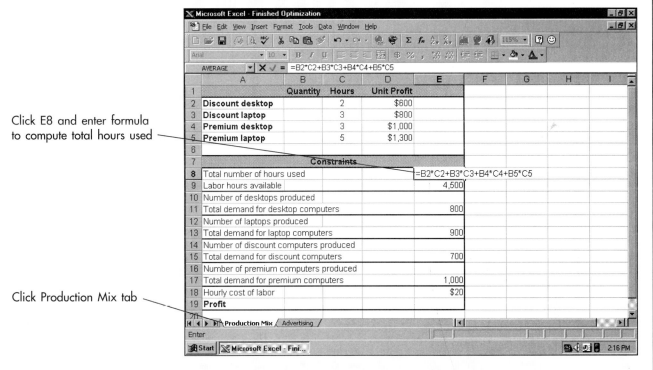

(a) Enter the Cell Formulas (step 1)

FIGURE C.4   Hands-on Exercise 1

USE POINTING TO ENTER CELL FORMULAS

A cell reference can be typed directly into a formula, or it can be entered more easily through pointing. The latter is also more accurate as you use the mouse or arrow keys to reference cells directly. To use pointing, select (click) the cell to contain the formula, type an equal sign to begin entering the formula, then click (or move to) the cell containing the value to be used. Type any arithmetic operator to place the cell reference in the formula, then continue pointing to additional cells. Press the enter key (instead of typing an arithmetic operator) to complete the formula.

STEP 2: Set the Target and Adjustable Cells

➤ Check that the formula in cell E19 is entered correctly as shown in Figure C.4b. Pull down the **Tools menu.** Click **Solver** to display the Solver Parameters dialog box shown in Figure C.4b.

➤ If necessary, click in the text box for Set Target cell. Click in cell **E19** to set the target cell. The **Max option button** is selected by default.

➤ Click in the **By Adjustable Cells** text box. Click and drag **cells B2** through **B5** in the worksheet to select these cells.

➤ Click the **Add command button** to add the first constraint as described in step 3.

Formula in E19

Target cell

Max option button is selected

Click in text box, then click and drag to select B2:B5

Click Add to add the first constraint

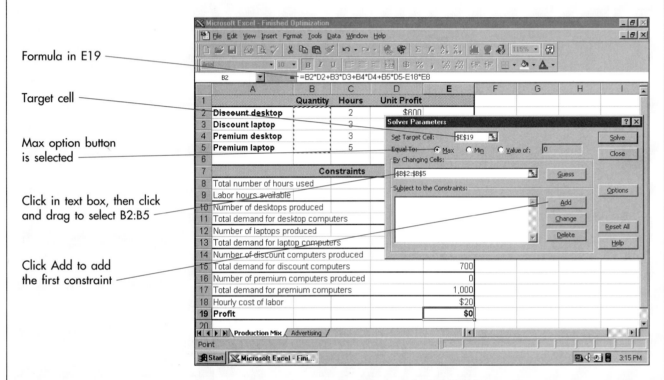

(b) Set the Target and Adjustable Cells (step 2)

FIGURE C.4   Hands-on Exercise 1 (continued)

MISSING SOLVER

Solver is an optional component of Excel and hence may not be loaded or installed on your system. Pull down the Tools menu and click Add-ins, then check the box next to Solver to load it. If Solver does not appear, you need to install it. Click the Windows 95 Start button, click Settings, then click Control Panel. Double click the icon to Add/Remove programs, click the Install/Uninstall tab, click Microsoft Office application, then click the Add/Remove command button and follow the instructions.

STEP 3: Add the Constraints

➤ You should see the Add Constraint dialog box in Figure C.4c with the insertion point (a flashing vertical line) in the Cell Reference text box.

- Click in **cell E8** (the cell containing the formula to compute the total number of hours used).

- The <= constraint is selected by default.

- Click in the **Constraint** text box, which will contain the value of the constraint, then click **cell E9** in the worksheet to enter the cell reference.

- Click **Add** to complete this constraint and add another.

➤ You will see a new (empty) Add Constraint dialog box, which enables you to enter additional constraints. Use pointing to enter each of the constraints shown below. (Solver automatically enters each reference as an absolute reference.):

- Enter the constraint **E10<=E11.** Click **Add.**

- Enter the constraint **E12<=E13.** Click **Add.**

- Enter the constraint **E14<=E15.** Click **Add.**

- Enter the constraint **E16<=E17.** Click **Add.**

➤ Add the last constraint. Click and drag to select **cells B2** through **B5.** Click the drop-down arrow for the relational operators and click the **>=** operator. Type **0** in the text box to indicate that the production quantities for all computers must be greater than zero. Click **OK** to return to the Solver Parameters dialog box.

Click in text box, then click E8

Click in text box, then click E9

Click Add

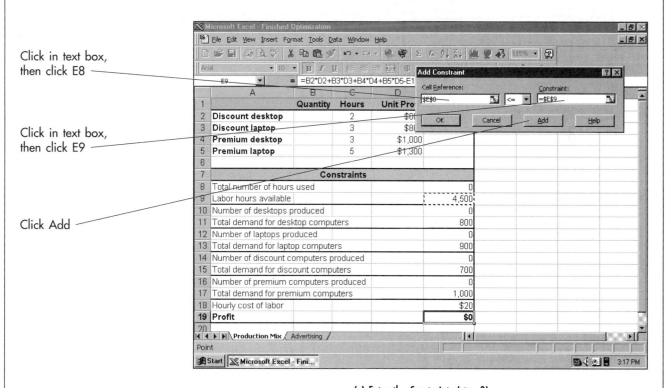

(c) Enter the Constraints (step 3)

FIGURE C.4   Hands-on Exercise 1 (continued)

STEP 4: Solve the Problem

➤ Check that the contents of the Solver Parameters dialog box match those of Figure C.4d. (The constraints appear in alphabetical order rather than the order in which they were entered.)

- To change the Target cell, click the **Set Target Cell** text box, then click the appropriate target cell in the worksheet.

- To change (edit) a constraint, select the constraint, then click the **Change button.**

- To delete a constraint, select the constraint and click the **Delete button.**

➤ Click the **Solve button** to solve the problem.

Click Solve button

Constraints are in alphabetical order

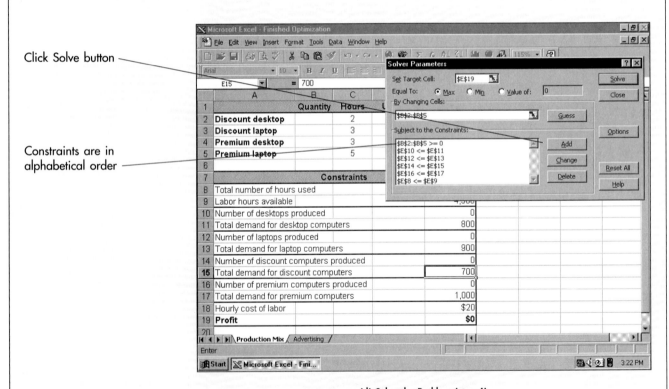

(d) Solve the Problem (step 4)

FIGURE C.4   Hands-on Exercise 1 (continued)

STEP 5: Create the Report

➤ You should see the Solver Results dialog box in Figure C.4e, indicating that Solver has found a solution. The option button to Keep Solver Solution is selected by default.

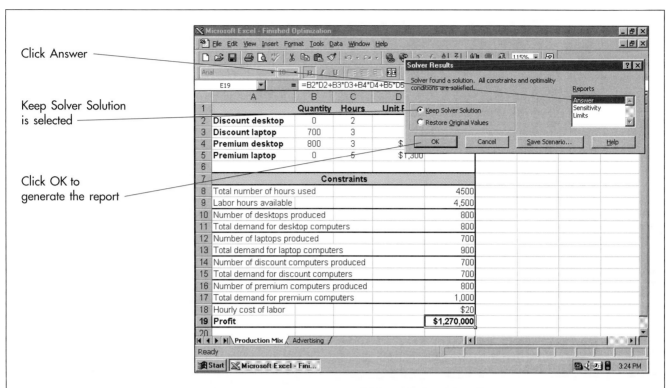

Click Answer

Keep Solver Solution is selected

Click OK to generate the report

(e) Create the Report (step 5)

FIGURE C.4   Hands-on Exercise 1 (continued)

➤ Click **Answer** in the Reports list box, then click **OK** to generate the report. You will see the report being generated, after which the Solver Results dialog box closes automatically.

➤ Save the workbook.

STEP 6: View the Report

➤ Click the **Answer Report 1 worksheet tab** to view the report as shown in Figure C.4f. Click in **cell A4,** the cell immediately under the entry showing the date and time the report was created. (The gridlines and row and column headings are suppressed by default for this worksheet.)

➤ Enter your name in boldface as shown in the figure, then press **enter** to complete the entry. Print the answer sheet and submit it to your instructor as proof you did the exercise.

➤ Exit Excel if you do not wish to continue with the next exercise at this time.

VIEW OPTIONS

Any worksheet used to create a spreadsheet model will display gridlines and row and column headers by default. Worksheets containing reports, however, especially reports generated by Excel, often suppress these elements to make the reports easier and more appealing to read. To suppress (display) these elements, pull down the Tools menu, click Options, click the View tab, then clear (check) the appropriate check boxes under Window options.

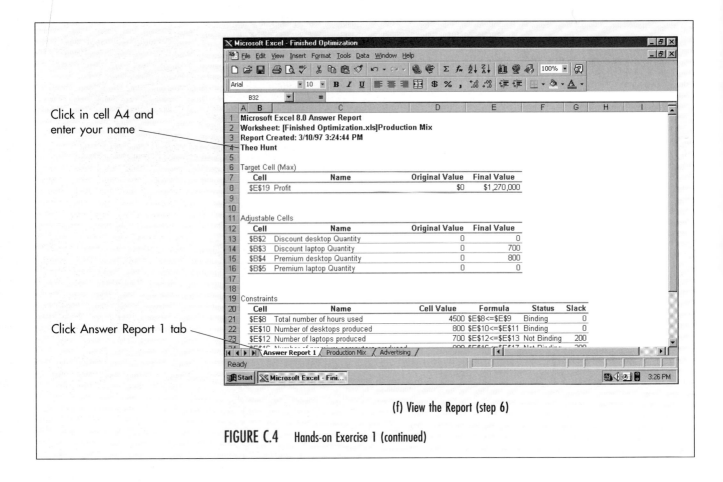

Click in cell A4 and enter your name

Click Answer Report 1 tab

(f) View the Report (step 6)

FIGURE C.4 Hands-on Exercise 1 (continued)

EXAMPLE 2—MINIMIZE COST

The example just concluded introduced you to the basics of Solver. We continue now with a second hands-on exercise, to provide additional practice, and to discuss various subtleties that can occur. This time we present a minimization problem in which we seek to minimize cost subject to a series of constraints. The problem will focus on the advertising campaign that will be conducted to sell the computers you have produced.

The director of marketing has allocated a total of $125,000 in his weekly advertising budget. He wants to establish a presence in both magazines and radio, and requires a minimum of four magazine ads and ten radio ads each week. Each magazine ad costs $10,000 and is seen by one million readers. Each radio commercial costs $5,000 and is heard by 250,000 listeners. How many ads of each type should be placed in order to reach at least 10 million customers at minimum cost?

All of the necessary information is contained within the previous paragraph. You must, however, display that information in a worksheet before you can ask Solver to find a solution. Accordingly, reread the previous paragraph, then try to set up a worksheet from which you can call Solver. (Our worksheet appears in step 1 of the following hands-on exercise. Try, however, to set up your own worksheet before you look at ours.)

FINER POINTS OF SOLVER

Figure C.5 displays the *Solver Options dialog box* that enables you to specify how Solver will approach the solution. The Max Time and Iterations entries determine

Settings determine how long Solver will work on finding a solution

Setting determines how close the computed value will come to the specified value

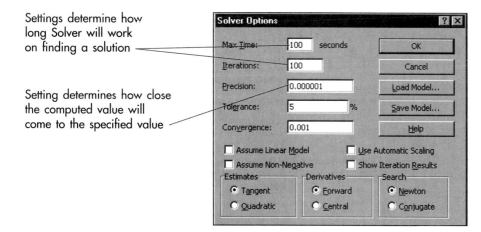

FIGURE C.5 Options Dialog Box

how long Solver will work on finding the solution. If either limit is reached before a solution is found, Solver will ask whether you want to continue. The default settings of 100 seconds and 100 iterations are sufficient for simpler problems, but may fall short for complex problems with multiple constraints.

The Precision setting determines how close the computed values in the constraint cells come to the specified value of the resource. The smaller the precision, the longer Solver will take in arriving at a solution. The default setting of .0000001 is adequate for most problems and should not be decreased. The remaining options are beyond the scope of our discussion.

HANDS-ON EXERCISE 2

Minimize Cost

Objective: To use Solver to minimize cost; to impose an integer constraint and examine its effect on the optimal solution; to relax a constraint in order to find a feasible solution. Use Figure C.6 as a guide in the exercise.

STEP 1: Enter the Cell Formulas

➤ Open the **Finished Optimization** workbook from the previous exercise.

➤ Click the tab for the **Advertising** worksheet, then click in **cell E6.** Enter the formula **=B2*C2+B3*C3** as shown in Figure C.6a.

➤ Click in **cell E10.** Enter the formula **=B2*D2+B3*D3** to compute the size of the audience. Save the workbook.

THE OFFICE ASSISTANT

The Office Assistant is common to all applications in Office 97 and is an invaluable source of help. You can activate the Assistant at any time by clicking its button on the Standard toolbar or from within a specialized dialog box. The Assistant also monitors your work and will indicate it has a suggestion by displaying a lightbulb on its button on the Standard toolbar.

Click E6 and enter the formula

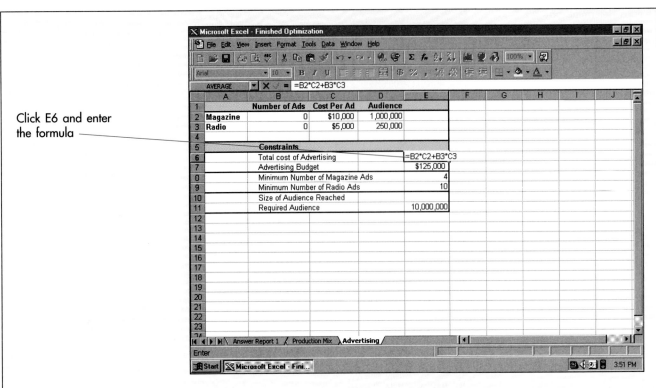

(a) Enter the Cell Formulas (step 1)

FIGURE C.6 Hands-on Exercise 2

STEP 2: Set the Target and Adjustable Cells

➤ Pull down the **Tools menu.** Click **Solver** to display the Solver Parameters dialog box shown in Figure C.6b.

➤ Set the target cell to **cell E6.** Click the **Min (Minimize) option button.** Click in the **By Changing Cells** text box.

➤ Click and drag **cells B2** and **B3** in the worksheet to select these cells as shown in Figure C.6b.

➤ Click the **Add command button** to add the first constraint as described in step 3.

STEP 3: Add the Constraints

➤ You should see the Add Constraint dialog box in Figure C.6c with the insertion point (a flashing vertical line) in the Cell Reference text box.

• Click in **cell E6** (the cell containing the formula to compute the total cost of advertising).

• The <= constraint is selected by default.

• Click in the text box to contain the value of the constraint, then click **cell E7** in the worksheet to enter the cell reference in the Add Constraint dialog box.

• Click **Add** to complete this constraint and add another.

Target cell is E6

Click Min

Click text box, then click
and drag to select B2:B3

Click Add button

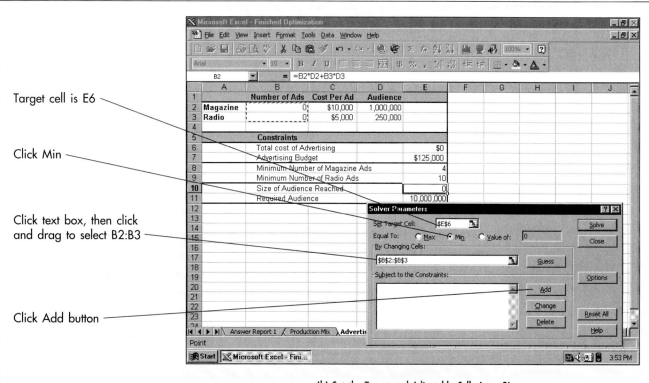

(b) Set the Target and Adjustable Cells (step 2)

Click text box, then click E6

Click text box, then click E7

Click Add button

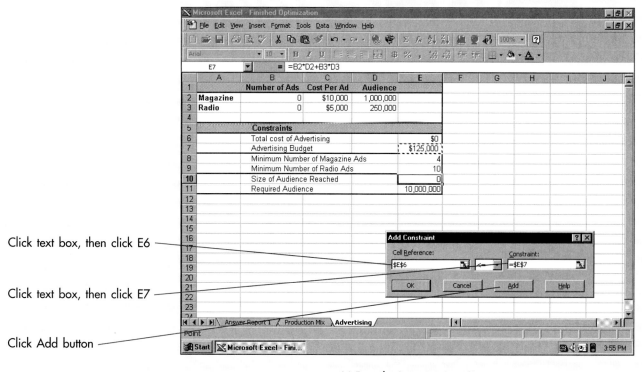

(c) Enter the Constraints (step 3)

FIGURE C.6   Hands-on Exercise 2 (continued)

➤ You will see a new (empty) Add Constraint dialog box, which enables you to enter additional constraints. Use pointing to enter each of the constraints shown below. (Solver automatically converts each reference to an absolute reference.)

- Enter the constraint **E10>=E11.** Click **Add.**
- Enter the constraint **B2>=E8.** Click **Add.**
- Enter the constraint **B3>=E9.** Click **OK** since this is the last constraint.

SHOW ITERATION RESULTS

Solver uses an iterative (repetitive) approach in which each iteration (trial solution) is one step closer to the optimal solution. It may be interesting, therefore, to examine the intermediate solutions, especially if you have a knowledge of optimization techniques, such as linear programming. Click the Options command button in the Solver Parameters dialog box, check the Show Iterations Results box, click OK to close the Solver Options dialog box, then click the Solve command button in the usual fashion. A Show Trial Solutions dialog box will appear as each intermediate solution is displayed in the worksheet. Click Continue to move from one iteration to the next until the optimal solution is reached.

STEP 4: Solve the Problem

➤ Check that the contents of the Solver Parameters dialog box match those in Figure C.6d. (The constraints appear in alphabetical order rather than the order in which they were entered.)

➤ Click the **Solve button** to solve the problem. The Solver Results dialog box appears and indicates that Solver has arrived at a solution.

➤ The option button to Keep Solver Solution is selected by default. Click **OK** to close the Solver Results dialog box and display the solution.

STEP 5: Impose an Integer Constraint

➤ The number of magazine ads in the solution is 7.5 as shown in Figure C.6e. This is a noninteger number, which is reasonable in the context of Solver but not in the "real world" as one cannot place half an ad.

➤ Pull down the **Tools menu.** Click **Solver** to once again display the Solver Parameters dialog box. Click the **Add button** to display the Add Constraint dialog box in Figure C.6e.

➤ The insertion point is already positioned in the Cell Reference text box. Click and drag to select **cells B2** through **B3.** Click the **drop-down arrow** in the Constraint list box and click **int** (for integer).

➤ Click **OK** to accept the constraint and close the Add Constraint dialog box.

➤ The Solver Parameters dialog box appears on your monitor with the integer constraint added. Click **Solve** to solve the problem.

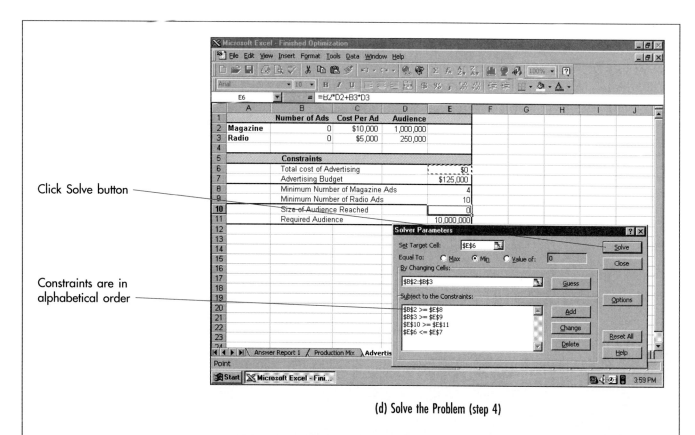

Click Solve button

Constraints are in alphabetical order

(d) Solve the Problem (step 4)

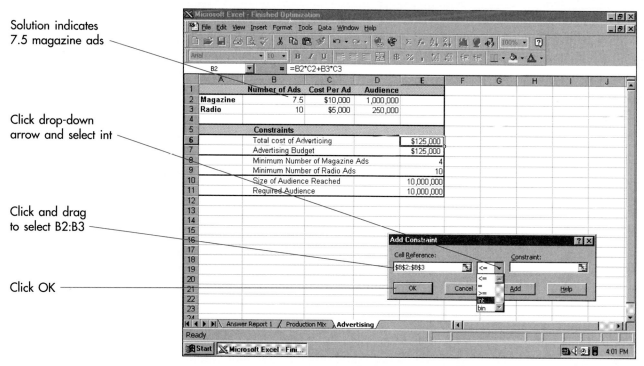

Solution indicates 7.5 magazine ads

Click drop-down arrow and select int

Click and drag to select B2:B3

Click OK

(e) Add the Integer Constraint (step 5)

FIGURE C.6   Hands-on Exercise 2 (continued)

DO YOU REALLY NEED AN INTEGER SOLUTION?

It seems like such a small change, but specifying an integer constraint can significantly increase the amount of time required for Solver to reach a solution. The examples in this chapter are relatively simple and did not take an inordinate amount of time to solve. Imposing an integer constraint on a more complex problem, however, especially on a slower microprocessor, may challenge your patience as Solver struggles to reach a solution.

STEP 6: The Infeasible Solution

➤ You should see the dialog box in Figure C.6f, indicating that Solver could *not* find a solution that satisfied the existing constraints. This is because the imposition of the integer constraint would raise the number of magazine ads from 7.5 to 8, which would increase the total cost of advertising to $130,000, exceeding the budget of $125,000.

➤ The desired audience can still be reached but only by relaxing one of the binding constraints. You can, for example, retain the requisite number of magazine and radio ads by increasing the budget. Alternatively, the budget can be held at $125,000, while still reaching the audience by decreasing the required number of radio ads.

➤ Click **Cancel** to exit the dialog box and return to the worksheet.

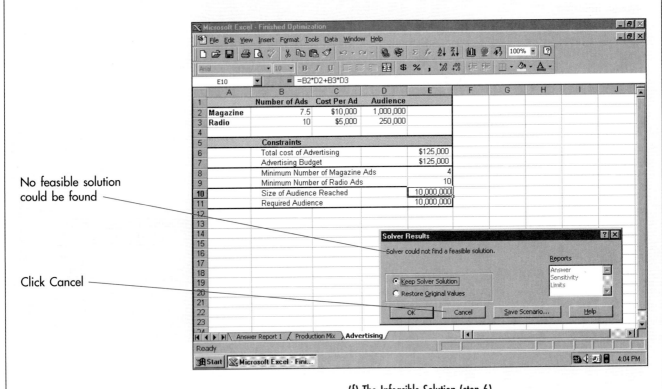

(f) The Infeasible Solution (step 6)

FIGURE C.6   Hands-on Exercise 2 (continued)

UNABLE TO FIND A SOLUTION

Solver is a powerful tool, but it cannot do the impossible. Some problems simply do not have a solution because the constraints may conflict with one another, and/or because the constraints exceed the available resources. Should this occur, and it will, check your constraints to make sure they were entered correctly. If Solver is still unable to reach a solution, it will be necessary to relax one or more of the constraints.

STEP 7: Relax a Constraint

➤ Click in **cell E9** (the cell containing the minimum number of radio ads). Enter **9** and press **enter.**

➤ Pull down the **Tools menu.** Click **Solver** to display the Solver Parameters dialog box. Click **Solve.** This time Solver finds a solution as shown in Figure C.6g.

➤ Click **Answer** in the Reports list box, then click **OK** to generate the report. You will see the report being generated, after which the Solver Results dialog box closes automatically.

➤ Click the **Answer Report 2 worksheet tab** to view the report. Add your name to the report, boldface your name, print the answer report, and submit it to your instructor.

➤ Save the workbook a final time. Exit Excel.

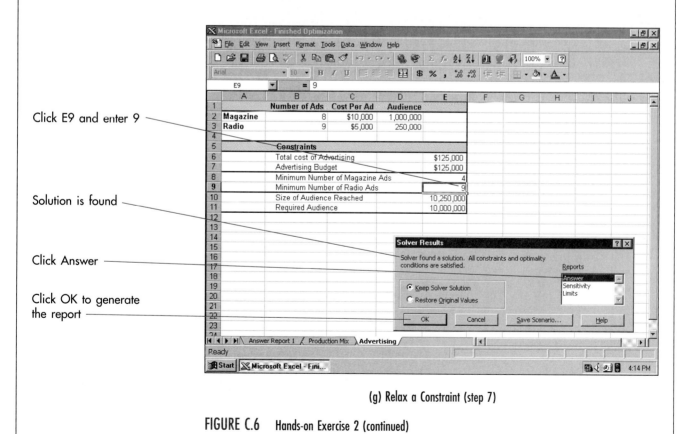

Click E9 and enter 9

Solution is found

Click Answer

Click OK to generate the report

(g) Relax a Constraint (step 7)

FIGURE C.6 Hands-on Exercise 2 (continued)

SUMMARY

Solver is an optimization and resource allocation tool that helps you achieve a desired goal, such as maximizing profit or minimizing cost. The information required by Solver is entered through the Solver Parameters dialog box, which is divided into three sections: the target cell, the adjustable cells, and the constraints.

The target cell identifies the goal (or objective function), which is the cell whose value you want to maximize, minimize, or set to a specific value. The adjustable cells are the cells whose values are changed until the constraints are satisfied and the target cell reaches its optimum value. The constraints specify the restrictions. Each constraint consists of a comparison containing a cell or cell range on the left, a relational operator, and a numeric value or cell reference on the right.

The Solver Options dialog box lets you specify how Solver will attempt to find a solution. The Max Time and Iterations entries determine how long Solver will work on finding a solution. If either limit is reached before a solution is found, Solver will ask whether you want to continue. The default settings of 100 seconds and 100 iterations are sufficient for simpler problems, but may not be enough for complex problems with multiple constraints.

KEY WORDS AND CONCEPTS

Adjustable cells
Answer Report
Binding constraint
Constraint
Feasible solution
Infeasible solution

Integer constraint
Iteration
Nonbinding constraint
Nonnegativity constraint
Precision

Solver Options dialog box
Solver Parameters dialog box
Target cell

APPENDIX D: DATA MAPPING

OVERVIEW

"A picture is worth 1,000 words." It is a well-documented fact that a chart can convey information more effectively than the corresponding table of numbers. You are probably familiar with the use of conventional charts (pie charts, bar charts, line charts, and so on) to represent the information in a worksheet. This appendix extends that discussion to the use of maps, a capability that is built into Microsoft Office 97.

Consider, for example, the worksheet and associated maps in Figure D.1, which display the results of the 1996 presidential election as well as a strategy for 2000. The worksheet in Figure D.1a contains the statistical data on which the maps are based. It lists the states in alphabetical order, and for each state, the number of electoral votes and the candidate who received those votes. The worksheet also shows the number of popular votes received by each candidate, although that information is not conveyed in either map. (The District of Columbia is not shown in the worksheet, but its three electoral votes are included in Mr. Clinton's total.)

The maps in Figures D.1b and D.1c display (some of the) information that is contained within the worksheet, but in a form that is more quickly grasped by the reader. Figure D.1b shows at a glance which candidate won which state by assigning different colors to each candidate. Figure D.1c groups the states according to the number of electoral votes in order to develop a strategy for the 2000 election.

This appendix shows you how to use the Data Mapping application in Microsoft Office to create the maps in Figure D.1. The appendix also introduces you to the Mapstats workbook that contains demographic information for the United States as well as several foreign countries, and enables you to create a variety of additional maps.

	A	B	C	D	E	F
1	State	Electoral Votes	Winner	Clinton	Dole	Perot
2	Alabama	9	Dole	664,503	782,029	92,010
3	Alaska	3	Dole	66,508	101,234	21,536
4	Arizona	8	Clinton	612,412	576,126	104,712
5	Arkansas	6	Clinton	469,164	322,349	66,997
6	California	54	Clinton	4,639,935	3,412,563	667,702
7	Colorado	8	Dole	670,854	691,291	99,509
8	Connecticut	8	Clinton	712,603	481,047	137,784
9	Delaware	3	Clinton	140,209	98,906	28,693
10	Florida	25	Clinton	2,533,502	2,226,117	482,237
11	Georgia	13	Dole	1,047,214	1,078,972	146,031
12	Hawaii	4	Clinton	205,012	113,943	27,358
13	Idaho	4	Dole	165,545	256,406	62,506
14	Illinois	22	Clinton	2,299,476	1,577,930	344,311
15	Indiana	12	Dole	874,668	995,082	218,739
16	Iowa	7	Clinton	615,732	490,949	104,462
17	Kansas	6	Dole	384,399	578,572	92,093
18	Kentucky	8	Clinton	635,804	622,339	118,768
19	Louisiana	9	Clinton	928,983	710,240	122,981
20	Maine	4	Clinton	311,092	185,133	85,290
21	Maryland	10	Clinton	924,284	651,682	113,684
22	Massachusetts	12	Clinton	1,567,223	717,622	225,594
23	Michigan	18	Clinton	1,941,126	1,440,977	326,751
24	Minnesota	10	Clinton	1,096,355	751,971	252,986
25	Mississippi	7	Dole	385,005	434,547	51,500
26	Missouri	11	Clinton	1,024,817	889,689	217,103
27	Montana	3	Dole	167,169	178,957	55,017
28	Nebraska	5	Dole	231,906	355,665	76,103
29	Nevada	4	Clinton	203,388	198,775	43,855
30	New Hampshire	4	Clinton	245,260	196,740	48,140
31	New Jersey	15	Clinton	1,599,932	1,080,041	257,979
32	New Mexico	5	Clinton	252,215	210,791	30,978
33	New York	33	Clinton	3,513,191	1,861,198	485,547
34	North Carolina	14	Dole	1,099,132	1,214,399	165,301
35	North Dakota	3	Dole	106,405	124,597	32,594
36	Ohio	21	Clinton	2,100,690	1,823,859	470,680
37	Oklahoma	8	Dole	488,102	582,310	130,788
38	Oregon	7	Clinton	326,099	256,105	73,265
39	Pennsylvania	23	Clinton	2,206,241	1,793,568	430,082
40	Rhode Island	4	Clinton	220,592	98,325	39,965
41	South Carolina	8	Dole	495,878	564,856	63,324
42	South Dakota	3	Dole	139,295	150,508	31,248
43	Tennessee	11	Clinton	905,599	860,809	105,577
44	Texas	32	Dole	2,455,735	2,731,998	377,530
45	Utah	5	Dole	220,197	359,394	66,100
46	Vermont	3	Clinton	138,400	80,043	30,912
47	Virginia	13	Dole	1,070,990	1,119,974	158,707
48	Washington	11	Clinton	899,645	639,743	161,642
49	West Virginia	5	Clinton	324,394	231,908	70,853
50	Wisconsin	11	Clinton	1,071,859	845,172	227,426
51	Wyoming	3	Dole	77,897	105,347	25,854
52						
53	Total			45,476,636	37,852,798	7,870,804
54						
55	Electoral Vote Totals					
56	Clinton	379				
57	Dole	159				

(a) Worksheet Data

FIGURE D.1   Data Mapping

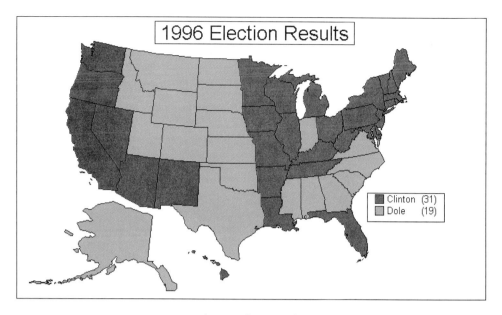

(b) 1996 Election Results

(c) Strategy for 2000

FIGURE D.1   Data Mapping (continued)

CREATING A MAP

The exercise that follows shortly illustrates the basic commands in the Data Mapping application and gives you an appreciation for its overall capability. Creating a map is easy provided you have a basic proficiency with Microsoft Excel. In essence, you do the following:

1. Select the cell range(s) containing the data for the map. (At least one column of the data must be recognizable as geographic names that are present in one of the available maps.)

2. Click the Map button on the Standard toolbar, then click and drag in the worksheet where you want the map to go.

3. Determine the type of map you want to create by selecting one of several formatting options. (The formatting options are specified in the Microsoft Map Control dialog box, which is described in greater detail on page 385.)

4. Add the finishing touches by changing the title, legend, or other features.

Each step displays a dialog box in which you specify the options you want. The best way to learn is to create a map. Let's begin.

HANDS-ON EXERCISE 1

Introduction to Data Mapping

Objective: To illustrate basic features of the Data Mapping application; to create a map showing the winning candidate in each state in the 1996 presidential election. Use Figure D.2 as a guide in the exercise.

STEP 1: Insert a Cell Note

➤ Start Excel. Open the **Presidential Election** workbook in the **Exploring Excel folder.** Save the workbook as **Finished Presidential Election** so that you can return to the original workbook if necessary.

➤ Press **Ctrl+End** to move to the end of the worksheet as shown in Figure D.2a. You can see the number of popular votes received by each candidate as well as the number of electoral votes.

➤ Click in **cell B56.** Pull down the **Insert menu.** Click **Comment.** A comment box opens as shown in Figure D.2a. Enter the text of your comment as shown in the figure, then click outside the comment when you are finished.

➤ The comment box closes, but a tiny red triangle appears in the upper corner of cell B51. (If you do not see the triangle, pull down the **Tools menu,** click **Options,** click the **View tab,** then click the option button in the Comments area to show **Comment Indicator only.**)

➤ Point to cell **B56** and the text of your comment appears as a ScreenTip. Point to a different cell and the comment disappears.

RESOLVE UNKNOWN GEOGRAPHIC DATA

The Data Mapping application uses its own version of a spell check to ensure that the selected data matches predefined geographic data. The states must be spelled correctly, for example, or else mapping is not possible. Any unrecognized entry is flagged as unknown geographic data. You may be offered suggestions for a simple misspelling, in which case you can accept the suggestion. A more serious error, however, such as including an extraneous row (e.g., totals) in the data range, requires you to discard the entry.

Map button ──────────

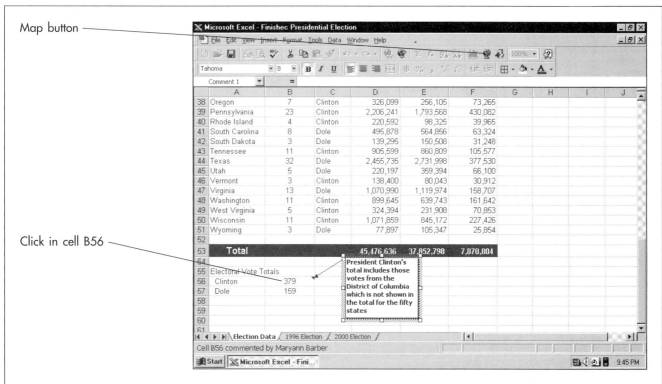

Click in cell B56 ──────

	A	B	C	D	E	F	G	H	I	J
38	Oregon	7	Clinton	326,099	256,105	73,265				
39	Pennsylvania	23	Clinton	2,206,241	1,793,568	430,082				
40	Rhode Island	4	Clinton	220,592	98,325	39,965				
41	South Carolina	8	Dole	495,878	564,856	63,324				
42	South Dakota	3	Dole	139,295	150,508	31,248				
43	Tennessee	11	Clinton	905,599	860,809	105,577				
44	Texas	32	Dole	2,455,735	2,731,998	377,530				
45	Utah	5	Dole	220,197	359,394	66,100				
46	Vermont	3	Clinton	138,400	80,043	30,912				
47	Virginia	13	Dole	1,070,990	1,119,974	158,707				
48	Washington	11	Clinton	899,645	639,743	161,642				
49	West Virginia	5	Clinton	324,394	231,908	70,853				
50	Wisconsin	11	Clinton	1,071,859	845,172	227,426				
51	Wyoming	3	Dole	77,897	105,347	25,854				
52										
53	**Total**			45,476,636	37,852,798	7,870,804				
54										
55	Electoral Vote Totals									
56	Clinton		379							
57	Dole		159							
58										
59										
60										
61										

President Clinton's total includes those votes from the District of Columbia which is not shown in the total for the fifty states

(a) Insert a Comment (step 1)

FIGURE D.2   Hands-on Exercise 1

STEP 2: Draw the Map

➤ Press **Ctrl+Home** to move to the beginning of the worksheet. Click and drag to select **cells A1** through **C51.** The AutoCalculate indicator on the status bar (see boxed tip) should display 535 as the total number of electoral votes in the selected range.

➤ Click the **Map button** on the Standard toolbar. Click the **down scroll arrow** until cell A59 comes into view. Click in **cell A59,** then click and drag as shown in Figure D.2b. (Excel requires that the map be created on the same sheet as the data. You can, however, move the map to a different sheet after it has been created to facilitate printing.) Release the mouse.

➤ A dialog box will appear on the screen with the message, "Retrieving current selection", followed by a second message, "Matching Data". You should then see the dialog box in Figure D.2b.

THE AUTOCALCULATE FEATURE

The AutoCalculate feature lets you check a total without having to use a calculator or enter a temporary formula in a worksheet. You can use the feature to check that you have selected all 50 states prior to drawing the map. Just select the range, and the status bar displays the result. You can change the AutoCalculate function (to display the count, average, maximum, or minimum value) by right clicking the AutoCalculate area of the status bar, then selecting the desired function.

Click OK to
create the map

Click to select
desired map

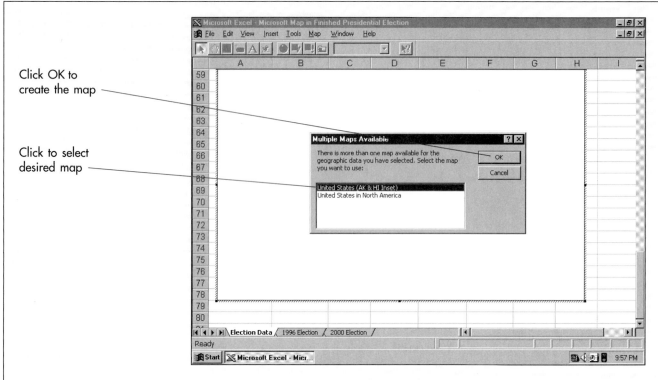

(b) Draw a Map (step 2)

FIGURE D.2   Hands-on Exercise 1 (continued)

➤ The program recognizes the state names in Column A and presents two options for U.S. maps. Click **United States (AK & HI Inset),** then click **OK** to create the map.

STEP 3: The Microsoft Map Control Dialog Box

➤ You should see the Microsoft Map Control dialog box in Figure D.2c. Excel has (by default) plotted the number of electoral votes, rather than the candidate who won the votes.

➤ Click and drag the **Electoral Votes button** out of the Map Control dialog box work area until you see a recycle bin. Release the mouse. The data disappears from the map, and all of the states appear in light green.

CHANGE THE CATEGORY COLORS

You can change the map colors when the Microsoft Map Control dialog box is displayed. To change the color for President Clinton, for example, double click the Winner button within the work area of the Map Control dialog box to display the Category Shading Options dialog box. Select the category (e.g., Clinton), then click the down arrow in the color list box to choose a different color. Click OK to accept the color change and close the Category Shading Options dialog box.

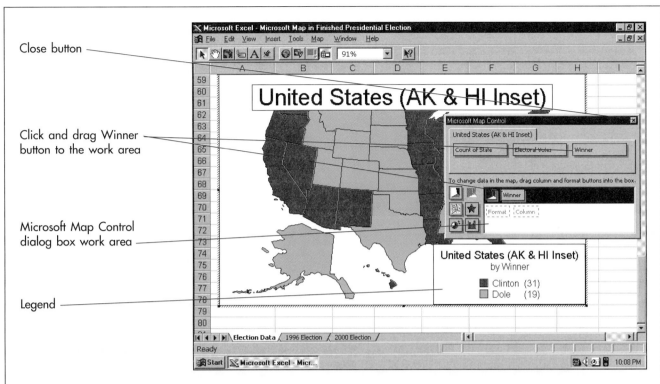

Close button

Click and drag Winner button to the work area

Microsoft Map Control dialog box work area

Legend

(c) Microsoft Map Control Dialog Box (step 3)

FIGURE D.2 Hands-on Exercise 1 (continued)

➤ Click and drag the **Winner button** (the name of the button corresponds to the column heading in the worksheet) to the work area in the dialog box. Release the mouse.

➤ A map is created with the various states shaded in red or green according to the winning candidate in each state. The significance of the different colors is determined from the legend as explained in step 4.

➤ Click the **Close button** to close the Microsoft Map Control dialog box.

STEP 4: Edit the Legend

➤ Your map should contain a legend with the candidates' names. If you do not see a legend, pull down the **View menu** and click **All Legends.**

➤ If you do not see the candidates' names, point to the legend, then click the **right mouse button** to display a shortcut menu. Click **Edit** to display the Edit Legend dialog box in Figure D.2d. Clear the Use Compact Format check box.

➤ Click and drag to select the contents of the legend Title text box. Press the **Del key.** Clear the contents of the Subtitle text box in similar fashion.

➤ Click **OK** to accept the changes and close the dialog box. The legend should consist of two lines, Dole and Clinton, with the numbers 19 and 31, respectively, indicating the number of states each candidate carried.

➤ Click inside the legend to select it. A shaded border appears around the legend. If necessary, click and drag the legend to position it within the map frame.

Click and drag to select title, then press Del key

Click and drag to select subtitle, then press Del key

Clear Compact Format check box

Click OK

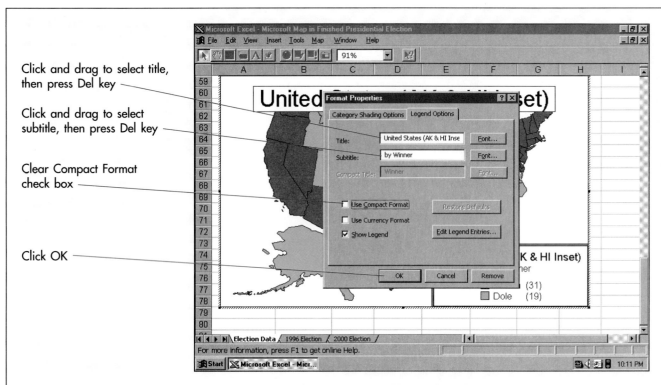

(d) Edit the Legend (step 4)

FIGURE D.2   Hands-on Exercise 1 (continued)

IN-PLACE EDITING

In-place editing enables you to edit an embedded object by using the toolbar and pull-down menus of the server application. Thus, when editing a map that has been embedded into an Excel worksheet, the title bar is that of the client application (Microsoft Excel), but the toolbars and pull-down menus reflect the server application (the Data Mapping application within Microsoft Office). There are, however, two exceptions; the File and Window menus are those of the client application (Excel). The File menu enables you to save the worksheet. The Window menu enables you to view (and edit) multiple workbooks in different windows.

STEP 5: The Finishing Touches
➤ Double click immediately in front of the "U" in "United States with AK and HI Insets" in order to edit the title. A flashing vertical line (the insertion point) will appear at the place where you double clicked.
➤ Click and drag to select the entire title, then type **1996 Election Results** as the new title. Press **enter** to complete the title.
➤ Point to the title, then click the **right mouse button** to display the shortcut menu shown in Figure D.2e.
➤ Click **Format Font** to display the Format Font dialog box. Change the font size to **20 points.** Change the other parameters (e.g., font color) as you see fit, then close the Format Font dialog box.

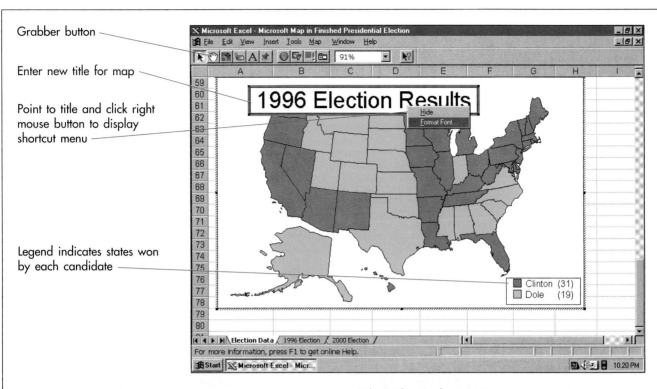

Grabber button

Enter new title for map

Point to title and click right
mouse button to display
shortcut menu

Legend indicates states won
by each candidate

(e) The Finishing Touches (step 5)

FIGURE D.2   Hands-on Exercise 1 (continued)

➤ You can position the title, legend, and map independently within the frame:
  • Click and drag the **title** to move the title anywhere within the frame.
  • Click and drag the **legend** to move the legend anywhere within the frame.
  • Click the **Grabber button** (a hand) on the Data Map toolbar to select it.
    Point to the map (the mouse pointer changes to a hand), then click and
    drag the **map** to move it within the frame.
  • Pull down the **File menu.** Click **Save** to save the worksheet.

TO CLICK OR DOUBLE CLICK

Clicking a map selects the map and displays the sizing handles that are
used to move or size the frame containing the map. Double clicking the
map loads the underlying Data Mapping application that created the map
and enables you to edit the map.

STEP 6: Place the Map in Its Own Worksheet
➤ Click outside the map to exit the Data Mapping application, then click anywhere on the map to select the map as an Excel object.
➤ Click the **Cut button.** The map is placed in the clipboard and disappears from
  the worksheet.
➤ Click the **1996 Election tab.** Click in **cell A1.** Click the **Paste button** to paste
  the map onto this worksheet.

STEP 7: The Print Preview Command

➤ Pull down the **File menu.** Click **Page Setup** to display the Page Setup dialog box.

- Click the **Page tab.** Click the **Landscape orientation button.**
- Click the option button to adjust **Scaling to 120%** of size.
- Click the **Margins tab.** Check the box to center the worksheet **Horizontally.**
- Click the **Sheet tab.** Clear the boxes to include Row and Column Headings and Gridlines.

➤ Click the **Print Preview button** to preview the map before printing as shown in Figure D.2f.

- If you are satisfied with the appearance of the worksheet, click the **Print button** within the Preview window, then click **OK** to print the worksheet.
- If you are not satisfied with the appearance of the map, click the **Setup button** within the Preview window to make the necessary changes, after which you can print the worksheet.

➤ Pull down the **File menu.** Click **Close.** Click **Yes** if prompted to save changes.

➤ Exit Excel if you do not want to continue with the next exercise at this time.

Click Print button

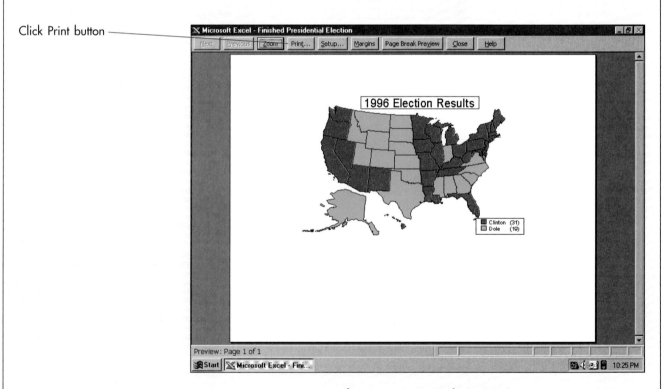

(f) Print Preview Command (step 7)

FIGURE D.2   Hands-on Exercise 1 (continued)

We trust you completed the hands-on exercise without difficulty. The exercise introduced you to the basic features in the Data Mapping application and enabled you to create a map showing the winning candidate in each state. The format of the map was chosen automatically according to the nature of the data. The exercise had you plot a qualitative variable (winner), which had one of two values (Dole or Clinton). The mapping program automatically selected *category shading* and assigned a different color to each value of a category, red to Mr. Clinton and green to Mr. Dole.

The next exercise directs you to plot a quantitative variable (the number of electoral votes in each state), then has you experiment with different formats for the resulting map. The selection is made in the *Microsoft Map Control dialog box* as shown in Figure D.3. Six formats are available, but not every format is suitable for every type of data. Figure D.3 illustrates three types of formatting.

Figure D.3a displays the Microsoft Map Control dialog box, which appears automatically as the map is created. The top half of the dialog box indicates the columns that have been selected from the associated worksheet. The bottom half of the dialog box (the work area) shows the data that is to be plotted and the type of formatting in effect.

Selected columns

Format in effect

Data to be plotted

Work area

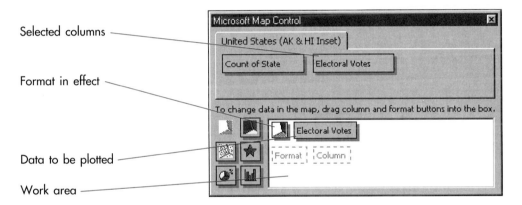

(a) Map Control Dialog Box

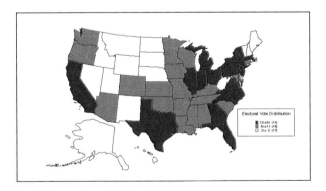

(b) Value Shading

FIGURE D.3 Microsoft Map Control

(c) Graduated Symbol

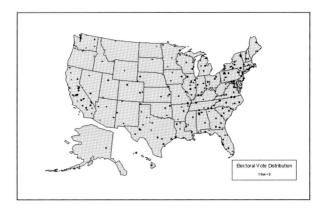

(d) Dot Density

FIGURE D.3   Microsoft Map Control (continued)

The maps in Figure D.3 plot the identical data (the number of electoral votes in each state), but in three different formats. Figure D.3b uses *value shading* to divide the states into groups and assign a different shade to each group. Figure D.3c uses the ***graduated symbol*** format to convey the same information. (The size of the symbol corresponds to the number of electoral votes.) Figure D.3d uses the ***dot density*** format to enable the user to see the actual number of electoral votes in each state. (Each dot corresponds to one electoral vote.) The choice between these maps is one of personal preference as will be seen in the next exercise.

HANDS-ON EXERCISE 2

Finer Points of Data Mapping

Objective: To create a map showing the distribution of electoral votes in the United States; to experiment with different formatting options in the Microsoft Map Control dialog box. Use Figure D.4 as a guide in the exercise.

STEP 1: Draw the Map

➤ Start Excel. Open the **Finished Presidential Election** workbook from the previous exercise. Click the **Election Data tab.**

➤ Click in **cell A1,** then click and drag to select **cells A1** through **B51.** (The AutoCalculate indicator on the status bar should display 535 as the total number of electoral votes in the selected range.)

➤ Click the **Map button** on the Standard toolbar. Click the **down scroll arrow** until cell A59 comes into view. Click in **cell A59,** then click and drag to draw the frame that will contain the map. Release the mouse.

➤ The program recognizes the state names in Column A and presents two options. Click **United States (AK & HI Inset),** then click **OK** to create the map as shown in Figure D.4a.

➤ Close the Microsoft Map Control dialog box. Pull down the **File menu.** Click **Save** to save the worksheet.

Click A59 and drag to draw frame to contain the map

Click to close the Microsoft Map Control dialog box

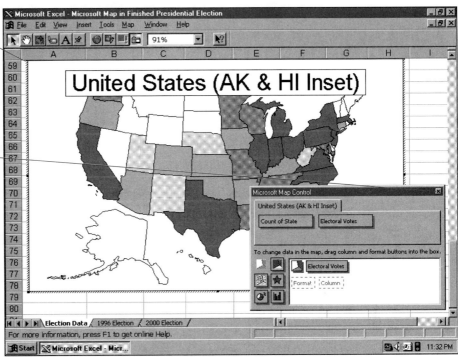

(a) Create the Map (step 1)

FIGURE D.4   Hands-on Exercise 2

STEP 2: Edit the Legend

➤ The various states are shaded according to the number of electoral votes in each state. To determine the meaning of the shadings, you need to display the complete (not the compact) legend.

• If you do not see any legend at all, pull down the **View menu** and click **All legends.**

• If you see a brief (compact) legend, point to the legend, then click the **right mouse button** to display a shortcut menu. Click the **Compact command** to toggle the compact legend off and display the complete legend.

➤ Point to the legend, click the **right mouse button** to display a shortcut menu, then click **Edit** to display the Format Properties dialog box.

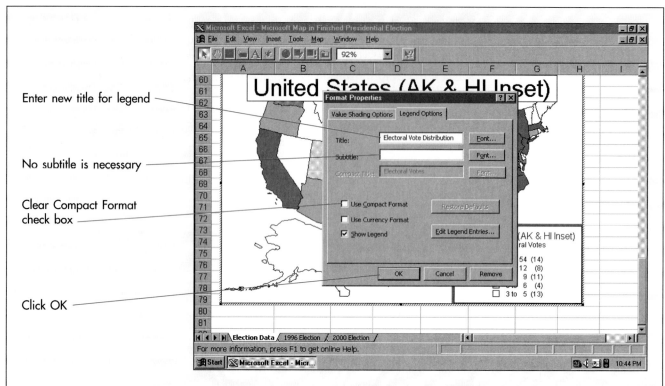

Enter new title for legend

No subtitle is necessary

Clear Compact Format
check box

Click OK

(b) Change the Legend (step 2)

FIGURE D.4   Hands-on Exercise 2 (continued)

➤ Click and drag to select the contents of the Title text box. Type **Electoral Vote Distribution** to replace the selected text. Clear the contents of the Subtitle text box as shown in Figure D.4b.

➤ Click **OK** to accept the changes and close the dialog box.

➤ Pull down the **File menu** and click the **Save command.**

STEP 3: Microsoft Map Control

➤ Click the **Show/Hide Microsoft Map Control button** to open the Map Control dialog box as shown in Figure D.4c.

• Click and drag the **Dot Density button** to a position next to the Electoral Votes button as shown in Figure D.4c. Click **OK** if asked to refresh the map. The shading on the map changes so that each state contains a number of dots proportional to its electoral votes.

• Click and drag the **Graduated Symbol button** to a position next to the Electoral Votes button. The map changes to place a graduated symbol (the same symbol in different sizes) in each state according to its number of electoral votes.

• Click and drag the **Category Shading button** to a position next to the Electoral Votes button. The states are displayed in a variety of colors, which is totally *inappropriate* for this map. (Category shading is used only when the number of distinct values is small; e.g., to indicate the winning candidate in each state as in the earlier map.)

• Click and drag the **Value Shading button** to a position next to the Electoral Votes button.

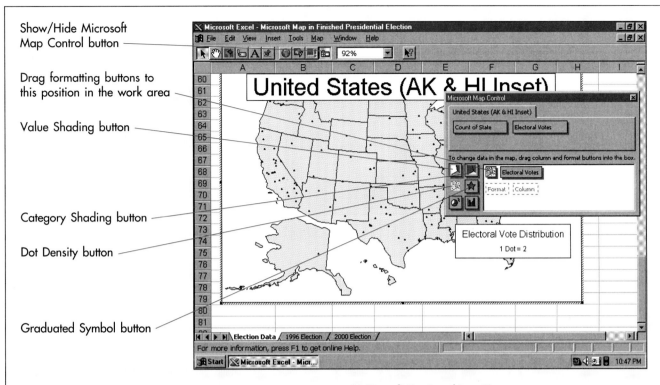

Show/Hide Microsoft
Map Control button

Drag formatting buttons to
this position in the work area

Value Shading button

Category Shading button

Dot Density button

Graduated Symbol button

(c) Microsoft Map Control (step 3)

FIGURE D.4   Hands-on Exercise 2 (continued)

➤ Close the Microsoft Map Control dialog box. Pull down the **File menu.** Click **Save** to save the worksheet.

CATEGORY SHADING VERSUS VALUE SHADING

Category shading is used with a nonquantitative variable (such as a candidate's name) and assigns a different color to each value of the category—for example, red to Mr. Clinton and green to Mr. Dole as was done in the map in exercise 1. Value shading is used with a quantitative variable (such as the number of electoral votes in each state) and is necessary when there are a large number of distinct values. Value shading divides the states into groups with a different shade assigned to each group.

STEP 4: Value Shading Options

➤ Pull down the **Map menu.** Click **Value Shading Options** to display the dialog box in Figure D.4d. (Click **OK** if asked to refresh the map.)

➤ Click the **drop-down arrow** to change the number of value ranges to **three.** Click the **drop-down arrow** in the **color** list box to change the color of the shading to **blue.**

➤ Click the option button for an equal number of items in each range of values. Click **OK** to close the Value Shading Options dialog box.

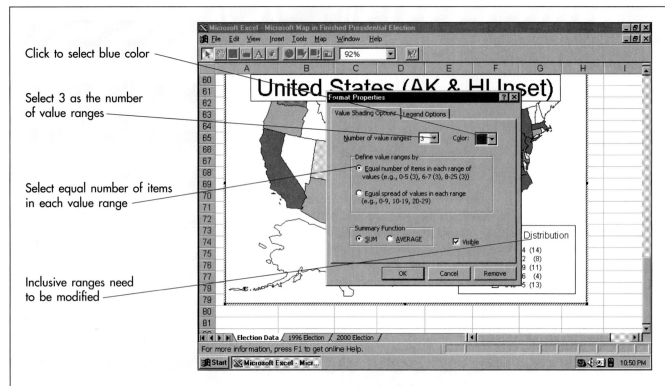

Click to select blue color

Select 3 as the number of value ranges

Select equal number of items in each value range

Inclusive ranges need to be modified

(d) Value Shading Options (step 4)

FIGURE D.4   Hands-on Exercise 2 (continued)

➤ The number of groups changes to three. The legend shows 14 states with 12 to 54 votes, 19 states with 6 to 12 votes, and 17 states with 3 to 6 votes. The legend uses *inclusive* ranges and needs to be modified.

➤ Point to the legend, click the **right mouse button** to display a shortcut menu, then click **Edit** to display the Edit Legend dialog box.

➤ Click the command button to **Edit Legend Entries,** then change the text for the latter two groups to read **6 to 11** and **3 to 5.** Click **OK** to close the Edit Legend Entries dialog box. Click **OK** to close the Edit Legend dialog box.

MISLEADING LEGEND

The legend created by the data mapping program incorrectly uses inclusive values, which need to be adjusted manually if the legend is to make sense. In creating groups for the electoral vote distribution, the number 12 is used as a break point in that there is a group of states with 12 to 54 electoral votes and a second group with 6 to 12 electoral votes. In actuality, the latter group consists of states with 6 to 11 electoral votes (i.e., the upper bound is less than 12).

STEP 5: Map Labels

➤ Click the **Map Labels button** to display the Map Labels dialog box. Click the option button to **Create labels from Values from Electoral Votes** (the only option in the drop-down list). Click **OK** to close the Map Labels dialog box.

➤ Point to a state (the mouse pointer changes to a crosshair), and you see the corresponding number of electoral votes. Point to California, for example, and you see 54. Point to Texas and you see 32.

➤ Point to a state, such as California, then **click the mouse** to create a label containing the number of electoral votes. The number 54 is entered on the map and surrounded in sizing handles to indicate that the label is currently selected.

➤ Click the **Select Objects button** (the arrow) on the Data Map toolbar to turn off the labeling feature so that we can change the color of the label and make it easier to read. Point to the number 54 and click the **right mouse button** to display a shortcut menu.

➤ Click **Format Font** to display the Font dialog box in Figure D.4e:

• Click the **drop-down arrow** on the **Color** list box. Click **aqua** as the color of the text.

• If necessary, change the type size to **8** points.

• Click **OK** to accept the color change and close the Font dialog box.

➤ Click the **Map Labels button,** click **OK** to close the Map Labels dialog box, then label all of the other states in the category with the highest numbers of electoral votes. When you are finished, click the **Select Objects button** (the arrow) on the Data Map toolbar to turn off the labeling feature.

➤ Pull down the **File menu** and click the **Save command.**

Map Labels button

Select Objects button

Point to a state, click the mouse to create a label

Point to the label and click right mouse button to display shortcut menu

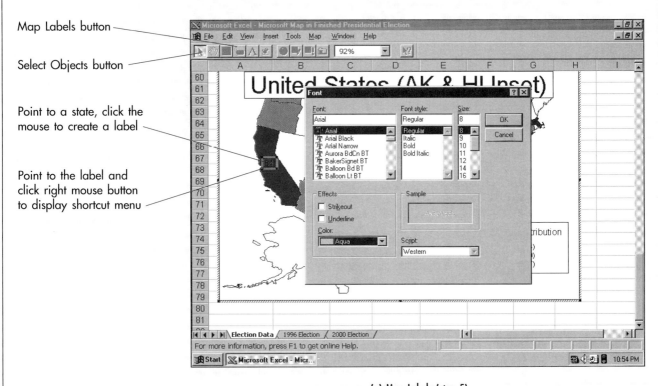

(e) Map Labels (step 5)

FIGURE D.4   Hands-on Exercise 2 (continued)

STEP 6: Complete the Map

➤ Click the **Text tool,** click at the bottom of the map as shown in Figure D.4f, then start to type the text shown in the figure. The text appears in aqua.

➤ Click the **right mouse button,** click **Format Font,** and change the color back to black. Click **OK** to close the Font dialog box, then finish entering the text.

➤ Click the title to select it. Click before the first character in the title, drag to select the entire title, then enter **Strategy for 2000** as shown in Figure D.4f.

➤ You can position the title, legend, and map independently within the frame:

  • Click and drag the **title** to move the title anywhere within the frame.

  • Click and drag the **legend** to move the legend anywhere within the frame.

  • Click the **Grabber button** on the Data Map toolbar to select it, then click and drag the **map** (the mouse pointer changes to a hand) to move it within the frame.

➤ Pull down the **File menu** and click the **Save command.**

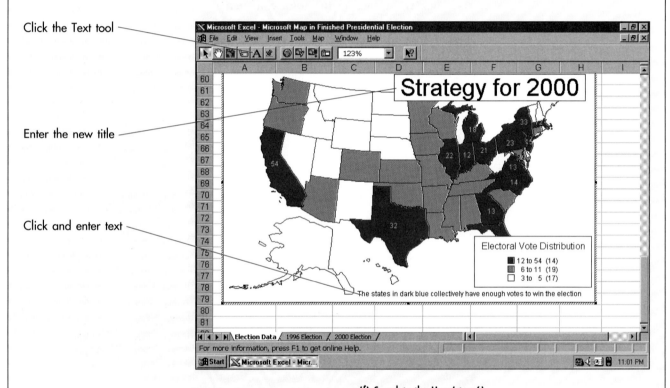

Click the Text tool

Enter the new title

Click and enter text

(f) Complete the Map (step 6)

FIGURE D.4   Hands-on Exercise 2 (continued)

STEP 7: Place the Map in Its Own Worksheet

➤ Click outside the map to exit the Data Mapping application, then click anywhere on the map to select it as an Excel object.

➤ Click the **Cut button.** The map is placed in the clipboard and disappears from the worksheet.

➤ Click the **Strategy for 2000 tab.** Click in **cell A1.** Click the **Paste button** to paste the map onto this worksheet.

➤ Print the map. Save the workbook a final time. Exit Excel.

Microsoft Excel comes with an assortment of maps, together with demographic data for each map. The demographic data is contained in the *Mapstats workbook* as shown in Figure D.5. The Table of Contents worksheet in Figure D.5a shows the countries for which a map and demographic data are supplied. Figure D.5b displays (some of) the demographic data for the United States.

The column headings in Figure D.5b are abbreviated, and hence the precise nature of the data is not immediately apparent. The cells containing the column headings are annotated, however (note the red dot in each cell), so that you can point to any heading and display the ScreenTip that fully describes the data. There are more than 30 categories of demographic data available for the United States. Similar, but not necessarily identical, data is available for the other countries in the workbook.

FINDING THE MAPSTATS WORKBOOK

The easiest way to open the Mapstats workbook is through the Windows 95 Find command. Click the Start button, click (or point to) the Find command, then click Files or Folders to display the Find dialog box. Enter Mapstats in the Named text box and My Computer in the Look In box. Click Find Now. Double click the icon next to the Mapstats workbook to start Excel and open the workbook. Save the workbook under a different name so that you can return to the original workbook should it become necessary.

Click USA Worksheet tab

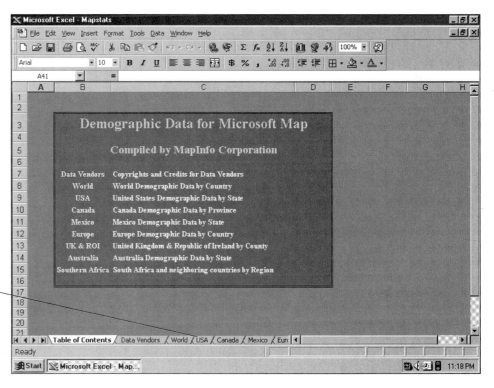

(a) Table of Contents Page

FIGURE D.5   The Mapstats Workbook

Map tool

Notes exist for all
column headings

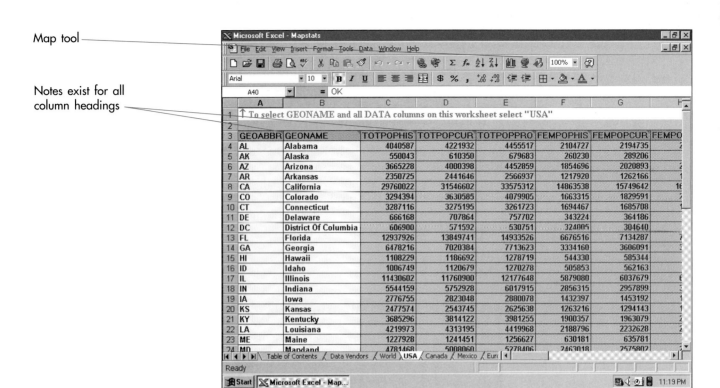

(b) USA Data Worksheet

FIGURE D.5   The Mapstats Workbook (continued)

You can create a map based on any column of demographic data by following the steps in the hands-on exercise. Just select the data, click the Map button on the Standard toolbar, then click in the worksheet where you want the map
to go. Choose the type of map you want, add the finishing touches as was done in
the exercises, and you will be able to create a variety of useful and attractive maps.
Cartography has never been so easy.

SUMMARY

Computer mapping enables you to visualize quantitative data and is made possible through the Data Mapping application included with Microsoft Office 97. Creation of a map is straightforward and consists of four general steps. You select the
data to be mapped, indicate where the map is to go, choose the type of map, then
apply the finishing touches.

The Microsoft Map Control dialog box determines the type of formatting in
effect. Category shading is always used with a nonquantitative variable and assigns
a different color to each value of a category. Value shading is one of several different formats that can be used with a quantitative variable and is used when many
outcomes are possible. The outcomes are divided into groups with a different
shade assigned to each group. Dot density and graduated symbol are other formats that can be used with a quantitative variable.

The mapping application includes an assortment of maps together with
demographic data for each map. The demographic data is contained in the Mapstats workbook (which can be located through the Windows 95 Find command).
Maps are available for the United States, Mexico, Canada, Australia, the United
Kingdom, and the world.

1

ONE-TO-MANY RELATIONSHIPS: SUBFORMS AND MULTIPLE TABLE QUERIES

OBJECTIVES

After reading this chapter you will be able to:

1. Explain how a one-to-many relationship is essential in the design of a database; differentiate between a primary key and a foreign key.
2. Use the Relationships window to implement a one-to-many relationship within an Access database.
3. Define referential integrity; explain how the enforcement of referential integrity maintains consistency within a database.
4. Distinguish between a main form and a subform; explain how a subform is used in conjunction with a one-to-many relationship.
5. Create a query based on multiple tables, then create a report based on that query.
6. Create a main form containing two subforms linked to one another

OVERVIEW

An Access database contains different types of objects: tables, forms, queries, and reports. A simple database may contain only one table, but the real power of Access stems from its use as a relational database, which contains multiple tables.

This chapter presents a new case study that focuses on a relational database. The case is that of a consumer loan system within a bank. The database contains two tables, one for customers and one for loans. There is a one-to-many relationship between the tables, in that one customer can have many loans, but a loan is tied to only one customer.

The case solution includes a discussion of database concepts. It reviews the definition of a primary key and explains how the primary

1

key of one table exists as a foreign key in a related table. It also introduces the concept of referential integrity, which ensures that the tables within the database are consistent with one another. And most important, it shows how to implement these concepts in an Access database.

The chapter builds on what you already know by expanding the earlier material on forms, queries, and reports. It describes how to create a main form and a corresponding subform that contains data from a related table. It develops a query that contains data from multiple tables, then creates a report based on that query.

Suffice it to say that this is a critically important chapter because it is built around a relational database, as opposed to a single table. Thus, when you complete the chapter, you will have a much better appreciation of what can be accomplished within Access. As always, the hands-on exercises are essential to your understanding of the material.

CASE STUDY: CONSUMER LOANS

Let us assume that you are in the Information Systems department of a commercial bank and are assigned the task of implementing a system for consumer loans. The bank needs complete data about every loan (the amount, interest rate, term, and so on). It also needs data about the customers holding those loans (name, address, telephone, etc.)

The problem is how to structure the data so that the bank will be able to obtain all of the information it needs from its database. The system must be able to supply the name and address of the person associated with a loan. The system must also be able to retrieve all of the loans for a specific individual.

The solution calls for a database with two tables, one for loans and one for customers. To appreciate the elegance of this approach, consider first a single table containing a combination of loan and customer data as shown in Figure 1.1. At first glance this solution appears to be satisfactory. You can, for example, search for a specific loan (e.g., L022) and determine that Lori Sangastiano is the customer associated with that loan. You can also search for a particular customer (e.g., Michelle Zacco) and find all of her loans (L028, L030, and L060).

There is a problem, however, in that the table duplicates customer data throughout the database. Thus, when one customer has multiple loans, the customer's name, address, and other data are stored multiple times. Maintaining the data in this form is a time-consuming and error-prone procedure, because any change to the customer's data has to be made in many places.

A second problem arises when you enter data for a new customer that occurs before a loan has been approved. The bank receives the customer's application data prior to granting a loan, and it wants to retain the customer data even if a loan is turned down. Adding a customer to the database in Figure 1.1 is awkward, however, because it requires the creation of a "dummy" loan record to hold the customer data.

The deletion (payoff) of a loan creates a third type of problem. What happens, for example, when Ted Myerson pays off loan L020? The loan record would be deleted, but so too would Ted's data as he has no other outstanding loans. The bank might want to contact Mr. Myerson about another loan in the future, but it would lose his data with the deletion of the existing loan.

The database in Figure 1.2 represents a much better design because it eliminates all three problems. It uses two different tables, a Loans table and a Customers table. Each record in the Loans table has data about a specific loan (LoanID, Date, Amount, Interest Rate, Term, Type, and CustomerID). Each record in the Customers table has data about a specific customer (CustomerID, First Name, Last Name, Address, City, State, Zip Code, and Phone Number). Each record in the Loans table is associated with a matching record in the Cus-

LoanID	Loan Data (Date, Amount, Interest Rate...)	Customer Data (First Name, Last Name, Address...)
L001	Loan Data for Loan L001	Customer data for Wendy Solomon
L004	Loan Data for Loan L004	Customer data for Wendy Solomon
L010	Loan Data for Loan L010	Customer data for Alex Rey
L014	Loan Data for Loan L014	Customer data for Wendy Solomon
L020	Loan Data for Loan L020	Customer data for Matt Hirsch
L022	Loan Data for Loan L022	Customer data for Lori Sangastiano
L026	Loan Data for Loan L026	Customer data for Matt Hirsch
L028	Loan Data for Loan L028	Customer data for Michelle Zacco
L030	Loan Data for Loan L030	Customer data for Michelle Zacco
L031	Loan Data for Loan L031	Customer data for Eileen Faulkner
L032	Loan Data for Loan L032	Customer data for Scott Wit
L033	Loan Data for Loan L033	Customer data for Alex Rey
L039	Loan Data for Loan L039	Customer data for David Powell
L040	Loan Data for Loan L040	Customer data for Matt Hirsch
L047	Loan Data for Loan L047	Customer data for Benjamin Grauer
L049	Loan Data for Loan L049	Customer data for Eileen Faulkner
L052	Loan Data for Loan L052	Customer data for Eileen Faulkner
L053	Loan Data for Loan L053	Customer data for Benjamin Grauer
L054	Loan Data for Loan L054	Customer data for Scott Wit
L057	Loan Data for Loan L057	Customer data for Benjamin Grauer
L060	Loan Data for Loan L060	Customer data for Michelle Zacco
L062	Loan Data for Loan L062	Customer data for Matt Hirsch
L100	Loan Data for Loan L100	Customer data for Benjamin Grauer
L109	Loan Data for Loan L109	Customer data for Wendy Solomon
L120	Loan Data for Loan L120	Customer data for Lori Sangastiano

FIGURE 1.1   Single Table Solution

tomers table through the CustomerID field common to both tables. This solution may seem complicated, but it is really quite simple and elegant.

Consider, for example, how easy it is to change a customer's address. If Michelle Zacco were to move, you would go into the Customers table, find her record (Customer C08), and make the necessary change. You would not have to change any of the records in the Loans table, because they do not contain customer data, but only a CustomerID that indicates who the customer is. In other words, you would change Michelle's address in only one place, and the change would be automatically reflected for every associated loan.

The addition of a new customer is done directly in the Customers table. This is much easier than the approach of Figure 1.1, which required an existing loan in order to add a new customer. And finally, the deletion of an existing loan is also easier than with the single table organization. A loan can be deleted from the Loans table without losing the corresponding customer data.

The database in Figure 1.2 is composed of two tables in which there is a **one-to-many relationship** between customers and loans. One customer (Michelle Zacco) can have many loans (Loan numbers L028, L030, and L060), but a specific loan (L028) is associated with only one customer (Michelle Zacco). The tables are related to one another by a common field (CustomerID) that is present in both the Customers and the Loans table.

Access enables you to create the one-to-many relationship between the tables, then uses that relationship to answer questions about the database. It can retrieve information about a specific loan, such as the name and address of the customer holding that loan. It can also find all of the loans for a particular customer, as illustrated in the queries that follow.

LoanID	Date	Amount	Interest Rate	Term	Type	CustomerID
L001	1/15/97	$475,000	6.90%	15	M	C04
L004	1/23/97	$35,000	7.20%	5	C	C04
L010	1/25/97	$10,000	5.50%	3	C	C05
L014	1/31/97	$12,000	9.50%	10	O	C04
L020	2/8/97	$525,000	6.50%	30	M	C06
L022	2/12/97	$10,500	7.50%	5	O	C07
L026	2/15/97	$35,000	6.50%	5	O	C10
L028	2/20/97	$250,000	8.80%	30	M	C08
L030	2/21/97	$5,000	10.00%	3	O	C08
L031	2/28/97	$200,000	7.00%	15	M	C01
L032	3/1/97	$25,000	10.00%	3	C	C02
L033	3/1/97	$20,000	9.50%	5	O	C05
L039	3/3/97	$56,000	7.50%	5	C	C09
L040	3/10/97	$129,000	8.50%	15	M	C10
L047	3/11/97	$200,000	7.25%	15	M	C03
L049	3/21/97	$150,000	7.50%	15	M	C01
L052	3/22/97	$100,000	7.00%	30	M	C01
L053	3/31/97	$15,000	6.50%	3	O	C03
L054	4/1/97	$10,000	8.00%	5	C	C02
L057	4/15/97	$25,000	8.50%	4	C	C03
L060	4/18/97	$41,000	9.90%	4	C	C08
L062	4/22/97	$350,000	7.50%	15	M	C10
L100	5/1/97	$150,000	6.00%	15	M	C03
L109	5/3/97	$350,000	8.20%	30	M	C04
L120	5/8/97	$275,000	9.20%	15	M	C07

(a) Loans Table

CustomerID	First Name	Last Name	Address	City	State	Zip Code	Phone Number
C01	Eileen	Faulkner	7245 NW 8 Street	Minneapolis	MN	55346	(612) 894-1511
C02	Scott	Wit	5660 NW 175 Terrace	Baltimore	MD	21224	(410) 753-0345
C03	Benjamin	Grauer	10000 Sample Road	Coral Springs	FL	33073	(305) 444-5555
C04	Wendy	Solomon	7500 Reno Road	Houston	TX	77090	(713) 427-3104
C05	Alex	Rey	3456 Main Highway	Denver	CO	80228	(303) 555-6666
C06	Ted	Myerson	6545 Stone Street	Chapel Hill	NC	27515	(919) 942-7654
C07	Lori	Sangastiano	4533 Aero Drive	Santa Rosa	CA	95403	(707) 542-3411
C08	Michelle	Zacco	488 Gold Street	Gainesville	FL	32601	(904) 374-5660
C09	David	Powell	5070 Battle Road	Decatur	GA	30034	(301) 345-6556
C10	Matt	Hirsch	777 NW 67 Avenue	Fort Lee	NJ	07624	(201) 664-3211

(b) Customers Table

FIGURE 1.2   Multiple Table Solution

Query: What are the name, address, and phone number of the customer associated with loan number L010?

Answer: Alex Rey, at 3456 Main Highway is the customer associated with loan L010. His phone number is (303) 555-6666.

To determine the answer, Access searches the Loans table for loan L010 to obtain the CustomerID (C05 in this example). It then searches the Customers table for the customer with the matching CustomerID and retrieves the name, address, and phone number. Consider a second example:

Query: What loans are associated with Wendy Solomon?
Answer: Wendy Solomon has four loans: loan L001 for $475,000, loan L004 for $35,000, loan L014 for $12,000, and loan L109 for $350,000.

This time Access begins in the Customers table and searches for Wendy Solomon to determine the CustomerID (C04). It then searches the Loans table for all records with a matching CustomerID.

PEDAGOGY VERSUS REALITY

Our design requires that the CustomerID and LoanID begin with the letters C and L, respectively, to emphasize the tables in which these fields are found and to facilitate data entry in the hands-on exercises. This convention places artificial limits on the number of customers and loans at 100 and 1000, respectively. (CustomerID goes from C00 to C99, and LoanID goes from L000 to L999.)

Implementation in Access

An Access database contains multiple tables. Each table stores data about a specific subject, such as customers or loans. Each table has a ***primary key,*** which is a field (or combination of fields) that uniquely identifies each record. CustomerID is the primary key in the Customers table. LoanID is the primary key in the Loans table.

A one-to-many relationship uses the primary key of the "one" table as a ***foreign key*** in the "many" table, and it is through the foreign key that the relationship is established. (A foreign key is simply the primary key of the related table.) The CustomerID appears in both the Customers table and the Loans table. It is the primary key in the Customers table, where its values are unique; it is a foreign key in the Loans table, where its values are not unique. Thus, multiple records in the Loans table can have the same CustomerID to implement the one-to-many relationship between customers and loans.

To create a one-to-many relationship, you open the ***Relationships window*** in Figure 1.3 and add the necessary tables. You then drag the field on which the relationship is built, from the field list of the "one" table (Customers) to the matching field in the ***related table*** (Loans). Once the relationship has been established, you will see a ***relationship line*** connecting the tables, which indicates the "one" and "many" sides of the relationship. The line extends from the primary key in the "one" table to the foreign key in the "many" table and uses the symbols 1 and ∞, respectively.

RELATED FIELDS AND DATA TYPES

The related fields must have the same data type—both text or both number. In addition, number fields must also have the same field size. The exception is an AutoNumber field in the primary table, which is related to a Number field with a Long Integer field size in the related table. AutoNumber fields are discussed in the next chapter.

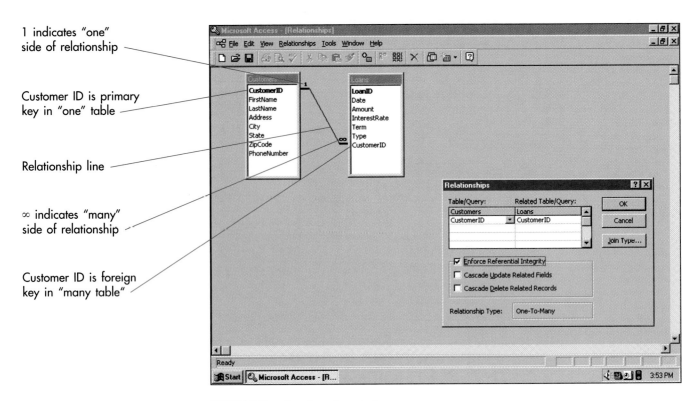

1 indicates "one" side of relationship

Customer ID is primary key in "one" table

Relationship line

∞ indicates "many" side of relationship

Customer ID is foreign key in "many table"

FIGURE 1.3   The Relationships Window

Referential Integrity

Referential integrity ensures that the records in related tables are consistent with one another. When enforcement of referential integrity is in effect, Access will prevent you from adding a record to the related table if that record contains an invalid foreign key. In other words, you cannot add a record to the Loans table if that record contains an invalid customer number. (Access will, however, let you leave the customer number blank unless it is specified as a required field or another validation rule is in effect.)

Enforcement of referential integrity will also prevent you from deleting a record in the primary (Customers) table if there is a corresponding record in the related (Loans) table. (Thus, to delete a customer, you would first have to delete all loans for that customer.) In similar fashion, you cannot change the primary key of a Customer record when there are matching Loan records. (These restrictions are relaxed if you check the Cascade Delete Related Records or Cascade Update Related Fields option in the Relationships dialog box. These options are discussed further in the next chapter.)

HANDS-ON EXERCISE 1

One-to-Many Relationships

Objective: To create a one-to-many relationship between existing tables in a database; to demonstrate referential integrity between the tables in a one-to-many relationship. Use Figure 1.4 as a guide in the exercise.

STEP 1: Open the National Bank Database

➤ Start Access. Open the **National Bank database** in the **Exploring Access folder.** The database contains three tables: for Customers, Loans, and Payments. (The Payments table will be used later in the chapter.)

➤ Pull down the **Tools menu** and click **Relationships** to open the Relationships window as shown in Figure 1.4a. (The Customers and Loans tables are not yet visible.) If you do not see the Show Table dialog box, pull down the **Relationships menu** and click the **Show Table command.**

➤ The **Tables tab** is selected within the Show Table dialog box. Click (select) the **Customers table,** then click the **Add Command button** to add the table to the Relationships window.

➤ Click the **Loans table,** then click the **Add Command button** (or simply double click the **Loans table**) to add this table to the Relationships window.

➤ Do *not* add the Payments table at this time. Click the **Close button** to close the Show Table dialog box.

Click to maximize window

Customers and Loans tables are added to Relationships window

Click Loans table

Click Add button

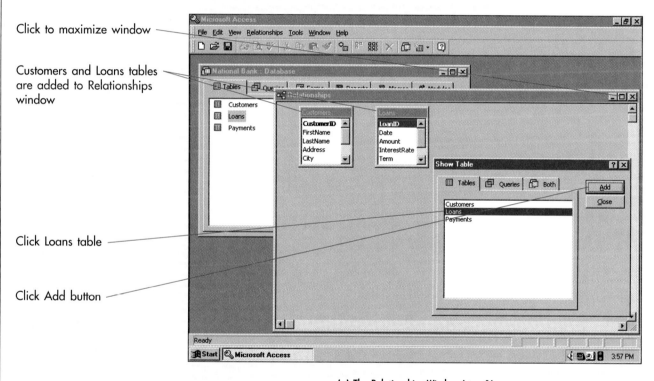

(a) The Relationships Window (step 1)

FIGURE 1.4   Hands-on Exercise 1

STEP 2: Create a Relationship

➤ Maximize the Relationships window so that you have more room in which to work. Point to the bottom border of the **Customers field list** (the mouse pointer changes to a double arrow), then click and drag the border until all of the fields are visible.

➤ Click and drag the bottom border of the **Loans field list** until all of the fields are visible.

➤ Click and drag the title bar of the **Loans field list** so that it is approximately one inch away from the Customers field list.

➤ Click and drag the **CustomerID field** in the Customers field list to the **CustomerID field** in the Loans field list. You will see the Relationships dialog box in Figure 1.4b.

➤ Check the **Enforce Referential Integrity** check box. (If necessary, clear the check boxes to Cascade Update Related Fields and Delete Related Records.)

➤ Click the **Create Command button** to establish the relationship and close the Relationships dialog box. You should see a line indicating a one-to-many relationship between the Customers and Loans tables.

THE RELATIONSHIPS ARE VISUAL

Access displays a relationship line between related tables to indicate the relationship between those tables. It uses the number 1 and the infinity symbol (∞) to indicate a one-to-many relationship in which referential integrity is enforced. The 1 appears at the end of the relationship line near the primary (one) table. The infinity symbol appears at the end nearest the related (many) table. Access shows the primary keys in each table in bold.

Click and drag title bar to move field list

Click and drag CustomerID to CustomerID field in Loans table

Click and drag bottom border until all fields are visible

Click check box to Enforce Referential Integrity

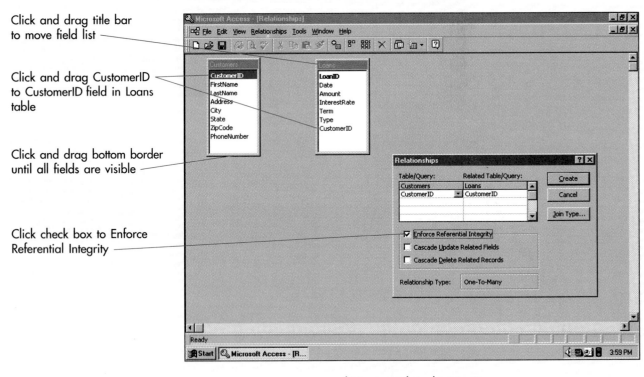

(b) Create a Relationship (step 2)

FIGURE 1.4   Hands-on Exercise 1 (continued)

STEP 3: Deleting a Relationship

➤ Point to the line indicating the relationship between the tables, then click the **right mouse button** to select the relationship and display a shortcut menu.

➤ Click the **Delete command.** You will see the dialog box in Figure 1.4c, asking whether you want to delete the relationship. Click **No** since you do *not* want to delete the relationship.

➤ Close the Relationships window. Click **Yes** when asked whether to save the layout changes.

Click to close Relationships window

Point to relationship line and click right mouse button to display shortcut menu

Click No

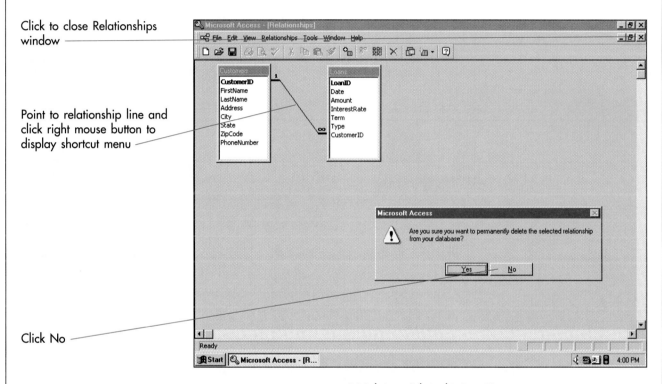

(c) Deleting a Relationship (step 3)

FIGURE 1.4   Hands-on Exercise 1 (continued)

STEP 4: Add a Customer Record

➤ The Database window is again visible with the Tables tab selected. Open the **Customers table.** If necessary, click the **Maximize button** to give yourself additional room when adding a record. Widen the fields as necessary to see the data.

➤ Click the **New Record button** on the toolbar. The record selector moves to the last record (record 11).

➤ Enter **C11** as the CustomerID as shown in Figure 1.4d. The record selector changes to a pencil as soon as you enter the first character.

➤ Enter data for yourself as the new customer. Data validation has been built into the Customers table, so you must enter the data correctly, or it will not be accepted.

• The message, *Customer ID must begin with the letter C followed by a two-digit number,* indicates that the CustomerID field is invalid.

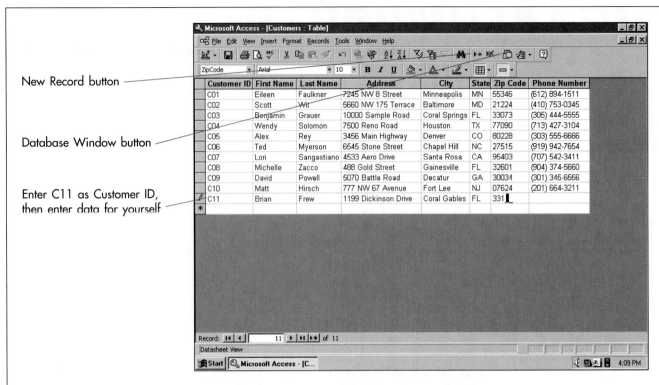

New Record button

Database Window button

Enter C11 as Customer ID,
then enter data for yourself

(d) Add a Customer Record (step 4)

FIGURE 1.4   Hands-on Exercise 1 (continued)

- The message, *The field 'Customers.LastName' can't contain a Null value because the Required property for this field is set to True,* indicates that you must enter a last name.
- A beep in either the ZipCode or PhoneNumber field indicates that you are entering a nonnumeric character.
- If you encounter a data validation error, press **Esc** (or Click **OK**), then reenter the data.

➤ Press **enter** when you have completed your record. Remember your CustomerID (C11) because you will need to enter it in the corresponding loan records.

THE RECORD SELECTOR

The record selector symbol indicates the status of the record. A triangle means the data in the current record has not changed. A pencil indicates you are in the process of entering (or changing) the data. An asterisk appears next to the blank record at the end of every table.

STEP 5: Add a Loan Record

➤ Click the **Database Window button** on the toolbar, then open the **Loans table.** Maximize the window containing the Loans table to give yourself additional room when adding a record.

➤ Click the **New Record button** on the toolbar. The record selector moves to the blank record at the end of the table. Add a new loan record as shown in Figure 1.4e.

- Use **L121** for the LoanID and enter the terms of the loan as you see fit.
- Data validation has been built into the Loans table so you will have to enter data correctly for it to be accepted. The term of the loan, for example, cannot exceed 30 years. The date of the loan cannot be set to a future date. The interest rate must be entered as a decimal. The type of the loan must be C, M, or O for Car, Mortgage, or Other. Enter **C** for a car loan.
- Be sure to enter **C11** as the CustomerID field. (This is your CustomerID from step 4.).

➤ Press **enter** when you have completed the loan record.

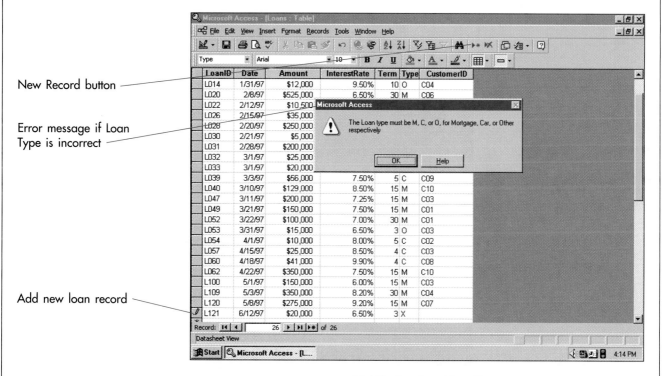

New Record button

Error message if Loan
Type is incorrect

Add new loan record

(e) Add a Loan Record (step 5)

FIGURE 1.4   Hands-on Exercise 1 (continued)

GARBAGE IN, GARBAGE OUT

The information produced by a system depends entirely on the quality of the data. It is important, therefore, that you validate data as it is being entered to ensure that the data is as accurate as possible. A well-designed system will anticipate errors that a user may make during data entry and will include data validation checks that will prevent invalid data from being accepted into the system.

STEP 6: Referential Integrity

➤ Pull down the **Window menu.** Click **Cascade** to cascade the open windows (the Database window, the Customers table, and the Loans table.)

➤ Click the **Database window,** then click the **Minimize button** to minimize this window. Move and size the Customers and Loans windows so that your desktop matches ours in Figure 1.4f.

➤ Click in the **Loans window.** Click the **CustomerID field** of your loan record and (attempt to) replace the CustomerID (C11) with **C88.** Press **enter.** You will see the dialog box in Figure 1.4f, indicating that referential integrity has been violated because there is no related record in the Customers table.

➤ Click **OK.** Reenter **C11** as the valid CustomerID. Press **enter.**

➤ Click the window for the **Customers table.** Click the **row selector** to select the first record (Customer C01). Press the **Del key** (in an attempt) to delete this record.

➤ Access indicates that you cannot delete this record because related records exist in the Loans table. Click **OK.**

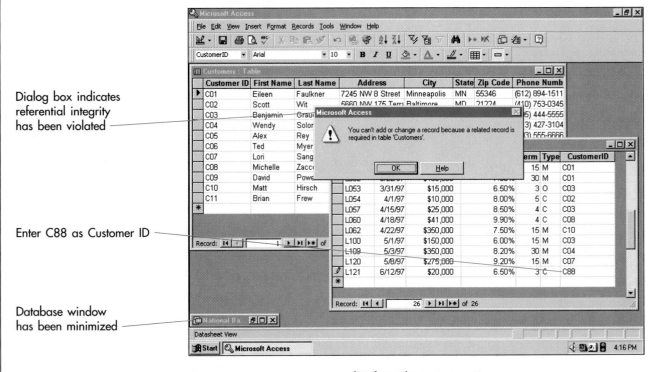

Dialog box indicates referential integrity has been violated

Enter C88 as Customer ID

Database window has been minimized

(f) Referential Integrity (step 6)

FIGURE 1.4   Hands-on Exercise 1 (continued)

STEP 7: Close the Database

➤ Close the Customers table. Close the Loans table.

➤ Close the Database window if you do not want to continue with the next hands-on exercise at this time.

SUBFORMS

A *subform* is a form within a form. It appears inside a main form to display records from a related table. A main form and its associated subform, to display the loans for one customer, are shown in Figure 1.5. The *main form* (also known as the primary form) is based on the *primary table* (the Customers table). The subform is based on the related table (the Loans table).

The main form and the subform are linked to one another so that the subform displays only the records related to the record currently displayed in the main form. The main form shows the "one" side of the relationship (the customer). The subform shows the "many" side of the relationship (the loans). The main form displays the customer data for one record (Eileen Faulkner with CustomerID C01). The subform shows the loans for that customer. The main form is displayed in the *Form view,* whereas the subform is displayed in the *Datasheet view.* (A subform can also be displayed in the Form view, in which case it would show one loan at a time.)

Each form in Figure 1.5a has its own status bar and associated navigation buttons. The status bar for the main form indicates that the active record is record 1 of 11 records in the Customers table. The status bar for the subform indicates record 1 of 3 records. (The latter shows the number of loans for this customer rather than the number of loans in the Loans table.) Click the navigation button to move to the next customer record, and you will automatically see the loans associated with that customer. If, for example, you were to move to the last customer record (C11, which contains the data you entered in the first hands-on exercise), you would see your loan information.

The Loans form also contains a calculated control, the payment due, which is based on the loan parameters. Loan L031, for example (a $200,000 mortgage with a 15-year term), has a monthly payment of $1,797.66. The amount of the payment is calculated using a predefined function, as will be described in the next hands-on exercise.

Figure 1.5b displays the Design view of the Customers form in Figure 1.5a. The Loans subform control is an object on the Customers form and can be moved and sized (or deleted) just like any other object. It should also be noted that the Loans subform is a form in and of itself, and can be opened in either the Datasheet

Calculated control

Main form is based
on primary table

Subform is based on related
table and displays only records
related to current record in main
form

Status bar for subform

Status bar for main form

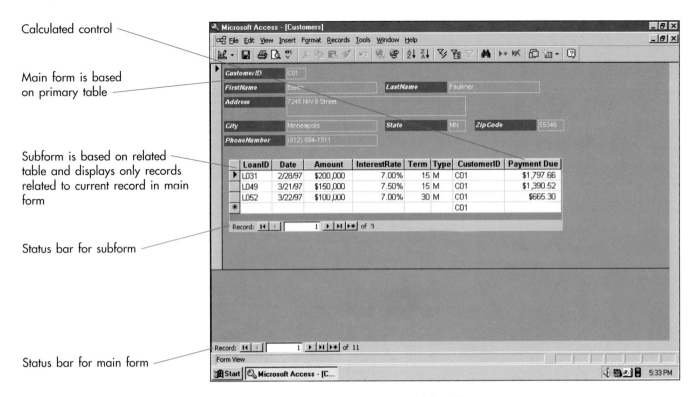

(a) Form View

Loans subform control

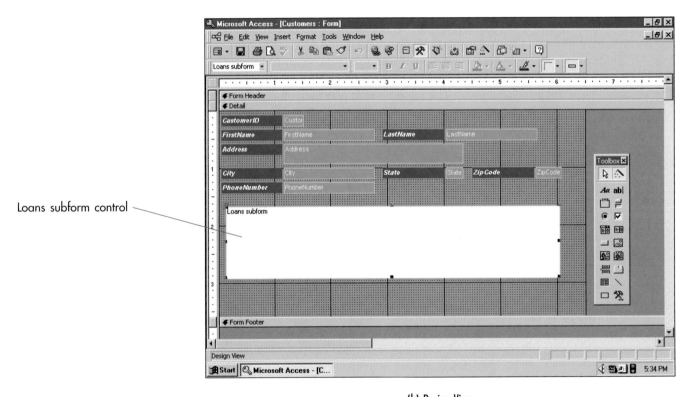

(b) Design View

FIGURE 1.5   A Main Form and a Subform

view or the Form view. It can also be opened in the Design view (to modify its appearance) as will be done in the next hands-on exercise.

THE PMT FUNCTION

The Pmt function is one of several predefined *functions* built into Access. It calculates the payment due on a loan based on the principal, interest rate, and term and is similar to the PMT function in Excel. The Pmt function is reached most easily through the Expression Builder and can be entered onto any form, query, or report. (See step 7 in the next hands-on exercise.)

The Subform Wizard

A subform can be created as a separate form, then dragged onto the main form. It can also be created directly on the main form by selecting the Subform/Subreport button, then clicking and dragging on the main form to size and position the subform. This in turn opens the ***Subform Wizard*** as shown in Figure 1.6. You specify whether to build the subform from an existing form or from a table or query

(a) Use an Existing Table/Query

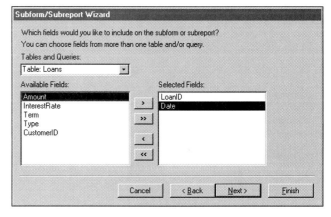

(b) Select the Fields

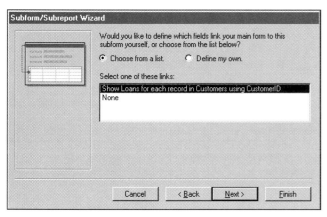

(c) Create the Link

(d) Save the Subform

FIGURE 1.6   The Subform Wizard

as shown in Figure 1.6a, then you select the desired fields in Figure 1.6b. Next, you specify the relationship between the main form and the subform as shown in Figure 1.6c. The subform in this example will show all of the loans for a particular customer. And finally, you specify the name for the subform as in Figure 1.6d to save the subform as an object within the database.

The Subform Wizard provides an excellent starting point, but as with the Form Wizard and a regular form, you usually need to customize the subform so that it meets your requirements. This is done using the identical techniques that were presented in Chapter 2 to move and size the controls and/or to modify their properties.

THE POWER OF SUBFORMS

A subform exists as a separate object within the database and can be opened or modified just like any other form. A main form can have any number of subforms, and a subform in turn can have its own subform. (See Hands-on Exercise 4 at the end of the chapter.)

HANDS-ON EXERCISE 2

Creating a Subform

Objective: To create a subform that displays the many records in a one-to-many relationship; to move and size controls in an existing form; to enter data in a subform. Use Figure 1.7 as a guide in doing the exercise.

STEP 1: Create the Customers Form
➤ Open the **National Bank database** from the previous exercise. Click the **Forms tab** in the Database window. Click **New** to display the New Form dialog box as shown in Figure 1.7a. Click **Form Wizard** in the list box.
➤ Click the **drop-down arrow** to display the available tables and queries in the database on which the form can be based. Click **Customers** to select the Customers table, then click **OK** to start the Form Wizard.

STEP 2: The Form Wizard
➤ You should see the dialog box in Figure 1.7b, which displays all of the fields in the Customers table. Click the **>> button** to enter all of the fields in the table on the form. Click **Next.**
➤ The **Columnar layout** is already selected. Click **Next.**
➤ Click **Colorful 1** as the style for your form. Click **Next.**
➤ The Form Wizard suggests **Customers** as the title of the form. (Keep this entry.) Click the option button to **Modify the form's design,** then click the **Finish Command button** to create the form and exit the Form Wizard.

Click Forms tab

Click Form Wizard

Click drop-down arrow

Click Customers

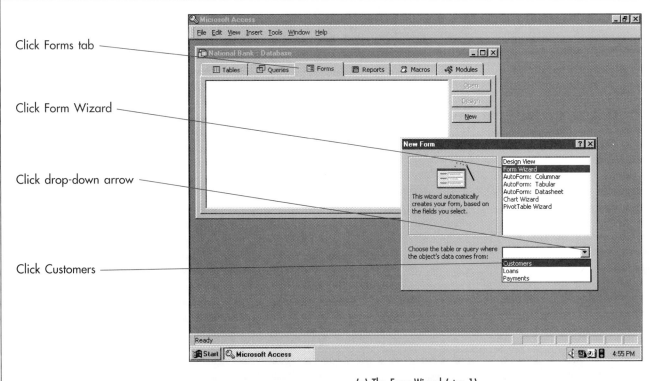

(a) The Form Wizard (step 1)

Click >> button to
select all fields

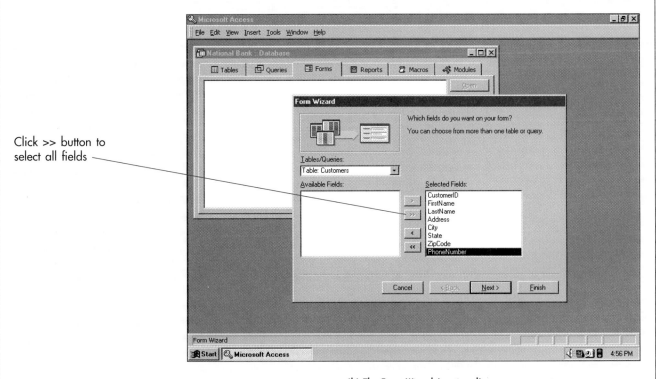

(b) The Form Wizard (continued)

FIGURE 1.7   Hands-on Exercise 2

THE NAME'S THE SAME

The Form Wizard automatically assigns the name of the underlying table (or query) to each form (subform) it creates. The Report Wizard works in similar fashion. The intent of the similar naming convention is to help you select the proper object from the Database window when you want to subsequently open the object. This becomes increasingly important in databases that contain a large number of objects.

STEP 3: Modify the Customers Form

➤ You should see the Customers form in Figure 1.7c. Maximize the window. Click and drag the right edge of the form to widen the form to **6½ inches.**

➤ Click the control for **LastName** to select the control and display the sizing handles, then drag the **LastName control** so that it is next to the FirstName control.

➤ Click and drag the other controls to complete the form:
  • Click and drag the **Address control** under the control for FirstName.
  • Place the controls for **City, State,** and **ZipCode** on the same line, then move these controls under the Address control.
  • Move the control for **PhoneNumber** under the control for City.

➤ Click the **Save button** to save the form.

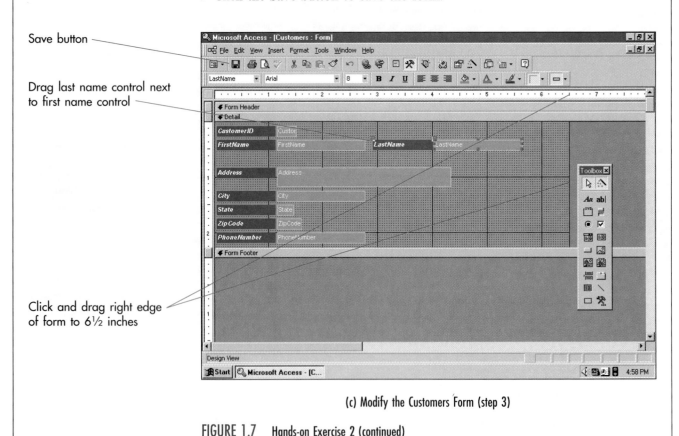

Save button

Drag last name control next to first name control

Click and drag right edge of form to 6½ inches

(c) Modify the Customers Form (step 3)

FIGURE 1.7   Hands-on Exercise 2 (continued)

ALIGN THE CONTROLS

To align labels or controls in a straight line (horizontally or vertically), press and hold the Shift key as you click the labels or the controls to be aligned. Pull down the Format menu and select the edge to align (Left, Right, Top, or Bottom). Click the Undo button if you are not satisfied with the result.

STEP 4: Create the Loans Subform

➤ Click and drag the bottom edge of the **Detail section** so that you have approximately 2 inches of blank space in the Detail section as shown in Figure 1.7d. (This is where the subform will go.)

➤ Click the **Subform/Subreport button** on the Toolbox toolbar, then click and drag in the Customers form where you want the subform to go. Release the mouse to start the Subform/Subreport Wizard.

➤ The **Table/Query Option button** is selected, indicating that we will build the subform from a table or query. Click **Next.**

➤ You should see the Subform/Subreport Wizard dialog box in Figure 1.7d. Click the **down arrow** on the Tables and Queries list box to select the **Loans table.** Click the **>> button** to enter all of the fields in the Loans table onto the subform. Click **Next.**

Subform/Subreport
Wizard button

Click >> button to
select all fields

Click and drag bottom
edge of Detail section

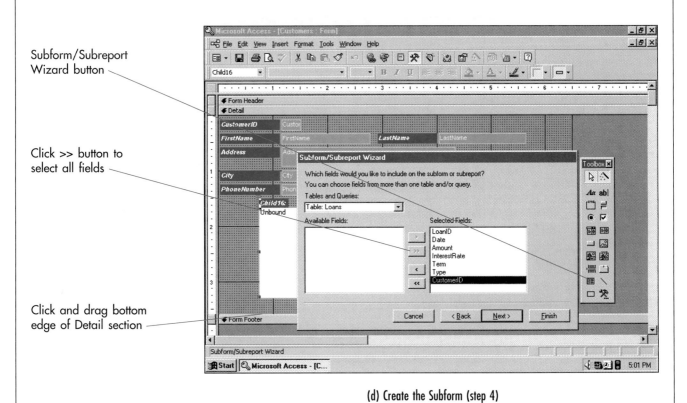

(d) Create the Subform (step 4)

FIGURE 1.7   Hands-on Exercise 2 (continued)

➤ The next step asks you to define the fields that link the main form to the subform. The option button to **Choose from a list** is selected. The selected link will **Show Loans for each record in Customers using CustomerID.** Click **Next.**

➤ The Wizard suggests **Loans subform** as the name of the subform. Click **Finish** to exit the Subform/Subreport wizard.

STEP 5: The Loans Subform (Datasheet view)

➤ You should be in the Design view for the Customers form, which contains a white rectangular area indicating the position of the Loans subform control. Maximize the window.

➤ Click the label attached to the subform control and press the **Del key.** Be sure you delete only the label and not the control for the subform.

➤ You need to open the Loans subform to check the column width of its fields. This is done in one of two ways:

• Deselect the Loans subform (by clicking anywhere in the main form), then double click the **Loans subform** to open it. Change to the **Datasheet view,** *or*

• Pull down the **Window menu** to change to the **Database window,** click the **Forms tab,** and open the **Loans subform.**

➤ You should see the Datasheet view of the Loans subform as shown in Figure 1.7e. Click and drag the various column headings to the approximate sizes shown in the figure so that you can see the complete field names.

➤ Save the Loans subform. Close the Loans subform.

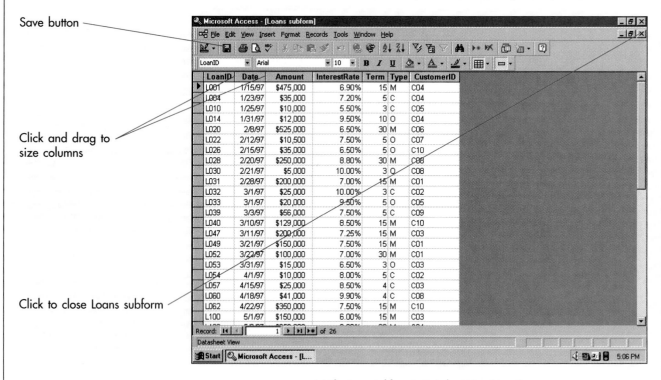

Save button

Click and drag to size columns

Click to close Loans subform

(e) The Loans Subform in Datasheet View (step 5)

FIGURE 1.7   Hands-on Exercise 2 (continued)

CHANGE THE VIEW

A subform can be displayed in either the Datasheet view or the Form view. To change the default view, open the subform in Design view, point to the Form Selection box in the upper-left corner, click the right mouse button to display a shortcut menu, and click Properties. Click the Default View box, click the drop-drop arrow, select the desired view, and close the Properties dialog box.

STEP 6: View the Customers Form

➤ You are either in the Database window or the Customers form, depending on how you opened the Loans subform. Use the **Window menu** to change to the Customers form (if necessary), then click the **Maximize button** so that the form takes the entire window.

➤ Change to the **Form view** as shown in Figure 1.7f. You may have to return to the Design view of the Customers form to increase the space allotted for the Loans subform. Size and/or move the subform control as necessary, then save the form. You may also have to reopen the Loans subform in the Datasheet view to adjust the column widths.

➤ Note the following:

- The customer information for the first customer (C01) is displayed in the main portion of the form. The loans for that customer are displayed in the subform.

Click to switch to Design view

Data for Customer C01 is displayed in main form

Loans for Customer C01 are displayed in subform

Status bar for subform

Status bar for main form

Click to move to next customer record

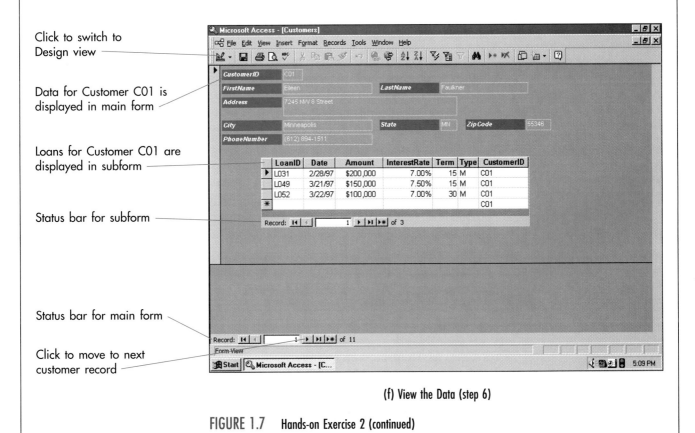

(f) View the Data (step 6)

FIGURE 1.7   Hands-on Exercise 2 (continued)

- The status bar at the bottom of the window (corresponding to the main form) displays record 1 of 11 records (you are looking at the first record in the Customers table).
- The status bar for the subform displays record 1 of 3 records (you are on the first of three loan records for this customer).

➤ Click the ▶ **button** on the status bar for the main form to move to the next customer record. The subform is updated automatically to display the two loans belonging to this customer.

➤ Press the **PgDn key** to move through the customer records until you come to your record in the Customers table.

WHY IT WORKS

The main form (Customers) and subform (Loans) work in conjunction with one another so that you always see all of the loans for a given customer. The link between the forms is established through a common field as described at the beginning of the chapter. To see how the link is actually implemented, change to the Design view of the Customers form and point anywhere inside the Loans subform. Click the right mouse button to display a shortcut menu, click Properties to display the Subform/Subreport properties dialog box, and if necessary, click the All tab within the dialog box. You should see CustomerID next to two properties (Link Child Fields and Link Master Fields), which define how the main and subforms are linked to one another.

STEP 7: Add the Payment Amount

➤ Click the **Database Window button,** click the **Forms tab,** select the **Loans subform,** then click the **Design button.** The Loans subform is open in the Design view as shown in Figure 1.7g. (The dialog boxes are not yet visible.)

➤ If necessary, maximize the window. Click and drag the right edge of the form to **6½ inches** to make room for a new control and its associated label.

➤ Click the **Label button,** then click and drag in the **Form Header** to create an unbound control. Enter **Payment Due** as the text for the label as shown in Figure 1.7g. Size and align the control to match the other labels.

➤ Click the **Textbox button** on the Toolbox toolbar, then click and drag in the **Detail section** to create an unbound control that will contain the amount of the monthly payment. Click the label for the control (e.g., Text 15), then press the **Del key** to delete the label.

➤ Point to the unbound control, click the **right mouse button** to display a shortcut menu, then click **Properties** to open the properties dialog box. Click the **All tab** to view all existing properties.

➤ Click the **Name property.** Enter **Payment Due** in place of the existing label (e.g., Text 15).

➤ Click the **Control Source property,** then click the **Build (...) button** to display the Expression Builder dialog box.

- Double click **Functions** (if there is a plus sign in its button), then click **Built-In Functions.** Click **Financial** in the second column, then double click **Pmt** to enter the Pmt function in the Expression Builder.

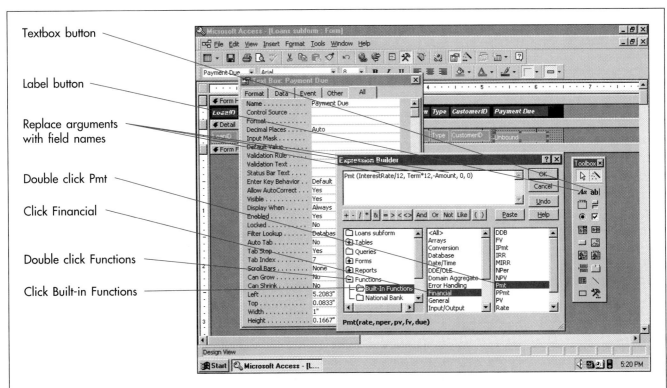

Textbox button

Label button

Replace arguments
with field names

Double click Pmt

Click Financial

Double click Functions

Click Built-in Functions

(g) Add the Payment Function (step 7)

FIGURE 1.7   Hands-on Exercise 2 (continued)

- You need to replace each of the arguments in the Pmt function with the appropriate field names from the Loans table. Select the arguments one at a time and enter the replacement for that argument exactly as shown in Figure 1.7g. Click **OK** when finished.

➤ Click the **Format property,** click the **down arrow,** and specify **Currency** (scrolling if necessary). Click the **Decimal Places property,** click the **down arrow,** and select **2.**

➤ Close the Properties dialog box. Size and align the control. Change to the Datasheet view and check the column widths, making adjustments as necessary. Close the Loans subform. Click **Yes** to save the changes.

THE ZOOM WINDOW

Trying to enter or edit a long expression directly in the Control Source properties box can be confusing in that you may not be able to see the entire expression. Access anticipates the situation and provides a Zoom window to increase the space in which you can work. Press Shift+F2 to open the Zoom window, enter or edit the expression as necessary, then click OK to accept the changes and close the Zoom window.

STEP 8: Enter a New Loan

➤ Pull down the **Window menu** and click **Customers** to return to the **Customers form** in the Form view as shown in Figure 1.7h. You may have to return to the Design view of the Customers form to increase the space allotted for the Loans subform. You may also have to reopen the Loans subform to adjust the column widths.

➤ Click the ▶| on the status bar of the main form to move to the last record (customer C11), which is the record you entered in the previous exercise. (Click the **PgUp key** if you are on a blank record.)

➤ Click the **LoanID field** next to the asterisk in the subform. The record selector changes to a triangle. Enter data for the new loan as shown in Figure 1.7h:

- The record selector changes to a pencil as soon as you begin to enter data.
- The payment due will be computed automatically as soon as you complete the Term field.
- You do *not* have to enter the CustomerID since it appears automatically due to the relationship between the Customers and Loans tables.

➤ Press the **down arrow** when you have entered the last field (Type), which saves the data in the current record. (The record selector symbol changes from a pencil to a triangle.)

Print Preview button

Selection area for current record

Enter data for new loan

Payment due is computed automatically

Click to move to last customer record (your record)

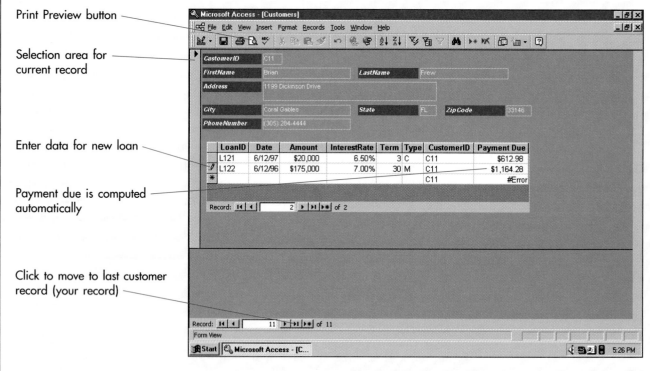

(h) Enter a New Loan (step 8)

FIGURE 1.7   Hands-on Exercise 2 (continued)

STEP 9: Print the Form

➤ Click the **Print Preview button** to view the form prior to printing to be sure that the form fits within the width of the page. (See boxed tip on the Page Setup command if the form does not fit.) Click the **Close button** to return to the Form view.

➤ Check that you are still on the record for customer 11 (the record containing your data), then click the **selection area** at the left of the form to select this record.

➤ Pull down the **File menu** and click **Print** to display the Print dialog box. Click the **Selected Record(s) option button.** Click **OK** to print the selected form.

➤ Close the Customers form. Click **Yes** if asked to save the changes to the form.

➤ Close the National Bank database and exit Access if you do not want to continue with the next hands-on exercise at this time.

MULTIPLE TABLE QUERIES

A relational database consists of multiple tables, each dealing with a specific subject. The related data can be displayed in a main form/subform combination as was done in the preceding exercise. It can also be displayed in a select query that is developed from multiple tables.

The real power of a select query is its ability to include fields from several tables. If, for example, you wanted the name and address of all customers holding a certain type of loan, you would need data from both the Customers table and the Loans table. Thus, you create the select query using the data from both tables. You would select the customer's name and address fields from the Customers table, and the various loan parameters from the Loans table.

Figure 1.8a shows the Design view of a query to select the 15-year mortgages (the term is 15 and the loan type is "M") issued after April 1, 1997. Figure 1.8b displays the resulting dynaset. You should recognize the design grid and the Field, Sort, Show, and Criteria rows from our earlier discussion. The *Table row* is new and displays the name of the table containing the field.

In Figure 1.8a the LastName and the FirstName fields are taken from the Customers table. All of the other fields are from the Loans table. The one-to-many relationship between the Customers table and the Loans table is shown graphically within the Query window. The tables are related through the CustomerID field, which is the primary key in the Customers table and a foreign key in the Loans table. The line between the two field lists is called a join line and tells Access how to relate the data in the tables.

Return for a moment to the discussion at the beginning of the chapter, where we asked the name and address of the customer holding loan L010 (Alex Rey at

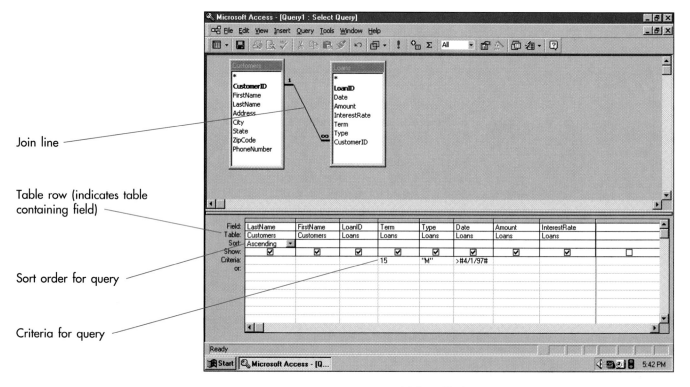

(a) Query Window

	Last Name	First Name	LoanID	Term	Type	Date	Amount	InterestRate
▶	Grauer	Benjamin	L100	15	M	5/1/97	$150,000	6.00%
	Hirsch	Matt	L062	15	M	4/22/97	$350,000	7.50%
	Sangastiano	Lori	L120	15	M	5/8/97	$275,000	9.20%
*								

(b) Dynaset

FIGURE 1.8   A Multitable Query

3456 Main Highway). Look at the data in Figure 1.2 at the beginning of the chapter and see how you have to consult both tables to answer the query. You do it intuitively; Access does it using a query containing fields from both tables.

Forms and reports become more interesting and contain more useful information when they are based on multiple table queries. The following exercise has you create a query similar to the one in Figure 1.8, then create a report based on that query.

THE JOIN LINE

Access joins the tables in a query automatically if a relationship exists between the tables. Access will also join the tables (even if no relationship exists) if both tables have a field with the same name and data type, and if one of the fields is a primary key. You can also create the join yourself by dragging a field from one table to the other, but this type of join applies only to the query in which it was created.

HANDS-ON EXERCISE 3

Queries and Reports

Objective: To create a query that relates two tables to one another, then create a report based on that query. Use Figure 1.9 as a guide in the exercise.

STEP 1: Create a Select Query

➤ Open the **National Bank database** from the previous exercise.

➤ Click the **Queries tab** in the Database window. Click the **New Command button** to display the New Query dialog box. **Design View** is already selected as the means of creating a query. Click **OK** to begin creating the query.

➤ The Show Table dialog box appears as shown in Figure 1.9a, with the Tables tab already selected. Click the **Customers table,** then click the **Add button** (or double click the **Customers table**) to add the Customers table to the query (the field list should appear within the Query window).

➤ Double click the **Loans table** to add the Loans table to the query.

➤ Click **Close** to close the Show Table dialog box.

ADDING AND DELETING TABLES

To add a table to an existing query, pull down the Query menu, click Show Table, then double click the name of the table from the Table/Query list. To delete a table, click anywhere in its field list and press the Del key, or pull down the Query menu and click Remove Table.

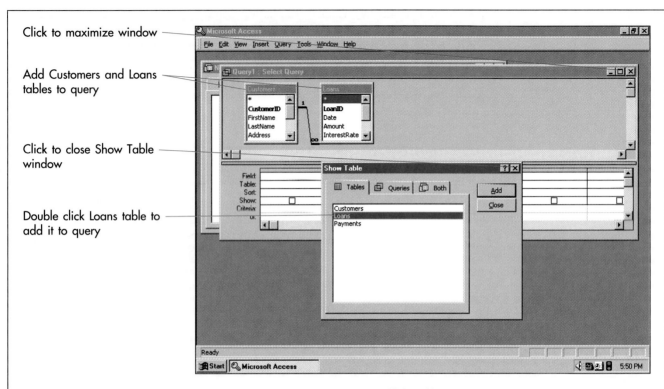

Click to maximize window

Add Customers and Loans tables to query

Click to close Show Table window

Double click Loans table to add it to query

(a) Add the Tables (step 1)

FIGURE 1.9   Hands-on Exercise 3

STEP 2: Move and Size the Field Lists

➤ Click the **Maximize button** so that the Query Design window takes the entire desktop.

➤ Point to the line separating the field lists from the design grid (the mouse pointer changes to a cross), then click and drag in a downward direction. This gives you more space to display the field lists for the tables in the query as shown in Figure 1.9b.

➤ Click and drag the bottom of the **Customers table field list** until you can see all of the fields in the Customers table. Click and drag the bottom of the **Loans table field list** until you can see all of the fields in the Loans table.

➤ Click and drag the title bar of the **Loans table** to the right until you are satisfied with the appearance of the line connecting the tables.

CONVERSION TO STANDARD FORMAT

Access is flexible in accepting text and date expressions in the Criteria row of a select query. A text entry can be entered with or without quotation marks (e.g., M or "M"). A date entry can be entered with or without pound signs (you can enter 1/1/96 or #1/1/96#). Access does, however, convert your entries to standard format as soon you move to the next cell in the design grid. Thus, text entries are always displayed in quotation marks, and dates are always enclosed in pound signs.

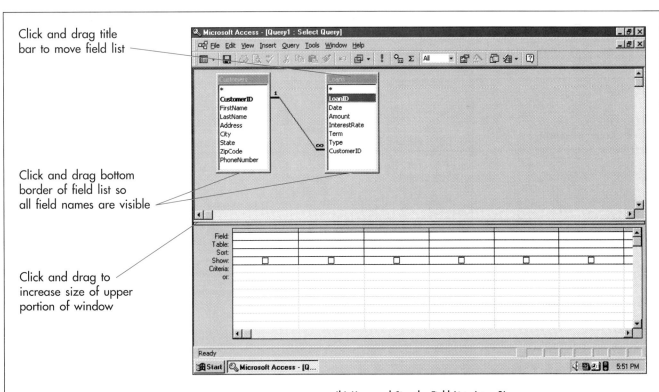

Click and drag title bar to move field list

Click and drag bottom border of field list so all field names are visible

Click and drag to increase size of upper portion of window

(b) Move and Size the Field Lists (step 2)

FIGURE 1.9   Hands-on Exercise 3 (continued)

STEP 3: Create the Query

➤ The Table row should be visible within the design grid. If not, pull down the **View menu** and click **Table Names** to display the Table row in the design grid as shown in Figure 1.9c.

➤ Double click the **LastName** and **FirstName fields,** in that order, from the Customers table to add these fields to the design grid. Double click the **title bar** of the Loans table to select all of the fields, then drag the selected group of fields to the design grid.

➤ Enter the selection criteria (scrolling if necessary) as follows:

• Click the **Criteria row** under the **Date field.** Type **Between 1/1/97 and 3/31/97.** (You do not have to type the pound signs.)

• Click the **Criteria row** for the **Amount field.** Type **>200000.**

• Type **M** in the Criteria row for the **Type field.** (You do not have to type the quotation marks.)

➤ Select all of the columns in the design grid by clicking the column selector in the first column, then pressing and holding the **Shift key** as you scroll to the last column and click its column selector. Double click the right edge of any column selector to adjust the column width of all the columns simultaneously.

➤ Click the **Sort row** under the LastName field, then click the **down arrow** to open the drop-down list box. Click **Ascending.**

➤ Click the **Save button** on the Query Design toolbar. Save the query as **First Quarter 1997 Jumbo Loans.**

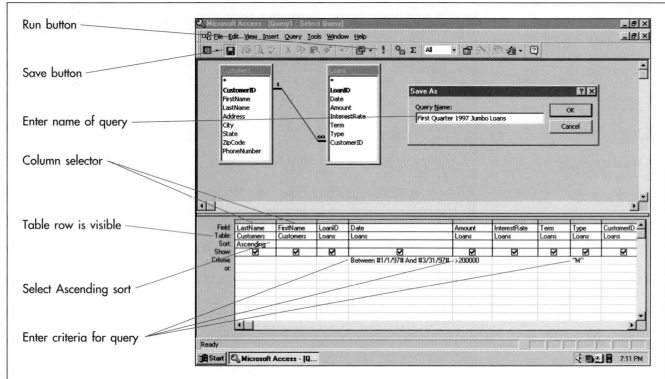

Run button

Save button

Enter name of query

Column selector

Table row is visible

Select Ascending sort

Enter criteria for query

(c) Create the Query (step 3)

FIGURE 1.9   Hands-on Exercise 3 (continued)

SORTING ON MULTIPLE FIELDS

A query can be sorted on more than one field, but you must be certain that the fields are in the proper order within the design grid. Access sorts from left to right (the leftmost field is the primary key), so the fields must be arranged in the desired sort sequence. To move a field within the design grid, click the column selector above the field name to select the column, then drag the column to its new position.

STEP 4: Run the Query

➤ Click the **Run button** (the exclamation point) to run the query and create the dynaset in Figure 1.9d. Three jumbo loans are listed.

➤ Click the **Amount field** for loan L028. Enter **100000** as the corrected amount and press **enter.** (This will reduce the number of jumbo loans in subsequent reports to two.)

➤ Click the **Close button** to close the query. Click **Yes** if asked whether to save the changes to the query.

Click to close query ————

Change Loan Amount
to 100000 ————

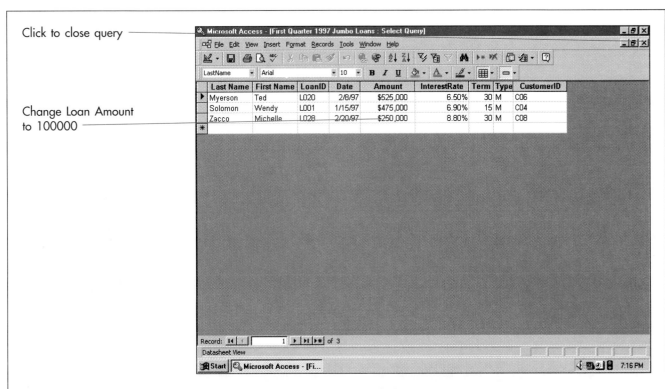

(d) The Dynaset (step 4)

FIGURE 1.9   Hands-on Exercise 3 (continued)

DATA TYPE MISMATCH

The data type determines the way in which criteria appear in the design grid. A text field is enclosed in quotation marks. Number, currency, and counter fields are shown as digits with or without a decimal point. Dates are enclosed in pound signs. A Yes/No field is entered as Yes or No without quotation marks. Entering criteria in the wrong form produces a Data Type Mismatch error when attempting to run the query.

STEP 5: Create a Report

➤ The National Bank database should still be open (although the size of your window may be different from the one in the figure).

➤ Click the **Reports tab** in the Database window, then click the **New command button** to display the New Report dialog box as shown in Figure 1.9e. Select the **Report Wizard** as the means of creating the report.

➤ Click the **drop-down arrow** to display the tables and queries in the database in order to select the one on which the report will be based. Select **First Quarter 1997 Jumbo Loans** (the query you just created) as the basis of your report. Click **OK** to start the Report Wizard.

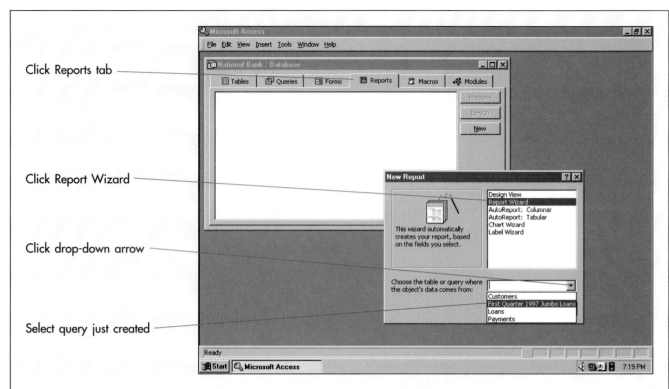

Click Reports tab

Click Report Wizard

Click drop-down arrow

Select query just created

(e) Create a Report (step 5)

FIGURE 1.9   Hands-on Exercise 3 (continued)

REPORTS WITHOUT QUERIES

You can create a report containing fields from multiple tables or queries without having to first create the underlying query. Use the Report Wizard as the basis for your design, and select fields from the first table or query in normal fashion. Click the down arrow in the Table/Query list box, select the next table or query, and enter the appropriate fields. Click the down arrow to select additional tables or queries as necessary, and continue in this fashion until you have selected all of the necessary fields.

STEP 6: The Report Wizard

➤ Double click **LoanID** from the Available Fields list box to add this field to the report. Add the **LastName, FirstName, Date,** and **Amount** fields as shown in Figure 1.9f. Click **Next.**

➤ The **by Loans option** is selected as the means of viewing your report. (This means that the report will display the loans in sequence by the LoanID field.) Click **Next.**

➤ There is no need to group the records. Click **Next.**

➤ There is no need to sort the records. Click **Next.**

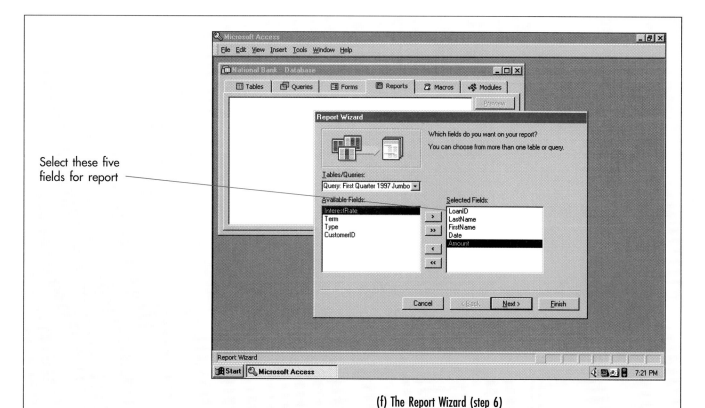

Select these five
fields for report

(f) The Report Wizard (step 6)

FIGURE 1.9   Hands-on Exercise 3 (continued)

➤ The **Tabular layout** is selected, as is **Portrait orientation.** Be sure the box is checked to **Adjust field width so all fields fit on a page.** Click **Next.**

➤ Choose **Soft Gray** as the style. Click **Next.**

➤ Enter **First Quarter 1997 Jumbo Loans** as the title for your report. The option button to **Preview the Report** is already selected.

➤ Click the **Finish Command button** to exit the Report Wizard and preview the report.

STEP 7: Print the Completed Report

➤ Click the **Maximize button.** If necessary, click the **Zoom button** in the Print Preview window so that you can see the whole report as in Figure 1.9g.

➤ The report is based on the query created earlier. Michelle Zacco is *not* in the report because the amount of her loan was updated in the query's dynaset in step 4.

➤ Click the **Print button** to print the report. Close the Preview window, then close the Report window. Click **Yes** if asked to save the changes.

➤ Close the National Bank database and exit Access if you do not want to continue with the next exercise at this time.

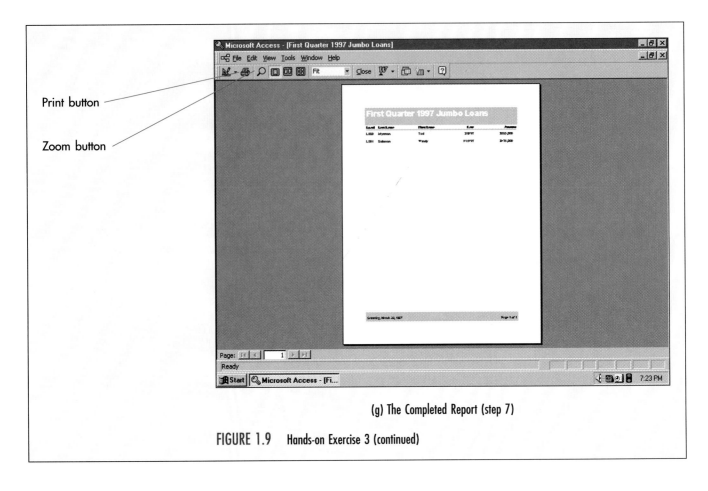

Print button

Zoom button

(g) The Completed Report (step 7)

FIGURE 1.9   Hands-on Exercise 3 (continued)

EXPANDING THE DATABASE

One of the advantages of a relational database is that it can be easily expanded to include additional tables without disturbing the existing tables. The database used throughout the chapter consisted of two tables: a Customers table and a Loans table. Figure 1.10 extends the database to include a partial listing of the Payments table containing the payments received by the bank. Each record in the Payments table has four fields: LoanID, PaymentNumber, Date (the date the payment was received), and PaymentReceived (the amount sent in).

The original database had a one-to-many relationship between customers and loans. One customer may have many loans, but a given loan is associated with only one customer. The expanded database contains a second one-to-many relationship between loans and payments. One loan has many payments, but a specific payment is associated with only one loan. Thus, the primary key of the Loans table (LoanID) appears as a foreign key in the Payments table.

Look carefully at the Payments table and note that it contains multiple records with the same payment number (e.g., every loan has a payment number 1). In similar fashion, there are multiple records with the same LoanID. Loan L001, for example, has five payments. The combination of LoanID and Payment-Number is unique, however (there is only one payment 1 for loan L001), and thus the combination of the two fields serves as the primary key in the Payments table.

We began the chapter by showing you hypothetical records in the database and asking you to answer queries based on that data. We end the chapter the same way, by asking you to reference one or more tables in Figure 1.10. As you consider each query, think of how it would appear in the design grid.

(a) Customers Table

CustomerID	First Name	Last Name	Address	City	State	Zip Code	Phone Number
C01	Eileen	Faulkner	7245 NW 8 Street	Minneapolis	MN	55346	(612) 894-1511
C02	Scott	Wit	5660 NW 175 Terrace	Baltimore	MD	21224	(410) 753-0345
C03	Benjamin	Grauer	10000 Sample Road	Coral Springs	FL	33073	(305) 444-5555
C04	Wendy	Solomon	7500 Reno Road	Houston	TX	77090	(713) 427-3104
C05	Alex	Rey	3456 Main Highway	Denver	CO	80228	(303) 555-6666
C06	Ted	Myerson	6545 Stone Street	Chapel Hill	NC	27515	(919) 942-7654
C07	Lori	Sangastiano	4533 Aero Drive	Santa Rosa	CA	95403	(707) 542-3411
C08	Michelle	Zacco	488 Gold Street	Gainesville	FL	32601	(904) 374-5660
C09	David	Powell	5070 Battle Road	Decatur	GA	30034	(301) 345-6556
C10	Matt	Hirsch	777 NW 67 Avenue	Fort Lee	NJ	07624	(201) 664-3211

(a) Customers Table

(b) Loans Table

LoanID	Date	Amount	Interest Rate	Term	Type	CustomerID
L001	1/15/97	$475,000	6.90%	15	M	C04
L004	1/23/97	$35,000	7.20%	5	C	C04
L010	1/25/97	$10,000	5.50%	3	C	C05
L014	1/31/97	$12,000	9.50%	10	O	C04
L020	2/8/97	$525,000	6.50%	30	M	C06
L022	2/12/97	$10,500	7.50%	5	O	C07
L026	2/15/97	$35,000	6.50%	5	O	C10
L028	2/20/97	$250,000	8.80%	30	M	C08
L030	2/21/97	$5,000	10.00%	3	O	C08
L031	2/28/97	$200,000	7.00%	15	M	C01
L032	3/1/97	$25,000	10.00%	3	C	C02
L033	3/1/97	$20,000	9.50%	5	O	C05
L039	3/3/97	$56,000	7.50%	5	C	C09
L040	3/10/97	$129,000	8.50%	15	M	C10
L047	3/11/97	$200,000	7.25%	15	M	C03
L049	3/21/97	$150,000	7.50%	15	M	C01
L052	3/22/97	$100,000	7.00%	30	M	C01
L053	3/31/97	$15,000	6.50%	3	O	C03
L054	4/1/97	$10,000	8.00%	5	C	C02
L057	4/15/97	$25,000	8.50%	4	C	C03
L060	4/18/97	$41,000	9.90%	4	C	C08
L062	4/22/97	$350,000	7.50%	15	M	C10
L100	5/1/97	$150,000	6.00%	15	M	C03
L109	5/3/97	$350,000	8.20%	30	M	C04
L120	5/8/97	$275,000	9.20%	15	M	C07

(b) Loans Table

(c) Payments Table (partial list)

LoanID	Payment Number	Date	Payment Received
L001	1	2/15/97	$4,242.92
L001	2	3/15/97	$4,242.92
L001	3	4/15/97	$4,242.92
L001	4	5/15/97	$4,242.92
L001	5	6/15/97	$4,242.92
L004	1	2/23/97	$696.35
L004	2	3/23/97	$696.35
L004	3	4/23/97	$696.35
L004	4	5/23/97	$696.35
L004	5	6/23/97	$696.35
L010	1	2/25/97	$301.96
L010	2	3/25/97	$301.96
L010	3	4/25/97	$301.96
L010	4	5/25/97	$301.96
L010	5	6/25/97	$301.96
L014	1	2/28/97	$155.28
L014	2	3/31/97	$155.28
L014	3	4/30/97	$155.28
L014	4	5/30/97	$155.28
L014	5	6/30/97	$155.28
L020	1	3/8/97	$3,318.36
L020	2	4/8/97	$3,318.36
L020	3	5/8/97	$3,318.36
L020	4	6/8/97	$3,318.36
L022	1	3/12/97	$210.40
L022	2	4/12/97	$210.40
L022	3	5/12/97	$210.40
L022	4	6/12/97	$210.40
L026	1	3/15/97	$684.82
L026	2	4/15/97	$684.82
L026	3	5/15/97	$684.82
L026	4	6/15/97	$684.82
L028	1	3/20/97	$1,975.69
L028	2	4/20/97	$1,975.69
L028	3	5/20/97	$1,975.69
L028	4	6/20/97	$1,975.69
L030	1	3/21/97	$161.34
L030	2	4/21/97	$161.34
L030	3	5/21/97	$161.34
L030	4	6/21/97	$161.34

(c) Payments Table (partial list)

FIGURE 1.10   Expanding the Database

Query: How many payments have been received for loan L022? What was the date of the most recent payment?

Answer: Four payments have been received for loan L022. The most recent payment was received on 6/12/97.

The query can be answered with reference to just the Payments table by finding all payments for loan L022. To determine the most recent payment, you would retrieve the records in descending order by Date and retrieve the first record.

Query: How many payments have been received from Michelle Zacco since May 1, 1997?

Answer: Four payments have been received. Two of the payments were for loan L028 on May 20th and June 20th. Two were for loan L030 on May 21st and June 21st.

To answer this query, you would look in the Customers table to determine the CustomerID for Ms. Zacco, search the Loans table for all loans for this customer, then retrieve the corresponding payments from the Payments table. (Michelle is also associated with loan L060. The Payments table, however, is truncated in Figure 1.10, and hence the payments for this loan are not visible.)

Multiple Subforms

Subforms were introduced earlier in the chapter as a means of displaying data from related tables. Figure 1.11 continues the discussion by showing a main form with two levels of subforms. The main (Customers) form has a one-to-many relationship with the first (Loans) subform. The Loans subform in turn has a one-to-many relationship with the second (Payments) subform. The Customers form and the Loans subform are the forms you created in the second hands-on exercise. (The Loans subform is displayed in the Form view as opposed to the Data sheet view.) The Payments subform is new and will be developed in our next exercise.

The records displayed in the three forms are linked to one another according to the relationships within the database. There is a one-to-many relationship between customers and loans so that the first subform displays all of the loans for one customer. There is also a one-to-many relationship between loans and payments so that the second subform (Payments) displays all of the payments for the selected loan. Click on a different loan (for the same customer), and the Payments subform is updated automatically to show all of the payments for that loan.

The status bar for the main form indicates record 5 of 11, meaning that you are viewing the fifth of 11 Customer records. The status bar for the Loans subform indicates record 2 of 2, corresponding to the second of two loan records for the fifth customer. The status bar for the Payments subform indicates record 1 of 3, corresponding to the first of three Payment records for this loan for this customer.

The three sets of navigation buttons enable you to advance to the next record(s) in any of the forms. The records move in conjunction with one another. Thus, if you advance to the next record in the Customers form you will automatically display a different set of records in the Loans subform, as well as a different set of Payment records in the Payments subform.

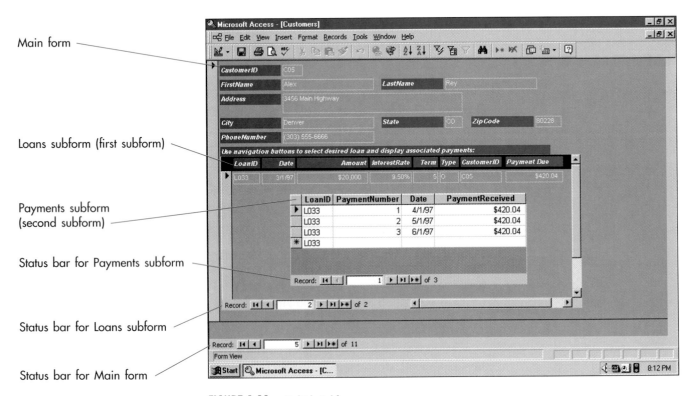

FIGURE 1.11   Multiple Subforms

Linked Subforms

Objective: To create a main form with two levels of subforms; to display a subform in Form view or Datasheet view. Use Figure 1.12 as a guide.

STEP 1: Add a Relationship

➤ Open the **National Bank database.** Pull down the **Tools menu.** Click **Relationships** to open the Relationships window as shown in Figure 1.12a. Maximize the Relationships window.

➤ Pull down the **Relationships menu.** Click **Show Table** to display the Show Table dialog box.

➤ The **Tables tab** is selected within the Show Table dialog box. Double click the **Payments table** to add the table to the Relationships window. Close the Show Table dialog box.

➤ Click and drag the title bar of the **Payments Field list** so that it is positioned approximately one inch from the Loans table.

➤ Click and drag the **LoanID field** in the Loans field list to the **LoanID field** in the Payments field list. You will see the Relationships dialog box.

➤ Check the **Enforce Referential Integrity** check box. (If necessary, clear the check boxes to Cascade Update Related Fields and Delete Related Records.)

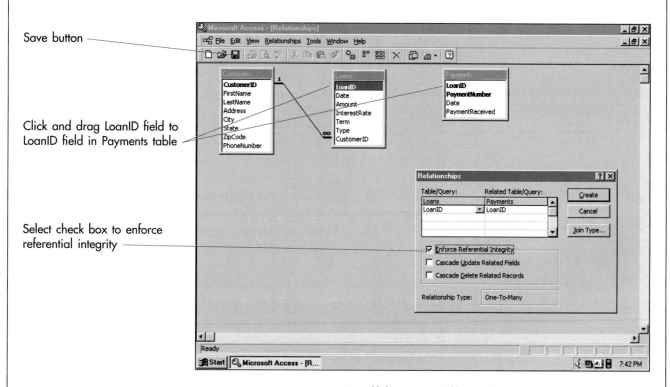

Save button

Click and drag LoanID field to LoanID field in Payments table

Select check box to enforce referential integrity

(a) Add the Payments Table (step 1)

FIGURE 1.12   Hands-on Exercise 4

➤ Click the **Create button** to establish the relationship. You should see a line indicating a one-to-many relationship between the Loans and Payments tables.

➤ Click the **Save button** to save the Relationships window, then close the Relationships window.

A CONCATENATED PRIMARY KEY

The primary key is defined as the field, or combination of fields, that is unique for every record in a table. The Payments table contains multiple records with the same payment number (i.e., every loan has a payment number 1, 2, 3, and so on) as well as multiple payments for the same LoanID. The combination of LoanID and PaymentNumber is unique, however, and serves as the primary key for the Payments table.

STEP 2: Create the Payments Subform

➤ You should be back in the Database window. Click the **Forms tab,** then open the **Loans subform** (from the second exercise) in Design view as shown in Figure 1.12b. If necessary, maximize the Form Design window.

➤ Click and drag the bottom edge of the **Details section** so that you have approximately 2 to 2½ inches of blank space in the Detail section. (This is where the Payments subform will go.)

➤ Click the **Subform/Subreport button** on the Toolbox toolbar, then click and drag in the Loans form to create the Payments subform. Release the mouse to begin the Subform/Subreport Wizard.

➤ The **Table/Query Option button** is selected, indicating that we will build the subform from a table or query. Click **Next.** You should see the Subform/Subreport dialog box in Figure 1.12b.

➤ Click the **drop-down arrow** on the Tables and Queries list box to select the **Payments table.** Click the **>> button** to add all of the fields in the Payments table to the subform. Click **Next.**

➤ The Subform Wizard asks you to define the fields that link the main form to the subform. The option button to **Choose from a list** is selected, as is **Show Payments for each record in <SQL Statement> using LoanID.** Click **Next.**

➤ The Wizard suggests **Payments subform** as the name of the subform. Click **Finish** to exit the Subform/Subreport wizard.

LINKING FIELDS, FORMS, AND SUBFORMS

Linking fields do not have to appear in the main form and subform but must be included in the underlying table or query. The LoanID, for example, is used to link the Loans form and the Payments form and need not appear in either form. We have, however, chosen to display the LoanID in both forms to emphasize the relationship between the corresponding tables.

Subform/Subreport button

Subform control

Click >> button to
select all fields

Click and drag bottom edge
of Detail section to increase
space in Detail section

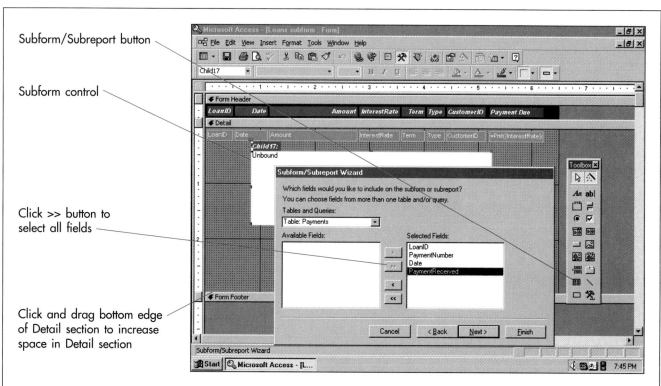

(b) Create the Payments Subform (step 2)

FIGURE 1.12   Hands-on Exercise 4 (continued)

STEP 3: Change the Default View

➤ Maximize the window. Point to the **Form Selector box** in the upper-left corner of the Design window, click the **right mouse button** to display a shortcut menu, and click **Properties** to display the Form Properties dialog box in Figure 1.12c.

➤ Click in the **Default View box,** click the **drop-down arrow** to display the views, then click **Single Form.** Close the Properties dialog box.

➤ Select the label for the Payments subform control, then press the **Del key** to delete the label. Save the form.

THE DEFAULT VIEW PROPERTY

The Default View property determines how a form is dislayed initially and is especially important when working with multiple forms. In general, the highest level form(s) is (are) displayed in the Single Form view and the lowest level in the Datasheet view. In this example, the Customers and Loans forms are both set to the Single Form view, whereas the Payment form is set to the Datasheet view.

Form View button

Form selector box

Click in Default View box

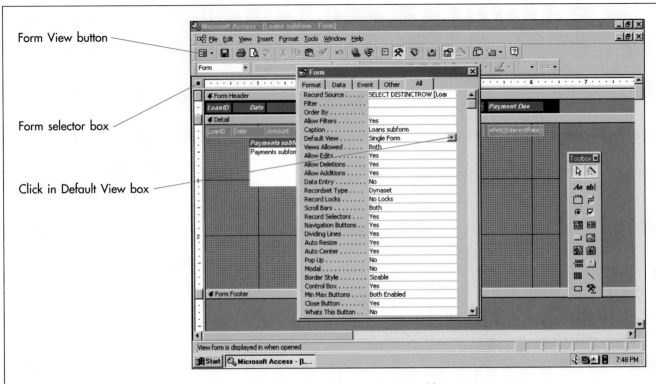

(c) Change the Loans Subform View (step 3)

FIGURE 1.12   Hands-on Exercise 4 (continued)

STEP 4: The Loans Subform in Form View

➤ Click the **Form View button** to switch to the Form view for the Loans sub-form as shown in Figure 1.12d.

➤ Do not be concerned if the size and/or position of your form is different from ours as you can return to the Design view in order to make the necessary changes.

• The status bar of the Loans form indicates record 1 of 27, meaning that you are positioned on the first of 27 records in the Loans table.

• The status bar for the Payments subform indicates record 1 of 5, corresponding to the first of five payment records for this loan.

➤ Change to the **Design view** to adjust the column widths within the Payments subform. This is accomplished by opening the subform in the Datasheet view (see boxed tip on page 177 on modifying a subform) and adjusting the column headings.

➤ You will most likely have to size and/or move the Payments subform control within the Loans subform. Click and drag the subform control as necessary.

➤ Save, then close, the Loans subform.

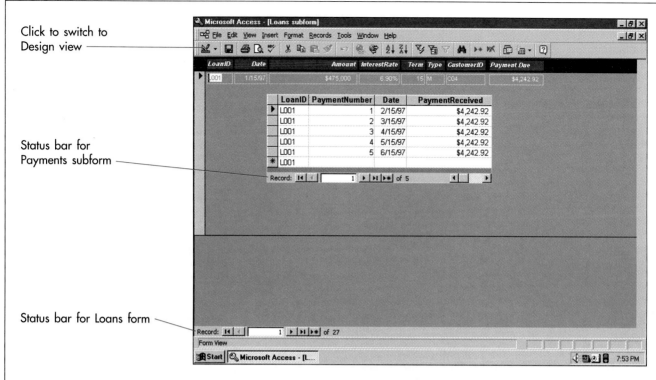

Click to switch to
Design view

Status bar for
Payments subform

Status bar for Loans form

(d) The Form View (step 4)

FIGURE 1.12   Hands-on Exercise 4 (continued)

STEP 5: The Customers Form

➤ You should be back in the Database window. Click the **Forms tab** (if necessary), then open the **Customers form** as shown in Figure 1.12e. Do not be concerned if the size of the Loans or Payments subforms are different from ours as you can return to the Design view to make the necessary changes.

- The status bar of the Customers form indicates record 1 of 11, meaning that you are positioned on the first of 11 records in the Customers table.
- The status bar for the Loans subform indicates record 1 of 3, corresponding to the first of three records for this customer.
- The status bar for the Payments subform indicates record 1 of 4, corresponding to the first of four payments for this loan.

➤ Change to the **Design view** to move and/or size the control for the Loans subform. You may also need to open the subform in the Datasheet view to adjust the column widths.

MODIFYING A SUBFORM

The Payment subform appears as an object in the Design view of the Loans form, but it can be opened and modified as an independent form. To open a subform, click outside the subform to deselect it, then double click the subform to open it.

Click to switch to
Design view

Status bar for
Payments subform

Status bar for Loans subform

Status bar for Customer
(main) form

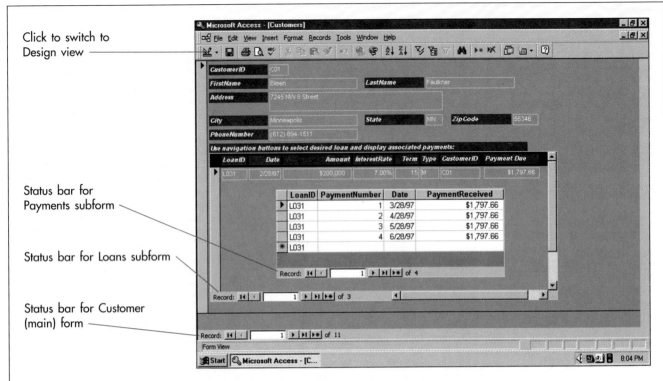

(e) The Customers Form (step 5)

FIGURE 1.12   Hands-on Exercise 4 (continued)

STEP 6: The Finishing Touches

➤ Point to the **Label tool,** then click and drag in the **Customers form** to create an unbound control as shown in Figure 1.12f.

➤ Release the mouse, then enter **Use navigation buttons to select desired loan and display associated payments.** Click outside the control when you have completed the text.

➤ Click the **Save button** to save the Customers form, which contains the two subforms.

USER-FRIENDLY FORMS

The phrase *user friendly* appears so frequently that we tend to take it for granted. The intention is clear, however, and you should strive to make your forms as clear as possible so that the user is provided with all the information he or she may need. It may be obvious to the designer that one has to click the Navigation buttons to move to a new loan, but a user unfamiliar with Access may not know that. Adding a descriptive label to the form goes a long way toward making the system successful.

Click to switch to Form view

Label tool

Create unbound control

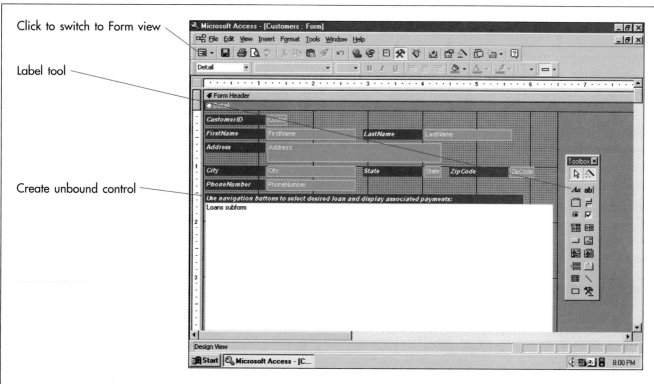

(f) The Finishing Touches (step 6)

FIGURE 1.12   Hands-on Exercise 4 (continued)

STEP 7: Make Your Payments

➤ Change to the **Form view.** Click the ▶| on the status bar for the Customers form to move to the last record as shown in Figure 1.12g. This should be Customer C11 (your record) that you entered in the earlier exercises in this chapter. You currently have two loans, L121 and L122, the first of which is displayed.

➤ Click in the **Payments subform.** Enter the payment number, press **Tab,** enter the date of your first payment, press **Tab,** then enter the amount paid. Press **enter** to move to the next payment record and enter this payment as well. Press **enter** and enter a third payment.

➤ Click the **selection area** at the left of the form to select this record. Pull down the **File menu** and click **Print** to display the Print dialog box. Click the **Selected Records Option button.** Click **OK** to print the selected form.

➤ Close the Customers form. Click **Yes** if asked to save the changes to the form.

➤ Close the National Bank database and exit Access.

THREE SETS OF NAVIGATION BUTTONS

Each form or subform has its own set of navigation buttons. Thus you are looking at record 11 of 11 in the Customers form, loan 1 of 2 in the Loans form for this customer, and payment 3 of 3 in the Payments form for this loan.

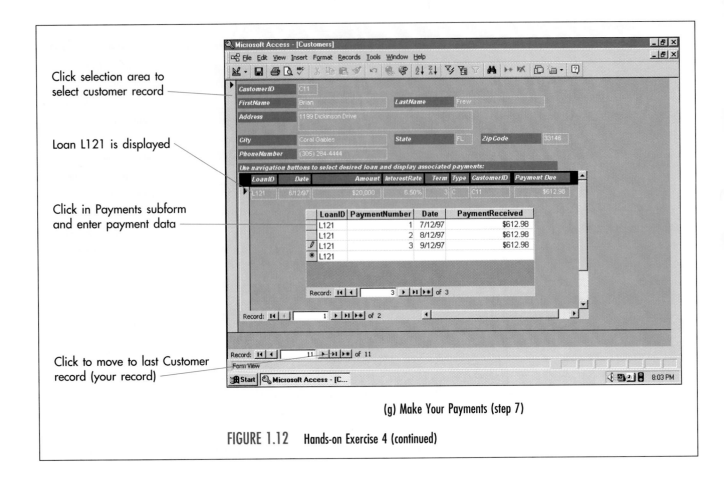

Click selection area to select customer record

Loan L121 is displayed

Click in Payments subform and enter payment data

Click to move to last Customer record (your record)

(g) Make Your Payments (step 7)

FIGURE 1.12   Hands-on Exercise 4 (continued)

SUMMARY

An Access database may contain multiple tables. Each table stores data about a specific subject. Each table has a primary key, which is a field (or combination of fields) that uniquely identifies each record.

A one-to-many relationship uses the primary key of the "one" table as a foreign key in the "many" table. (A foreign key is simply the primary key of the related table.) The Relationships window enables you to graphically create a one-to-many relationship by dragging the join field from one table to the other.

Referential integrity ensures that the tables in a database are consistent with one another. When referential integrity is enforced, Access prevents you from adding a record to a related table if that record contains an invalid foreign key. It also prevents you from deleting a record in the primary table if there is a corresponding record in the related table.

A subform is a form within a form and is used to display data from a related table. It is created most easily with the Form Wizard, then modified in the Form Design view just as any other form. A main form can have any number of subforms. Subforms can extend to two levels, enabling a subform to be created within a subform.

The power of a select query lies in its ability to include fields from several tables. The query shows the relationships that exist between the tables by drawing a join line that indicates how to relate the data. The Tables row displays the name of the table containing the corresponding field. Once created, a multiple table query can be the basis for a form or report.

Tables can be added to a relational database without disturbing the data in existing tables. A database can have several one-to-many relationships.

Build button

Control Source property

Datasheet view

Foreign key

Form view

Function

Main form

One-to-many relationship

Primary key

Primary table

Referential integrity

Related table

Relationship line

Relationships window

Subform

Subform Wizard

Table row

MULTIPLE CHOICE

1. Which of the following will cause a problem of referential integrity when there is a one-to-many relationship between customers and loans?
   (a) The deletion of a customer record that has corresponding loan records
   (b) The deletion of a customer record that has no corresponding loan records
   (c) The deletion of a loan record with a corresponding customer record
   (d) All of the above

2. Which of the following will cause a problem of referential integrity when there is a one-to-many relationship between customers and loans?
   (a) The addition of a new customer prior to entering loans for that customer
   (b) The addition of a new loan that references an invalid customer
   (c) Both (a) and (b)
   (d) Neither (a) nor (b)

3. Which of the following is true about a database that monitors players and the teams to which those players are assigned?
   (a) The PlayerID will be defined as a primary key within the Teams table
   (b) The TeamID will be defined as a primary key within the Players table
   (c) The PlayerID will appear as a foreign key within the Teams table
   (d) The TeamID will appear as a foreign key within the Players table

4. Which of the following best expresses the relationships within the expanded National Bank database as it appeared at the end of the chapter?
   (a) There is a one-to-many relationship between customers and loans
   (b) There is a one-to-many relationship between loans and payments
   (c) Both (a) and (b)
   (d) Neither (a) nor (b)

5. A database has a one-to-many relationship between branches and employees (one branch can have many employees). Which of the following is true?
   (a) The EmployeeID will be defined as a primary key within the Branches table
   (b) The BranchID will be defined as a primary key within the Employees table
   (c) The EmployeeID will appear as a foreign key within the Branches table
   (d) The BranchID will appear as a foreign key within the Employees table

6. Every table in an Access database:
   (a) Must be related to every other table
   (b) Must have one or more foreign keys
   (c) Both (a) and (b)
   (d) Neither (a) nor (b)

7. Which of the following is true of a main form and subform that are created in conjunction with the one-to-many relationship between customers and loans?
   (a) The main form should be based on the Customers table
   (b) The subform should be based on the Loans table
   (c) Both (a) and (b)
   (d) Neither (a) nor (b)

8. Which of the following is true regarding the navigation buttons for a main form and its associated subform?
   (a) The navigation buttons pertain to just the main form
   (b) The navigation buttons pertain to just the subform
   (c) There are separate navigation buttons for each form
   (d) There are no navigation buttons at all

9. How do you open a subform?
   (a) Go to the Design view of the associated main form, click anywhere in the main form to deselect the subform, then double click the subform
   (b) Go to the Database window, select the subform, then click the Open or Design buttons, depending on the desired view
   (c) Both (a) and (b)
   (d) Neither (a) nor (b)

10. Which of the following is true?
    (a) A main form may contain multiple subforms
    (b) A subform may contain another subform
    (c) Both (a) and (b)
    (d) Neither (a) nor (b)

11. Which command displays the open tables in an Access database in equal-sized windows one on top of another?
    (a) The Tile command in the Window menu
    (b) The Cascade command in the Window menu
    (c) The Tile command in the Relationships menu
    (d) The Cascade command in the Relationships menu

12. Which of the following describes how to move and size a field list within the Relationships window?
    (a) Click and drag the title bar to size the field list
    (b) Click and drag a border or corner to move the field list
    (c) Both (a) and (b)
    (d) Neither (a) nor (b)

13. Which of the following is true regarding entries in a Criteria row of a select query?
    (a) A text field may be entered with or without quotation marks
    (b) A date field may be entered with or without surrounding number (pound) signs
    (c) Both (a) and (b)
    (d) Neither (a) nor (b)

14. Which of the following is true about a select query?

(a) It may reference fields in one or more tables

(b) It may have one or more criteria rows

(c) It may sort on one or more fields

(d) All of the above

15. A report may be based on:

(a) A table

(b) A query

(c) Both (a) and (b)

(d) Neither (a) nor (b)

ANSWERS

1. a	**6.** d	**11.** b
2. b	**7.** c	**12.** d
3. d	**8.** c	**13.** c
4. c	**9.** c	**14.** d
5. d	**10.** c	**15.** c

PRACTICE WITH ACCESS 97

1. Figure 1.13 contains a modified version of the Customers form and its associated subforms. Complete the hands-on exercises in the chapter, then modify the completed Customers form so that it matches Figure 1.13. (The easiest way to add the label at the top of the form is to create a form header.) Follow the steps below to add the clip art image. (The faster your machine, the more you will enjoy the exercise.)

a. Open the Customers form in the Design view. Double click the Loans subform control to open the Loans subform in the Design view. Move the control for the Payments subform to the left to allow room for the OLE object.

b. Click the Unbound Object Frame tool on the toolbox. (If you are unsure as to which tool to click, just point to the tool to display the name of the tool.)

c. Click and drag in the Loans subform to size the frame, then release the mouse to display an Insert Object dialog box.

d. Click the Create New Option button. Select the Microsoft Clip Gallery as the object type. Click OK.

e. Click the ClipArt tab. Choose the category and picture you want from within the Clip Gallery. Click the Insert button to insert the picture into the Access form and simultaneously close the Clip Gallery dialog box. Do *not* be concerned if only a portion of the picture appears on the form.

f. Right click the newly inserted object to display a shortcut menu, then click Properties to display the Properties dialog box. Click the Format tab, then select (click) the Size Mode property and select Stretch from the associated list. Change the Back Style property to Transparent, the Special Effect property to Flat, and the Border Style property to Transparent. Close the Properties dialog box.

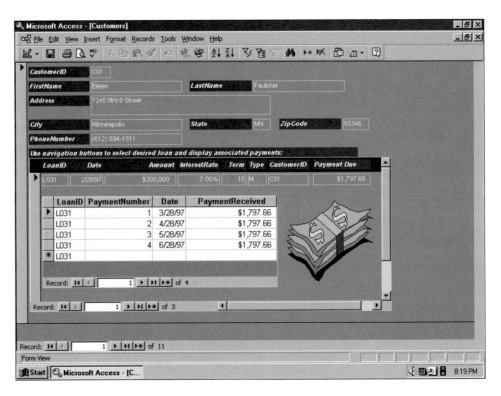

FIGURE 1.13   Screen for Practice Exercise 1

g. You should see the entire clip art image, although it may be distorted because the size and shape of the frame you inserted in steps (a) and (b) does not match the image you selected. Click and drag the sizing handles on the frame to size the object so that its proportions are correct. Click anywhere in the middle of the frame (the mouse pointer changes to a hand) to move the frame elsewhere in the form.

h. If you want to display a different object, double click the clip art image to return to the Clip Gallery in order to select another object. View the completed form, then make any final changes.

i. Print the completed form with your customer information. Remember to click the selection area prior to printing. (You are still customer C11.)

2. Interest rates have come down and National Bank has decided to run a promotion on car loans. The loan officer would like to contact all existing customers with a car loan to inform them of their new rates. Create a report similar to the one in Figure 1.14 in response to the request from the loan officer.

The report may be based on a query that contains fields from both the Customers and the Loans tables, or it may be created directly in the Report Wizard. Note, too, the clip art image, which is required in the Report heading and which can be added using the techniques described in the previous problem. Be sure to add your name to the heading so that your instructor will know the report came from you.

3. Use the Employee database in the Exploring Access folder on the data disk to create the main form and subform combination shown in Figure 1.15. There is a one-to-many relationship between locations and employees (one location contains many employees), and you need to define this relationship prior to creating the form.

Customers with Car Loans

Prepared by Brian Frew

Last Name	First	Address	Phone Number
Frew	Brian	1199 Dickinson Drive Coral Gables FL 33146	(305) 284-4444
Grauer	Benjamin	10000 Sample Road Coral Springs FL 33073	(305) 444-5555
Powell	David	5070 Battle Road Decatur GA 30034	(301) 345-6556
Rey	Alex	3456 Main Highway Denver CO 80228	(303) 555-6666
Solomon	Wendy	7500 Reno Road Houston TX 77090	(713) 427-3104
Wit	Scott	5660 NW 175 Terrace Baltimore MD 21224	(410) 753-0345
Wit	Scott	5660 NW 175 Terrace Baltimore MD 21224	(410) 753-0345
Zacco	Michelle	488 Gold Street Gainesville FL 32601	(904) 374-5660

Thursday, June 10, 1997   **Page 1 of 1**

FIGURE 1.14   Report for Practice Exercise 2

You also need to modify the underlying Employee table to use a Location code rather than the Location name. (The change in design was requested by the end-user after the initial database was completed. This is not a trivial task, and you will see how important it is to arrive at a satisfactory design as early as possible in a project.)

In creating the form we used the Colorful 2 style, but you are free to use any style you like. You can create the forms using the techniques in the second hands-on exercise. Alternatively, you can access the Subform/Subreport Wizard directly from the Form Wizard by following the steps on the next page.

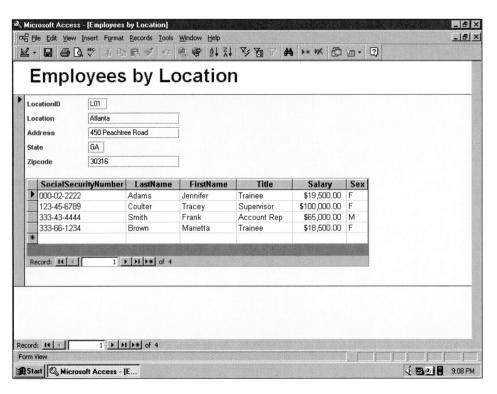

FIGURE 1.15   Screen for Practice Exercise 3

a. Click the Forms tab in the Database window, click New to display the New Form dialog box, then click Form Wizard as the means of creating the form. Select Locations as the table on which to base the main form, and click OK to start the Form Wizard.

b. Click the >> button to select all of the fields in the Locations table for the form. Do *not,* however, click Next at this time as you will select additional fields from the Employees table for inclusion on the form.

c. Click the drop-down arrow on the Tables/Queries list box, select the Employees table, then add all of the fields in the Employees table except Location ID. Click Next.

d. View your data by Locations and be sure the Form with subform(s) option button is selected. Click Next.

e. Choose the Datasheet layout for your subform, then answer the remaining questions to complete the forms.

f. Add your name as an Account Rep in Miami at a salary of $50,000. Print the location form for the Miami location only, and submit it to your instructor as proof you did this exercise.

4. The Titles form in Figure 1.16 is based on the Employees database referenced in problem 3. Open the Employee database and add the one-to-many relationship between titles and employees, then create the form in Figure 1.16. As in the previous exercise, you will need to change the Employees table to accommodate a Title code rather than a Title description.

Use the technique described in problem 1 to add a clip art logo of your choice to the form. (You can download additional clipart from the site www.clipart.com).

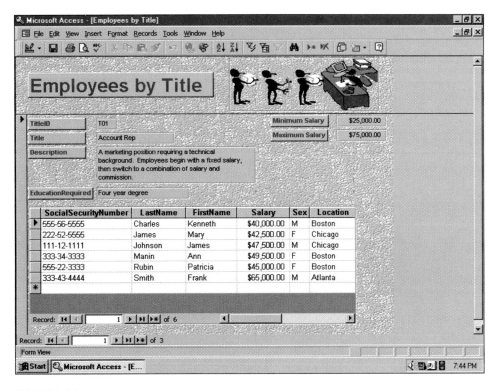

FIGURE 1.16   Report for Practice Exercise 4

Case Studies

Recreational Sports League

Design a database for a recreational sports league that will monitor players, coaches, and sponsors. There may be any number of teams in the league, with each team having any number of players. A player is associated with only one team.

Each team has at least one coach. The league also imposes the rule that a person may not coach more than one team. Each team has a sponsor such as a local business. One sponsor can be associated with multiple teams.

Your solution should make the system as realistic as possible. The player table, for example, requires not only the identifying information for each player (name, address, phone, and so on) but additional fields such as birth date (to implement age limits on various teams), ability ratings, and so on. Your system should be capable of producing reports that will display all information about a specific team, such as its players, coach, and sponsor. The league administrators would also like master lists of all teams, players, coaches, and sponsors.

Show the required tables in the database, being sure to indicate the primary key and foreign keys in each table. Indicate one or two other fields in each table (you need not list them all).

The Personnel Director

You have been hired as a personnel director for a medium-sized company with offices in several cities. You require the usual personal data for each employee (birth date, hire date, home address, and so on.) You also need to reach an employee at work, and must be able to retrieve the office address, office phone number, and office fax number for each employee. Each employee is assigned to only one branch office.

Your duties also include the administration of various health plans offered by the company. Each employee is given his or her choice of several health plans. Each plan has a monthly premium and deductible amount. Once the deductible is reached, each plan pays a designated percentage of all subsequent expenses.

Design a database that will include the necessary data to provide all of the information you need. Show the required tables in the database, being sure to indicate the primary key and foreign keys in each table. Indicate one or two other fields in each table (you need not list them all).

The Franchise

The management of a national restaurant chain is automating its procedure for monitoring its restaurants, restaurant owners (franchisees), and the contracts that govern the two. Each restaurant has one owner (franchisee). There is no limit on the number of restaurants an individual may own, and franchisees are encouraged to apply for multiple restaurants.

The payment from the franchisee to the company varies according to the contract in effect for the particular restaurant. The company offers a choice of contracts, which vary according to the length of the contract, the franchise fee, and the percentage of the restaurant's sales paid to the company for marketing and royalty fees. Each restaurant has one contract, but a given contract may pertain to many restaurants.

The company needs a database capable of retrieving all data for a given restaurant, such as its annual sales, location, phone number, owner, and type of contract in effect. It would also like to know all restaurants owned by one person as well as all restaurants governed by a specific contract type.

Widgets of America

Widgets of America gives its sales staff exclusive rights to specific customers. Each sales person has many customers, but a specific customer always deals with the same sales representative. The company needs to know all of the orders placed by a specific customer as well as the total business generated by each sales representative. The data for each order includes the date the order was placed and the amount of the order. Design a database capable of producing the information required by the company.

Show the required tables in the database, being sure to indicate the primary key and foreign keys in each table. Indicate one or two other fields in each table (you need not list them all).

MANY-TO-MANY RELATIONSHIPS: A MORE COMPLEX SYSTEM

After reading this chapter you will be able to:

1. Define a many-to-many relationship and explain how it is implemented in Access.
2. Use the Cascade Update and Cascade Delete options in the Relationships window to relax enforcement of referential integrity.
3. Explain how the AutoNumber field type simplifies the entry of a primary key for a new record.
4. Create a main and subform based on a query; discuss the advantage of using queries rather than tables as the basis for a form or report.
5. Create a parameter query; explain how a parameter query can be made to accept multiple parameters.
6. Use aggregate functions in a select query to perform calculations on groups of records.
7. Use the Get External Data command to add external tables to an existing database.

OVERVIEW

This chapter introduces a new case study to give you additional practice in database design. The system extends the concept of a relational database that was introduced in the previous chapter to include both a one-to-many and a many-to-many relationship. The case solution reviews earlier material on establishing relationships in Access and the importance of referential integrity. Another point of particular interest is the use of an AutoNumber field to facilitate the addition of new records.

The chapter extends what you already know about subforms and queries, and uses both to present information from related tables. The forms created in this chapter are based on multiple table queries rather than tables. The queries themselves are of a more advanced nature. We show you how to create a parameter query, where the user is prompted to enter the criteria when the query is run. We also show you how to create queries that use the aggregate functions built into Access to perform calculations on groups of records.

The chapter contains four hands-on exercises to implement the case study. We think you will be pleased with what you have accomplished by the end of the chapter, working with a sophisticated system that is typical of real-world applications.

CASE STUDY: THE COMPUTER SUPER STORE

The case study in this chapter is set within the context of a computer store that requires a database for its customers, products, and orders. The store maintains the usual customer data (name, address, phone, etc.). It also keeps data about the products it sells, storing for each product a product ID, description, quantity on hand, quantity on order, and unit price. And finally, the store has to track its orders. It needs to know the date an order was received, the customer who placed it, the products that were ordered, and the quantity of each product ordered.

Think, for a moment, about the tables that are necessary and the relationships between those tables, then compare your thoughts to our solution in Figure 2.1. You probably have no trouble recognizing the need for the Customers, Products, and Orders tables. Initially, you may be puzzled by the Order Details table, but you will soon appreciate why it is there and how powerful it is.

You can use the Customers, Products, and Orders tables individually to obtain information about a specific customer, product, or order, respectively. For example:

Query: What is Jeffrey Muddell's phone number?
Answer: Jeffrey Muddell's phone is (305) 253-3909.

Query: What is the price of a Pentium laptop/133? How many are in stock?
Answer: A Pentium laptop/133 sells for $2,599. Fifteen systems are in stock.

Query: When was order O0003 placed?
Answer: Order O0003 was placed on April 18, 1997.

Other queries require you to relate the tables to one another. There is, for example, a *one-to-many relationship* between customers and orders. One customer can place many orders, but a specific order can be associated with only one customer. The tables are related through the CustomerID, which appears as the *primary key* in the Customers table and as a *foreign key* in the Orders table. Consider:

Query: What is the name of the customer who placed order number O0003?
Answer: Order O0003 was placed by Jeffrey Muddell.

Query: How many orders were placed by Jeffrey Muddell?
Answer: Jeffrey Muddell placed five orders: O0003, O0014, O0016, O0024, and O0025.

These queries require you to use two tables. To answer the first query, you would search the Orders table to find order O0003 and obtain the CustomerID (C0006 in this example). You would then search the Customers table for the customer with this CustomerID and retrieve the customer's name. To answer the

Customer ID	First Name	Last Name	Address	City	State	Zip Code	Phone Number
C0001	Benjamin	Lee	1000 Call Street	Tallahassee	FL	33340	(904) 327-4124
C0002	Eleanor	Milgrom	7245 NW 8 Street	Margate	FL	33065	(305) 974-1234
C0003	Neil	Goodman	4215 South 81 Street	Margate	FL	33065	(305) 444-5555
C0004	Nicholas	Colon	9020 N.W. 75 Street	Coral Springs	FL	33065	(305) 753-9887
C0005	Michael	Ware	276 Brickell Avenue	Miami	FL	33131	(305) 444-3980
C0006	Jeffrey	Muddell	9522 N.W. 142 Street	Miami	FL	33176	(305) 253-3909
C0007	Ashley	Geoghegan	7500 Center Lane	Coral Springs	FL	33070	(305) 753-7830
C0008	Serena	Sherard	5000 Jefferson Lane	Gainesville	FL	32601	(904) 375-6442
C0009	Luis	Couto	455 Bargello Avenue	Coral Gables	FL	33146	(305) 666-4801
C0010	Derek	Anderson	6000 Tigertail Avenue	Coconut Grove	FL	33120	(305) 446-8900
C0011	Lauren	Center	12380 S.W. 137 Avenue	Miami	FL	33186	(305) 385-4432
C0012	Robert	Slane	4508 N.W. 7 Street	Miami	FL	33131	(305) 635-3454

(a) Customers Table

Product ID	Product Name	Units In Stock	Units On Order	Unit Price
P0001	Pentium desktop/166 with MMX	50	0	$1,899.00
P0002	Pentium desktop/200 with MMX	25	5	$1,999.00
P0003	Pentium Pro desktop/180	125	15	$2,099.00
P0004	Pentium Pro desktop/200	25	50	$2,299.00
P0005	Pentium laptop/133	15	25	$2,599.00
P0006	15" SVGA Monitor	50	0	$499.00
P0007	17" SVGA Monitor	25	10	$899.00
P0008	20" Multisync Monitor	50	20	$1,599.00
P0009	2.5 Gb IDE Hard Drive	15	20	$399.00
P0010	2 Gb SCSI Hard Drive	25	15	$799.00
P0011	4 Gb SCSI Hard Drive	10	0	$1,245.00
P0012	CD-ROM: 8X	40	0	$249.00
P0013	CD-ROM: 12X	50	15	$449.95
P0014	HD Floppy Disks	500	200	$9.99
P0015	HD Data Cartridges	100	50	$14.79
P0016	2 Gb Tape Backup	15	3	$179.95
P0017	Serial Mouse	150	50	$69.95
P0018	Trackball	55	0	$59.95
P0019	Joystick	250	100	$39.95
P0020	Fax/Modem 56 Kbps	35	10	$189.95
P0021	Fax/Modem 33.6 Kbps	20	0	$65.95
P0022	Laser Printer	100	15	$1,395.00
P0023	Ink Jet Printer	50	50	$249.95
P0024	Color Ink Jet Printer	125	25	$569.95
P0025	Windows 95	400	200	$95.95
P0026	Norton Anti-Virus	150	50	$75.95
P0027	Norton Utilities	150	50	$115.95
P0028	Microsoft Scenes Screen Saver	75	25	$29.95
P0029	Microsoft Bookshelf	250	100	$129.95
P0030	Microsoft Cinemania	25	10	$59.95
P0031	Professional Photos on CD-ROM	15	0	$45.95

(b) Products Table

Order ID	Customer ID	Order Date
O0001	C0004	4/15/97
O0002	C0003	4/18/97
O0003	C0006	4/18/97
O0004	C0007	4/18/97
O0005	C0001	4/20/97
O0006	C0001	4/21/97
O0007	C0002	4/21/97
O0008	C0002	4/22/97
O0009	C0001	4/22/97
O0010	C0002	4/22/97
O0011	C0001	4/24/97
O0012	C0007	4/24/97
O0013	C0004	4/24/97
O0014	C0006	4/25/97
O0015	C0009	4/25/97
O0016	C0006	4/26/97
O0017	C0011	4/26/97
O0018	C0011	4/26/97
O0019	C0012	4/27/97
O0020	C0012	4/28/97
O0021	C0010	4/29/97
O0022	C0010	4/29/97
O0023	C0008	4/30/97
O0024	C0006	5/1/97
O0025	C0006	5/1/97

(c) Orders Table

Order ID	Product ID	Quantity
O0001	P0013	1
O0001	P0014	4
O0001	P0027	1
O0002	P0001	1
O0002	P0006	1
O0002	P0020	1
O0002	P0022	1
O0003	P0005	1
O0003	P0020	1
O0003	P0022	1
O0004	P0003	1
O0004	P0010	1
O0004	P0022	2
O0005	P0003	2
O0005	P0012	2
O0005	P0016	2
O0006	P0007	1
O0006	P0014	10
O0007	P0028	1
O0007	P0030	3
O0008	P0001	1
O0008	P0004	3
O0008	P0008	4
O0008	P0011	2
O0008	P0012	1
O0009	P0006	1
O0010	P0002	2
O0010	P0022	1
O0010	P0023	1
O0011	P0016	2
O0011	P0020	2
O0012	P0021	10
O0012	P0029	10
O0012	P0030	10
O0013	P0009	4
O0013	P0016	10
O0013	P0024	2
O0014	P0019	2
O0014	P0028	1
O0015	P0018	1
O0015	P0020	1
O0016	P0029	2
O0017	P0019	2
O0018	P0009	1
O0018	P0025	2
O0018	P0026	2
O0019	P0014	25
O0020	P0024	1
O0021	P0004	1
O0022	P0027	1
O0023	P0021	1
O0023	P0028	1
O0023	P0029	1
O0024	P0007	1
O0024	P0013	5
O0024	P0014	3
O0024	P0016	1
O0025	P0012	2
O0025	P0029	2

(d) Order Details Table

FIGURE 2.1   Super Store Database

second query, you would begin in the Customers table and search for Jeffrey Muddell to determine the CustomerID (C0006), then search the Orders table for all records with this CustomerID.

The system is more complicated than earlier examples in that there is a ***many-to-many relationship*** between orders and products. One order can include many products, and at the same time a specific product can appear in many orders. The implementation of a many-to-many relationship requires an additional table, the Order Details table, containing (at a minimum) the primary keys of the individual tables.

The Order Details table will contain many records with the same OrderID, because there is a separate record for each product in a given order. It will also contain many records with the same ProductID, because there is a separate record for every order containing that product. However, the *combination* of OrderID and ProductID is unique, and this ***combined key*** becomes the primary key in the Order Details table. The Order Details table also contains an additional field (Quantity) whose value depends on the primary key (the *combination* of OrderID and ProductID). Thus:

Query: How many units of product P0014 were included in order O0001?
Answer: Order O0001 included four units of product P0014. (The order also included one unit of Product P0013 and one unit of P0027.)

The Order Details table has four records with a ProductID of P0014. It also has three records with an OrderID of O0001. There is, however, only one record with a ProductID P0014 *and* an OrderID O0001, which is for four units.

The Order Details table makes it possible to determine all products in one order or all orders for one product. You can also use the Products table in conjunction with the Order Details table to determine the names of those products. Consider:

Query: Which orders include a Pentium desktop/166 with MMX?
Answer: A Pentium desktop/166 with MMX is found in orders O0002 and O0008.

Query: Which products were included in Order O0003?
Answer: Order O0003 consisted of products P0005 (a Pentium laptop/133), P0020 (a 56Kbps fax/modem), and P0022 (a laser printer).

To answer the first query, you would begin in the Products table to find the ProductID for a Pentium desktop/166 with MMX (P0001). You would then search the Order Details table for records containing a ProductID of P0001, which in turn identifies orders O0002 and O0008. The second query is processed in similar fashion except that you would search the Order Details table for an OrderID of O0003. This time you would find three records with ProductIDs P0005, P0020, and P0022, respectively. You would then go to the Products table to look up the ProductIDs to return the name of each product.

We've emphasized that the power of a relational database comes from the inclusion of multiple tables and the relationships between those tables. As you already know, you can use data from several tables to compute the answer to more complex queries. For example:

Query: What is the total cost of order O0006?
Answer: Order O0006 costs $998.90.

To determine the cost of an order, you must first identify all of the products associated with that order, the quantity of each product, and the price of each product. The previous queries have shown how you would find the products in an order and the associated quantities. The price of a specific product is obtained from the Products table, which enables you to compute the invoice by multiplying the price of each product by the quantity. Thus, the total cost of order O0006 is $998.90. (One unit of P0007 at $899.00 and ten units of product P0014 at $9.99.)

PRACTICE WITH DATABASE DESIGN

An Access database consists of multiple tables, each of which stores data about a specific subject. To use Access effectively, you must be able to relate the tables to one another, which in turn requires a knowledge of database design. Appendix B provides additional examples that enable you to master the principles of a relational database.

The AutoNumber Field Type

Look carefully at the Customer, Order, and Product numbers in their respective tables and note that each set of numbers is consecutive. This is accomplished by specifying the *AutoNumber field* type for each of these fields in the design of the individual tables. The AutoNumber specification automatically assigns the next sequential number to the primary key of a new record. If, for example, you were to add a new customer to the existing Customers table, that customer would be assigned the number 13. In similar fashion, the next order will be order number 26, and the next product will be product number 32. (Deleting a record does not, however, renumber the remaining records in the table; that is, once a value is assigned to a primary key, the primary key will always retain that value.)

The C, O, and P that appear as the initial character of each field, as well as the high-order zeros, are *not* part of the fields themselves, but are displayed through the *Format property* associated with each field. In other words, the internal value of the first CustomerID is the number 1 (not C0001). The letters function as a prefix and identify the table to which the field belongs; for example, C0001, O0001, and P0001 correspond to the first record in the Customers, Orders, and Products tables, respectively. The zeros provide a uniform appearance for that field throughout the table.

SIMPLIFIED DATA ENTRY

The AutoNumber field type is often assigned to the primary key of a table to ensure a unique value (the next consecutive number) in each new record. This simplifies data entry in situations where the user has no knowledge of what the primary key should be, as in the case of a customer number other than a social security number. The Format property can be used in conjunction with an AutoNumber field to improve its appearance through the addition of a letter prefix and/or high-order zeros.

The Relationships Window

The Relationships window in Figure 2.2 shows the Computer Store database as it will be implemented in Access. The database contains the Customers, Orders,

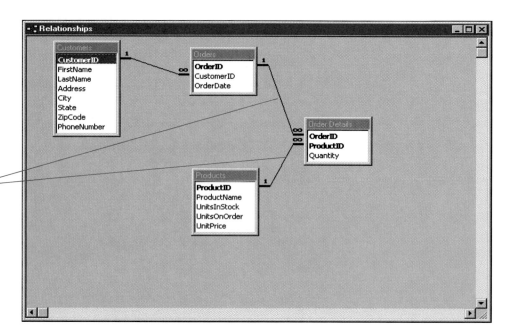

Many-to-many relationship implemented by a pair of one-to-many relationships

FIGURE 2.2   The Relationships Window

Products, and Order Details tables as per the previous discussion. The field lists display the fields within each table, with the primary key shown in bold. The OrderID and ProductID are both shown in bold in the Order Details table, to indicate that the primary key consists of the combination of these fields.

The many-to-many relationship between Orders and Products is implemented by a *pair* of one-to-many relationships. There is a one-to-many relationship between the Orders table and the Order Details table. There is a second one-to-many relationship between the Products table and the Order Details table. In other words, the Orders and Products tables are not related to each other directly, but indirectly through the pair of one-to-many relationships with the Order Details table.

The ***relationship lines*** show the relationships between the tables. The number 1 appears next to the Orders table on the relationship line connecting the Orders table and the Order Details table. The infinity symbol appears at the end of the line next to the Order Details table. The one-to-many relationship between these tables means that each record in the Orders table can be associated with many records in the Order Details table. Each record in the Order Details table, however, can be associated with only one record in the Orders table.

In similar fashion, there is also a one-to-many relationship between the Products table and the Order Details table. The number 1 appears on the relationship line next to the Products table. The infinity symbol appears at the end of the relationship line next to the Order Details table. Each record in the Products table can be associated with many records in the Order Details table, but each record in the Order Details table is associated with only one product.

Referential Integrity

The concept of ***referential integrity,*** which was introduced in the previous chapter, ensures that the records in related tables are consistent with one another. Enforcement of referential integrity prevents you from adding a record to the related table with an invalid foreign key. It means, for example, that you cannot add a record to the Orders table that references a nonexistent customer. Access will, however, let you add an order without referencing a specific customer, unless the CustomerID is a required field or some other validation rule is in effect.

Enforcement of referential integrity will also prevent you from deleting a record in the primary (Customers) table when there are corresponding records in the related (Orders) table. Nor will it let you change the primary key of a record in the primary (Customers) table if there are matching records in the related (Orders) table.

Consider, for example, the application of referential integrity to the one-to-many relationship between the Orders table and the Order Details table. Referential integrity prevents the addition of a record to the related (Order Details) table with a specific value of OrderID unless there is a corresponding record in the primary (Orders) table. It prevents the deletion of a record in the Orders table when there are corresponding records in the Order Details table. And finally, it prevents the modification of the OrderID in any record in the Orders table when there are matching records in the Order Details table.

There may be times, however, when you want to delete an order and simultaneously delete the corresponding records in the Order Details table. This is accomplished by enabling the *cascaded deletion* of related records, so that when you delete a record in the Orders table, Access automatically deletes the associated records in the Order Details table.

You might also want to enable the *cascaded updating* of related fields to correct the value of an OrderID. Enforcement of referential integrity would ordinarily prevent you from changing the value of the OrderID field in the Orders table when there are corresponding records in the Order Details table. You could, however, specify the cascaded updating of related fields so that if you were to change the OrderID in the Orders table, the corresponding fields in the Order Details table would also change.

USE WITH CAUTION

The cascaded deletion of related records relaxes referential integrity and eliminates errors that would otherwise occur during data entry. That does not mean, however, that the option should always be selected, and in fact, most of the time it is disabled. What would happen, for example, in an employee database with a one-to-many relationship between branch offices and employees, if cascade deleted records was in effect and a branch office was eliminated?

HANDS-ON EXERCISE 1

Relationships and Referential Integrity

Objective: To create relationships between existing tables in order to demonstrate referential integrity; to edit an existing relationship to allow the cascaded deletion of related records. Use Figure 2.3 as a guide in the exercise.

STEP 1: Add a Customer (the AutoNumber field type)
➤ Start Access. Open the **Computer Store database** in the **Exploring Access folder.**

➤ The **Tables tab** is already selected in the Database window. Open the **Customers table,** then click the **Maximize button** (if necessary) so that the table takes the entire screen as shown in Figure 2.3a.

➤ Click the **New Record button,** then click in the **First Name field.** Enter the first letter of your first name (e.g., "J" as shown in the figure:

- The record selector changes to a pencil to indicate that you are in the process of entering a record.

- The CustomerID is assigned automatically as soon as you begin to enter data. *Remember your customer number as you will use it throughout the chapter.* (Your CustomerID is 13, not C0013. The prefix and high-order zeros are displayed through the Format property. See boxed tip.)

THE AUTONUMBER FIELD TYPE AND FORMAT PROPERTY

The Format property can enhance the appearance of an AutoNumber field by displaying a prefix and/or high-order zeros. To view (or assign) the Format property of a field, open the table in Design view, select (click) the field name in the upper part of the window, then click the Format property and enter the desired format. Our Customers table, for example, uses the format \C0000, which displays a C in front of the field and pads it with high-order zeros. The Format property determines how a value is displayed, but does not affect how it is stored in the table. The CustomerID of the first customer, for example, is stored as the number 1, rather than C0001.

New Record button

CustomerID assigned automatically as soon as you begin to enter data

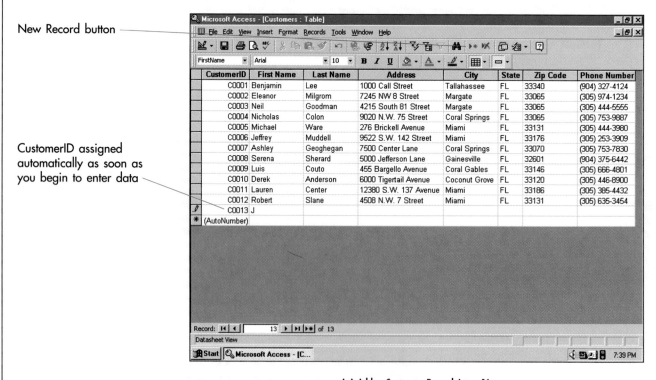

CustomerID	First Name	Last Name	Address	City	State	Zip Code	Phone Number
C0001	Benjamin	Lee	1000 Call Street	Tallahassee	FL	33340	(904) 327-4124
C0002	Eleanor	Milgrom	7245 NW 8 Street	Margate	FL	33065	(305) 974-1234
C0003	Neil	Goodman	4215 South 81 Street	Margate	FL	33065	(305) 444-5555
C0004	Nicholas	Colon	9020 N.W. 75 Street	Coral Springs	FL	33065	(305) 753-9887
C0005	Michael	Ware	276 Brickell Avenue	Miami	FL	33131	(305) 444-3980
C0006	Jeffrey	Muddell	9522 S.W. 142 Street	Miami	FL	33176	(305) 253-3909
C0007	Ashley	Geoghegan	7500 Center Lane	Coral Springs	FL	33070	(305) 753-7830
C0008	Serena	Sherard	5000 Jefferson Lane	Gainesville	FL	32601	(904) 375-6442
C0009	Luis	Couto	455 Bargello Avenue	Coral Gables	FL	33146	(305) 666-4801
C0010	Derek	Anderson	6000 Tigertail Avenue	Coconut Grove	FL	33120	(305) 446-8900
C0011	Lauren	Center	12380 S.W. 137 Avenue	Miami	FL	33186	(305) 385-4432
C0012	Robert	Slane	4508 N.W. 7 Street	Miami	FL	33131	(305) 635-3454
C0013	J						
(AutoNumber)							

Record: 13 of 13

(a) Add a Customer Record (step 1)

FIGURE 2.3   Hands-on Exercise 1

➤ Complete your customer record, pressing the **Tab key** to move from one field to the next. Press **Tab** after you have entered the last field (phone number) to complete the record.

➤ Close the Customers table.

STEP 2: The Relationships Window

➤ Pull down the **Tools menu** and click **Relationships** to open the Relationships window as shown in Figure 2.3b. (The tables are not yet visible.) Maximize the Relationships window so that you have more room in which to work.

➤ Pull down the **Relationships menu** and click **Show Table** (or click the **Show Table button** on the Relationships toolbar) to display the Show Table dialog box.

➤ The **Tables tab** is selected within the Show Table dialog box, and the **Customers table** is selected. Click the **Add Command button** (or double click the **table name**) to add the Customers table to the Relationships window.

➤ Add the **Order Details, Orders,** and **Products** tables in similar fashion. Close the Show Table dialog box.

➤ Point to the bottom border of the **Customers field list** (the mouse pointer changes to a double arrow), then click and drag the border until all of the fields are visible. (The vertical scroll bar will disappear.)

➤ If necessary, click and drag the bottom border of the other tables until all of their fields are visible.

➤ Click and drag the title bars to move the field lists so that they are positioned as in Figure 2.3b.

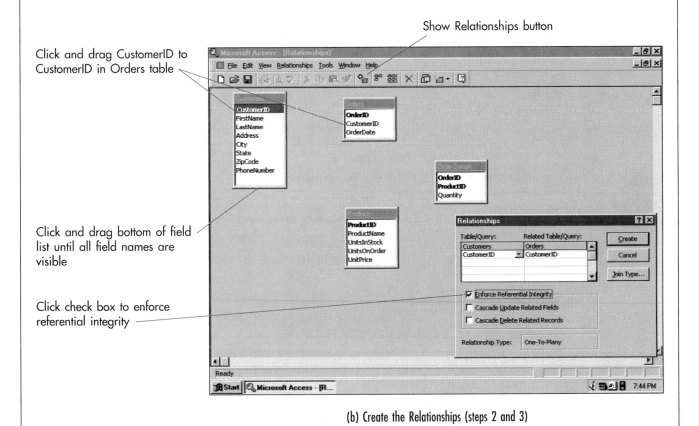

Show Relationships button

Click and drag CustomerID to CustomerID in Orders table

Click and drag bottom of field list until all field names are visible

Click check box to enforce referential integrity

(b) Create the Relationships (steps 2 and 3)

FIGURE 2.3   Hands-on Exercise 1 (continued)

STEP 3: Create the Relationships

➤ Click and drag the **CustomerID field** in the Customers field list to the **CustomerID field** in the Orders field list. You will see the Relationships dialog box in Figure 2.3b when you release the mouse.

➤ Click the **Enforce Referential Integrity** check box. Click the **Create Command button** to establish the relationship and close the Relationships dialog box. You should see a line indicating a one-to-many relationship between the Customers and Orders tables.

➤ Click and drag the **OrderID field** in the Orders field list to the **OrderID field** in the Order Details field list. Click the **Enforce Referential Integrity** check box, then click the **Create Command button.**

➤ Click and drag the **ProductID field** in the Products field list to the **ProductID field** in the Order Details field list. Click the **Enforce Referential Integrity** check box, then click the **Create Command button.**

➤ Click the **Save button** to save the relationships, then close the Relationships window.

RELATED FIELDS AND DATA TYPE

The related fields on both sides of a relationship must be the same data type—for example, both number fields or both text fields. (Number fields must also have the same field size setting.) You cannot, however, specify an AutoNumber field on both sides of a relationship. Accordingly, if the related field in the primary table is an AutoNumber field, the related field in the related table must be specified as a number field, with the Field Size property set to Long Integer.

STEP 4: Open the Orders and Order Details Tables

➤ You should be in the Database window. Click the **Restore button** to return the window to its previous size, then click the **Tables tab** (if necessary) and open the **Orders table.**

➤ Return to the Database window:
  • Click in the **Database window** (if it is visible), *or*
  • Click the **Database Window button** on the toolbar, *or*
  • Pull down the **Window menu** and click **Computer Store: Database.**

➤ Open the **Order Details table.** Your desktop should resemble Figure 2.3c although the precise arrangement of the open windows will be different.

➤ Return to the Database window, then click the **Minimize button** to lessen the clutter on the desktop.

STEP 5: Delete an Order Details Record

➤ Pull down the **Window menu.** Click **Tile Vertically** to display the Orders table and the Order Details table side by side as in Figure 2.3d. (It doesn't matter whether the Orders table appears on the left or right.)

➤ Click the **Order Details window.** Click the row selector column for the last Order Details record for order O0005. You should have selected the record for product **P0016** in order **O0005.**

Click to minimize
database window

Open the Orders table

Open the Order Details table

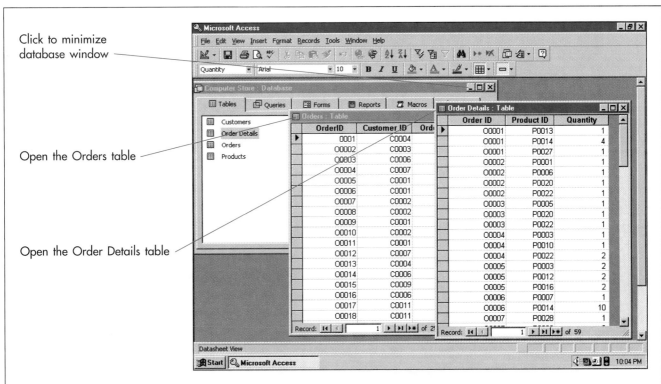

(c) Arranging the Desktop (step 4)

Click row selector for
last Order Details record
for Order O0005

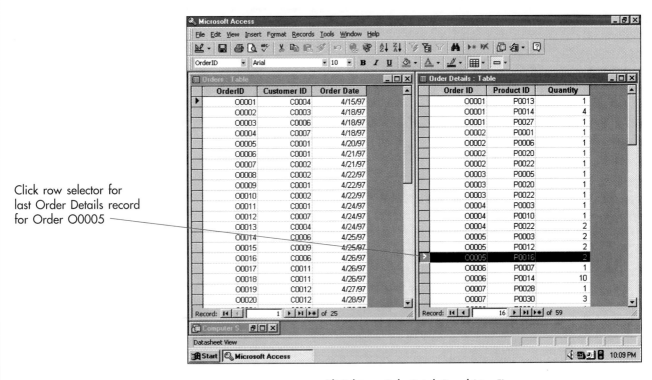

(d) Delete an Order Details Record (step 5)

FIGURE 2.3   Hands-on Exercise 1 (continued)

➤ Press the **Del key.** You will see a message indicating that you have just deleted one record. Click **Yes** to delete the record. The Delete command works because you are deleting a "many record" in a one-to-many relationship.

STEP 6: Referential Integrity

➤ Click the **Orders window.** Click the row selector column for **Order O0005** as shown in Figure 2.3e. Press the **Del key** to (attempt to) delete the record.

➤ You will see the message in Figure 2.3e, indicating that you cannot delete the record. The Delete command does not work because you are attempting to delete the "one record" in a one-to-many relationship. Click **OK.**

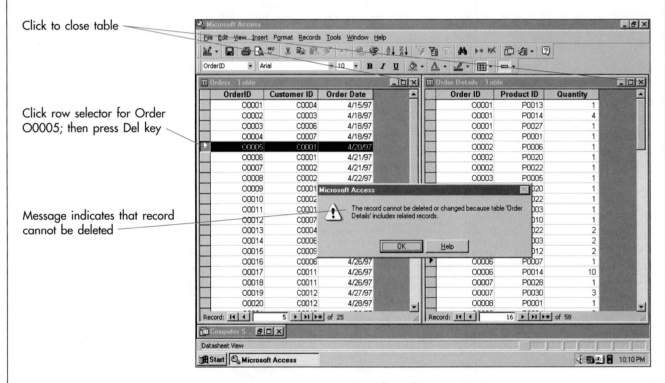

Click to close table

Click row selector for Order O0005; then press Del key

Message indicates that record cannot be deleted

(e) Referential Integrity (step 6)

FIGURE 2.3   Hands-on Exercise 1 (continued)

STEP 7: Edit a Relationship

➤ Close the Orders table. Close the Order Details table. (The tables in a relationship must be closed before the relationship can be edited.)

➤ Pull down the **Tools menu** and click **Relationships** to reopen the Relationships window (or click the **Relationships button** on the toolbar). Maximize the window.

➤ Point to the line connecting the Orders and Order Details tables, then click the **right mouse button** to display a shortcut menu. Click **Edit Relationship** to display the Relationships dialog box in Figure 2.3f.

➤ Check the box to **Cascade Delete Related Records,** then click **OK** to accept the change and close the dialog box.

➤ Click the **Save button** to save the edited relationship. Close the Relationships window.

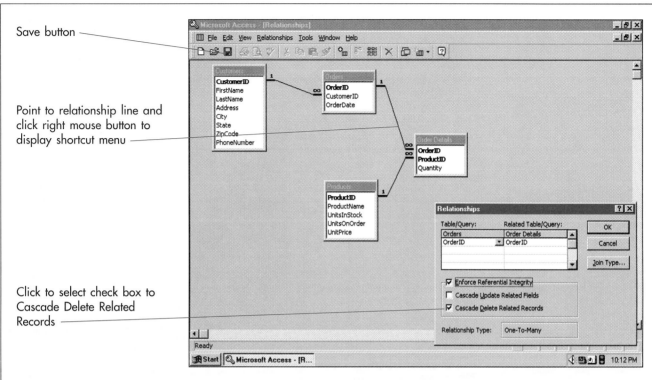

Save button

Point to relationship line and click right mouse button to display shortcut menu

Click to select check box to Cascade Delete Related Records

(f) Edit a Relationship (step 7)

FIGURE 2.3   Hands-on Exercise 1 (continued)

TO CLICK OR DOUBLE CLICK

Click the relationship line connecting two tables to select the relationship, then press the Del key to delete the relationship. Double click the relationship line to select the relationship and bring up the Relationships window to edit the relationship.

STEP 8: Delete the Related Records

➤ If necessary, restore the Database window, then open the **Orders table** and the **Order Details table.** Minimize the Database window, then tile the open windows vertically as shown in Figure 2.3g.

➤ Click the **Orders window** and select the record for **Order O0005.** Press the **Del key** to delete the record.

➤ You will see a message about cascaded deletes, indicating that records in the Orders table as well as related tables are about to be deleted. Click **Yes.** Order O0005 is gone from the Orders table.

➤ The related records in the Order Details table have also been deleted but are displayed with the #Deleted indicator as shown in Figure 2.3g. (The records will be gone the next time the Order Details table is opened.)

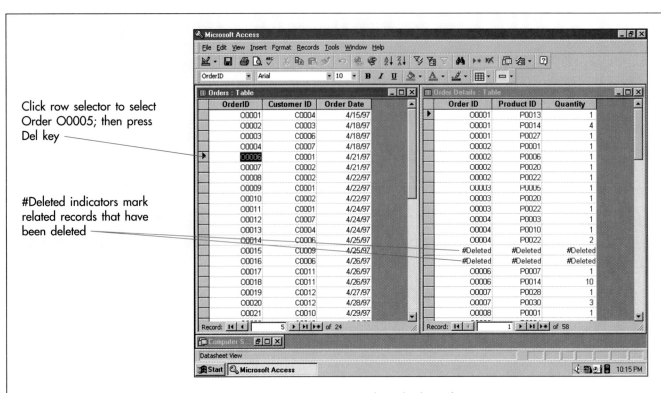

Click row selector to select Order O0005; then press Del key

#Deleted indicators mark related records that have been deleted

(g) Delete Related Records (step 8)

FIGURE 2.3   Hands-on Exercise 1 (continued)

➤ The Delete command works this time (unlike the previous attempt in step 5) because the relationship was changed to permit the deletion of related records.

➤ Close the Orders table. Close the Order Details table.

STEP 9: Document the Relationships

➤ Pull down the **Tools menu,** click (or point to) **Analyze,** then click **Documenter** to display the Database Documenter dialog box.

➤ Click the **Current database tab,** then check the box for **Relationships.** Click **OK.**

➤ Be patient as it takes a little while for Access to check the relationships within the database and to display the Object Definition window in Figure 2.3h. Maximize the window.

➤ Scroll through the report to note the relationship between the Orders and Order Details tables (one-to-many; enforced, cascade deletes), which is consistent with the edited relationship.

➤ Click the **Print button** to print the definition. Close the Object Definition window to continue.

➤ Close the database. Click **Yes** if prompted to save the tables or relationships.

➤ Exit Access if you do not want to continue with the next exercise at this time.

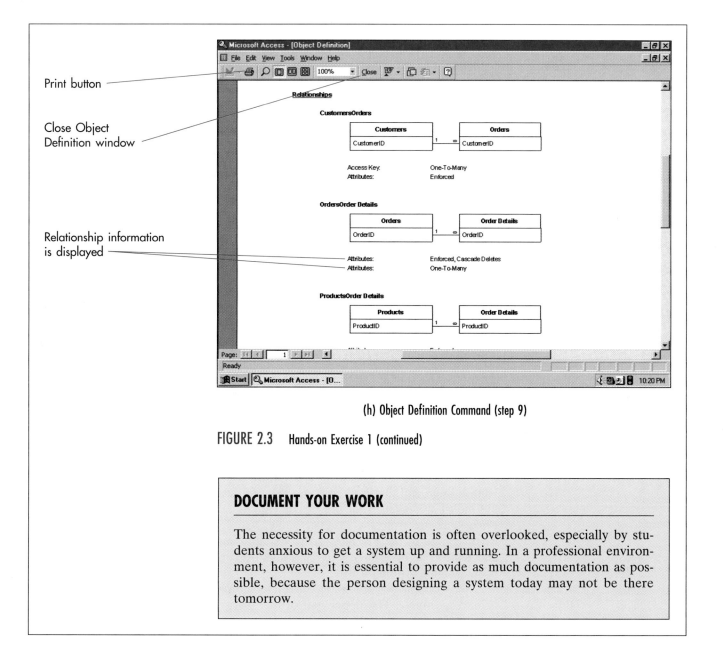

Print button

Close Object
Definition window

Relationship information
is displayed

(h) Object Definition Command (step 9)

FIGURE 2.3   Hands-on Exercise 1 (continued)

DOCUMENT YOUR WORK

The necessity for documentation is often overlooked, especially by students anxious to get a system up and running. In a professional environment, however, it is essential to provide as much documentation as possible, because the person designing a system today may not be there tomorrow.

SUBFORMS, QUERIES, AND AUTOLOOKUP

The main and subform combination in Figure 2.4 is used by the store to enter a new order for an existing customer. The forms are based on queries (rather than tables) for several reasons. A query enables you to display data from multiple tables, to display a calculated field, and to take advantage of AutoLookup, a feature that is explained shortly. A query also lets you display records in a sequence other than by primary key.

The main form contains fields from both the Orders table and the Customers table. The OrderID, OrderDate, and CustomerID (the join field) are taken from the Orders table. The other fields are taken from the Customers table. The query is designed so that you do not have to enter any customer information other than the CustomerID; that is, you enter the CustomerID, and Access will automatically look up (*AutoLookup*) the corresponding customer data.

Main form has fields from both
Orders and Customers tables

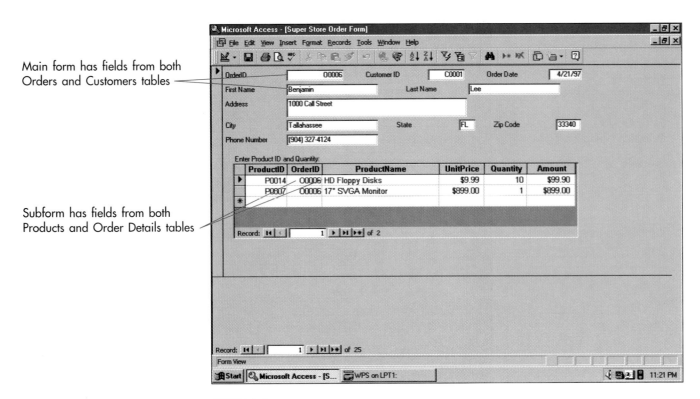

Subform has fields from both
Products and Order Details tables

FIGURE 2.4 The Super Store Order Form

The subform is based on a second query containing fields from the Order Details table and the Products table. The OrderID, Quantity, and ProductID (the join field) are taken from the Order Details table. The ProductName and Unit-Price fields are from the Products table. AutoLookup works here as well so that when you enter the ProductID, Access automatically displays the Product Name and Unit Price. You then enter the quantity, and the amount (a calculated field) is determined automatically.

The queries for the main form and subform are shown in Figures 2.5a and 2.5b, respectively. The upper half of the Query window displays the field list for each table and the relationship between the tables. The lower half of the Query window contains the design grid. Any query intended to take advantage of AutoLookup must adhere to the following:

1. The tables in the query must have a one-to-many relationship, such as customers to orders in Figure 2.5a or products to order details in Figure 2.5b.
2. The join field on the "one" side of the relationship must have a unique value in the primary table. The CustomerID in Figure 2.5a and the ProductID in Figure 2.5b are primary keys in their respective tables and therefore unique.
3. The join field in the query must be taken from the "many" side of the relationship. Thus, CustomerID is from the Orders table in Figure 2.5a rather than from the Customers table. In similar fashion, ProductID is taken from the Order Details table in Figure 2.5b, not from the Products table.

The following exercise has you create the main and subform in Figure 2.4. We supply the query for the main form (Figure 2.5a), but we ask you to create the query for the subform (Figure 2.5b).

Join field in "one"
table is unique

Tables have a one-to-many
relationship

Join field in query is
from "many" table

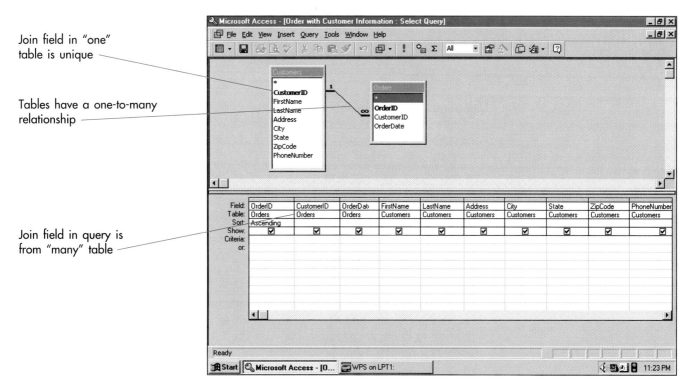

(a) Order with Customer Information Query (used for the main form)

Join field in "one"
table is unique

Tables have a one-to-many
relationship

Join field in query is
from "many" table

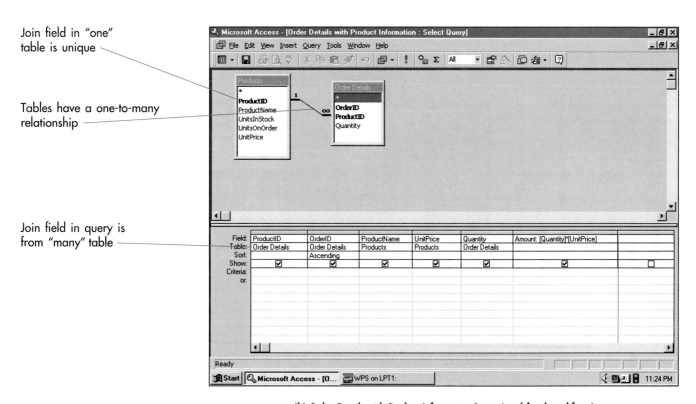

(b) Order Details with Product Information Query (used for the subform)

FIGURE 2.5   Multiple Table Queries

Subforms and Multiple Table Queries

Objective: To use multiple table queries as the basis for a main form and its associated subform; to create the link between a main form and subform manually. Use Figure 2.6 as a guide in the exercise.

STEP 1: Create the Subform Query

➤ Open the **Computer Store database** from the previous exercise. Click the **Queries tab** in the Database window, click **New** to display the New Query dialog box, select **Design View** as the means of creating the query, then click **OK.**

➤ The Show Table dialog box appears in Figure 2.6a with the Tables tab already selected.

➤ Double click the **Products table** to add this table to the query. Double click the **Order Details table** to add this table to the query. A join line showing the one-to-many relationship between the Products and Order Details table appears automatically.

➤ Click **Close** to close the Show Table dialog box. If necessary, click the **Maximize button.**

Double click Order Details table to add it to the query

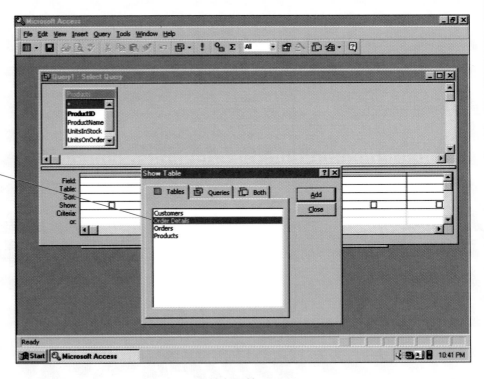

(a) Add the Tables (step 1)

FIGURE 2.6 Hands-on Exercise 2

STEP 2: Create the Subform Query (continued)

➤ Add the fields to the query as follows:

- Double click the **ProductID** and **OrderID fields** in that order from the Order Details table.
- Double click the **ProductName** and **UnitPrice fields** in that order from the Products table.
- Double click the **Quantity field** from the Order Details table.

➤ Click the **Sort row** under the **OrderID field.** Click the **drop-down arrow,** then specify an **ascending** sequence.

➤ Click the first available cell in the Field row. Type **=[Quantity]*[UnitPrice].** Do not be concerned if you cannot see the entire expression, but be sure you put square brackets around each field name.

➤ Press **enter.** Access has substituted Expr1: for the equal sign you typed. Drag the column boundary so that the entire expression is visible as in Figure 2.6b. (You may need to make the other columns narrower in order to see all of the fields in the design grid.)

➤ Click and drag to select **Expr1.** (Do not select the colon.) Type **Amount** to substitute a more meaningful field name.

➤ Point to the expression and click the **right mouse button** to display a shortcut menu. Click **Properties** to display the Field Properties dialog box in Figure 2.6b.

➤ Click the box for the **Format property.** Click the **drop-down arrow,** then scroll until you can click **Currency.** Close the Properties dialog box.

➤ Save the query as **Order Details with Product Information.** Click the **Run button** to test the query so that you know the query works prior to using it as the basis of a form.

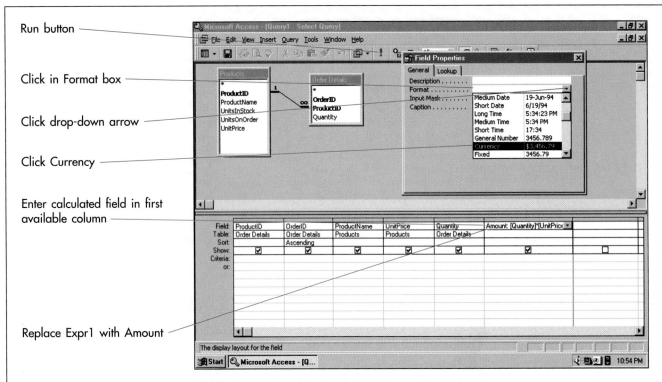

Run button

Click in Format box

Click drop-down arrow

Click Currency

Enter calculated field in first
available column

Replace Expr1 with Amount

(b) Create the Subform Query (step 2)

FIGURE 2.6 Hands-on Exercise 2 (continued)

STEP 3: Test the Query

➤ You should see the dynaset shown in Figure 2.6c. (See the boxed tip below if the dynaset does not appear.)

➤ Enter **1** (not P0001) to change the ProductID to 1 (from 14) in the very first record. (The Format property automatically displays the letter P and the high-order zeros.)

➤ Press **enter.** The Product Name changes to a Pentium desktop/166 with MMX system as you hit the enter key. The unit price also changes, as does the computed amount.

➤ Click the **Undo button** to cancel the change. The ProductID returns to P0014, and the Product Name changes back to HD Floppy Disks. The unit price also changes, as does the computed amount.

➤ Close the query.

A PUZZLING ERROR

If you are unable to run a query, it is most likely because you misspelled a field name in the design grid. Access interprets the misspelling as a parameter query (see page 79) and asks you to enter a parameter value (the erroneous field name is displayed in the dialog box). Press the Esc key to exit the query and return to the Design view. Click the field row for the problem field and make the necessary correction.

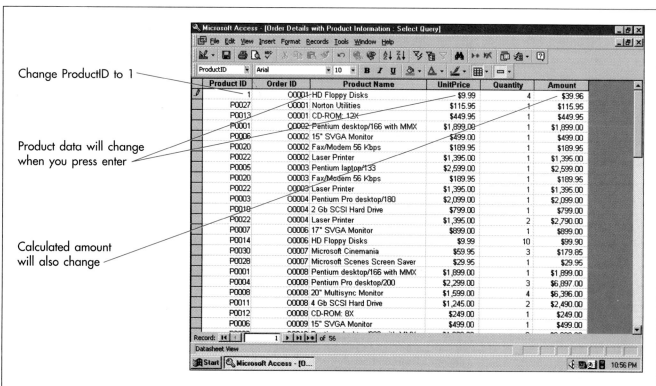

Change ProductID to 1

Product data will change when you press enter

Calculated amount will also change

(c) Test the Query (step 3)

FIGURE 2.6   Hands-on Exercise 2 (continued)

STEP 4: Create the Orders Form

➤ You should be back in the Database window. Click the **Forms tab.** Click the **New Command button** to display the New Form dialog box, click **Form Wizard** in the list box, then click the **drop-down arrow** to display the available tables and queries.

➤ Select the **Order with Customer Information query** (the query we provided) as the basis for the form, then click **OK** to start the Form Wizard.

➤ You should see the Form Wizard dialog box, which displays all of the fields in the selected query. Click the **>> button** to enter all of the fields onto the form. Click **Next.**

➤ **By Orders** is selected as the means of viewing your data. Click **Next.** The **Columnar layout** is already selected. Click **Next.** Click **Standard** as the style for your form. Click **Next.**

➤ Save the form as **Super Store Order Form.** Click the option button to **Modify the form's design,** then click the **Finish Command button** to create the form and exit the Form Wizard.

STEP 5: Modify the Orders Form

➤ You should see the Super Store Order Form in Figure 2.6d. Click the **CustomerID control** to select the control and display the sizing handles, then drag the **CustomerID control** so that it is next to the OrderID.

➤ Click and drag the **OrderDate control** so that it is next to the CustomerID. (The width of the form will change automatically, but you will need to extend the width a little further when you release the mouse.)

Save button

Click CustomerID control,
then drag it next to OrderID
control

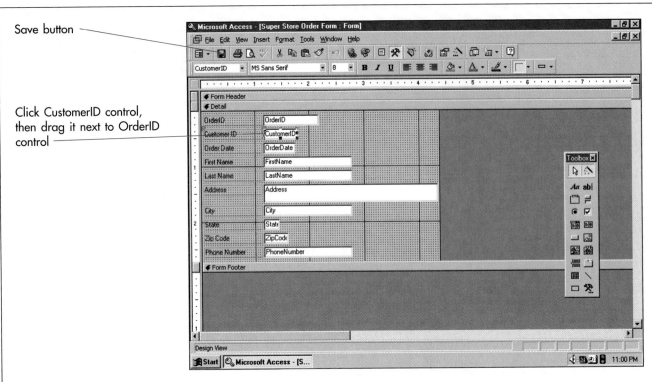

(d) Create the Super Store Order Form (steps 4 and 5)

FIGURE 2.6   Hands-on Exercise 2 (continued)

➤ Click and drag the other controls to complete the form:
  • Click and drag the **LastName control** so that it is next to the FirstName control.
  • Click and drag the **Address control** under the control for FirstName.
  • Place the controls for **City, State,** and **ZipCode** on the same line and move them under the Address control.
  • Move the control for **PhoneNumber** under the control for City.
  • Move all of the controls under the OrderID control.
➤ Click the **Save button** to save the form.

SIZING OR MOVING A CONTROL AND ITS LABEL

A bound control is created with an attached label. Select (click) the control, and the control has sizing handles and a move handle, but the label has only a move handle. Select the label (instead of the control) and the opposite occurs: The control has only a move handle, but the label will have both sizing handles and a move handle. To move a control and its label, click and drag the border of either object. To move either the control or its label, click and drag the move handle (a tiny square in the upper-left corner) of the appropriate object.

STEP 6: Create the Order Details Subform

➤ Click and drag the bottom edge of the **Detail section** so that you have approximately 2 inches of blank space as shown in Figure 2.6e. (This is where the subform will go.)

➤ Click the **Subform/Subreport button** on the Toolbox toolbar, then click and drag in the **Orders form** where you want the subform to go. Release the mouse to begin the Subform/Subreport Wizard.

➤ The **Table/Query option button** is selected, indicating that we will build the subform from a table or query. Click **Next.**

➤ You should see the Subform/Subreport dialog box. Click the **drop-down arrow** on the Tables and Queries list box to select the **Order Details with Product Information query** as shown in Figure 2.6e. (This is the query you created in steps 1 and 2.)

➤ Click the **>> button** to enter all of the fields in the query onto the subform. Click **Next.**

➤ The next step asks you to define the fields that link the main form to the subform: The option button to **Choose from a list** is selected. The selected link will **Show Order Details with Product Information.** Click **Next.**

➤ The Wizard suggests **Order Details with Product Information subform** as the name of the subform. Click **Finish** to exit the Subform/Subreport wizard.

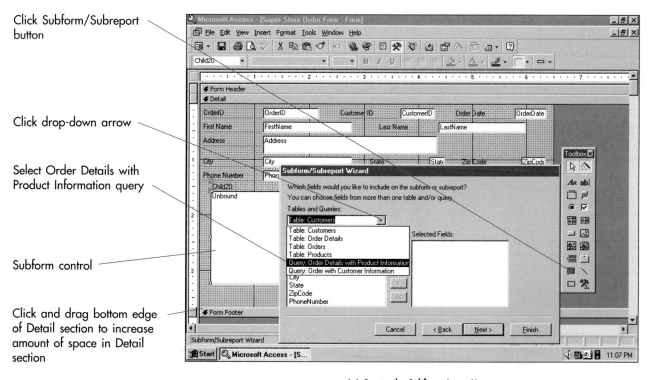

Click Subform/Subreport button

Click drop-down arrow

Select Order Details with Product Information query

Subform control

Click and drag bottom edge of Detail section to increase amount of space in Detail section

(e) Create the Subform (step 6)

FIGURE 2.6   Hands-on Exercise 2 (continued)

STEP 7: The Order Details Subform (Datasheet view)

➤ You should be in the Design view for the Super Store Order Form. The white rectangular control indicates the position of the Order Details with Product Information subform within the main form. Maximize the window.

➤ You need to open the **Order Details with Product Information subform** to check the column width of its columns. Accordingly:

• Deselect the Order Details subform (by clicking anywhere in the main form), then double click the **Order Details with Product Information subform** to open it. Change to the Datasheet view, *or*

• Change to the **Database window,** click the **Forms tab,** and open the **Order Details subform.**

➤ You should see the Datasheet view of the Order Details with Product Information subform as shown in Figure 2.6f. Click and drag the various column headings until you can read all of the information.

➤ Click the **Save button** to save the new layout, then close the subform. This returns you to the Design view of the Orders form. (Alternatively, you may be back in the Database window, in which case you need to pull down the Window menu to return to the Super Store Order Form.)

➤ Select (click) the label of the **subform control,** then click and drag to select the existing text (Order Details with Product Information subform). Type **Enter Product ID and Quantity** (to provide descriptive help to the user).

➤ Save the completed form.

Save button

Click and drag to size columns

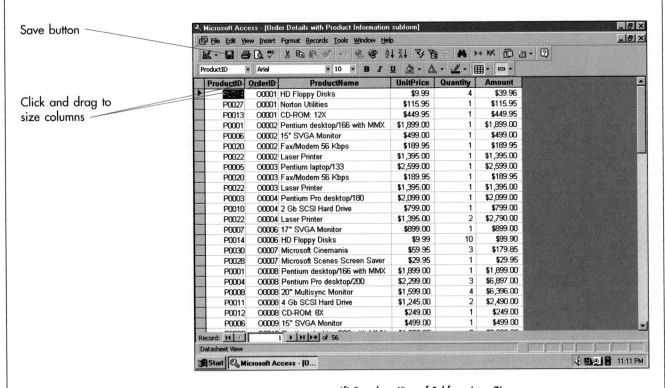

(f) Datasheet View of Subform (step 7)

FIGURE 2.6   Hands-on Exercise 2 (continued)

STEP 8: Enter a New Order

➤ Change to the **Form view** of the Orders form as shown in Figure 2.6g. (You will probably need to return to the Design view to move and/or size the sub-form control.)

➤ Click the **New Record button** to display a blank form so that you can place an order.

➤ Click in the **Customer ID text box.** Enter **13** (your customer number from the first exercise), then press the **Tab** or **enter key** to move to the next field.

  • The OrderID is entered automatically as it is an AutoNumber field and assigned the next sequential number.

  • All of your customer information (your name, address, and phone number) is entered automatically because of the AutoLookup feature that is built into the underlying query.

  • Today's date is entered automatically because of the default value (=Date()) that is built into the Orders table.

➤ Click the **ProductID text box** in the subform. Enter **1** (not P0001) and press the **enter key** to move to the next field. The OrderID (O0026) is entered automatically, as is the Product Name and Unit Price.

➤ Press the **Tab key** three times to move to the Quantity field, enter **1,** and press the **Tab key** twice more to move to the ProductID field for the next item. (The amount is calculated automatically.)

➤ Complete your order as shown in Figure 2.6g. (If necessary, re-open the sub-form in the Datasheet view as described in step 7 to adjust the column widths.)

Click to change to Design view

New Record button

Enter 13 as CustomerID

Enter products for order

Amount is calculated automatically

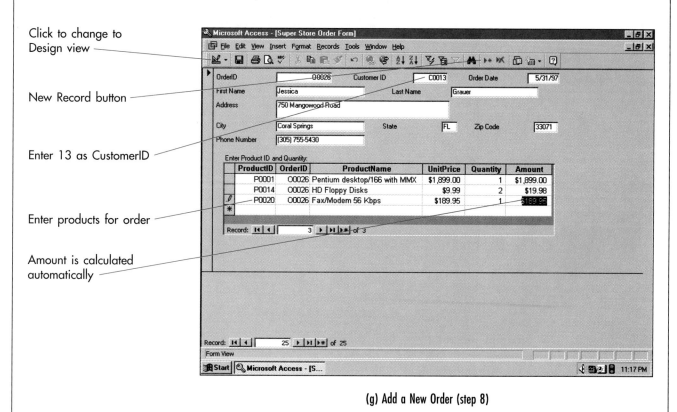

(g) Add a New Order (step 8)

FIGURE 2.6   Hands-on Exercise 2 (continued)

AUTOLOOKUP—WHY IT WORKS

The main form is based on a query containing a one-to-many relationship between Customers and Orders, in which CustomerID is the join field and appears in both tables. The CustomerID is the primary key in the Customers table and is unique in that table. The query, however, must contain the CustomerID field from the Orders table for the AutoLookup feature to take effect. AutoLookup is implemented in similar fashion in the subform, which is based on a query containing a one-to-many relationship between the Products and Order Details tables. The ProductID field is common to both tables and must be taken from the Order Details table (the "many" table) in order for AutoLookup to work.

STEP 9: Print the Completed Order

➤ Click the **Selection Area** to select the current record (the order you just completed). This is done to print only the current record.

➤ Pull down the **File menu.** Click **Page Setup** to display the Page Setup dialog box as shown in Figure 2.6h. Click the **Page tab,** then click the **Landscape option button** so that your form will fit on the page. (Alternatively, you could click the **Margins tab** and decrease the left and right margins.) Click **OK** to close the Page Setup dialog box.

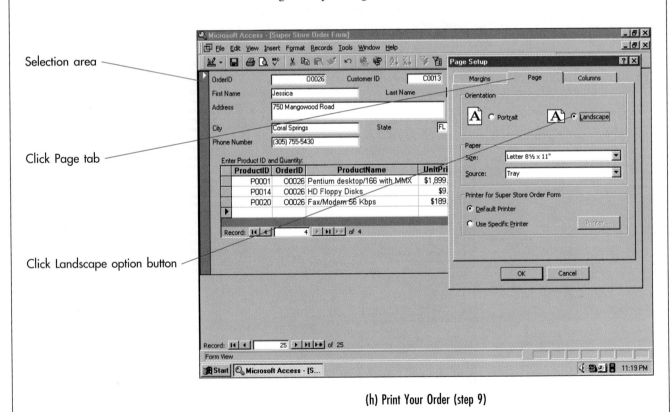

(h) Print Your Order (step 9)

FIGURE 2.6   Hands-on Exercise 2 (continued)

➤ Pull down the **File menu,** click **Print** to display the Print dialog box, then click the option button to specify **Selected Record(s)** as the print range. (You cannot click the Print button on the toolbar as that will print every record.)

➤ Click **OK** to print the form and submit it to your instructor as proof that you did this exercise. Close the form, then close the database. Answer **Yes** if asked to save the changes.

➤ Exit Access if you do not want to continue with the next exercise at this time.

ADDING CUSTOMERS

The form that you just created enables you to add an order for an existing customer, provided you know the CustomerID. It does not, however, let you add an order for a new customer because the underlying query does not contain the primary key from the Customers table. See practice exercises 3 and 4 at the end of the chapter for instructions on how to overcome these limitations.

ADVANCED QUERIES

A select query, powerful as it is, has its limitations. It requires you to enter the criteria directly in the query, which means you have to change the query every time you vary the criteria. What if you wanted to use a different set of criteria (e.g., a different customer's name) every time you ran the "same" query?

A second limitation of select queries is that they do not produce summary information about groups of records. How many orders have we received this month? What was the largest order? What was the smallest order? This section introduces two additional types of queries to overcome both limitations.

Parameter Queries

A *parameter query* prompts you for the criteria each time you execute the query. It is created in similar fashion to a select query and is illustrated in Figure 2.7. The difference between a parameter query and an ordinary select query is the way in which the criteria are specified. A select query contains the actual criteria. A parameter query, however, contains a *prompt* (message) that will request the criteria when the query is executed.

The design grid in Figure 2.7a creates a parameter query that will display the orders for a particular customer. The query does not contain the customer's name, but a prompt for that name. The prompt is enclosed in square brackets and is displayed in a dialog box in which the user enters the requested data when the query is executed. Thus, the user supplies the customer's name in Figure 2.7b, and the query displays the resulting dynaset in Figure 2.7c. This enables you to run the same query with different criteria; that is, you can enter a different customer name every time you execute the query.

A parameter query may prompt for any number of variables (parameters), which are entered in successive dialog boxes. The parameters are requested in order from left to right, according to the way in which they appear in the design grid.

Prompt for customer's name (indicates a parameter query)

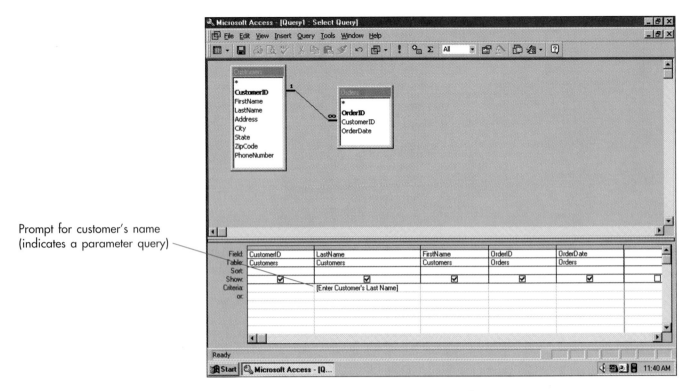

(a) Design Grid

User supplies customer name

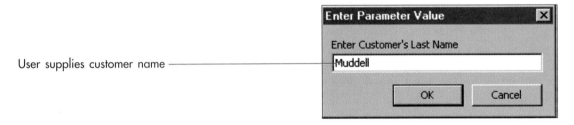

(b) Dialog Box

Dynaset contains records for Muddell only

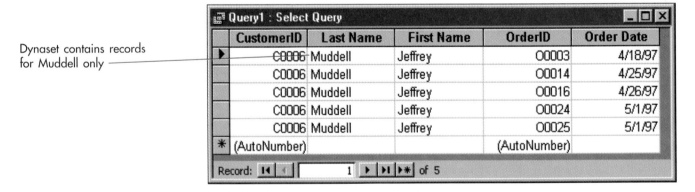

(c) Dynaset

FIGURE 2.7   Parameter Query

Total Queries

A *total query* performs calculations on a *group* of records using one of several summary (aggregate) functions available within Access. These include the Sum, Count, Avg, Max, and Min functions to determine the total, number of, average, maximum, and minimum values, respectively. Figure 2.8 illustrates the use of a total query to compute the total amount for each order.

Figure 2.8a displays the dynaset from a select query with fields from both the Products and Order Details tables. (The dynaset contains one record for each product in each order and enables us to verify the results of the total query in Figure 2.8c.) Each record in Figure 2.8a contains the price of the product, the quantity ordered, and the amount for that product. There are, for example, three products in order O0001. The first product costs $449.95, the second product costs $39.96 (four units at $9.99 each), and the third product costs $115.95). The total for the order comes to $605.86, which is obtained by (manually) adding the amount field in each of the records for this order.

Figure 2.8b shows the Design view of the total query to calculate the cost of each order. The query contains only two fields, OrderID and Amount. The QBE grid also displays a *Total row* in which each field in the query has either a Group By or aggregate entry. The *Group By* entry under OrderID indicates that the records in the dynaset are to be grouped (aggregated) according to the like values of OrderID; that is, there will be one record in the total query for each distinct value of OrderID. The *Sum function* specifies the arithmetic operation to be performed on each group of records.

The dynaset in Figure 2.8c displays the result of the total query and contains *aggregate* records, as opposed to *individual* records. There are, for example, three records for order O0001 in Figure 2.8a, but only one record in Figure 2.8c. This is because each record in a total query contains a calculated result for a group of records.

Contains multiple records for order O0001

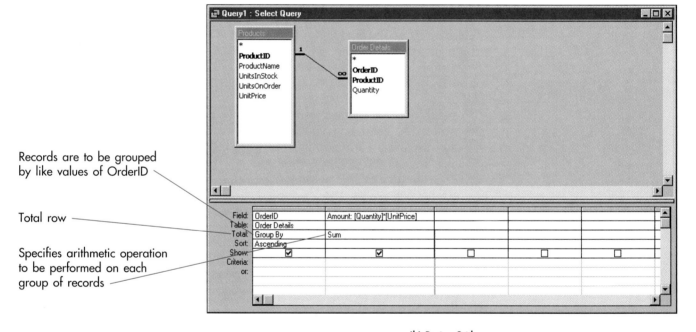

(a) Order Details with Product Information Dynaset

Records are to be grouped by like values of OrderID

Total row

Specifies arithmetic operation to be performed on each group of records

(b) Design Grid

Reflects the total cost for order O0001

(c) Dynaset

FIGURE 2.8   Total Query

The exercise that follows begins by having you create the report in Figure 2.9. The report is a detailed analysis of all orders, listing every product in every order. The report is based on a query containing fields from the Orders, Customers, Products, and Order Details tables. The exercise also provides practice in creating parameter queries and total queries.

Sales Analysis by Order

Prepared by: Jessica Grauer

			Product Name	Quantity	UnitPrice	Amount
O0001	Colon	4/15/97				
			CD-ROM: 12X	1	$449.95	$449.95
			HD Floppy Disks	4	$9.99	$39.96
			Norton Utilities	1	$115.95	$115.95
					Sum	$605.86
O0002	Goodman	4/18/97				
			15" SVGA Monitor	1	$499.00	$499.00
			Fax/Modem 56 Kbps	1	$189.95	$189.95
			Laser Printer	1	$1,395.00	$1,395.00
			Pentium desktop/166 with MMX	1	$1,899.00	$1,899.00
					Sum	$3,982.95
O0003	Muddell	4/18/97				
			Fax/Modem 56 Kbps	1	$189.95	$189.95
			Laser Printer	1	$1,395.00	$1,395.00
			Pentium laptop/133	1	$2,599.00	$2,599.00
					Sum	$4,183.95
O0004	Geoghegan	4/18/97				
			2 Gb SCSI Hard Drive	1	$799.00	$799.00
			Laser Printer	2	$1,395.00	$2,790.00
			Pentium Pro desktop/180	1	$2,099.00	$2,099.00
					Sum	$5,688.00
O0006	Lee	4/21/97				
			17" SVGA Monitor	1	$899.00	$899.00
			HD Floppy Disks	10	$9.99	$99.90
					Sum	$998.90
O0007	Milgrom	4/21/97				
			Microsoft Cinemania	3	$59.95	$179.85
			Microsoft Scenes Screen Saver	1	$29.95	$29.95
					Sum	$209.80

Saturday, May 31, 1997   **Page 1 of 4**

FIGURE 2.9   Sales Analysis by Order

Objective: To copy an existing query; to create a parameter query; to create a total query using the aggregate Sum function. Use Figure 2.10 as a guide.

STEP 1: Create the Query

➤ Open the **Computer Store database** from the previous exercise. Click the **Queries tab** in the Database window, click **New** to display the New Query dialog box, select **Design View,** then click **OK.**

➤ By now you have had sufficient practice creating a query, so we will just outline the steps:

• Add the **Customers, Orders, Products,** and **Order Details** tables. Move and size the field lists within the Query window to match Figure 2.10a. Maximize the window.

• Add the indicated fields to the design grid. Be sure to take each field from the appropriate table.

• Add the calculated field to compute the amount by multiplying the quantity by the unit price. Point to the expression, click the **right mouse button** to display a shortcut menu, then change the Format property to **Currency.**

• Check that your query matches Figure 2.10a. Save the query as **Sales Analysis by Order.**

➤ Click the **Run button** (the exclamation point) to run the query. The dynaset contains one record for every item in every order. Close the query.

Run button

Add all four tables to query

Table row indicates which table field is from

Enter calculated field

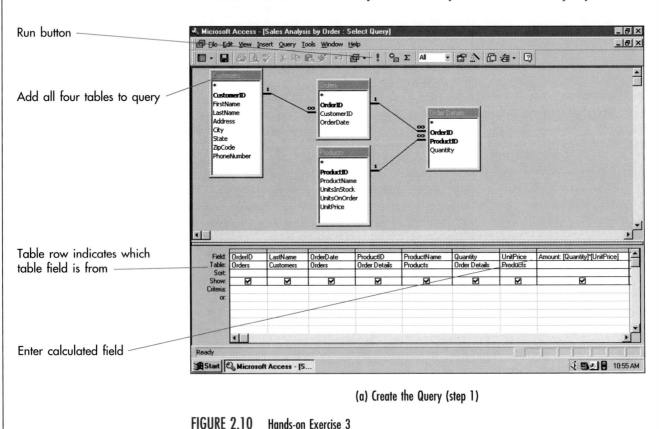

(a) Create the Query (step 1)

FIGURE 2.10   Hands-on Exercise 3

STEP 2: The Report Wizard

➤ Click the **Reports tab** in the Database window, then click the **New Command button** to display the New Report dialog box. Select the **Report Wizard.**

➤ Click the **drop-down arrow** to display the tables and queries in the database, then select **Sales Analysis by Order** (the query you just created). Click **OK.**

➤ By now you have had sufficient practice using the Report Wizard, so we will just outline the steps:

• Select all of the fields in the query *except* the ProductID. Click the **>> button** to move every field in the Available Fields list box to the Selected Fields list, then select the **ProductID field** within the Selected Fields list and click the **< button** to remove this field. Click **Next.**

• Group the report by **OrderID.** Click **Next.**

• Sort the report by **ProductName.** Click the **Summary Options button** to display the Summary Options dialog box in Figure 2.10b. Check **Sum** under the Amount field. The option button to **Show Detail and Summary** is selected. Click **OK** to close the Summary Options dialog box. Click **Next.**

• The **Stepped Layout** is selected, as is **Portrait orientation.** Be sure the box is checked to **Adjust field width so all fields fit on a page.** Click **Next.**

• Choose **Bold** as the style. Click **Next.**

• **Sales Analysis by Order** is entered as the title of the report. The option button to **Preview the Report** is selected. Click **Finish.**

➤ The report you see approximates the finished report, but requires several modifications to improve the formatting. The OrderDate and LastName, for example, are repeated for every product in an order, when they should appear only once in the group (OrderID) header.

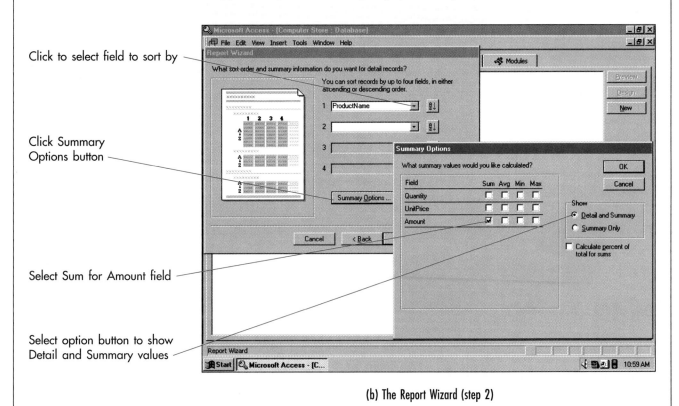

(b) The Report Wizard (step 2)

FIGURE 2.10   Hands-on Exercise 3 (continued)

STEP 3: Modify the Report

➤ Click the **Close button** to change to the Design view to modify the report as shown in Figure 2.10c.

➤ Press and hold the **Shift key** as you click the **OrderDate** and **LastName** controls to select both controls, then drag the controls to the group header next to the OrderID.

➤ Click anywhere in the report to deselect the controls after they have been moved. Press and hold the **Shift key** to select the **OrderID, OrderDate,** and **LastName** labels in the Page Header. Press the **Del key** to delete the labels.

➤ Size the **Quantity, UnitPrice,** and **Amount controls** (and their **labels**). Move the **ProductName control** and its **label** closer to the other controls.

➤ Click the **OrderID control** in the OrderID header. Click the **right mouse button,** click **Properties,** and change the Border Style to **Transparent.** Close the Properties dialog box.

➤ Click the **Label tool,** then click and drag in the report header to create an unbound control under the title of the report. Type **Prepared by:** followed by your name as shown in Figure 2.10c.

➤ Select (click) the first control in the OrderID footer (which begins with "Summary for). Press the **Del key.** Click and drag the unbound control containing the word **Sum** to the right of the group footer so that the label is next to the computed total for each order. Do the same for the Grand Total label in the Report footer.

➤ Click the **Save button** to save the report, then click the **View button** to preview the report.

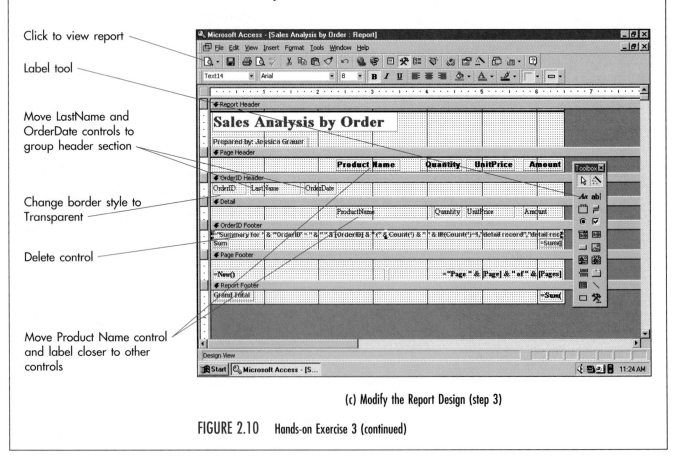

Click to view report

Label tool

Move LastName and OrderDate controls to group header section

Change border style to Transparent

Delete control

Move Product Name control and label closer to other controls

(c) Modify the Report Design (step 3)

FIGURE 2.10   Hands-on Exercise 3 (continued)

STEP 4: Print the Report

➤ You should see the report in Figure 2.10d, which groups the reports by Order ID. The products are in alphabetical order within each order.

➤ Click the **Zoom button** to see the entire page. Click the **Zoom button** a second time to return to the higher magnification.

➤ Click the **Printer button** if you are satisfied with the appearance of the report, or return to the Design view to make any needed changes.

➤ Pull down the **File menu** and click **Close** to close the report. Click **Yes** if asked whether to save the changes.

Zoom button

Report is grouped by OrderID

Products are in alphabetical order

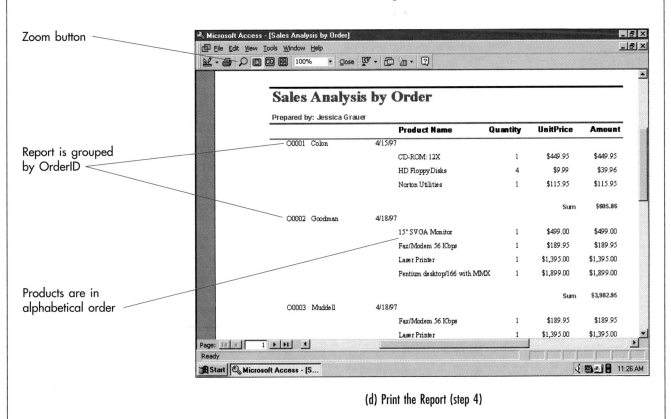

(d) Print the Report (step 4)

FIGURE 2.10   Hands-on Exercise 3 (continued)

STEP 5: Copy a Query

➤ If necessary, return to the Database window, then click the **Queries tab** in the Database window.

➤ Click the **Sales Analysis by Order query** to select the query as shown in Figure 2.10e.

➤ Pull down the **Edit menu.** Click **Copy** to copy the query to the clipboard.

➤ Pull down the **Edit menu.** Click **Paste** to produce the Paste As dialog box in Figure 2.10e. Type **Sales Totals.** Click **OK.** The Database window contains the original query (Sales Analysis by Order) as well as the copied version (Sales Totals) you just created.

COPY, DELETE, OR RENAME A REPORT

The Database window enables you to copy, delete, or rename any object (a table, form, query, or report) in an Access database. To copy an object, select the object, pull down the Edit menu, and click Copy. Pull down the Edit menu a second time, click Paste, then enter the name of the copied object. To delete or rename an object, point to the object, then click the right mouse button to display a shortcut menu, and select the desired operation.

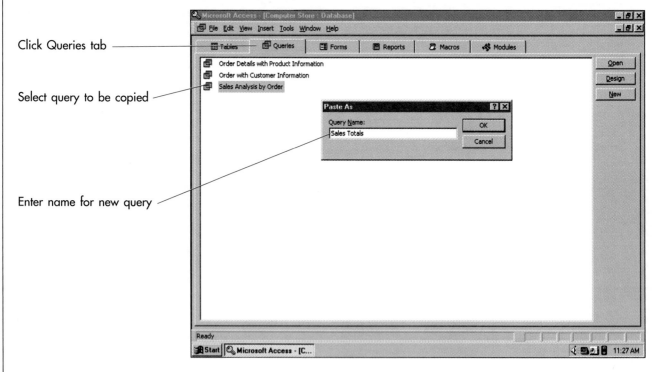

Click Queries tab

Select query to be copied

Enter name for new query

(e) Copy an Existing Query (step 5)

FIGURE 2.10 Hands-on Exercise 3 (continued)

STEP 6: Create a Total Query

➤ Select the newly created **Sales Totals query.** Click the **Design button** to open the Query Design window in Figure 2.10f.

➤ Click the **column selector** for the **OrderDate field** to select the column. Press the **Del key** to delete the field from the query. Delete the **ProductID, ProductName, Quantity,** and **UnitPrice fields** in similar fashion.

➤ Pull down the **View menu** and click **Totals** to display the Total row (or click the **Totals button** on the toolbar).

➤ Click the **Total row** under the Amount field, then click the **drop-down arrow** to display the summary functions. Click **Sum** as shown in the figure.

➤ Save the query.

THE DESCRIPTION PROPERTY

A working database will contain many different objects of the same type, making it all too easy to forget the purpose of the individual objects. The Description property helps you to remember. Point to any object within the Database window, click the right mouse button to display a shortcut menu, click Properties to display the Properties dialog box, enter an appropriate description, then click OK to close the Properties sheet. Once a description has been created, you can right click any object in the Database window, then click the Properties command from the shortcut menu to display the information.

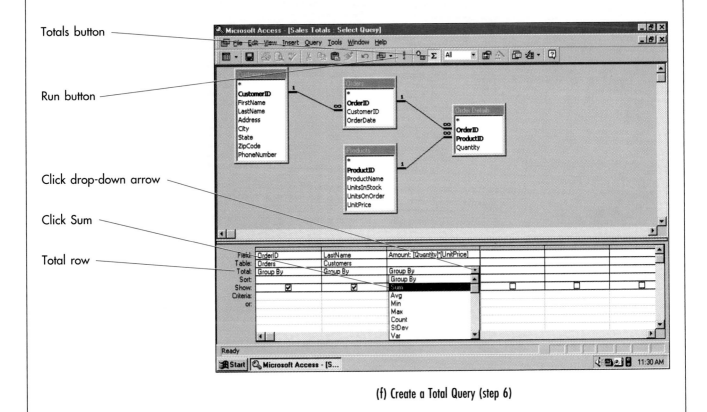

(f) Create a Total Query (step 6)

FIGURE 2.10   Hands-on Exercise 3 (continued)

STEP 7: Run the Query

➤ Pull down the **Query menu** and click **Run** (or click the **Run button**) to run the query. You should see the datasheet in Figure 2.10g, which contains one record for each order with the total amount of that order.

➤ Click any field and attempt to change its value. You will be unable to do so as indicated by the beep and the message in the status bar, indicating that the recordset is not updatable.

➤ Click the **Design View button** to return to the Query Design view.

UPDATING THE QUERY

The changes made to a query's dynaset are automatically made in the underlying table(s). Not every field in a query is updatable, however, and the easiest way to determine if you can change a value is to run the query, view the dynaset, and attempt to edit the field. Access will prevent you from updating a calculated field, a field based on an aggregate function (such as Sum or Count), or the join field on the "one side" of a one-to-many relationship. If you attempt to update a field you cannot change, the status bar will display a message indicating why the change is not allowed.

Design View button

Attempt to change any entry

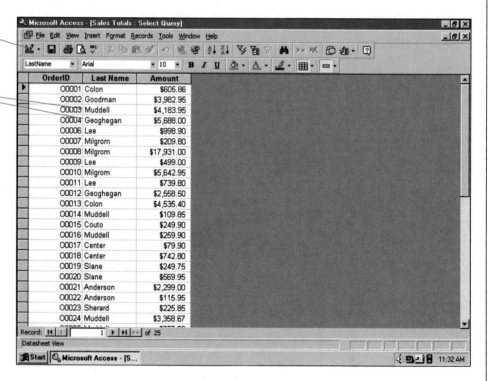

(g) The Total Query (step 7)

FIGURE 2.10   Hands-on Exercise 3 (continued)

STEP 8: Create a Parameter Query

➤ Click the **Criteria row** under **LastName.** Type **[Enter Customer's Last Name].** Be sure to enclose the entry in square brackets.

➤ Pull down the **File menu.** Click **Save As/Export.** Save the query as **Customer Parameter Query.**

➤ Run the query. Access will display the dialog box in Figure 2.10h, asking for the Customer's last name. Type **your name** and press **enter.** Access displays the information for your order(s). Close the query.

THE TOPVALUES PROPERTY

The TopValues property returns a designated number of records rather than the entire dynaset. Open the query in Design view, then click the right mouse button *outside* the design grid to display a shortcut menu. Click Properties, click the box for TopValues, and enter the desired value as either a number or a percent; for example, 5 to list the top five records, or 5% to display the records that make up the top five percent. The dynaset must be in sequence according to the desired field in order for the TopValues property to work properly.

Run button

Save button

Enter your name

Enter prompt for customer's name in square brackets

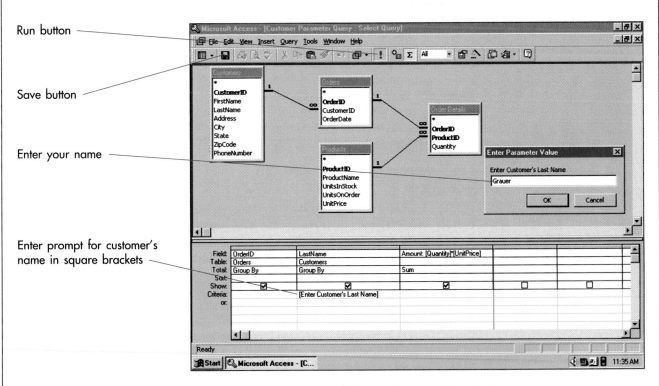

(h) Create a Parameter Query (step 8)

FIGURE 2.10   Hands-on Exercise 3 (continued)

STEP 9: Exit Access

➤ Exit Access if you do not want to continue with the next exercise. (Do not be concerned if Access indicates it will empty the clipboard.)

One of the advantages of an Access database is that it can be easily expanded to include additional data without disturbing the existing tables. The database used throughout the chapter consisted of four tables: a Customers table, a Products table, an Orders table, and an Order Details table. Figure 2.11 extends the database to include a Sales Persons table with data about each member of the sales staff.

The salesperson helps the customer as he or she comes into the store, then receives a commission based on the order. There is a one-to-many relationship between the salesperson and orders. One salesperson can generate many orders, but an order can have only one salesperson. The Sales Persons and Orders tables are joined by the SalesPersonID field, which is common to both tables.

Figure 2.11 is similar to Figure 2.1 at the beginning of the chapter except that the Sales Persons table has been added and the Orders table has been expanded to include a SalesPersonID. This enables management to monitor the performance of the sales staff. Consider:

Query: How many orders has Cori Rice taken?
Answer: Cori has taken five orders.

The query is straightforward and easily answered. You would search the Sales Persons table for Cori Rice to determine her SalesPersonID (S03). You would then search the Orders table and count the records containing S03 in the SalesPersonID field.

The Sales Persons table is also used to generate a report listing the commissions due to each salesperson. The store pays a 5% commission on every sale. Consider:

Query: Which salesperson is associated with order O0003? When was this person hired?
Answer: Cori Rice is the salesperson for order O0003. Ms. Rice was hired on March 15, 1993.

The determination of the salesperson is straightforward, as all you have to do is search the Orders table to locate the order and obtain the SalesPersonID (S03). You then search the Sales Persons table for this value (S03) and find the corresponding name (Cori Rice) and hire date (3/15/93).

Query: What is the commission on order O0003?
Answer: The commission on order O0003 is $209.20.

The calculation of the commission requires a fair amount of arithmetic. First, you need to compute the total amount of the order. Thus, you would begin in the Order Details table, find each product in order O0003, and multiply the quantity of that product by its unit price. The total cost of order O0003 is $4,183.95, based on one unit of product P0005 at $2,599, one unit of product P0020 at $189.95, and one unit of product P0022 at $1,395. (You can also refer to the sales report in Figure 2.9 that was developed in the previous exercise to check these calculations.)

Now that you know the total cost of the order, you can compute the commission, which is 5% of the total order, or $209.20 (.05 × $4,183.95). The complete calculation is lengthy, but Access does it automatically, and therein lies the beauty of a relational database.

(a) Customers Table

CustomerID	First Name	Last Name	Address	City	State	Zip Code	Phone Number
C0001	Benjamin	Lee	1000 Call Street	Tallahassee	FL	33340	(904) 327-4124
C0002	Eleanor	Milgrom	7245 NW 8 Street	Margate	FL	33065	(305) 974-1234
C0003	Neil	Goodman	4215 South 81 Street	Margate	FL	33065	(305) 444-5555
C0004	Nicholas	Colon	9020 N.W. 75 Street	Coral Springs	FL	33065	(305) 753-9887
C0005	Michael	Ware	276 Brickell Avenue	Miami	FL	33131	(305) 444-3980
C0006	Jeffrey	Muddell	9522 S.W. 142 Street	Miami	FL	33176	(305) 253-3909
C0007	Ashley	Geoghegan	7500 Center Lane	Coral Springs	FL	33070	(305) 753-7830
C0008	Serena	Sherard	5000 Jefferson Lane	Gainesville	FL	32601	(904) 375-6442
C0009	Luis	Couto	455 Bargello Avenue	Coral Gables	FL	33146	(305) 666-4801
C0010	Derek	Anderson	6000 Tigertail Avenue	Coconut Grove	FL	33120	(305) 446-8900
C0011	Lauren	Center	12380 S.W. 137 Avenue	Miami	FL	33186	(305) 385-4432
C0012	Robert	Slane	4508 N.W. 7 Street	Miami	FL	33131	(305) 635-3454
C0013	Jessica	Grauer	758 Mangowood Road	Coral Springs	FL	33071	(305) 755-5430

(a) Customers Table

(b) Products Table

Product ID	Product Name	Units In Stock	Units On Order	Unit Price
P0001	Pentium desktop/166 with MMX	50	0	$1,899.00
P0002	Pentium desktop/200 with MMX	25	5	$1,999.00
P0003	Pentium Pro desktop/180	125	15	$2,099.00
P0004	Pentium Pro desktop/200	25	50	$2,299.00
P0005	Pentium laptop/133	15	25	$2,599.00
P0006	15" SVGA Monitor	50	0	$499.00
P0007	17" SVGA Monitor	25	10	$899.00
P0008	20" Multisync Monitor	50	20	$1,599.00
P0009	2.5 Gb IDE Hard Drive	15	20	$399.00
P0010	2 Gb SCSI Hard Drive	25	15	$799.00
P0011	4 Gb SCSI Hard Drive	10	0	$1,245.00
P0012	CD-ROM: 8X	40	0	$249.00
P0013	CD-ROM: 12X	50	15	$449.95
P0014	HD Floppy Disks	500	200	$9.99
P0015	HD Data Cartridges	100	50	$14.79
P0016	2 Gb Tape Backup	15	3	$179.95
P0017	Serial Mouse	150	50	$69.95
P0018	Trackball	55	0	$59.95
P0019	Joystick	250	100	$39.95
P0020	Fax/Modem 56 Kbps	35	10	$189.95
P0021	Fax/Modem 33.6 Kbps	20	0	$65.95
P0022	Laser Printer	100	15	$1,395.00
P0023	Ink Jet Printer	50	50	$249.95
P0024	Color Ink Jet Printer	125	25	$569.95
P0025	Windows 95	400	200	$95.95
P0026	Norton Anti-Virus	150	50	$75.95
P0027	Norton Utilities	150	50	$115.95
P0028	Microsoft Scenes Screen Saver	75	25	$29.95
P0029	Microsoft Bookshelf	250	100	$129.95
P0030	Microsoft Cinemania	25	10	$59.95
P0031	Professional Photos on CD-ROM	15	0	$45.95

(b) Products Table

(c) Orders Table

Order ID	Customer ID	Order Date	SalesPerson ID
O0001	C0004	4/15/97	S01
O0002	C0003	4/18/97	S02
O0003	C0006	4/18/97	S03
O0004	C0007	4/18/97	S04
O0006	C0001	4/21/97	S05
O0007	C0002	4/21/97	S01
O0008	C0002	4/22/97	S02
O0009	C0001	4/22/97	S03
O0010	C0002	4/22/97	S04
O0011	C0001	4/24/97	S05
O0012	C0007	4/24/97	S01
O0013	C0004	4/24/97	S02
O0014	C0006	4/25/97	S03
O0015	C0009	4/25/97	S04
O0016	C0006	4/26/97	S05
O0017	C0011	4/26/97	S01
O0018	C0011	4/26/97	S02
O0019	C0012	4/27/97	S03
O0020	C0012	4/28/97	S04
O0021	C0010	4/29/97	S05
O0022	C0010	4/29/97	S01
O0023	C0008	4/30/97	S02
O0024	C0006	5/1/97	S03
O0025	C0006	5/1/97	S04
O0026	C0013	5/31/97	S05

(c) Orders Table

(d) Order Details Table

Order ID	Product ID	Quantity
O0001	P0013	1
O0001	P0014	4
O0001	P0027	1
O0002	P0001	1
O0002	P0006	1
O0002	P0020	1
O0002	P0022	1
O0003	P0005	1
O0003	P0020	1
O0003	P0022	1
O0004	P0003	1
O0004	P0010	1
O0004	P0022	2
O0006	P0007	1
O0006	P0014	10
O0007	P0028	1
O0007	P0030	3
O0008	P0001	1
O0008	P0004	3
O0008	P0008	4
O0008	P0011	2
O0008	P0012	1
O0009	P0006	1
O0010	P0002	2
O0010	P0022	1
O0010	P0023	1
O0011	P0016	2
O0011	P0020	2
O0012	P0021	10
O0012	P0029	10
O0012	P0030	10
O0013	P0009	4
O0013	P0016	10
O0013	P0024	2
O0014	P0019	2
O0014	P0028	1
O0015	P0018	1
O0015	P0020	1
O0016	P0029	2
O0017	P0019	2
O0018	P0009	1
O0018	P0025	2
O0018	P0026	2
O0019	P0014	25
O0020	P0024	1
O0021	P0004	1
O0022	P0027	1
O0023	P0021	1
O0023	P0028	1
O0023	P0029	1
O0024	P0007	1
O0024	P0013	5
O0024	P0014	3
O0024	P0016	1
O0025	P0012	2
O0025	P0029	2
O0026	P0001	1
O0026	P0014	2
O0026	P0020	1

(d) Order Details Table

(e) Sales Persons Table

SalesPersonID	FirstName	LastName	WorkPhone	HireDate
S01	Linda	Black	(305) 284-6105	2/3/93
S02	Michael	Vaughn	(305) 284-3993	2/10/93
S03	Cori	Rice	(305) 284-2557	3/15/93
S04	Karen	Ruenheck	(305) 284-4641	1/31/94
S05	Richard	Linger	(305) 284-4662	1/31/94

(e) Sales Persons Table

FIGURE 2.11   Super Store Database

The Sales Commission Query

We think it important that you understand how the tables in a database are related to one another and that you can answer conceptual questions such as obtaining the commission for a specific order. Practically speaking, however, you would not do the calculations yourself, but would create the necessary queries to let Access do the work for you.

Consider, for example, Figure 2.12a, which displays the design view of a parameter query to calculate the commissions for a specific salesperson. (This query determines the commissions for Cori Rice, which you computed manually in the previous discussion.) Enter the last name of the sales associate, Rice, and the query returns the dynaset in Figure 2.12b, showing all of her commissions. Note, too, that the commission returned for order O0003 is $209.20, which corresponds to the amount we arrived at earlier.

Rice is entered as
name of salesperson

Prompt in square brackets
indicates a parameter query

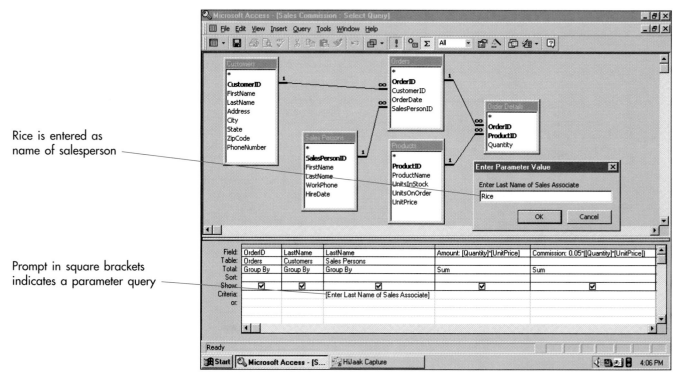

(a) Design View

Commission earned
on Order O0003

(b) Dynaset

FIGURE 2.12   Sales Commissions

The query in Figure 2.12a includes fields from all five tables in the database. The relationships are shown graphically in the top half of the query window and reflect the earlier discussion—for example, the one-to-many relationship between salespersons and orders. These tables are joined through the SalesPersonID field, which is the primary key in the Sales Persons table but a foreign key in the Orders table. (The Orders table has been modified to include this field.) Each field in the Total row contains either a Group By entry or an aggregate function, as explained in the previous discussion on total queries.

The Get External Data Command

The Computer Store database that you have been using in the hands-on exercises does not include the Sales Persons table. You could, of course, create the table manually, just as you would enter any other table. Alternatively, you could import the table from an external database, if it (the Sales Persons table) had been created independently. This is accomplished through the ***Get External Data command,*** which imports an object (a table, query, form, or report) from another database.

One benefit of this approach is that you can take advantage of any work that was previously done. The Sales Persons table, for example, may be part of an employee database in a completely different application. The Get External Data command also enables you to divide a large project (perhaps a class project) among many individuals, then subsequently put the objects back into a common database when the individual work is completed.

The following exercise has you import the Sales Persons table from another Access database. It then directs you to modify the existing Orders table to include a SalesPersonID, which references the records in the Sales Persons table, and to modify the Super Store Order Form to include the salesperson data.

HANDS-ON EXERCISE 4

Expanding the Database

Objective: To import a table from another database; to modify the design of an existing table. Use Figure 2.13 as a guide in the exercise.

STEP 1: Import the Sales Persons Table

➤ Open the **Computer Store database.** Click the **Tables tab.**

➤ Pull down the **File menu.** Click **Get External Data** to display a cascaded menu, then click **Import** to display the Import dialog box.

➤ Click (select) the **Sales Persons database** from the **Exploring Access folder,** then click **Import** to display the Import Objects dialog box in Figure 2.13a.

➤ If necessary, click the **Tables tab,** click **Sales Persons** (the only table in this database), then click **OK.** A dialog box will appear briefly on your screen as the Sales Persons table is imported into the Computer Store database.

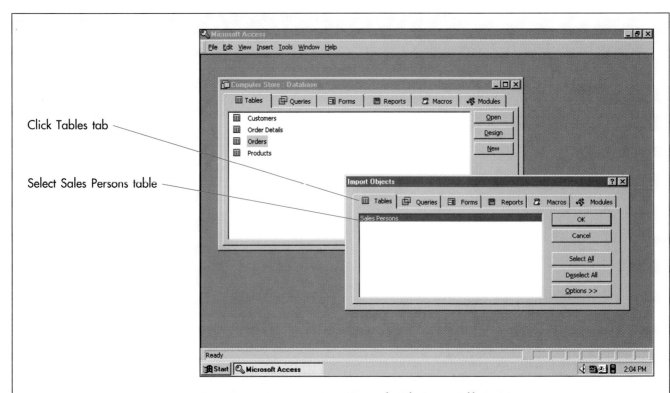

(a) Import the Sales Persons Table (step 1)

FIGURE 2.13   Hands-on Exercise 4

THE DOCUMENTS SUBMENU

One of the fastest ways to get to a recently used file, regardless of the application, is through the Windows 95 Start menu, which includes a Documents submenu containing the last 15 files that were opened. Click the Start button, click (or point to) the Documents submenu, then click the document you wish to open (e.g., Computer Store), assuming that it appears on the submenu. Windows will start the application, then open the indicated document.

STEP 2: Modify the Orders Table Design

➤ Select the **Orders table** from the Database window as shown in Figure 2.13b. Click the **Design button.**

➤ Click in the first available row in the **Field Name** column. Enter **SalesPersonID** as shown in Figure 2.13b. Choose **Number** as the data type. The Field Size property changes to Long Integer by default.

• Click the **Format** property. Enter **\S00.**

• Click the **Default Value** property and delete the **0.**

➤ Click the **Save button** to save the modified design of the Orders table.

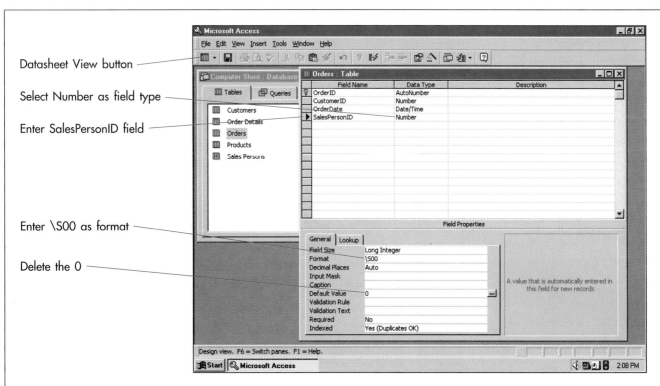

Datasheet View button

Select Number as field type

Enter SalesPersonID field

Enter \S00 as format

Delete the 0

(b) Modify the Orders Table (step 2)

FIGURE 2.13   Hands-on Exercise 4 (continued)

RELATIONSHIPS AND THE AUTONUMBER FIELD TYPE

The join fields on both sides of a relationship must be the same data type—for example, both number fields or both text fields. The Auto-Number field type, however, cannot be specified on both sides of a relationship. Thus, if the join field (SalesPersonID) in the primary table (Sales Persons) is an AutoNumber field, the join field in the related table (Orders) must be specified as a Number field, with the Field Size property set to Long Integer.

STEP 3: Add the Sales Person to Existing Orders

➤ Click the **Datasheet View button** to change to the Datasheet view as shown in Figure 2.13c. Maximize the window.

➤ Enter the **SalesPersonID** for each existing order as shown in Figure 2.13c. Enter only the number (e.g., 1, rather than S01) as the S and leading 0 are displayed automatically through the Format property. (Orders O0001 and O0002 have salespersons 1 and 2 respectively, and are not visible in the figure.)

➤ Close the Orders table.

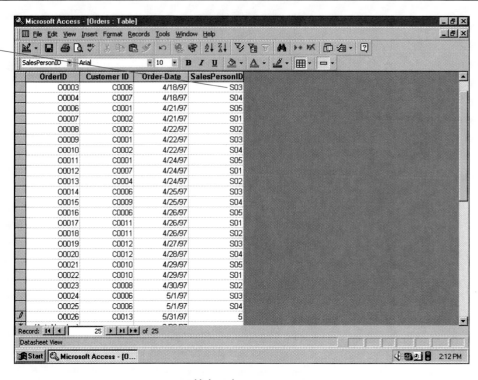

Enter SalesPersonID for each order (enter number only)

(c) Add the Sales Person (step 3)

FIGURE 2.13 Hands-on Exercise 4 (continued)

HIDE THE WINDOWS 95 TASKBAR

The Windows 95 taskbar is great for novices because it makes task switching as easy as changing channels on a TV. It also takes up valuable real estate on the desktop, and hence you may want to hide the taskbar when you don't need it. Point to an empty area on the taskbar, click the right mouse button to display a shortcut menu, and click Properties to display the Taskbar Properties dialog box. Click the Taskbar Options tab (if necessary), check the box to Auto hide the taskbar, and click OK. The taskbar should disappear. Now point to the bottom of the screen (or the edge where the taskbar was last displayed), and it will reappear.

STEP 4: Add a Relationship

➤ Pull down the **Tools menu.** Click **Relationships** to open the Relationships window as shown in Figure 2.13d. (The Sales Persons table is not yet visible.) Click the **Maximize button.**

➤ If necessary, drag the bottom border of the **Orders table** until you see the SalesPersonID (the field you added in step 2).

➤ Pull down the **Relationships menu.** Click **Show Table.** Click the **Tables tab** if necessary, select the **Sales Persons table,** then click the **Add button** to add the Sales Persons table to the Relationships window. Close the Show Table dialog box.

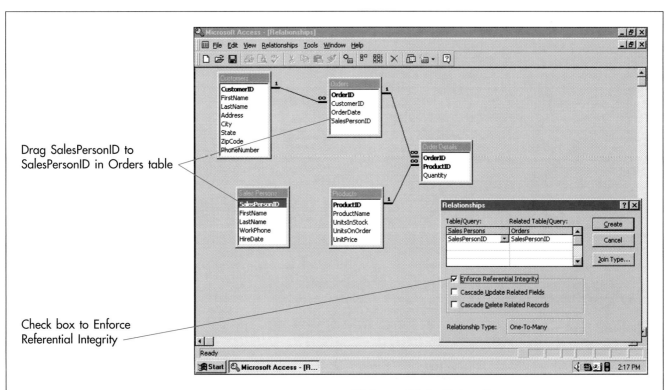

Drag SalesPersonID to
SalesPersonID in Orders table

Check box to Enforce
Referential Integrity

(d) Create a Relationship (step 4)

FIGURE 2.13   Hands-on Exercise 4 (continued)

> Drag the title bar of the **Sales Persons table** to position the table as shown
  in Figure 2.13d. Drag the **SalesPersonID field** from the Sales Persons table
  to the SalesPersonID in the Orders table. You will see the Relationships dialog box.

> Check the box to **Enforce Referential Integrity.** Click the **Create Command
  button** to create the relationship.

> Click the **Save button** to save the Relationships window. Close the Rela-
  tionships window.

STEP 5: Modify the Order with Customer Information Query

> You should be back in the Database window. Click the **Queries tab,** select
  the **Order with Customer Information query,** then click the **Design button** to
  open the query in the Design view as shown in Figure 2.13e.

> If necessary, click and drag the border of the **Orders table** so that the newly
  added SalesPersonID field is displayed. Click the **horizontal scroll arrow** until
  a blank column in the design grid is visible.

> Click and drag the **SalesPersonID** from the Orders table to the last column
  in the design grid.

> Save the query. Close the query.

Drag SalesPersonID
to design grid

Click until blank column
is visible

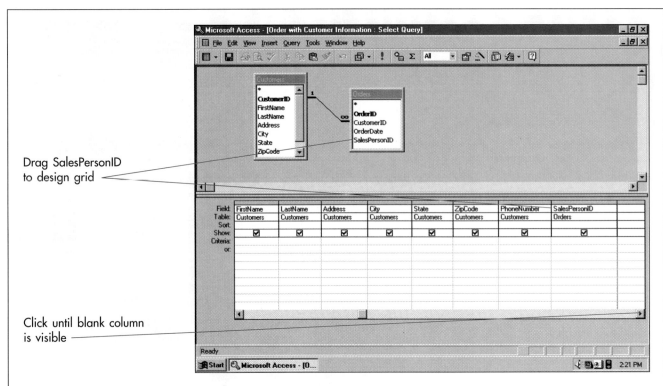

(e) Modify the Order with Customer Information Query (step 5)

FIGURE 2.13 Hands-on Exercise 4 (continued)

STEP 6: Modify the Order Form

➤ You should be back in the Database window. Click the **Forms tab,** select the **Super Store Order Form,** then click the **Design** button to open the form in the Design view.

➤ Right click the **form selector box** and click **Properties** to display the Form Properties box. Click the **Data tab,** click the **Record Source property,** click the **drop-down arrow,** then select **Order with Customer Information.** This updates the form so that it looks for information from the modified (rather than the original) query. Close the Properties box.

➤ Move and size the controls so that there is room to add a control for the salesperson as shown in Figure 2.13f.

➤ Click the **Combo Box tool** on the Toolbox toolbar. Click and drag in the form where you want the combo box to go. Release the mouse. You will see the first step in the Combo Box Wizard.

• Check the option button that indicates you want the combo box to look up values in a table or query. Click **Next.**

• Choose the **Sales Persons table** in the next screen. Click **Next.**

• Select the **SalesPersonID** and **LastName** from the Available Fields list box for inclusion in the Combo box columns list. Click **Next.**

• Adjust the column widths if necessary. Be sure the box to hide the key column is checked. Click **Next.**

• Click the option button to store the value in the field. Click the **drop-down arrow** to display the fields in the query and select the **SalesPersonID** field. Click **Next.**

• Enter **Salesperson** as the label for the combo box. Click **Finish.**

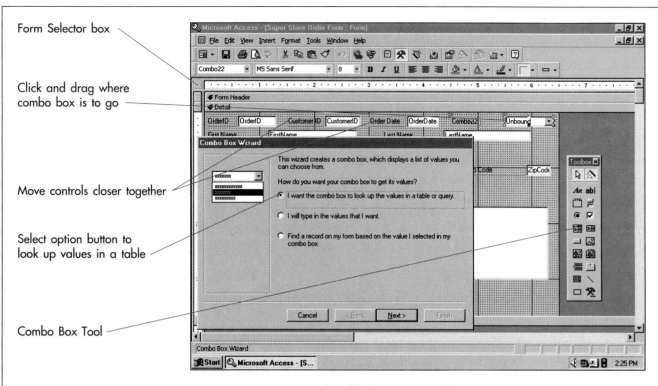

Form Selector box

Click and drag where
combo box is to go

Move controls closer together

Select option button to
look up values in a table

Combo Box Tool

(f) Modify the Super Store Order Form (step 6)

FIGURE 2.13   Hands-on Exercise 4 (continued)

➤ Move and/or size the combo box and its label so that it is spaced attractively
on the form.
➤ Point to the combo box, click the **right mouse button** to display a shortcut
menu, and click **Properties.**
➤ Click the **Other tab.** Change the name of the box to **Sales Person.** Close the
dialog box.
➤ Pull down the **View menu** and click **Tab Order.** Click the **AutoOrder button**
to change the tab order so that the combo box is accessed in sequence. Click
OK.
➤ Save the form. Change to the Form view.

STRUCTURED QUERY LANGUAGE

Structured Query Language (SQL) was developed by IBM during the
1970s and has since become the standard language for accessing a relational database. Access shields you from the subtleties of the SQL syntax through the design grid, which creates the equivalent SQL statement
for you. An SQL statement may appear, however, as the record source
property within the form and can be confusing if you are not familiar with
SQL. Click the Record Source property, click the drop-down arrow to
display the list of queries within the database, then click the desired query
to replace the SQL statement.

STEP 7: The Completed Order Form

➤ You should see the completed form as shown in Figure 2.13g. Click the **New Record button** to display a blank form so that you can place an order.

➤ Click in the **Customer ID text box.** Enter **13** (your customer number from the first exercise), then press the **Tab key** to move to the next field.

• The OrderID is entered automatically as it is an AutoNumber field and assigned the next sequential number.

• All of your customer information (your name, address, and phone number) is entered automatically because of the AutoLookup feature that is built into the underlying query.

• Today's date is entered automatically because of the default value (=Date()) that is built into the Orders table.

➤ Click the **drop-down arrow** on the Sales Person combo box. Select **Black** (or click in the box and type **B**), and the complete name is entered automatically.

➤ Click the **ProductID text box** in the subform. Enter **2** (not P0002) and press the **enter key** to move to the next field. The OrderID (O0027) is entered automatically, as is the Product Name and Unit Price.

➤ Press the **Tab key** three times to move to the Quantity field, enter **1,** and press the **Tab key** twice more to move to the ProductID field for the next item.

➤ Close the Order form.

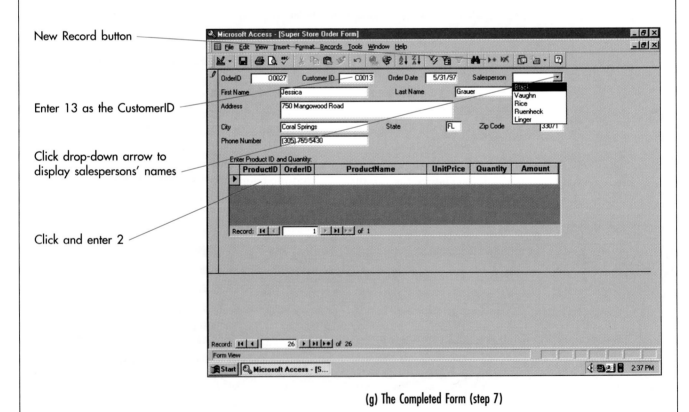

New Record button ——

Enter 13 as the CustomerID ——

Click drop-down arrow to display salespersons' names ——

Click and enter 2 ——

(g) The Completed Form (step 7)

FIGURE 2.13   Hands-on Exercise 4 (continued)

THE STARTUP PROPERTY

The Startup property determines how a database will appear when it is opened. One very common option is to open a form automatically so that the user is presented with the form without having to navigate through the Database window. Pull down the Tools menu, click Startup to display the Startup dialog box, then click the drop-down arrow in the Display Form list box. Select the desired form (e.g., the Super Store Order form developed in this exercise), then click OK. The next time you open the database the designated form will be opened automatically.

STEP 8: Database Properties

➤ You should be back in the Database window. Pull down the **File menu** and click **Database Properties** to display the dialog box in Figure 2.13h.

➤ Click the **Contents tab** to display the contents of the Computer Store database on which you have been working:

- There are five tables (Customers, Order Details, Orders, Products, and Sales Persons).

- There are five queries, which include the Total and Parameter queries you created in exercise 3.

- There are two forms—the main form, which you have completed in this exercise, and the associated subform.

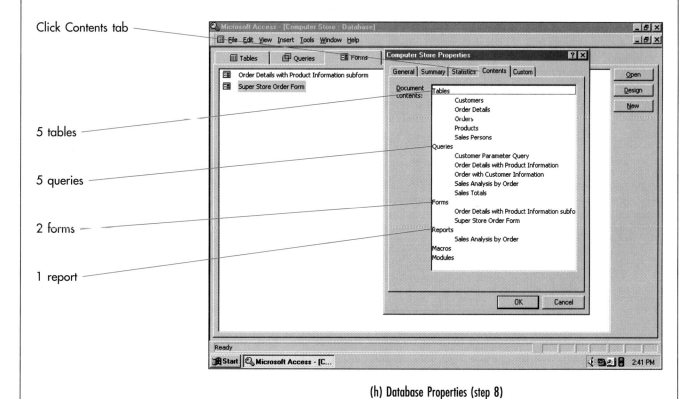

Click Contents tab

5 tables

5 queries

2 forms

1 report

(h) Database Properties (step 8)

FIGURE 2.13   Hands-on Exercise 4 (continued)

- There is one report, the report you created in exercise 3.
- There are no macros or modules. (Macros are covered in the next chapter.)

➤ Close the Properties window.

COMPACTING A DATABASE

The size of an Access database with multiple objects is quite large even if the database contains only a limited number of records. It is important, therefore, to compact the database periodically so that it is stored as efficiently as possible. Close the open database, but remain in Access. Pull down the Tools menu, click Database utilities, then click Compact Database to display a dialog box similar to the Open box. Select (click) the database you wish to compact, then enter a *different file name* for the compacted base. (This ensures that you still have the original database if there is a problem.) Click the Save button to compact the database and close the dialog box. Check that the compacted database is OK, delete the original database, then rename the compacted database to the original name. See online Help for additional information.

STEP 9: Exit Access

➤ Click OK to close the dialog box. Close the Computer Store database. Exit Access. Congratulations on a job well done.

SUMMARY

The implementation of a many-to-many relationship requires an additional table whose primary key consists of (at least) the primary keys of the individual tables. The many-to-many table may also contain additional fields whose values are dependent on the combined key. All relationships are created in the Relationships window by dragging the join field from the primary table to the related table. A many-to-many relationship is implemented by a pair of one-to-many relationships.

Enforcement of referential integrity prevents you from adding a record to the related table if that record contains an invalid value of the foreign key. It also prevents the deletion and/or updating of records on the "one" side of a one-to-many relationship when there are matching records in the related table. The deletion (updating) can take place, however, if the relationship is modified to allow the cascaded deletion (updating) of related records (fields).

There are several reasons to base a form (or subform) on a query rather than a table. A query can contain a calculated field; a table cannot. A query can contain fields from more than one table and take advantage of AutoLookup. A query can also contain selected records from a table and/or display those records in a different sequence from that of the table on which it is based.

A parameter query prompts you for the criteria each time you execute the query. The prompt is enclosed in square brackets and is entered in the Criteria row within the Query Design view. Multiple parameters may be specified within the same query.

Aggregate functions (Avg, Min, Max, Sum, and Count) perform calculations on groups of records. Execution of the query displays an aggregate record for each group, and individual records do not appear. Updating of individual records is not possible in this type of query.

Tables may be added to an Access database without disturbing the data in existing tables. The Get External Data command enables you to import an object(s) from another database.

KEY WORDS AND CONCEPTS

AutoLookup	Join field	Startup property
AutoNumber field	Join line	Sum function
Cascaded deletion	Main form	Table row
Cascaded updating	Many-to-many	TopValues property
Combined key	relationship	Total query
Description property	One-to-many	Total row
Foreign key	relationship	Unmatched Query
Format property	Parameter query	Wizard
Get External Data	Primary key	Zoom box
command	Prompt	
Group By	Referential integrity	

MULTIPLE CHOICE

1. Which tables are necessary to implement a many-to-many relationship between students and the courses they take?
   (a) A Students table
   (b) A Courses table
   (c) A Students-Courses table
   (d) All of the above

2. Which of the following would be suitable as the primary key in a Students-Courses table, where there is a many-to-many relationship between Students and Courses, and further, when a student is allowed to repeat a course?
   (a) The combination of StudentID and CourseID
   (b) The combination of StudentID, CourseID, and semester
   (c) The combination of StudentID, CourseID, semester, and grade
   (d) All of the above are equally appropriate

3. Which of the following is necessary to add a record to the "one" side in a one-to-many relationship in which referential integrity is enforced?
   (a) A unique primary key for the new record
   (b) One or more matching records in the many table
   (c) Both (a) and (b)
   (d) Neither (a) nor (b)

4. Which of the following is necessary to add a record to the "many" side in a one-to-many relationship in which referential integrity is enforced?
   (a) A unique primary key for the new record
   (b) A matching record in the primary table
   (c) Both (a) and (b)
   (d) Neither (a) nor (b)

5. Under which circumstances can you delete a "many" record in a one-to-many relationship?
   (a) Under all circumstances
   (b) Under no circumstances
   (c) By enforcing referential integrity
   (d) By enforcing referential integrity with the cascaded deletion of related records

6. Under which circumstances can you delete the "one" record in a one-to-many relationship?
   (a) Under all circumstances
   (b) Under no circumstances
   (c) By enforcing referential integrity
   (d) By enforcing referential integrity with the cascaded deletion of related records

7. Which of the following would be suitable as the primary key in a Patients-Doctors table, where there is a many-to-many relationship between patients and doctors, and where the same patient can see the same doctor on different visits?
   (a) The combination of PatientID and DoctorID
   (b) The combination of PatientID, DoctorID, and the date of the visit
   (c) Either (a) or (b)
   (d) Neither (a) nor (b)

8. How do you implement the many-to-many relationship between patients and doctors described in the previous question?
   (a) Through a one-to-many relationship between the Patients table and the Patients-Doctors table
   (b) Through a one-to-many relationship between the Doctors table and the Patients-Doctors table
   (c) Both (a) and (b)
   (d) Neither (a) nor (b)

9. A database has a one-to-many relationship between teams and players, which is implemented through a common TeamID field. Which data type and field size should be assigned to the TeamID field in the Players table, if TeamID is defined as an AutoNumber field in the Teams table?
   (a) AutoNumber and Long Integer
   (b) Number and Long Integer
   (c) Text and Long Integer
   (d) Lookup Wizard and Long Integer

10. Which of the following is true about a main form and an associated subform?
   (a) The main form can be based on a query
   (b) The subform can be based on a query
   (c) Both (a) and (b)
   (d) Neither (a) nor (b)

11. A parameter query:
   (a) Displays a prompt within brackets in the Criteria row of the query
   (b) Is limited to a single parameter
   (c) Both (a) and (b)
   (d) Neither (a) nor (b)

12. Which of the following is available as an aggregate function within a select query?
   (a) Sum and Avg
   (b) Min and Max
   (c) Both (a) and (b)
   (d) Neither (a) nor (b)

13. A query designed to take advantage of AutoLookup requires:
   (a) A unique value for the join field in the "one" side of a one-to-many relationship
   (b) The join field to be taken from the "many" side of a one-to-many relationship
   (c) Both (a) and (b)
   (d) Neither (a) nor (b)

14. Which of the following can be imported from another Access database?
   (a) Tables and forms
   (b) Queries and reports
   (c) Both (a) and (b)
   (d) Neither (a) nor (b)

15. Which of the following is true of the TopValues query property?
   (a) It can be used to display the top 10 records in a dynaset
   (b) It can be used to display the top 10 percent of the records in a dynaset
   (c) Both (a) and (b)
   (d) Neither (a) nor (b)

ANSWERS

1. d	**6.** d	**11.** a
2. b	**7.** b	**12.** c
3. a	**8.** c	**13.** c
4. a	**9.** b	**14.** c
5. a	**10.** c	**15.** c

PRACTICE WITH ACCESS 97

1. The Sales Commission report in Figure 2.14 is based on a query similar to the parameter query used to determine the commissions for a particular salesperson. Create the necessary query, then use the Report Wizard to create the report in Figure 2.14. This exercise illustrates the power of Access as both the report and underlying query are based on five different tables.

Sales Commission Report

	Order ID	Order Date	Last Name	Amount	Commission
Black					
	O0001	4/15/97	Colon	$605.86	$30.29
	O0007	4/21/97	Milgrom	$209.80	$10.49
	O0012	4/24/97	Geoghegan	$2,558.50	$127.93
	O0017	4/26/97	Center	$79.90	$4.00
	O0022	4/29/97	Anderson	$115.95	$5.80
	O0027	5/31/97	Grauer	$1,999.00	$99.95
			Sum:	$5,569.01	$278.45
Linger					
	O0006	4/21/97	Lee	$998.90	$49.95
	O0011	4/24/97	Lee	$739.80	$36.99
	O0016	4/26/97	Muddell	$259.90	$13.00
	O0021	4/29/97	Anderson	$2,299.00	$114.95
	O0026	5/31/97	Grauer	$2,108.93	$105.45
			Sum:	$6,406.53	$320.33
Rice					
	O0003	4/18/97	Muddell	$4,183.95	$209.20
	O0009	4/22/97	Lee	$499.00	$24.95
	O0014	4/25/97	Muddell	$109.85	$5.49
	O0019	4/27/97	Slane	$249.75	$12.49
	O0024	5/ 1/97	Muddell	$3,358.67	$167.93
			Sum:	$8,401.22	$420.06
Ruenheck					
	O0004	4/18/97	Geoghegan	$5,688.00	$284.40
	O0010	4/22/97	Milgrom	$5,642.95	$282.15
	O0015	4/25/97	Couto	$249.90	$12.50
	O0020	4/28/97	Slane	$569.95	$28.50
	O0025	5/ 1/97	Muddell	$757.90	$37.90
			Sum:	$12,908.70	$645.43

Saturday, May 31, 1997   **Page 1 of 2**

FIGURE 2.14   Report for Practice Exercise 1

2. The query in Figure 2.15 identifies products that have never been ordered. The query was created through the Unmatched Query Wizard according to the instructions below.

   a. Click the Queries tab in the Database window. Click New, select the Find Unmatched Query Wizard, then click OK.

   b. Choose Products as the table whose records you want to see in the query results. Click Next.

   c. Choose Order Details as the table that contains the related records. Click Next.

   d. ProductID is automatically selected as the matching field. Click Next.

   e. Select every field from the Available Fields list. Click Next.

   f. Products without Matching Order Details is entered as the name of the query. Click the Finish Command button to exit the Wizard and see the results of the query.

   g. What advice will you give to management regarding unnecessary inventory?

   h. What advantage (if any) is there in using the Find Unmatched Query Wizard to create the query, as opposed to creating the query by entering the information directly in the Query Design view?

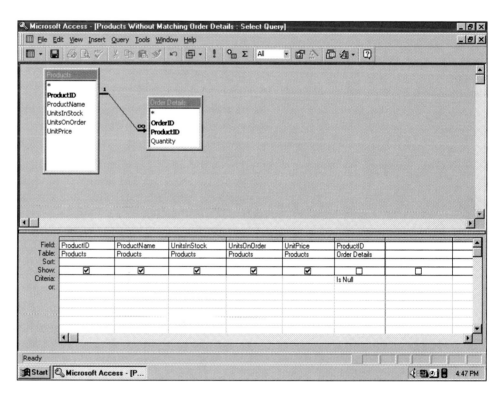

FIGURE 2.15   Screen for Practice Exercise 2

3. Create the form in Figure 2.16, which displays either the information for an existing customer or a blank form to add a new customer. This is accomplished by basing the form on a parameter query rather than the Customers table. Execution of the query displays a blank form when the customer's name is not in the database (as in Figure 2.16), or it will display a completed form when it finds the name. Create the necessary parameter query that

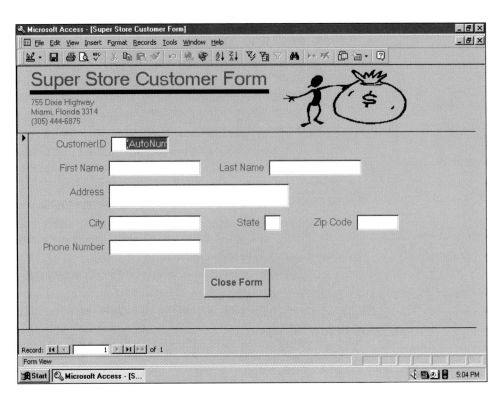

FIGURE 2.16   Screen for Practice Exercise 3

requests the customer's last name followed by the customer's first name, then create the form based on the parameter query. You are free to improve upon our design.

4. The best way to open the Customer form that was created in the previous exercise is by adding a command button to the Super Store Order form as shown in Figure 2.17. The user would click the Find/Add Command button to display the Parameter Value dialog box, then he or she would enter the customer's last name as indicated. The system would return a completed Customer form for an existing customer (from which to obtain the CustomerID) or a blank form to add a new customer. Closing the customer form, in either case, would return you to the Order form where you can enter the CustomerID and the data for the new order.

   a. Open the Super Store Order form that was completed in Hands-on Exercise 4, then use the Command Button Wizard to add the buttons in Figure 2.17. The Find/Add a Customer button should open the form from the previous problem. The Add Order button should add a new order, and the Close Form button should close the Order form.

   b. You can improve the form further by modifying the subform to display a combo box for the product name. This way, the user clicks on the combo box within an order, and selects the products by name rather than having to enter a ProductID. Open the subform in Design view, delete the existing ProductID and ProductName controls, then follow the procedure that was used to add a combo box for the salesperson (see step 6 on page 236). Remember to change the Tab order.

   c. Add the Form Header to improve the appearance of the form.

   d. Add a new order for yourself consisting of a Pentium 133, 17-inch monitor, laser printer, and 28.8 bps modem. Print this order (be sure to print only a single order) and submit it to your instructor.

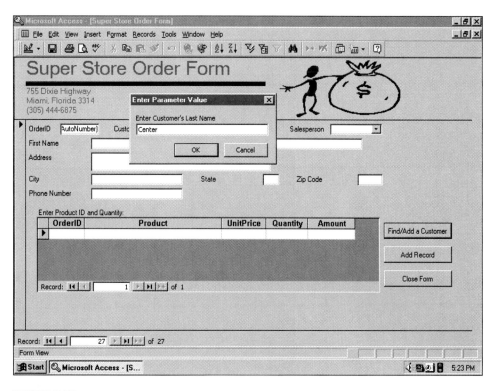

FIGURE 2.17   Screen for Practice Exercise 4

5. Figure 2.18 displays the final version of our Super Store Order form, which contains one additional element—the total amount for the displayed order. Proceed as follows:

   a. Open the Super Store Order form in Design view. Click the Subform/Subreport Wizard tool, then click and drag on the design grid under the existing subform control to create a new subform to display the total amount of the order. The subform should be based on the Sales Total query that was created in the third hands-on exercise.

   b. Add the OrderID and Amount fields to the new form. Select the option to Show Sales Totals for each record in the Order with Customer Information. Accept the suggested name for the subform.

   c. Click off the newly created subform control, then double click the subform to open it. Delete the OrderID controls in the header and detail sections. Delete the Amount label in the Form header. Close the Form header, then size the Amount control to make it smaller.

   d. Right click the Form Selector box to display the Properties dialog box. Change the Default View property to Single Form and the Scroll Bars property to Neither. Suppress the record selectors and the navigation buttons. Save the form.

   e. Size and move the Sales Total subform within the Order Form. Delete the current label and add a new label for the Order total. Save the form.

   f. Change to the Form view, then use the Navigation buttons to move from one order to the next. Each time you view a new order, the total amount is visible at the bottom of the screen.

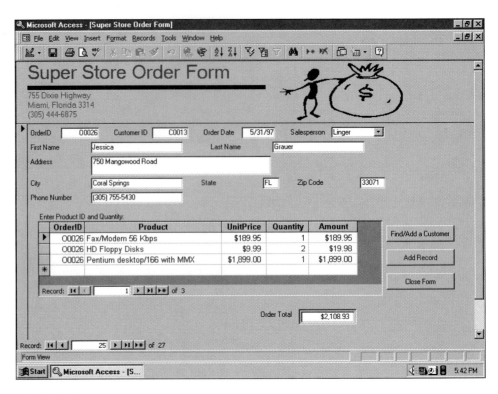

FIGURE 2.18 Screen for Practice Exercise 5

Case Studies

Medical Research

Design a database for a medical research project that will track specific volunteers and/or specific studies. A study will require several subjects, but a specific person may participate in only one study. The system should also be able to track physicians. Many physicians can work on the same study. A given physician may also work on multiple studies.

The system should be able to display all facts about a particular volunteer (subject) such as name, birth date, sex, height, weight, blood pressure, and cholesterol level. It should be able to display all characteristics associated with a particular study—for example, the title, beginning date, ending date, as well as the names of all physicians who work on that study. It should also show whether the physician is a primary or secondary investigator in each study.

Show the required tables in the database, being sure to indicate the primary key and foreign keys in each table. Indicate one or two other fields in each table as appropriate. (You need not list them all.)

The Stock Broker

You have been hired as a consultant to a securities firm that wants to track its clients and the stocks they own. The firm prides itself on its research and maintains a detailed file for the stocks it follows. Among the data for each stock are its symbol (ideal for the primary key), the industry it is in, its earnings, dividend, etc.

The firm requires the usual client data (name, address, phone number, social security number, etc.). One client can hold many different stocks, and the same stock can be held by different clients. The firm needs to know the date the client purchased the stock, the number of shares that were purchased, and the purchase price.

Show the required tables in the database, being sure to indicate the primary key and foreign keys in each table. Indicate one or two other fields in each table (you need not list them all).

The Video Store

You have been hired as a database consultant to the local video store, which rents and/or sells tapes to customers. The store maintains the usual information about every customer (name, address, phone number, and so on). It also has detailed information about every movie, such as its duration, rating, rental price, and purchase price. One customer can rent several tapes, and the same tape will (over time) be rented to many customers.

The owner of the store needs a detailed record of every rental that identifies the movie, the customer, the date the rental was made, and the number of days the customer may keep the movie without penalty.

Class Scheduling

Class scheduling represents a major undertaking at any university. It entails the coordination of course offerings as published in a registration schedule together with faculty assignments. All courses have a formal title but are more commonly known by a six-position course-id. Microcomputer Applications, for example, is better known as CIS120. The first three characters in the course-id denote the department (e.g., CIS stands for Computer Information Systems). The last three indicate the particular course.

The university may offer multiple sections of any given course at different times. CIS120, for example, is offered at four different times: at 9:00, 10:00, 11:00, and 12:00, with all sections meeting three days a week (Mondays, Wednesdays, and Fridays). The information about when a class meets is summarized in the one-letter section designation; for example, section A meets from 9:00 to 9:50 on Mondays, Wednesdays, and Fridays.

The published schedule should list every section of every course together with the days, times, and room assignments. It should also display the complete course title, number of credits, and the name of the faculty member assigned to that section. It should be able to list all classes taught by a particular faculty member or all sections of a particular course. Design a relational database to satisfy these requirements.

BUILDING APPLICATIONS: INTRODUCTION TO MACROS AND PROTOTYPING

After reading this chapter you will be able to:

1. Explain how forms are used to develop an automated user interface; create a form with multiple command buttons to serve as a menu.
2. Use the Link Tables command to associate tables in one database with objects in a different database.
3. Describe how macros are used to automate an application; explain the special role of the AutoExec macro.
4. Describe the components of the Macro window; distinguish between a macro action and an argument.
5. Use the On Click property to change the action associated with a command button.
6. Use the Find Unmatched Query Wizard to identify records in one table that do not have a corresponding record in another table.
7. Explain how prototyping facilitates the development of an application; use the MsgBox action as the basis of a prototype macro.
8. Create a macro group; explain how macro groups simplify the organization of macros within a database.

OVERVIEW

You have completed several chapters in our text and have developed some impressive databases. You have created systems with multiple tables that contained both one-to-many and many-to-many relationships. You have created sophisticated forms and queries that relate data from several tables to one another. In short, you have become proficient in Microsoft Access and have learned how to create the objects (tables, forms, queries, and reports) that comprise a database.

You have not, however, developed a user interface that ties the objects together so that the database is easy to use. In other words, you have created a database, but have not yet created an application. An application contains the same objects as a database. The difference is subtle and has to do with how the objects are presented to the user. An application has an intuitive user interface that does not require a knowledge of Microsoft Access on the part of the user.

This chapter has you develop an application for the Coral Springs Soccer Association. The discussion starts with an existing database that is expanded to include a user interface that enables a nontechnical person to use the application. The application includes macros that automate common command sequences and further simplify the system for the end user. And finally, the application includes the concept of prototyping, which enables you to demonstrate its "look and feel" to potential users, even before the application is complete.

Four hands-on exercises are included that progressively build the application. The end result is a system that is fully functional and one that can be used by any youth-oriented sports league.

THE CORAL SPRINGS SOCCER ASSOCIATION

The Coral Springs Soccer Association (CSSA) has approximately three thousand players organized into teams in various age groups. The Association registers the players and coaches, then holds a draft (among the coaches) to divide the players into teams. The Association has designed a database with three tables (Teams, Players, and Coaches) and has implemented the following relationships:

- A one-to-many relationship between teams and players (one team has many players, but a player is assigned to only one team).
- A one-to-many relationship between teams and coaches (one team has many coaches, but a coach is assigned to only one team).

The Access database developed by the CSSA contains multiple forms, queries, and reports based on these tables. There is a Players form through which you add a new player, or edit or delete the record of an existing player. A similar form exists for the Coaches table. There is also a sophisticated main and subform combination for the Teams table that displays the players and coaches on each team, and through which data for any table (Team, Player, or Coach) can be added, edited, or deleted.

The CSSA database contains a variety of reports, including a master list of players in alphabetical order, mailing labels for all coaches and players, a list of players according to their ability rating, and printed team rosters. The CSSA database also contains queries to find a specific player or coach, and to locate all players and/or coaches who have not been assigned to a team.

It would not be difficult for a person knowledgeable in Access to open the database and then select the various objects from the Database window as the need arose. The Soccer database, however, is used by nontechnical volunteers during registration, at which time hundreds of players (accompanied by their parents) sign up for the coming season. It is essential, therefore, that the database be easy to use, and that a nontechnical person be able to register the players and produce the queries and reports. This gives rise to the menu-driven system in Figure 3.1.

The *user interface* (the screens the user sees) is the most important part of any system, at least from the viewpoint of the end-user. A system that is intuitive and easy to use will be successful. Conversely, a system that is difficult to use or visually unappealing is sure to fail. You don't have to know anything about soccer or the workings of our system to use the menu in Figure 3.1.

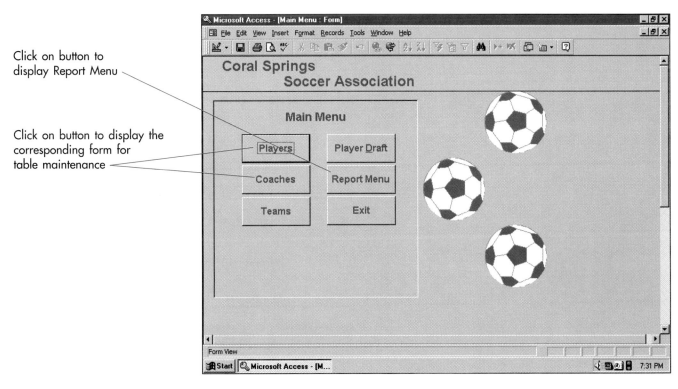

Click on button to display Report Menu

Click on button to display the corresponding form for table maintenance

FIGURE 3.1   A User Interface

You would, for example, click the Players, Coaches, or Teams command buttons and expect a screen that would enable you to maintain records in the corresponding table. In similar fashion, you would click the Report Menu button to display a menu listing the various reports, each of which could be produced by clicking the corresponding button. You would click the Player Draft button to assign players to teams after registration has taken place.

The menu in Figure 3.1 is a form similar to those that you have developed in other chapters. Each of the command buttons was created through the Command Button Wizard. The form is created in such a way that when a user clicks a button, Access interprets the click as an *event* and responds with an action that has been assigned to that event. Clicking the Teams button, for example, causes Access to open the Teams form. Clicking the Players button is a different event and causes Access to open the Players form.

To develop a menu, you create a form, then add command buttons through the Command Button Wizard. The Wizard prompts you for the action you want to take in response to the event (e.g., clicking the button), then creates an *event procedure* for you. The event procedure is a Visual Basic program that executes automatically each time the event occurs. Eventually, you may want to learn Access Basic so that you can develop more advanced applications and create your own procedures. Access Basic is, however, beyond the scope of this text.

THE LINK TABLES COMMAND

All applications consist of tables *and* objects (forms, queries, reports, macros, and modules) based on those tables. The tables and objects may be stored in the same database (as was done throughout the book), or they may be stored in separate databases, as shown in Figure 3.2. In this example the tables are stored in one database (the Soccer Tables database), while the objects are stored in a different database (the Soccer Objects database).

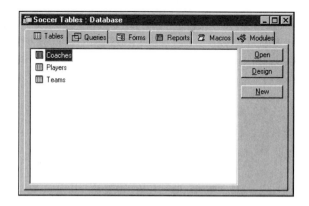

(a) Soccer Tables Database (contains only the tables)

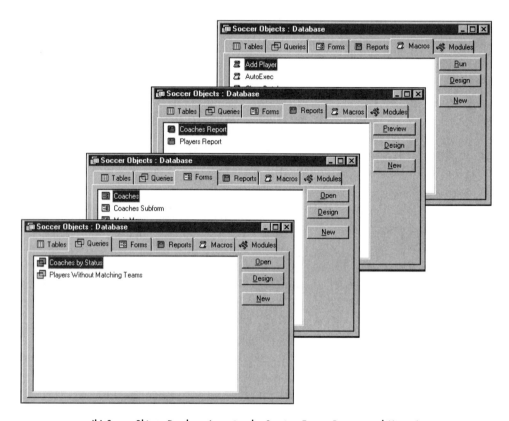

(b) Soccer Objects Database (contains the Queries, Forms, Reports, and Macros)

FIGURE 3.2   Separating the Tables and Objects

One advantage of separating the data from the other objects is that you can create new versions of an application *without* disturbing the data. In other words, you can develop an upgraded release of the application (Soccer Objects Two) and distribute it to the users without affecting the various tables. The new version contains additional and/or improved features (e.g., new reports and queries) but attaches to the original data, and thus retains all of the transactions that have been processed.

The approach also provides flexibility with respect to where the tables and the associated objects are stored. It is common, for example, to store the tables on a network drive, which can be accessed by multiple users. The other objects, however, would be stored on the users' local drives. Thus, you could create different sets of objects for different users. The Director, for example, may be given access to all tables within the database where he or she can perform any type of operation. Other users, however, may be given only restricted access, such as being able to add players or coaches, but prevented from making team assignments.

The tables and objects are tied to one another through the **Link Tables command,** which is executed from within the Soccer Objects database. The command associates the tables in one database (Soccer Tables) with the objects in another database (Soccer Objects). Once the Link Tables command has been executed, it is as though the tables were in the Soccer Objects database with respect to maintaining the data. You can add, edit, and delete a record in any (linked) table; you cannot, however, change the design of a linked table from within the Soccer Objects database.

The following exercise has you link the tables from one database to the objects in a different database, then develop the Main Menu (shown earlier in Figure 3.1) for the Coral Springs Soccer Association.

HANDS-ON EXERCISE 1

Creating a User Interface

Objective: To use the Link Tables command to associate tables in one database with the objects in a different database. To create a form with multiple command buttons to provide the user with a menu. Use Figure 3.3 as a guide in the exercise.

STEP 1: Open the Soccer Objects Database

➤ Start Access. Change to the **Exploring Access folder** as you have been doing throughout the text.

➤ Open the **Soccer Objects database** as shown in Figure 3.3a, then click the various tabs in the Database window to view the contents of this database. This database contains the various objects (forms, queries, and reports) in the soccer application, but not the tables.

- Click the **Tables tab.** There are currently no tables in the database.
- Click the **Forms tab.** There are six forms in the database.
- Click the **Queries tab.** There is one query in the database.
- Click the **Reports tab.** There are currently no reports in the database.

➤ Pull down the **File menu,** click **Database Properties,** then click the **Contents tab** to see the contents of the database as shown in Figure 3.3a. Click **OK** to close the dialog box.

DATABASE PROPERTIES

The tabs within the Database window display the objects within a database, but show only one type of object at a time. You can, for example, see all of the reports or all of the queries, but you cannot see the reports and queries at the same time. There is another way. Pull down the File menu, click Database Properties, then click the Contents tab to display the contents (objects) in the database. You cannot, however, use the Database Properties dialog box to open those objects.

No tables

One query

Six forms

No reports

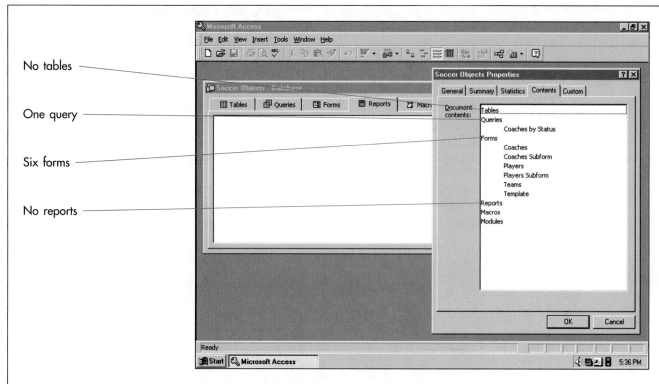

(a) The Soccer Objects Database (step 1)

FIGURE 3.3   Hands-on Exercise 1

STEP 2: The Link Tables Command

➤ Pull down the **File menu.** Click **Get External Data,** then click **Link Tables** from the submenu. You should see the Link dialog box.

➤ Select the **Exploring Access folder.** Scroll (if necessary) until you can select the **Soccer Tables database,** then click the **Link Command button.**

➤ You should see the Link Tables dialog box in Figure 3.3b. Click the **Select All Command button** to select all three tables, then click **OK.**

➤ The system (briefly) displays a message indicating that it is linking the tables, after which the tables should appear in the Database window. (If necessary, click the **Tables tab** in the Database window.) The arrow next to each table indicates that the table physically resides in another database.

IMPORTING VERSUS LINKING

The Get External Data command displays a cascaded menu to import or link an object from another database. (Any type of object can be imported. A table is the only type of object that can be linked.) Importing an object brings a copy of the object into the current database and does not maintain a tie to the original object. Thus, any changes to the object in the current database are not reflected in the original object. Linking, on the other hand, does not bring the table into the database but only a pointer to the table. Any changes to the data in the linked table are reflected in the original table as well as any other databases that are linked to that table.

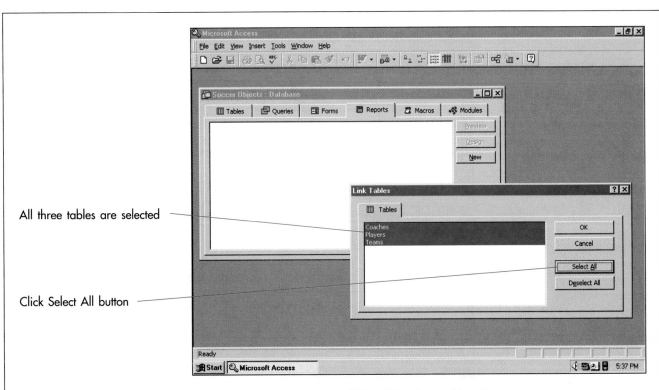

All three tables are selected

Click Select All button

(b) Link Tables Command (step 2)

FIGURE 3.3   Hands-on Exercise 1 (continued)

STEP 3: Add a New Player

➤ Click the **Forms tab** to display the available forms, then double click the **Players form** to open the form. Click the **Maximize button** so that the form takes the entire window as shown in Figure 3.3c.

➤ Click the **Add Player Command button** on the bottom of the form. Click the **text box** to enter your first name. (The PlayerID is an AutoNumber field that is updated automatically.) Enter your name, then press the **Tab key** to move to the next field.

➤ Continue to enter the appropriate data for yourself, but please assign yourself to the **Comets team.** Note, too, that various defaults and data validation have been built into the system:

- As soon as you begin to enter data, a unique PlayerID is assigned automatically since PlayerID is an AutoNumber field.

- The phone number must be numeric and must contain both the area code and phone number.

- Coral Springs and FL are entered as default values for city and state, respectively, but can be changed by entering new values.

- The team is entered via a drop-down list. Type **C** (the first letter in Comets) and Comets is entered automatically from the drop-down list for teams.

- The player rating is a required field (all players are evaluated for ability in order to balance the teams) and must be A, B, C, or D.

➤ Click the **Close Form Command button** to complete the data entry and return to the Database window.

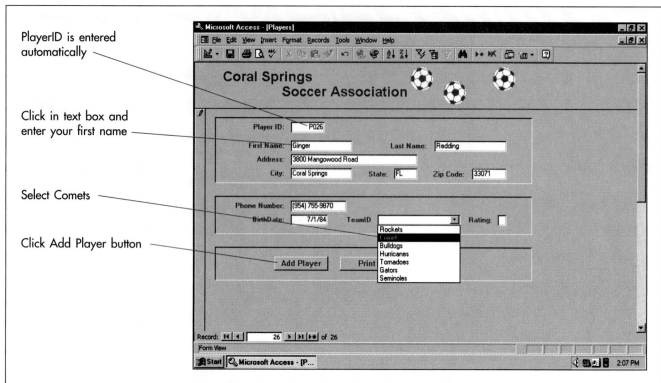

PlayerID is entered automatically

Click in text box and enter your first name

Select Comets

Click Add Player button

(c) Add a Player (step 3)

FIGURE 3.3   Hands-on Exercise 1 (continued)

A LOOK AHEAD

The Add Record button in the Players form was created through the Command Button Wizard. The Wizard creates an *event procedure* that creates a blank record at the end of the underlying table and enables you to add a new player. The procedure does not, however, position you at a specific control within the Players form; that is, you still have to click in the First Name text box to start entering the data. You can, however, create a macro that displays a blank record *and* automatically moves to the First Name control. See steps 7 and 8 in the next hands-on exercise.

STEP 4: View the Team Form

➤ Double click the **Teams form** to open this form. You will see the players and coaches for Team T01 (Rockets).

➤ Click the ▶ on the Team status bar (or press the **PgDn key**) to move to the next team, which is team T02 (Comets) as shown in Figure 3.3d.

➤ Your name has been added as the last player on this team because of the team assignment you made in the previous step. Don't be concerned that your team doesn't have a coach, as we will take care of that in step 9.

➤ Click the **Close Form Command button** to return to the Database window.

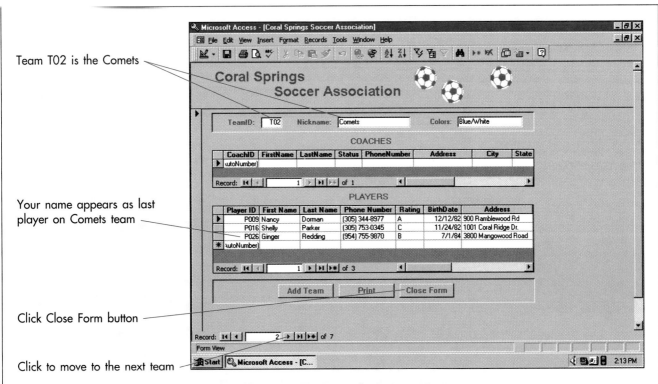

Team T02 is the Comets

Your name appears as last player on Comets team

Click Close Form button

Click to move to the next team

(d) View a Team Roster (step 4)

FIGURE 3.3 Hands-on Exercise 1 (continued)

STEP 5: Create the Main Menu Form

➤ Select (click) the **Template form,** but do *not* open the form. Pull down the **Edit menu** and click **Copy** (or click the **Copy button** on the Database toolbar). The form has been copied to the clipboard, although there is no visible indication that this has been accomplished.

➤ Pull down the **Edit menu** and click **Paste** (or click the **Paste button** on the Database toolbar). You will see the Paste As dialog box in Figure 3.3e.

➤ Type **Main Menu** as the name of the form. Press **enter** or click **OK.** The Database window should now contain the Main Menu form you just created.

USE A TEMPLATE

Avoid the routine and repetitive work of creating a new form by basing all forms for a given application on the same template. A template is a partially completed form that contains graphic elements and other formatting specifications. A template does not, however, have an underlying table or query. We suggest that you create a template for your application and store it within the database, then use that template whenever you need to create a new form. (All you do is copy the template.) It saves you time and trouble. It also promotes a consistent look that is critical to the application's overall success.

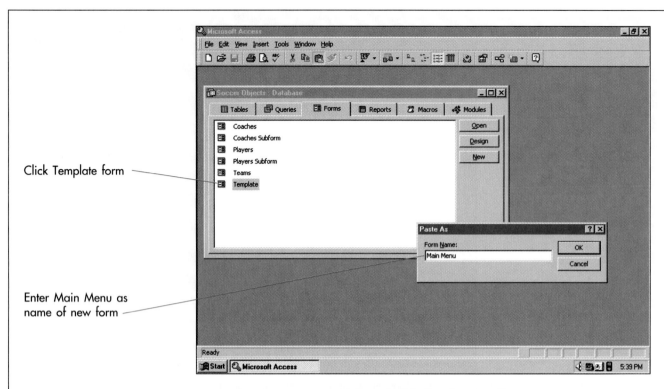

Click Template form

Enter Main Menu as name of new form

(e) Create the Main Menu Form (step 5)

FIGURE 3.3 Hands-on Exercise 1 (continued)

STEP 6: Add the Player Command Button

➤ Click the newly created **Main Menu form.** Click the **Design button** to open the form in Design view, then maximize the window.

➤ Click the text box containing the label, **Enter menu name here,** then click and drag to select the text. Enter **Main Menu** to replace the selected text as shown in Figure 3.3f.

➤ Check that the Form Design, Formatting (Form/Report), and Toolbox toolbars are all visible. (See boxed tip to display a missing toolbar.)

➤ Click the **Command button tool.** (The mouse pointer changes to a tiny crosshair attached to a command button when you point anywhere in the form.)

➤ Click and drag in the form where you want the button to go, then release the mouse. This draws a button and simultaneously opens the Command Button Wizard as shown in Figure 3.3f. (The number on your button may be different from ours.)

• Click **Form Operations** in the Categories list box. Select **Open Form** from the list of actions. Click **Next.**

• Select **Players** from the list of available forms. Click **Next.**

• Click the option button to **Open the form and show all the records.** Click **Next.**

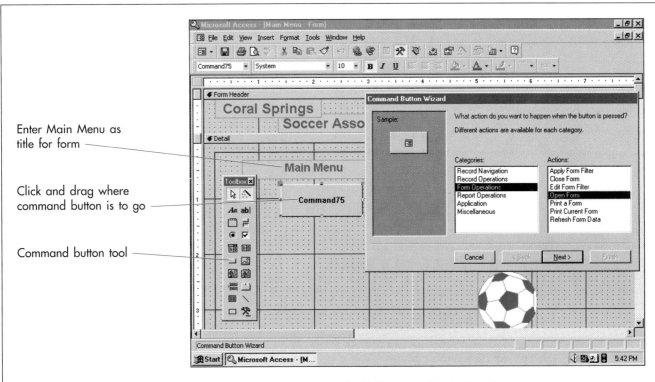

Enter Main Menu as title for form

Click and drag where command button is to go

Command button tool

(f) Add the Command Button (step 6)

FIGURE 3.3   Hands-on Exercise 1 (continued)

- Click the **Text option button,** then click and drag to select the default text (Open Form). Type **Players** in the text box next to the option button. Click **Next.**
- Enter **Players** (in place of the button number) as the name of the button, then click the **Finish Command button.**
➤ The completed command button should appear on your form. This button will open the Players form when clicked.

FIXED VERSUS FLOATING TOOLBARS

A toolbar can be docked (fixed) along the edge of a window, or it can be displayed as a floating toolbar within the window. To move a docked toolbar, drag the move handle in the toolbar background. To move a floating toolbar, drag its title bar. If a desired toolbar is not visible, point to any visible toolbar and click the right mouse button to display a shortcut menu from which you can display other toolbars.

STEP 7: Add the Remaining Command Buttons
➤ Add a command button to open the **Coaches form** following the procedure in the previous step. Click the **Command button tool,** click and drag in the form where you want the button to go, then release the mouse. Choose **Form Operations** in the Categories list box, select **Open Form,** and click **Next.**

- Choose **Coaches** from the list of available forms and click **Next.** Click the option button to **Open the form and show all the records.** Click **Next.**
- Click the **Text Option button,** enter **Coaches** in the text box, and click **Next.** Enter **Coaches** as the name of the button and click the **Finish Command button.**
- Add a **Teams button** in similar fashion.
- Add a fourth (and final) command button to close the Main Menu form. Choose **Form Operations,** then select **Close Form** as the action when the button is pressed.
- Enter **Exit** as the text to display on the button, and use **Exit** as the name of the button. Save the completed form.

THE FORMAT PAINTER

The Format Painter (common to all Office applications) copies the formatting of the selected object, such as a command button, to another object. Select (click) the object whose formatting you want to copy, then click or double click the Format Painter button. (Clicking the Format Painter will paint only one object. Double clicking will paint continuously until the feature is disabled by clicking the Format Painter button a second time.) Either way, the mouse pointer changes to a paintbrush to indicate that you can paint other objects with the current formatting. Just click the target object, which will assume the identical formatting characteristics as the original object.

STEP 8: Size and Align the Buttons

- Your form should contain four command buttons as shown in Figure 3.3g. Size one of the buttons to the height and width you want, then select all four command buttons by pressing and holding the **Shift key** as you click each button.
- Pull down the **Format menu.** Click **Size** to display the cascade menu shown in Figure 3.3g. Click **To Widest** to set a uniform width for the selected buttons.
- Pull down the **Format menu** a second time, click **Size** to display the cascade menu, and click **To Tallest** to set a uniform height for the selected buttons.
- Pull down the **Format menu** once again, click **Vertical Spacing,** then click **Make Equal.**
- Pull down the **Format menu** a final time, click **Align,** then click **Left** to complete the alignment.
- Click the **drop-down arrow** on the **Font/Fore Color button** on the Formatting toolbar to display the available colors, then click **Blue** to change the text color of all four buttons.
- If necessary, move the buttons so they are centered under the Main Menu title. Change the font on the buttons to Arial 12 pt. Make other changes in the formatting and/or spacing of the buttons as necessary.
- Save the form.

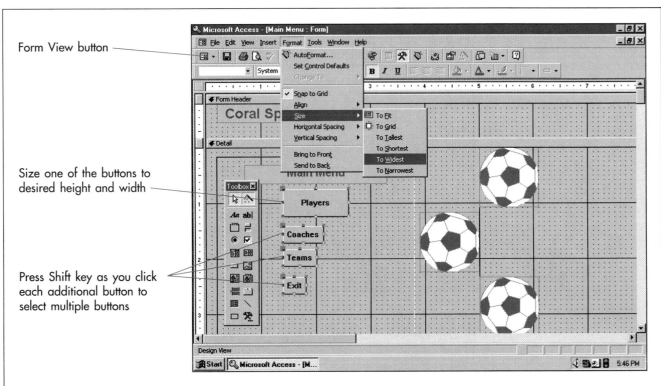

Form View button

Size one of the buttons to desired height and width

Press Shift key as you click each additional button to select multiple buttons

(g) Size and Align the Buttons (step 8)

FIGURE 3.3   Hands-on Exercise 1 (continued)

AVOID CLUTTER

Don't clutter a screen by displaying too much information or too many command buttons. (Seven or eight is the maximum that most people can handle comfortably.) Develop subservient (lower-level) menus if you find yourself with too many buttons on one screen. Don't crowd the command buttons. Make the buttons large enough (and of a uniform size) so that the text within a button is easy to read. Use sufficient blank space around the buttons so that they stand out from the rest of the screen.

STEP 9: Test the Menu

➤ Click the **Form View button** on the Form Design toolbar to switch to the Form view and view the completed menu in Figure 3.3h.

➤ Click the **Coaches Command button** to open this form. You should see a Coaches form similar to the Players and Teams forms.

➤ Click the **Add Coach Command button** at the bottom of the form. Click the text box to enter the coach's first name. (The CoachID is entered automatically as an AutoNumber field.)

➤ Enter data for your instructor as the coach. Click the appropriate **Option button** to make your instructor a **Head Coach.** Assign your instructor to the Comets (Team T02), which is the same team you joined in step 3.

➤ Click the **Close Form Command button** to complete data entry.

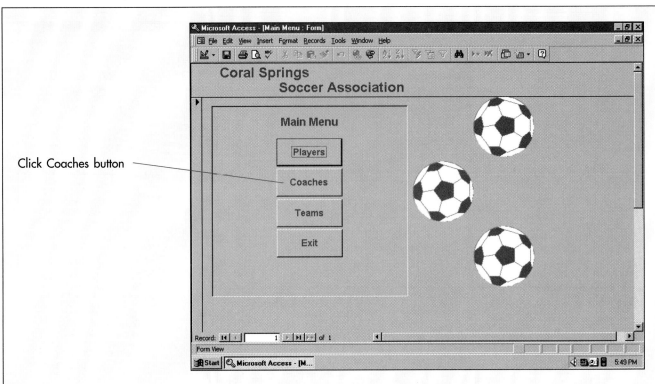

Click Coaches button

(h) The Completed Form (step 9)

FIGURE 3.3 Hands-on Exercise 1 (continued)

➤ Click the **Teams Command button** to open the Teams form, then click the ▶ (next record) or ◀ (previous record) button on the Teams status bar to move to Team T02 (the Comets). You should see your instructor as the head coach and yourself as a player.

➤ Pull down the **Edit menu,** click **Select Record** to select the record for your team, then click the **Print button** on the form to print the roster and prove to your instructor that you have completed the exercise. Click the **Close Form button** to close the Teams form and return to the Main Menu.

SUPPRESS THE RECORD SELECTOR AND NAVIGATION BUTTONS

The Main Menu form is not based on an underlying table and thus the record selector and navigation buttons have no meaning. Change to the Design view for the Main Menu, right click the Form selector box to the left of the ruler, then click the Properties command to display the Properties dialog box. Click the Record Selector text box and click No to disable the Record Selector. Click the Navigation Buttons Text box and click No to disable the buttons. Close the Properties dialog box. Return to the Form view to see the effect of these changes, which are subtle but worthwhile.

STEP 10: Exit Access

➤ Click the **Exit button** to close the Main Menu form. Click **Yes** if asked to save changes to the design of the Main Menu form.

➤ Exit Access if you do not want to continue with the next exercise at this time.

The exercise just completed created a user interface that enables a nontechnical user to maintain the tables in the Soccer application. It did not, however, automate the system completely in that the user still has to open the form containing the Main Menu to get started, and further, has to close the same form at the end of a session to exit Access. You can make the application even easier to use by including macros that perform these tasks automatically.

A *macro* automates a command sequence. Thus, instead of using the mouse or keyboard to execute a series of commands, you store the commands (actions) in a macro and execute the macro. You can create a macro to open a table, query, form, or report. You can create a macro to display an informational message, then beep to call attention to that message. You can create a macro to move or size a window, or to minimize, maximize, or restore a window. In short, you can create a macro to execute any command in any Access menu and thus make an application easy to use.

The Macro Window

A macro is created in the *Macro window* as shown in Figure 3.4. The Macro window has two sections. You enter the *actions* (commands) that make up the macro and any optional comments in the upper section. You supply the additional information (*arguments*) for those actions in the lower section.

The macro in Figure 3.4 consists of a single action (MsgBox), which has four arguments (Message, Beep, Type, and Title). The *MsgBox action* displays a dialog box with the message you define. It's an ideal way to display an informational message to a user and is illustrated later in the chapter. The help area at the bottom right of the Macro window displays help information; the specific help information depends on where you are in the Macro window.

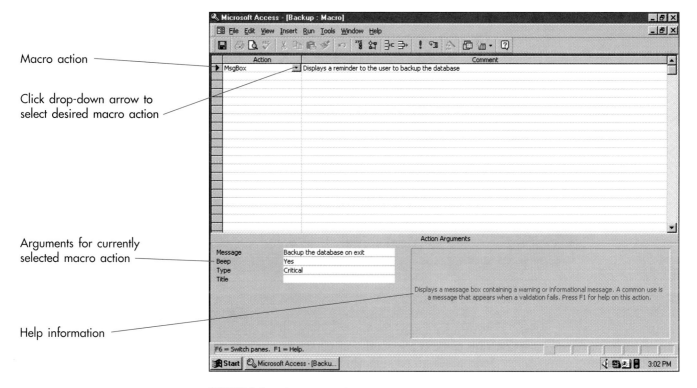

FIGURE 3.4   The Macro Window

A macro is created from the Database window by selecting the Macros tab and clicking the New button. It is stored as an object in the database in the same fashion as a form or report. Actions are added to a macro by choosing the action from a drop-down list or by typing the name of the action. The arguments for an action are entered in similar fashion; that is, by choosing from a drop-down list (when available) or by typing the argument directly. After a macro has been saved, it can be run from the Macro window or the Database window or it can be assigned to run as a response to an event (e.g., clicking a command button) in a form or report.

The *macro toolbar* is displayed at the top of the Macro window and contains buttons that help create and test a macro. Many of the buttons (e.g., the Database Window, Save, and Office Assistant buttons) are common to other toolbars you have used in conjunction with other objects. Other buttons are specific to the Macro window and are referenced in the hands-on exercises as necessary. As with other toolbars, you can point to a button to display its ScreenTip and determine its purpose.

ACCESS MACROS ARE DIFFERENT

Access lacks the macro recorder that is common to Word and Excel. This means that you have to explicitly enter the actions in the Macro window rather than have the recorder do it for you. Nevertheless, you can still create an Access macro to do virtually anything you would do via the keyboard or mouse.

The AutoExec Macro

After a macro is created, it is saved so that it can be run (executed) at a later time. A macro name can contain up to 64 characters (letters and numbers) and may include spaces. The name of the macro appears in the title bar of the Macro window (e.g., Backup in Figure 3.4). You can use any name at all for a macro, as long as you adhere to these simple rules.

One macro name, however, *AutoExec,* is reserved, and this macro has a unique function. The *AutoExec macro* (if it exists) is executed automatically whenever the database in which it is stored is opened. In other words, whenever you open a database, Access looks to see if the database contains an AutoExec macro, and if so, Access runs the macro for you.

The AutoExec macro is essential to automating a system for the end-user. It typically contains an OpenForm action to load the form containing the main (start-up) menu. The AutoExec macro may also perform other housekeeping chores to get the database ready to use, such as maximizing the current window.

Every database can have its own AutoExec macro, but there is no requirement for the AutoExec macro to be present. We recommend, however, that you include an AutoExec macro in every application to help the user get started quickly.

Debugging

Writing a macro is similar to writing a program in that mistakes are virtually certain to be made, and you need a way to correct those mistakes. Should Access encounter an error during the execution of a macro, it displays as much information as it can to help you determine the reason for the error—to assist you in *debugging* your program.

Figure 3.5a contains an erroneous version of the AutoExec macro that will be developed in the exercise that follows shortly. The macro contains two actions, Maximize and OpenForm. The Maximize action maximizes the Database window and affects all subsequent screens that will be displayed in the application. The OpenForm macro opens the form containing the menu developed in the previous exercise. The name of the form is deliberately misspelled to produce the error in Figure 3.5b.

When the AutoExec macro is executed, Access attempts to open the Main Menus form but is unable to do so. It displays the informational message in Figure 3.5b, followed by the Action Failed dialog box in Figure 3.5c. The latter is displayed whenever a macro is unable to execute successfully. Your only course of action is to click the Halt Command button, then attempt to correct the error using the displayed information.

Two macro actions are included

Name of form to be opened is misspelled

Arguments for currently selected macro action (OpenForm)

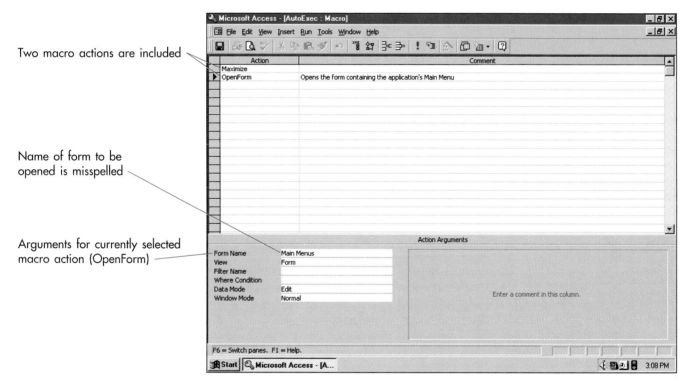

(a) AutoExec Macro

(b) Informational Message

FIGURE 3.5   Debugging

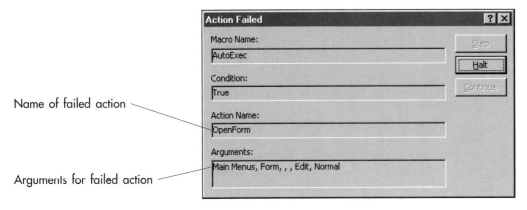

Name of failed action

Arguments for failed action

(c) Action Failed Dialog Box

FIGURE 3.5   Debugging (continued)

The Action Failed dialog box indicates the name of the failed macro (AutoExec). The Action Name indicates the failed action (OpenForm) within the macro, and the Arguments box shows the corresponding values. In this example the error is easy to find. The name of the form should have been Main Menu rather than Main Menus.

THE FIRST BUG

A bug is a mistake in a computer program; hence debugging refers to the process of correcting program errors. According to legend, the first bug was an unlucky moth crushed to death on one of the relays of the electro-mechanical Mark II computer, bringing the machine's operation to a halt. The cause of the failure was discovered by Grace Hopper, who promptly taped the moth to her logbook, noting, *"First actual case of bug being found."*

HANDS-ON EXERCISE 2

Introduction to Macros

Objective: To create an AutoExec macro to open a form automatically; to create a Close Database macro to close the database and exit from the system. To use the On Click property to change the action associated with a command button. Use Figure 3.6 as a guide in the exercise.

STEP 1: Create the AutoExec Macro
➤ Start Access. Open the **Soccer Objects database** from the previous exercise.
➤ Click the **Macros tab** in the Database window (there are currently no macros in the database). Click the **New button** to create a new macro. If necessary, click the **Maximize button** so that the Macro window takes the entire screen as in Figure 3.6a.

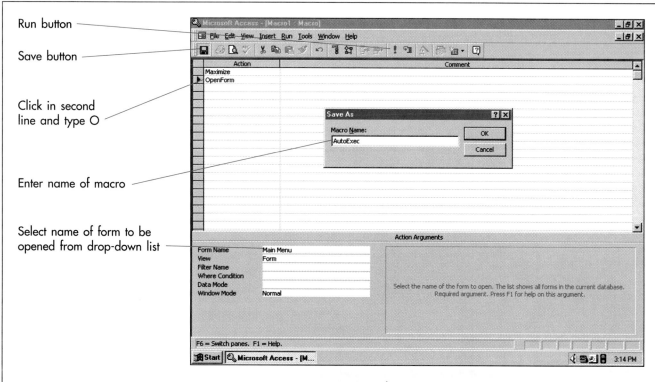

Run button

Save button

Click in second
line and type O

Enter name of macro

Select name of form to be
opened from drop-down list

(a) Create the AutoExec Macro (step 1)

FIGURE 3.6   Hands-on Exercise 2

> Click the **drop-down arrow** to display the available macro actions. Scroll through the list until you can select **Maximize.**

> Click the **Action box** on the second line. Type the letter **O,** and the Open-Form action appears automatically. Press **enter** to accept this action, then click the text box for the **Form Name** argument in the lower section of the Macro window.

> Click the **drop-down arrow** to display the list of existing forms and select **Main Menu** (the form you created in the previous exercise).

> Click the **Save button** to display the Save As dialog box in Figure 3.6a. Type **AutoExec** as the macro name and click **OK.**

> Click the **Run button** to run the macro, which displays the Main Menu from the previous exercise. (The window is maximized on the screen.) Click the **Exit button** on the Main Menu to close the menu and return to the macro.

> Pull down the **File menu.** Click **Close** to close the AutoExec macro.

TYPE ONLY THE FIRST LETTER(S)

Click the Action box, then type the first letter of a macro action to move immediately to the first macro action beginning with that letter. Type an M, for example, and Access automatically enters the Maximize action. If necessary, type the second letter of the desired action; for example, type the letter I (after typing an M), and Access selects the Minimize action, which begins with the letters M and I.

STEP 2: The MsgBox Action

➤ You should be back in the Database window, which should display the name of the AutoExec macro. Click the **New button** to create a second macro, which automatically positions you at the first action.

➤ Type **MS** (the first two letters in the MsgBox action), then press **enter** to accept this action.

➤ Click the text box for the **Type** argument in the lower section of the Macro window. Click the **drop-down arrow** to display the list of message types. Select **Critical.**

➤ Click the text box for the **Message** argument. Press **Shift+F2** to display the zoom box so that you can see the contents of your entire message, then enter the message in Figure 3.6b. Click **OK.**

Run button

Click and type MS

Zoom box

Click and enter
message to be displayed

Click and press Shift+F2
to display zoom box

Click and select Critical
from drop-down list

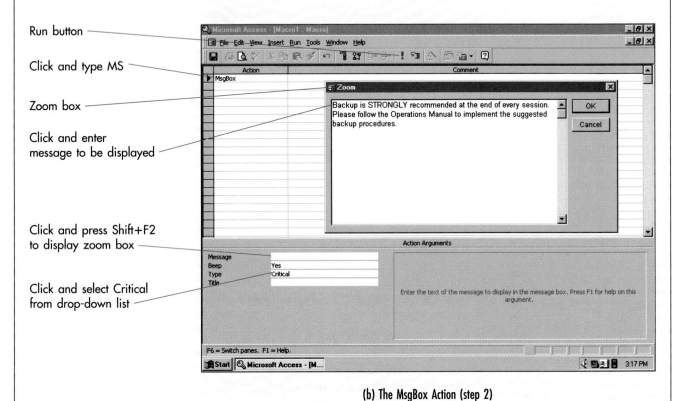

(b) The MsgBox Action (step 2)

FIGURE 3.6   Hands-on Exercise 2 (continued)

BACK UP YOUR DATABASE

It's not a question of if it will happen, but when. Hard disks die, files are lost, and viruses infect a system. Take our word for it, there are few things more unpleasant than searching for a file that isn't there or discovering that the file you do retrieve is missing most of its data. Adequate backup is the only insurance you can obtain against data loss. Backing up a system is easy, but you must remember to do it, and you must do it faithfully, without fail.

➤ Click the **Run button** to test the macro. You will see a message indicating that you have to save the macro. Click **Yes** to save the macro, type **Close Database** as the name of the macro, and click **OK.**

➤ You will see a dialog box containing the text of the message you just created. Click **OK** after you have read the message so that you can continue working on the macro.

STEP 3: Complete the Close Database Macro

➤ Click the **Action box** on the second line. Type **Cl** (the first two letters in *Close*) and press **enter.**

➤ Click the text box for the **Object Type** argument. Click the **drop-down arrow.** Choose **Form** as the Object type. Click the **Object Name** argument, click the **drop-down arrow,** and choose **Main Menu** as the Object (form) name.

➤ Click the **comment line** for this action. Type **Close the Main Menu form** as shown in Figure 3.6c.

➤ Click the **Action box** on the third line. Type **Cl** (the first two letters in *Close*) and press **enter.**

➤ This time no arguments are necessary. The Close command will affect the current window (i.e., the Database window), which closes the database.

➤ Click the **comments line** for this macro action and enter the comment shown in the figure.

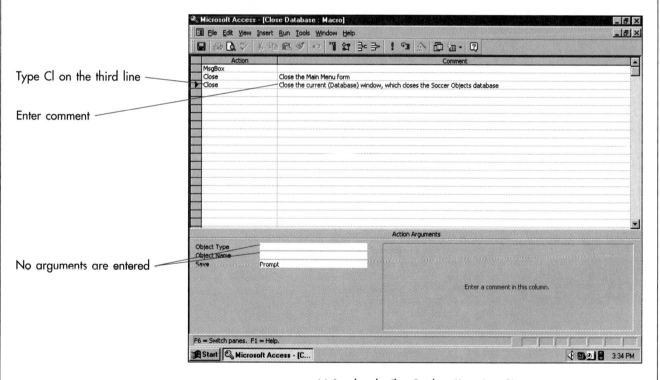

(c) Complete the Close Database Macro (step 3)

FIGURE 3.6 Hands-on Exercise 2 (continued)

> Pull down the **File menu** and click **Close** to close the macro. Click **Yes** when prompted whether to save the changes to the Close Database macro.
> If necessary, press the **F11 key** to switch to the Database window. You should see the names of both macros (AutoExec and Close Database).

THE F6 KEY

Press the F6 key to move back and forth between the top and bottom halves of the Macro window. You can also use the F6 key to move between the top and bottom portions of the Table and Query windows when they are open in Design view.

STEP 4: The On Click Property
> Click the **Forms tab,** select the **Main Menu form,** then click the **Design button** to open the form in Design view. If necessary, maximize the window.
> Point to the **Exit command button** (that was created in the first exercise) and click the **right mouse button** to display a shortcut menu. Click **Properties** to display the Properties dialog box in Figure 3.6d. Click the **Event tab.**
> Click the **On Click box,** which is currently set to [Event Procedure]. This was set automatically when you used the Command Button Wizard to create the button in step 7 of the previous exercise.

Form View button

Click in box, then click drop-down arrow to display macro names

Point to Exit button, click right mouse button to display shortcut menu

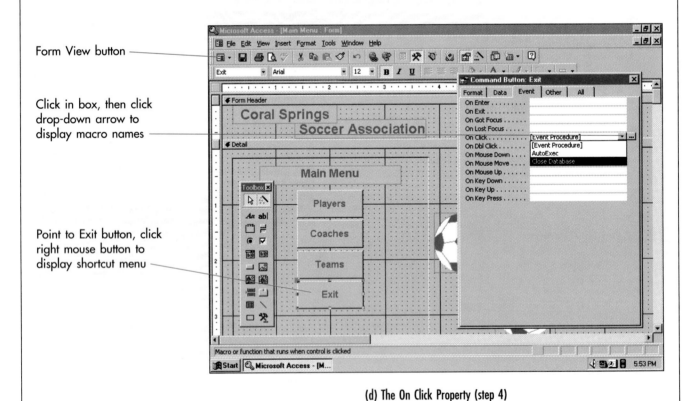

(d) The On Click Property (step 4)

FIGURE 3.6   Hands-on Exercise 2 (continued)

➤ Click the **drop-down arrow** to display the existing macros. Click **Close Database** (the macro you just created). Close the Properties dialog box.

➤ Save the form. Click the **Form View button** to switch to Form view so that you can test the macros you just created.

CREATE A HELP BUTTON

One of the nicest features you can provide your users is a means of obtaining technical support either by telephone or via e-mail. Use the MsgBox action to create a simple macro that displays your phone number and e-mail address, then assign that macro to a Help button on your Main Menu. See practice exercise 1 at the end of the chapter.

STEP 5: Test the AutoExec and Close Database Macros

➤ You should see the Main Menu form displayed in Figure 3.6e. Click the **Exit Command button,** which executes the Close Database macro you assigned to the button.

• You should see the informational message shown in the figure. (The message is displayed by the MsgBox action in the Close Database macro.)

• Click **OK** to accept the message. The Close Database macro then closes the database.

Informational message

Click Exit button

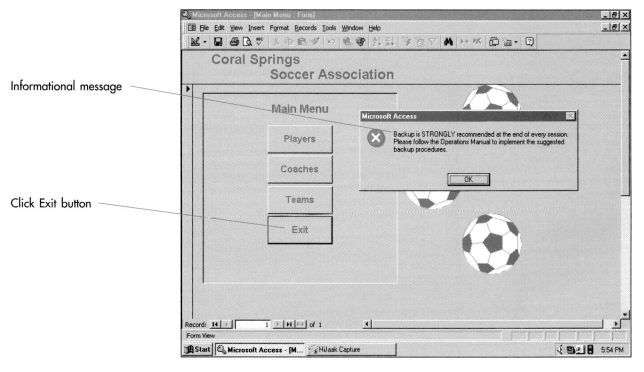

(e) Test the Macro (step 5)

FIGURE 3.6   Hands-on Exercise 2 (continued)

STEP 6: Reopen the Database

➤ Pull down the **File menu,** then click **Soccer Objects** from the list of recently opened databases. The AutoExec macro executes automatically, maximizes the current window, and displays the Main Menu.

➤ Pull down the **File menu** and click **Close** to close the form and continue working on this database. (You cannot click the Exit command button as that would close the database.) You should be back in the Database window.

STEP 7: Create the Add Player Macro

➤ Click the **Forms tab** in the Database window. Double click the **Players form** to open this form.

➤ Click the **Add Player button** on the Players form and note that in order to add a player, you must first click the First Name text box. We will correct this by creating an Add Player macro that will automatically move to the First Name text box. Click the **Close Form button** to exit the Players form.

➤ Click the **Macros tab** in the Database window. Click **New** to create a new macro, then create the Add Player macro as shown in Figure 3.6f:

- Use the **F6 key** to switch between the top and bottom halves of the Macro window.
- The first action, **Go To Record,** has three arguments we must enter: Object Type, Object Name, and Record. Click in the Object Type box, click the drop-down arrow, and select **Form.** Click in the Object Name box, click the drop-down arrow, and select **Players.** Click in the Record box, click the drop-down arrow, and select **New.** The macro action and corresponding arguments are equivalent to moving to the end of the Player table in order to add a new record.

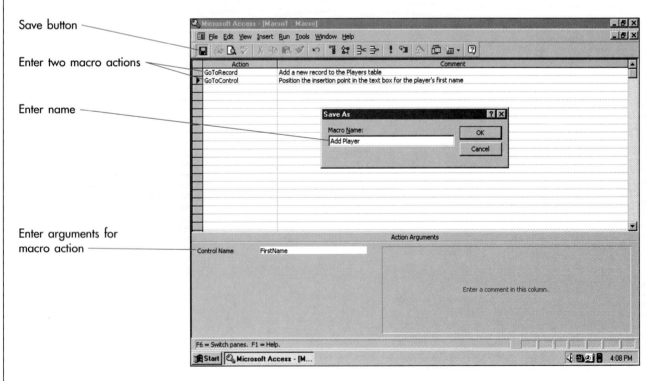

Save button

Enter two macro actions

Enter name

Enter arguments for
macro action

(f) The Add Player Macro (step 7)

FIGURE 3.6   Hands-on Exercise 2 (continued)

- The **GoToControl** action has a single argument, which is the name of the control on the Players form. Type **FirstName** (there is no space in the control name).
- Add the comments as shown.

> Save the macro as **Add Player.** Do *not* attempt to run the macro at this time.
> Pull down the **File menu** and click **Close** to exit the macro and return to the Database window.

THE DISPLAY WHEN PROPERTY

The Add, Print, and Close Form Command buttons appear on the various forms (Team, Player, or Coach) when the forms are displayed on the screen, but not when the forms are printed. This was accomplished by setting the Display When property of the individual command buttons when the forms were created. Open a form in Design view, point to an existing command button, then click the right mouse button to display a shortcut menu. Click on the line for the Display When property and set the property accordingly.

STEP 8: The On Click Property

> Click the **Forms tab** in the Database window and select the **Players form.** Click the **Design button** to open the form in Design view as shown in Figure 3.6g.

Click in On Click box, then click drop-down arrow to display macro names

Point to Add Player button, click right mouse button to display shortcut menu

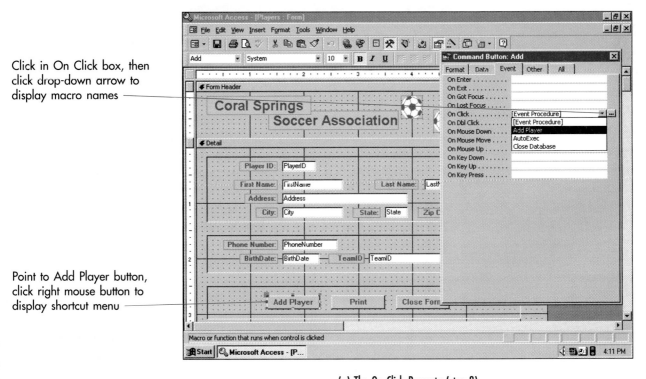

(g) The On Click Property (step 8)

FIGURE 3.6   Hands-on Exercise 2 (continued)

➤ Point to the **Add Player command button,** then click the **right mouse button** to display a shortcut menu. Click **Properties** to display the Properties dialog box.

➤ Click the **Event tab.** You will see the On Click property, which is currently set to [Event Procedure]. Click the **On Click property box,** then click the **drop-down arrow** to display the existing macros.

➤ Click **Add Player** (the macro you just created). Close the Properties dialog box.

➤ Click the **Form View button** to switch to Form view and test the Add Player macro.

  • Click the **Add Player command button.** You are automatically positioned in the First Name box (because of the Add Player macro) and can start typing immediately.

  • Enter data for a friend of yours. Assign your friend to the **Comets** (your team).

➤ Click the **Close Form command button** when you have completed the record. Click **Yes** if prompted to save the changes to the Players form.

THE CONTROLTIP TEXT PROPERTY

Point to any button on any Office toolbar and you see a ScreenTip that describes the purpose of that button. Access enables you to create your own ScreenTips through the ControlTip Text property. Open a form in Design view, right click the control for which you want to create a tip, then click the Properties command to open the Properties dialog box. Click the Other (or All) tab, click the ControlTip text box to enter the desired text, then close the dialog box. Change to Form view and point to the control. You will see the ToolTip you just created.

STEP 9: Close the Database

➤ You can close the database in one of two ways:

  • You should be back in the Database window. Pull down the **File menu** and click **Close** to close the Soccer Objects database, *or*

  • Click the **Forms tab,** double click the **Main Menu form** to open this form, click the **Exit button** on the form, then click **OK** in response to the message reminding you to back up the system.

➤ Pull down the **File menu.** Click **Exit** if you do not want to continue with the next exercise at this time.

THE PLAYER DRAFT

The implementation of a player draft is essential to the Soccer Association. Players sign up for the coming season at registration, after which the coaches meet to select players for their teams. All players are rated as to ability, and the CSSA strives to maintain a competitive balance between teams.

The coaches take turns selecting players from the pool of unassigned players as displayed in the form shown in Figure 3.7. The form is based on a query that identifies the players who have not yet been drafted. To aid in the selection process, the unassigned players are listed by ability and alphabetically within ability. Note, too, the use of a **combo box** to simplify data entry in conjunction with the team assignment. The user is able to click the drop-down arrow to display a list of team nicknames (or enter the nickname directly) rather than having to remember the associated team number.

In addition to displaying the list of unassigned players, the form in Figure 3.7 also contains three command buttons that are used during the player draft. The Find Player button moves directly to a specific player, and enables a coach to see whether a specific player has been assigned to a team, and if so, to which team. The Update List button refreshes the underlying query on which the list of unassigned players is based. It is used periodically during the draft as players are assigned to teams, to remove those players from the list of unassigned players. The End Draft button closes the form and returns to the Main Menu.

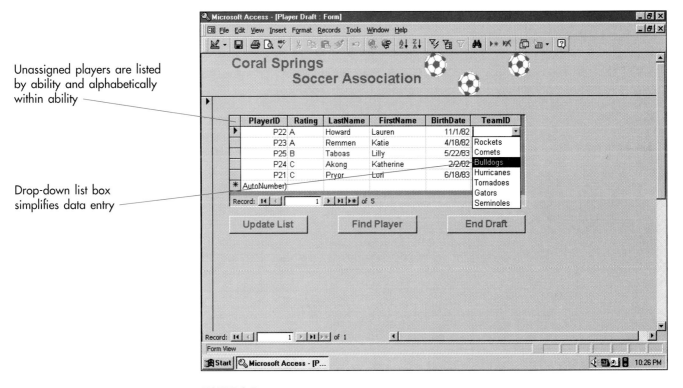

Unassigned players are listed by ability and alphabetically within ability

Drop-down list box simplifies data entry

FIGURE 3.7   The Player Draft

SIMPLIFY DATA ENTRY

A drop-down list box simplifies data entry as it lets you select a value from a list, such as a team nickname, rather than having to remember the corresponding team number. A combo box combines the properties of a text box and a list box; that is, you can enter a new value directly in the box, or you can click the drop-down arrow to display a list of values from which to choose.

The Find Unmatched Query Wizard

Think, for a moment, how Access is able to display the list of unassigned players. You need to remember the one-to-many relationship between teams and players (one team has many players, but a player has only one team). Remember, too, that this relationship is implemented through the common TeamID field, which appears in both tables. The TeamID is the primary key in the Teams table and it is a foreign key in the Players table. A player is assigned to a team by entering the team number into the TeamID field in the Players table. Conversely, any player without a value in his or her TeamID field is an unassigned player.

To display a list of unassigned players, you need to create a query, based on the Players table, which selects records without an entry for TeamID. This can be done by creating the query explicitly (and specifying the Null criterion for TeamID) or more easily through the Find Unmatched Query Wizard, which creates the query for you. The Wizard asks the questions in Figure 3.8, then generates the query.

The *Find Unmatched Query Wizard* identifies the records in one table (e.g., the Players table) that do not have matching records in another table (e.g., the Teams table). The wizard begins by asking for the table that contains the unmatched records (Figure 3.8a) and for the related table (Figure 3.8b). It identifies the join field (TeamID in Figure 3.8c), then gives you the opportunity to select the fields you want to see in the query results (Figure 3.8d). The Wizard even suggests a name for the query (Players Without Matching Teams in Figure 3.8e), then displays the dynaset in Figure 3.8f.

The Find Unmatched Query Wizard has multiple applications within the CSSA database. It can identify players without teams (as in Figure 3.8), or conversely, teams without players. It can also identify coaches who have not been assigned to a team, and, conversely, teams without coaches.

Macro Groups

Implementation of the player draft requires three macros, one for each command button. Although you could create a separate macro for each button, it is convenient to create a *macro group* that contains the individual macros. The macro group has a name, as does each macro in the group. Only the name of the macro group appears in the Database window.

Figure 3.9 displays a Player Draft macro group containing three individual macros (Update List, Find Player, and End Draft), which run independently of one another. The name of each macro appears in the Macro Name column (which is displayed by clicking the Macro Names button on the Macro toolbar). The actions and comments for each macro are shown in the corresponding columns to the right of the macro name.

The advantage of storing related macros in a macro group, as opposed to storing them individually, is purely organizational. Large systems often contain many macros, which can overwhelm the developer as he or she tries to locate a specific macro. Storing related macros in macro groups limits the entries in the Database window, since only the (name of the) macro group is displayed. Thus, the Database window would contain a single entry (Player Draft, which is the name of the macro group), as opposed to three individual entries (Update List, Find Player, and End Draft, which correspond to the macros in the group).

Access must still be able to identify the individual macros so that each macro can be executed at the appropriate time. If, for example, a macro is to be executed when the user clicks a command button, the *On Click property* of that command button must specify both the individual macro and the macro group to which it belongs. The two names are separated by a period—for example, Player Draft.Update List—to indicate the Update List macro in the Player Draft group.

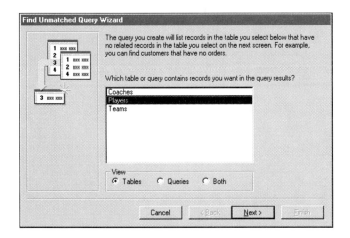

(a) Table Containing the Unmatched Records

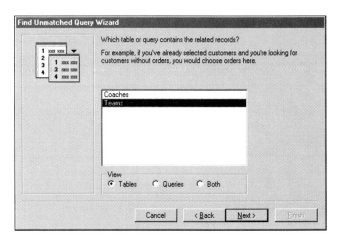

(b) The Related Table

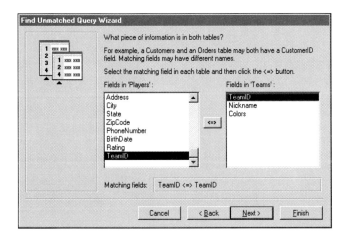

(c) Join Field

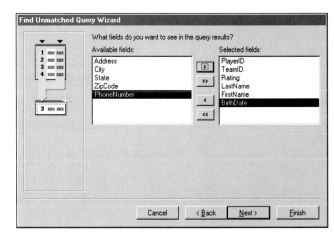

(d) Fields for Dynaset

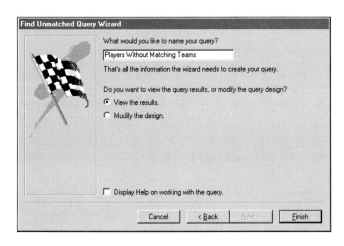

(e) Suggested Name

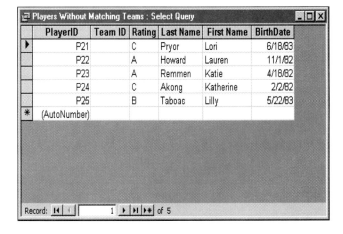

(f) Dynaset

FIGURE 3.8   The Find Unmatched Query Wizard

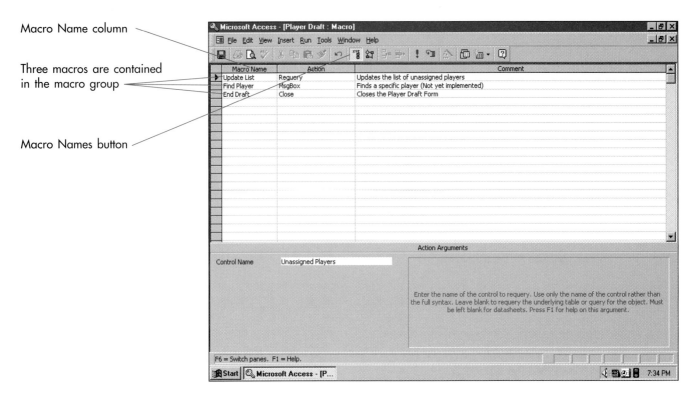

Macro Name column

Three macros are contained in the macro group

Macro Names button

FIGURE 3.9   Macro Groups

As indicated, each macro in Figure 3.9 is assigned to a command button in the Player Draft form of Figure 3.7. The macros are created in the following hands-on exercise, which implements the player draft.

THE MACRO TOOLBAR

The Macro Name and Conditions buttons on the Macro toolbar toggle the corresponding columns on and off. Click either button to display (hide) the indicated column. See practice exercise 3 at the end of the chapter for additional information on the Conditions column.

HANDS-ON EXERCISE 3

The Player Draft

Objective: To create a macro group containing three macros to implement a player draft. Use Figure 3.10 as a guide in the exercise.

STEP 1: The Unmatched Query Wizard

➤ Start Access and open the **Soccer Objects database.** Pull down the **File menu** and click **Close** (or click the **Close button**) to close the Main Menu form but leave the database open. (You *cannot* click the Exit command button as that would close the database.)

➤ Click the **Queries tab** in the Database window. Click **New,** select the **Find Unmatched Query Wizard,** then click **OK** to start the Wizard:

  • Select **Players** as the table whose records you want to see in the query results. Click **Next.**

  • Select **Teams** as the table that contains the related records. Click **Next.**

  • **TeamID** is automatically selected as the matching field. Click **Next.**

  • Select the following fields from the Available Fields list: **PlayerID, Rating, LastName, FirstName, BirthDate,** and **TeamID.** Click **Next.**

  • **Players Without Matching Teams** is entered as the name of the query. Check that the option button to **View the results** is selected, then click **Finish** to exit the Wizard and see the results of the query.

➤ You should see a dynaset containing five players (Pryor, Howard, Remmen, Akong, and Taboas) as shown in Figure 3.10a. The TeamID field for each of these players is blank, indicating these players are not on a team.

Click to switch to
Design view

TeamID field is blank

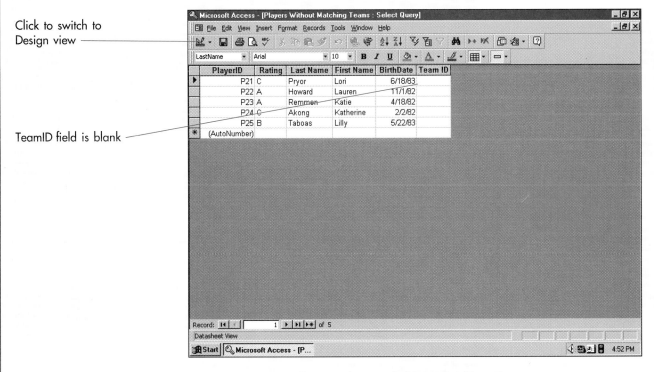

(a) The Unmatched Query Wizard (step 1)

FIGURE 3.10   Hands-on Exercise 3

THE MOST RECENTLY OPENED FILE LIST

An easy way to open a recently used database is to select it from the Microsoft Access dialog box that appears when Access is first started. Check to see if your database appears on the list of the most recently opened databases, and if so, simply double click the database to open it.

STEP 2: Modify the Unmatched Query

➤ Change to Design view to see the underlying query as displayed in Figure 3.10b.

➤ Click and drag the line separating the upper and lower portions of the window. If necessary, click and drag the field lists to match the figure.

➤ Click in the **Sort row** for **Rating,** then click **Ascending** from the drop-down list. Click in the **Sort row** for **LastName,** then click **Ascending** from the drop-down list.

➤ Click the **Run button** to view the revised query, which lists players according to their player rating and alphabetically within rating.

➤ Close the query. Click **Yes** if asked whether to save the changes to the Players Without Matching Teams query.

Run button

Click and drag to increase size in upper portion of window

Select sort sequences

Is Null criterion entered automatically

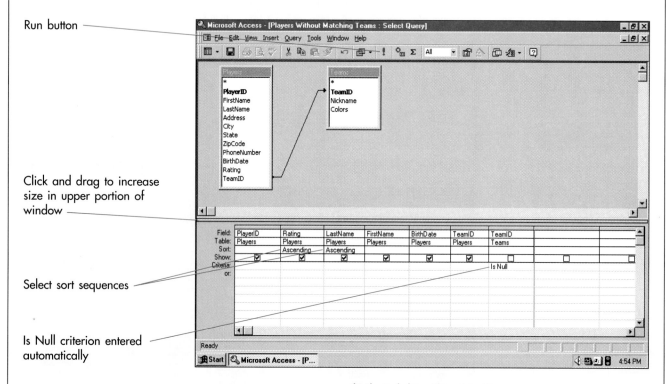

(b) The Underlying Query (step 2)

FIGURE 3.10   Hands-on Exercise 3 (continued)

THE IS NULL CRITERION

The Is Null criterion selects those records that do not have a value in the designated field. It is the essence of the Unmatched Query Wizard, which uses the criterion to identify the records in one table that do not have a matching record in another table. The NOT operator can be combined with the Is Null criterion to produce the opposite effect; that is, the criterion Is Not Null will select records with any type of entry (including spaces) in the specified field.

STEP 3: Create the Unmatched Players Form

➤ Click the **Forms tab** in the Database window, click **New** to display the New Form dialog box, and select **AutoForm:Datasheet.**

➤ Click the **drop-down arrow** to choose a table or query. Select the **Players Without Matching Teams** (the query created in step 2). Click **OK.**

➤ Wait a few seconds as Access creates a form that lists the players who are not currently assigned to a team. The form is displayed in the Datasheet view and resembles the dynaset shown earlier.

➤ Maximize the form if necessary, then change to the Design view as shown in Figure 3.10c. Select the **TeamID control** in the Detail section, then press the **Del key** to delete the TeamID (which will be replaced with a combo box).

➤ Click the **Combo Box tool** on the Toolbox toolbar. Click and drag in the form where you want the combo box to go. Release the mouse. You will see the first step in the Combo Box Wizard:

- Check the **Option button** that indicates you want the combo box to **look up values in a table or query.** Click **Next.**

- Choose the **Teams table** in the next screen. Click **Next.**

- Select the **TeamID** and **Nickname** from the Available Fields list box for inclusion in the combo box columns list. Click **Next.**

- Adjust the column widths if necessary. Be sure the box to **Hide the key column** is checked. Click **Next.**

- Click the **Option button** to store the value in the field. Click the **drop-down arrow** to display the fields in the query and select the **TeamID field.** Click **Next.**

- Enter **TeamID** as the label for the combo box. Click **Finish.**

➤ Click (select) the label next to the control you just created. Press the **Del key** to delete the label.

➤ Point to the combo box, click the **right mouse button** to display a shortcut menu, and click **Properties.** Change the name of the control to **TeamID.** Close the Properties box.

➤ Click the **Save button** to display the Save As dialog box in Figure 3.10c. (Players Without Matching Teams is already entered as the default name.)

➤ Click **OK** to save the form, then close the form.

LIST BOXES VERSUS COMBO BOXES

The choice between a list box and a combo box depends on how you want the control to appear in the form. The advantage of a list box is that it is always visible, and further, that the user is restricted to selecting a value from the list. The advantage of a combo box is that it takes less space because its values are not displayed until you open it. A combo box also enables you to control whether the user can select just the values in the list or whether additional values are permitted. (The Limit to List property is set to Yes and No, respectively.) And finally, a combo box permits you to enter the first few characters in a value to move directly to that value. A list box, however, accepts only the first letter.

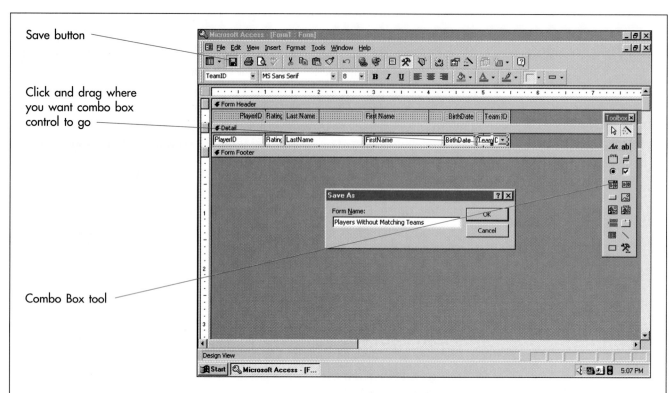

Save button

Click and drag where
you want combo box
control to go

Combo Box tool

(c) Create the Unmatched Players Form (step 3)

FIGURE 3.10   Hands-on Exercise 3 (continued)

STEP 4: Create the Player Draft Macro Group

➤ Click the **Macros tab** in the Database window. Click **New** to create a new macro, and if necessary, click the **Maximize button** to maximize the Macro window.

➤ If you do not see the Macro Names column, pull down the **View menu** and click **Macro Names** to display the column. (Alternatively, you can click the **Macro Names button** on the Macro toolbar.)

➤ Enter the macro names, actions, and comments as shown in Figure 3.10d. Supply the arguments for each action as indicated below:

  • The Requery action (in the Update List macro) has a single argument in which you specify the control name (the name of the query). Type **Players Without Matching Teams,** which is the query you created earlier in step 1.

  • The Find Player macro will be implemented as an assignment (see practice exercise 4), but in the interim, it will display a message and contain only the MsgBox action. Enter **Not Yet Implemented** as the text of the message. Select **Information** as the type of message.

  • The arguments for the End Draft macro are visible in Figure 3.10d. The Player Draft form will be created in the next step. Thus, you need to enter the form name explicitly since it will not appear in the drop-down list.

➤ Save the Macro group as **Player Draft** as shown in Figure 3.10d. Close the Macro window.

Macro Names button

Save button

Enter macro names
and actions

Enter arguments for
macro action

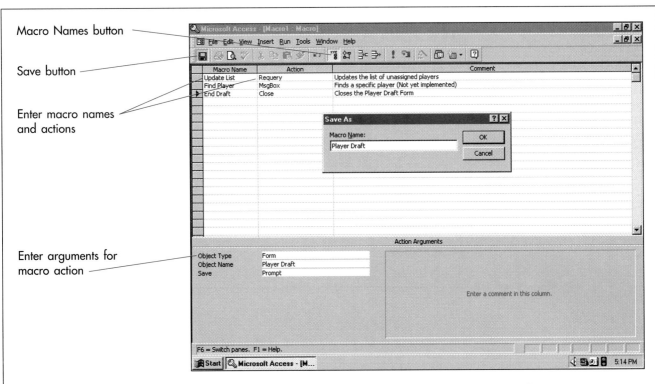

(d) Create the Player Draft Macro Group (step 4)

FIGURE 3.10   Hands-on Exercise 3 (continued)

REQUERY COMMAND NOT AVAILABLE

Most macros are designed to run at specified times and will fail if tested in isolation. The macros in the Player Draft group, for example, are designed to run only when the Player Draft form is open. Do not be concerned, therefore, if you attempt to test the macros at this time and the Action Failed dialog box appears. The macros will work correctly at the end of the exercise, when the entire player draft is in place. See problem 2 at the end of the chapter.

STEP 5: Create the Player Draft Form

➤ Click the **Forms tab** in the Database window. Select the **Template form,** click the **Copy button** to copy the form to the clipboard, then click the **Paste button** to complete the copy operation. Type **Player Draft** as the name of the copied form. Click **OK.**

➤ Open the **Player Draft form** in Design view. Delete the label and the rectangle from the Details section. Size the soccer balls, then move them to the Form Header section as shown in Figure 3.10e.

➤ Click the **Restore button,** then move and size the windows as shown in Figure 3.10e.

➤ Click the **Database window.** Click and drag the **Players Without Matching Teams form** onto the Player Draft form as shown in Figure 3.10e. Maximize the window.

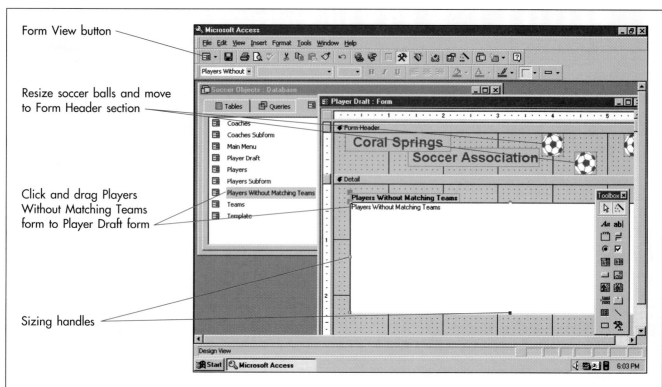

Form View button

Resize soccer balls and move to Form Header section

Click and drag Players Without Matching Teams form to Player Draft form

Sizing handles

(e) Create the Player Draft Form (step 5)

FIGURE 3.10   Hands-on Exercise 3 (continued)

➤ Click and drag the **sizing handles** in the Players Without Matching Team form so that its size approximates the form in Figure 3.10e.

➤ Click the **Form View button** to view your progress. You should see the Datasheet view of the subform, which displays the players who have not yet been assigned to a team.

➤ Click the **Form Design button** to continue working on the form. If necessary, click off the subform control, then double click the subform control to open the subform in Design view. Switch to the Datasheet view to change the width of the columns within the form.

➤ Continue to switch back and forth between the Form view and the Design view until you are satisfied with the appearance of the subform. Close the form. Click **Yes** when asked whether to save the changes.

➤ Select (click) the **label** of the subform (Players Without Matching Teams), then press the **Del key** to delete the label. Be sure you delete the label and not the subform. (Click the **Undo button** if you make a mistake.) Save the form.

MODIFYING A SUBFORM

To modify the subform, click outside the subform to deselect it, then double click the subform to open it. Once the subform is open, you can change to the Design, Datasheet, or Form view by clicking the drop-down arrow on the Form View button on the Form Design toolbar.

STEP 6: Create the Command Buttons

➤ Click and drag the **Command Button tool** to create a command button, as shown in Figure 3.10f.

➤ Click **Miscellaneous** in the Categories list box. Select **Run Macro** from the list of actions. Click the **Next Command button.**

➤ Select **Player Draft.Update List** from the list of existing macros. Click the **Next Command button.**

➤ Click the **Text Option button.** Click and drag to select the default text (Run Macro), then type **Update List** as the text to display on the button. Click the **Next Command button.**

➤ Enter **Update List** (in place of the button number) and click the **Finish Command button.**

➤ Repeat these steps to create the additional command buttons shown in Figure 3.10f. Assign the Find Player and End Draft macros from the Player Draft group to the additional command buttons.

➤ Size, align, space, and color the command buttons as in the previous exercise. Save the completed form.

➤ Close the form.

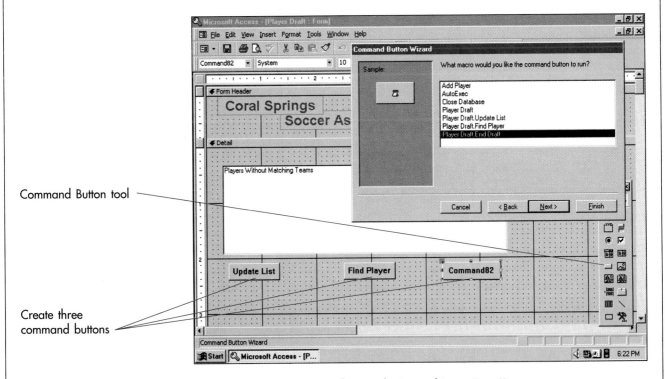

(f) Create the Command Buttons (step 6)

FIGURE 3.10   Hands-on Exercise 3 (continued)

UNIFORM COMMAND BUTTONS

Press and hold the Shift key to select multiple command buttons so that they can be formatted, sized, and aligned in a single command. After the buttons are selected, click the appropriate button on the Formatting toolbar to change the color, font, or point size, or to specify boldface or italics. Check that buttons are still selected, then pull down the Format menu to execute the Size and Alignment commands to arrange the buttons attractively on the form.

STEP 7: Modify the Main Menu

➤ You're almost finished. Open the **Main Menu form** in Design view. Move the four existing buttons to the left.

➤ Click and drag the **Command Button tool** to create the fifth command button as shown in Figure 3.10g. (Your button will display a different number.)

➤ Supply the necessary information to the Command Button Wizard so that the new button opens the Player Draft form just created. The text on the button should read **Player Draft.**

➤ Size, align, space, and color the command buttons as in the previous exercise. (Press and hold the **Shift key** to select multiple command buttons.)

➤ Save the completed form. Close the form, which returns you to the Database window.

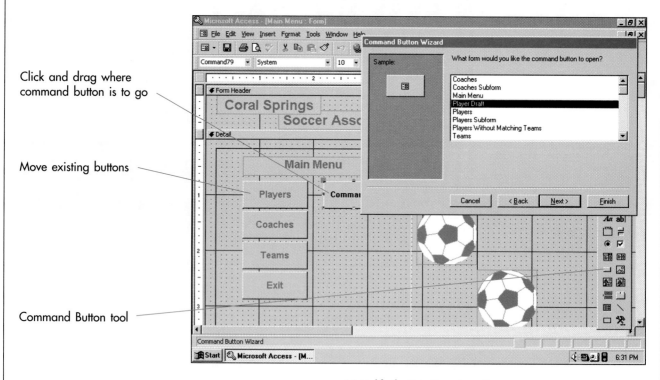

Click and drag where command button is to go

Move existing buttons

Command Button tool

(g) Modify the Main Menu (step 7)

FIGURE 3.10   Hands-on Exercise 3 (continued)

THE F11 KEY

It's easy to lose the Database window, especially when you are maximizing objects within a database. Press the F11 key at any time to make the Database window the active window and place it in front of all the other open objects.

STEP 8: Test the Completed System

➤ Click the **Macros tab** in the Database window. Double click the **AutoExec macro** to execute this macro, as though you just opened the Soccer Objects database.

➤ Click the **Player Draft button** in the Main Menu to display the form you just created, as shown in Figure 3.10h. The Players are listed according to their ratings.

➤ Click the **TeamID field** for Katie Remmen. Type **R** (the first letter in Rockets) and Katie is assigned automatically to this team.

➤ Click the **Update List Command button.** Katie disappears from the list of unassigned players as she has just been drafted by the Rockets.

➤ Click the **End Draft button** to (temporarily) end the draft and return to the Main Menu.

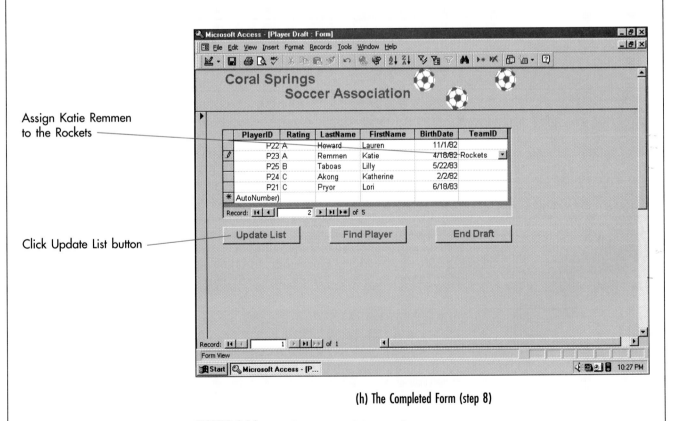

(h) The Completed Form (step 8)

FIGURE 3.10   Hands-on Exercise 3 (continued)

➤ Click the **Teams Command button** to view the team rosters. Team T01 (Rockets) is the first team you see, and Katie Remmen is on the roster. Click the **Close Form button** to return to the Main Menu.

➤ Click the **Exit Command button** to leave the system. Click **OK** in response to the message reminding you to back up the system.

A SIMPLE STRATEGY FOR BACKUP

We cannot overemphasize the importance of adequate backup. Backup procedures are personal and vary from individual to individual as well as installation to installation. Our suggested strategy is very simple, namely, that you back up whatever you cannot afford to lose and that you do so at the end of every session. Be sure to store the backup at a different location from the original file.

PROTOTYPING

Today's competitive environment demands that you develop applications quickly. This is especially true if you are creating an application for a client, where it is important for that person to see a working system as soon as possible. Prototyping enables you to do precisely that. Not only will the client appreciate your sense of urgency, but the sooner the client sees the initial version, the easier it is for you to make the necessary corrections.

A **prototype** is a partially completed version of an application that demonstrates the "look and feel" of the finished system. Consider, for example, Figure 3.11, which applies prototyping to the soccer application. The Main Menu in Figure 3.11a now includes a command button to display the Report Menu in Figure 3.11b. The Report Menu then enables a user to select any of the available reports.

The reports, however, have not yet been created; that is, clicking any of the command buttons in Figure 3.11b displays a message indicating that the report is not available. Nevertheless, the user has a better appreciation for how the eventual system will work and can provide immediate feedback on the portion of the system that has been completed. He or she may request changes in the user interface, the addition or deletion of reports, and so on. And, as indicated, the sooner the user communicates the requested changes to you, the easier it is for you to make those corrections. Once the prototype has been approved, the individual reports can be implemented one at a time, until the system is complete.

TOP-DOWN IMPLEMENTATION

An application should be developed in stages, beginning at the top (the form containing the Main Menu) and working toward the bottom (subsidiary forms, reports, and queries). Testing should go on continually, even before all of the objects are completed. This is accomplished through prototyping, which always presents a working application to the user, in which lower-level objects need not be completed. Development continues in top-down fashion, with each new version of the application containing additional objects until the system is finished.

New button displays a
Report Menu

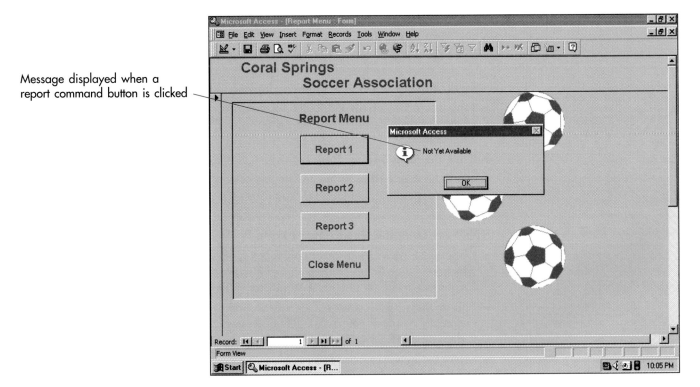

(a) Main Menu

Message displayed when a
report command button is clicked

(b) Report Menu

FIGURE 3.11   Prototyping

Realize, too, how easy it is to produce the prototype shown in Figure 3.11. You need to create a macro (containing the MsgBox action) that will display the appropriate message when a report is not available. You also need to create a form that displays the Report Menu, and that form is easily created using the same template you used to create the Main Menu. And finally, you need to add a command button to the Main Menu to display the Report Menu. All of these steps are detailed in the following hands-on exercise.

HANDS-ON EXERCISE 4

Prototyping

Objective: To create a subsidiary Report Menu that is not fully implemented; to use the MsgBox action as the basis of a prototyping macro. Use Figure 3.12 as a guide in the exercise.

STEP 1: Create the Prototype Macro

➤ Start Access and open the **Soccer Objects database.** Pull down the **File menu** and click **Close** (or click the **Close button**) to close the Main Menu form but leave the database open. (You *cannot* click the Exit command button as that would close the database.)

➤ Click the **Macros tab** in the Database window, which contains the four macros from the previous exercise. Click the **New button,** which opens the Macro window and automatically positions you at the first action. If necessary, click the **Maximize button** so that the Macro window takes the entire screen.

➤ Type **MS** (the first two letters in the MsgBox action), then press **enter** to accept this action. Press the **F6 key** or click the **box for the Message argument.** Type **Not Yet Available** as shown in Figure 3.12a.

➤ Press the **down arrow key** twice to move to the box for the **Type argument.** Click the **drop-down arrow** to display the list of message types and select **Information.**

➤ Click the **Save button.** Save the macro as **Prototype.**

➤ Click the **Run button** to test the macro, which displays the informational message in Figure 3.12a. Click **OK** to accept the message. Close the Macro window.

STEP 2: Create the Report Menu Form

➤ Click the **Forms tab** in the Database window. Click the **Template form** (on which all other forms are based), pull down the **Edit menu,** and click **Copy** (or press **Ctrl+C,** a universal Windows shortcut).

➤ Pull down the **Edit menu** a second time and click **Paste** (or click **Ctrl+V,** a universal Windows shortcut). Enter **Report Menu** as the name of the new form. Click **OK.**

➤ Select the newly created **Report Menu form.** Click the **Design button** to open the form in Design view as shown in Figure 3.12b.

➤ Click the **Restore button,** then size and/or move the Database and Form windows so that your desktop matches the arrangement in Figure 3.12b.

➤ Click the **label** in the Detail section, then click and drag to select the text **Enter Menu Name Here.** Enter **Report Menu** to replace the selected text. Save the form.

Run button

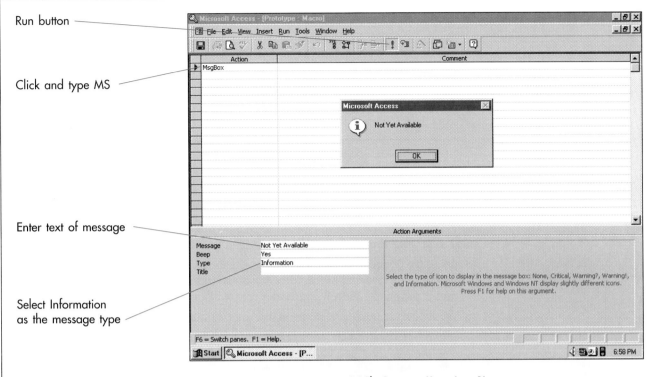

Click and type MS

Enter text of message

Select Information
as the message type

(a) The Prototype Macro (step 1)

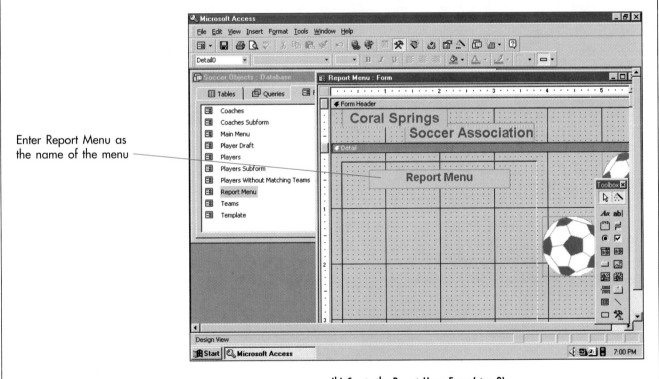

Enter Report Menu as
the name of the menu

(b) Create the Report Menu Form (step 2)

FIGURE 3.12   Hands-on Exercise 4

ARRANGE THE DESKTOP

To size a window, point to any border (the mouse pointer changes to a double arrow), then drag the border in the direction you want to go: inward to shrink the window or outward to enlarge it. Alternatively, you can drag a corner to change both dimensions at the same time. To move a window while retaining its size, point to its title bar, then drag the window to its new position. Remember, too, that you cannot size a maximized window; that is, you must restore a maximized window if you want to change its size.

STEP 3: Add the Command Buttons

➤ Click the **Macros tab** in the Database window. Click and drag the **Prototype macro** to the Report Menu form as shown in Figure 3.12c. Release the mouse, and a command button is created that will execute the Prototype macro.

➤ Click and drag to select the name of the button (Prototype), which corresponds to the name of the macro. Type **Report 1** as the new name. (Clicking this button in Form view will still execute the Prototype macro as you have changed only the text of the button, not the underlying macro.)

➤ Repeat these steps to create two additional buttons, **Report 2** and **Report 3,** as shown in Figure 3.12c. Do not worry about the size or position of the buttons at this time.

Click to maximize the
Form window

Click and drag Prototype
macro to form

Change name of button
to Report 3

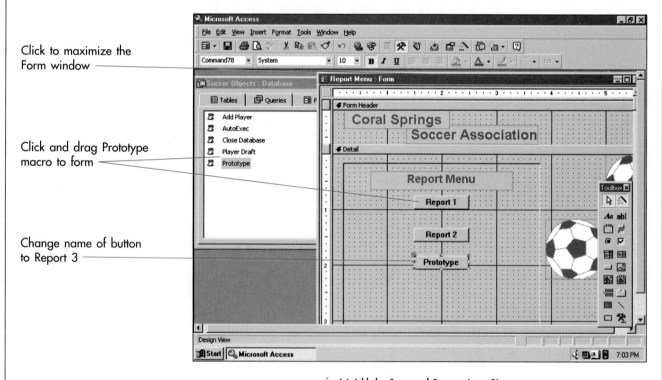

(c) Add the Command Buttons (step 3)

FIGURE 3.12   Hands-on Exercise 4 (continued)

STEP 4: Complete the Report Menu

➤ Maximize the Form window.

➤ Click the **Command Button tool** on the Toolbox toolbar, then click and drag in the form to create the command button shown in Figure 3.12d. (The number of your button will be different from ours.)

➤ The Command Button Wizard prompts you for the next several responses. Choose **Form operations** from the Categories list. Select **Close Form** as shown in Figure 3.12d. Click **Next.**

➤ Click the **Text option,** type **Close Menu** in the text box, and click **Next.** Type **Close Menu** as the name of the button. Click **Finish.**

➤ Size, align, color, and/or move the command buttons as you have done throughout the chapter.

➤ Click the **Form View button** to test the menu. Click the **Report 1 button,** which displays a message indicating that the report is not yet available. Click **OK** in response to the message.

➤ Click the buttons for **Report 2** and **Report 3,** then click **OK** as you see each informational message.

➤ Click the **Close Menu Command button** to close the Report Menu. Click **Yes** when asked whether to save the form.

Command Button Wizard creates the button for you

Form View button

Click and drag where command button is to go

Command Button tool

(d) Complete the Report Menu (step 4)

FIGURE 3.12   Hands-on Exercise 4 (continued)

GIVE YOUR USERS WHAT THEY WANT

Talk to the people who will eventually use your application to determine what they expect from the system. Ask for copies of the (paper) forms they currently have and aim for a similar look in your application. Try to obtain copies of the reports they currently prepare to be sure that your system produces the information expected from it.

STEP 5: Modify the Main Menu

➤ If necessary, click the **Forms tab** in the Database window. Select the **Main Menu form,** then click the **Design button** to open the form in Design view as shown in Figure 3.12e.

➤ Click the **Command Button tool** on the Forms Design toolbar, then click and drag in the form to create the command button shown in Figure 3.12e. (The number of your button will be different from ours.)

➤ The Command Button Wizard prompts you for several responses. Choose **Form operations** from the Categories list. Select **Open Form.** Click **Next.**

➤ Choose **Report Menu** as the name of the form. Click **Next.**

➤ Click the **Text option,** type **Report Menu** in the text box, and click **Next.** Type **Report Menu** as the name of the button. Click **Finish.**

Form View button

Select Report Menu as the name of the form

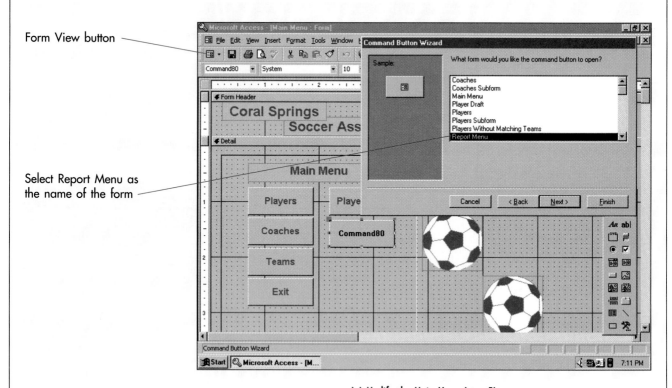

(e) Modify the Main Menu (step 5)

FIGURE 3.12   Hands-on Exercise 4 (continued)

BE CONSISTENT

Consistency within an application is essential to its success. Similar functions should be done in similar ways to facilitate learning and to build confidence in the application. The soccer application, for example, has similar screens for the Players, Coaches, and Teams forms, each of which contains the identical command buttons to add or print a record and close the form. The interface and means of navigation are consistent from one screen to the next.

STEP 6: Test the Completed System

➤ Click the **Form View button** to switch to the Form view and test the system. Click the **Report Menu button** on the Main Menu to display the Report Menu in Figure 3.12f.

➤ Click the command buttons for any of the reports, then click **OK** in response to the informational message.

➤ Click the **Close Menu Command button** to exit the Report Menu and return to the Main Menu.

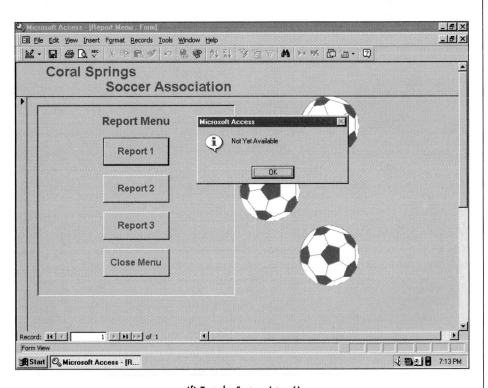

(f) Test the System (step 6)

FIGURE 3.12   Hands-on Exercise 4 (continued)

STEP 7: Additional Properties

➤ Return to the Design view for the Main Menu. Point to the **Form Selector box** to the left of the ruler, click the **right mouse button**, then click the **Properties command** to display the Properties dialog box for the form as shown in Figure 3.12g.

➤ Click the **Format tab** (if necessary), then click in the **Record Selectors text box** to display the drop-down list shown in Figure 3.12g. Click **No** to disable the Record Selector.

➤ Click in the **Navigation Buttons text box** to display its drop-down list, then click **No** to suppress the display of the navigation buttons.

➤ Click the **Player Draft button.** The Properties box displays the properties of the selected object.

➤ Click the **All tab,** then change the caption property to **Player &Draft** by placing an ampersand in front of the "D" in "Draft."

➤ Scroll down to the **ControlTip Text** property and enter **Click this button or press Alt+D** to assign players to teams. Close the Properties box.

➤ If necessary, size and align the command button within the Main Menu. (Press and hold the **Shift key** to select multiple buttons, then use the Size and Align commands on the Format menu.)

➤ Save the completed form.

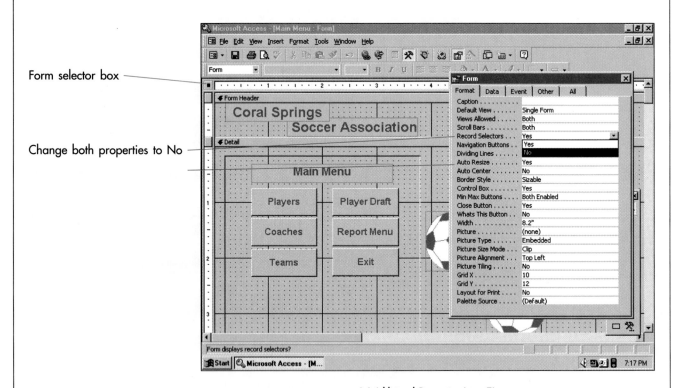

(g) Additional Properties (step 7)

FIGURE 3.12   Hands-on Exercise 4 (continued)

KEYBOARD SHORTCUTS—THE CAPTION PROPERTY

The Caption Property enables you to create a keyboard shortcut for a command button. Right click the button in the Form Design view to display the Properties dialog box for the command button. Click the All tab, then modify the Caption Property to include an ampersand immediately in front of the letter that will become part of the shortcut (e.g., &Help if you have a Help button). Close the dialog box, then go to the Form view. The command button will contain an underlined letter (e.g., Help), which can be activated in conjunction with the Alt key (e.g. Alt+H).

STEP 8: The Finished Form

➤ Return to the Form view to view the finished menu. Neither the Selection Area nor the Navigation buttons are visible in accordance with the property settings in the previous step.

➤ Point to the Player Draft button, which displays the ScreenTip shown in Figure 3.12h. Press **Alt+D** (the keyboard shortcut created in step 7) to return to the player draft that was created earlier in the exercise. Click the **End Draft button** to return to the main form.

➤ Click the **Exit command button** to close the database. Click **Yes** if prompted to save any of the objects created in this exercise.

➤ Exit Access. Congratulations on a job well done.

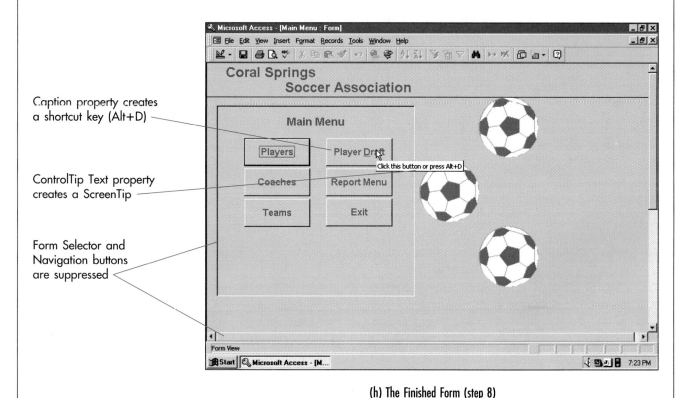

(h) The Finished Form (step 8)

FIGURE 3.12   Hands-on Exercise 4 (continued)

An application contains the same objects as a database. The difference is in how the objects are presented to the user. An application has an intuitive user interface that does not require a knowledge of Microsoft Access on the part of the user.

The tables in a database can be separated from the other objects to enable the distribution of updated versions of the application without disturbing the data. The tables are stored in one database and the objects in another. The Link Tables command associates the tables with the objects.

A form is the basis of a user interface. The form contains text or list boxes in which to enter or edit data, and command buttons to move from one screen to the next. Clicking a command button causes Access to execute the underlying macro or event procedure.

A macro automates a command sequence and consists of one or more actions. An action is a command that performs a specific operation, such as opening a form or running a select query. A macro action has one or more arguments that supply information about how the command is to be executed.

The Macro window has two sections. The upper section contains the name (if any) of the macro, the condition (if any) under which it is executed, and most important, the actions (commands) that make up the macro. The lower section specifies the arguments for the various actions. A macro group consists of multiple macros and is used for organizational purposes.

The AutoExec macro is executed automatically whenever the database in which it is stored is opened. Each database can have its own AutoExec macro, but there is no requirement for an AutoExec macro to be present.

The Unmatched Query Wizard identifies the records in one table (e.g., the Players table) that do not have matching records in another table (e.g., the Teams table).

A prototype is a model (mockup) of a completed application that demonstrates the "look and feel" of the application. Prototypes can be developed quickly and easily through the use of simple macros containing the MsgBox action.

KEY WORDS AND CONCEPTS

Action
Application
Argument
AutoExec macro
Combo box
Command button
Database properties
Debugging
Display When property
Event

Event procedure
Find Unmatched Query
    Wizard
Get External Data
Is Null criterion
Link Tables command
List box
Macro
Macro group
Macro toolbar

Macro window
MsgBox action
On Click property
Prototype
Requery command
Template
Top-down
    implementation
User interface
Zoom box

MULTIPLE CHOICE

1. The user interface of an application is based on a:
   (a) Table
   (b) Form
   (c) Query
   (d) Report

2. Which of the following describes the storage of the tables and objects for the application developed in the chapter?
   (a) Each table is stored in its own database
   (b) Each object is stored in its own database
   (c) The tables are stored in one database and the objects in a different database
   (d) The tables and objects are stored in the same database

3. Which of the following is true regarding the Link Tables command as it was used in the chapter?
   (a) It was executed from the Soccer Objects database
   (b) It was executed from the Soccer Tables database
   (c) Both (a) and (b)
   (d) Neither (a) nor (b)

4. What happens when an Access database is initially opened?
   (a) Access executes the AutoExec macro if the macro exists
   (b) Access opens the AutoExec form if the form exists
   (c) Both (a) and (b)
   (d) Neither (a) nor (b)

5. Which statement is true regarding the AutoExec macro?
   (a) Every database must have an AutoExec macro
   (b) A database may have more than one AutoExec macro
   (c) Both (a) and (b)
   (d) Neither (a) nor (b)

6. Which of the following are examples of arguments?
   (a) MsgBox and OpenForm
   (b) Message type (e.g., critical) and Form name
   (c) Both (a) and (b)
   (d) Neither (a) nor (b)

7. What happens if you drag a macro from the Database window onto a form?
   (a) A command button is created that opens the form
   (b) A command button is created that runs the macro
   (c) Both (a) and (b)
   (d) Neither (a) nor (b)

8. How do you change the properties of a command button on an existing form?
   (a) Open the form in Form view, then click the left mouse button to display a shortcut menu
   (b) Open the form in Form view, then click the right mouse button to display a shortcut menu
   (c) Open the form in Form Design view, then click the left mouse button to display a shortcut menu
   (d) Open the form in Form Design view, then click the right mouse button to display a shortcut menu

9. Which of the following is true regarding the Unmatched Query Wizard with respect to the CSSA database?
   (a) It can be used to identify teams without players
   (b) It can be used to identify players without teams
   (c) Both (a) and (b)
   (d) Neither (a) nor (b)

10. Which of the following can be associated with the On Click property of a command button?
   (a) An event procedure created by the Command Button Wizard
   (b) A macro created by the user
   (c) Either (a) or (b)
   (d) Neither (a) nor (b)

11. Which of the following was suggested as essential to a backup strategy?
   (a) Backing up files at the end of every session
   (b) Storing the backup file(s) at another location
   (c) Both (a) and (b)
   (d) Neither (a) nor (b)

12. The On Click property of a command button contains the entry, *Player Draft.Update List*. Which of the following is true?
   (a) Update List is an event procedure
   (b) Player Draft is an event procedure
   (c) Player Draft is a macro in the Update List macro group
   (d) Update List is a macro in the Player Draft macro group

13. Which columns are always visible in the Macro window?
   (a) Action and Comments
   (b) Macro Name and Conditions
   (c) Both (a) and (b)
   (d) Neither (a) nor (b)

14. The F6 and F11 function keys were introduced as shortcuts. Which of the following is true about these keys?
   (a) The F6 key switches between the top and bottom sections of the Macro window
   (b) The F11 key makes the Database window the active window
   (c) Both (a) and (b)
   (d) Neither (a) nor (b)

15. Which of the following was suggested as a way to organize macros and thus limit the number of macros that are displayed in the Database window?

(a) Avoid macro actions that have only a single argument

(b) Avoid macros that contain only a single action

(c) Create a macro group

(d) All of the above

ANSWERS

1. b	**6.** b	**11.** c
2. c	**7.** b	**12.** d
3. a	**8.** d	**13.** a
4. a	**9.** c	**14.** c
5. d	**10.** c	**15.** c

PRACTICE WITH ACCESS 97

1. Prototyping was demonstrated in the fourth hands-on exercise to create the "look and feel" of the soccer application. It remains, however, to create the three reports in the Report Menu, to create a macro to open each of these reports, and finally to assign each macro to the appropriate command button. Create the following reports:

a. Report 1 is a master list of all players in alphabetical order. Include the player's first and last names, date of birth, rating, phone, and address in that order. Create the report in landscape rather than portrait orientation.

b. Report 2 is a master list of all coaches in alphabetical order. Include the coach's first and last names, phone, and address in that order. Create the report in landscape rather than portrait orientation.

c. Report 3 is to print the team rosters in sequence by TeamID. Each roster is to begin on a new page. The header line should contain the TeamID, nickname, and team colors as well as the name and phone number of the head coach. A detail line—containing the player's first and last names, telephone number, and date of birth—is to appear for each player. Players are to be listed alphabetically.

d. Submit a disk with the CSSA database to your instructor.

2. Figure 3.13 displays a modified version of the Main Menu for the CSSA database, which has been enhanced through the addition of a Help button. The user clicks the Help button to execute a macro, which in turn displays the dialog box shown in the figure.

a. Complete all of the hands-on exercises in the chapter, then add a Help macro containing your telephone and e-mail address. (The macro consists of a single MsgBox action.)

b. Modify the existing Main Menu to include the Help button shown in Figure 3.13, which runs the macro you just created.

c. Submit a disk with the CSSA database to your instructor.

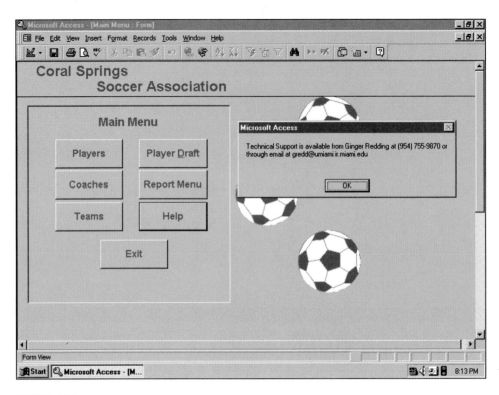

FIGURE 3.13   Screen for Practice Exercise 2

3. Figure 3.14 illustrates the use of the Condition column in the Macro window. The intent of the macro in Figure 3.14 is to display a message to "A"-rated players inviting them to try out for an All-City competitive team that plays against teams from other cities.

   a. Create the macro shown in Figure 3.14. (Click the Conditions button on the Macro toolbar to display the Conditions column in the Macro window.)

   b. Open the Players form in Design view. Right click the Rating control to display its Property sheet, then assign the macro you just created to the On Exit property.

   c. Prove to yourself that the macro works. Change to Form view, then move to the record containing the information you entered for yourself in step 3 of the first hands-on exercise. Click the text box containing the player rating, enter "A", then press the Tab key to move to the next control. You should see a message inviting you to try for the competitive team. Change your rating to a "B" and press the Tab key a second time. This time there is no message.

   d. Submit a disk with the CSSA database to your instructor.

4. The player draft was only partially completed in the fourth hands-on exercise and still requires the completion of the Find Player function. After this has been accomplished, you will be able to click the Find Player button in Figure 3.15 to display the Find Parameter Value dialog box to enter a player's name, and then view the information for that player. Accordingly:

   a. Create a parameter query that requests the last name of a player, then returns *all* fields for that player.

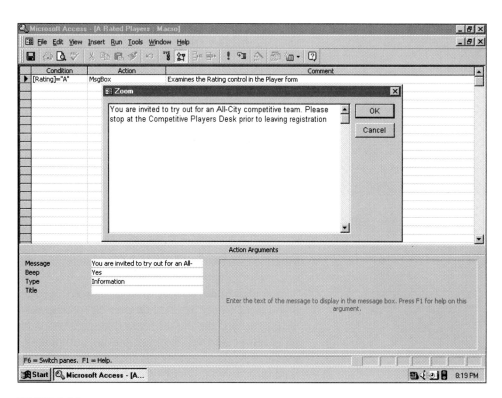

FIGURE 3.14   Screen for Practice Exercise 3

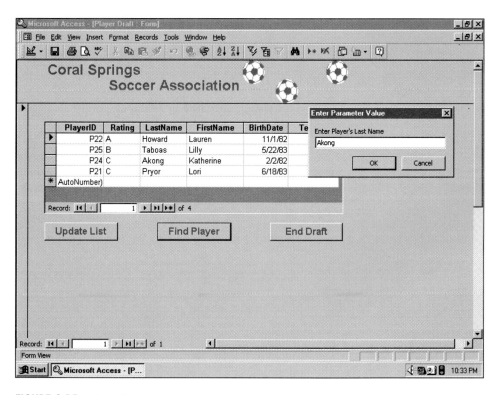

FIGURE 3.15   Screen for Practice Exercise 4

b. Copy the existing Players Form to a new form called Find Player. Change the Record Source property of the Find Player form to the parameter query you created in part a.

c. Change the Find Player macro in the Player Draft group so that it opens the Find Player form you just created.

d. Add the Help button to the Player Draft menu as described in practice exercise 2. Submit the completed disk to your instructor.

CASE STUDIES

Client/Server Applications

The application for the Coral Springs Soccer Association was developed to run on a single PC; in practice, however, it would most likely be implemented on a network. Investigate the additional steps needed to load the Soccer Tables database on a server and enable multiple users (clients) to access the database simultaneously. How does Access prevent two users from modifying the same record simultaneously? What security features are available? How would backup be implemented? Where would the Soccer Objects database be stored?

A Project for the Semester

Choose any of the eight cases at the end of the two previous chapters (with the exception of the Recreational Sports League) and develop a complete system. Design the tables and relationships and provide a representative series of forms to enter and edit the data. Create a representative set of queries and reports. And finally, tie the system together via a system of menus similar to those that were developed in this chapter.

The Database Wizard

The Database Wizard provides an easy way to create a database as it creates the database for you. The advantage of the Wizard is that it creates the tables, forms, and reports, together with a Main Menu (called a switchboard) in one operation. The disadvantage is that the Wizard is inflexible compared to creating the database yourself. Use the online Help facility to learn about the Database Wizard, then use the Wizard to create a simple database for your music collection. Is the Wizard a useful shortcut, or is it easier to create the database yourself?

Compacting versus Compressing

The importance of adequate backup has been stressed throughout the text. As a student, however, your backup may be limited to what you can fit on a single floppy disk, which in turn creates a problem if the size of your database grows beyond 1.4Mb. Two potential solutions involve compacting and/or compressing the database. Compacting is done from within Access, whereas compressing requires additional software. Investigate both of these techniques with respect to the CSSA database created in the chapter. Be sure to indicate to your instructor the reduction in file size that you were able to achieve.

APPENDIX A: TOOLBARS

OVERVIEW

Microsoft Access has 20 predefined toolbars that provide access to commonly used commands. Twelve of the toolbars are tied to a specific view and are displayed automatically when you work in that view. These twelve toolbars are shown in Figure A.1 and are listed here for convenience: the Database, Relationships, Table Design, Table Datasheet, Query Design, Query Datasheet, Form Design, Form View, Report Design, Print Preview, Macro Design, and Visual Basic toolbars.

The remaining toolbars are shown in Figure A.2. The Toolbox and Formatting (Form/Report Design) toolbars are displayed by default in both the Form Design and Report Design views. The Formatting (Datasheet) toolbar is displayed by default in both the Table Datasheet and Query Datasheet views. The Web toolbar can be displayed (hidden) in any view at the discretion of the user. The Filter/Sort toolbar is displayed at the discretion of the user.

Database Toolbar

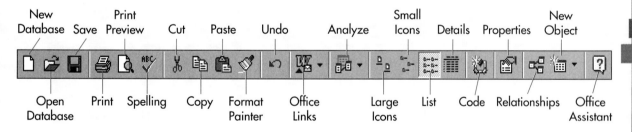

Relationships Toolbar

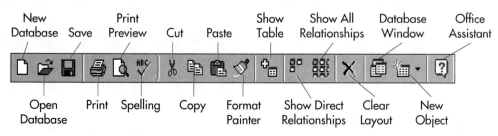

FIGURE A.1 Access Toolbars Tied to Specific Views

Table Design Toolbar

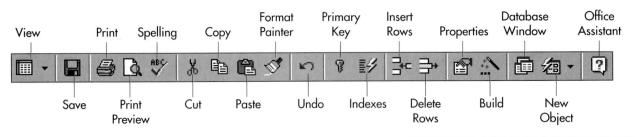

Table Datasheet Toolbar

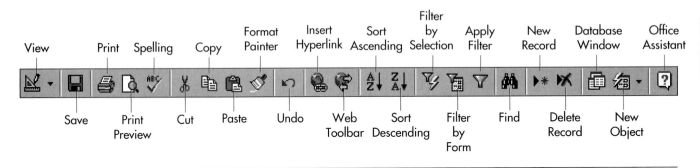

Query Design Toolbar

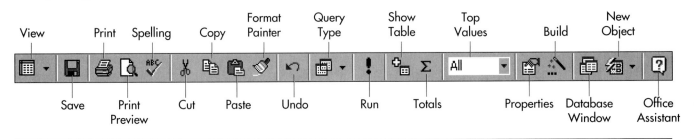

Query Datasheet Toolbar

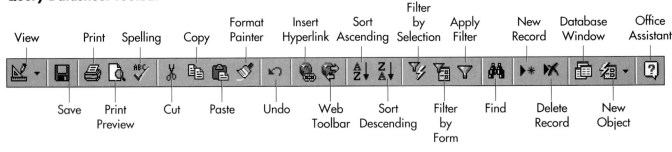

Form Design Toolbar

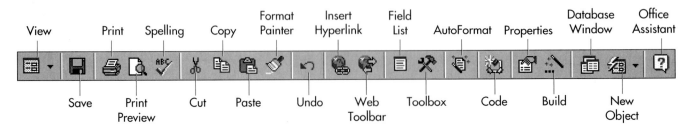

FIGURE A.1   Access Toolbars Tied to Specific Views (continued)

Form View Toolbar

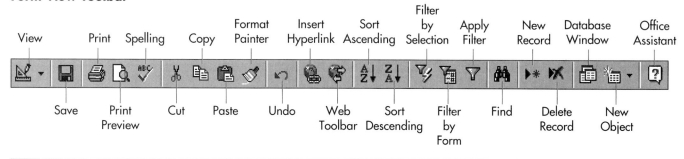

Report Design Toolbar

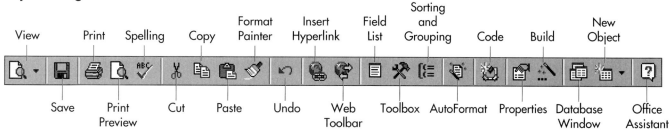

Print Preview Toolbar

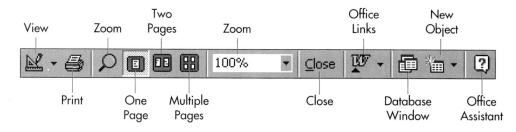

Macro Design Toolbar

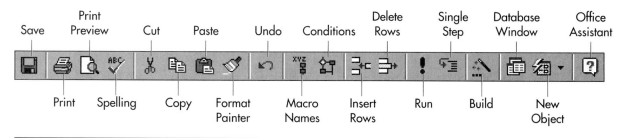

Visual Basic Toolbar

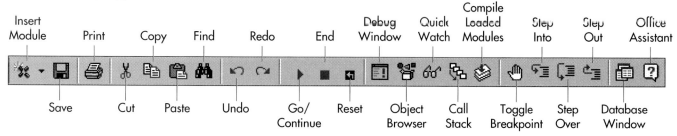

FIGURE A.1   Access Toolbars Tied to Specific Views (continued)

Toolbox Toolbar

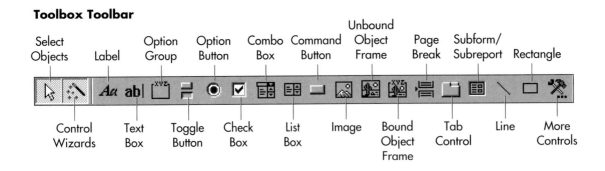

Formatting (Form/Report) Toolbar

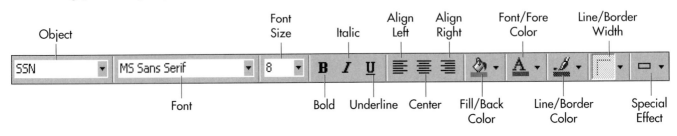

Formatting (Datasheet) Toolbar

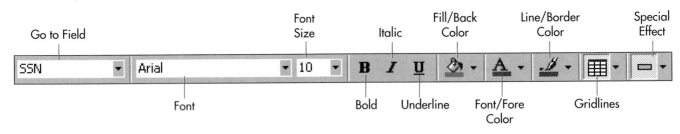

Web Toolbar

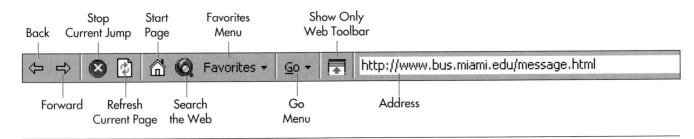

Filter/Sort Toolbar

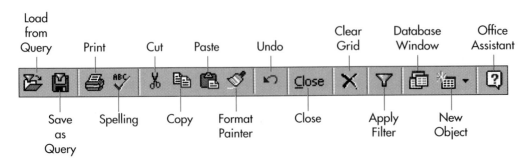

FIGURE A.2   Other Access Toolbars

APPENDIX B: DESIGNING A RELATIONAL DATABASE

OVERVIEW

An Access database consists of multiple tables, each of which stores data about a specific subject. To use Access effectively, you must relate the tables to one another. This in turn requires a knowledge of database design and an understanding of the principles of a relational database under which Access operates.

Our approach to teaching database design is to present two case studies, each of which covers a common application. The first case centers on franchises for fast food restaurants and incorporates the concept of a one-to-many relationship. One person can own many restaurants, but a given restaurant is owned by only one person. The second case is based on a system for student transcripts and incorporates a many-to-many relationship. One student takes many courses, and one course is taken by many students. The intent in both cases is to design a database capable of producing the desired information.

CASE STUDY: FAST FOOD FRANCHISES

The case you are about to read is set within the context of a national corporation offering franchises for fast food restaurants. The concept of a franchise operation is a familiar one and exists within many industries. The parent organization develops a model operation, then franchises that concept to qualified individuals (franchisees) seeking to operate their own businesses. The national company teaches the franchisee to run the business, aids the person in site selection and staffing, coordinates national advertising, and so on. The franchisee pays an initial fee to open the business followed by subsequent royalties and marketing fees to the parent corporation.

The essence of the case is how to relate the data for the various entities (the restaurants, franchisees, and contracts) to one another. One approach is to develop a single restaurant table, with each restaurant record containing data about the owner and contract arrangement. As we shall see, that design leads to problems of redundancy whenever the same person owns more than one restaurant or when several restaurants are governed by the same contract type. A better approach is to develop separate tables, one for each of the objects (restaurants, franchisees, and contracts).

The entities in the case have a definite relationship to one another, which must be reflected in the database design. The corporation encourages individuals to own multiple restaurants, creating a *one-to-many relationship* between franchisees and restaurants. One person can own many restaurants, but a given restaurant is owned by only one person. There is also a one-to-many relationship between contracts and restaurants because the corporation offers a choice of contracts to each restaurant.

The company wants a database that can retrieve all data for a given restaurant, such as the annual sales, type of contract in effect (contract types are described below), and/or detailed information about the restaurant owner. The company also needs reports that reflect the location of each restaurant, all restaurants in a given state, and all restaurants managed by a particular contract type. The various contract arrangements are described below:

Contract 1: 99-year term, requiring a one-time fee of $250,000 payable at the time the franchise is awarded. In addition, the franchisee must pay a royalty of 2 percent of the restaurant's gross sales to the parent corporation, and contribute an additional 2 percent of sales to the parent corporation for advertising.

Contract 2: 5-year term (renewable at franchisee's option), requiring an initial payment of $50,000. In addition, the franchisee must pay a royalty of 4 percent of the restaurant's gross sales to the parent corporation, and contribute an additional 3 percent of sales to the parent corporation for advertising.

Contract 3: 10-year term (renewable at franchisee's option), requiring an initial payment of $75,000. In addition, the franchisee must pay a royalty of 3 percent of the restaurant's gross sales to the parent corporation, and contribute an additional 3 percent of sales to the parent corporation for advertising.

Other contract types may be offered in the future. The company currently has 500 restaurants, of which 200 are company owned. Expansion plans call for opening an additional 200 restaurants each year for the next three years, all of which are to be franchised. There is no limit on the number of restaurants an individual may own, and franchisees are encouraged to apply for multiple restaurants.

Single Table Solution

The initial concern in this, or any other, system is how best to structure the data so that the solution satisfies the information requirements of the client. We present two solutions. The first is based on a single restaurant table and will be shown to have several limitations. The second introduces the concept of a relational database and consists of three tables (for the restaurants, franchisee, and contracts).

The single table solution is shown in Figure B.1a. Each record within the table contains data about a particular restaurant, its franchisees (owner), and contract type. There are five restaurants in our example, each with a *unique* restaurant number. At first glance, Figure B.1a appears satisfactory; yet there are three specific types of problems associated with this solution. These are:

1. Difficulties in the modification of data for an existing franchisee or contract type, in that the same change may be made in multiple places.

Restaurant Number	Restaurant Data (Address, annual sales . . .)	Franchisee Data (Name, telephone, address . . .)	Contract Data (Type, term, initial fee . . .)
R1	Restaurant data for Miami . . .	Franchisee data (Grauer . . .)	Contract data (Type 1 . . .)
R2	Restaurant data for Coral Gables . . .	Franchisee data (Moldof . . .)	Contract data (Type 1 . . .)
R3	Restaurant data for Fort Lauderdale. . .	Franchisee data (Grauer . . .)	Contract data (Type 2 . . .)
R4	Restaurant data for New York . . .	Franchisee data (Glassman . . .)	Contract data (Type 1 . . .)
R5	Restaurant data for Coral Springs . . .	Franchisee data (Coulter . . .)	Contract data (Type 3 . . .)

(a) Single Table Solution

Restaurant Number	Restaurant Data	Franchisee Number	Contract Type
R1	Restaurant data for Miami . . .	F1	C1
R2	Restaurant data for Coral Gables . . .	F2	C1
R3	Restaurant data for Fort Lauderdale. . .	F1	C2
R4	Restaurant data for New York . . .	F3	C1
R5	Restaurant data for Coral Springs . . .	F4	C3

Contract Type	Contract Data
C1	Contract data. . .
C2	Contract data. . .
C3	Contract data. . .

Franchisee Number	Franchisee Data (Name, telephone, address, . . .)
F1	Grauer. . .
F2	Moldof. . .
F3	Glassman. . .
F4	Coulter. . .

(b) Multiple Table Solution

FIGURE B.1   Single versus Multiple Table Solution

2. Difficulties in the addition of a new franchisee or contract type, in that these entities must first be associated with a particular restaurant.

3. Difficulties in the deletion of a restaurant, in that data for a particular franchisee or contract type may be deleted as well.

The first problem, modification of data about an existing franchisee or contract type, stems from *redundancy,* which in turn requires that any change to duplicated data be made in several places. In other words, any modification to a duplicated entry, such as a change in data for a franchisee with multiple restaurants (e.g., Grauer, who owns restaurants in Miami and Fort Lauderdale), requires a search through the entire table to find all instances of that data so that the identical modification can be made to each of the records. A similar procedure would have to be followed should data change about a duplicated contract (e.g., a change in the royalty percentage for contract Type 1, which applies to restaurants R1, R2, and R4). This is, to say the least, a time-consuming and error-prone procedure.

The addition of a new franchisee or contract type poses a different type of problem. It is quite logical, for example, that potential franchisees must apply to the corporation and qualify for ownership before having a restaurant assigned to them. It is also likely that the corporation would develop a new contract type prior to offering that contract to an existing restaurant. Neither of these events is easily accommodated in the table structure of Figure B.1a, which would require the creation of a dummy restaurant record to accommodate the new franchisee or contract type.

The deletion of a restaurant creates yet another type of difficulty. What happens, for example, if the company decides to close restaurant R5 because of insufficient sales? The record for this restaurant would disappear as expected, but so too would the data for the franchisee (Coulter) and the contract type (C3), which is not intended. The corporation might want to award Coulter another restaurant in the future and/or offer this contract type to other restaurants. Neither situation would be possible as the relevant data has been lost with the deletion of the restaurant record.

Multiple Table Solution

A much better solution appears in Figure B.1b, which uses a different table for each of the entities (restaurants, franchisees, and contracts) that exist in the system. Every record in the restaurant table is assigned a unique restaurant number (e.g., R1 or R2), just as every record in the franchisee table is given a unique franchisee number (e.g., F1 or F2), and every contract record a unique contract number (e.g., C1 or C2).

The tables are linked to one another through the franchisee and/or contract numbers, which also appear in the restaurant table. Every record in the restaurant table is associated with its appropriate record in the franchisee table through the franchisee number common to both tables. In similar fashion, every restaurant is tied to its appropriate contract through the contract number, which appears in the restaurant record. This solution may seem complicated, but it is really quite simple and elegant.

Assume, for example, that we want the name of the franchisee for restaurant R5, and further, that we need the details of the contract type for this restaurant. We retrieve the appropriate restaurant record, which contains franchisee and contract numbers of F4 and C3, respectively. We then search through the franchisee table for franchisee F4 (obtaining all necessary information about Coulter) and search again through the contract table for contract C3 (obtaining the data for this contract type). The process is depicted graphically in Figure B.1b.

The multiple table solution may require slightly more effort to retrieve information, but this is more than offset by the advantages of table maintenance. Consider, for example, a change in data for contract C1, which currently governs restaurants R1, R2, and R4. All that is necessary is to go into the contract table, find record C1, and make the changes. The records in the restaurant table are *not* affected because the restaurant records do not contain contract data per se, only the number of the corresponding contract record. In other words, the change in data for contract C1 is made in one place (the contract table), yet that change would be reflected for all affected restaurants. This is in contrast to the single table solution of Figure B.1a, which would require the identical modification in three places.

The addition of new records for franchisees or contracts is done immediately in the appropriate tables of Figure B.1b. The corporation simply adds a franchisee or contract record as these events occur, without the necessity of a corresponding restaurant record. This is much easier than the approach of Figure B.1a, which required an existing restaurant in order to add one of the other entities.

The deletion of a restaurant is also easier than with the single table organization. You could, for example, delete restaurant R5 without losing the associated franchisee and contract data as these records exist in different tables.

Queries to the Database

By now you should be convinced of the need for multiple tables within a database and that this type of design facilitates all types of table maintenance. However, the ultimate objective of any system is to produce information, and it is in this area that the design excels. Consider now Figure B.2, which expands upon the multiple table solution to include additional data for the respective tables.

To be absolutely sure you understand the multiple table solution of Figure B.2, use it to answer the questions at the top of the next page. Check your answers with those provided.

Restaurant Number	Street Address	City	State	Zip Code	Annual Sales	Franchisee Number	Contract Type
R1	1001 Ponce de Leon Blvd	Miami	FL	33361	$600,000	F1	C1
R2	31 West Rivo Alto Road	Coral Gables	FL	33139	$450,000	F2	C1
R3	333 Las Olas Blvd	Fort Lauderdale	FL	33033	$250,000	F1	C2
R4	1700 Broadway	New York	NY	10293	$1,750,000	F3	C1
R5	1300 Sample Road	Coral Springs	FL	33071	$50,000	F4	C3

(a) Restaurant Table

Franchisee Number	Franchisee Name	Telephone	Street Address	City	State	Zip Code
F1	Grauer	(305) 755-1000	2133 NW 102 Terrace	Coral Springs	FL	33071
F2	Moldof	(305) 753-4614	1400 Lejeune Blvd	Miami	FL	33365
F3	Glassman	(212) 458-5054	555 Fifth Avenue	New York	NY	10024
F4	Coulter	(305) 755-0910	1000 Federal Highway	Fort Lauderdale	FL	33033

(b) Franchisee Table

Contract Type	Term (years)	Initial Fee	Royalty Pct	Advertising Pct
C1	99	$250,000	2%	2%
C2	5	$50,000	4%	3%
C3	10	$75,000	3%	3%

(c) Contract Table

FIGURE B.2   Fast Food Franchises

Questions

1. Who owns restaurant R2? What contract type is in effect for this restaurant?
2. What is the address of restaurant R4?
3. Which restaurant(s) are owned by Mr. Grauer?
4. List all restaurants with a contract type of C1.
5. Which restaurants in Florida have gross sales over $300,000?
6. List all contract types.
7. Which contract type has the lowest initial fee? How much is the initial fee? Which restaurant(s) are governed by this contract?
8. How many franchisees are there? What are their names?
9. What are the royalty and advertising percentages for restaurant R3?

Answers

1. Restaurant R2 is owned by Moldof and governed by contract C1.
2. Restaurant R4 is located at 1700 Broadway, New York, NY 10293.
3. Mr. Grauer owns restaurants R1 and R3.
4. R1, R2, and R4 are governed by contract C1.
5. The restaurants in Florida with gross sales over $300,000 are R1 ($600,000) and R2 ($450,000).
6. The existing contract types are C1, C2, and C3.
7. Contract C2 has the lowest initial fee ($50,000); restaurant R3 is governed by this contract type.
8. There are four franchisees: Grauer, Moldof, Glassman, and Coulter.
9. Restaurant R3 is governed by contract C2 with royalty and advertising percentages of four and three percent, respectively.

THE RELATIONAL MODEL

The restaurant case study illustrates a *relational database,* which requires a separate table for every entity in the physical system (restaurants, franchisees, and contracts). Each occurrence of an entity (a specific restaurant, franchisee, or contract type) appears as a *row* within a table. The properties of an entity (a restaurant's address, owner, or sales) appear as *columns* within a table.

Every row in every table of a relational database must be distinct. This is accomplished by including a column (or combination of columns) to uniquely identify the row. The unique identifier is known as the *primary key.* The restaurant number, for example, is different for every restaurant in the restaurant table. The franchisee number is unique in the franchisee table. The contract type is unique in the contract table.

The same column can, however, appear in multiple tables. The franchisee number, for example, appears in both the franchisee table, where its values are unique, and in the restaurant table, where they are not. The franchisee number is the primary key in the franchisee table, but it is a *foreign key* in the restaurant table. (A foreign key is simply the primary key of a related table.)

The inclusion of a foreign key in the restaurant table enables us to implement the one-to-many relationship between franchisees and restaurants. We enter the franchisee number (the primary key in the franchisee table) as a column in the restaurant table, where it (the franchisee number) is a foreign key. In similar fashion, contract type (the primary key in the contract table) appears as a foreign key in the restaurant table to implement the one-to-many relationship between contracts and restaurants.

It is helpful perhaps to restate these observations about a relational database in general terms:

1. Every entity in a physical system requires its own table in a database.
2. Each row in a table is different from every other row because of a unique column (or combination of columns) known as a primary key.
3. The primary key of one table can appear as a foreign key in another table.
4. The order of rows in a table is immaterial.
5. The order of columns in a table is immaterial, although the primary key is generally listed first.
6. The number of columns is the same in every row of the table.

THE KEY, THE WHOLE KEY, AND NOTHING BUT THE KEY

The theory of a relational database was developed by Dr. Edgar Codd, giving rise to the phrase, "*The key, the whole key, and nothing but the key . . . so help me Codd.*" The sentence effectively summarizes the concepts behind a relational database and helps to ensure the validity of a design. Simply stated, the value of every column other than the primary key depends on the key in that row, on the entire key, and on nothing but that key.

Referential Integrity

The concept of *referential integrity* requires that the tables in a database be consistent with one another. Consider once again the first row in the restaurant table of Figure B.2a, which indicates that the restaurant is owned by franchisee F1 and governed by contract Type C1. Recall also how these values are used to obtain additional information about the franchisee or contract type from the appropriate tables in Figures B.2b and B.2c, respectively.

What if, however, the restaurant table referred to franchisee number F1000 or contract C9, neither of which exists in the database of Figure B.2? There would be a problem because the tables would be inconsistent with one another; that is, the restaurant table would refer to rows in the franchisee and contract tables that do not exist. It is important, therefore, that referential integrity be strictly enforced and that such inconsistencies be prevented from occurring. Suffice it to say that data validation is critical when establishing or maintaining a database, and that no system, relational or otherwise, can compensate for inaccurate or incomplete data.

CASE STUDY: STUDENT TRANSCRIPTS

Our second case is set within the context of student transcripts and expands the concept of a relational database to implement a *many-to-many relationship*. The system is intended to track students and the courses they take. The many-to-many relationship occurs because one student takes many courses, while at the same time, one course is taken by many students. The objective of this case is to relate the student and course tables to one another to produce the desired information.

The system should be able to display information about a particular student as well as information about a particular course. It should also display information about a student-course combination, such as when a student took the course and the grade he or she received.

Solution

The (intuitive and incorrect) solution of Figure B.3 consists of two tables, one for courses and one for students, corresponding to the two entities in the physical system. The student table contains the student's name, address, major, date of entry into the school, cumulative credits, and cumulative quality points. The course table contains the unique six-character course identifier, the course title, and the number of credits.

There are no problems of redundancy. The data for a particular course (its description and number of credits) appears only once in the course table, just as the data for a particular student appears only once in the student table. New courses will be added directly to the course table, just as new students will be added to the student table.

The design of the student table makes it easy to list all courses for one student. It is more difficult, however, to list all students in one course. Even if this were not the case, the solution is complicated by the irregular shape of the student table. The rows in the table are of variable length, according to the number of courses taken by each student. Not only is this design awkward, but how do we know in advance how much space to allocate for each student?

Course Number	Course Description	Credits
ACC101	Introduction to Accounting	3
CHM100	Survey of Chemistry	3
CHM101	Chemistry Lab	1
CIS120	Microcomputer Applications	3
ENG100	Freshman English	3
MTH100	Calculus with Analytic Geometry	4
MUS110	Music Appreciation	2
SPN100	Spanish I	3

(a) Course Table

Student Number	Student Data	Courses Taken with Grade and Semester											
S1	Student data (Adams. . .)	ACC101	SP95	A	CIS120	FA94	A	MU100	SP94	B			
S2	Student data (Fox. . .)	ENG100	SP95	B	MTH100	SP95	B	SPN100	SP95	B	CIS120	FA94	A
S3	Student data (Baker. . .)	ACC101	SP95	C	ENG100	SP95	B	MTH100	FA94	C	CIS120	FA94	B
S4	Student data (Jones. . .)	ENG100	SP95	A	MTH100	SP95	A						
S5	Student data (Smith. . .)	CIS120	SP95	C	ENG100	SP95	B	CIS120	FA94	F			

(b) Student Table

FIGURE B.3   Student Transcripts (repeating groups)

The problems inherent in Figure B.3 stem from the many-to-many relationship that exists between students and courses. The solution is to eliminate the *repeating groups* (course number, semester, and grade), which occur in each row of the student table in Figure B.3, in favor of the additional table shown in Figure B.4. Each row in the new table is unique because the *combination* of student number, course number, and semester is unique. Semester must be included since students are allowed to repeat a course. Smith (student number S5), for example, took CIS120 a second time after failing it initially.

The implementation of a many-to-many relationship requires an additional table, with a **combined key** consisting of (at least) the keys of the individual entities. The many-to-many table may also contain additional columns, which exist as a result of the combination (intersection) of the individual keys. The combination of student S5, course CIS120, and semester SP95 is unique and results in a grade of C.

Note, too, how the design in Figure B.4 facilitates table maintenance as discussed in the previous case. A change in student data is made in only one place (the student table) regardless of how many courses the student has taken. A new student may be added to the student table prior to taking any courses. In similar fashion, a new course can be added to the course table before any students have taken the course.

Review once more the properties of a relational database, then verify that the solution in Figure B.4 adheres to these requirements. To be absolutely sure

Course Number	Course Description	Credits
ACC101	Introduction to Accounting	3
CHM100	Survey of Chemistry	3
CHM101	Chemistry Lab	1
CIS120	Microcomputer Applications	3
ENG100	Freshman English	3
MTH100	Calculus with Analytic Geometry	4
MUS110	Music Appreciation	2
SPN100	Spanish I	3

(a) Course Table

Student Number	Student Data
S1	Student data (Adams. . .)
S2	Student data (Fox. . .)
S3	Student data (Baker. . .)
S4	Student data (Jones. . .)
S5	Student data (Smith. . .)

(b) Student Table

Student Number	Course Number	Semester	Grade
S1	ACC101	SP95	A
S1	CIS120	FA94	A
S1	MU100	SP94	B
S2	ENG100	SP95	B
S2	MTH100	SP95	B
S2	SPN100	SP95	B
S2	CIS120	FA94	A
S3	ACC101	SP95	C
S3	ENG100	SP95	B
S3	MTH100	FA94	C
S3	CIS120	FA94	B
S4	ENG100	SP95	A
S4	MTH100	SP95	A
S5	CIS120	SP95	C
S5	ENG100	SP95	B
S5	CIS120	FA94	F

(c) Student-Course Table

FIGURE B.4 Student Transcripts (improved design)

that you understand the solution, and to illustrate once again the power of the relational model, use Figure B.4 to answer the following questions about the student database.

Questions

1. How many courses are currently offered?
2. List all three-credit courses.
3. Which courses has Smith taken during his stay at the university?
4. Which students have taken MTH100?
5. Which courses did Adams take during the Fall 1994 semester?
6. Which students took Microcomputer Applications in the Fall 1994 semester?
7. Which students received an A in Freshman English during the Spring 1995 semester?

Answers

1. Eight courses are offered.
2. The three-credit courses are ACC101, CHM100, CIS120, ENG100, and SPN100.
3. Smith has taken CIS120 (twice) and ENG100.
4. Fox, Baker, and Jones have taken MTH100.
5. Adams took CIS120 during the Fall 1994 semester.
6. Adams, Fox, Baker, and Smith took Microcomputer Applications in the Fall 1994 semester.
7. Jones was the only student to receive an A in Freshman English during the Spring 1995 semester.

SUMMARY

A relational database consists of multiple two-dimensional tables. Each entity in a physical system requires its own table in the database. Every row in a table is unique due to the existence of a primary key. The order of the rows and columns in a table is immaterial. Every row in a table contains the same columns in the same order as every other row.

A one-to-many relationship is implemented by including the primary key of one table as a foreign key in the other table. Implementation of a many-to-many relationship requires an additional table whose primary key combines (at a minimum) the primary keys of the individual tables. Referential integrity ensures that the information in a database is internally consistent.

KEY WORDS AND CONCEPTS

Column
Combined key
Entity
Foreign key
Many-to-many
  relationship

One-to-many
  relationship
Primary key
Query
Redundancy
Referential integrity

Relational database
Repeating group
Row
Table

APPENDIX C: COMBINING AN ACCESS DATABASE WITH A WORD FORM LETTER

OVERVIEW

One of the greatest benefits of using the Microsoft Office suite is the ability to combine data from one application with another. An excellent example is a *mail merge,* in which data from an Access *table* or *query* are input into a Word document to produce a set of individualized form letters. You create the *form letter* using Microsoft Word, then you merge the letter with the *records* in the Access table or query. The merge process creates the individual letters, changing the name, address, and other information as appropriate from letter to letter. The concept is illustrated in Figure C.1, in which John Smith uses a mail merge to seek a job upon graduation. John writes the letter describing his qualifications, then merges that letter with a set of names and addresses to produce the individual letters.

The mail merge process uses two input files (a main document and a data source) and produces a third file as output (the set of form letters). The *main document* (e.g., the cover letter in Figure C.1a) contains standardized text together with one or more *merge fields* that indicate where the variable information is to be inserted in the individual letters. The *data source* (the set of names and addresses in Figure C.1b) contains the data that varies from letter to letter and is a table (or query) within an Access database. (The data source may also be taken from an Excel list, or alternatively it can be created as a table in Microsoft Word.)

The main document and the data source work in conjunction with one another, with the merge fields in the main document referencing the corresponding fields in the data source. The first line in the address of Figure C.1a, for example, contains three merge fields, each of which is enclosed in angle brackets, *<<Title>> <<FirstName>> <<LastName>>.* (These entries are not typed explicitly but are entered through special commands as described in the hands-on exercise that follows shortly.) The merge process examines each record in the data

John H. Smith

426 Jenny Lake Drive • Coral Gables, FL 33146 • (305) 666-4801

April 13, 1997

<<Title>> <<FirstName>> <<LastName>>
<<JobTitle>>
<<Company>>
<<Address1>>
<<City>>, <<State>> <<PostalCode>>

Dear <<Title>> <<LastName>>:

I am writing to inquire about a position with <<Company>> as an entry-level computer programmer. I have just graduated from the University of Miami with a bachelor's degree in Computer Information Systems (May 1997), and I am very interested in working for you. I have a background in both microcomputer applications (Windows 95, Word, Excel, PowerPoint, and Access) as well as extensive experience with programming languages (Visual Basic, C++, and COBOL). I feel that I am well qualified to join your staff as over the past two years I have had a great deal of experience designing and implementing computer programs, both as a part of my educational program and during my internship with Personalized Computer Designs, Inc.

I am eager to put my skills to work and would like to talk with you at your earliest convenience. I have enclosed a copy of my résumé and will be happy to furnish the names and addresses of my references, if you so desire. You may reach me at the above address and phone number. I look forward to hearing from you.

Sincerely,

John H. Smith

(a) The Form Letter (a Word document)

FIGURE C.1   The Mail Merge

source and substitutes the appropriate field values for the corresponding merge fields as it creates the individual form letters. For example, the first three fields in the first record will produce *Mr. Jason Frasher;* the same fields in the second record will produce, *Ms. Lauren Howard,* and so on.

In similar fashion, the second line in the address contains the *<<JobTitle>>* field. The third line contains the *<<Company>>* field. The fourth line references the *<<Address1>>* field, and the last line contains the *<<City>>, <<State>>,* and *<<Postalcode>>* fields. The salutation repeats the *<<Title>>* and *<<LastName>>* fields. The first sentence in the letter uses the *<<Company>>* field a second time. The mail merge prepares the letters one at a time, with one letter created for every record in the data source until the file of names and addresses is exhausted. The individual form letters are shown in Figure C.1c. Each letter begins automatically on a new page.

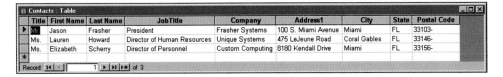

Title	First Name	Last Name	JobTitle	Company	Address1	City	State	Postal Code
Mr.	Jason	Frasher	President	Frasher Systems	100 S. Miami Avenue	Miami	FL	33103-
Ms.	Lauren	Howard	Director of Human Resources	Unique Systems	475 LeJeune Road	Coral Gables	FL	33146-
Ms.	Elizabeth	Scherry	Director of Personnel	Custom Computing	8180 Kendall Drive	Miami	FL	33156-

Record: 1 of 3

(b) The Data Source (an Access Table or Query)

John H. Smith

426 Jenny Lake Drive • Coral Gables, FL 33146 • (305) 666-4801

April 13, 1997

Ms. Elizabeth Scherry
Director of Personnel
Custom Computing
8180 Kendall Drive
Miami, FL 33156

Dear Ms. Scherry:

I am writing to inquire about a position with Custom Computing as an entry-level computer programmer. I have just graduated from the U... Computer Information Systems (May 1997), a... background in both microcomputer applicatio... Access) as well as extensive experience with p... COBOL). I feel that I am well qualified to jo... great deal of experience designing and imple... educational program and during my internshi...

I am eager to put my skills to work and woul... have enclosed a copy of my résumé and will b... references, if you so desire. You may reach m... forward to hearing from you.

Sincerely,

John H. Smith

John H. Smith

426 Jenny Lake Drive • Coral Gables, FL 33146 • (305) 666-4801

April 13, 1997

Ms. Lauren Howard
Director of Human Resources
Unique Systems
475 LeJeune Road
Coral Gables, FL 33146

Dear Ms. Howard:

I am writing to inquire about a position with Unique Systems as an entry-level computer programmer. I have just graduated from th... Computer Information Systems (May 1997... background in both microcomputer applica... Access) as well as extensive experience wi... COBOL). I feel that I am well qualified to... great deal of experience designing and imp... educational program and during my intern...

I am eager to put my skills to work and w... have enclosed a copy of my résumé and w... references, if you so desire. You may reac... forward to hearing from you.

Sincerely,

John H Smith

John H. Smith

426 Jenny Lake Drive • Coral Gables, FL 33146 • (305) 666-4801

April 13, 1997

Mr. Jason Frasher
President
Frasher Systems
100 S. Miami Avenue
Miami, FL 33103

Dear Mr. Frasher:

I am writing to inquire about a position with Frasher Systems as an entry-level computer programmer. I have just graduated from the University of Miami with a bachelor's degree in Computer Information Systems (May 1997), and I am very interested in working for you. I have a background in both microcomputer applications (Windows 95, Word, Excel, PowerPoint, and Access) as well as extensive experience with programming languages (Visual Basic, C++, and COBOL). I feel that I am well qualified to join your staff as over the past two years I have had a great deal of experience designing and implementing computer programs, both as a part of my educational program and during my internship with Personalized Computer Designs, Inc.

I am eager to put my skills to work and would like to talk with you at your earliest convenience. I have enclosed a copy of my résumé and will be happy to furnish the names and addresses of my references, if you so desire. You may reach me at the above address and phone number. I look forward to hearing from you.

Sincerely,

John H. Smith

(c) The Printed Letters

FIGURE C.1   The Mail Merge (continued)

Mail Merge Helper

A mail merge can be started from either *Microsoft Word* or *Microsoft Access.* Either way two input files are required—the form letter (main document) and the data source. The order in which these files are created depends on how the merge is initiated. When starting in Microsoft Word, you begin with the form letter, then create the data source. The process is reversed in Access—you start with a table or query, then exit to Word to create the form letter. The merge itself, however, is always performed from within Microsoft Word through the *Mail Merge Helper* as indicated in the next hands-on exercise.

The Mail Merge Helper guides you through the process. It enables you to create (or edit) the main document, to create or edit the data source, and finally, it enables you to merge the two.

PAPER MAKES A DIFFERENCE

Most of us take paper for granted, but the right paper can make a significant difference in the effectiveness of the document. Reports and formal correspondence are usually printed on white paper, but you would be surprised how many different shades of white there are. Other types of documents lend themselves to colored paper for additional impact. In short, the paper you use is far from an automatic decision. Our favorite source for paper is a company called Paper Direct (1-800-APAPERS). Ask for a catalog, then consider the use of a specialty paper the next time you have an important project, such as the cover letter for your résumé.

HANDS-ON EXERCISE 1

Mail Merge

Objective: To combine an Access table and a Word form letter to implement a mail merge and produce a set of form letters. Use Figure C.2 as a guide in the exercise.

STEP 1: Open the Names and Addresses Database

➤ Start Access. Open the **Names and Addresses** database in the **Exploring Access folder.** The **Tables tab** is selected. The **Contacts table** is the only table within the database.

➤ Pull down the **Tools menu,** click **Office Links** to display a cascaded menu in Figure C.2a, then click **Merge It with MS Word** to begin the mail merge.

➤ The dialog box for the Microsoft Word Mail Merge Wizard appears after a few seconds.

➤ The option button to link your data to an existing Microsoft Word document is already selected. (We have created the form letter for you on the data disk.) Click **OK.**

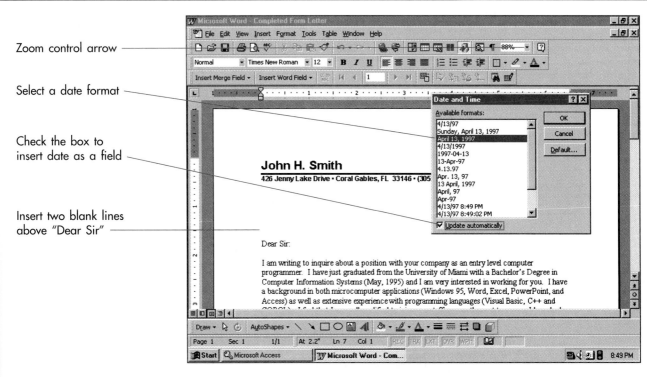

Zoom control arrow ────────────

Select a date format ────────────

Check the box to
insert date as a field ──────────

Insert two blank lines
above "Dear Sir" ────────────

(c) Insert the Date (step 3)

FIGURE C.2   Hands-on Exercise 1 (continued)

STEP 4: Insert the Merge Fields

➤ Click in the document immediately below the date. Press **enter** to leave a blank line between the date and the first line of the address.

➤ Click the **Insert Merge Field** button on the Mail Merge toolbar to display the fields within the data source, then select (click) **Title** from the list of fields. The title field is inserted into the main document and enclosed in angle brackets as shown in Figure C.2d.

➤ Press the **space bar** to add a space between the words. Click the **Insert Merge Field** button a second time. Click **FirstName.** Press the **space bar.**

➤ Click the **Insert Merge Field** button again. Click **LastName.**

➤ Press **enter** to move to the next line. Enter the remaining fields in the address as shown in Figure C.2d. Be sure to add a comma as well as a space after the **City field.**

➤ Delete the word "Sir" in the salutation and replace it with the **Title** and **Last Name fields** separated by spaces. Delete the words "your company" in the first sentence and replace them with the **Company field.**

➤ Save the document.

STEP 5: The Mail Merge Toolbar

➤ The Mail Merge toolbar enables you to preview the form letters before they are created. Click the **<<abc>> button** on the Mail Merge toolbar to display field values rather than field codes.

➤ You will see, for example, Mr. Jason Frasher (instead of <<Title>> <<First-Name>> <<LastName>>) as shown in Figure C.2e

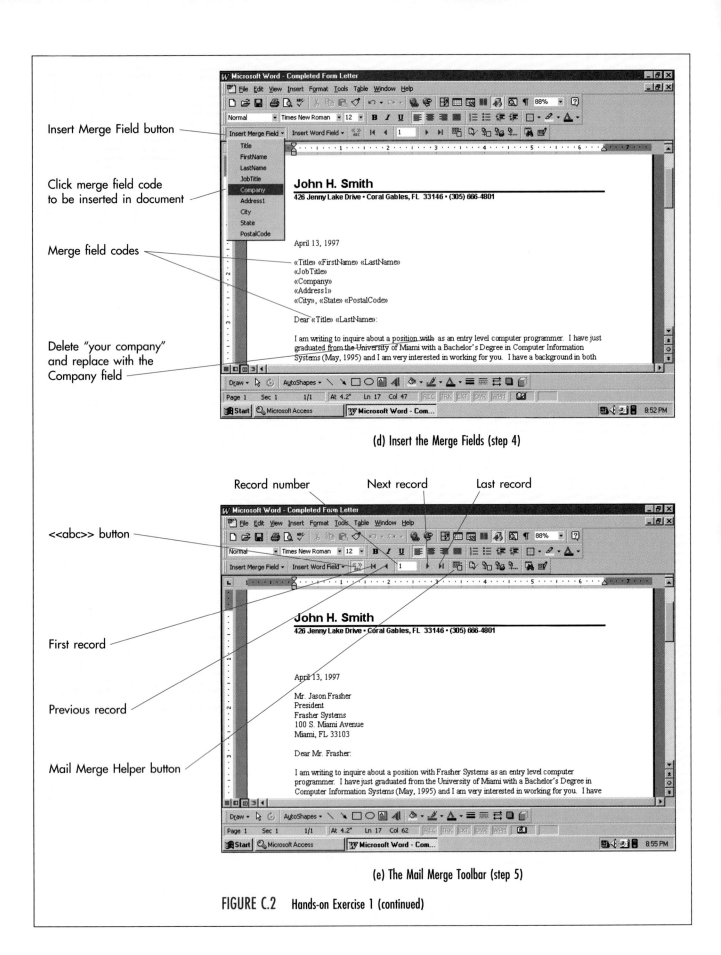

Insert Merge Field button

Click merge field code
to be inserted in document

Merge field codes

Delete "your company"
and replace with the
Company field

(d) Insert the Merge Fields (step 4)

Record number   Next record   Last record

<<abc>> button

First record

Previous record

Mail Merge Helper button

(e) The Mail Merge Toolbar (step 5)

FIGURE C.2   Hands-on Exercise 1 (continued)

➤ The **<<abc>> button** functions as a toggle switch. Click it once and you switch from field codes to field values; click it a second time and you go from field values back to field codes. End with the field values displayed.

➤ Look at the text box on the Mail Merge toolbar, which displays the number 1 to indicate that the first record is displayed. Click the ► **button** to display the form letter for the next record (Ms. Lauren Howard, in our example).

➤ Click the ► **button** again to display the form letter for the next record (Ms. Elizabeth Scherry). The toolbar indicates you are on the third record. Click the ◄ **button** to return to the previous (second) record.

➤ Click the |◄ **button** to move directly to the first record (Jason Frasher). Click the ►| **button** to display the form letter for the last record (Elizabeth Scherry).

➤ Toggle the **<<abc>> button** to display the field codes.

STEP 6: The Mail Merge Helper

➤ Click the **Mail Merge Helper button** on the Merge toolbar to display the dialog box in Figure C.2f.

➤ The Mail Merge Helper shows your progress thus far:

  • The main document has been created and saved as Completed Form Letter on drive C.

  • The data source is the Contacts table within the Names and Addresses database.

➤ Click the **Merge command button** to display the Merge dialog box in Figure C.2f. The selected options should already be set, but if necessary, change your options to match those in the figure.

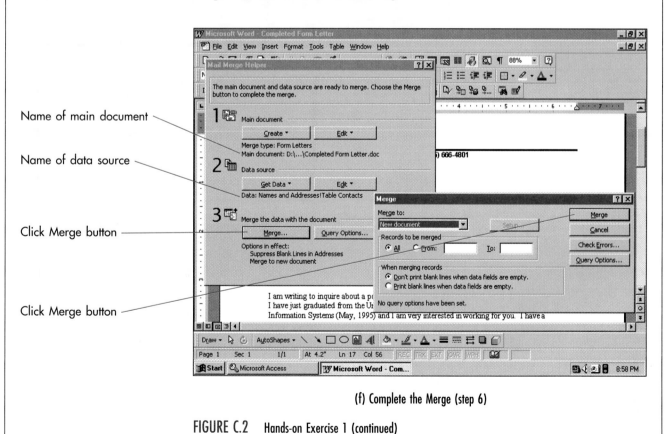

Name of main document

Name of data source

Click Merge button

Click Merge button

(f) Complete the Merge (step 6)

FIGURE C.2   Hands-on Exercise 1 (continued)

➤ Click the **Merge command button.** Word pauses momentarily, then generates the three form letters in a new document, which becomes the active document and is displayed on the monitor. The title bar of the active window changes to Form Letters1.

STEP 7: The Form Letters

➤ Scroll through the individual letters in the FormLetters1 document to review the letters one at a time.

➤ Pull down the **View menu.** Click **Zoom.** Click **Many Pages.** Click the **monitor icon,** then click and drag the icon within the resulting dialog box to display three pages side by side. Click **OK.** You should see the three form letters as shown in Figure C.2g.

➤ Print the letters to prove to your instructor that you did this exercise.

➤ Pull down the **File menu** and click **Exit** to exit Word. Pay close attention to the informational messages that ask whether to save the modified file(s):

- There is no need to save the merged document (Form Letters1) because you can always re-create the merged letters, provided you have saved the main document and data source.

- Save the Completed Form Letter if you are asked to do so.

➤ Exit Access. Congratulations on a job well done. We wish you good luck in your job hunting!

Title bar shows a new document

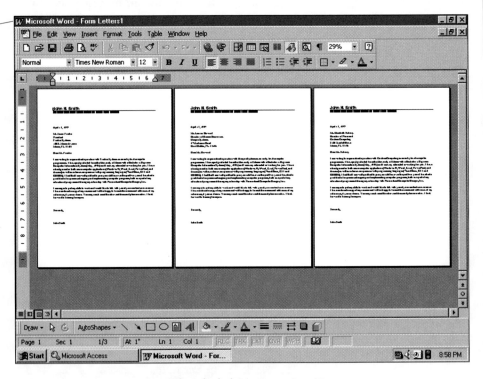

(g) The Individual Form Letters (step 7)

FIGURE C.2   Hands-on Exercise 1 (continued)

APPENDIX D:
A SEMESTER PROJECT

OVERVIEW

This appendix describes the student project we require in our introductory course in Microsoft Access at the University of Miami. It is intended for both students and instructors as it describes the various milestones in the administration of a class project. Our experience has been uniformly positive. Students work hard, but they are proud of the end result, and we are continually impressed at the diversity and quality of student projects. The project is what students remember most about our course and it truly enhances the learning experience.

We begin our course with detailed coverage of Access as it pertains to a single table so that students can develop proficiency with basic skills. Once this is accomplished, we move into a discussion of database design and relational databases. It is at this point that we introduce the class project, which becomes the focal point of our course for the rest of the semester. The class is divided into groups of three or four students each, and students work together to submit a collective project.

It is important that the groups be balanced with respect to student abilities. Our groups are always formed after the first exam, when we have additional information with which to create the groups. We distribute a questionnaire in which we ask students who they want to work with (and conversely, if there is anyone they would be uncomfortable working with). We always honor the latter request and do our best to honor the former as well. We also make continual use of peer evaluations so that the groups work as smoothly as possible.

Once the groups have been formed, we establish a series of milestones that are described in the remainder of the appendix. There is absolutely no requirement for you or your class to follow our milestones exactly. We have found, however, that providing detailed feedback through a series of continual assignments is very effective in moving the groups toward their final goal. We hope this appendix is useful to you and we look forward to receiving your comments.

Phase I—Preliminary Design

Describe, in a one- or two-page narrative, the relational database that your group will design and implement. You can select any of the case studies at the end of the chapters on one-to-many or many-to-many relationships, or alternatively, you can choose an entirely different system. Regardless of which system you choose, however, the preliminary design is one of the most important aspects of the entire project as it is the basis for the eventual Access database. A good design will enable you to implement the project successfully, and hence you should give considerable thought to the document you prepare. Your project need not be unduly complex, but it must include at least three tables. The relationships between the tables can be one-to-many or many-to-many. Your document should describe the physical system for which you will create the database. It should also contain a "wish list" describing in general terms the information the system is to produce.

Phase II—Detailed Design

Implement the refinements (if any) to the preliminary design from Phase I, then expand that design to include all of the necessary fields in each table. You also need to develop the properties for each field at this time. Be sure to include adequate data validation and to use input masks as appropriate. One additional requirement is that the primary key of at least one table be an AutoNumber field.

After you have completed the design, create an Access database containing the necessary tables, with all the fields in each table, but no other objects. You do not have to enter any data at this time, but you are required to document your work. To do so, pull down the Tools menu, click the Relationships command, define the various relationships, then press the PrintScreen key to capture the screen to the clipboard. Start Word, then paste the contents of the clipboard (containing the relationships diagram) into your Word document. This creates a one-page document that gives you a visual overview of your database. Submit this document to your instructor.

You are also asked to provide detailed documentation for each table. Pull down the Tools menu, click Analyze, then click Documentor. Select Tables in the Object Type drop-down list box, then select all of the tables. Click the Options button, then include for each table the Properties and Relationships but not the Permissions by User and Group. Include for each field Names, Data types, Sizes, and Properties. Do not include any information on indexes. Print the information for each table in the database and submit it to your instructor for review.

Phase III—The User Interface

Phase III focuses on the development of a template, which will be replicated throughout the system. The template, or user interface, is critical to the success of any system as a user spends his or her day in front of the screen. The interface must be functional and it helps if it is visually compelling. We have found that the best way for the group to arrive at a template is for each member to submit a design independently, after which the group can select the best design.

Your template should contain a logo for the project and establish a color scheme. You do *not* have to put actual command buttons on the template, but you are to use the rectangle tool to indicate the placement of the buttons. Use clip art as appropriate, but clip art for the sake of clip art is often juvenile. You may want to use different fonts and/or simple graphics (e.g., horizontal or vertical lines are often quite effective). A simple design is generally the best design.

After the individual templates have been created, they are to be merged into a database, which consists solely of the four individual templates; there will be no tables or other objects in the database. (This is accomplished through the File Import command.) Bring this database to class and be prepared to show off the competing designs for your project. Choose the winning template for your system, then use that design as the basis for the remainder of the project.

Phase IV—Create the Forms and Enter Test Data

Phase IV has you create the forms in which to enter test data based on the template of Phase III. You need a form (or subform) for every table to add, edit, and delete records in that table. You are required, however, to have at least one subform, and you must structure your forms to facilitate data entry in a logical way. All forms should have a consistent look (via a common template).

The forms should be user friendly and display command buttons so that there is no requirement on the part of the end user to know Access. Each form is to include buttons to add, delete, find and print a record, and to close the form. A Help button is a nice touch. Include drop-down list boxes to facilitate data entry in at least two places. The forms should be designed so that they fit on one screen and do not require the user to scroll to access all of the fields and/or the command buttons. Design for the lowest common denominator (e.g., 640 × 480).

Once they have been created, use the forms to enter test data for each table. (Each table should contain 10 to 15 records.) Be sure that the data will adequately test all of the queries and reports that will be in your final system. Submit a print-out of the data in each table to your instructor. (You can print the Datasheet view of each table.) In addition, submit a printed copy of each form to your instructor.

Phase V—Prototyping

Phase V has you develop a "complete" system using the prototyping described in the text. The main menu should be displayed automatically (via an AutoExec macro) when the database is opened, and the user should be able to step through the entire system. The final reports and queries need not be implemented at this time (a "not yet implemented" message is fine at this stage). The user should, however, be able to go from one form to the next, without encountering an error message. Realize, too, that the main menu is not based on a table or query, and thus it should not display the Record Selector and Navigation buttons.

Phase VI—The Completed System

Submit the completed Access database on disk. You will be judged on whether your system actually works; that is, the instructor will enter and/or modify data at random. The effects of the new data should be manifest in the various reports and queries. To obtain a grade of A, you will need to satisfy the following requirements (many of which have been completed) in the earlier phases:

1. Use of the Data Validation and Input Mask properties to validate and facilitate data entry. In addition, at least one table is to contain an AutoNumber field as its primary key.
2. Existing data in all tables, with 10 to 15 records in each table.
3. An AutoExec macro to load the main menu and maximize the window.
4. A help button on one or more screens that displays the name of the group and an appropriate help message (e.g., a phone number).
5. A working form (or subform) for each table in the database so that you can maintain each table. You must have at least one subform in your system. The forms should have a consistent look (via a common template). The system

and especially the forms should make sense; just because you have all of the forms does not mean you satisfy the requirements of the project. Your forms should be designed to facilitate data entry in a logical way.

6. The forms should be user friendly so that there is no requirement on the part of the end user to know Access. Each form is to include buttons to add, delete, find and print a record, and to close the form. Include drop-down list boxes to facilitate data entry in at least two places.

7. All forms should be designed for the lowest common denominator (640 × 480). The screens should be sufficiently compact so that no scrolling is required.

8. Five working reports, at least one of which is a group/total report.

9. Inclusion of a parameter query to drive a form or report.

10. At least one unmatched query and one top-value query.

11. The completed system should be as visually compelling as possible. Clip art for the sake of clip art tends to dilute the desired effect. In general, a consistent logo (one image) is much better from slide to slide than multiple images. No clip art is better than poor clip art or too much clip art.

The Written Document

In addition to demonstrating a working system, you are to submit a written document. The submission of the written project will be an impressive (lengthy) document, but easily generated as much of the material is created directly from Access. The objective is for you to have a project of which you will be proud and something that you can demonstrate in the future. Include the following:

1. Title page plus table (list) of the contents; pages need not be numbered, but please include "loose-leaf" dividers for each section.

2. A one- or two-page description of the system.

3. Technical documentation. Pull down the Tools menu, click Analyze, then click the Documentor command to print the definition of each table. Include the Properties and Relationships, but do *not* include Permissions by User and Group. Choose the option to print the Names, Data types, Sizes, and Properties for each field. Do not print anything for the indexes.

4. Hard copy of each form (one per page).

5. Hard copy of each report (one per page).

6. A working disk.

A Final Word

Throughout the project, you will be working with different versions of your database on different machines. You will also need to share your work with other members of your group. And, of course, you need to back up your work. The floppy disk is the medium of choice but its capacity is only 1.4MB and an Access database can quickly exceed that.

It is important, therefore, that you master certain skills as early as possible. In particular, you should learn how to *compact* an Access database, after which you can take advantage of a *file compression program* to reduce the size even further. You might also explore the use of *FTP* as an alternate means of transferring a file. You should also learn how to separate the data from the other objects in a database to further reduce storage requirements.

ENHANCING A PRESENTATION: THE WEB AND OTHER RESOURCES

After reading this chapter you will be able to:

1. Use Microsoft Graph to create and edit a graph within a presentation.
2. Use the Drawing toolbar to modify existing clip art; describe the function of at least four different drawing tools.
3. Use Microsoft Organization Chart to embed an organization chart into a presentation.
4. Use Microsoft WordArt to embed a WordArt object into a presentation.
5. Link an Excel worksheet to a PowerPoint presentation.
6. Distinguish between linking and embedding; explain how in-place editing is used to modify an embedded object.
7. Embed a sound file into a PowerPoint presentation.
8. Describe the Internet and World Wide Web; explain how to display the Web toolbar in PowerPoint.
9. Download a photograph from the Web and include it in a Power-Point presentation.

OVERVIEW

Thus far we have focused on presentations that consisted largely of text. PowerPoint also enables you to include a variety of visual elements that add impact to your presentation. You can add clip art or photographs from within PowerPoint through the Microsoft Clip Gallery, or you can include these elements from other sources. You can use the supplementary applications that are included with Microsoft Office to add graphs, organization charts, and WordArt. You can insert objects created in other applications, such as a worksheet from Microsoft Excel or a table from Microsoft Word. And best of all, you can download resources from the World Wide Web for inclusion in a PowerPoint presentation.

We begin by introducing Microsoft Graph, an application that creates (and modifies) a graph based on data in an associated datasheet. We show you how to use the Drawing toolbar to modify existing clip art and/or develop original images, even if you are not artistic by nature. We describe how to create special text effects through WordArt, how to create organization charts, and how to include sound in a presentation. We describe the Internet and World Wide Web, explain how to display the Web toolbar, and show you how to download resources from the Web.

All told, we think you will be quite impressed with what you can do. As always, the hands-on exercises are essential to our learn-by-doing philosophy.

MICROSOFT GRAPH

The Microsoft Office suite includes a supplementary application called **Microsoft Graph,** which enables you to insert a graph into a presentation in support of numeric data. The program is called from within PowerPoint by choosing an Auto-Layout containing a graph placeholder, then double clicking the placeholder to start Microsoft Graph. You create the graph using commands within Microsoft Graph, then you exit Microsoft Graph and return to your presentation.

Figure 1.1 illustrates the basics of the Microsoft Graph program as it will be used in a hands-on exercise later in the chapter. The program has many of the same commands and capabilities as the charting component of Microsoft Excel. (See Grauer and Barber, *Exploring Microsoft Excel 97,* pages 133–178, Prentice Hall, 1997, for additional information on graphs and charting.)

The **datasheet** in Figure 1.1a displays the quarterly sales for each of three salesmen: Tom, Dick, and Harry. The datasheet contains 12 **data points** (four quarterly values for each of three salesmen). The data points are grouped into **data series,** which appear as rows or columns in the datasheet.

The graph in Figure 1.1b plots the data by row so that you can see the relative performance of each salesman in each quarter. There are three data series (Sales for Tom, Sales for Dick, and Sales for Harry), each with four data points (1st Qtr, 2nd Qtr, 3rd Qtr, and 4th Qtr). The text entries in the first row of the datasheet appear on the X axis as the category names. The text entries in the first column of the datasheet appear as a legend to indicate the name associated with each series.

Figure 1.1c, on the other hand, plots the data by column, making it easy to see the progress of each salesman over the course of the year. This time there are four data series (Sales for 1st Qtr, Sales for 2nd Qtr, Sales for 3rd Qtr, and Sales for 4th Qtr), each with three data points (one each for Tom, Dick, and Harry). The text entries in the first column of the datasheet appear on the X axis as the category names. The text entries in the first row of the datasheet appear in the legend to indicate the name associated with each series.

Figure 1.1d also displays the data series in columns, but uses a different graph type, a stacked column rather than side-by-side columns as in Figure 1.1c. The choice between the two types of graphs depends on your message. If, for example, you want your audience to see each individual's sales in each quarter, the side-by-side graph is more appropriate. If, on the other hand, you want to emphasize the total sales for each salesperson, the stacked column graph is preferable. Note, too, the different scale on the Y axis in the two graphs. The side-by-side graph in Figure 1.1c shows the sales in each quarter and so the Y axis goes only to $90,000. The stacked bars in Figure 1.1d, however, reflect the total sales for each salesperson and thus the scale goes to $250,000.

All three graphs contain the same number of data points (12 in all) but plot them differently to emphasize different information. All three graphs are equally correct, and the choice depends on the message you want to convey.

EMPHASIZE YOUR MESSAGE

A graph is used to deliver a message, and you want that message to be as clear as possible. One way to help put your point across is to choose a title that leads the audience. A neutral title such as *Revenue by Quarter* is vague and requires the audience to reach its own conclusion. A better title might be *Tom Is the Leading Sales Associate* if the objective were to emphasize Tom's contribution. A well-chosen title emphasizes your message.

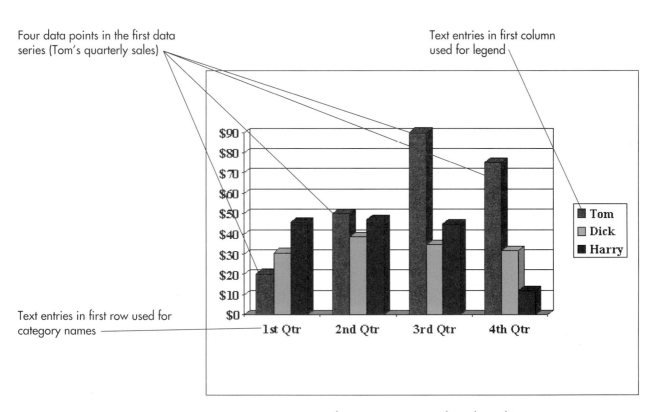

(a) The Datasheet (sales in thousands)

Four data points in the first data series (Tom's quarterly sales)

Text entries in first column used for legend

Text entries in first row used for category names

(b) Data Series in Rows (sales in thousands)

FIGURE 1.1   Microsoft Graph

Three data points in first data series (1st quarter sales)

Text entries in first row used for legend

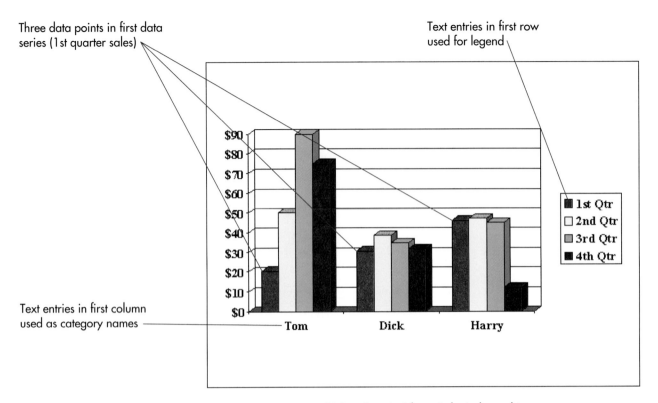

Text entries in first column used as category names

(c) Data Series in Columns (sales in thousands)

Columns reflect total sales for each salesperson

Scale on Y axis goes to $250,000

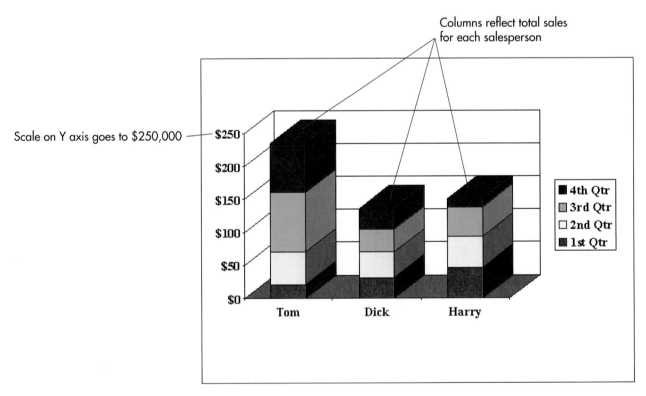

(d) Stacked Column Chart (sales in thousands)

FIGURE 1.1   Microsoft Graph (continued)

Microsoft Graph

Objective: To use Microsoft Graph to insert a graph into a presentation; to modify the graph to display the data in rows or columns; to change the graph format and underlying data. Use Figure 1.2 as a guide in the exercise.

STEP 1: Start Microsoft Graph

➤ Start PowerPoint. Click the option button to create a new presentation using a **Blank Presentation.** Click **OK.** You should see the New Slide dialog box.

➤ Select (click) the AutoLayout for a chart (it is the AutoLayout at the end of the second row), then click **OK** to add the slide as shown in Figure 1.2a. If necessary, maximize the document window.

Double click chart placeholder ─────

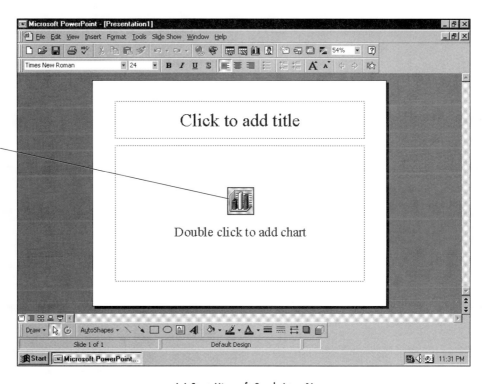

(a) Start Microsoft Graph (step 1)

FIGURE 1.2   Hands-on Exercise 1

INSERTING A GRAPH

There are several ways to insert a graph into a presentation. You can choose one of three AutoLayouts containing a placeholder for a graph. You can also pull down the Insert menu and select Chart, or you can click the Insert Chart button on the Standard toolbar. You can also insert a graph created in another application by executing the Insert Object command and selecting the appropriate object, such as a Microsoft Excel chart.

➤ Double click the placeholder to add a chart, which starts the Microsoft Graph application.

STEP 2: The Default Graph

➤ The default datasheet and graph should be displayed on your monitor, as shown in Figure 1.2b. The menus and toolbar have changed to reflect the Microsoft Graph application.

➤ Do not be concerned if the numbers in your datasheet are different from those in the figure. (You can create your own graph simply by editing the text and numeric values, as will be described in the next step.)

➤ Click and drag the **title bar** of the datasheet so that you can see more of the graph, as in the figure.

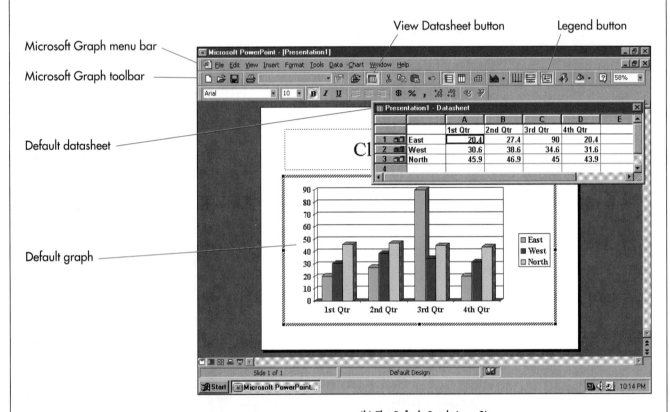

(b) The Default Graph (step 2)

FIGURE 1.2   Hands-on Exercise 1 (continued)

IN-PLACE EDITING

Microsoft Graph enables in-place editing as you create and/or modify a graph; that is, you remain in PowerPoint, but the toolbars and pull-down menus are those of Microsoft Graph. The File and Window menus are exceptions, however, and contain PowerPoint commands (so that you can save the presentation and/or view multiple presentations). In-place editing requires that both applications support the Microsoft specification for Object Linking and Embedding 2.0.

➤ Click the **View Datasheet button** on the (Microsoft Graph) Standard toolbar to close the datasheet. Click the **View Datasheet button** a second time to open the datasheet.

➤ Click the **Legend button** on the Standard toolbar to suppress the legend on the graph. Click the **Legend button** a second time to display the legend.

STEP 3: Change the Data

➤ Click in **cell B1** of the datasheet (the value for East in the 2nd Quarter). Type **50** and press **enter.** The graph changes automatically to reflect the new data.

➤ Change the values of the following cells as follows:

- Click in **cell D1.** Type **75.**
- Click in **cell D3.** Type **12.**
- Click in the cell containing **East.** Type **Tom.**
- Press the **down arrow key** to move to the cell containing **West.** Type **Dick.**
- Press the **down arrow key** to move to the cell containing **North.** Type **Harry.**

➤ Check that all of the values in your datasheet match those in Figure 1.2c. Click the **Close button** to close the datasheet.

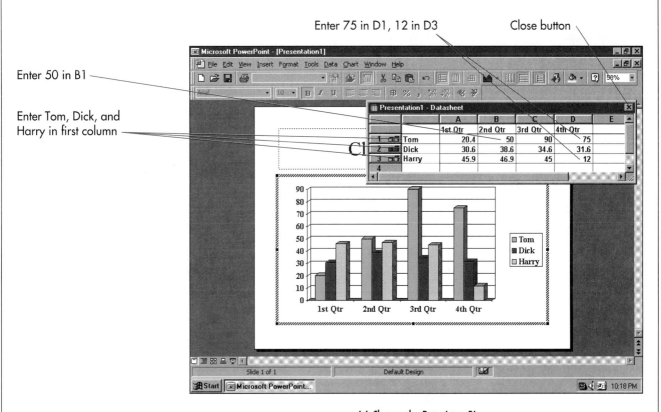

(c) Change the Data (step 3)

FIGURE 1.2   Hands-on Exercise 1 (continued)

STEP 4: Change the Orientation and Format

➤ Click the **By Column button** on the Standard toolbar to change the data series from rows to columns as shown in Figure 1.2d. The X axis changes to display the names of the salespersons, and the legend indicates the quarter.

➤ Click the **By Row button** on the Standard toolbar to change the data series back to rows.

➤ Click the **By Column button** a second time to match the orientation in Figure 1.2d.

➤ Pull down the **Chart menu.** Click **Chart Type** to display the Chart Type.

➤ If necessary, click **Column** in the Chart Type list box. Select the stacked column with 3-D visual effect as the Chart subtype. Click **OK.**

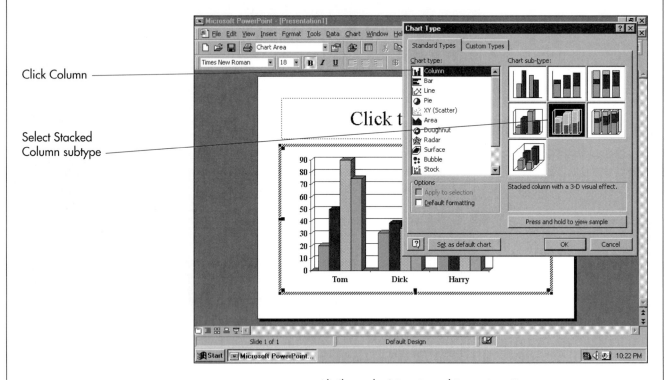

Click Column

Select Stacked
Column subtype

(d) Change the Orientation and Format (step 4)

FIGURE 1.2   Hands-on Exercise 1 (continued)

DON'T FORGET HELP

Microsoft Graph includes its own Help system, which functions identically to the Help in any other application. Pull down the Help menu and search on any topic for which you want additional information. Remember, too, that you can print the contents of a Help screen by clicking the Print button in the Help window.

STEP 5: Return to PowerPoint

➤ Click outside the chart to exit Microsoft Graph and return to PowerPoint. You should see the stacked column graph in Figure 1.2e.

➤ Click inside the graph, and the sizing handles appear to indicate the graph is selected. Click and drag a corner sizing handle to increase (decrease) the size of the graph within the slide.

➤ Click the **title placeholder,** which deselects the graph and positions the insertion point to enter the title. Type **Tom is the Top Sales Associate.**

➤ Pull down the **File menu** and click **Save** (or click the **Save button** on the Standard toolbar). Save the presentation as **My Chart** in the **Exploring Power-Point folder.**

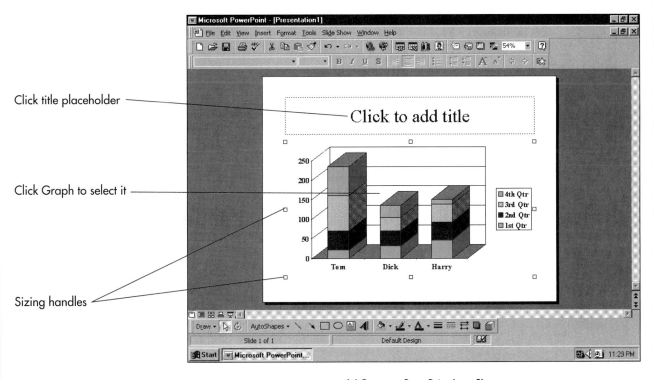

(e) Return to PowerPoint (step 5)

FIGURE 1.2   Hands-on Exercise 1 (continued)

STEP 6: Add a Data Series

➤ Point to the graph and click the **right mouse button** to display a shortcut menu, then click **Edit Chart Object.** (You can also double click the graph as described in the previous tip.)

➤ Once again you are in Microsoft Graph, and the menus and toolbar have changed to reflect this application.

➤ Click the **View Datasheet button** to reopen the datasheet. If necessary, click and drag the title bar of the datasheet so you can see more of the graph.

➤ Add an additional data series as follows:

• Click in the cell under Harry. Type **George,** then press the **right arrow key** to move to cell A4. George appears as a category name on the X axis.

• Enter **10, 15, 20,** and **25** in cells A4, B4, C4, and D4, respectively. Notice that as you complete each entry, the graph adjusts automatically to reflect the value you just entered.

➤ The data for George is plotted automatically as shown in Figure 1.2f. Close the datasheet.

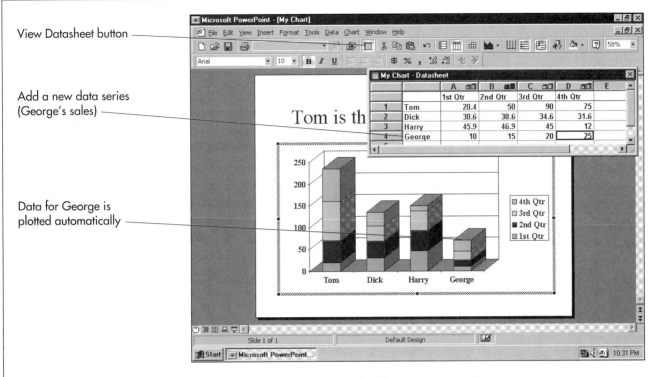

Labels pointing to the figure:
- View Datasheet button
- Add a new data series (George's sales)
- Data for George is plotted automatically

(f) Add a Data Series (step 6)

FIGURE 1.2   Hands-on Exercise 1 (continued)

STEP 7: The Finishing Touches

➤ You can customize every object within a chart (the legend, axis, plot area, and so on) by pointing to the object and clicking the right mouse button to display a shortcut menu.

➤ Point to the gray section (4th Qtr Sales) of any column and click the **right mouse button** to display a shortcut menu. Click **Format Data Series.**

➤ Click the **Patterns tab** (if necessary) in the Format Data Series dialog box and click **red** as the new color. Click **OK** to close the dialog box. The data series for the fourth quarter has been changed to red as shown in Figure 1.2g.

➤ Point to any value on the vertical axis, then click the **right mouse button** to display the shortcut menu in Figure 1.2g. Click **Format Axis.**

➤ Click the **Number tab** in the Format Number dialog box, then select the **Currency format** within the Category list box. Change the decimal places to 0. Click **OK.** The format of the axis has been changed to include the dollar sign.

STEP 8: Save the Presentation

➤ Click outside the chart to exit Microsoft Graph and return to PowerPoint. Save the presentation.

➤ Pull down the **File menu** and click **Print** (or click the **Print button**). Click **OK** to print the slide.

➤ Exit PowerPoint if you do not want to continue with the next exercise at this time. Click **Yes** if prompted to save the changes to the presentation.

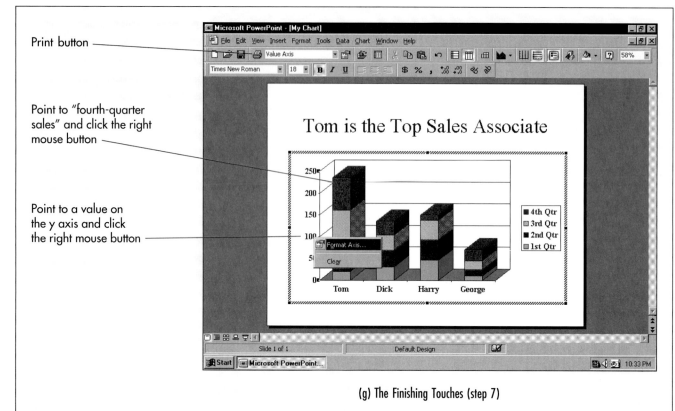

Print button

Point to "fourth-quarter sales" and click the right mouse button

Point to a value on the y axis and click the right mouse button

(g) The Finishing Touches (step 7)

FIGURE 1.2 Hands-on Exercise 1 (continued)

THE 3-D VIEW COMMAND

The 3-D View command enables you to fine-tune the appearance of a graph by controlling the rotation, elevation, and other parameters found within its dialog box. The rotation controls the rotation around the vertical axis and determines how much of the stacked bars you see. The elevation controls the height at which you view the graph. Pull down the Chart menu, select the 3-D View command, then set these parameters as you see fit.

OFFICE ART

Office 97 contains a powerful set of drawing tools that are collectively known as **Office Art.** Even if you are not an artist, you can use these tools to modify existing clip art and thus create new and very different illustrations. Consider, for example, Figure 1.3, which contains an original piece of clip art and five variations. (The clip art was taken from the Cartoons category of the Microsoft Clip Gallery.) We are not artistic by nature and there is no way that we could have created the original duck. We did, however, create all of the variations. All it took was a little imagination and a sense of what can be done.

The tools in Office Art are accessed through the **Drawing toolbar,** which is displayed by default in the Slide view and illustrated in Figure 1.4. As with the

The Original Clip Art

Flip Vertically

Copy and Flip Horizontally

Change Colors

Ungroup and Resize

Get Your Ducks in a Row

FIGURE 1.3   What You Can Do with Clip Art

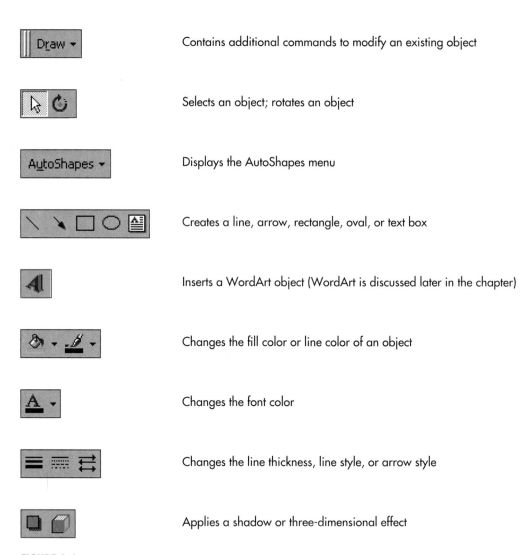

Draw ▾	Contains additional commands to modify an existing object
▯ ⟳	Selects an object; rotates an object
AutoShapes ▾	Displays the AutoShapes menu
╲ ╲ ▢ ◯ ▤	Creates a line, arrow, rectangle, oval, or text box
◀	Inserts a WordArt object (WordArt is discussed later in the chapter)
◇ ▾ ✎ ▾	Changes the fill color or line color of an object
A ▾	Changes the font color
≡ ≣ ⇄	Changes the line thickness, line style, or arrow style
▢ ◰	Applies a shadow or three-dimensional effect

FIGURE 1.4   The Drawing Toolbar

other toolbars, there is no need to memorize what the individual buttons do. You can, however, gain a better appreciation of their function by viewing the tools in groups, as is done in Figure 1.4. And, as with all toolbars, you can point to any tool and PowerPoint will display the name of the tool. You can also access the Help menu for detailed information on a specific tool.

The various tools are used to create or modify the objects that appear on a PowerPoint slide. An *object* is anything you put on a slide. Select the Line tool, for example, then click and drag to create the line. Once the line is created, you can select it, then change its properties (such as its thickness or style) by using other tools on the Drawing toolbar. Objects (such as lines and arcs) are the building blocks of any drawing. You can create an original drawing of your own, or you can modify an existing drawing (as we did with the ducks) by manipulating its objects to create an entirely different drawing.

The ***Draw menu*** provides access to additional commands that let you modify an object in various ways. The ***Ungroup command*** breaks an object into smaller objects (e.g., it separates the duck and the computer) so you can work with each object on an individual basis. The ***Group command*** does the opposite and combines multiple objects into a single object. The **Rotate or Flip command** enables you to change the orientation of an object (e.g., make the duck face left or right or turn him upside down).

The following exercise has you insert a clip art image into a presentation, then modify that image using various tools on the Drawing toolbar. Be flexible and willing to experiment. Try, and try again, and don't be discouraged if you don't succeed initially. Just keep trying, and you will be amazed at what you will be able to do.

HANDS-ON EXERCISE 2

You Don't Have to Be an Artist

Objective: To insert clip art into a presentation, then use various tools on the Drawing toolbar to modify the clip art. Use Figure 1.5 as a guide in the exercise.

STEP 1: Create the Title Slide

➤ Create a new presentation:

- If necessary, start PowerPoint. Click the option button to create a **Blank Presentation** as you have been doing throughout the text. Click **OK.**

- If PowerPoint is already started, pull down the **File menu** and click **New** (or click the **New button** on the Standard toolbar). If necessary, double click the **Blank Presentation icon** to display the New Slide dialog box.

➤ You should see the New Slide dialog box with the **AutoLayout** for the title slide already selected. Click **OK** to create the title slide. Click the placeholder for the title. Type **What You Can Do With Clip Art** as shown in Figure 1.5a.

➤ Click the placeholder for the subtitle. Enter your name.

➤ Click the **Save button** on the Standard toolbar. Save the presentation as **You Don't Have to Be an Artist** in the **Exploring PowerPoint folder.**

STEP 2: Add the Clip Art

➤ Pull down the **Insert menu** and click **New Slide** (or click the **New Slide button** on the Standard toolbar).

➤ Select (click) the **Title Only layout.** (This is AutoLayout number 11 and is the third layout in the third row.) Click **OK.**

➤ Click the **Insert Clip Art button** on the Standard toolbar to display the Microsoft Clip Gallery as shown in Figure 1.5b. Click **OK** if you see a dialog box reminding you that additional clip art is available on a CD-ROM.

➤ If necessary, click the **Clip Art tab** and select (click) the **Cartoons category.** Select the **Duck and Computer,** then click the **Insert button** to insert the picture into the presentation.

➤ Close the Picture toolbar if it appears since we do not need to use any of its tools in this exercise.

➤ Click anywhere on the slide (other than the clip art) to deselect the clip art.

➤ Click the placeholder for the title. Enter **The Original Clip Art** as the title for the slide. Save the presentation.

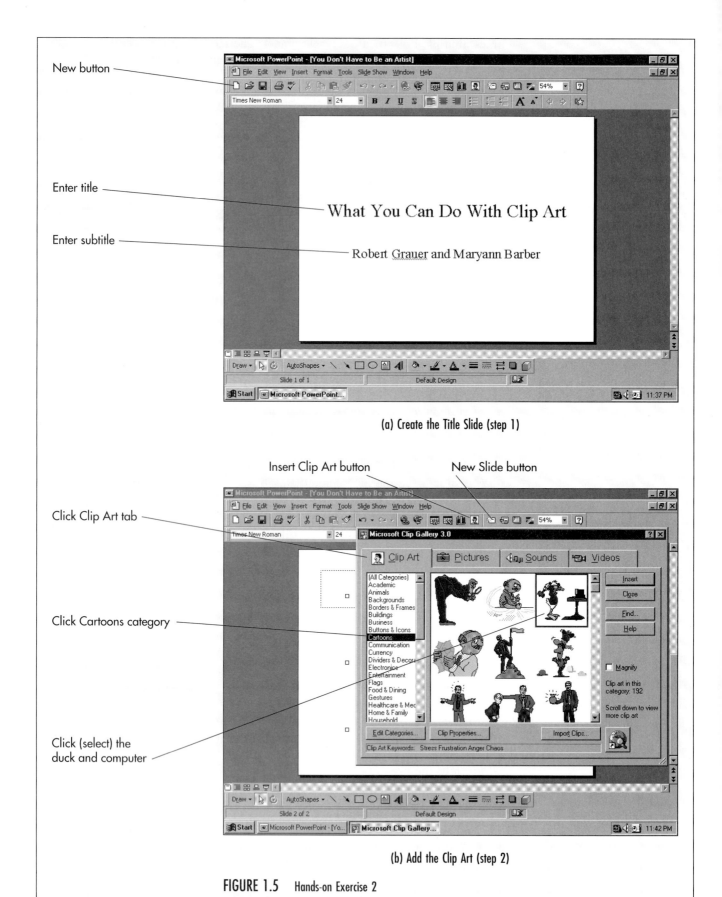

New button

Enter title

Enter subtitle

What You Can Do With Clip Art

Robert Grauer and Maryann Barber

(a) Create the Title Slide (step 1)

Insert Clip Art button   New Slide button

Click Clip Art tab

Click Cartoons category

Click (select) the
duck and computer

(b) Add the Clip Art (step 2)

FIGURE 1.5   Hands-on Exercise 2

THE PICTURE TOOLBAR

The Picture toolbar is displayed automatically when a picture (or clip art image) is selected; otherwise it is suppressed. It contains a button to format the picture (which lets you change its size or position, or add a border) as well as a button to crop (erase) part of a picture. As with any toolbar, you can point to a button to display a ScreenTip containing the name of the button, which is indicative of its function.

STEP 3: Copy the Slide

➤ Click the **Slide Sorter View button** on the status bar to change to the view in Figure 1.5c. Slide 2, the slide with the duck, is selected.

➤ Click the **Copy button** on the Standard toolbar (or press **Ctrl+C**) to copy the slide to the clipboard.

➤ Click the **Paste button** on the Standard toolbar (or press **Ctrl+V**) to paste the contents of the clipboard into the presentation. This creates a new slide (slide 3), which is identical to slide 2.

➤ Click the **Paste button** four additional times so that you wind up with seven slides in all, as shown in Figure 1.5c. There are now six identical slides of the duck smashing the computer.

➤ Save the presentation.

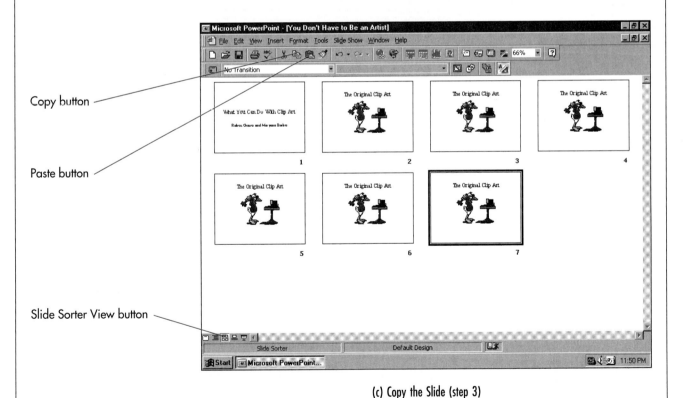

(c) Copy the Slide (step 3)

FIGURE 1.5 Hands-on Exercise 2 (continued)

CUT, COPY, AND PASTE

Ctrl+X (the X is supposed to remind you of a pair of scissors), Ctrl+C, and Ctrl+V are keyboard equivalents to cut, copy, and paste, respectively, and apply to each application in Microsoft Office, as well as Windows applications in general. (The keystrokes are easier to remember when you realize that the operative letters—X, C, and V—are next to each other at the bottom left side of the keyboard.) Alternatively, you can use the Cut, Copy, and Paste buttons on the Standard toolbar.

STEP 4: The Ungroup Command

➤ Double click **slide 3** to simultaneously select the slide and change to the Slide view, as shown in Figure 1.5d. The status bar should indicate that slide 3 is the current slide.

➤ Click and drag to select the text of the slide title, then type **Flip Vertically** as the new title.

➤ Click anywhere on the clip art to select the entire image. You should see eight sizing handles around the image as shown in the figure.

➤ Click the **Draw menu** on the Drawing toolbar to display additional commands. Click **Ungroup.**

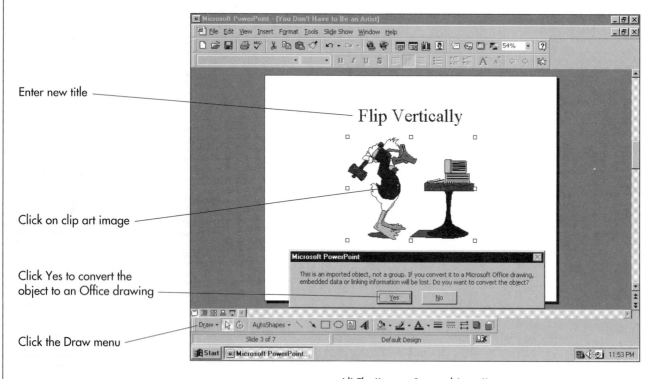

(d) The Ungroup Command (step 4)

FIGURE 1.5   Hands-on Exercise 2 (continued)

- ➤ You will see the message in Figure 1.5d. Click **Yes** to convert the object to a Microsoft Office drawing, allowing you to use the PowerPoint tools to edit the image.
- ➤ You should see two sets of sizing handles: one set surrounding the duck, and the other set around the computer and the table.
- ➤ Click outside the selected area, then click anywhere on the duck to select just the duck.
- ➤ Click the **Draw menu** on the Drawing toolbar. Click **Rotate or Flip,** then click the **Flip Vertical command.** The duck is now upside down.
- ➤ Save the presentation.

DISPLAY THE ROTATE OR FLIP TOOLBAR

The exercise makes frequent use of the Flip Horizontal and Flip Vertical commands that can be accessed more easily from a toolbar. Click the Draw menu on the Drawing toolbar, then click the Rotate or Flip command to display the Rotate or Flip menu. Point to the top of the menu (which is actually a title bar), then click and drag to display the Rotate or Flip toolbar. You can leave the toolbar floating on the desktop or you can anchor it along an edge. (Double click the gray background of the toolbar to toggle between a docked or floating toolbar.)

STEP 5: Copy and Flip Horizontally

- ➤ Press the **PgDn key** (or click the **Next Slide button** at the bottom of the scroll bar) to move to slide 4. (You can also drag the scroll box (slide elevator) on the vertical scroll bar to move to slide 4.)
- ➤ Click and drag to select the slide title, then type **Copy and Flip Horizontally** as the new title as shown in Figure 1.5e.
- ➤ Click the clip art to select it, then drag the clip art to the left edge of the slide. Ungroup the duck and the computer as in the previous step.
- ➤ Click outside the selected objects. Select just the duck. Click the **Copy button** on the Standard toolbar (which copies the duck to the clipboard).
- ➤ Click the **Paste button** on the Standard toolbar. You should see a second duck on top of the first duck.
- ➤ Click and drag the second duck past the computer all the way to the right of the slide as shown in Figure 1.5e.
- ➤ Click the **Draw menu** on the Drawing toolbar, click **Rotate or Flip,** then click **Flip Horizontal.** Move the table and/or the ducks to adjust the spacing as desired.
- ➤ Save the presentation.

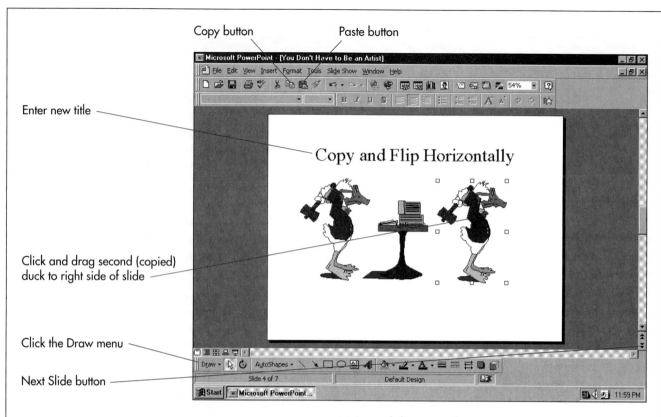

Copy button   Paste button

Enter new title

Click and drag second (copied) duck to right side of slide

Click the Draw menu

Next Slide button

(e) Copy and Flip Horizontally (step 5)

FIGURE 1.5   Hands-on Exercise 2 (continued)

ALIGNING OBJECTS

You can improve the appearance of any slide by precisely aligning the objects it contains. Press and hold the Shift key to select the objects you want to align. Click the Draw menu on the Drawing toolbar, click Align or Distribute, then choose the alignment you want (left, center, right, top, middle, or bottom) from the cascade menu.

STEP 6: Change Colors

➤ Press the **PgDn key** to move to slide 5. Click and drag to select the text of the slide title, then type **Change Colors** as the new title as shown in Figure 1.5f.

➤ Repeat the actions from the previous step to copy the duck and flip him horizontally:

• Click and drag the clip art to the left side of the slide, then **ungroup** the duck and the computer.

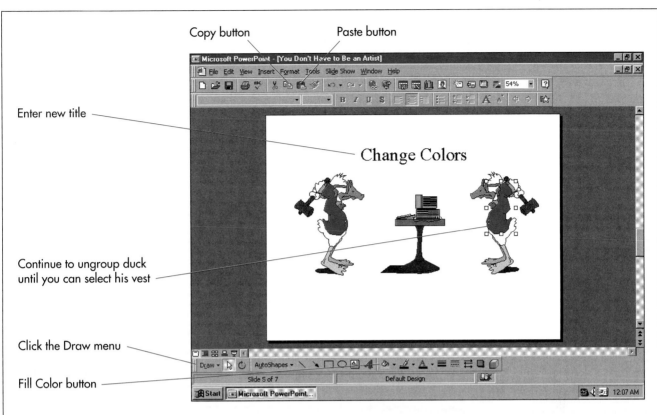

Copy button   Paste button

Enter new title

Continue to ungroup duck
until you can select his vest

Click the Draw menu

Fill Color button

(f) Change Colors (step 6)

FIGURE 1.5   Hands-on Exercise 2 (continued)

- • Click outside the selected area to deselect both objects. Select the duck, click the **Copy button,** click the **Paste button,** then drag the second duck to the right of the computer.
  - • Click the **Draw button** on the Drawing toolbar, click **Rotate or Flip,** and click **Flip Horizontal.**
- ➤ Check that the duck on the right is still selected, then execute the **Ungroup Command** to ungroup the objects that make up this duck and his hammer. The duck is now a separate object; the hammer and shadow are a second object.
- ➤ Click outside the selected objects, then click the duck. Execute the **Ungroup Command** to ungroup the objects that make up the duck.
- ➤ Continue to ungroup the duck until you have separated his vest from his tie. Click outside the selected objects, then click the **duck's vest** to select just the vest as shown in Figure 1.5f.
- ➤ Click the **down arrow** on the **Fill Color button** on the Drawing toolbar, then click **More Fill Colors.** Choose a shade of green to change the vest to green.
- ➤ Repeat these steps to change the costume of the other duck to a black vest with a blue tie.
- ➤ Save the presentation.

FILL, LINE, AND SHADOW

All drawn objects have attributes (characteristics) that determine the appearance of the object. To change an attribute, select the object, then click the appropriate tool on the Drawing toolbar. You can apply a shadow. You can change the style of the exterior line and/or the color of the line. You can also change the interior (fill) color of the object and/or the fill pattern.

STEP 7: Ungroup and Resize

➤ Press the **PgDn key** to move to slide 6. Click and drag to select the text of the slide title, then type **Ungroup and Resize** as the new title.

➤ Check that the title is still selected. Pull down the **Format menu.** Click **Alignment.** Click **Right** to move the slide title to the right as shown in Figure 1.5g.

➤ Ungroup the duck and computer. Click outside the selected areas, then select the duck. Click and drag the duck to the upper left part of the slide.

➤ Click the computer and table, and upgroup these objects.

➤ Click outside the selected items, then click and drag the table under the duck.

➤ Click the computer. Drag a **corner handle** to increase the size of the computer, then click and drag to position the computer closer to the duck.

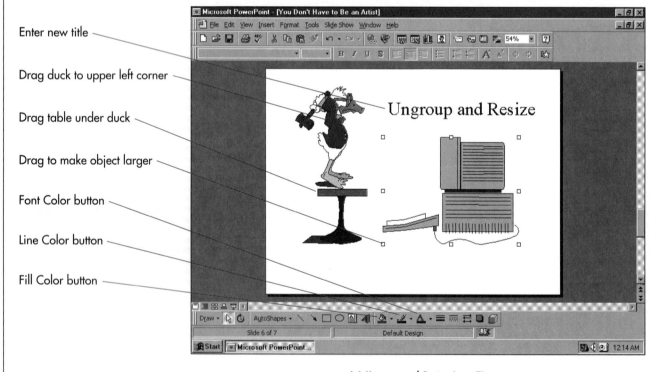

Enter new title

Drag duck to upper left corner

Drag table under duck

Drag to make object larger

Font Color button

Line Color button

Fill Color button

(g) Ungroup and Resize (step 7)

FIGURE 1.5   Hands-on Exercise 2 (continued)

PICK UP THE MOUSE

You always seem to run out of room on your real desk just when you need to move the mouse a little further. The solution is to pick up the mouse and move it closer to you—the pointer will stay in its present position on the screen, but when you put the mouse down you will have more room on your desk in which to work.

STEP 8: The Duplicate Command

➤ Press the **PgDn key** to move to slide 7. Click and drag to select the slide title, then type **Get Your Ducks in a Row** as the new title as shown in Figure 1.5h.

➤ Click and drag the clip art to the left side of the slide, then **ungroup** the duck and the computer. Click outside the selection to deselect both items, then click and drag the computer and table to the right of the slide.

➤ Select the duck. Pull down the **Edit menu** and click **Duplicate** (a combination of the Copy and Paste commands). You will see a second duck to the right of the first. Drag the second duck to the right until the ducks are separated as shown in Figure 1.5h.

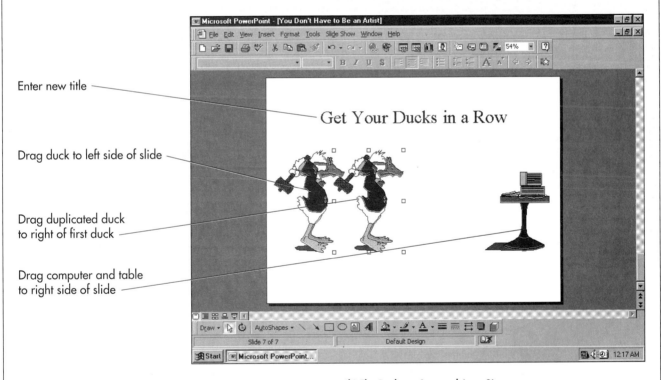

Enter new title

Drag duck to left side of slide

Drag duplicated duck to right of first duck

Drag computer and table to right side of slide

(h) The Duplicate Command (step 8)

FIGURE 1.5 Hands-on Exercise 2 (continued)

> Pull down the **Edit menu** a second time and click the **Duplicate command** a second time. A third duck will appear. (The distance between the second and third ducks is equal to the distance between the first and second ducks.)

> Execute the **Duplicate command** a third time to create the fourth and final duck. Change the vest colors as you see fit.

> Save the presentation.

STEP 10: Print the Audience Handouts

> Pull down the **File menu.** Click **Page Setup.** If necessary, click the **Portrait option button** to change the orientation for the Notes, Handouts, and Outline. Click **OK.**

> Pull down the **File menu.** Click **Print** to produce the Print dialog box. Click the **drop-down arrow** in the Print What list box. Click **Handouts (2 slides per page).**

> Check that the **All option button** is selected. Check the box to **Frame Slides.** Click **OK** to print the handouts.

> Save the presentation. Exit PowerPoint if you do not want to continue with the next exercise at this time.

OBJECT LINKING AND EMBEDDING

One of the primary advantages of the Windows environment is the ability to create a document containing data from multiple applications. This is accomplished through *Object Linking and Embedding* (OLE, pronounced "oh-lay") and it enables you to insert data (objects) from other applications into a PowerPoint presentation. You have, in fact, used OLE every time you inserted a clip art object into a presentation. You used it again at the beginning of this chapter to insert a chart created with the Microsoft Graph application. The next several pages describe other types of objects you can use to enhance a presentation.

In actuality, linking and embedding are two different techniques. The essential difference between the two is that embedding places the object into the presentation, whereas linking does not. In other words, an *embedded object* is stored within the presentation, and the presentation, in turn, becomes the only user (container) of that object. A *linked object,* on the other hand, is stored in its own file, and the presentation is one of many potential containers of that object. The presentation does not contain the object per se, but only a representation of the object as well as a pointer (link) to the file containing the object (the source document). The advantage of linking is that the presentation is updated automatically if the object is changed in the source document.

The choice between linking and embedding depends on how the object will be used. Linking is preferable if the object is likely to change and your presentation requires the latest version. Linking should also be used when the same object is placed in many documents, so that any change to the object has to be made in only one place (the source document). Embedding should be used if you need to take the presentation with you—for example, if you intend to show the presentation on a different computer.

The easiest way to link or embed an object is through the appropriate Auto-Layout as shown in Figure 1.6. Choose the AutoLayout for an Object slide as shown in Figure 1.6a, then double click the object placeholder to display the Insert Object dialog box in Figure 1.6b. The object types displayed within the dialog box depend on the applications that are installed on your system.

Click on Object slide

Name of selected slide

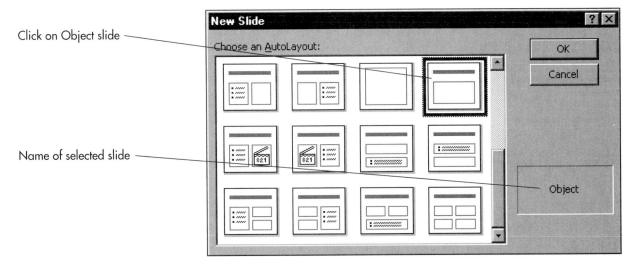

(a) The AutoLayout

Embedding allows
selection of either option

Linking requires selection
of Create from File option

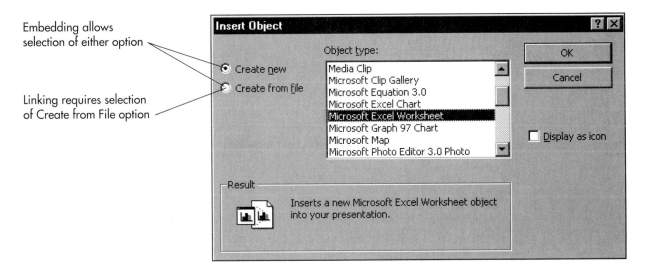

(b) Insert Object Dialog Box

Object will come
from an existing file

Name of file containing the object

Object is to be linked

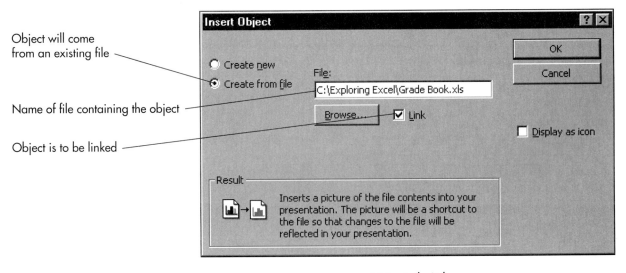

(c) Create the Link

FIGURE 1.6   Object Linking and Embedding

The option buttons to create a new object or to create the object from an existing file are mutually exclusive, in that you choose one or the other. If you embed an object, you can choose either option. If you link, however, you must choose the Create from File option because a linked object has to exist in its own file. This in turn produces the dialog box in Figure 1.6c, in which you must enter the source file name as well as check the box to create a link. The example links the Excel workbook, Grade Book in the Exploring Excel folder, to the Power-Point presentation and is illustrated in the next hands-on exercise.

Microsoft WordArt

Microsoft WordArt enables you to create decorative text to add interest to a presentation. It is available from every Office application and is called by clicking the Insert WordArt button on the Drawing toolbar.

WordArt is intuitive and easy to use. In essence, you choose a style for the text from among the selections in the dialog box of Figure 1.7a, then you enter the specific text as shown in Figure 1.7b. Figure 1.7c shows the completed Word-Art object, which can be moved and sized just like any other Windows object.

WordArt even has its own toolbar, which enables you to modify a WordArt object in subtle ways. You can rotate text in any direction, add three-dimensional effects, display the text vertically down the page, shade it, slant it, arch it, or even print it upside down. You're limited only by your imagination. It's fun, it's easy, and you can create some truly dynamite documents. (See practice exercise 1 at the end of the chapter.)

Organization Charts

Microsoft Organization Chart is yet another application included with Microsoft Office; it enables you to create an organization chart and embed it into a presentation. You start the application by choosing the AutoLayout containing an organization chart or by creating an object slide and choosing Microsoft Organization Chart as the object.

A partially completed organization chart is shown in Figure 1.8. To add additional boxes, you just click the appropriate command button at the top of the window. The coworker buttons create a box on the same level to the left or right of the current box. The subordinate command button creates a box under the current box, while the manager button creates a box above the current box. To delete a box, select the box, then press the Del key.

You can change the design of the connecting lines and/or the boxes in the chart, as well as their color. You can also change the font and/or alignment of the text within the individual boxes. Microsoft Organization Chart is illustrated in the hands-on exercise that follows shortly.

Sound

Sound can be linked or embedded into a presentation just like any other object. Realize, however, that sound requires additional hardware, namely a sound card and speakers, and we urge you to include these options on any machine you buy. (Sound may not be available in a laboratory setting for obvious reasons.)

Sounds exist as separate files that are inserted into a presentation through the Insert Object command as illustrated in the following hands-on exercise. Additional information about the different types of sound files is found in Appendix B, Introduction to Multimedia.

Selected style

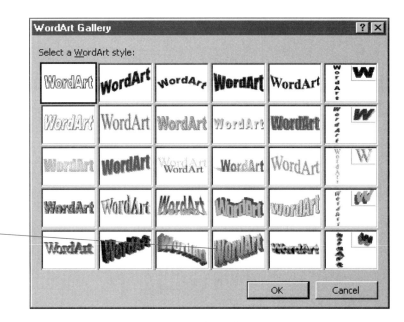

(a) WordArt Gallery

Enter text

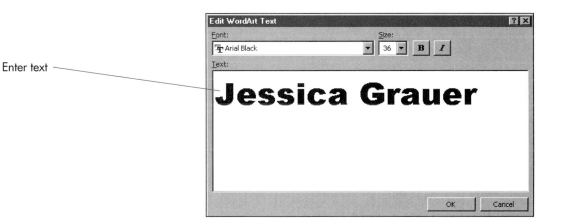

(b) Enter the Text

(c) The Completed WordArt Object

FIGURE 1.7   WordArt

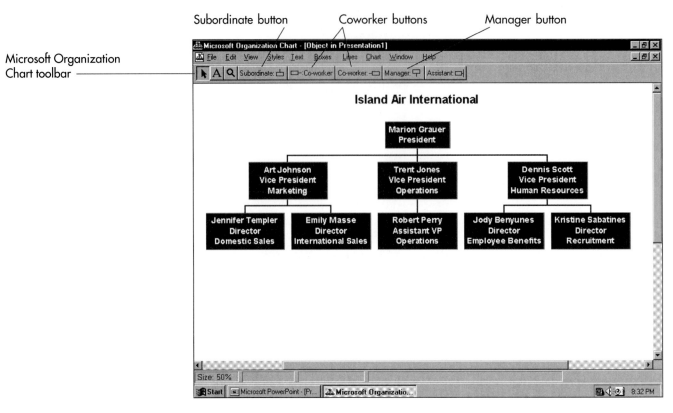

Subordinate button   Coworker buttons   Manager button

Microsoft Organization
Chart toolbar

FIGURE 1.8   Organization Chart

HANDS-ON EXERCISE 3

Object Linking and Embedding

Objective: To link an Excel worksheet to a PowerPoint presentation; to embed an organization chart, a WordArt object, and a sound file into a PowerPoint presentation. Use Figure 1.9 as a guide in doing the exercise. Completion of the exercise requires that Microsoft Excel be installed on your system.

STEP 1: Create the Title Slide

➤ Create a new presentation:

- If necessary, start PowerPoint. Click the option button to create a **Blank Presentation,** then click **OK.**

- If PowerPoint is already started, pull down the **File menu** and click **New** (or click the **New button** on the Standard toolbar). If necessary, double click the **Blank Presentation icon** to display the New Slide dialog box.

➤ You should see the New Slide dialog box with the AutoLayout for the title slide already selected. Click **OK** to create the title slide.

➤ Click the placeholder for the title and enter **Object Linking and Embedding** as the title of the presentation. Click the placeholder for the subtitle. Enter your name as indicated.

STEP 2: Add an Object Slide

➤ Click the **Save button** on the Standard toolbar. Save the presentation as **Object Linking and Embedding** in the **Exploring PowerPoint folder.**

➤ Click the **New Slide button** on the Standard toolbar to add a second slide. You should see the New Slide dialog box.

➤ Click the **down arrow** and scroll through the available slide layouts until you can select the **Object slide** (AutoLayout number 16). Click **OK.**

➤ You should see the slide in Figure 1.9a.

New Slide button

New button

Double click the object placeholder

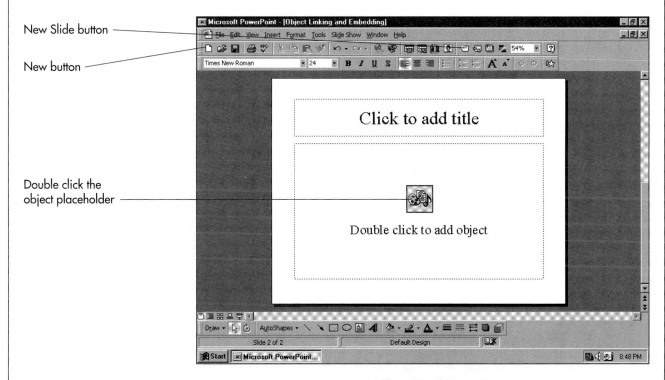

(a) Add an Object Slide (step 2)

FIGURE 1.9   Hands-on Exercise 3

THE AUTOLAYOUTS ARE NUMBERED

Each of the 24 AutoLayouts has an assigned number, corresponding to its position within the New Slide dialog box. (The layouts are numbered consecutively from left to right and top to bottom.) The number can be used as a shortcut to select the AutoLayout in lieu of clicking; type 2, for example, to select a bulleted list (the second slide in row 1). Other frequently used AutoLayouts include a title slide (number 1), a graph and title (number 8), an organization chart and title (number 7), an object and title (number 16), and a blank slide (number 12).

STEP 3: Insert the Excel Worksheet

➤ Double click the **placeholder** to add an object, which displays the Insert Object dialog box. Scroll through the **Object Type** list box until you can select **Microsoft Excel Worksheet.**

➤ Click the option button for **Create from File** to display the dialog box in Figure 1.9b.

➤ Click the **Browse button** to display the Browse dialog box. Click the **down arrow** on the Look In list box and select the **Exploring PowerPoint folder.**

➤ Select the **Grade Book workbook** from within the Exploring PowerPoint folder. Click **OK** to close the Browse dialog box.

➤ If necessary, clear the Link check box as we want to embed (rather than link) the worksheet into the presentation. Click **OK** to insert the worksheet into the presentation.

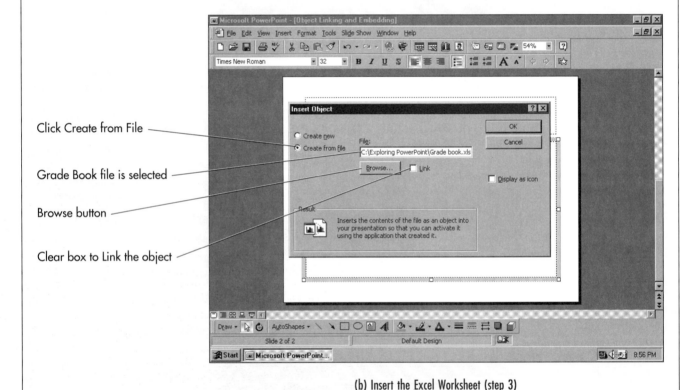

Click Create from File

Grade Book file is selected

Browse button

Clear box to Link the object

(b) Insert the Excel Worksheet (step 3)

FIGURE 1.9   Hands-on Exercise 3 (continued)

IN-PLACE EDITING

In-place editing enables you to double click an Excel worksheet in order to edit the object. You remain in PowerPoint, but the toolbars and pull-down menus are those of Excel. The File and Window menus are exceptions, however, and contain PowerPoint commands to save the presentation and/or view multiple presentations.

STEP 4: Complete the Slide

➤ You should see the worksheet in Figure 1.9c. The sizing handles indicate that the worksheet is currently selected and can be moved and sized like any other Windows object.

➤ Click anywhere outside the worksheet to deselect it. The sizing handles disappear.

➤ Click the **title placeholder** and type **CIS120 Grade Book** as the title of the slide.

➤ Save the presentation.

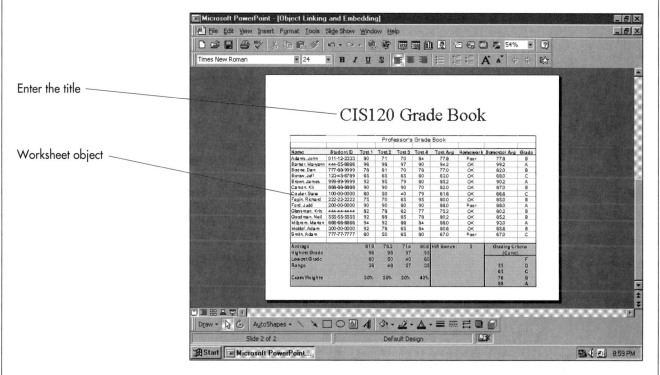

(c) Complete the Slide (step 4)

FIGURE 1.9 Hands-on Exercise 3 (continued)

LINKING VERSUS EMBEDDING

Linking is very different from embedding as it provides a dynamic connection between the source and destination documents. A linked object (e.g., an Excel worksheet) is tied to the destination document (e.g., a PowerPoint presentation) in such a way that any changes to the source file are automatically reflected in the destination document. Linking is especially useful when the same object is inserted in multiple documents, as changes to the object are made in only one place (in the source file). A linked object must be saved as a separate file. An embedded object, on the other hand, is inserted directly into a document and need not exist in its own file.

STEP 5: Create the Organization Chart

➤ Click the **New Slide button** on the Standard toolbar. Click the AutoLayout for an **Organization chart.**

➤ Click **OK** to add the slide, then double click the placeholder to add the organization chart.

➤ You should see a window titled **Microsoft Organization Chart** open within the PowerPoint window, as shown in Figure 1.9d. Click the **Maximize button** of the Microsoft Organization Chart window.

➤ The text in the first box is already selected. Type your name and press **enter** to move to the second line. Type **President** for your title.

➤ Click in the first box in the second row. Enter the name of a friend as Vice President of Marketing. (Press **enter** to move to a second line.) Add two additional friends as Vice Presidents of Operations and Human Resources.

Microsoft Organization Chart toolbar

Subordinate button

Enter your name and title

Click and enter a friend's name

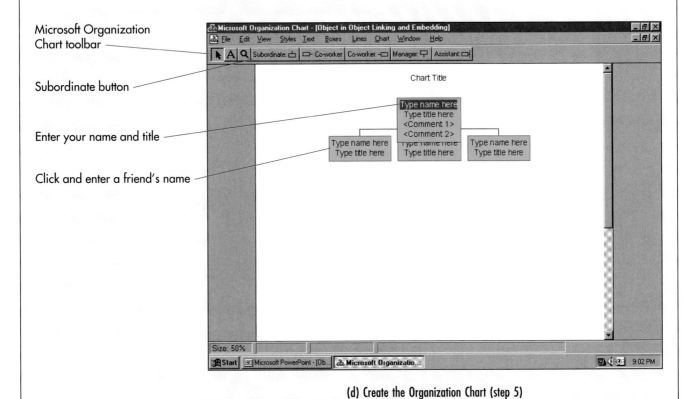

(d) Create the Organization Chart (step 5)

FIGURE 1.9   Hands-on Exercise 3 (continued)

STEP 6: Complete the Organization Chart

➤ You can add detail to the chart by entering additional boxes for subordinates or coworkers. Enter the subordinates as shown in Figure 1.9e:

• To add a subordinate, click the subordinate button on the Organization Chart toolbar, then click the box under which the subordinate is to appear.

• To add a coworker, manager, or assistant, follow the same procedure as for a subordinate.

• To enter a person's name and title in an existing box, click in the box, then enter the text. Press the **enter key** to go from line to line.

• To delete a box, click in the box to select it, then press the **Del key.**

New Slide button

Enter new title

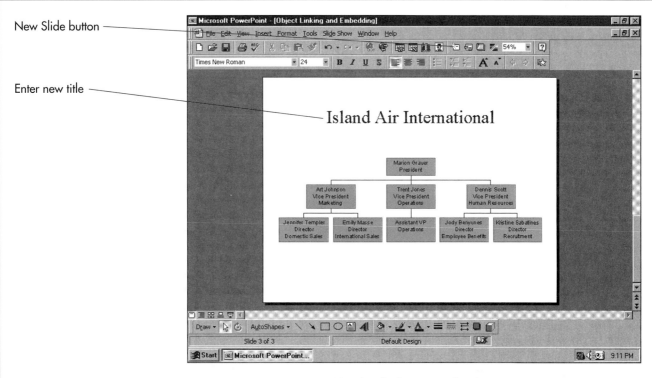

(e) Complete the Organization Chart (step 6)

FIGURE 1.9   Hands-on Exercise 3 (continued)

➤ Pull down the **File menu.** Click **Exit and Return to Object Linking and Embedding** (the name of the presentation).
➤ Click **Yes** when asked whether to update the object. You should see an organization chart similar to the one in Figure 1.9e.
➤ Click the placeholder for the slide title. Enter the name of your organization.
➤ Save the presentation

CUSTOMIZE THE ORGANIZATION CHART

You can change the appearance of an organization chart by selecting a box or line, then executing the appropriate formatting command. It's generally best, however, to retain a uniform appearance by formatting the entire chart at one time. Press Ctrl+A to select the chart, pull down the Boxes menu, then select the command to change the box color, border style, border color, or border line style. To change the line color, style, or thickness, select all of the lines (pull down the Edit menu, click Select, and click Connecting lines), then choose the desired commands from the Lines menu.

STEP 7: Clip Art and AutoShapes

➤ Click the **New Slide button,** then do one of the following:

• Click **AutoLayout Number 11** (Title only), click **OK** to add the slide to the presentation, then click the **Insert Clip Art button** on the Standard toolbar to display the Microsoft Clip Gallery dialog box, *or*

• Click **AutoLayout Number 16** (Object), click **OK** to add the slide to the presentation, then double click the placeholder to add the object. Choose **Microsoft Clip Gallery** from the list of available objects and click **OK** to display the Clip Gallery dialog box.

➤ Choose an appropriate clip art image. Click **Insert,** then move and size the clip art so that it is positioned as shown in Figure 1.9f. Click in the title placeholder, then enter **Clip Art and AutoShapes** as the title for this slide.

➤ Click the **down arrow** on the **AutoShapes button** on the Drawing toolbar to display the AutoShapes menu. Select (click) **Callouts,** then select the **Cloud callout** at the end of the first row. Click and drag on the slide where you want the callout to go. Release the mouse.

➤ The callout should be selected automatically:

• Type **I can do this!** as the caption. (You must enter the text when the callout is selected.)

• If necessary, click and drag the callout to adjust its size or position.

• To change the Fill color or Line color, click the appropriate tool on the Drawing toolbar, then select one of the displayed colors.

➤ Click outside the callout to deselect it.

➤ Save the presentation.

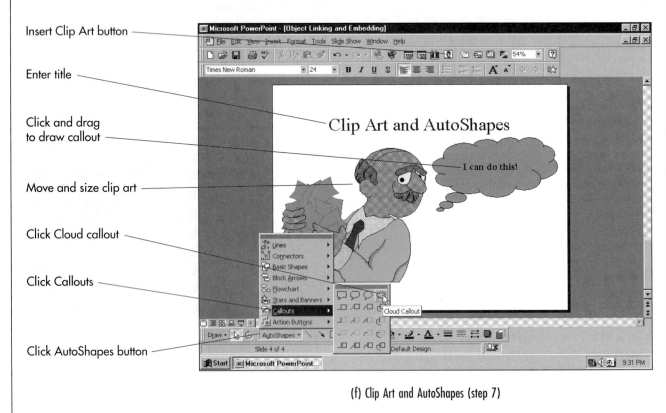

(f) Clip Art and AutoShapes (step 7)

FIGURE 1.9 Hands-on Exercise 3 (continued)

AUTOSHAPES

An AutoShape is a predefined shape that is drawn automatically when you select its icon from the AutoShapes menu, then click and drag in the slide. (To display the AutoShapes menu, click the AutoShape tool on the Drawing toolbar.) To place text inside an AutoShape, select the shape and start typing. You can also change the fill color or line thickness by selecting the shape, then clicking the appropriate button on the Drawing toolbar. See practice exercise 3 at the end of the chapter.

STEP 8: The Slide Finder

➤ You can insert slides from other presentations into the current presentation. Pull down the **Insert menu.** Click **Slides from Files** to display the Slide Finder dialog box in Figure 1.9g. (The My Chart presentation is not yet visible.)

➤ Click the **Browse button,** then select the **Exploring PowerPoint folder** where you have been saving your work. Select (click) the **My Chart presentation** that you created in the first hands-on exercise.

➤ Click the **Open button,** then click the **Display button** to view the slides in this presentation (there is only one slide).

➤ Select the slide, then click the **Insert button** to insert the slide containing the chart into this presentation. (The new slide is inserted after the current slide.) Close the Slide Finder dialog box.

➤ Save the presentation.

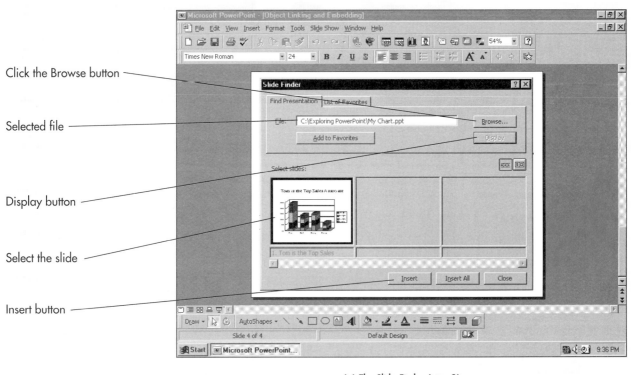

Click the Browse button

Selected file

Display button

Select the slide

Insert button

(g) The Slide Finder (step 8)

FIGURE 1.9   Hands-on Exercise 3 (continued)

THE SLIDE FINDER

You work hard to develop individual slides and thus you may find it useful to reuse a slide from one presentation to the next. Pull down the Insert menu, click the Slides from Files command to display the Slide Finder dialog box, then browse until you locate the presentation containing the slide or slides you want to use. Open the presentation, then click the Display button to view the slides it contains. Select the slides individually, or press and hold the Shift key to select multiple slides, click Insert, then close the Slide Finder dialog box.

STEP 9: WordArt

➤ You should be on the fifth (of five) slides. Click the **New Slide button** on the status bar, click the AutoLayout for a **blank slide** (or type **12** as the number of the desired layout), then click **OK** to add the slide.

➤ Click the **Insert WordArt button** on the Drawing toolbar to display the WordArt Gallery dialog box. Choose any style you like (we took the fourth style from the left in the first row). Click **OK.**

➤ You should see the Edit WordArt text box as shown in Figure 1.9h. Enter **The End** as the text for your WordArt object.

➤ Click **OK** to close the Edit WordArt text box and insert the WordArt into your presentation. Save the presentation.

New Slide button

Enter text

Insert WordArt button

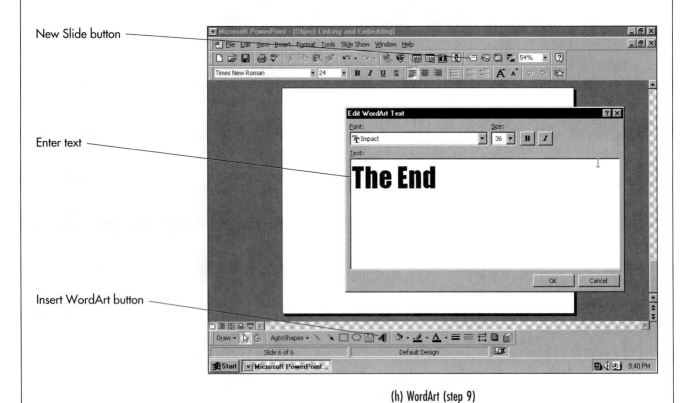

(h) WordArt (step 9)

FIGURE 1.9 Hands-on Exercise 3 (continued)

THE WORDART TOOLBAR

The WordArt toolbar is the easiest way to change an existing WordArt object. It is displayed automatically when a WordArt object is selected; otherwise it is suppressed. As with any toolbar, you can point to a button to display a ScreenTip containing the name of the button, which is indicative of its function. You will find buttons to display the text vertically, change the style or shape, and/or edit the text.

STEP 10: WordArt Continued

➤ Move and size the WordArt object just as you would any other Windows object:

- Click and drag a corner sizing handle to increase the size of the WordArt until it takes the entire slide.
- Point to the middle of the WordArt object (the mouse pointer changes to a double cross), then click and drag to position the WordArt in the middle of the slide.

➤ Click the **drop-down arrow** for the **Fill Color tool** on the Drawing toolbar to display the available fill colors as shown in Figure 1.9i. Select (click) **blue** to change the color of the WordArt object.

➤ Experiment with other tools, on either or both the Drawing and WordArt toolbars, to enhance the WordArt image.

➤ Save the presentation.

Click and drag to size the WordArt object

Click and drag to move WordArt object

Click Blue

Fill Color button

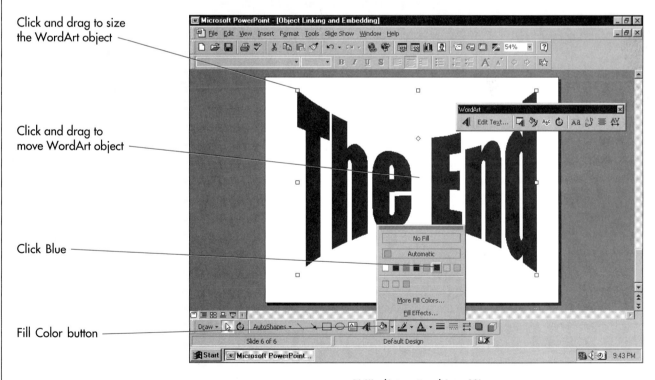

(i) WordArt continued (step 10)

FIGURE 1.9   Hands-on Exercise 3 (continued)

THE THIRD DIMENSION

You can make your WordArt images even more dramatic by adding 3-D effects. You can tilt the text up or down, right or left, increase or decrease the depth, and change the shading. Pull down the View menu, click Toolbars, click Customize to display the complete list of toolbars, then check the box to display the 3-D Settings toolbar. Select the WordArt object, then experiment with various tools and special effects. The results are even better if you have a color printer.

STEP 11: Insert a Sound

➤ Pull down the Insert menu. Click **Movies and Sound,** then click **Sound from File** to display the Insert Sound dialog box in Figure 1.9j.

➤ Change to the Exploring PowerPoint folder if you cannot locate the Office97 folder, which comes up by default.

➤ Select (click) the **Applause sound,** then click **OK** to insert the file into the presentation.

➤ A tiny microphone should appear in the middle of the slide to indicate that the sound file has been embedded on the slide. Double click the microphone to play the sound and hear the applause. (Your machine has to have a sound card if you are to actually hear the applause.)

➤ Save the presentation.

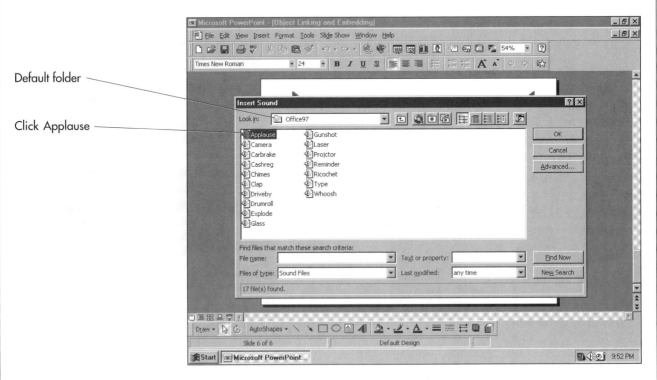

(j) Insert a Sound (step 11)

FIGURE 1.9   Hands-on Exercise 3 (continued)

THE WINDOWS 95 FIND COMMAND

We supplied the sound of applause, but you are likely to have many other sound files on your system, any one of which can be embedded into a presentation. The easiest way to locate these files is through the Windows 95 Find command. Click the Start button, click (or point to) the Find command, then click Files or Folders to display the Find dialog box. Enter *.wav (the "wav" indicates a sound file) in the Named text box and My Computer in the Look In box. Click Find Now. Use the right mouse button to click and drag a file from the Find Files window onto your presentation. Release the mouse, then click the Copy Here command to embed the sound onto the slide.

STEP 12: Custom Animation

➤ Click and drag the sound icon to the upper right portion of the slide. Point to the icon, click the **right mouse button** to display a shortcut menu, then click **Custom Animation** to display the Custom Animation dialog box in Figure 1.9k.

➤ Click the **Timing tab.** Select the **Media 2 object,** click the **Animate option button,** then click the **Automatically option button.** Enter **1** second in the associated list box to play the applause automatically one second after the slide appears. Click **OK** to accept the settings and close the dialog box.

➤ Save the presentation.

Click and drag Sound icon to upper right

Media Object becomes an animated object

Timing tab

Click Animate button

Enter 1 second

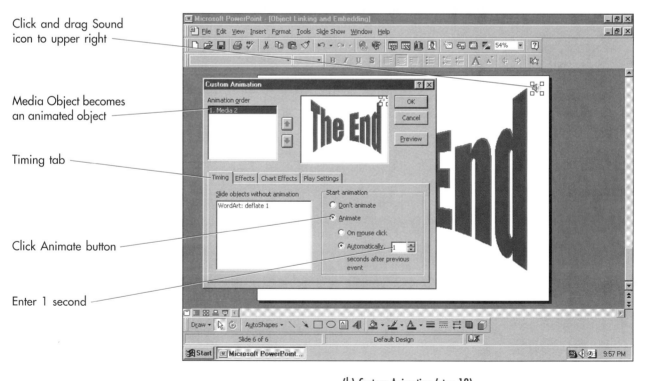

(k) Custom Animation (step 12)

FIGURE 1.9 Hands-on Exercise 3 (continued)

STEP 13: Applause, Applause

➤ Press **Ctrl+Home** to move to the first slide in the presentation, then click the **Slide Show button** to view the presentation.

➤ Click the **left mouse button** (or press the **PgDn key**) to move from slide to slide until you come to the end of the presentation. The applause you hear on the last slide is for your efforts in this exercise.

➤ Click the mouse a final time to return to the Slide view. Exit PowerPoint if you do not want to continue with the next exercise at this time.

RESOURCES FROM THE INTERNET AND WORLD WIDE WEB

The resources in the Microsoft Clip Gallery in Office 97 are impressive when compared to previous versions of Microsoft Office, but pale in comparison to what is available on the Internet and World Wide Web. Hence, any discussion of enhancing a presentation through clip art and/or photographs must also include the Internet. We begin with a brief description of the Internet and World Wide Web, then we describe how to incorporate these resources into a PowerPoint presentation.

The ***Internet*** is a network of networks that connects computers across the country and around the world. It grew out of a U.S. Department of Defense (DOD) experimental project begun in 1969 to test the feasibility of a wide area (long distance) computer network over which scientists and military personnel could share messages and data.

The ***World Wide Web*** (WWW, or simply, the Web) is a very large subset of the Internet, consisting of those computers containing hypertext and/or hypermedia documents. A ***hypertext document*** is a document that contains a link (reference) to another document, which may be on the same computer or even on a different computer, with the latter located anywhere in the world. ***Hypermedia*** is similar in concept, except that it also provides links to graphic, sound, and video files.

Either type of document enables you to move effortlessly from one document (or computer) to another. And therein lies the fascination of the Web, in that you simply click on link after link to go from one document to the next. You can start your journey at your professor's home page in New York, for example, which may contain a link to the Library of Congress, which in turn may contain links to other documents. So, off you go to Washington D.C., and from there to a different document on a different computer across the country or perhaps around the world.

Figure 1.10 depicts how the Internet can be used in conjunction with a PowerPoint presentation. The first task is to locate the resource, which in this example is a photograph from the Dinosaur Hall at the National Museum of

URL address

Right click on photograph
to display a shortcut menu

Click Save Picture as

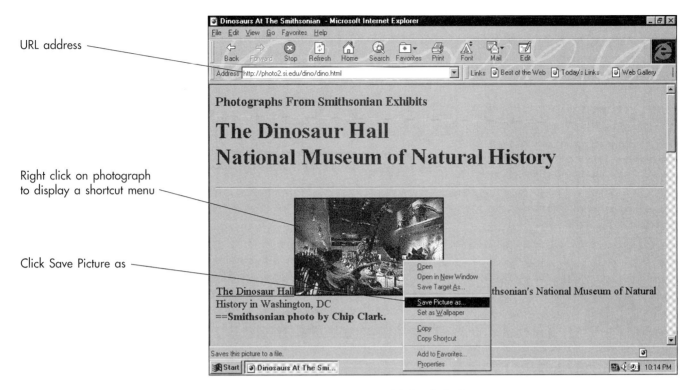

(a) Identify the Resources

Insert Hyperlink button

URL address of Web page
or local document

Web toolbar

Back button

Forward button

Hyperlink

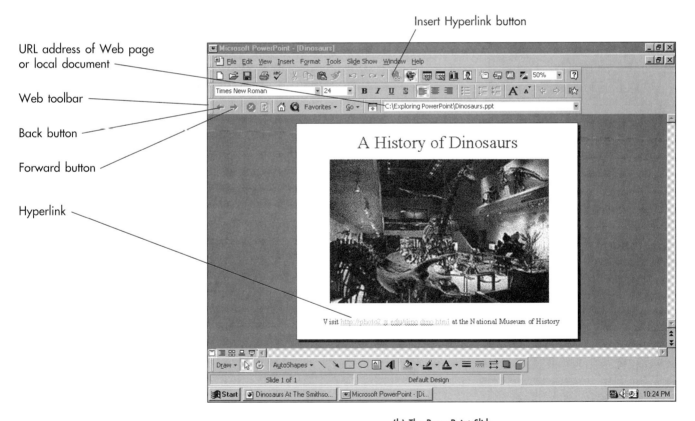

(b) The PowerPoint Slide

FIGURE 1.10   The Internet as a Resource

Natural History. To do this you start your Web browser (e.g., Internet Explorer), then you use your favorite search engine to locate the required information (perhaps a photograph of a dinosaur). Once this is done, right click on the photograph to display the context-sensitive menu in the figure, then click the Save Picture as command to download the file to your hard drive.

Next, you start PowerPoint, using the **Insert Picture command** to insert the picture that was just downloaded into a presentation. You can also use the **Insert Hyperlink command** to insert a hyperlink onto a slide, which you can click during the slide show, and provided you have an Internet connection, your Web browser will display the associated page.

Look carefully at the screen in Figure 1.10b, which displays the **Web toolbar** immediately under the Formatting toolbar. (The Web toolbar is displayed by executing the Toolbars command from the View menu.) The Web toolbar contains buttons similar to those on the toolbar in Internet Explorer. You can, for example, enter the address (URL) of a Web page (or a local document) to activate your browser and access the page. You can use the Favorites button to add a page to your list of favorites, and/or open a previously added page. You can click the Back and Forward buttons to move between previously displayed pages. And, as with any toolbar, ScreenTips are displayed when you point to a button to display the name of the button, which is indicative of its function.

MULTITASKING

Multitasking, the ability to run multiple applications at the same time, is one of the primary advantages of the Windows environment. Entering a Web address within the Web toolbar automatically opens Internet Explorer so that both applications (PowerPoint and Internet Explorer) are open on your desktop. You can maximize both windows, then switch back and forth between the open applications by clicking the appropriate button on the Windows taskbar.

Copyright Protection

A *copyright* provides legal protection to a written or artistic work, giving the author exclusive rights to its use and reproduction, except as governed under the fair use exclusion as explained below. Anything on the Internet or World Wide Web should be considered copyrighted unless the document specifically says it is in the *public domain,* in which case the author is giving everyone the right to freely reproduce and distribute the material.

Does this mean you cannot use statistics and other facts that you find while browsing the Web? Does it mean you cannot download an image to include in a report? The answer to both questions depends on the amount of the material and on your intended use of the information. It is considered *fair use,* and thus not an infringement of copyright, to use a portion of the work for educational, nonprofit purposes, or for the purpose of critical review or commentary. In other words, you can use a quote, downloaded image, or other information from the Web, provided you cite the original work in your footnotes and/or bibliography. Facts themselves are not covered by copyright, so you can use statistical and other data without fear of infringement. Be sure, however, to cite the original source in your document.

The following exercise takes you to the home page of the **National Aeronautics and Space Administration (NASA),** where you will download an image for inclusion into a PowerPoint presentation.

The Internet as a Resource

Objective: To download a picture from the Internet and use it in a PowerPoint presentation. Use Figure 1.11 as a guide in the exercise. The exercise requires that you have an Internet connection.

STEP 1: The Web Toolbar

➤ Start PowerPoint. Click the option button to create a **Blank Presentation,** then enter the title slide for your presentation as shown in Figure 1.11a. Drag the title placeholder to the top of the slide.

➤ Save the presentation as **The Web as a Resource** in the **Exploring Power-Point folder** that you have used throughout the text.

➤ Point to any toolbar, then click the **right mouse button** to display a context-sensitive menu, which lists the available toolbars. Click **Web** to display the Web toolbar. Do not be concerned if the position of your toolbars is different from ours.

➤ Click the **Address box.** Enter **www.nasa.gov** (the http:// is assumed), then press the **enter key** to connect to this site. Your Web browser (e.g., Internet Explorer) will open automatically after which you should be connected to NASA's home page. If necessary, maximize the Internet Explorer window.

Enter www.nasa.gov in Address box

Display the Web toolbar

Web browser opens on desktop

URL address of site

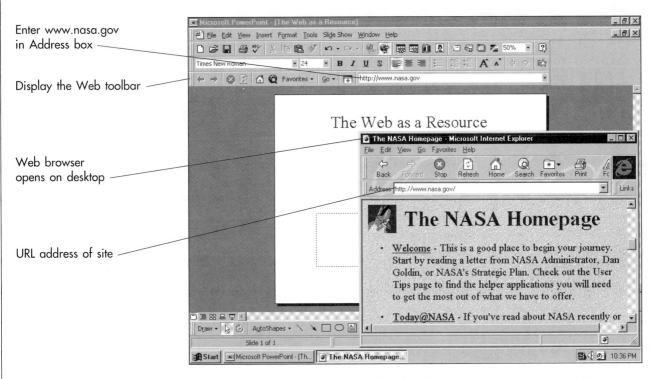

(a) The Web Toolbar (step 1)

FIGURE 1.11   Hands-on Exercise 4

STEP 2: Download the Picture

➤ Scroll down NASA's home page to see the descriptions of the various links, then click the link to **Today@NASA** to view current information. Scroll down the page of today's stories until you find a link that interests you. It does not matter which link you choose.

➤ We chose the link to **Updated Photo and Video Galleries Online,** which led eventually to pictures from the various Apollo missions as shown in Figure 1.11b. (The site is changing continually, however, and you may not be able to locate our exact picture. It doesn't matter.)

➤ Select any picture on the NASA site, click the **right mouse button** to display a shortcut menu, then click the **Save Picture as command** to display the Save As dialog box.

 • Click the **drop-down arrow** in the Save in list box to specify the drive and folder in which you want to save the graphic (e.g., the Exploring Power-Point folder on drive C).

 • The file name and file type are entered automatically by Internet Explorer. (You may change the name, but don't change the file type.) Click the **Save button** to download the image. Remember the file name and location as you will need to access the file in the next step.

➤ The Save As dialog box closes automatically as soon as the picture has been downloaded to your PC.

➤ Click the link that says **Select here if you wish to read the caption.** You will need the descriptive information later in the exercise.

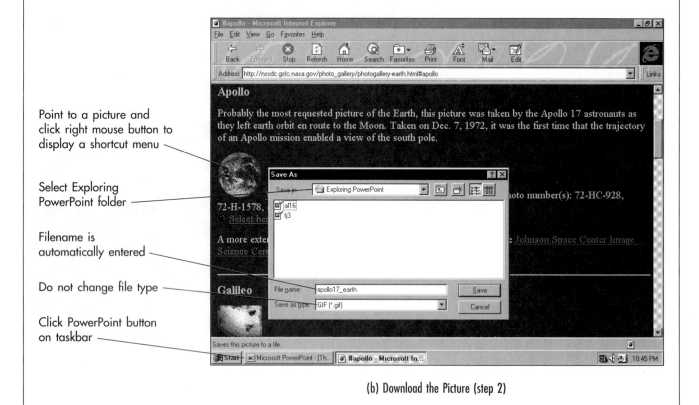

Point to a picture and click right mouse button to display a shortcut menu

Select Exploring PowerPoint folder

Filename is automatically entered

Do not change file type

Click PowerPoint button on taskbar

(b) Download the Picture (step 2)

FIGURE 1.11   Hands-on Exercise 4 (continued)

THE THUMBNAIL SKETCH

Graphics add to the visual appeal of a Web page, but they also add significantly to the time required to display the page. Hence, many Web designers include a thumbnail sketch (a small version of the larger image) to preview the picture without having to wait the extra time to display the entire image. The user can click the thumbnail sketch to see the complete image if he or she desires to do so.

STEP 3: Insert the Picture

➤ Click the **PowerPoint button** on the Windows taskbar to return to Power-Point. Click the **New Slide button** on the Standard toolbar to display the New Slide dialog box, then choose a blank slide and click **OK.**

➤ Pull down the **Insert menu,** point to (or click) **Picture,** then click **From File** to display the Insert Picture dialog box shown in Figure 1.11c.

➤ Click the **drop-down arrow** on the Look in text box to select the drive and folder where you previously saved the picture (e.g., the Exploring Word folder on drive C).

➤ Select (click) **APOLLO17_EARTH,** which is the file containing the picture of the earth as seen from Apollo 17. Click **Insert** and the picture will appear in your presentation.

➤ Save the presentation.

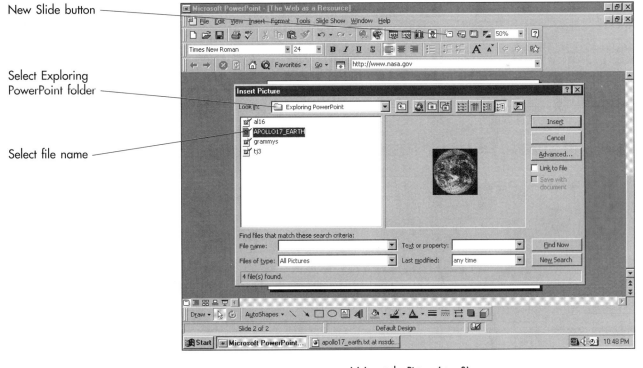

(c) Insert the Picture (step 3)

FIGURE 1.11   Hands-on Exercise 4 (continued)

THE CLIPBOARD

Use the Windows clipboard (an area of memory available to every application) to copy text from one application to another. Go to the Web page containing the text you want to copy (e.g., the descriptive information about the photograph), click and drag within Internet Explorer to select the text, then press Ctrl+C to copy the selected text to the Windows clipboard. Switch to PowerPoint, click on the slide where you want the text to go, then press Ctrl+V to paste the text into the presentation. Be sure to credit your sources.

STEP 4: Add Text to the Slide

➤ Move and/or size the picture so that your slide is similar to Figure 1.11d. Click the **Textbox tool** on the Drawing toolbar, then click and drag on the right side of the slide to create a text box.

➤ Enter the text as shown in Figure 1.11d. If necessary, change to an appropriate font and point size such as **24 point Times New Roman.**

➤ Click the **Textbox tool** a second time, then click and drag below the picture to create a second text box. Enter the text as shown in the figure. We used the same font as in the previous text box (Times New Roman), but chose a smaller size **(18 point).**

➤ Save the presentation.

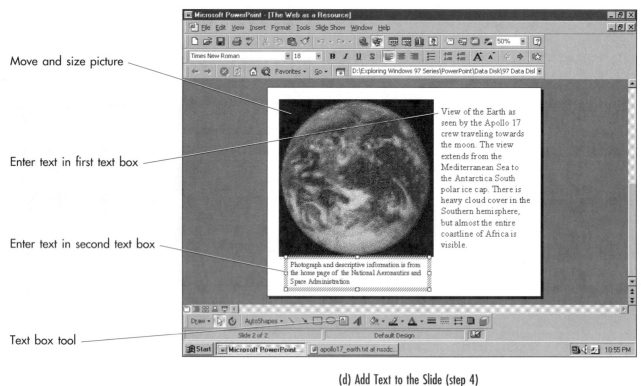

Move and size picture

Enter text in first text box

Enter text in second text box

Text box tool

(d) Add Text to the Slide (step 4)

FIGURE 1.11   Hands-on Exercise 4 (continued)

CROPPING A PICTURE

The picture of the earth is perfect for this exercise. Other times, however, you may want to crop (erase) part of a picture. To do so, select the picture to display the Picture toolbar and the sizing handles. Click the Cropping tool (the ScreenTip will display the name of the tool), then click and drag a sizing handle to crop the part of the picture you want to erase. Click elsewhere in the document to deselect the picture.

STEP 5: Insert a Hyperlink

➤ Click and drag to select the text, **National Aeronautics and Space Administration,** as shown in Figure 1.11e.

➤ Pull down the **Insert menu** and click **Hyperlink** (or click the **Insert Hyperlink button** on the Standard toolbar) to display the Insert Hyperlink dialog box. Type **www.nasa.gov** (the http:// is assumed). Click **OK** to close the Insert Hyperlink dialog box.

➤ Click elsewhere in the slide to deselect the text, which now appears as a hyperlink (i.e., it will be underlined in a different color).

➤ Save the presentation.

Insert Hyperlink button

Enter URL address

Click and drag to select text

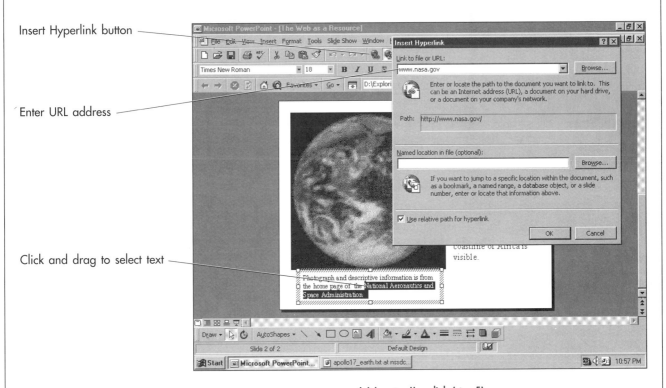

(e) Insert a Hyperlink (step 5)

FIGURE 1.11   Hands-on Exercise 4 (continued)

STEP 6: Test the Hyperlink

➤ Change to the **Slide Show view.** Point to the hyperlink. The mouse pointer changes to a hand and you see a ScreenTip indicating the associated Web address as shown in Figure 1.11f.

➤ Click the hyperlink to open (reactivate) Internet Explorer and branch to the indicated Web page. Take a few minutes to explore NASA's home page, then close Internet Explorer.

➤ Exit PowerPoint. Click **Yes** if asked to save the presentation.

Point to the hyperlink; click to open Web browser and go to specified Web page

View of the Earth as seen by the Apollo 17 crew traveling towards the moon. The view extends from the Mediterranean Sea to the Antarctica South polar ice cap. There is heavy cloud cover in the Southern hemisphere, but almost the entire coastline of Africa is visible.

Photograph and descriptive information is from the home page of the National Aeronautics and Space Administration

http://www.nasa.gov/

(f) Test the Hyperlink (step 6)

FIGURE 1.11   Hands-on Exercise 4 (continued)

SUMMARY

Microsoft Graph has many of the same commands and capabilities as the charting component of Microsoft Excel. After a graph has been inserted into a presentation, it becomes an embedded object that retains its connection to Microsoft Graph. Thus, you can double click the graph to restart Microsoft Graph and edit the graph. You can also click the graph to select it as an object on a PowerPoint slide, then move or size the graph just as you would any other Windows object.

Office 97 contains a powerful set of drawing tools that are collectively known as Office Art. Even if you are not an artist, you can use these tools to modify existing clip art and thus create new and very different illustrations.

Object Linking and Embedding (OLE) enables you to link or embed information (objects) created in other applications. The choice between linking and embedding depends on how the object will be used. Linking is preferable if the object is likely to change and your presentation requires the latest version, or when the same object is shared among many destination documents. Embedding should be used if you plan to show the presentation on a different computer from the one used to create the presentation.

Microsoft WordArt enables you to add special effects to text, then embed the text object into a presentation. WordArt is called from within PowerPoint by clicking the Insert WordArt tool on the Drawing toolbar.

Microsoft Organization Chart enables you to create an organization chart and embed it into a presentation. The application is called from within Power-Point by choosing the AutoLayout containing an organization chart or by creating an object slide and choosing Microsoft Organization Chart as the object type.

PowerPoint enables you to embed a sound file or a video clip (a movie) into a presentation. Movies do not require additional hardware. Sound requires a sound board and speakers.

Resources from the Internet and World Wide Web can be downloaded for inclusion in a PowerPoint presentation. Hyperlinks can be added to any slide, which when clicked during a slide show will open a Web browser to display the associated page. The Web toolbar contains buttons similar to those on the toolbar in Internet Explorer.

KEY WORDS AND CONCEPTS

AutoShape	Hypertext document	Microsoft WordArt
Category names	In-place editing	Object
Copyright	Insert Hyperlink command	Object Linking and Embedding
Data points	Insert Picture command	Office Art
Data series	Internet	Public domain
Datasheet	Linked object	Sound
Destination document	Microsoft Clip Gallery	Source document
Drawing toolbar	Microsoft Graph	Ungroup command
Embedded object	Microsoft Organization Chart	Web toolbar
Group command		World Wide Web
Hypermedia document		

MULTIPLE CHOICE

1. What happens if you click the Datasheet button on the Microsoft Graph toolbar twice in a row?
   (a) The datasheet is closed (hidden)
   (b) The datasheet is opened (displayed)
   (c) The datasheet is in the same status (either opened or closed) as it was before it was clicked
   (d) Impossible to determine

2. Which of the following is true of data series that are plotted in rows?
   (a) The first row in the datasheet contains the category names for the X axis
   (b) The first column in the datasheet contains the legend
   (c) Both (a) and (b)
   (d) Neither (a) nor (b)

3. Which of the following is true of data series that are plotted in columns?
   (a) The first column in the datasheet contains the category names for the X axis
   (b) The first row in the datasheet contains the legend
   (c) Both (a) and (b)
   (d) Neither (a) nor (b)

4. What happens if you select a slide in the Slide Sorter view, click the Copy button, then click the Paste button twice in a row?
   (a) You have made one additional copy of the slide
   (b) You have made two additional copies of the slide
   (c) You have made three additional copies of the slide
   (d) The situation is impossible because you cannot execute the Paste command twice in a row

5. How do you size an object so that it maintains the original proportion between height and width?
   (a) Drag a sizing handle on the left or right side of the object to change its width, then drag a sizing handle on the top or bottom edge to change the height
   (b) Drag a sizing handle on any of the corners
   (c) Both (a) and (b)
   (d) Neither (a) nor (b)

6. What happens if you select an object, then execute the Flip Vertical command twice in a row?
   (a) The object has been rotated 90 degrees
   (b) The object has been rotated 180 degrees (turned upside down)
   (c) The object has been rotated 270 degrees
   (d) The object has been rotated 360 degrees and is in the same position as when you started

7. What is the difference between clicking and double clicking an embedded object?
   (a) Clicking selects the object; double clicking starts the application that created the object
   (b) Double clicking selects the object; clicking starts the application that create the object
   (c) Clicking changes to the Slide Sorter view; double clicking changes to the Outline view
   (d) Double clicking changes to the Slide Sorter view; clicking changes to the Outline view

8. Under which circumstances would you choose linking over embedding?
   (a) When the same object is referenced in many different documents
   (b) When an object is constantly changing and you need the latest version
   (c) Both (a) and (b)
   (d) Neither (a) nor (b)

9. Under which circumstances would you choose embedding over linking?
   (a) When you need to show a presentation on a different computer
   (b) When the same object is referenced in many different documents
   (c) Both (a) and (b)
   (d) Neither (a) nor (b)

10. Which of the following can be created as an embedded object?
    (a) A graph created by Microsoft Graph
    (b) Text created by Microsoft WordArt
    (c) Clip art
    (d) All of the above

11. Which of the following is true regarding the Web toolbar?
    (a) It enables you to enter the address of a Web page from within a PowerPoint presentation
    (b) It enables you to add a Web page to a list of favorite pages
    (c) It contains a button to return to previous Web pages
    (d) All of the above

12. How do you insert clip art onto an existing slide?
    (a) Pull down the Insert menu, click Object, then choose Microsoft Clip Gallery from the list of available objects
    (b) Click the Insert Clip Art button on the Standard toolbar
    (c) Pull down the Insert menu, click Picture, and click the Clip Art command
    (d) All of the above

13. How do you create a new slide containing a graph?
    (a) Create a blank slide, then pull down the Insert menu and click the Chart command
    (b) Create a blank slide, then click the Insert Chart button on the Standard toolbar
    (c) Click the New Slide button, select an AutoLayout containing a chart, then double click the placeholder for the chart in the Slide view
    (d) All of the above

14. What happens if you select an object, click the Copy command, move to a new slide, and click the Paste command?
    (a) Nothing because you cannot copy and paste an object on two different slides
    (b) The selected object has been moved from the first slide to the second slide
    (c) The selected object has been copied from the first slide to the second slide
    (d) The selected object has been copied from the first slide to the second slide, and in addition, remains on the clipboard from where it can be pasted onto another slide

15. What happens if you select an object, click the Cut command, move to a new slide, and click the Paste command?
    (a) Nothing because you cannot copy and paste an object on two different slides
    (b) The selected object has been moved from the first slide to the second slide
    (c) The selected object has been copied from the first slide to the second slide
    (d) The selected object has been copied from the first slide to the second slide, and in addition, remains on the clipboard from where it can be pasted onto another slide

PRACTICE WITH POWERPOINT 97

1. Microsoft WordArt is an ideal tool to create the title slide of a presentation, as can be seen from Figure 1.12. Open the Object Linking and Embedding presentation created in the third hands-on exercise and do the following:

   a. Switch to the Slide Sorter view. Select the Title Slide, then press the Del key to delete the slide.

   b. Click the New Slide button on the Standard toolbar to insert a new slide. Choose AutoLayout 12 for a blank slide. Click OK.

   c. Double click the new slide to change to the slide view. Click the Insert WordArt button on the Drawing toolbar to start WordArt.

   d. You're on your own. Duplicate our slide or, better yet, create your own. Let's see how creative you can be and how much impact you can add.

FIGURE 1.12   Screen for Practice Exercise 1

2. Microsoft Organization Chart offers considerable flexibility in the appearance of an organization chart as shown by the chart in Figure 1.13. You can change the line thickness, style, or color for the boxes or connecting lines. You can change the shape of a border and/or add a shadow effect. You can change the font and/or color of text within a box.

All of these changes are done within the context of *select-then-do;* that is, you select the box (or boxes) for which the change is to apply, then you execute the appropriate command. (To select multiple boxes, press and hold the Shift key as you click additional boxes. You can also use the Select commands in the Edit menu.) Open the Object Linking and Embedding presentation created in the third hands-on exercise and do the following:

a. Switch to the Slide Sorter view. Select the slide with the organization chart.

b. Double click the slide to change to the Slide view. Double click the Organization Chart to edit the chart so that it matches Figure 1.13.

c. Change the box and/or line style as you see fit.

d. Print a full-page version of the revised slide and submit it to your instructor as proof you did the exercise.

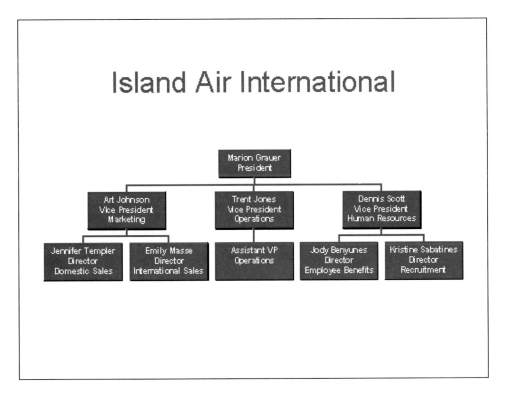

FIGURE 1.13   Screen for Practice Exercise 2

3. Exploring AutoShapes: Figure 1.14 displays a single slide containing a variety of AutoShapes. Open the presentation created in the third hands-on exercise and do the following:

a. Add a blank slide immediately before the last slide.

b. Click the AutoShapes tool on the Drawing toolbar to display the AutoShapes menu. Click and drag the top of the menu to make it a floating toolbar.

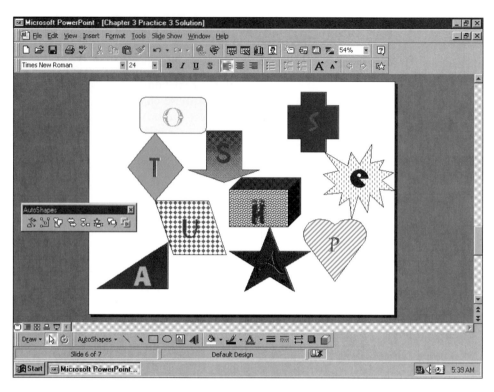

FIGURE 1.14 Screen for Practice Exercise 3

   c. Point to an AutoShape, then click and drag in the slide to create the shape on the slide. (You can press and hold the Shift key as you drag for special effects; for example, press and hold the Shift key as you drag the ellipse or rectangle tool to draw a circle or square, respectively. You can also use the Shift key in conjunction with the Line tool to draw a perfect horizontal or vertical line, or a line at a 45-degree angle.)

   d. To place text inside a shape, select the shape and start typing.

   e. To change the fill color or line thickness, select the shape, then click the appropriate button on the Drawing toolbar.

   f. Use these techniques to duplicate Figure 1.14, or better yet, create your own design. Add your name to the completed slide and submit it to your instructor.

4. Figure 1.15 shows two additional examples of what you can do with clip art. The smaller slide on the edge of the page contains the original clip art image. The full-size slide shows the modified slide and is the objective of the exercise. To create Figure 1.15a:

   a. Create a blank slide in any presentation. Click the Insert Clip Art button on the Standard toolbar to open the Microsoft Clip Gallery. Add the image from the Cartoons category.

   b. Select the clip art image and move it to the right side of the slide. Click the Copy and Paste buttons on the Standard toolbar to copy the image, then drag the copied image to the left side of the slide.

   c. Select the image on the right, then ungroup the clip art to convert it to a Microsoft Office drawing. Click the Draw button on the Drawing toolbar, click Rotate or Flip, and click Flip Horizontal.

   d. Continue to ungroup the image, changing various colors as appropriate.

   e. Click and drag the Rectangle tool to draw a rectangle under our demanding friends. Do not be concerned if the rectangle is on top of the men and you cannot see their elbows. Check that the rectangle is still selected, then click the Fill Color button on the Drawing toolbar to change the color of the rectangle to brown. You can also change the texture (fill color).

f. Click the rectangle to select it. Click the Draw button on the Drawing toolbar, click Order, and click Send to back.

g. Add the AutoShape with the indicated text. Add your name to the slide.

(a) Clip Art 1

(b) Clip Art 2

FIGURE 1.15   Screens for Practice Exercise 4

To create Figure 1.15b:

h. Create a blank slide in any presentation. Click the Insert Clip Art button on the Standard toolbar to open the Microsoft Clip Gallery. Add the image from the Cartoons category.

i. Click and drag the image to size and position it as shown in Figure 1.15b.

j. Copy the clip art image, then click and drag the copied image so that the figures are separated from one another.

k. Ungroup all of the elements in the copied image. Select just the smile, then flip and resize the smile to change it to a frown. (This takes a little practice.)

l. Use the Fill Color tool on the Drawing toolbar to recolor the clothing.

m. Click and drag the Text tool on the Drawing toolbar to create the first text box, then type *There's Good News* in the text box. Be sure the text is still selected, then change the font, size, and color as you see fit.

n. Repeat step (m) to create the second text box. Print both slides and submit them to your instructor.

5. Every sport, and indeed every team, has its own home page. Basketball and football fans, for example, can visit www.nba.com and www.nfl.com, respectively, from where you can click links to your local teams. Similar pages exist for other leagues as well. And if you don't know where to start, consider the ESPN home page in Figure 1.16.

Choose your favorite sport, team, or player, then create a presentation of six to ten slides. You can create a presentation to announce your own All Star team, with pictures and statistics for each player. Alternatively, you could focus on the career of a specific player. The possibilities are endless.

FIGURE 1.16 Screen for Practice Exercise 5

Case Studies

Before and After

As you already know, PowerPoint provides a set of drawing tools to develop virtually any type of illustration. Even if you are not artistic, you can use these tools to modify existing clip art and thus create new and very different illustrations. All it takes is a little imagination and a sense of what can be done. Choose any clip art image(s), then modify that image(s) to create an entirely different effect. Present your results in a three-slide presentation consisting of a title slide, a "before slide" showing the original image(s), and an "after slide" showing the modifications. Print the audience handouts for your presentation, three slides per page, and be sure to check the box to frame the slides. Ask your instructor to hold a class contest in which the class votes to determine the most creative application.

Photographs versus Clip Art

The right clip art can enhance a presentation, but there are times when clip art just won't do. It may be too juvenile or simply inappropriate. Photographs offer an alternative and are inserted into a presentation through the Insert Picture command. Once inserted into a presentation, photographs can be moved or sized just like any other Windows object. The CD-ROM version of the Clip Gallery contains a series of photographs. We invite you to explore these photographs, then report back to the class on their quality and cost.

The National Debt

The national debt is staggering—more than $5 trillion, or approximately $20,000 for every man, woman, and child in the United States. The annual budget is approximately $1.5 trillion, and Congress has yet to eliminate the deficit, which exceeds $100 billion annually.

Use the Internet to obtain exact figures for the current year, then use this information to create a presentation pleading for fiscal sanity. Do some additional research and obtain data on the budget, the deficit, and the national debt for the years 1945, 1967, and 1980. The numbers may surprise you. For example, how does the interest expense for the current year compare to the total budget in 1967 (at the height of the Viet Nam War)? To the total budget in 1945 (at the end of World War II)?

File Compression

Photographs add significantly to the appearance of a presentation, but they also add to its size. Accordingly, you might want to consider acquiring a file compression program to facilitate copying large files to a floppy disk in order to transport your presentations to and from school, home, or work. You can download an evaluation copy of the popular WinZip program at www.winzip.com. Investigate the subject of file compression, then submit a summary of your findings to your instructor.

Copyright Infringement

It's fun to download images from the Web for inclusion in a presentation, but is it legal? Copyright protection (infringement) is one of the most pressing legal issues on the Web. Search the Web for sites that provide information on current copyright law. One excellent site is the copyright page at the Institute for Learning Technologies at www.ilt.columbia.edu/projects/copyright. Another excellent reference is the page at www.benedict.com. Research these and other sites, then summarize your findings in a short note to your instructor.

Our Last Case

Once again we refer you to the Valupack on the CD-ROM version of Microsoft Office to view a 45-slide presentation that introduces (and reviews) the major features in PowerPoint. The presentation is called "QuikStrt" and is found in the Tutorial folder within the Valupack folder on the CD-ROM. It is a multimedia presentation that incorporates music, video, as well as the various other features discussed in this chapter. Sit back, relax, and enjoy the show.

APPENDIX A: TOOLBARS

OVERVIEW

Microsoft PowerPoint has fourteen predefined toolbars that provide access to commonly used commands. The toolbars are displayed in Figure A.1 and are listed here for convenience. They are: the Standard, Formatting, Animation Effects, Common Tasks, Control Toolbox, Drawing, Picture, Reviewing, Shadow Settings, Stop Recording, Visual Basic, Web, WordArt, and 3-D Settings toolbars. The Standard and Formatting toolbars are displayed by default and appear immediately below the menu bar. The other predefined toolbars are displayed (hidden) at the discretion of the user.

The buttons on the toolbars indicate their functions. Clicking the Printer button, for example (the fourth button from the left on the Standard toolbar), executes the Print command. If you are unsure of the purpose of any toolbar button, point to it, and a ScreenTip will appear that displays its name.

You can display multiple toolbars at one time, move them to a new location, customize their appearance, or suppress their display.

- To display or hide a toolbar, pull down the View menu and click the Toolbars command. Select (deselect) the toolbar(s) that you want to display (hide). The selected toolbar(s) will be displayed in the same position as when last displayed. You may also point to any toolbar and click with the right mouse button to bring up a shortcut menu that lets you select the toolbar to be displayed (hidden). In either case, if you do not see the desired toolbar listed, click the Customize command to display the list of all available toolbars. Click the check box for the desired toolbar(s) and then click Close.

- To change the size of the buttons, suppress the display of the ScreenTips, or display the associated shortcut key (if available) with the ScreenTips, pull down the View menu, click Toolbars, and click Customize to display the Customize dialog box. If necessary, click the Options tab, then select (deselect) the appropriate check box.

- Toolbars are either docked (along the edge of the window) or floating (in their own window). A toolbar moved to the edge of the window will dock along that edge. A toolbar moved anywhere else in the window will float in its own window. Docked toolbars are one tool wide (high), whereas floating toolbars can be resized by clicking and dragging a border or corner as you would with any window.
  - To move a docked toolbar, click anywhere in the gray background area and drag the toolbar to its new location. You can also click and drag the move handle (the pair of parallel lines) at the left of the toolbar.
  - To move a floating toolbar, drag its title bar to its new location.
- To customize one or more toolbars, display the toolbar(s) on the screen. Then pull down the View menu, click Toolbars, click Customize to display the Customize dialog box, and select the Toolbars tab. Alternatively, you can click on any toolbar with the right mouse button, select Customize from the shortcut menu, and then click the Toolbars tab.
  - To move a button, drag the button to its new location on that toolbar or any other displayed toolbar.
  - To copy a button, press the Ctrl key as you drag the button to its new location on that toolbar or any other displayed toolbar.
  - To delete a button, drag the button off the toolbar and release the mouse button.
  - To add a button, click the Commands tab in the Customize dialog box, select the category from the Categories list box that contains the button you want to add, then drag the button to the desired location on the toolbar. (To see a description of a tool's function before adding it to a toolbar, select the tool, then click the Description command button.)
  - To restore a predefined toolbar to its default appearance, pull down the View menu, click Toolbars, click Customize, click the Toolbars tab, select (highlight) the desired toolbar, and click the Reset command button.
- Buttons can also be moved, copied, or deleted without displaying the Customize dialog box.
  - To move a button, press the Alt key as you drag the button to the new location.
  - To copy a button, press the Alt and Ctrl keys as you drag the button to the new location.
  - To delete a button, press the Alt key as you drag the button off the toolbar.
- To create your own toolbar, pull down the View menu, click Toolbars, click Customize, click the Toolbars tab, then click the New command button. Alternatively, you can click on any toolbar with the right mouse button, select Customize from the shortcut menu, click the Toolbars tab, and then click the New command button.
  - Enter a name for the toolbar in the dialog box that follows. The name can be any length and can contain spaces.
  - The new toolbar will appear on the screen. Initially it will be big enough to hold only one button. Add, move, and delete buttons following the same procedures as outlined above. The toolbar will automatically size itself as new buttons are added and deleted.
  - To delete a custom toolbar, pull down the View menu, click Toolbars, click Customize, and click the Toolbars tab. *Verify that the custom toolbar to be deleted is the only one selected (highlighted).* Click the Delete command button. Click Yes to confirm the deletion. (Note that a predefined toolbar cannot be deleted.)

Standard Toolbar

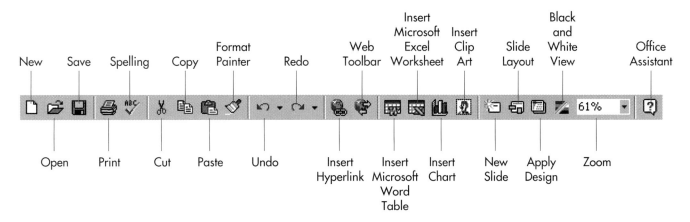

New · Save · Spelling · Copy · Format Painter · Redo · Web Toolbar · Insert Microsoft Excel Worksheet · Insert Clip Art · Slide Layout · Black and White View · Office Assistant

Open · Print · Cut · Paste · Undo · Insert Hyperlink · Insert Microsoft Word Table · Insert Chart · New Slide · Apply Design · Zoom

Formatting Toolbar

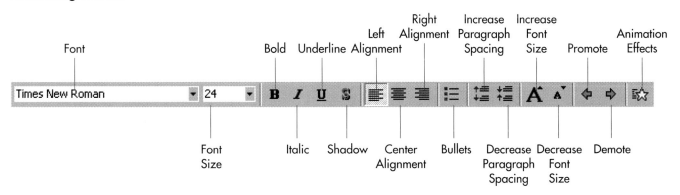

Font · Bold · Underline · Left Alignment · Right Alignment · Increase Paragraph Spacing · Increase Font Size · Promote · Animation Effects

Times New Roman · 24

Font Size · Italic · Shadow · Center Alignment · Bullets · Decrease Paragraph Spacing · Decrease Font Size · Demote

Animation Effects Toolbar

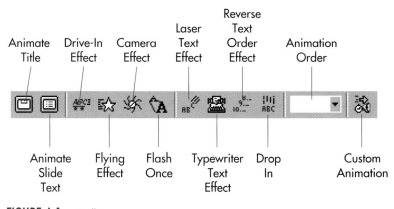

Animate Title · Drive-In Effect · Camera Effect · Laser Text Effect · Reverse Text Order Effect · Animation Order

Animate Slide Text · Flying Effect · Flash Once · Typewriter Text Effect · Drop In · Custom Animation

FIGURE A.1   Toolbars

Common Tasks Toolbar

New Slide
Dialog Box

Apply Design
Dialog Box

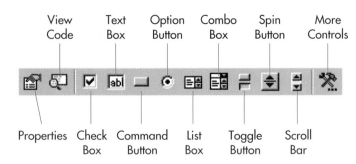

Slide Layout
Dialog Box

Control Toolbox Toolbar

View
Code

Text
Box

Option
Button

Combo
Box

Spin
Button

More
Controls

Properties

Check
Box

Command
Button

List
Box

Toggle
Button

Scroll
Bar

Drawing Toolbar

Draw
Menu

Free
Rotate

Line

Rectangle

Text
Box

Fill
Color

Font
Color

Dash
Style

Shadow

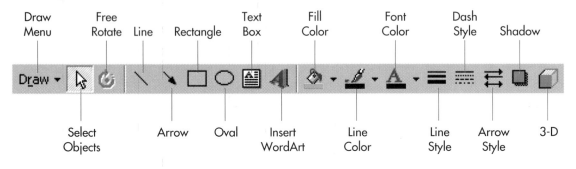

Select
Objects

Arrow

Oval

Insert
WordArt

Line
Color

Line
Style

Arrow
Style

3-D

Picture Toolbar

Insert
Picture
from File

More
Contrast

More
Brightness

Crop

Recolor
Picture

Set
Transparent
Color

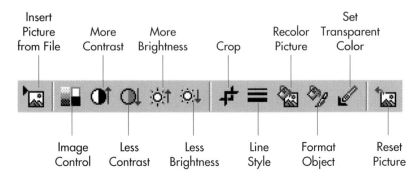

Image
Control

Less
Contrast

Less
Brightness

Line
Style

Format
Object

Reset
Picture

Reviewing Toolbar

Insert
Comment

Create
Microsoft
Outlook Task

Show/Hide
Comment

Mail
Recipient

Shadow Settings Toolbar

Shadow
On/Off

Nudge
Shadow
Down

Nudge
Shadow
Right

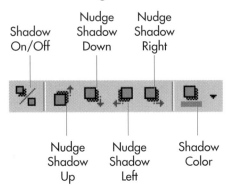

Nudge
Shadow
Up

Nudge
Shadow
Left

Shadow
Color

FIGURE A.1   Toolbars (continued)

Stop Recording Toolbar

Stop
Recording

Visual Basic Toolbar

Run   Visual Basic
Macro   Editor

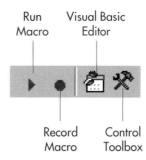

Record   Control
Macro   Toolbox

Web Toolbar

Back   Stop   Start   Favorites   Show Only
    Current   Page   Menu   Web Toolbar
    Jump

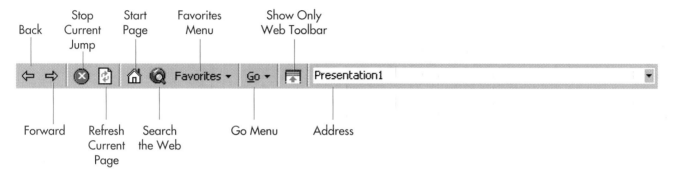

Forward   Refresh   Search   Go Menu   Address
    Current   the Web
    Page

WordArt Toolbar

Insert   WordArt   WordArt   WordArt   WordArt
WordArt   Gallery   Shape   Same   Alignment
    Letter
    Heights

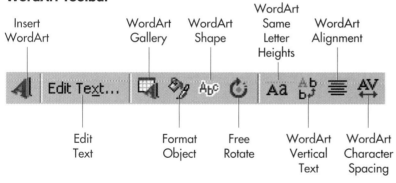

Edit   Format   Free   WordArt   WordArt
Text   Object   Rotate   Vertical   Character
    Text   Spacing

3-D Settings Toolbar

3-D   Tilt   Tilt
On/Off   Up   Right   Direction   Surface

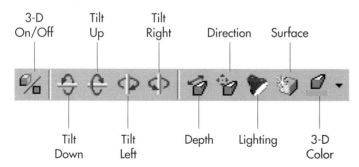

Tilt   Tilt   Depth   Lighting   3-D
Down   Left   Color

FIGURE A.1   Toolbars (continued)

APPENDIX B: INTRODUCTION TO MULTIMEDIA

B

OVERVIEW

Multimedia combines the text and graphics capability of the PC with high-quality sound and video. The combination of different media, under the control of the PC, has opened up a new world of education and entertainment. This appendix introduces you to the basics of multimedia and shows you how to incorporate sound and video into a PowerPoint presentation.

We begin with a brief discussion of the hardware requirements needed to run multimedia applications. We explain the various file types that are associated with multimedia and discuss the support that is built into Windows 95. The appendix also contains two hands-on exercises that let you apply the conceptual material. The first exercise is independent of PowerPoint and has you experiment with various sound and video files to better acquaint you with the capabilities of multimedia. The second exercise shows you how to create your own multimedia presentation.

THE MULTIMEDIA COMPUTER

Multimedia is possible only because of recent advances in technology that include faster microprocessors, CD-ROM, and sophisticated sound and video boards. But how fast a microprocessor do you really need? What type of CD-ROM and sound card should you consider? The answer is critical to both the consumer and the developer. The consumer wants a system that is capable of running "typical" multimedia applications. The developer, on the other hand, wants to appeal to the widest possible audience and must write an application so that it runs on the "typical" configuration.

To guide developers, and to let the public know about the specific hardware needed, the Multimedia PC Working Group of the Software Publishers Association was established to determine the suggested minimum specification for a multimedia computer. Three standards have been published to date—MPC-1, MPC-2, and MPC-3, in 1991, 1993, and 1995, respectively, as shown in Figure B.1. Implicit in each standard is the requirement that the system retail for less than $2,000. Technology has advanced so quickly, however, that the current standard (MPC-3) is well below today's entry-level computer. MPC-4 was not available at the time we went to press (June 1997) but you can check the Web site (www.spa.org/mpc) for additional information. Realize also that in addition to the equipment listed in the table, you will need speakers to amplify the sound, a microphone if you want to record your own sounds, and a joystick for games.

	MPC-1 (1991)	MPC-2 (1993)	MPC-3 (1995)
CPU	80386 16MHz	80486SX 25MHz	75MHz Pentium
RAM	2MB	4MB	8MB
Disk capacity	30MB	160MB	540MB
Sound card	8 bit	8 bit	16 bit with multivoice internal synthesizer
CD-ROM	Single speed	Double speed	Quadruple speed
Video system	VGA (640 × 480)	SVGA (800 × 600)	30 frames/second at 320 × 240 pixels

FIGURE B.1   The Multimedia PC

WHAT IS MMX TECHNOLOGY?

Intel has enhanced its Pentium processor through an additional set of 57 instructions that are collectively known as MMX technology. The instructions are designed to process video, audio, and graphical data more efficiently and increase the speed of a Pentium processor by approximately 20 percent. You do not need an MMX processor to run multimedia applications; it helps significantly, however, and you should not purchase a computer without it.

THE BASICS OF MULTIMEDIA

A few years ago, multimedia was an extra. Today, it is a virtual standard and everyone has a favorite multimedia application. But did you ever stop to think of how the application was created? Or of the large number of individual files that are needed for the sound and visual effects that are at the heart of the application? In this section we look at the individual components—the sound and video files—that comprise a multimedia application.

Sound

The sound you hear from your PC is the result of a sound file (stored on disk or a CD-ROM) being played through the sound card in your system. There are, however, two very different types of sound files—a WAV file and a MIDI file. Each is discussed in turn.

A **WAV file** is a digitized recording of an actual sound (a voice, music, or special effects). It is created by a chip in the sound card that converts a recorded sound (e.g., your voice by way of a microphone) into a file on disk. The sound card divides the sound wave into tiny segments (known as samples) and stores each sample as a binary number. The quality of the sound is determined by two factors—the sampling rate and the resolution of each sample. The higher each of these values, the better the quality, and the larger the corresponding file.

The **sampling rate** (or frequency) is the number of samples per second and is expressed in KHz (thousands of samples per second). The higher the sampling rate, the more accurately the sound will be represented in the wave file. Common sampling rates are 11KHz, 22KHz, and 44KHz. The **resolution** is the number of bits (binary digits) used to store each sample. The more bits the better. The first sound cards provided for only eight bits and are obsolete. Sixteen bits are standard in today's environment.

WAV files, even those that last only a few seconds, grow large very quickly. Eight-bit sound, for example, at a sampling rate of 11KHz (11,000 samples a second) requires approximately 11KB of disk space per second. Thirty seconds of sound at this sampling rate will take some 330KB. If you improve the quality by using a 16-bit sound card, and by doubling the sampling rate to 22KHz, the same 30 seconds of sound will consume 1.3MB, or almost an entire high-density floppy disk!

A **MIDI file** (Musical Instrument Digital Interface) is very different from a WAV file and is used only to create music. It does not store an actual sound (as does a WAV file), but rather the instructions to create that sound. In other words, a MIDI file is the electronic equivalent of sheet music. The advantage of a MIDI file is that it is much more compact than a WAV file because it stores instructions to create the sound rather than the sound itself.

Video

An **AVI** (Audi-Video Interleaved) **file** is the Microsoft standard for a digital video (i.e., a multimedia) file. It takes approximately 4.5MB to store one second of *uncompressed* color video in the AVI format. That may sound unbelievable, but you can verify the number with a little arithmetic.

A single VGA screen contains approximately 300,000 (640 × 480) pixels, each of which requires (at least) one byte of storage to store the color associated with that pixel. Allocating one byte (or 8 bits) per pixel yields only 256 (or 2^8) different colors. It is more common, therefore, to define color palettes based on two or even three bytes per pixel, which yield 65,536 (2^{16}) and 16,777,216 (2^{24}) colors, respectively. The more colors you have, the better the picture, but the larger the file.

In addition, to fool the eye and create the effect of motion, the screen must display at least 15 screens (frames) a second. If we multiply 300,000 bytes per frame times 15 frames per second, we arrive at the earlier number of 4.5MB of data for each second of video. Storage requirements of this magnitude are clearly prohibitive, in that an entire 640MB CD would hold less than three minutes of video. And even if storage capacity were not a problem, it's simply not possible for a CD-ROM to deliver almost 5MB of data per second to the PC. Clearly something had to be done to deliver video to the PC market.

Full-motion video is made possible in two ways, by reducing the size of the window in which the movie clip is displayed, and through file compression. Think, for a moment, of the movie clips you have seen (or consider the Basket.AVI file in Figure B.2) and realize that it is displayed in a window that is only 240 × 180 as opposed to a full (640 × 480) VGA screen. The smaller window immediately reduces the storage requirements.

Even more significant than a reduced window is the availability of sophisticated compression-decompression algorithms that dramatically reduce the storage requirements. In essence, these algorithms do not store every pixel in every frame, but only information about how pixels change from frame to frame. The details of file compression are not important at this time. What is important is that you appreciate the amount of data that is required for multimedia applications.

Realize, too, that even with the smaller window and file compression, AVI files are still inordinately large. The 3½-second movie clip in Figure B.2, for example, requires 670KB. Nevertheless, compare this requirement to our earlier calculations, which showed that an uncompressed video running on a VGA screen would take approximately 4.5MB per second!

THE AVI (AUDIO VIDEO INTERLEAVED) STANDARD

The AVI format was introduced in 1992 and specified a standard video clip of 160 × 120 pixels, or one-sixteenth of a VGA screen. The tiny screen was not overly impressive to the public at large, but it represented a significant technical achievement. Improved technology such as the local bus, multi-speed CDs, better compression algorithms, and faster microprocessors have resulted in today's superior video clips.

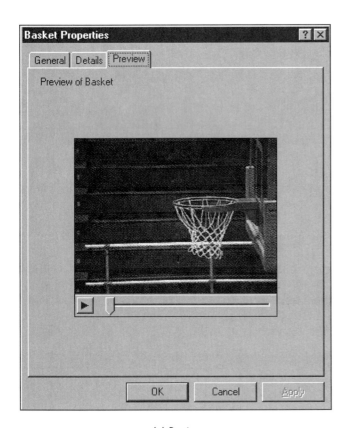

(a) Preview

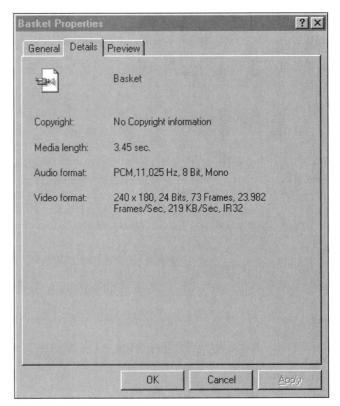

(b) Details

FIGURE B.2   Movie Clip

Windows 95 Support

Windows 95 includes the necessary software (in the form of accessories) to play the various types of multimedia files. The appropriate accessory is opened automatically when you double click a media file type from within Windows Explorer or My Computer. The software can also be accessed from the Start button by clicking Programs, then Accessories, then Multimedia. Each accessory is described briefly below, then illustrated in a hands-on exercise.

The **Sound Recorder** is used to record and/or play a WAV file. Options within the Sound Recorder let you record at different qualities (such as CD or radio), add special effects such as an echo, or change the speed. You can even play the sound backwards.

The **Media Player** lets you play audio (MIDI), video, or animation files. **Volume Control** enables you to control the volume and/or balance of your sound card. The **CD Player** enables you to play audio CDs in a CD-ROM drive while you work on your PC. The controls on the Windows CD player look just like those on a regular CD player. It also has many of the same features, such as random play, and a programmable playback order.

The following exercise lets you experiment with the various types of multimedia files we have described.

ORDINARY FILES

A multimedia file is just like any other file with respect to ordinary file operations. Thus, you can point to the file in My Computer or Windows Explorer, then click the right mouse button to display a menu to cut or copy the file, rename or delete the file, or display its properties. You can also use the right mouse button to click and drag the file to a different drive or folder or to create a shortcut on the desktop.

HANDS-ON EXERCISE 1

Introduction to Multimedia

Objective: To locate and play WAV, MIDI and AVI files. The exercise requires a sound card but can be done without a CD-ROM. Use Figure B.3 as a guide in the exercise.

STEP 1: A WAV File

➤ Click the **Start button** on the Windows 95 taskbar. Click (or point to) **Programs,** then click **Windows Explorer.** Click the **maximize button** so that Windows Explorer takes the entire desktop as shown in Figure B.3a.

➤ Select the **Exploring PowerPoint folder** that you have been using throughout the text. If necessary, pull down the **View menu** and click **Details.**

➤ Pull down the **View menu** a second time. Click **Options,** then click the **View tab** in the Options dialog box. Clear the box (if necessary) to **Hide MS-DOS file extensions.** Click **OK.**

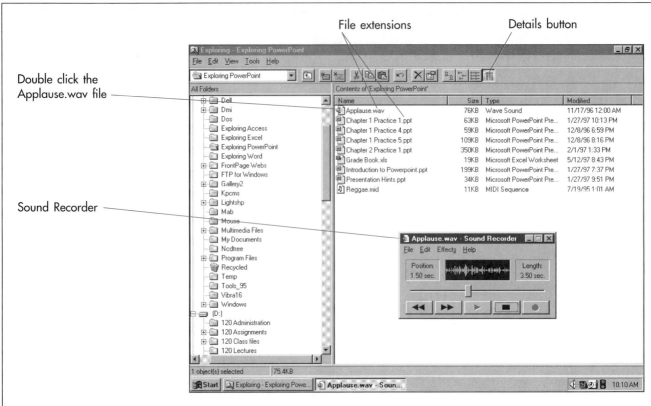

File extensions   Details button

Double click the
Applause.wav file

Sound Recorder

(a) A WAV File (step 1)

FIGURE B.3   Hands-on Exercise 1

➤ Double click the **Applause.wav file** to play the file. The Sound Recorder opens automatically as you hear the applause, then closes after the sound is complete.

➤ Point to the **Applause.wav file,** then click the **right mouse button** to display a context-sensitive menu. Click **Properties** to display the Properties dialog box, then click the **Details tab** to see additional information about this file.

➤ Close the Properties dialog box.

RECORD YOUR OWN WAV FILES

You can record your own WAV files, provided you have a microphone; then you can link or embed those files in a PowerPoint presentation. To create a new sound (WAV) file, right click in the folder that is to contain the file, click New, then click Wave Sound to specify the type of object you want to create. Change the default file name, then double click the file to open the Sound Recorder. Click the Record button to start recording and the Stop button when you have finished. Click the Play button to hear the recorded sound. Close the Sound Recorder, then use the Insert Sound command in PowerPoint to insert the sound file into a presentation.

STEP 2: A MIDI File

➤ Double click the **Reggae file** to listen to the sound of Reggae music. The Media Player opens automatically as shown in Figure B.3b. Unlike the Wav files, which typically last only a few seconds, the MIDI files are musical compositions that play for longer periods.

➤ Experiment with the controls on the Media Player:

- Click the **Pause button** to suspend playing.
- Click the **Play button** (which appears after you click the Pause button) to resume playing.
- Click the **Stop button** to stop playing.
- Click the **Rewind button** to return to the beginning of the recording.

➤ Close the Media Player when you are finished listening.

Double click the
Reggae.mid file

Click to close
the Media Player

Pause (Play) button

Stop button

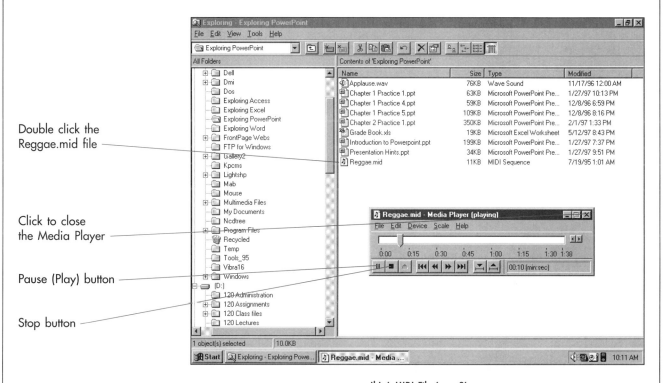

(b) A MIDI File (step 2)

FIGURE B.3   Hands-on Exercise 1 (continued)

WAV FILES VERSUS MIDI FILES

A WAV file stores an actual sound whereas a MIDI file stores the instructions to create the sound. Because a WAV file stores a recorded sound, it can represent any type of sound—a voice, music, or special effects. A MIDI file can store only music. WAV files, even those that last only a few seconds, are very large because the sound is sampled thousands of times a second to create the file. MIDI files, however, are much more compact because they store the instructions to create the sound rather than the sound itself.

STEP 3: The Find Command

➤ Movie clips (AVI files) are quite large, and hence we did not include any of these files in the Exploring PowerPoint folder. Thus, you need to search for an AVI file in order to play it.

➤ Click the **Start button** on the Windows 95 taskbar. Click (or point to) the **Find command,** then click **Files or Folders** to display the dialog box in Figure B.3c. The size and/or position of the dialog box may be different from the one in the figure.

- Enter ***.AVI** (the type of file you are searching for) in the Named text box.
- Click the **drop-down arrow** in the **Look in** list box and select drive C.
- Be sure the **Include subfolders** box is checked.

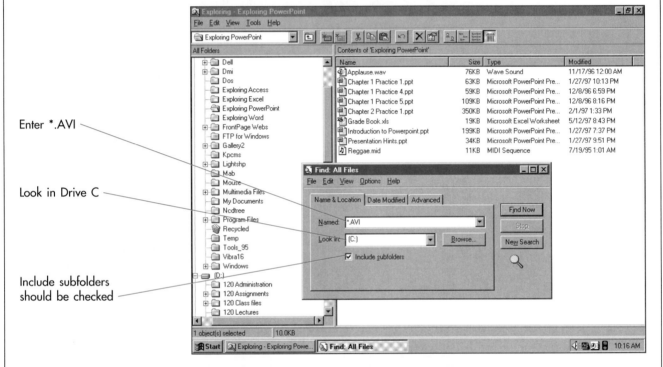

Enter *.AVI

Look in Drive C

Include subfolders
should be checked

(c) The Find Command (step 3)

FIGURE B.3   Hands-on Exercise 1 (continued)

FILE EXTENSIONS

Long-time DOS users will recognize the three-character extension at the end of a file name, which indicates the file type. The extensions are displayed or hidden according to an option in the View menu in My Computer or the Windows Explorer. Windows 95 maintains the file extension for compatibility, and in addition, displays an icon next to the file name to indicate the file type. The icons are more easily recognized in the Large Icons view as opposed to the Details view. Extensions of WAV and MID denote a wave form and MIDI file, respectively. An AVI (Audio-Video Interleaved) file is the Microsoft standard for a multimedia file with video and sound.

- Click the **Find Now button** to begin the search, then watch the status bar as Windows searches for the specified files and folders.
➤ The results of the search are displayed within the Find Files dialog box and should contain multiple AVI files. If you do not see any files at all, check the search parameters, then repeat the search.

STEP 4: Play an AVI File
➤ Maximize the Find Files dialog box as shown in Figure B.3d. The results of your search may be different from ours, but at the very least you should see various AVI files from the Windows Help folder.
➤ Double click the **Taskswch.avi** file to play this movie as shown in Figure B.3d.

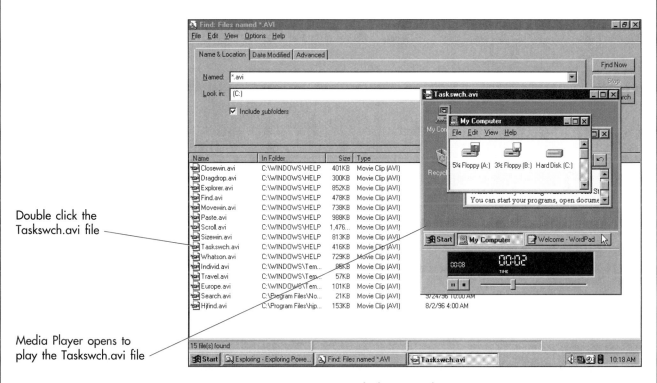

Double click the
Taskswch.avi file

Media Player opens to
play the Taskswch.avi file

(d) Play an AVI File (step 4)

FIGURE B.3   Hands-on Exercise 1 (continued)

THE WINDOWS 95 HELP COMMAND

The answer to almost anything you need to know about Windows is available through the Help command if only you take the trouble to look. Click the Start button, then click Help to display the Help topics dialog box. Click the Index tab, type *ta* (the first two letters in *task switching*), double click *task switching* when it appears in the open list box, then double click *The Basics* in the Topics Found dialog box to display a help screen for the Windows desktop. Click any of the indicated topics and follow the on-screen instructions to play the AVI files in the Windows Help folder.

➤ The movie is relatively unimpressive—it takes only a few seconds and illustrates the use of the taskbar to switch between open applications. Nevertheless, it is more than 400KB in size and illustrates the complexity of creating a movie clip.

➤ View as many movie clips as you like, then close the Find Files dialog box when you are finished.

STEP 5: A More Interesting AVI File

➤ This step requires the Office 97 CD as the best AVI files, for purposes of demonstration, are found on this CD.

➤ Click the **Start button** on the Windows 95 taskbar. Click the **Find command,** then click **Files or Folders** to display the Find Files dialog box.

➤ Enter ***.avi** (the type of file you are searching for) in the Named text box. Click the **drop-down arrow** in the **Look in** list box and select the drive for your CD (drive F on our system).

➤ Check the **Include subfolders** box, then click the **Find Now button** to begin the search.

➤ The results of the search should reference multiple files in the Books folder from the Office 97 CD as shown in Figure B.3e. Double click one or more files to view a movie clip.

➤ Close the Find Files dialog box. Close the Windows Explorer.

➤ Exit Windows if you do not want to continue with the next exercise at this time.

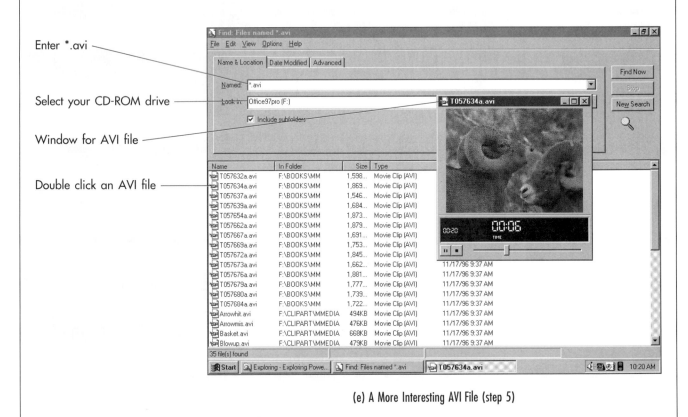

(e) A More Interesting AVI File (step 5)

FIGURE B.3 Hands-on Exercise 1 (continued)

The exercise just completed had you explore the elements of multimedia and experiment with individual files. You learned about the different types of sound files and saw the impact of a movie clip. The effectiveness of multimedia, however, depends on integrating the various elements into a cohesive unit.

A multimedia presentation is a show, and like any show it requires careful planning if it is to be successful. The actors in a show, or the objects on a PowerPoint slide, must be thoroughly scripted so that the performance is as effective as possible. Consider now Figure B.4, which contains one of the slides in the presentation you will create.

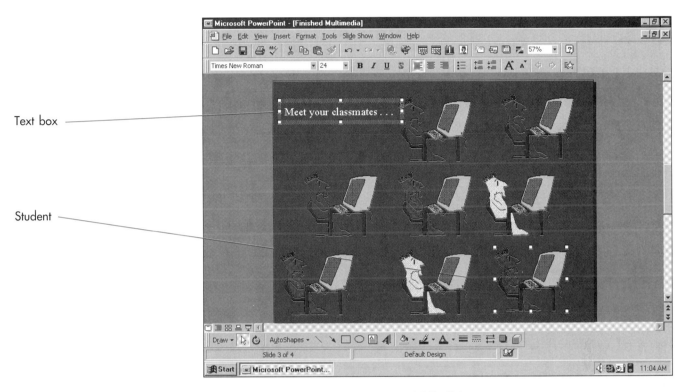

Text box

Student

(a) The Slide

FIGURE B.4   Animation Settings

THE MICROSOFT CLIP GALLERY

The Microsoft Clip Gallery contains over 100MB including 3,000 clip art images, 100 photographs, 28 sounds, and 20 movie clips. To insert a movie clip into a PowerPoint presentation, click the Insert Clip Art button on the Standard toolbar to display the Clip Gallery dialog box, click the Video tab, select the desired file (such as the basket clip shown earlier in the chapter), and click the Insert button. To play the clip, change to the Slide Show view, then click the object.

Text object is selected

Text will appear
one letter at a time

Text will fly in from left

Sound effect will
play as text appears

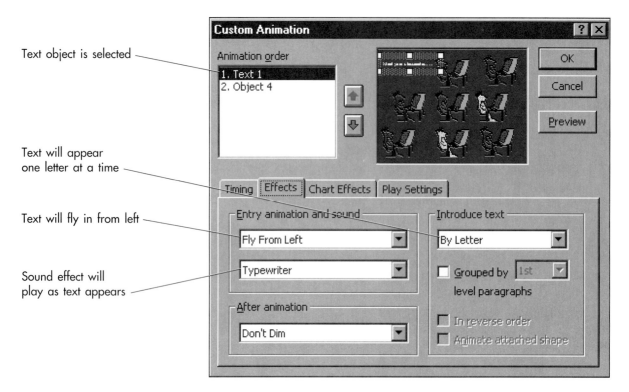

(b) Text Object

Student is selected (it
was the fourth object
placed on the slide)

Object will fly in
from top-left corner

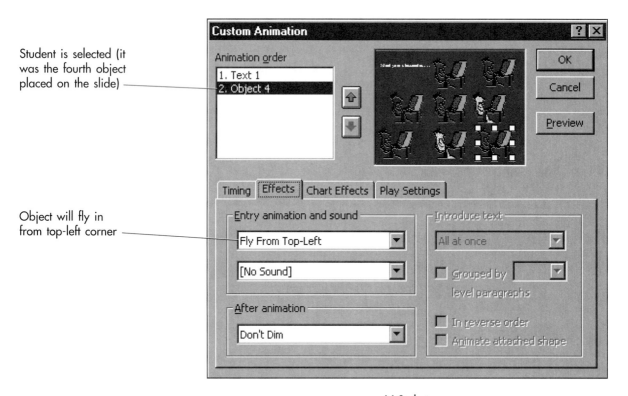

(c) Student

FIGURE B.4   Animation Settings (continued)

Figure B.4a contains the actual slide, whereas Figure B.4b and B.4c show the dialog boxes associated with two of the objects on the slide. The slide contains a total of nine objects (a single text box and eight students). Each of these objects is an "actor" in the presentation and requires instructions as to when to appear on stage and how to make that entrance.

You, as director, have decided that seven of the students will be in place on the slide when it is shown initially. The text will then enter from the left, after which the last student will appear from the top left. The *Custom Animation command* (in the Slide Show menu) is the means by which you convey your directions. Figure B.4b displays the Custom Animation dialog box for the text that is to fly in from the left, letter by letter, accompanied by the sound of a typewriter. The text is shown first in the animation order list box since it is to appear before the student.

Figure B.4c shows the dialog box for the student in the lower right corner (which is designated as object 4 because it was the fourth student placed on the slide when it was created). The Student is to fly in silently from the top left. No other objects (students) appear in the animation order list box, since there are no animation effects for the other students (they are in place when the slide is first shown). These instructions may sound complicated, but they work beautifully, as you will see in the next hands-on exercise.

HANDS-ON EXERCISE 2

Creating a Multimedia Presentation

Objective: To add music (a MIDI file) to the first slide of a presentation so that it plays continually throughout the presentation; to use the Custom Animation command to control the appearance of objects on a slide. Use Figure B.5 as a guide in the exercise.

STEP 1: Add the Music

➤ Open the **Multimedia** presentation in the **Exploring PowerPoint folder** as shown in Figure B.5a. Save the presentation as **Finished Multimedia.**

➤ Pull down the **Insert menu.** Click **Movies and Sounds,** then click **Sound from File** to display the Insert Sound dialog box in Figure B.5a.

➤ Click the **down arrow** in the Look in text box to select the **Exploring Power-Point folder.** Select **Reggae,** then click **OK** to insert the sound file.

LOOK FOR OTHER MUSIC

Click the Start button on the Windows 95 taskbar, click (or point to) the Find command, then click Files or Folders to display the Find All Files dialog box. Click the Name & Location tab, click in the Named text box, and enter *.MID (the file type you are searching for). Click the drop-down arrow in the Look in list box and select My Computer to search all of the drives on your system. Be sure the Include subfolders box is checked, then click the Find Now button to begin the search. Once a MIDI file is found, you can right click and drag the file from the Find All Files dialog box to the PowerPoint slide.

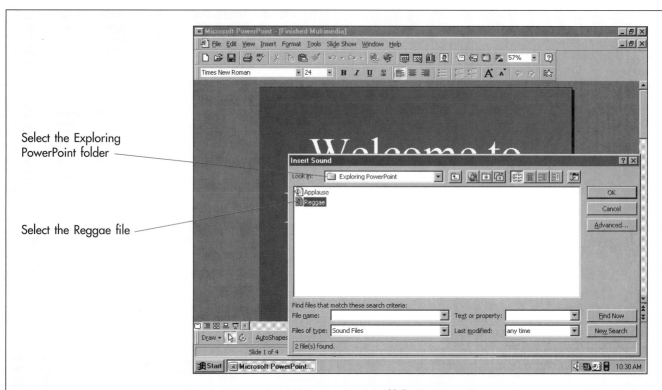

(a) Add the Music (step 1)

FIGURE B.5   Hands-on Exercise 2

STEP 2: Set the Music Options

➤ You should see a small microphone in the middle of the title slide indicating that a sound file has been embedded on this slide.

➤ Click and drag the **sound icon** (the microphone corresponding to the Reggae sound file) to the bottom left of the slide. Pull down the **Slide Show menu** and click **Custom Animation** to display the Custom Animation dialog box.

➤ Select the options shown in Figure B.5b. Thus, click the check box to **Play using animation order,** click the option button to **Continue slide show,** click the option button to stop playing after the specified number of slides, then enter **4 slides** in the associated text box.

➤ Click the **More options command button** to display the Play Options dialog box. Check the box to **loop until stopped.** Verify that your settings match those in Figure B.5b. Click **OK** to close the Play Options dialog box.

➤ Click the **Timing tab,** then click the option button to animate automatically after zero seconds. Click **OK** to close the Custom Animation dialog box.

➤ Click the **Slide Show button** above the status bar to begin the show. The music should begin to play automatically because of the previous command.

➤ Click the mouse to move to the next slide (with a clip art image of an instructor). The music continues to play as you move from one slide to the next.

➤ Press the **Esc key** to stop the music. Press the **Esc key** a second time to cancel the slide show and return to the Slide view.

➤ Save the presentation.

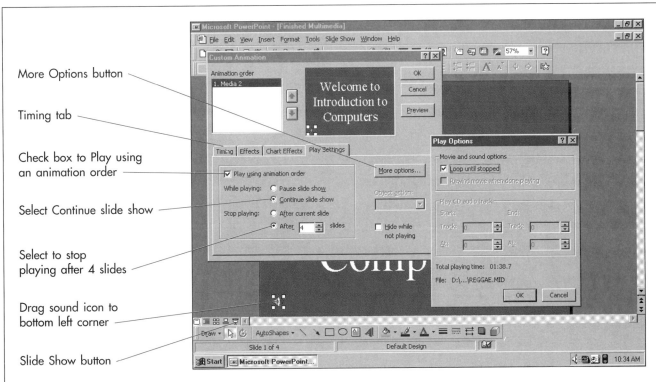

More Options button

Timing tab

Check box to Play using
an animation order

Select Continue slide show

Select to stop
playing after 4 slides

Drag sound icon to
bottom left corner

Slide Show button

(b) Set the Music Options (step 2)

FIGURE B.5   Hands-on Exercise 2 (continued)

THE VOICE OVER

Use the Sound Recorder to create a voice-over narration that you can play
during a self-running presentation. Music and/or narration are especially
effective in standalone presentations such as those found in a kiosk or
demonstration booth. The only disadvantage is the large file size. The
Sound Recorder creates a WAV file, which requires a minimum of
11KB/second. Thus a 30-second sound byte results in a 330KB file.

STEP 3: Animate the Title Slide

➤ Press **Ctrl+Home** to move to the first slide, then click anywhere within the
title to select the title as shown in Figure B.5c. Pull down the **Slide Show
menu** and click **Custom Animation** to display the Custom Animation dialog
box.

➤ Click the **Timing tab.** Text 1 (corresponding to the title) is selected automatically and appears initially as an object without animation. Click the **Animate option button,** which moves the text under Media 2 in the animation
order. In other words, the music will play before the animation effect for the
text.

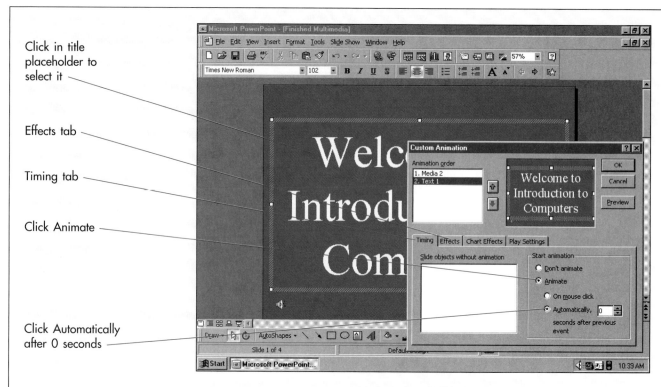

Click in title placeholder to select it

Effects tab

Timing tab

Click Animate

Click Automatically after 0 seconds

(c) Animate the Title Slide (step 3)

FIGURE B.5   Hands-on Exercise 2 (continued)

➤ Click the option button to animate **Automatically** after zero seconds. This will display the title without your having to click the mouse.

➤ Click the **Effects tab.** Click the **down arrow** in the first Entry animation and sound list box. Select **Fly from Left** as the desired effect. Click the **down arrow** on the Introduce Text list box and select **By Letter.** Click **OK.**

➤ Click the **Slide Show button** above the status bar. This time you will not only hear the music, but you will also see the letters fly in from the left.

➤ Press the **Esc key** after you see the title to stop the music, then press the **Esc key** a second time to return to the Slide view and continue working.

➤ Save the presentation.

YOU'RE THE DIRECTOR

No one ever said that multimedia was quick or easy. Creating an effective presentation takes time, much more time than you might expect initially, as each slide has to be choreographed in detail. Think of yourself as the director who must tell the actors (the objects on a slide) when to come on stage and how to make their entrance. It takes a lot of patience and practice.

STEP 4: Animate the Student Slide

➤ Use the Slide Elevator (or press the **PgDn key** twice) to select the third slide as shown in Figure B.5d.

➤ Click the **Slide Show button** to view this slide as it will appear in the slide show. There are no animation effects and all of the students appear at the same time. Press **Esc** to return to the slide view.

➤ Pull down the **Edit menu** and click **Select All** (or press **Ctrl+A**) to select all of the objects (the text and the eight students) on this slide. Pull down the **Slide Show menu** and click **Custom Animation** to display the Custom Animation dialog box.

➤ Click the **Timing tab.** Click the **Animate** option button, which moves the objects to the Animation order list at the top of the dialog box. Click the option button to animate **Automatically** after zero seconds.

➤ Click the **Effects tab.** Click the **down arrow** in the first Entry animation and sound list box. Select **Fly from Right** as the desired effect.

➤ Click the up or down arrow on the scroll bar in the Animation order list box, then click **Text 1,** which deselects all of the other objects. Select **Fly from Left** as the effect for the text. Select **By Letter.**

➤ Click **OK** to accept these settings and close the dialog box.

➤ Click the **Slide Show button** to view this slide with the animation effects you added. The text should appear first, followed by the students in the order they were added to the slide when the slide was created initially. Press **Esc** to return to the slide view.

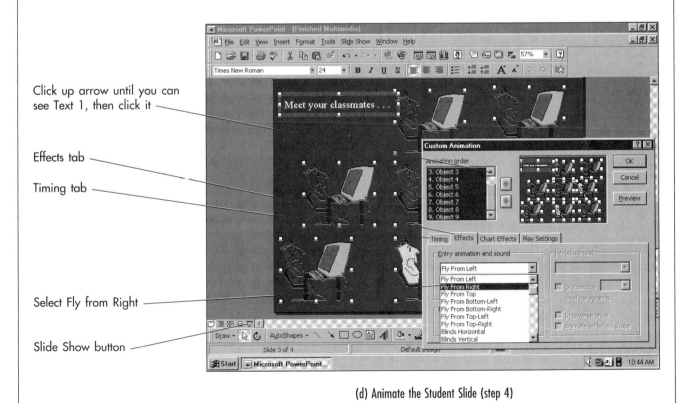

(d) Animate the Student Slide (step 4)

FIGURE B.5 Hands-on Exercise 2 (continued)

THE ANIMATION EFFECTS TOOLBAR

The Animation Effects toolbar is the easiest way to change the order in which objects appear on a slide. Point to any visible toolbar, click the right mouse button, then click Animation Effects to display (hide) the toolbar. Select the object on the slide, click the drop-down arrow on the Animation Order list box, then choose the appropriate number (e.g., 1, if the object is to appear first).

STEP 5: Rehearse the Timings

➤ Press **Ctrl+Home** to return to the first slide. Pull down the **Slide Show menu.** Click the **Rehearse Timings command.**

➤ The first slide appears in the Slide Show view, and the Rehearsal dialog box is displayed in the lower right corner of the screen. Click the mouse to register the elapsed time and move to the next slide.

➤ The second slide in the presentation should appear as shown in Figure B.5e with the animation effects built in. The cumulative time appears on the left (00:01:06 seconds). The time for this specific slide (00:00:16 seconds) is shown at the right.

• Click the **Repeat button** to redo the timing for the slide. (You won't see the new timing until the slide concludes.)

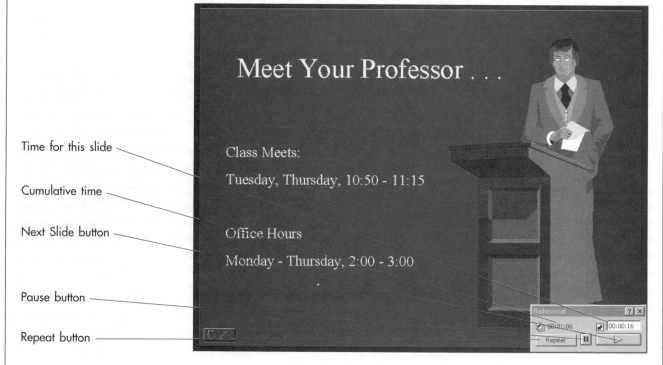

(e) Rehearse the Timings (step 5)

FIGURE B.5   Hands-on Exercise 2 (continued)

- Click the **Pause button** to (temporarily) stop the clock. Click the Pause button a second time to resume the clock. (The music continues to play.)
- Click the **Next slide button** to record the timing and move to the next slide.
- Continue rehearsing the show until you reach the last slide (containing the PC and other equipment), then click on this last slide to end the presentation. Be sure to click the mouse so it will record the timing for the last slide.

➤ You should see a dialog box at the end of the presentation that indicates the total time of the slide show. Click **Yes** when asked whether you want to record the new timings. Click **Yes** when asked if you want to review the timings in the Slide Sorter view.

➤ Save the presentation.

STEP 6: Set Up the Show

➤ You should be back in the Slide Sorter view, with the timings recorded under each slide. Pull down the **Slide Show menu** and click **Set Up show** to display the Set Up show dialog box as shown in Figure B.5f.

➤ Check the box to **Loop continuously until Esc.**

➤ Click the **All option button** under Slides, click the **Using timings if present** option button under Advance slides. Click **OK** to accept the settings and close the Set Up show dialog box.

➤ Press **Ctrl+Home** to move to the first slide. Click the **Slide Show button** to view the show one last time. End the show by clicking at the appropriate place in the last slide or by pressing the **Esc key.**

➤ Save the presentation. Exit PowerPoint. Welcome to Multimedia!!

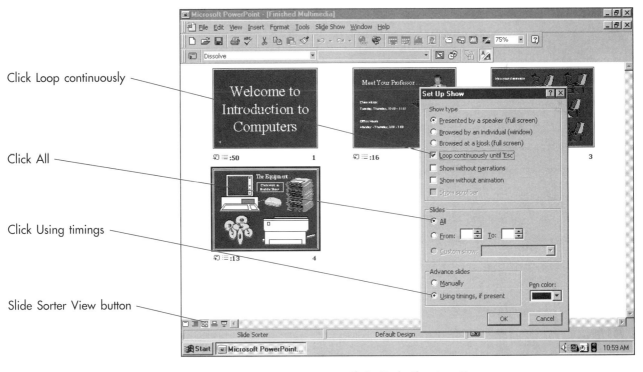

(f) Set Up the Show (step 6)

FIGURE B.5   Hands-on Exercise 2 (continued)

SUMMARY

The Multimedia PC Marketing Council has established a minimum specification for a multimedia computer that is intended to guide both the consumer and the developer. Three standards—MPC-1, MPC-2, and MPC-3—have been published to date.

There are two types of sound files, WAV files and MIDI files. A WAV file records an actual sound and requires large amounts of disk space because the sound is sampled several times a second to create the file. A MIDI file is much more compact than a WAV file because it stores the instructions to create the sound rather than the actual sound. A WAV file can represent any type of sound (a voice, music, or special effects) because it is a recorded sound. A MIDI file is the electronic equivalent of sheet music and can store only music. An AVI (Audi-Video Interleaved) file is the Microsoft standard for a digital video (multimedia) file.

Windows 95 provides the software tools necessary to play the various types of multimedia files. The accessories can be accessed through the Start button or through shortcuts in the Multimedia folder.

The slides in a multimedia production must be carefully scripted with respect to when and how each object is to appear. The Custom Animation command is the means by which the information is specified.

KEY WORDS AND CONCEPTS

Animation settings
AVI file
CD Player
Custom Animation command
File compression
File extensions
Media player

MIDI file
MPC-1
MPC-2
MPC-3
Multimedia
PowerPoint Multimedia CD
Resolution

Sampling rate
Sound recorder
Volume Control
WAV file

MICROSOFT OUTLOOK 97: A DESKTOP INFORMATION MANAGER

OVERVIEW

Microsoft Outlook is a very worthwhile addition to Office 97. It can be used on a standalone PC to manage your own work, or on a network to facilitate communication with others in your organization. Think of Outlook as a personal assistant, or desktop manager, that keeps track of all types of information for you. You can use it to maintain an address book, schedule appointments, create a task list, write notes to yourself, or send and receive e-mail.

Outlook also monitors your work and automatically creates a journal of everything you do on your computer. The journal is in essence a log that tracks every document you access. You can then

1

reference the journal to find out when you last worked on a document and even to find lost documents on your system.

This appendix introduces you to the basic functions in Microsoft Outlook. We begin with a brief overview of each component, then present a hands-on exercise so that you can put the material to practical use. Intuitively, however, you already know how Outlook works. Do you carry an address book or an appointment book? Do you write yourself a list of things to do? Outlook simply automates the process and in so doing adds considerable flexibility to the way you enter and reference your data.

The second half of the appendix focuses on e-mail, perhaps the most widely used function in Outlook. Our discussion introduces (or reviews) the basic commands used in any e-mail system to compose, send, read, and reply to e-mail messages. We show you how to attach files to an e-mail message and how to create various folders so that you can organize the messages you send and receive. As always, the hands-on exercises are essential to the learn-by-doing philosophy we follow throughout the text.

INTRODUCTION TO OUTLOOK

Figure 1 displays the Outlook window, which is similar in appearance to that of the other applications in Microsoft Office. There is one significant difference, however, and that is the *Outlook bar,* which appears at the left of the window. The Outlook bar contains icons corresponding to various folders that are created in Outlook. The icons are divided into groups. The *Mail group* is selected in Figure 1a. The *Outlook group* is selected in all other parts of Figure 1.

Take a quick look at each screen in Figure 1 and you gain an appreciation for each of Outlook's major capabilities. The *Inbox folder* (one of several e-mail folders) in the Mail group is selected in Figure 1a. The contents of the selected folder (the inbox in this example) are displayed in the right pane of the Outlook window. As you can see, the inbox lists all incoming messages (including faxes), the person who sent the message, the subject of the message, and the date and time the message was received. E-mail is covered in depth in the second half of the appendix.

The *Calendar folder* (within the Outlook group) is selected in Figure 1b. The calendar function enables you to create a detailed appointment book, and to display those appointments in different views (daily, weekly, or monthly). You can create recurring appointments (e.g., the same appointment on different days) and you can instruct Outlook to remind you prior to each appointment. You can also print your appointment book and take it with you.

The *Contacts folder* is selected in Figure 1c. As with the calendar, contacts can be displayed in different views (the detailed view is selected in Figure 1c). You can enter as much (or as little) information for each contact as you like. And once created, the Contacts folder becomes the basis for other Office functions. E-mail addresses, for example, can be selected automatically from the Contacts folder. Regular (postal) addresses can also be selected from the Contacts folder, a feature we use all the time from Microsoft Word when we are addressing a letter. And as with all Outlook functions, you can print the contents of the Contacts folder, something we do to create a hard copy of our telephone directory.

The *Journal* in Figure 1d is a log of the activity on your computer. An entry in the Journal is generated automatically by Outlook every time you access an Office document or use your computer to place a phone call. As with the other functions, the Journal can be displayed in different views (for example, weekly in Figure 1d). You can collapse or expand the entries for different activities. The entries for Microsoft Access, for example, are expanded in Figure 1d, which shows

Mail group is selected

Inbox folder is selected

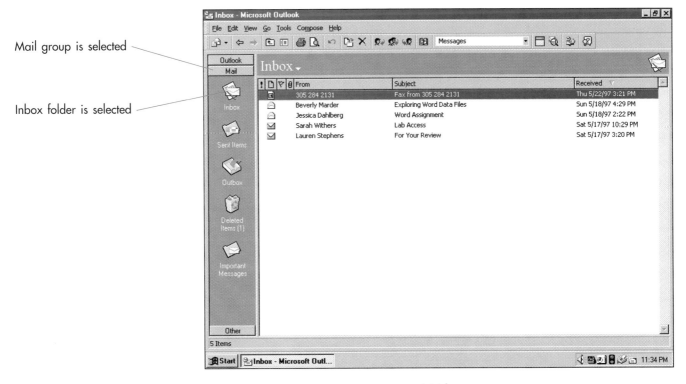

(a) Inbox

Calendar is selected

Appointments are
displayed monthly

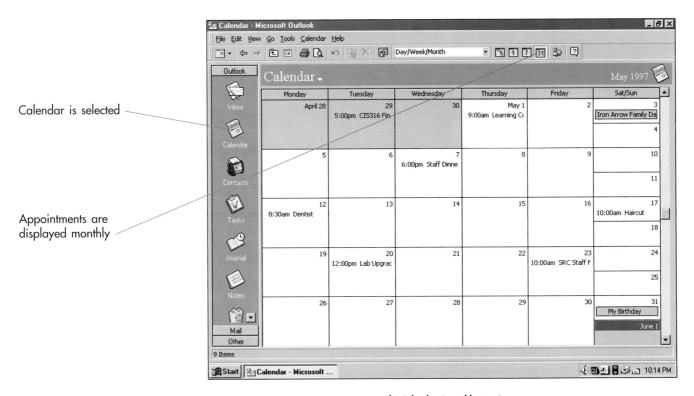

(b) Calendar (monthly view)

FIGURE 1   Microsoft Outlook 97

Contacts folder is selected

Detailed information is displayed for each contact

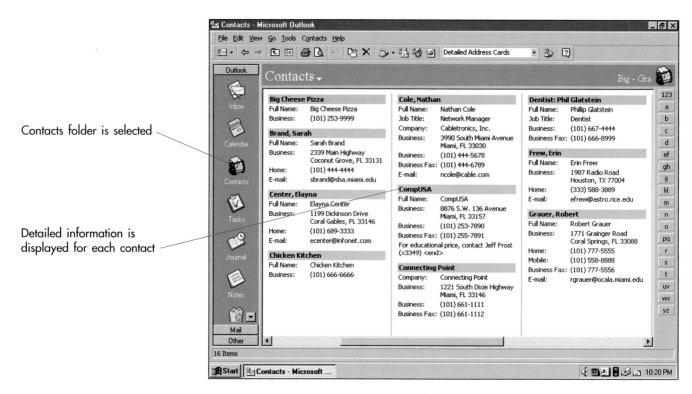

(c) Contacts (detailed address cards)

Access entries are expanded

Journal is selected

Phone calls are logged automatically

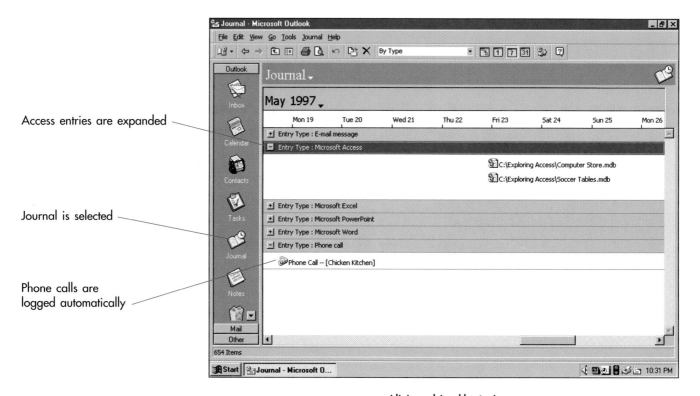

(d) Journal (weekly view)

FIGURE 1   Microsoft Outlook 97 (continued)

Indicates completed task

Tasks are selected

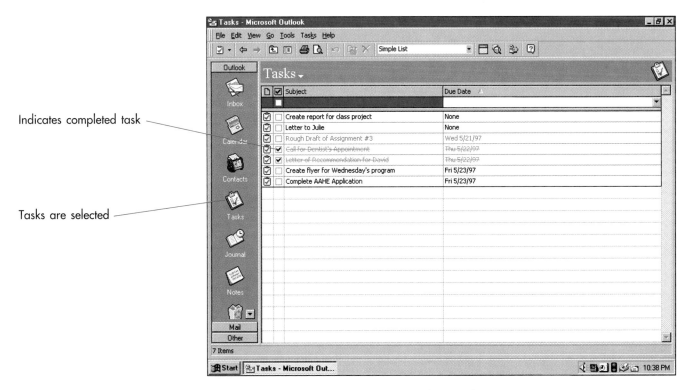

(e) Tasks (To Do list)

Double click to open the note

Notes folder is selected

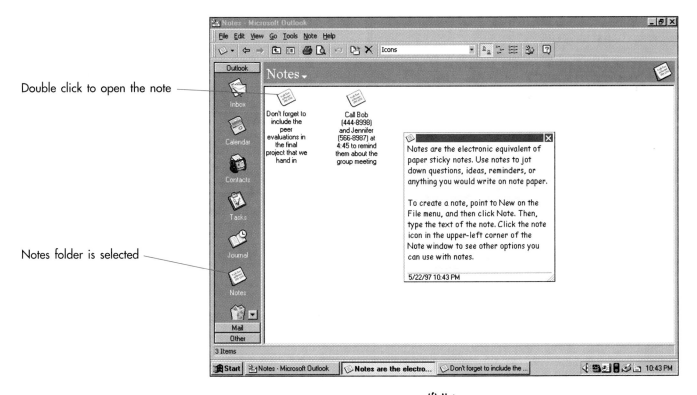

(f) Notes

FIGURE 1   Microsoft Outlook 97 (continued)

that you accessed the Computer Store and Soccer Tables databases on Friday, May 23. This is very useful information, especially if you need to retrace the steps you took on a specific day. Note, too, that the Journal also provides shortcut icons to reopen the documents it displays.

The *Task list* in Figure 1e is a simple but effective way to organize the work you have to do. We're fond of making lists, and the Tasks folder in Outlook makes it easy. You can check off a task (just as you can with pencil and paper). And unlike pencil and paper, overdue tasks are shown in red, reminding you to get busy.

The *Notes folder* in Figure 1f is the electronic version of the ubiquitous yellow "Post-it" notes. You can use it any time to store any type of information. And as with all Outlook functions, you can use the Print command to obtain hard copy.

IT'S SYNERGISTIC

The functions in Outlook are thoroughly integrated with one another, making each function more valuable as a part of the whole. E-mail, for example, can be generated automatically from appointments on the calendar (perhaps to remind attendees of a scheduled meeting) using entries in the address book. You can also go in the other direction and create entries in your address book or events on your calendar directly from an e-mail message. Look for other examples of how the individual applications enhance one another as you read this appendix.

HANDS-ON EXERCISE 1

Introduction to Outlook

Objective: To create and print a contact list; to enter appointments and print the resulting schedule; to examine the Outlook Journal. Use Figure 2 as a guide in the exercise. (This exercise does not require an Internet connection.)

STEP 1: Start Outlook

➤ Click the **Start button** to display the Start menu. Click (or point to) the **Programs menu,** then click **Microsoft Outlook** to start the program.

➤ If necessary, click the **maximize button** so that Outlook takes the entire desktop. Do not be concerned about the presence (or absence) of the Office Assistant.

➤ The Outlook bar should be displayed by default. If not, pull down the **View menu** and click **Outlook bar** to display the bar. If necessary, pull down the **View menu** a second time, and toggle the **Folder list** off so that your display matches Figure 2a.

➤ If necessary, click the **Office Assistant button** on the Standard toolbar to display the Office Assistant. Enter your question—for example, **How do I get help?**—as shown in Figure 2a, then click the **Search button** to look for the answer.

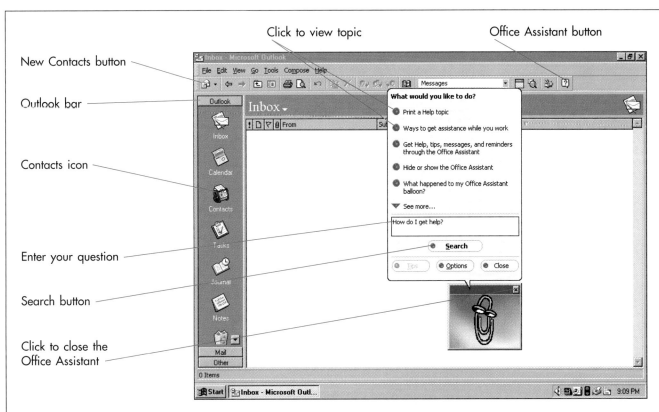

New Contacts button

Outlook bar

Contacts icon

Enter your question

Search button

Click to close the
Office Assistant

Click to view topic

Office Assistant button

(a) Start Outlook (step 1)

FIGURE 2   Hands-on Exercise 1

➤ Read through the various Help topics to get a feel for the Office Assistant and how it can provide help to you during an Outlook session. Close the Assistant when you are finished.

THE OFFICE ASSISTANT

The Office Assistant is common to all applications in Office 97 and is activated by clicking the Office Assistant button on the Standard toolbar or by pressing the F1 function key. The Assistant also monitors your work and will suggest more efficient ways of accomplishing a task by displaying a lightbulb. Click the lightbulb to display the tip, then click the Back or Next button to view additional tips.

STEP 2: Create a Contact

➤ Click the **Contacts icon** on the Outlook bar to change to the Contacts folder.

➤ Click the **New Contacts button** on the Standard toolbar to open the Contact window in Figure 2b. If necessary, click the **maximize button** to give yourself additional room in which to work.

➤ Enter your friend's **full name, address,** and **home telephone number.** Be sure to include his or her **e-mail address** as we will use this information in the next hands-on exercise.

Enter phone number   Click to select File As option

Save and New button

Enter name

Enter address

Enter e-mail address

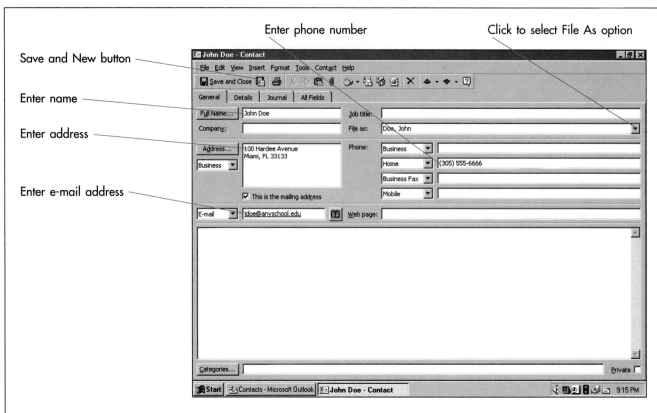

(b) Create a Contact (step 2)

FIGURE 2   Hands-on Exercise 1 (continued)

➤ Click the **drop-down arrow** in the File as list box, then choose how you want to file the contact in the Contacts folder. (You can file by first name, last name, or enter an entirely different entry.)

➤ Click the **Save and New button** to save the information for your friend and simultaneously open a New contact window.

➤ Enter information for yourself as a second contact. Be sure to include your **e-mail address,** which will be used in the next hands-on exercise.

➤ Click the **Save and Close icon** to save the information and return to the Contacts folder.

THE AUTODIALER

You cannot use the AutoDialer in school, but it is a wonderful feature if you are working at home. Select a contact, then click the AutoDialer button on the Standard toolbar to display the New Call dialog box. Select a phone number (business or home), check the box to have Outlook create a journal entry for you, then click the Start Call button. Not only will Outlook dial the call for you, but it will create a journal entry in which you can enter pertinent information about the call.

STEP 3: Print the Contact List

➤ You should see the Contacts folder. Pull down the **View menu,** click **Current view,** then click (if necessary) **Detailed Address cards** to match the view in Figure 2c.

➤ Click the tab containing the first letter of your friend's last name (for example, D for John Doe) corresponding to the contact you entered in the previous step. The information should be correct, but if not, click the line(s) containing the invalid data to make the correction directly in this view.

➤ Pull down the **File menu,** click the **Print command,** click the **down arrow** in the Print style list box, and select **Phone Directory Style.** Click the option button to select **All items,** then click **OK.**

➤ Outlook will print a phone directory consisting of every phone number for every contact, a list we find very helpful.

John Doe's contact information

Calendar icon

Click tab for letter d

Select Phone Directory style

Click All items

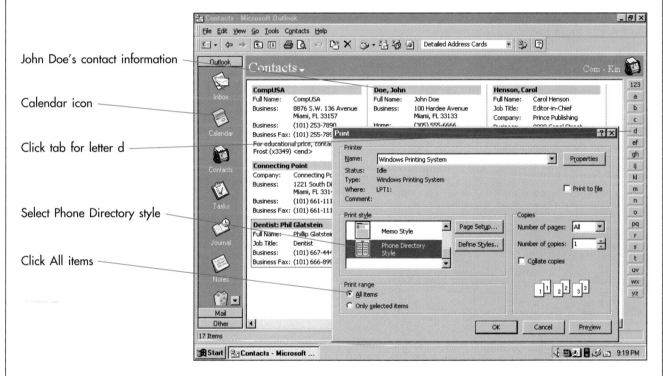

(c) Print the Contact List (step 3)

FIGURE 2   Hands-on Exercise 1 (continued)

THE PAGE SETUP COMMAND

Outlook is very flexible in the way it displays and prints information. Pull down the File menu, click the Page Setup command, and click Define Print Styles to display the Define Print Styles dialog box. Choose the style you want, such as Phone Directory, then click the Edit button to display the Page Setup dialog box. You can change the number of columns for your directory, print headers or footers, and/or print letter tabs at the edge of the page.

STEP 4: Enter an Appointment

➤ Click the **Calendar icon** on the Outlook bar to change to the Calendar folder. Pull down the **View menu** and click the **Day view** (or click the **Day button** on the Standard toolbar). You should see your schedule for today. No events have been entered as yet.

➤ Click the **New Appointment button** on the Standard toolbar to open the Appointment dialog box as shown in Figure 2d.

➤ Enter the subject and location of the appointment such as a Group meeting at Bob's house. If necessary, clear the **All day event** check box, then enter the starting time of your appointment as beginning 20 minutes from now. Enter the ending time one hour after that.

➤ Check the **Reminder box** to be notified 15 minutes before the appointment is to begin. Click the **Save and Close button** to save the appointment.

New Appointment button

Enter subject

Enter location

Enter start and end dates/times

Check Reminder option

Select 15 minutes

All day event check box

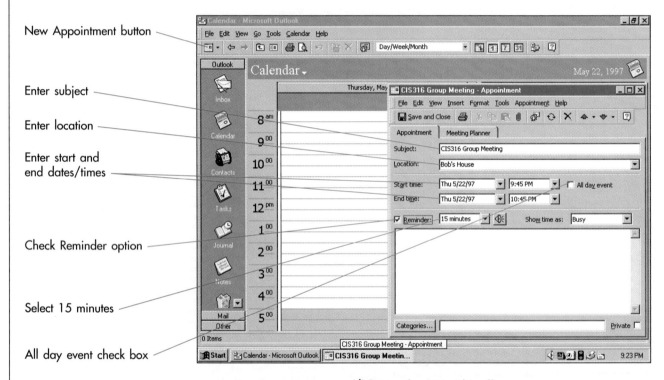

(d) Enter an Appointment (step 4)

FIGURE 2   Hands-on Exercise 1 (continued)

INVITE THE ATTENDEES

You can send e-mail automatically in conjunction with scheduling a meeting on your calendar. Invitations can be sent when the meeting is scheduled initially, or any time after the meeting appears on your calendar. If necessary, double click the event to reopen the Appointment dialog box, then click the Invite Attendees button to create an e-mail message. E-mail is discussed in detail in the second half of this appendix.

STEP 5: Create a Task List

➤ Your appointment should appear in today's calendar as shown in Figure 2e. (You can double click the appointment at any time to reopen the Appointment window and change the information.)

➤ Five minutes from now you will see a simple dialog box reminding you of this hypothetical appointment. Click the **Dismiss button** when this occurs, to close the Reminder dialog box and continue working.

➤ The Daily view should also display a mini calendar and a TaskPad. If these elements are not visible on your screen, point to the right border of the Outlook window (the mouse pointer changes to small parallel lines), then click and drag the border to the left.

➤ Click in the **TaskPad entry area** to the right of today's calendar.

➤ Type **Create a new contact** and press the **enter key** to create the first task and move to the next. (A task is simpler than an appointment and is not associated with a specific date or time.) Think of the Tasks folder as containing a simple "to do" list.

➤ Add the other tasks as shown in Figure 2e. Press **enter** after you type each task in order to move automatically from one task to the next. Leave all tasks open at this time.

(e) Create a Task List (step 5)

FIGURE 2   Hands-on Exercise 1 (continued)

➤ Click tomorrow's date in the mini calendar at the right of the Outlook window to display the schedule for tomorrow. You will see the identical task list, but there are no appointments scheduled yet.

➤ Right click next to any time slot to display a context-sensitive menu, click **New Appointment** to open the Appointment dialog box, then enter an appointment for tomorrow.

➤ Click the **Save and Close button** to close the Appointment dialog box and save the appointment.

THE REMINDER

Schedule or not, it's easy to become absorbed in what you are doing, lose track of the time, and thereby miss an important appointment. We suggest, therefore, that you check the reminder box whenever you create an appointment so that Outlook will notify you of it. Of course, Outlook won't remind you of anything unless it is running, so you must remember to start Outlook at the beginning of every session. (You can add a shortcut to Outlook in the Start Up folder. Click the Windows 95 Start button, click Help, click the Index tab, then search for help on the Start Up folder.)

STEP 6: The Print Preview Command

➤ Pull down the **View menu** and click the **Week view** (or click the **Week button** on the Standard toolbar). You should see your schedule for the week, which includes the two appointments added in the previous step.

➤ Pull down the **File menu,** click **Print** to display the Print dialog box, then click **Weekly style** in the Print style list box. Click the **Page Setup button** to display the Page Setup dialog box, click the **dropdown arrow** in the Layout list box, and select **2 pages/week.** Click **OK** to close the Page Setup dialog box.

➤ Click the **Preview button** to preview your schedule. Click the **Multiple Pages** button so that the display on your monitor matches Figure 2f.

➤ Click the **Print button** to close the Print preview, then click **OK** to print your schedule for this week.

THE RECURRING APPOINTMENT

You can schedule all occurrences of a recurring appointment (such as a class or weekly office meeting) when you enter the first appointment. Create the appointment as you usually do, then pull down the Appointment menu and click Recurrence to display the Recurring Appointment dialog box. Enter the pattern (say, daily or weekly) and the number of occurrences or the starting and ending date, then click OK to make the appointment and close the dialog box. Change to a weekly or monthly view in the Schedule folder to see how the multiple appointments were entered.

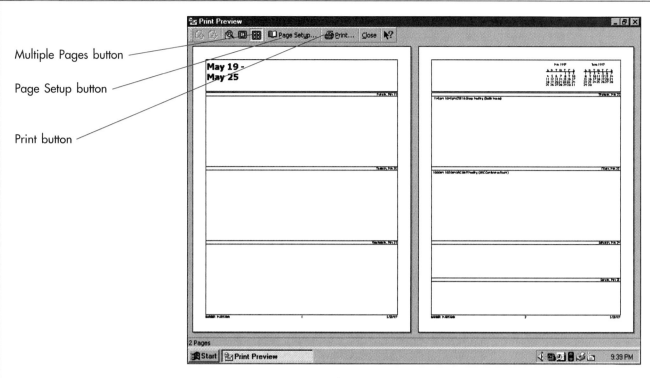

Multiple Pages button

Page Setup button

Print button

(f) The Print Preview Command (step 6)

FIGURE 2   Hands-on Exercise 1 (continued)

STEP 7: Modify the Task List

➤ Click the **Tasks icon** on the Outlook bar to change to the Tasks folder as shown in Figure 2g.

➤ Click the check box in the last item (Create a new contact). A line appears through the item to indicate that the task has been completed.

➤ Click the check boxes next to the two other tasks you have finished so far.

➤ Click in the area to add a new task. Enter **This task is late.** Click in the **Due Date text box,** click the **drop down arrow,** which appears when you click this box, then click yesterday's date. Press **enter** to complete the task and enter it in the task list.

ASSIGN A TASK TO SOMEONE ELSE

A task can be as simple as an item on a "To Do" list. It can also contain significantly more information such as whether or not the task has been started and if so, the percentage of the task that has been completed. And best of all, you can assign a task to someone else. Double click an existing task to open a task dialog box, then click the Assign Task button to create an e-mail message in which you request help from a friend or colleague.

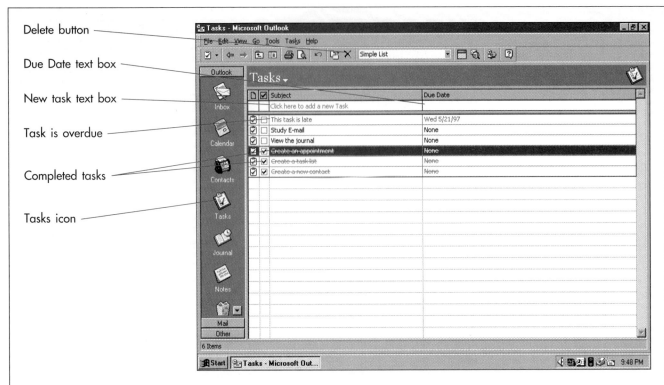

Delete button
Due Date text box
New task text box
Task is overdue
Completed tasks
Tasks icon

(g) Modify the Task List (step 7)

FIGURE 2 Hands-on Exercise 1 (continued)

➤ Click any other task in the list to deselect the current task. The task that you just created appears in red to remind you it is overdue.

➤ Press and hold the **Ctrl key** to select the tasks you want to delete from your list. Press the **Delete button** on the Standard toolbar to remove these tasks from the list.

STEP 8: The Journal

➤ Click the **Journal icon** on the Outlook bar to change to the Journal folder. Click the **Day button** on the Standard toolbar to change to this view, then click the **Go to Today button** to see the events for today.

➤ Click the **plus sign** next to an entry type such as Microsoft Word to see the various Word documents that have been opened. If you do not see any documents, it is because you have not worked on Word today, or because the documents are not being recorded.

➤ Pull down the **Tools menu,** click **Options** to display the Options dialog box, then click the **Journal tab** as shown in Figure 2h. Verify that there is a check next to each of the applications, then click **OK** to close the Options dialog box. All subsequent events will be recorded in the journal.

➤ Do *not* print the journal, as it runs to many pages and in general does not provide useful output.

➤ Close Outlook if you do not want to continue with the next exercise at this time.

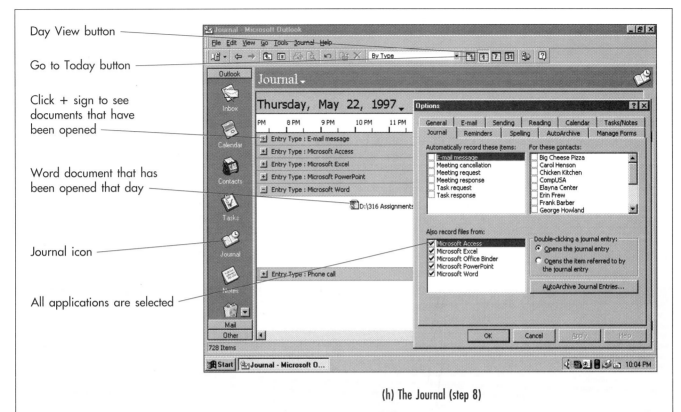

Day View button

Go to Today button

Click + sign to see documents that have been opened

Word document that has been opened that day

Journal icon

All applications are selected

(h) The Journal (step 8)

FIGURE 2   Hands-on Exercise 1 (continued)

FIND THAT MISSING DOCUMENT

You know a file is on your computer, you can't remember its name or the folder where it's saved, but you know you worked on it last Monday. The Outlook Journal will help. Open the Journal, change to the Week or Month view, then go to the day when you last worked on the document. Double click the shortcut in the Journal to open the document and retrieve your work.

INTRODUCTION TO E-MAIL

Electronic mail, or *e-mail,* is conceptually the same as writing a letter and sending it through the U.S. Postal Service with one very significant advantage—e-mail messages are delivered almost instantly as opposed to regular (snail) mail, which requires several days. E-mail was unknown to the general public only a few years ago, but it has become an integral part of American culture. Indeed, the business community has embraced e-mail (and the fax) to such an extent that the number of first-class letters sent between businesses through the U.S. Postal Service is significantly smaller than it was a decade ago.

All Windows-based e-mail systems work basically the same way. You need access to a *mail server* (a computer with a network connection) to receive your incoming messages and to deliver the messages you send. You also need a *mail client,* a program such as Microsoft Outlook in order to read and compose e-mail messages, and to transfer mail back and forth to the server.

The mail server functions as a central post office and provides private mailboxes to persons authorized to use its services. It receives mail around the clock and will hold it for you until you sign on to retrieve it. You gain access to your mailbox (inbox) via a ***username*** and a ***password.*** The username identifies you to the server. The password protects your account from unauthorized use by others. Once you log on to the server, incoming mail is downloaded from the server and stored in the inbox on your PC. Outgoing mail is uploaded from your PC to the server, where it is sent on its way across a local area network to another person within your organization or across the Internet to the world at large.

Figure 3 displays a typical inbox as it appears in Microsoft Outlook. The inbox lists all incoming messages (including faxes), the person who sent the message, the subject of the message, and the date and time the message was received. The messages are listed in order according to when they were received (the most recent message appears at the top of the list).

Unread messages are in bold

Incoming fax

Flagged message

Attachment

High priority message

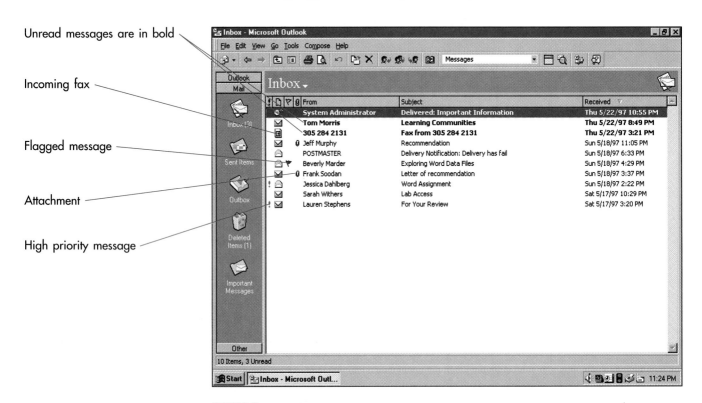

FIGURE 3   The Inbox

NO MORE TELEPHONE TAG

E-mail has changed the way we communicate and in many ways is superior to the telephone. You send a message when it is convenient for you. The recipient reads the message when it is convenient to do so. Neither person has to be online for the other to access his or her e-mail system. You can send the same message to many people as opposed to having to call them individually. And best of all, e-mail is a lot cheaper than a long-distance phone call.

Look carefully at the messages in the inbox to learn more about their status and contents. Three messages have not yet been read and appear in bold. (The Inbox icon on the Outlook bar also indicates that there are three unread messages.) All other messages have been read and appear in regular type. Two of the messages came with attachments (from Jeff Murphy and Frank Soodan). Two other messages (from Jessica Dahlberg and Lauren Stephens) were flagged by their senders as high priority. The message from Beverly Marder has also been flagged (but by the recipient, rather than the sender) to indicate it needs further attention.

Mail Folders

Think, for a moment, about how you process your regular mail. You bring it into your house from the mailbox and read it at your leisure. Some mail is junk mail, which you immediately throw away. Other mail is important and you file it away with other important papers. And some mail you want to share with others in your household; you leave it on the kitchen table to reread at a later time.

E-mail is very similar. You will probably throw away many if not most of the messages you receive. Even if you save only the most important, after you have been receiving e-mail for some time you will discover that there is too much mail to keep in your inbox—like the kitchen table, the inbox simply gets too crowded. You can alleviate the mess by setting up different folders for the various types of mail you receive, then moving each message you want to save to the appropriate folder.

The inbox is one of four folders created by Outlook for use with Internet mail. Only one folder can be selected at a time, however (for example, the Inbox in Figure 3), and its contents are displayed in the right pane of the Outlook window. Click a different folder on the Outlook bar and its contents will be displayed in the right pane.

The purpose of the other folders can be inferred from their names. The **Outbox folder** contains all of the messages you have written that have not yet been sent (uploaded) to the server. Once a message has been sent, however, it is moved automatically to the **Sent Items folder.** Messages will remain indefinitely in both the Inbox and Sent Items folders unless you delete them, in which case they are moved to the **Deleted Items folder.**

Messages can be moved or copied from one mail folder to another just as you can move and copy files with any Windows folder. Simply follow the same conventions as you do in the Windows Explorer; that is, click and drag to move a message from one folder to another. You can also create additional folders of your own such as an Important Message folder to hold messages of a special nature.

IT'S NOT AS PRIVATE AS YOU THINK

One of the most significant differences between e-mail and regular mail is privacy—or the lack thereof. When you receive a sealed letter through the mail, you can assume that no one else has read the letter. Not so with e-mail. The network administrator can read the messages in your inbox, and indeed, many employers maintain that they have the legal right to read their employees' e-mail. And don't assume that deleting a message protects its privacy, since most organizations maintain extensive backup and can recover a deleted message. In other words, never put anything in an e-mail message that you would be uncomfortable seeing in tomorrow's newspaper.

Anatomy of an E-Mail Message

Now that you know about the various e-mail folders, you need to learn about the messages themselves. Specifically you need to know how to create a new message and how to reply to messages that you receive. Creating a message is easy. Just click the **New Mail Message button** on the Standard toolbar to display a window similar to Figure 4.

The function of the various text boxes at the top of the message is apparent from their names. The To text box, for example, contains the address of the recipient(s). The Cc (courtesy or carbon copy) text box indicates the names of other people who are to receive copies of the message. The format of the address depends on the location of the recipient. If, for example, the person is on the same local area network or mail server as you are, then you only need to enter the individual's username such as "rgrauer". If, however, you are sending mail to a person outside your network or information service, you need to use the individual's complete Internet address—for example, rgrauer@umiami.miami.edu.

The message itself appears in the message area below the subject line. Enter the text of the message, then click the Send button to mail it. That's it. The message itself can be simple or more sophisticated, such as our example in Figure 4. Note, for example, that Outlook documents are Web-enabled, meaning that you (or the recipient) can click a hyperlink within an e-mail message and, provided you have an Internet connection, be connected automatically to the Web page.

The message in Figure 4 also contains three **attached files**—a Word document, a PowerPoint presentation, and an Excel workbook. The recipient reads the message as usual, then has the ability to view and/or edit the attached file on his or her machine in its native format. Both capabilities are illustrated in our next hands-on exercise.

Replying to an existing message is similar in concept to creating a new message except that Outlook automatically enters the addressee for you. You open a message from the inbox to read it, click the Reply button to open a window sim-

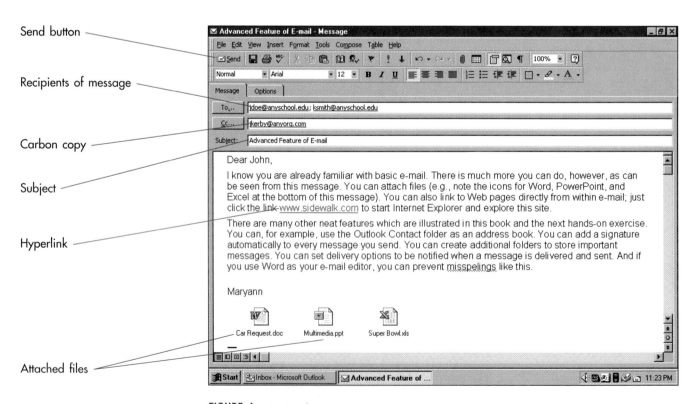

FIGURE 4   An E-mail Message

ilar to Figure 4, then enter the text of your message. You can enter additional recipients of your reply and/or forward the original message to someone else.

As with any Office application, Outlook commands are executed in a variety of ways. You can execute a command by pulling down a menu, by clicking a button on a toolbar, or by a keyboard shortcut. It is the underlying capabilities that are important, however, rather than the specific means of execution.

FINDING AN E-MAIL ADDRESS

What happens if you want to send an e-mail message to a friend or colleague, but you don't know the e-mail address? One solution is to consult an e-mail directory (or Internet White Pages). Start Internet Explorer, then link to www.whowhere.com or www.four11.com, then enter the name of the person and any additional information you have. The directory will then return the e-mail address, provided the person is listed.

LEARNING BY DOING

As always, learning is best accomplished by doing, and it is time for you to apply what we have discussed. One of the best ways to experiment with e-mail is to send yourself a message (or a copy of a message you send to someone else). Not only does this give you practice with the editor, but it also lets you check that the message is actually delivered to its intended recipient. You open your inbox to view the message, and then use the Reply command to send yourself an answer, or the Forward command to send the same message to someone else.

FIND A PEN PAL

Everyone likes to get mail, especially when using e-mail for the first time. Find a classmate and exchange e-mail addresses so that you can practice sending and receiving mail. If you have access to the Internet, find another pen pal outside of class so that you can practice sending mail across the Internet. Try a friend who attends a different school or who has a different Internet provider.

HANDS-ON EXERCISE 2

Welcome to E-mail

Objective: To send and receive an e-mail message. This exercise requires you to have an e-mail account and a network connection, either to a local area network or to an Internet service provider. Use Figure 5 as a guide in doing the exercise.

STEP 1: Establish the Network Connection
➤ You need to initiate a network connection in order to send and receive e-mail. The precise directions depend on where you are doing the exercise.

- If you are using a local area network at school your instructor will provide an account (username) and a password, and you will be connected automatically to the network.
- If you are doing the exercise at home, you will need to sign up (and pay) for the service in order to obtain an account and username, and you will need to connect by modem.

➤ Start Outlook. Close the Office Assistant if it appears. If necessary, maximize the Outlook window so that it takes the entire desktop.

➤ Click the **Mail button** on the Outlook bar to display the mail folders. The Inbox folder is selected by default, as shown in Figure 5a. There are no messages in our inbox.

New Mail Message button

Mail button

Inbox is current folder

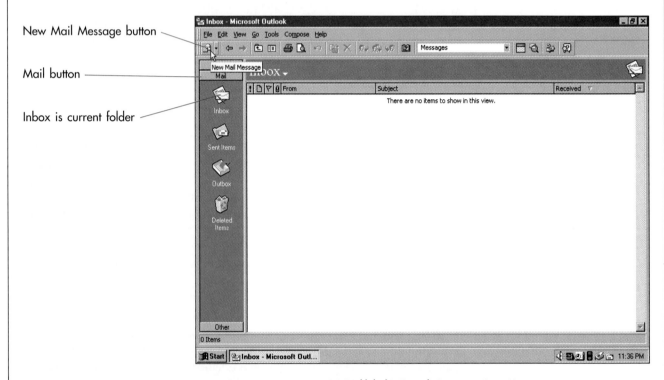

(a) Establish the Network Connection (step 1)

FIGURE 5   Hands-on Exercise 2

PROTECT YOUR PASSWORD

Many people choose passwords that are easy to remember, but what is easy for you is also easy for someone trying to break into your account. Avoid proper names and common words, as a hacker will use a program that goes through the dictionary trying common words until it finds one that lets the hacker in. Keep the password to yourself and change it periodically. Do your LAN administrator a favor, and remember your password. If every user frequently forgets his or her password, the academic computing staff will have time to do little else but reset user passwords.

STEP 2: Send a Message

➤ Click the **New Mail Message button** on the Standard toolbar to display the editing window in Figure 5b. Maximize the window so you have more room to work.

➤ The insertion point should be blinking in the To text box. Enter the Internet address(es) of the person(s) to whom you are sending the message. E-mail addresses may be case-sensitive, so use lowercase unless you are instructed otherwise.

   • If you have not made arrangements to send a message to a classmate, enter your own e-mail address in the To field.

   • If you are sending the message to more than one person, separate the e-mail addresses with a semicolon followed by a space.

   • If the recipient is on the same local area network or Internet server, enter just the username. You must, however, enter the complete Internet address if the recipient is on a different e-mail server.

➤ Press the **Tab key** to move the insertion point to the Cc (Courtesy or Carbon Copy) text box. Enter your e-mail address so you will get a copy of the message.

➤ Press the **Tab key** to move the insertion point to (or click in) the Subject field. Type the subject of your message and press the **Tab key** again to move to the message area. Note that as soon as you enter the subject, the title bar changes to reflect this information.

➤ Enter the text of your message as you would using any word processor, pressing the enter key only at the end of a paragraph. Check your message for errors and correct any mistakes.

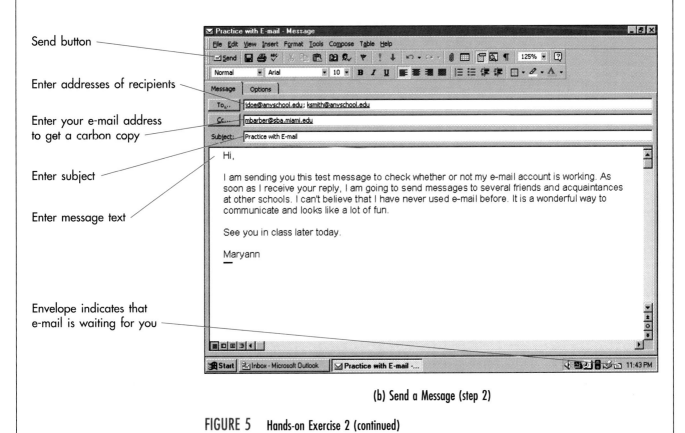

(b) Send a Message (step 2)

FIGURE 5   Hands-on Exercise 2 (continued)

➤ Click the **Send button** when you have completed your message. (You may be prompted to correct a spelling error if you have misspelled a word and are using Word as your e-mail editor.)

➤ The editing window closes automatically, and you are returned to the Inbox folder.

USE WORD AS YOUR E-MAIL EDITOR

Outlook is part of Office 97, and thus we encourage you to use Microsoft Word as your e-mail editor to take advantage of its powerful editing and other capabilities. Pull down the Tools menu, click Options, click the E-mail tab, then (if necessary) check the box to Use Microsoft Word as the e-mail editor. Click OK to accept the settings and close the Options dialog box. One immediate benefit of using Word is the automatic spell check, which takes place after you click the Send button but prior to actually sending the message.

STEP 3: Check Your Folders

➤ The way in which Outlook notifies you that mail has arrived depends on the options in effect:

- You may see the dialog box in Figure 5c. You can click Yes to read the mail immediately or No to close the dialog box and continue working. Click **No** if the message appears before we are ready for it.

- You may hear a sound and/or see an envelope icon at the extreme right of the status bar.

➤ Click the **Outbox icon** on the Outlook bar. You should see the message you just created unless your mail server is extremely fast, in which case the message will have already been moved to the Sent Items folder.

➤ Wait until the message disappears from the Outbox folder, then click the **Sent Items icon** on the Outlook bar. The message has been moved automatically to this folder and serves as a permanent record until you delete it.

➤ Click the **Inbox icon** on the Outlook bar. By now, you should see the notification that new mail has arrived (assuming that you sent a copy of the message to yourself or that a friend has previously sent you mail).

➤ Double click the icon next to the message in the inbox to open the message and read your mail. If the mail has still not arrived, pull down the **Tools menu** and click the **Check for New Mail command.**

DELIVERY HAS FAILED

There is no room for error in an Internet address. Thus, you must obtain the correct address from the intended recipient, and further, you must enter the address exactly in an e-mail message or else it will not be delivered. Failure to do so results in a message from your mail server indicating that delivery was unsuccessful. Open the message from the mail server, double check the address and make the necessary correction, then resend the corrected message.

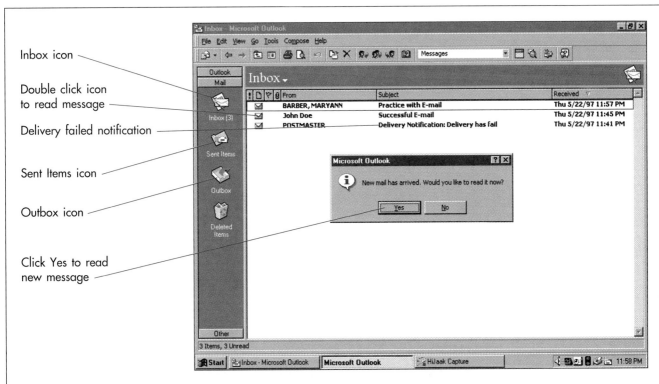

Inbox icon

Double click icon
to read message

Delivery failed notification

Sent Items icon

Outbox icon

Click Yes to read
new message

(c) Check Your Folders (step 3)

FIGURE 5   Hands-on Exercise 2 (continued)

STEP 4: Read Your Mail

➤ The text of the message you see will depend on the sender. If you are working with a friend in the class, then you may see a message similar to that in
Figure 5d. Alternatively, if you are working alone, you will see the message
you created.

➤ Click the **Next Item button** (if you have multiple messages) until you come
to the message to which you want to reply. (Clicking the Next Item button
after you have read the last message takes you back to the Inbox, where you
can double click a message to reopen it.)

➤ Click the **Reply button** to reply to the message.

PRINT ONLY WHEN NECESSARY

There is absolutely no need to print every message you receive. You can,
however, print a message at any time by selecting the message and clicking the Print button on the toolbar. You can also access the Print command through the File menu. And, as with any other Windows application, the File menu contains the Page Setup command to change margins
and/or other characteristics of the printed page.

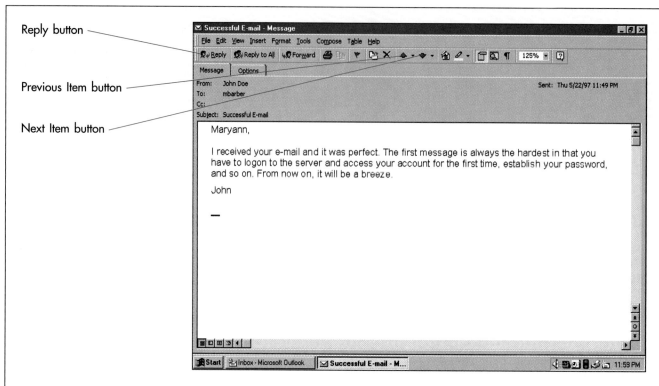

Reply button

Previous Item button

Next Item button

(d) Read Your Mail (step 4)

FIGURE 5 Hands-on Exercise 2 (continued)

STEP 5: Reply to a Message

➤ You should see a screen similar to Figure 5e. The recipient's e-mail address and the subject are entered automatically. The original e-mail message may (or may not) appear, depending on the options that have been set as described in the tip below.

➤ Enter the text of your reply using the same editing commands as when you created the original message earlier in the exercise.

➤ Click the **High Importance** or **Low Importance button** (as you deem appropriate) to flag your reply when it appears in the recipient's inbox.

➤ Click the **Send button** when you have completed your reply. Close the window containing the original message to return to your inbox.

THE OPTIONS MENU

The Options menu enables you to customize virtually every feature in Outlook. To determine whether or not the original message is included in a reply, go to the Outlook window, pull down the Tools menu, click the Options command, then click the Reading tab. Click the down arrow in the When Replying to a Message list box, and choose the desired option. Use the other tabs in the Options dialog box to customize other features in Outlook.

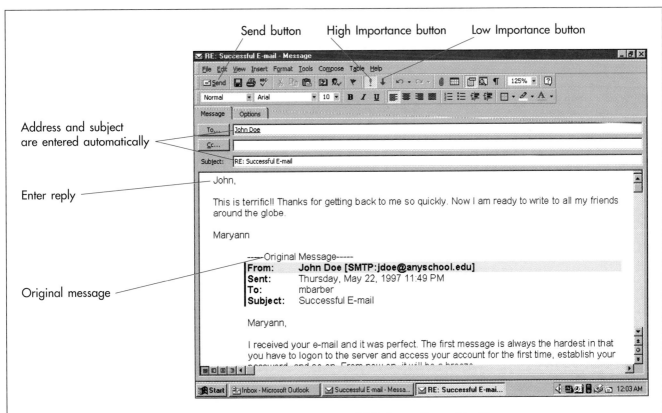

Send button   High Importance button   Low Importance button

Address and subject
are entered automatically

Enter reply

Original message

(e) Reply to a Message (step 5)

FIGURE 5   Hands-on Exercise 2 (continued)

STEP 6: Use the Address Book

➤ Click the **New Mail Message button** on the Standard toolbar to display the editing window. Click the **To button** to display the Select Names dialog box in Figure 5f.

➤ If necessary, click the **down arrow** on the Show Names from the list box, then select **Contacts** as the source of the address book.

➤ Select the individual who is to receive this message (e.g., the contact you entered in the first hands-on exercise). Click the **To button** to add your friend to the list of message recipients.

➤ Select your name within the list of contacts, then click the **Cc button** to add your name to the list of recipients.

➤ Continue to add names to either the To or Cc field as appropriate. (The names of multiple recipients are separated automatically by a semicolon and a space.) Click **OK** to close the Select Names dialog box when you are finished.

➤ Press the **Tab key** to move to the Subject dialog box. Enter **Advanced Features** as the subject of your message.

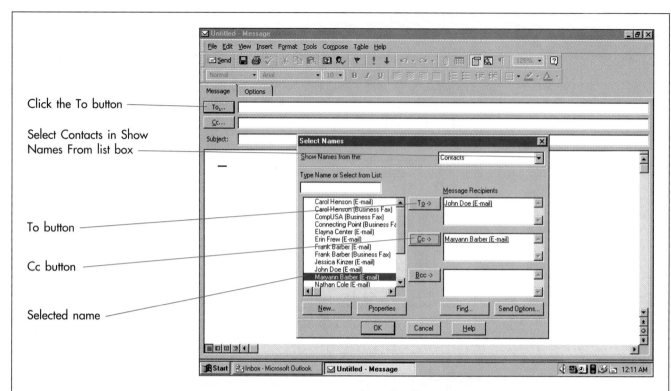

Click the To button

Select Contacts in Show Names From list box

To button

Cc button

Selected name

(f) Use the Address Book (step 6)

FIGURE 5   Hands-on Exercise 2 (continued)

INSTANT ADDRESS BOOK

Use Outlook to create the entries in your address book based on the content of an e-mail message. Click Mail on the Outlook bar, then select the folder on the Outlook bar that contains the message. Click the Outlook button on the Outlook bar so that the Contacts icon is visible, then click and drag the message from the selected folder to the Contacts icon on the Outlook bar. Outlook will create the contact automatically and display the New Contact window, where you can edit the information or add new information as appropriate. Click the Save and Close button.

STEP 7: Attach a File

➤ Enter the text of a new message as shown in Figure 5g. Be sure to enter the Web addresses exactly as they appear in the figure (**www.aprilfool.com** and **www.foundmoney.com**).

➤ Pull down the **Insert menu** and click **File** (or click the **Insert File button** on the Standard toolbar) to display the Insert file dialog box.

➤ Click the **down arrow** on the Look in text box and select any folder on your system, then select a file within that folder. Click **OK** to insert the file. You will see an application icon at the point where the file has been inserted.

➤ Click the **Send button** to send the message. The editing window closes automatically, and you are once again returned to the Inbox folder.

Insert File button

Enter text of message

Enter Web addresses

Click to select drive and folder

Select file

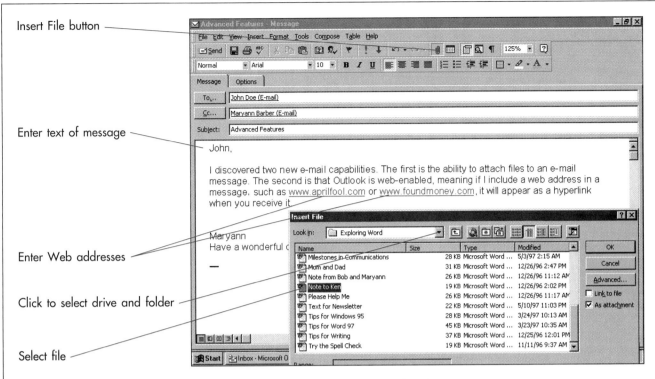

(g) Attach a File (step 7)

FIGURE 5   Hands-on Exercise 2 (continued)

CREATE A SIGNATURE FILE

Many people end their e-mail messages with a consistent closing (known as a signature), consisting of their name, title, address, telephone, and/or a closing phrase. To create a signature for yourself, enter the desired signature at the end of an e-mail message, then click and drag to select the text. Pull down the Tools menu, select the AutoSignature command, then click Yes when asked whether you want to save the current selection. Your signature will be entered automatically into every subsequent message. To delete an existing signature, deselect any selected text, pull down the Tools menu, click AutoSignature, then click Yes when asked if you want to delete the AutoSignature file.

STEP 8: Open an Attachment

➤ Double click the message you just created when it appears in your Inbox to display the screen in Figure 5h. (Be patient, as it may take a few minutes for the message to appear. If you are truly in a rush, however, you can open the message from the Sent Items folder rather than your inbox.)

➤ Look carefully at the displayed message and note that the hyperlinks are underlined and appear in blue. Outlook, like all Office 97 applications, is Web-enabled, meaning that you can click on a link to start Internet Explorer and connect to the site. Consider:

Close button —

Hyperlink —

Point to attached file icon
and click right mouse button
to display shortcut menu —

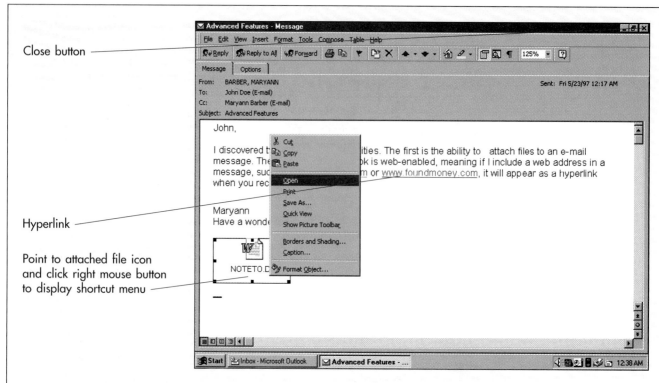

(h) Open an Attachment (step 8)

FIGURE 5 Hands-on Exercise 2 (continued)

- *www.aprilfool.com* is a favorite site any day of the year. We suggest you click the Headline News button to create a news story, then e-mail that to a friend with a sense of humor.
- *www.foundmoney.com* is a clever site that enables you to search publicly available archives for money that has been unknowingly abandoned, such as a closed bank account or an unrefunded security deposit.

➤ Point to the icon indicating the attached file and click the **right mouse button** to display the context-sensitive menu.

➤ Press the **Esc key** to suppress the menu as you need not do anything with the file at this time. (You could also click the Open command to read the file, or the Save As command to save the file to your hard drive for later access.)

➤ Click the **Close button** to return to the main Outlook window.

STAY CURRENT

Go to www.microsoft.com/outlook for the latest information about Outlook. You will find tips for beginners as well as advanced information for developers. You will also find news of additional software to download, typically to correct a reported problem.

FORWARDING MAIL

The ability to forward an e-mail message to a third party is quite useful. Open the message as you normally do, click the Forward button to open the editing window, then enter the recipient's e-mail address. The subject is entered automatically and begins with the letters FW to indicate the message has been forwarded. The text of the original message appears in the editing window where you can edit the message. Click the Send button when you are finished.

STEP 9: Create a New Folder

➤ Click the **Outlook button** on the Outlook bar to display all of your folders. If necessary, click the **Inbox icon** to select this folder and display its messages.

➤ Pull down the **File menu,** click (or point to) **New,** then click **Folder** to display the Create New Folder dialog box in Figure 5i.

➤ Enter **Important Messages** as the name of the new folder. Select the **Personal Folders** as the parent folder. Check the box to **Create a shortcut to the new folder on the Outlook bar.** Click **OK.**

➤ Click the **down arrow** on the Outlook bar to scroll to (but do not click) the icon for the newly created Important Messages folder.

➤ Click and drag all of the messages from the Inbox folder to the Important Messages icon on the Outlook bar. The messages disappear from your Inbox because they have been moved to the new folder.

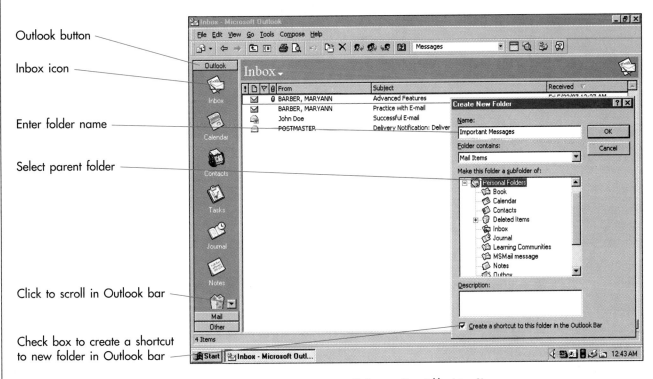

Outlook button

Inbox icon

Enter folder name

Select parent folder

Click to scroll in Outlook bar

Check box to create a shortcut to new folder in Outlook bar

(i) Create a New Folder (step 9)

FIGURE 5   Hands-on Exercise 2 (continued)

MAINTAIN YOUR INBOX

You don't let regular mail sit indefinitely on the kitchen table and you shouldn't let it accumulate in your inbox either. Delete messages that you don't need and move messages that you want to keep to a new folder. Depending on the amount of mail you receive, you may want to set up multiple folders for different correspondents or categories of mail.

STEP 10: Exit Outlook

➤ Click the icon for the **Important Messages folder** as shown in Figure 5j. You should see all of the messages that were previously in the inbox.

➤ Select a message that you decide is no longer important, then click the **Delete button** on the Standard toolbar to delete this message. The message disappears from the Important Messages folder and is moved automatically to the Deleted Items folder.

➤ Pull down the **File menu** and click **Exit,** or click the **Close button** to exit Outlook. Click **Yes** if you see the dialog box in Figure 5j to permanently delete the contents of the Deleted Items folder.

➤ Congratulations on a job well done.

Close button

Delete button

Important Messages icon

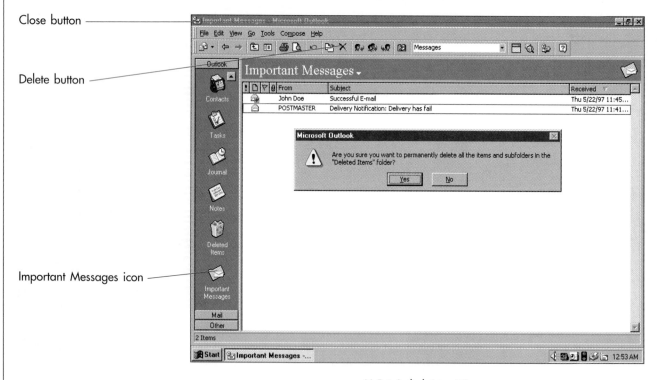

(j) Exit Outlook (step 10)

FIGURE 5   Hands-on Exercise 2 (continued)

The only difficulty you are likely to have with e-mail is establishing an initial connection with the mail server. This will not be a problem if you are doing the exercise from school. If you are connecting from home, however, you may have to experiment until your settings are correct.

The Internet Mail dialog box in Figures 6a and 6b is displayed through the Services command in the Tools menu. Figure 6a displays the General Properties tab in which you enter your name and e-mail address (as it will appear in your e-mail messages). The mailbox information specifies the address of your mail server, your account name, and your password. The Connection tab in Figure 6b indicates how you will connect to the mail server, and specifies the name of the dial-up connection (for example, My Connection) that is established through Windows 95. The Connect To dialog box in Figure 6c (which is accessed from the Dial-Up Networking folder in My Computer) displays the parameters for the actual connection. (The username and password for your Internet provider need not be the same as for your mailbox.)

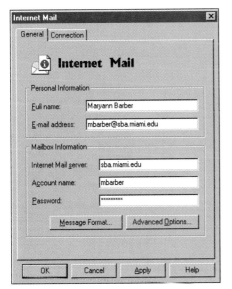

(a) General Properties Tab

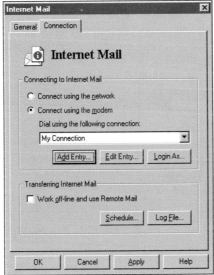

(b Connection Tab

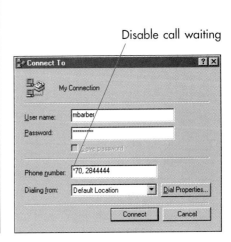

(c) Dial-up Networking

FIGURE 6   Connecting from Home

DISABLE CALL WAITING

Your friend may understand if you excuse yourself in the middle of a conversation to answer another incoming call. A computer, however, is not so tolerant and will often break the current connection if another call comes in. Accordingly, check the settings of your communications program to disable call waiting prior to connecting to the Internet (typically by entering *70 in front of the phone number). Your friends may complain of a busy signal, but you will be able to work without interruption.

Microsoft Outlook is a desktop information manager that keeps track of all types of information. You can use it to maintain an address book, schedule appointments, create a task list, write notes to yourself, create a journal that monitors the activity on your PC, or send and receive e-mail. Microsoft Outlook is included in the Professional Edition of Office 97.

The Outlook bar appears at the left of the Outlook window and provides the easiest way to switch from one function to another. The icons on the Outlook bar are divided into groups. The Outlook group contains an icon for each major function (Inbox, Calendar, Contacts, Tasks, Journal, and Notes). The Mail group contains an icon for each mail folder (Inbox, Sent Items, Outbox, and Deleted Items).

The functions in Outlook are thoroughly integrated with one another, making each function more valuable as a part of the whole. An e-mail message, for example, can be generated automatically from appointments on the calendar (perhaps to remind attendees of a scheduled meeting) using entries in the address book. You can also go in the other direction and create entries in your address book or events on your calendar directly from an e-mail message.

The Options command in the Tools menu lets you customize virtually every aspect of Outlook. The meaning of each option is generally apparent from its name, but you can click the What's This button (the question mark) at the right of the title bar) for a detailed explanation.

KEY WORDS AND CONCEPTS

Attached file	Mail group	Password
Calendar folder	Mail server	Reply command
Contacts folder	Mailbox	Send command
Deleted Items folder	New Mail Message	Sent Items folder
E-mail	button	Server
Folder	Notes folder	Signature
Inbox folder	Options command	Task list
Internet address	Outbox folder	Username
Journal	Outlook bar	
Mail client	Outlook group	

Index

A = Access
E = Excel
O = Outlook
P = PowerPoint
W = Word

#VALUE error, E164

A

Absolute reference
   shortcut for, E81
   in VBA, E106–E107
Action, A129
Address book, O25
Adjustable cells, E173, E176, E182
Advanced Filter command, E18,
   E26–E27, E121–E122
Animation settings, P76–P77
Application, A116
Argument, A129
Arrange command, E56, E69
Ascending sequence, E5
Assumptions, isolation of, E161
Attached file, O18, O26–O27
Audience handouts, printing of, P24
Audit, E157–E169
Auditing toolbar, E159, E164–E165
AutoCalculate, E193
AutoCorrect, E11
AutoDialer, O8
AutoExec macro, A130, A132–A133
AutoFill command, E67, E80
AutoFilter command, E17–E18,
   E24–E25
AutoFormat command, W24–W26,
   W38
AutoLayouts, numbering of, P29
AutoLookup, A67–A68, A78
AutoNumber field, A57, A59–A61
   with relationships, A97
AutoShape, P34–P35
AutoSum button, E72
AVI file, P67–P68, P73–P74

B

Background, of HTML document,
   W116–W117
Binding constraint, E172
Body Text style, W22
   with AutoFormat command, W24
Bookmark, in HTML document,
   W110, W121–W123
Borders and Shading command, W56,
   W78–W79
Browse object, W44
Build button, A22
Bulleted list, W2–W5, W56, W75
Bullets and Numbering command,
   W2–W5

C

Calendar folder, O2–O3, O10
Call waiting, disabling of, O31
Caption property, A163
Cascade Delete, A59
Cascade Update, A59
Category Shading, E199, E203
CD Player, P69
Cell, in a Word table, W11
Character style, W21
Clip art, W19–W20, W56, W76–W77,
   P13, P15–P16
Clipboard, P46
Codd, Edgar, A181
Code window, E94–E95
Collapse Dialog button, E29
Columns command, W58–W59,
   W63–W64, W74
Combined key, A56, A183

K

Key, E2
Keyboard shortcut
  creation of, A163
  trouble with, E103

L

Leader character, W36–W37
Legend, in Data Mapping, E201–E202
Letter Wizard, W161
Link Tables command, A117–A119,
  A120
Linked object, P24, W133
Linked subforms, A36–A44
Linking, W141–W150
  versus embedding, P31, W146
Linking workbooks, E78–E84
List box, versus combo box, A147
List management, E1–E42
  macros for, E115–E143

M

Macro, A129–A140, E93–E143
  execution of, E124
  name of, E97
Macro button, E130–E131
Macro group, A142, A144
Macro recorder, E94, E96–E98
Macro toolbar, A130, A144
Macro virus, E126
Macro window, A129
Mail client, O15
Mail folders, O17
Mail group, O2
Mail merge, A185–A194, W157–W168
Mail Merge Helper, A188, A193,
  W160–W161, W166
Mail Merge toolbar, A189, A191–A192,
  W166
Mail server, O15
Main document, A185, W157–W159,
  W162
Main form, A13
Many-to-many relationship,
  A53–A104, A181
MapStats Workbook, E207–E208
Margins, changing of, W61
Masthead, W56, W65–W66

Media player, P69
Merge and Center button, E28
Merge field, A185, W157
Microsoft Clip Gallery, P75, W56
Microsoft Graph, P2–P12
Microsoft Map Control dialog box,
  E194–E195, E199–E200,
  E202–E203
Microsoft Multimedia Gallery,
  W112–W114
Microsoft Organization Chart, P26,
  P28, P32–P33
Microsoft Outlook, O1–O31
Microsoft Word, as e-mail editor,
  O22
Microsoft WordArt, P26–P27,
  P36–P38
MIDI file, P67, P71
MMX technology, P66
MPC standards, P66
MsgBox Action, A129, A134
Multimedia, P65–P84
Multitasking, P42, W98, W145

N

Name box, E27, E119
Named range, E118
Navigation buttons
  with subforms, A43
  suppression of, A128, A162
New Window command, E56
Newsletter Wizard, W59–W61
Nonbinding constraint, E172
Nonnegativity constraint, E174
Normal style, W21–W22
Notes, O5–O6
Null criterion, A146
Numbered list, W2–W5, W56, W75

O

Object Linking and Embedding,
  P24–P40, W133–W150
Office Art, P12–P14
Offset, in VBA, E106–E107
OLE. *See* Object Linking and
  Embedding
On Click property, A136, A139–A140
One-to-many relationship, A1–A44,
  A176